MATTERS OF ENGAGEMENT

By drawing on a broad range of disciplinary and cross-disciplinary expertise, this study addresses the history of emotions in relation to cross-cultural movement, exchange, contact, and changing connections in the later medieval and early modern periods.

All essays in this volume focus on the performance and negotiation of identity in situations of cultural contact, with particular emphasis on emotional practices. They cover a wide range of thematic and disciplinary areas and are organized around the primary sources on which they are based. The edited volume brings together two major areas in contemporary humanities: the study of how emotions were understood, expressed, and performed in shaping premodern transcultural relations, and the study of premodern cultural movements, contacts, exchanges, and understandings as emotionally charged encounters. In discussing these hitherto separated historiographies together, this study sheds new light on the role of emotions within Europe and amongst non-Europeans and Europeans between 1100 and 1800.

The discussion of emotions in a wide range of sources including letters, images, material culture, travel writing, and literary accounts makes *Matters of Engagement* an invaluable source for both scholars and students concerned with the history of premodern emotions.

Daniela Hacke is an internationally renowned cultural historian and Full Professor of Early Modern History at *Freie Universität Berlin*.

Claudia Jarzebowski, partner investigator at the Centre of Excellence for the History of Emotions since its founding in 2011, researches and publishes on early modern global history and applies polycentric perspectives with a focus on agency, gender, and ethnic and religious/spiritual creolization. Her second book, *Childhood and Emotion. Children in Early Modern Europe*, was published (in German) in 2018.

Hannes Ziegler is Research Fellow in early modern history at the German Historical Institute London.

MATTERS OF ENGAGEMENT

Emotions, Identity, and Cultural Contact in the Premodern World

Edited by Daniela Hacke, Claudia Jarzebowski, and Hannes Ziegler

LONDON AND NEW YORK

First published 2021
by Routledge
2 Park Square, Milton Park, Abingdon, Oxon OX14 4RN

and by Routledge
52 Vanderbilt Avenue, New York, NY 10017

Routledge is an imprint of the Taylor & Francis Group, an informa business

© 2021 selection and editorial matter, Daniela Hacke, Claudia Jarzebowski and Hannes Ziegler, individual chapters, the contributors

The right of Daniela Hacke, Claudia Jarzebowski, and Hannes Ziegler to be identified as the authors of the editorial material, and of the authors for their individual chapters, has been asserted in accordance with sections 77 and 78 of the Copyright, Designs and Patents Act 1988.

All rights reserved. No part of this book may be reprinted or reproduced or utilised in any form or by any electronic, mechanical, or other means, now known or hereafter invented, including photocopying and recording, or in any information storage or retrieval system, without permission in writing from the publishers.

Trademark notice: Product or corporate names may be trademarks or registered trademarks, and are used only for identification and explanation without intent to infringe.

British Library Cataloguing-in-Publication Data
A catalogue record for this book is available from the British Library

Library of Congress Cataloging-in-Publication Data
Names: Ziegler, Hannes, editor. | Hacke, Daniela, editor. | Jarzebowski, Claudia, editor.
Title: Matters of engagement: emotions, identity, and cultural contact in the premodern world / edited by Hannes Ziegler, Daniela Hacke, Claudia Jarzebowski.
Description: 1 Edition. | New York: Routledge, 2020. | Includes bibliographical references and index.
Identifiers: LCCN 2020022902 | ISBN 9781138594654 (hardback) | ISBN 9781138594678 (paperback) | ISBN 9780429488689 (ebook)
Subjects: LCSH: Emotions—History. | Culture.
Classification: LCC BF531 .M328 2020 | DDC 152.409—dc23
LC record available at https://lccn.loc.gov/2020022902

ISBN: 978-1-138-59465-4 (hbk)
ISBN: 978-1-138-59467-8 (pbk)
ISBN: 978-0-429-48868-9 (ebk)

Typeset in Bembo
by codeMantra

CONTENTS

List of figures   *viii*
Acknowledgements   *x*
List of contributors   *xi*

1 Matters of engagement. Emotions, identity, and cultural contact in the premodern world: an introduction   1
Daniela Hacke, Claudia Jarzebowski, and Hannes Ziegler

PART I
Letters   15

2 Bridging the gap: techniques of appresentation and familiar(izing) narratives in eighteenth-century transmaritime family correspondence   17
Christina Beckers

3 An emotional company: mobility, community, and control in the records of the English East India Company   48
Mark Williams

PART II
Images   71

4 Lust, love and curiosity: the emotional threads in the Dutch encounter with an exotic East   73
Natsuko Akagawa

5 Santiago Matamoros/Mataindios: adopting an Old World battlefield apparition as a New World representation of triumph 95
Heather Dalton

6 Riding the juggernaut: embodied emotions and 'Indian' ritual processions through European eyes, c. 1300–1600 123
Jennifer Spinks

PART III
Materials **151**

7 Robbing the grave: stealing the remains of the blessed John of Matha from the church of S. Tommaso in Formis in 1655 153
Lisa Beaven

8 Days of wrath, days of friendships: the materiality of anger and love in early modern Denmark 172
Jette Linaa

PART IV
Travel writing **195**

9 "A country where reason does not rule the heart": Spanish exuberance and the traveller's gaze 197
Thomas C. Devaney

10 Sensible distances: the colonial projections of Therese Huber and E. G. Wakefield 216
Lisa O'Connell

11 Animals and emotions in the early modern world 231
Margaret R. Hunt

Part V
Literary accounts **257**

12 Travel, emotions and timelessness: on otherworldly encounters in medieval narratives 259
Jutta Eming

13 "Always fleeing away": emotion, exile and rest in the Old
English *Life of St Mary of Egypt* 276
Andrew Lynch

14 From Aaron to Othello: the changing emotional register of
blackness in Shakespeare 290
Bríd Phillips

15 Emotions, identity and propaganda: Ottoman threat and
confessional divide in later sixteenth-century Germany 311
Hannes Ziegler

Index *333*

FIGURES

5.1	Statue of Santiago Matamoros, Catedral de Nuestra Señora de la Asunción, Cordoba, Spain	98
5.2	Cross of the Order of Santiago with scallop shells, Santiago Apóstol, Málaga, Spain	99
5.3	Effigy, alabaster, of Don García de Osorio, in the tradition of the work of Gil de Siloe, Spanish (Castilian), perhaps Toledo, c. 1499–1505	100
5.4	Upper title band, Monogramist S.M.D., woodcut, 1534. Frontispiece, published by Juan Cromberger, Seville, Spain, 1535	102
5.5	Miguel Mauricio, painted carved panel, Iglesia de Santiago Tlatelolco, Mexico, 1604–10	104
5.6	Felipe Guaman Poma de Ayala, 'El primer Nueva coronica y buen gobierno' (Peru, 1584–1615)	106
5.7	'Diego Muñoz Camargo, *Historia de Tlaxcala* (Mexico, 1585) 'Battle of Guatemala'	109
5.8	Santiago Mataindios, Cuzco School, Peru, oil on canvas, 1690–1720	110
6.1	Johann Theodor de Bry, image of the 'juggernaut', engraving, 1598	124
6.2	Anonymous artist, depiction of the tomb of Saint Thomas and of the 'juggernaut', woodcut, in John Mandeville, *Das buch des ritters herr hannsen von monte villa*, 1481	130
6.3	Anonymous artist, depiction of the 'juggernaut', manuscript, Codex Casantense 1889	131
6.4	Anonymous artist, image of the 'juggernaut', engraving in André Thevet, *La Cosmographie Universelle*	133
6.5	Philips Galle, after a drawing by Maarten van Heemskerck, 'The Triumph of Death', engraving, c. 1565	138

6.6	Anonymous artist, 'Triumph of Fame over Death', tapestry, c. 1500–1530	138
6.7	Maerten van Heemskerck, 'Triumph of Bacchus', oil on wood, c. 1536/37	140
7.1	Anonymous illustration of a Trinitarian habit	154
7.2	Relic of the scapula of St. John of Matha, Church of S. Crisogono, Rome	162
8.1	*Helsingör med sine Gader og Stræder, Cronborg Slot ved Siden, Peder Hansen Resen, 1677*	174
8.2	Results of network analysis based on the debts registered in 48 probate inventories in Elsinore 1590–1600	180
8.3	Prosperous Calvinist family. Anonymous, 1627	188

ACKNOWLEDGEMENTS

This volume evolved from the International Conference "Emotions: Movement, Cultural Contact, and Exchange – 1100–1800" that took place in Berlin in 2016 (30 June–2 July). The wide-ranging conference had been generously funded by the Centre of Excellence for the History of Emotions, 1100–1800 (Australian Research Council), and the Centre for International Cooperation (FU Berlin). This volume owes its inspiration and existence to the splendid papers discussed at the conference. As editors, we wish to express our gratitude to all speakers and to those who agreed to develop their papers into chapters under the thematic umbrella that gave us the idea to edit this book. We especially thank Andrew Lynch (Western Australia), Charles Zika (Melbourne) and Jaqueline Van Gent (Western Australia) who have served on the conference committee and supported the idea of this book *ab initio*. Valuable discussions have also taken place with the plenary speakers Lyndal Roper (Oxford), Monique Scheer (Tübingen) and Laura M. Stevens (Tulsa) before, during and after the conference.

Eventually, Routledge has once more proved an outstandingly supportive publishing house. Many thanks especially to Laura Pilsworth, Morwenna Scott and Isabel Voice, who have guided the manuscript to the press. Important input came from both anonymous reviewers. If the reviewers happen to read this: Thank you for that! A heartfelt thank you also to Jan Becker, Paul Grimm, Florian Wieser and Man Zheng, who have spent many an hour in the preparation of the manuscript, and to Friederike Philippe for her help with Japanese translations.

As the history of emotions is "ambiguous territory", as Philippa Maddern (+ 2014) has termed it pointedly very early in the process of establishing the "Centre of Excellence for the History of Emotions, 1100–1800", we are delighted to present a selection of contributions to the vibrant history of emotions in connection to recent issues of early modern global history.

CONTRIBUTORS

Natsuko Akagawa is Senior Lecturer at the University of Queensland. She researches the history and politics of heritage, and entangled emotion and memory in a global context. She was an associate investigator for the ARC Centre of Excellence for the History of Emotions (University of Western Australia) and is the Series General Editor for *Routledge Research on Museums and Heritage in Asia*. Her books include *Heritage Conservation and Cultural Diplomacy* (Routledge 2015), *Safeguarding Intangible Heritage* (Routledge 2019) and *Intangible Heritage* (Routledge 2009).

Lisa Beaven is Senior Lecturer in art history and visual culture at La Trobe University, Australia. From 2014 to 2018, she was a post-doctoral research fellow in the ARC Centre of Excellence for the History of Emotions at the University of Melbourne. Her research interests are concentrated on seventeenth-century Italian art patronage and in collecting and digital mapping, religious emotion and the reception of devotional art in early modern Italy. She has contributed to books such as *Possessions of a Cardinal: Politics, Piety and Art* (2010), *The Early Modern Villa* (2017), *The Routledge History of Emotions in Europe: 1100–1700* (2019), and *The Early Modern Companion to Rome* (2019). Her book, *An Ardent Patron: Cardinal Camillo Massimo and his artistic and antiquarian circle: Claude Lorrain, Nicolas Poussin and Diego Velazquez,* was published by Paul Holberton Press, London and CEEH, Madrid in 2010, and she is editor (with Angela Ndalianis) of *Emotion and the Seduction of the Senses, baroque to neo-Baroque* (2018).

Christina Beckers is project coordinator of the Prize Papers Database project (Göttingen Academy of Sciences and Humanities/ University of Oldenburg in cooperation with The National Archives, UK, and the GHI London). After graduating in 2008 with a thesis on language acquisition in the seventeenth and eighteenth centuries, she was research assistant to Professor Dr Dagmar Freist, chair of Early Modern History at the Carl von Ossietzky University of Oldenburg from 2009 to 2018. In her research, she has been focusing on networks and the negotiation of family relations in the eighteenth century. Moreover, she has been particularly interested in the interplay of theoretical impulses from material culture studies and sensory history with digital methods and approaches to (digital) archives.

Heather Dalton is an Honorary Fellow in the School of Historical & Philosophical Studies, University of Melbourne. She is the author of *Merchants and Explorers: Roger Barlow, Sebastian Cabot and Networks of Atlantic Exchange, 1500–1560* (OUP, 2016); and "A Sulphur-crested Cockatoo in fifteenth century Mantua: Rethinking symbols of sanctity and patterns of trade", *Renaissance Studies* 28/5 (2014), which won the ANZAMEMS' inaugural Philippa Maddern Early Career Researcher Publication Prize in 2016. Dr Dalton's most recent publication is the edited volume: *Keeping Family in an Age of Long Distance Trade, Imperial Expansion and Exile, 1550–1850* (AUP, 2020).

Thomas C. Devaney (Associate Professor, University of Rochester) is a scholar of late medieval and early modern cultural history who has published multiple articles in *Speculum, Medieval Encounters, Viator*, and elsewhere as well as a monograph titled *Enemies in the Plaza: Urban Spectacle and the End of Spanish Frontier Culture, 1460–1492*, with the University of Pennsylvania Press. Currently, he is engaged in a project examining the emotional, sensory, and cognitive experience of *romerías*, or pilgrimages to local shrines, in early modern Iberia. The goals of this project include contributing to the methodologies of the history of emotions and clarifying the often-contradictory history of interfaith relations in Iberia.

Jutta Eming is a Professor of Medieval German Literature and Language at the Institute for German and Dutch Philology, Freie Universität Berlin. Jutta Eming's research interests include romances from the high to the late Middle Ages, genre theory and gender, emotionality, performativity, premodern drama, adventure narratives and hybrid temporalities. She has published the monographs *Emotion und Expression. Untersuchungen zu deutschen und französischen Liebes- und Abenteuerromanen des 12.-16. Jahrhunderts*, Berlin/New York: De Gruyter 2006, and *Emotionen im 'Tristan'. Untersuchungen zu ihrer Paradigmatik*, Göttingen: v & r unipress 2015, as well as several articles on emotionality in medieval and early modern literature.

Daniela Hacke is Full Professor of Early Modern History at the *Freie Universität Berlin*. Her major publications include *Women, Sex, and Marriage in Counterreformation Venice* (Ashgate 2004) and *Konfession und Kommunikation. Religiöse Koexistenz und Politik in der Alten Eidgenossenschaft, 1531–1712* (Böhlau 2017). Her most recent book (co-edited with P. Musselwhite) is focused on the importance of the senses in intercultural settings and colonial projects; it is titled: *Empire of the Senses: Sensory Practices of Colonialism in Early America* (Brill 2018).

Contributors **xiii**

Margaret R. Hunt is Professor of History at Uppsala University. She is the author of *The Middling Sort: Commerce, Gender and the Family in England 1680–1780* (1996) and *Women in Eighteenth-century Europe* (2010), and co-author of *The 1689 Siege of Bombay: The East India Company at the Height of Mughal Expansion* (2017). She has also written numerous articles on gender, law, travel, race, sexuality and maritime history and is currently working on projects related to English East India Company, English and Northwest Indian maritime communities and Scandinavian shipping in the early modern period.

Claudia Jarzebowski is an Assistant Professor of Early Modern History in the History Department, Free University Berlin. She has served as a partner investigator at the Centre for the History of Emotions and has recently published a book on *Kindheit und Emotion. Kinder und ihre Lebenswelten in der europäischen Frühen Neuzeit* (DE Gruyter: 2018). Her focus has now shifted to emotions within global history with a focus on material culture, family and work relations. In her upcoming chapter "Towards a World History. Youth in the Age of Enlightenment" (Bloomsbury 2021), she explores how and why education has become a paradigm of European enlightenment and at what intellectual cost, still relevant in present times.

Jette Linaa is curator of Historical Archaeology at Moesgaard Museum Denmark, and adjunct associate professor at Department of Archaeology and Heritage Studies, Aarhus University. Linaa´s research interests concentrate on community formation, social networks and dark heritage. Linaa is head of the collective research project "Urban Diaspora" on migration and mobility in the early modern period, funded by the Danish Council for Independent Research/Humanities.

Andrew Lynch is Emeritus Professor of English and Literary Studies at The University of Western Australia, and a former director of the Australian Research Council Centre of Excellence for the History of Emotions. His recent publications as co-editor and contributor include *The Routledge History of Emotions in Europe, 1100–1700* (2019) and *A Cultural History of Emotions*, 6 vols (Bloomsbury, 2019). He is an editor of the journal *Emotions: History, Culture, Society* (Brill).

Lisa O'Connell is Associate Professor in English at the University of Queensland. She is the author of *The Origins of the English Marriage Plot: Literature, Politics and Religion in the Eighteenth Century* (Cambridge UP, 2019) and co-editor of *Libertine Enlightenment* (2004). Her current research focuses on the secularization and worlding of eighteenth-century fiction.

Bríd Phillips is a Lecturer in health humanities with a particular interest in Shakespeare, emotions and narrative medicine. Her most recent publication is a co-edited volume *Hamlet and Emotions* (editors Paul Megna, Bríd Phillips, and R. S. White, Palgrave 2019). She writes regularly for the online publication

Synapsis: A Health Humanities Journals, and her current research involves staged readings for health humanities students.

Jennifer Spinks is Hansen Senior Lecturer in History at the University of Melbourne. She works on print culture and religious identity, and has co-curated exhibitions at the National Gallery of Victoria in Melbourne and the John Rylands Library in Manchester. Her publications include *Monstrous Births and Visual Culture in Sixteenth-Century Germany* (2009, pbk 2016) and the recent article "Karlstadt's *Wagen*: The first visual propaganda for the Reformation" (*Art History*, 2017; co-authored with Lyndal Roper).

Mark Williams is Senior Lecturer in Early Modern History at Cardiff University. Broadly interested in the history of early modern mobility, he is currently working on a cultural history of the English East India Company in the early modern period.

Hannes Ziegler is a Research Fellow in early modern history at the German Historical Institute London. He earned his PhD from the University of Munich (LMU) on trust in political relations in the Holy Roman Empire and has subsequently worked on the history of emotions for a time. He is currently conducting research on eighteenth-century Britain.

1

MATTERS OF ENGAGEMENT. EMOTIONS, IDENTITY, AND CULTURAL CONTACT IN THE PREMODERN WORLD

An introduction

Daniela Hacke, Claudia Jarzebowski, and Hannes Ziegler

Aims of the volume

When asked what he thought of Western civilization, Mahatma Gandhi replied: "I think that would be a fabulous idea". This story is told by Kwame Anthony Appiah in his book *The Lies that Bind. Rethinking Identity*.[1] It is particularly telling in regard to the purpose of this book: to start investigations in the history of emotions as investigations in identity-building and cultural encounters, cognizant of the increasing fragility of formerly and reputedly cemented paradigms such as the West and "the rest". Therefore, cultural encounters in this book are not per se defined as encounters across cultures insinuating a European/non-European divide, but also within cultures, approving of the notion of cultural heterogeneity in early modern history in Europe as much as in all other regions of the world. Culture is therefore – throughout the volume – understood as a multitude of interdependent processes and practices.[2]

Recent studies from the field of the history of emotions have convincingly shown that emotions played out in all kinds of cultural contact and that they did, and still do, for all who are part of such processes. If one looks at recent debates on migration, population policies, and immigration policies – whether in Great Britain, the USA or the majority of European countries– this insight does not come as a surprise. People react emotionally to – in their view – unexpected and unnecessary challenges of social life and cultural discourse. However, the myth of the West is built upon an ideal of self-controlled, emotionally regulated, and civilized individuals who, as a matter of fact, turn out to be male, white, Christian, and well off. One source of reference still in use can be identified as Norbert Elias' *Civilizing Process*.[3] Intended to explain the atrocities of German *Nationalsozialismus* as a fall-back into purportedly uncivilized habits of former times, it has soon become a leading paradigm among the first generation of historians of emotions such as Lucien Febvre (who would not, of course, have called himself a historian of emotions). These were historians and sociologists who were mainly interested in collective emotions and manipulative forces.[4] This line of thinking operated with different degrees of civilization according to the capacity of emotional control a given society could perform, with Western civilization the ultimate benchmark. The difficulties of this kind of approach are obvious.

In line with sociologists such as Paul Ekman, emotions have for long been conceptualized as universal human features – which is, of course, true. But this argument has been taken one step further: seven emotions have subsequently been established as universally comparable (if not equal) and universally recognizable,[5] leaving no space for historical change and cultural appropriation.[6] This is where the second generation of historians of emotions steps in. Based on the assumption that emotions have been important modes of interaction, understanding, and discourse; and are factors in negotiating conflicts, hierarchies, and power relations at all times and in all regions, the analytical power of investigating differences now prevails over the often fruitless search for similarities. Especially when it comes to cultural encounters across regions, religions, languages, hierarchies, beliefs, and also modes of communication in general, it is of utmost importance not to presuppose any kind of human and/or anthropological sameness but to be conscious of emotions as structuring elements in perceiving and establishing relations, differences, and hierarchies.

In a recent article, Fatima Mernissi (+ 2015) shares a story of emotional alienation during a book tour of her autobiographical account *Dreams of Trespass: Tales of a Harem Girlhood*.[7] Whenever she read the first line "I was born in a harem" aloud, people smiled in different ways and, as Mernissi came to find out, with constitutively different intentions – referencing their specific cultural background that included specific, often unconscious, notions of what a harem was:

> The American men, upon hearing the word 'harem', smiled with unadulterated and straightforward embarrassment. Whatever the word means for Americans hinges on something linked to shame. The Europeans, in contrast, responded with smiles that varied from polite reserve in the North to merry exuberance in the South [...] French, Spanish, and Italian men had a flirtatious, amused light in their eyes. Scandinavians and Germans, with the exception of the Danes, had astonishment in theirs, astonishment tinged with shock: 'Were you really born in a harem?', they would ask, looking intently at me with a mixture of apprehension and puzzlement.[8]

This could simply be a witty story, had it not dramatically illustrated some of the problems historians face when investigating cultural encounters with a focus on emotions. Mernissi was able to reflect upon her audience's prejudices, suppressed visions of lust and desire and their cultural heritage as represented in paintings of the harem, as produced by, for example, Paul Ingrès. She was able to argue for her own stand, perception and (mis)-understandings of her life and work, and of the life and work of innumerable women born in a harem, whether in Morocco, as in Mernissi's case, or in the Ottoman Empire of the sixteenth or seventeenth century. This example, therefore, strikingly illustrates some of the major questions and topics in this volume.

Firstly, emotions are a matter of cultural and personal engagement. What a person felt at any given point of time in history and how this imagined person perceived his or her feelings and subtle reactions to a situation or encounter have always been prefigured by normative frames, or, as William Reddy has put it, regimes. As the editors of this volume, we share the conviction that the history of emotions cannot be told as a history of increasing control but rather as a history of emotional patchwork with different highpoints and conditions of aggregation. People have always encountered people, cultures, texts, customs, beliefs, and religions they were not familiar with. Similarly, people have always encountered cultural conflict and social hierarchies on local and global scales. If cultural encounters are the main focus throughout this volume, we speak of cultural encounters that could have taken place all over the world. Depending on where they took place, however, the cultural encounters were enacted and perceived in different ways. Space and time mattered, and still matter, for how emotions played out.

Secondly, emotions had, and still have, a strong impact on identity-building. For pre-modernity, Rosenwein suggested a focus on communities and group identities built through and upon emotions. Still highly influential in its basic approach, it soon became clear that differentiation was required, especially in terms of how emotions were used and performed in order to bridge and overcome strangeness and difference, as well as hierarchies. For example, any given relation of a European king or a queen, that is of worldly authority to their subjects, was shaped after the model of God loving all people.[9] Of course, this love could be unequally distributed and/or exclusive. It limited the normative legitimacy of cruel behaviour against subordinates, but for instance regularly excluded enslaved people. The interest of this book is directed at emotionally charged practices in moral and social norms and expectations and – to a smaller extent – discourses of identity-building.

Thirdly, sources are a key element for an in-depth study in the history of emotions. The second generation of historians of emotions – scholars such as Peter and Carol Z. Stearns or William Reddy and Barbara Rosenwein – mainly read manuals, literature (fiction and advice literature), legal documents, and orders and, step by step, based their research on new sources such as ego documents (letters, memoirs, autobiographies, chronicles, entries in books and Bible).[10] Material culture has only recently begun to be considered as a subject in the study of emotions. A few examples of material culture are gravestones, their inscriptions, and how and where they are placed; paintings; toys; pieces of fabric;[11] presents; and assignments from testaments.[12]

Fourthly, the study and research of the history of emotions always deals with temporalities and timelines. Elizabeth Freeman has convincingly underlined the importance of acknowledging the significance of different, conflicting, and affirmative time regimes according to age, gender, and social and cultural origin.[13] In her study on emotions of the nineteenth and twentieth centuries, emotions emerge as the potential extra resource in surmounting – what she calls – chrononormativity.[14] With regard to this volume, it is important to be aware of temporalities as culturally and socially constructed and at the same time bound to normative regimes intended to incorporate the human body into historically and culturally specific logics of productivity such as work, and reproductivity such as giving birth and raising children. Investigating how emotions played out in cultural encounters, therefore, also means to place and understand them in their respective temporal implications. In the example given by Mernissi, two conflicting temporalities could be named as the supposed ahistorical, anthropomorphic notion of a harem: one as a static space of erotic services on the "Western side", and the other as a place of birth, of socialization and as starting point into a professional career outside it, pointing to its temporal progressiveness.

Thus, all these examples from both history and historiography lead to the following conclusion: from a historical point of view, emotions and identity-building practices among human beings of all kinds – among members of homogenous religious, social or gender groups, and among representatives of different levels even in competing hierarchies (i.e. the Indian Moghul and the Queen of England) – were, and are, inseparably interconnected. In 1641, René Descartes spoke the following groundbreaking words, "Cogito, ergo sum", which were to become emblematic for modern enlightened philosophy; however, Western identity politics today can be summarized in the following sentence: "Sentio, ergo sum". For the purpose of this book, we suggest to not make this into a question of "either – or" but to take these two statements as possible extremes in the field of emotions and identity-building in cultural encounters. However, the underlying concept is not one of linear time but – in the sense of Reinhart Koselleck – one that values the *Gleichzeitigkeit des Ungleichzeitigen*, the "Cogito" and the "Sensio" as equal options within and across cultures.

Emotions and cultural encounters: historiography

The volume presents case studies within a period of history (1100–1800) which saw a vast expansion of cultural movement through travel, trade and exploration, migration, mercantile and missionary activities, and colonial ventures. From pilgrimage routes to slave routes, European culture was on the move and opened up to incomers, bringing people, goods, and material objects from different backgrounds into close contact, often for the first time. Individuals and societies had unprecedented opportunities for new forms of cultural encounter and conflict. The contributions of this volume are concerned with the role emotions played in this varied history. They furthermore seek to understand the role of emotions for the negotiation of identity in processes and situations of cultural contact.

This endeavour is firmly grounded in recent developments in the history of emotions and profits from methodological advances in this field. As mentioned above, the history of emotions has successfully challenged the idea of emotions being a timeless and natural feature of human protagonists. Emotions, much like beliefs, have consequently emerged as historically changing and culturally contingent.[15] And yet historical actors have always relied on emotions as a way to express oneself to others. Instead of taking these expressions at face value, however, the methodology of the history of emotions allows historians to explore their dynamics and functions in communicative settings.[16] The attribution and the portrayal of emotions can thus be understood as a means to establish, to ascertain, and to communicate identities. This was especially relevant during the period under study, since any kind of cultural encounter potentially entailed a questioning of customary beliefs and a challenge to established identities. In recognizing emotions as a means of communication and exploring their meaning in a methodological approach that prioritizes social practices and performances over norms and rules, this volume aims at a deeper understanding of the dynamics in cultural contact in the medieval and early modern societies. The pathway that most contributions in this volume follow leads from European territories to colonial settings and thus looks at the situation from a double-bind point of view. It is especially this field of rearranging complex historical settings as they connect to questions of "Europeanness"[17] and its constituents in situations of cultural encounter (and situations of cultural mingling) that has recently challenged historiography and the layout of historical and epistemological points of departure. The contributors in this book claim that emotions are fundamental, first, to detangle the complexities that came with colonial settings and cultural encounters and/or cultural minglings, and, secondly, to regain intellectual spaces for rearranging agency within the historical setting. In doing so, the edited volume brings together two major areas in contemporary humanities: the study of how emotions were understood, expressed, and performed in shaping premodern transcultural relations and identities, both by individuals and by larger groups and communities; and the study of premodern cultural movements, contacts, exchanges, and understandings as emotionally charged processes.

Although the field of the history of emotions is constantly growing, research has only started to investigate the role that emotions played for individuals, groups, and/or different ethnicities in cultural encounters.[18] Religion has provided one of the most important overarching frameworks for perceiving and enacting cultural encounters and processes of emotional appropriation. And yet, overwhelmingly, research has focused on missions and missionaries. Jacqueline Van Gent, for instance, has stressed the relevance of emotions for conversion narratives and the emotional practices of converts in global encounters.[19] Rather than a simple display of inner turmoil, Van Gent, together with Spencer Young, has, in fact, argued that emotions occupy a central place in shaping encounters and changing doctrinal beliefs as well as religious practices.

Violent and hierarchically organized encounters framed as religious encounters have attracted the most interest, in particular from Western scholars of the history of emotion. In this respect, Van Gent's various explorations have also shown the difficulties that came with deviant notions of spirituality and Christianity. What has been considered a success by a missionary might have been a functional adaptation to an imposed regime of accessibility to resources and communities, thus communities constituted by outwardly shared emotional practices by those who were to be converted.[20] Such an approach, however, ignores indigenous people and their bodies, minds and hearts.[21] The documentation of indigenous conversion, historians of missionary movements argue, offers important insights into the ways such communities and their individuals' identities are formed and negotiated.[22] Such processes had allegedly been particularly visible in the public display and the ceremonial rites of conversion. Francois Soyer has demonstrated that the violently enforced public baptisms of Muslims and Jews in Spain and Portugal during Inquisition was intended to provoke and shape the emotional responses of the old and new Christian audience, thereby forging "a sense of collective identity based upon emotional norms".[23]

Such forced encounters often did not, however, remain restricted to the religious sphere, but routinely extended to other forms of identity such as family, gender, class or ethnic descent.[24] In many instances, moreover, they were intrinsically connected to seemingly secular agendas, as Susan Broomhall's work on the Dutch East India Company's encounters with the South Lands and its stance on conversion attests. For the VOC, for instance, religious ideas were closely connected to social, political and economic motives.[25] Religious encounters thus offer an important way of addressing the questions of community and identity in global encounters during the period under study, even if, as Robin MacDonald has argued, the study of such encounters remains "challenging" because of the methodological difficulties and the "complexity, as well as the fluidity, of spiritual identities in the medieval and early modern world".[26]

If important work has been done on the role of emotions in religious encounters, there is currently less work on other kinds of encounters.[27] Therefore, postcolonial studies such as a recent description of cross-cultural violence in Dutch-Amerindian encounters, a study of European-Oceanic encounters, the accounts of imperial exploration in late eighteenth-century Pacific and a recent monograph of the emotional aspects of the encounter between the Spanish and indigenous peoples of Mesoamerica are thus particularly valuable.[28] A question that comes to the fore immediately is how to investigate emotions in all kinds of encounters and how to make sense of their significance if they are not explicitly mentioned.[29] From a conceptual point of view, a chapter by Nicholas Dean Broadie offers helpful guidance both on the crucial importance of emotion in such encounters and, again, the methodological difficulties in making sense of their role. Broadie stresses the ambiguity of emotional responses in maritime encounters of Europeans with other non-European cultures. More importantly, however, Broadie argues that emotions are not merely a reaction to what is encountered, but very often can and must be attributed a "causal" role in determining "the nature and outcome of encounters for all sides". "Emotion itself", he contends, "thereby becomes an element of the maritime encounter that, like text and transmission, is worth examining for a fuller understanding of events and their narration". Though it was only a handful of representatives of any given European or non-European culture that partook in the encounter, Broadie suggests that such contact offered sites for "emotional introspection on a wide cultural scale", with the emotional community on board the ship potentially representing the emotional community of a nation and an empire. For the participants as well as the recipients of the original events, there was thus more at stake in the encounter "than the events of any given beach".[30] The study of emotions in such encounters thus gives new meaning and new perspectives to well-established stories and, perhaps more importantly, shows the necessity to question "well-worn assumptions about European exploration as a predominantly 'rational' and 'intellectual' enterprise", as Maria Nugent has put it.[31] Different notions and practices of temporalities and gender prove meaningful strands into histories of emotional and cultural entanglements that enable historians, both of global history and the history of emotions, to find out more about what Homi Bhabha has termed the "third space".[32] Nadine Amsler's study on Jesuit missionaries and domestic religious communities in early modern China is one such example. "A focus on gender relations", she argues, "has the potential to add a new perspective". Next to cultural and social differences, her book shows that "the ways societies imagined and practiced differences between the sexes" was just as important for local forms of religion. More relevant still for the context of this volume is that such an approach often helps bringing neglected groups into sharper focus. In Amsler's case: the non-European and the female that were "frequently less visible in the dominant European discourse."[33] Elizabeth A. Povinelli's book *The Empire of Love* is another such example as it thematizes the intricate connections made between temporal and emotional orders that enhanced patterns of domination and resistance. The

> attempt to provide some preliminary flesh to an intuition about how a set of ethical and normative claims about the governance of love, sociality, and the body circulate in *liberal settler colonies* in such a way that life and death, rights and recognition, goods and resources are unevenly distributed there,

opens up a whole new agenda of where investigations as the ones presented in this book could lead to in future research.[34]

A similar contention is also at the heart of a recently published edited volume focusing on "Encounters with Emotions". In a wide chronological and geographical framework, spanning from the seventeenth century to the present and encompassing regions in Europe, Asia, and the Pacific, the volume approaches the subject of cultural encounters and the mediating role of emotions from the point of view of individual social groups such as diplomats, missionaries, or travellers, and aims to explore the social, cultural, and political repercussions of such encounters. Much like the present volume, the collection by Gammerl, Nielsen, and Pernau starts from the observation that the history of emotions and the research on cross-cultural encounters have so far received too little attention. Unlike many other approaches in the history of emotions, the volume and its contributions do so by integrating perspectives on the history of the body. Moreover, investigating the significance of emotions in human interaction and assuming its historical and cultural flexibility in situations and processes of cultural encounter, appropriation, suppression, and mingling are inclined to, in the best case, enable historians "to scrutinize in greater detail how feelings impacted the very production and the shifting organization of cultural differences".[35]

What these first explorations into the role of emotions in cultural encounters perhaps most clearly show is that the history of emotions has as much to tell us about the way in which mobility and cultural encounter was conceived as about the process through which it was enacted. The present collection thus operates on the crucial contention that emotions were not merely off-shoots in a premodern global history, but were essential tools to establish inner and outer certainty, perhaps reliability also in a non-verbal dimension, in times of growing uncertainty – just as in present times. According to Nicholas Dean Brodie, they are considered "causal" factors rather than merely "reactive" phenomena. In doing so, however, the volume does not confine itself to religious encounters but seeks to deepen the history of cross-cultural encounters beyond the seventeenth century. The volume, moreover, adopts a particularly wide outlook as to the potential sources for the study of emotions in cultural encounters. Unlike traditional accounts, in which one particular set of sources such as self-narratives has taken centre stage, this volume seeks to integrate and interrelate a wide variety of sources.[36] In order to analyse emotional practices, identity-building and representations as part of cultural encounters that extended beyond the pragmatic process of establishing and defining intercultural communications, we think it is crucial to read emotions from different perspectives and materials at the same time and regarding a specific setting to be researched, that is, the Dutch-Amerindian trade and others.[37] Therefore, the different authors draw on a broad range of disciplinary and cross-disciplinary expertise in addressing the history of emotions in relation to cultural movement, exchange, contact and changing interrelations in the late medieval and early modern periods. Such encounters took place within a context of beliefs – popular, religious, and scientific – that were propagated in literary, historical, material, and visual sources, with a heritage reaching back to the classical period, and with a long religious and/or spiritual tradition. Literary works (travel narratives, histories, epics, romances, hagiography), letters, material culture, and visual artefacts were highly important in forming the emotional character of cross-cultural contacts, and the nature of literary, visual, and performance culture. They responded to new cultural influences and created the emotional habits and practices through which cultural understandings were received and interpreted. In studying these emotional representations of cross-cultural encounters, the exceedingly wide range of possible responses and coping mechanisms will, hopefully, come to the fore.

Emotions and cultural encounters: methodology

In keeping with the aforementioned research into the role of emotions and cultural encounters, the volume follows the recent praxeological trend in the field. Unlike other, more lexical explorations into the history of emotions, it does not stop at the language of emotions as expressed in societal norms and rules of conduct to study their role in cross-cultural encounters, but aims to study the "doing" of emotions and their performance as crucial elements in the negotiation of communal and individual identities.[38] But although there is certainly no lack of discussion on the methodology of emotions in more general terms, appropriations for the field of cross-cultural encounters are much rarer: "Only recently have there been efforts to theorize the work of emotion and affect within cross-cultural relations in the context of expanding European exploration".[39] As is generally the case for the entire field, however, the popular concepts by Barbara Rosenwein and Monique Scheer have received great attention, and there have been several attempts at enabling the study of cross-cultural emotional encounters from these vantage points.

Barbara Rosenwein's idea of emotional communities revolves around the observation that emotions, and more specifically their modes of expression, are usually shared within a wider group of people and often meant to establish that very group in the first place. These need not be entire cultural formations, but can extend to much smaller units such as the family or urban or monastic communities. In her own words, emotional communities "are groups – usually but not always social groups – that have their own particular values, modes of feeling, and ways to express those feelings". Thus, they "share important norms concerning the emotions that they value and deplore and the modes of expressing them".[40] Rosenwein's concept has subsequently gained much attention, and though occasionally criticized for being centred on norms and thus relatively static elements of social formations, it remains one of the most quoted concepts in the history of emotions.[41] Perhaps unsurprisingly given that this was the empirical context of its original formulation, this has made it particularly relevant to the study of religious communities. Exemplified by Susan Karant-Nunn for the reformation period, this also applies to religious communities in the context of religious encounters.[42] The religious community of the Moravians, for instance, has been described "as a utopian emotional community where identities are created in daily practice and in epistolary exchanges across the Atlantic".[43] In the context of trading companies, too, the concept has been convincingly employed. Susan Broomhall, in particular, has tried to make sense of modes of feeling and their ritualized expression within the context of the Dutch East India Company and its often violent endeavours by considering the company an imagined emotional community.[44] From here, questions can be asked such as the following: how did the actual encounter with groups and individuals who did not genuinely belong to that community challenge the emotional patterns, regimes, and practices within the community and how did these experiences in turn change the community?

The idea of emotional communities alone has not fully satisfied scholars working in the field. Building on both Rosenwein and Benedict Anderson's *Imagined Communities* addressing modern societies and processes of globalization, the concept has been further developed. Going beyond the somewhat static original concept of Rosenwein, Monique Scheer explores the role of emotions in actively creating and negotiating identity across social and emotional communities. To understand emotions as part of a process and as a tool of power has become the basis of respective research ever since. Stressing their inherently "performative power and their potential ability to contribute to, or even trigger, the creation of communities", links emotions to the shape and the very existence of not just emotional, but also social, communities.[45] Belonging as well as identity has never been and is not static. Especially in situations of encounter with the alleged other, emotions and emotional regimes are subject to processes of adaptation and negotiation. Emotions, in this view, are an important vehicle of such processes. They "do" things.[46]

Such reconsideration is potentially wider and more apt to enhance an understanding of emotional ambiguity and instability in that it allows for emotional practices as a factor in such situations. These emotional practices have been theorized in various forms, whether in the concept of "emotionology" or in the idea of "emotives", and are turn modelled on Austin's idea of the speech act.[47] Perhaps most prominent in recent years, however, has been Monique Scheer's formulation of emotions as social practices.[48] Based on the sociology of Pierre Bourdieu and his concept of the habitus, Scheer has argued for an understanding of emotions as part of the self that is continuously enacted not only by what one says but also by what one does. It thus extends beyond speech acts and fully encompasses the body and its expressions. She conceptualizes emotions not as an effect of what people did and do, but as themselves a form of practice. Most importantly, perhaps, Scheer argues that the "feeling subject is not prior to but emerges in the doing of emotion".[49] Next to firmly historicizing emotions beyond the more static realm of societal rules and norms, this approach also allows for a wider set of sources for the history of emotions beyond written texts. More immediately relevant for the present discussion, however, is the fact that such an approach allows for a study of identity as being continually enacted and negotiated in the "doing" of emotions rather than merely expressed in emotional language. Rather than being able to describe the formation and negotiation of identity with emotion words in hindsight, in other words, this process actively involves emotions in the form of emotional practices. Unsurprisingly, this concept has been instructive for many scholars and has also resonated in the field of cultural encounters. "Understanding emotions 'as a kind of practice' allows for the exploration of cultural and historical practices that shaped emotions in diverse locales" by providing a tool to study something that was "constantly in flux".[50]

Despite the variety of approaches, contextual framing, geographical area, and time period, the contributors in the present volume are interested in the ways that emotions (understood to be encapsulated in a variety of practices, materials, performances and discourses) are instrumental in negotiating and performing premodern cultural encounters. More precisely, they share a number of key questions which concern, firstly, the observation that cultural encounters led to emotional responses on behalf of those that were exposed to new, often unknown and unexpected, cultural and emotional regimes. Secondly, emotions were at times instrumental in absorbing and mediating those encounters. Thus, the contributors are interested in the way (and if) emotions helped to negotiate, perform, and structure cross-cultural encounters. Thirdly, the contributors are interested in whether these encounters prompted responses in different forms of writing, and if so, how they were enshrined in different forms of objects and necessitated distinct forms of narratives. We ask what genres were used in what ways to negotiate the confrontation between deviant emotional regimes connected to distinct cultural contexts. And eventually, the aspect of "identity" and its correspondence to emotional practices is central to this volume. The authors of *Matters of Engagement* reflect on how the negotiation, experience, and performance of emotions contributed to the volatile and indeed situational process of constructing identities in the face of encounters with people, materials, and practices that were new, often frightening, producing and increasing a sense of uncertainty and unsettledness. Emotions could, for instance, also be understood to minimize differences since they offer creative modes of interaction and, at best, mutual comprehension. Ultimately, it is our contention that these questions have theoretical and methodological implications for the study of cultural encounters as well as the history of emotions. Organized around the primary sources on which they are based, all the essays focus on comparable questions, namely, the performativity and negotiation of identity in situations of cultural contact with a particular emphasis on emotional practices and capacities of understanding.

Notes

1 Kwame Anthony Appiah, *The Lies that Bind. Rethinking Identity* (New York: Liveright, 2018), 189–190.
2 Homi K. Bhabha, *The Location of Culture* (London/New York: Routledge, 1994), especially his chapter on: Articulating the archaic: Cultural difference and colonial nonsense.
3 Norbert Elias, *The Civilizing Process. Vol 1: History of Manners* (Oxford: Blackwell, 1969).
4 Lucien Febvre, 'Sensibility and History: How to Reconstitute the Emotional Life of the Past', in *A New Kind of History: From the Writings of Febvre*, ed. Peter Burke, trans. K. Folca (New York: Routledge, 1973), 12–26.
5 Shame, Anger, Fear, Joy, Disgust, Sadness, Surprise, Disdain/Contempt. See Paul Ekman, 'Universals and Cultural Differences in Facial Expressions of Emotion', in

Nebraska Symposium on Motivation, ed. James K. Cole (Lincoln: University of Nebraska Press, 1972), 207–282.
6 A sound critique has recently been formulated by Christian von Scheve, Anna Lea Berg, Meike Haken and Nur Yasemin Ural (eds.), *Affect and Emotion in Multireligious Secular Societies* (London/New York: Routledge 2020).
7 Fatima Mernissi, 'Scheherazade goes West: Different Cultures, Different Harems', in *Emotions. A Cultural Studies Reader*, eds. Jennifer Harding and E. Deirdre Pribram (London/New York: Routledge, 2009), 365–374.
8 Mernissi, 'Schherazade goes West', 365.
9 Claudia Jarzebowski, 'Lieben und Herrschen. Fürstenerziehung im späten 15. und 16. Jahrhundert', *Saeculum. Jahrbuch für Universalgeschichte* 61 (2011), 39–56.
10 An important effort in this regard has been made by the Centre of Excellence for the History of Emotions, 1100–1800, by which the conference preceding this volume has been intellectually and financially enabled.
11 John Styles (ed.), *Threads of Feeling. The London Foundling Hospital's Textile Tokens, 1740–1770* (London: The Foundling Museum, 2010).
12 Anna Moran and Sorcha O'Brian, *Love Objects. Emotion, Design and Material Culture* (London et al: Bloomsbury, 2014); O. Harris and T. Sørensen, 'Rethinking Emotion and Material Culture', *Archaeological Dialogues* 17.2 (2010), 145–163.
13 Elizabeth Freeman, *Time Binds. Queer Temporalities, Queer Histories* (Durham, NC: Duke University Press, 2010).
14 Freeman, *Time Binds*, 3.
15 Particularly instructive are the recent overviews by Barbara Rosenwein, *Generations of Feeling: A History of Emotions, 600–1700* (Cambridge: Cambridge University Press, 2016); Susan Broomhall (ed.), *Early Modern Emotions: An Introduction* (London/New York: Routledge, 2017); Damien Boquet, Piroska Nagy, *Medieval Sensibilities: A History of Emotions in the Middle Ages* (Cambridge: Polity Press, 2018).
16 Jan Plamper, *The History of Emotions: An Introduction* (Oxford: Oxford University Press, 2017).
17 Ann Laura Stoler, 'A Sentimental Education. Native Servants and the Cultivation of European Children in the Netherlands's Indies', in *Fantasizing the Feminine in Indonesia*, ed. Laurie J. Sears (Durham, NC/London: Duke University Press, 1996), 71–92, at 72–73.
18 See S. Broomhall and A. Lynch (eds.) *The Routledge History of Emotions in Europe, 1100–1700* (London: Routledge, 2020).
19 Jacqueline Van Gent, 'Sarah and Her Sisters: Letters, Emotions, and Colonial Identities in the Early Modern Atlantic World', *Journal of Religious History* 38.1 (2014), 71–90; Jacqueline Van Gent, 'The Burden of Love: Moravian Conversions and Emotions in Eighteenth-Century Labrador', *Journal of Religious History* 39.4 (2015), 557–574; Jacqueline Van Gent, 'Moravian Memoirs and the Emotional Salience of Conversion Rituals', in *Emotion, Ritual and Power in Europe, 1200–1920*, eds. M.L. Bailey and K. Barclay (Basingstoke: Palgrave Macmillan, 2017), 241–260. On emotions and religious encounters, see also C. McLisky, D. Midena and K. Vallgårda (eds.), *Emotions and Christian Missions: Historical Perspectives* (London: Palgrave Macmillan, 2015).
20 See also Robin MacDonald, 'Christian Missions and Global Encounters', in *The Routledge History of Emotions in Europe, 1100–1700*, eds. Susan Broomhall and Andrew Lynch (London: Routledge, 2020), 320–334.
21 Emma Anderson, *Betrayal of Faith: The Tragic Journey of a Colonial Native Convert* (Cambridge, MA: Harvard University Press, 2007).
22 Jacqueline Van Gent and Spencer E. Young, 'Introduction: Emotions and Conversion', *Journal of Religious History* 39.4 (2015), 461–467.
23 Francois Soyer, 'The Public Baptism of Muslim in Early Modern Spain and Portugal: Forging Communal Identity through Collective Emotional Display', *Journal of Religious History* 39.4 (2015), 506–523, at 509.

24 Van Gent, Young, 'Introduction.'
25 Susan Broomhall, '"Quite Indifferent to These Things": The Role of Emotions and Conversion in the Dutch East India Company's Interactions with the South Lands', *Journal of Religious History* 39.4 (2015), 524–544.
26 Robin MacDonald, 'Christian Missions and Global Encounters', in *The Routledge History of Emotions in Europe, 1100–1700*, eds. Susan Broomhall and Andrew Lynch (London: Routledge, 2020), 320-334.
27 See the short essays by Donna Merwick, 'Colonialism' and Maria Nugent, 'Indigenous/European Encounters', in *Early Modern Emotions: An Introduction*, ed. Susan Broomhall (London/New York: Routledge, 2017), 316–320 and 323–326.
28 Donna Merwick, *The Shame and the Sorrow: Dutch-Amerindian Encounters in New Netherland* (Princeton, NJ: Princeton University Press, 2006); Vanessa Smith, *Intimate Strangers: Friendship, Exchange and Pacific Encounters* (Cambridge: Cambridge University Press, 2010); Manuel Kohlert, *Ideale Balance: Die politische Ökonomie der Emotionen während der spanischen Expansion* (Frankfurt/Main: Campus, 2019).
29 Nicholas Dean Brodie gives interesting examples from maritime encounters: 'Maritime Encounters and Global History', in *The Routledge History of Emotions in Europe, 1100–1700*, eds. Susan Broomhall and Andrew Lynch (London: Routledge, 2020), 335–350.
30 Brodie, 'Maritime Encounters and Global History.'
31 Maria Nugent, 'Indigenous/European Encounters', in *Early Modern Emotions: An Introduction*, ed. Susan Broomhall (London/New York: Routledge, 2017), 323–326, at 323.
32 Bhabha, *Location of Culture*.
33 Nadine Amsler, *Jesuits and Matriarchs. Domestic Worship in Early Modern China* (Seattle: University of Washington Press, 2018), 155. In her study, Amsler not only reverses the perspective on missionary efforts from the missionary agents to those intended to become proselytized but also from the male dominance to female agency.
34 Elizabeth A. Povinelli, *Empire of Love. Towards a Theory of Intimacy, Genealogy, and Carnality* (Durham, NC: Duke University Press, 2006), 3.
35 Benno Gammerl, Philipp Nielsen, Margrit Pernau, 'Introduction: Encountering Feelings – Feeling Encounters', in *Encounters with Emotions: Negotiating Cultural Differences since Early Modernity*, eds. Benno Gammerl, Philipp Nielsen and Margrit Pernau (New York: Berghahn, 2019), 1–35.
36 Angelika Schaser, Claudia Ulbrich and Hans Medick (eds.), *Selbstzeugnis und Person. Transkulturelle Perspektiven* (Wien/Weimar/Cologne: Böhlau, 2012).
37 Donna Merwick, *The Shame and the Sorrow: Dutch-Amerindian Encounters in New Netherland* (Princeton, NJ: Princeton University Press, 2006); Linda Colley, *The Ordeal of Elizabeth Marsh: A Woman in World History* (London: Harper, 2007).
38 For a thorough discussion of methodological trends, see Plamper, *History of Emotions* as well as the methodological section in Broomhall, *Early Modern Emotions*, 1–30. Still helpful is Bettina Hitzer's overview from 2011: 'Emotionsgeschichte - ein Anfang mit Folgen. Forschungsbericht', in http://hsozkult.geschichte.hu-berlin.de/forum/2011-11-001.pdf (published: 23.11.2011). See also the 2010 essay by Barbara Rosenwein, 'Problems and Methods in the History of Emotions', *Passions in Context: Journal of the History and Philosophy of the Emotions* 1.1 (2010): 1–32. A more lexical approach is, for instance, represented by Ute Frevert et al., *Emotional Lexicons: Continuity and Change in the Vocabulary of Feeling 1700–2000* (Oxford: Oxford University Press, 2014).
39 See Nugent, 'Indigenous/European Encounters', 323. This sentiment is also reflected by other authors in the section on "The World Beyond Europe", 304–326.
40 Rosenwein, *Generations of Feeling*, 3. For earlier formulations of the same idea, see also Barbara Rosenwein, *Emotional Communities in the Early Middle Ages* (Ithaca, NY: Cornell University Press, 2006) and Rosenwein, 'Problems and Methods'.
41 Andrew Lynch, 'Emotional Community', in *Early Modern Emotions: An Introduction*, ed. Susan Broomhall (London/New York, Routledge, 2017), 3–6.

42 Susan Karant-Nunn, *The Reformation of Feeling: Shaping the Religious Emotions in Early Modern Germany* (Oxford: Oxford University Press, 2010).
43 Gent, 'Sarah and Her Sisters', 75.
44 Susan Broomhall, 'Shipwrecks, Sorrow, Shame, and the Great Southland: The Use of Emotions in Seventeenth-Century Dutch East India Company Communicative Ritual', in *Emotion, Ritual and Power in Europe, 1200–1900: Family, State and Church*, eds. M. L. Bailey and K. Barclay (Houndmills: Palgrave, 2016), 83–102.
45 Margrit Pernau, 'Feeling Communities: Introduction', *The Indian Economic and Social History Review* 54.1 (2017), 1–20, at 10.
46 Monique Scheer, 'Are Emotions a Kind of Practice (and Is That What Makes Them Have a History?) A Bourdieuian Approach to Understanding Emotion', *History and Theory* 51.2 (2012), 193–220.
47 Peter Stearns and Carol Stearns, 'Emotionology: Clarifying the History of Emotions and Emotional Standards', *American Historical Review* 90.4 (1985), 813–836; William Reddy, *The Navigation of Feeling: A Framework for the History of Emotions* (Cambridge: Cambridge University Press, 2001).
48 Scheer, 'Are Emotions a Kind of Practice'.
49 Scheer, 'Are Emotions a Kind of Practice', 220.
50 MacDonald, 'Christian Missions and Global Encounters'.

PART I
Letters

2

BRIDGING THE GAP

Techniques of appresentation and familiar(izing) narratives in eighteenth-century transmaritime family correspondence

Christina Beckers

Family in remote – identifying the gap(s)

In 1755, one Mr. Kello writes home from Southampton, Virginia, to his brother in London:

> Dear brother [...] I've a thousand adventures to tell you of [...] but [fear I must disappoint] you as I've lately had a very bad fever and cannot write my hand shakes so bad this is [what] is called a seasoning - [...] you must stay a little longer for particulars of that sort tho' I know thou has a natural curiosity to all at new [...][1]

In the following, Kello spreads news about relatives in Virginia, asks for commodities, and inquires about family and friends at home. Apparently, the history of his passage from London to Virginia as well as descriptions of a supposedly unfamiliar environment and people remains untold. Why would Kello ignore his brother's "natural curiosity to all new" – a curiosity one anticipates and sympathizes with, given the circumstances? While his family – and most of his friends – stayed in London, Kello set out to an overseas colony at war.[2] Even if one was not to expect the urge of the traveler to share his experiences and potential encounters with everything unknown with his own peer community, trying to integrate his experiences into accustomed schemes of knowledge and interpretation of the world, Kello himself generates and supports this expectation when he mentions "a thousand adventures to tell."[3]

J.C. Metzendorff gives a fine example of such a narration. On his journey from Copenhagen to the Cape of Good Hope and Tranquebar in 1777/1778, he reports to his parents and friends

> "[...] Auch giebt es unter der Linie weder giftige Nebel noch giftigen Regen, wie einige Lügenhafte Reisebeschreiber versichern, wenigstens habe

ich davon keines auf der See angetroffen"[4] and "[...] Ich habe nun tausend schöne Sachen gesehen, als: Die Orcadischen Inseln, die Insel Madeira, den Pico von Tennerifa und Palma, Gomera und Ferro. Bonitos, Albicoren, fliegende Fische, Heyen, Wallfische, Meerschweine, tropische Vögel und was dem mehr ist. Ich bin beyde Wendezirkel und die Linie paßiert, und stehe nun auf dem Vorgebürge der Hoffnung, werde den Tafelberg besteigen, und das große Indianische Meer zur linken und den Ozean zur rechten haben – ist das nicht beneidenswerth?"[5]

This excitement for the unfamiliar, or rather exotic, is also vibrant, when soldiers on overseas duty promise to "[...] bring [...] sum fine things home, sum yankey things,"[6] or having "[...] a fin Parot for Dock Geans family if Ever my I leve [live] to Come to Ingland [England] and it to."[7]

Against this background, it is striking to the reader of the twenty-first century how these examples of narrating unusual encounters (from a European perspective) stick to "home" and "family and relations left behind" as major points of reference; accordingly, the unfamiliar is repressed and reduced to the niche of being a souvenir or travel excitement, eventually limited to accounts of wartime events, rather than allowing for encounters to challenge given understandings and interpretations. Metzendorff's travel account and William Hodgeon's and George Brown's promises to bring souvenirs are all directed toward a return (i.e. Metzendorff: "So Gott will bin ich über 2 Jahre von heute schon wieder längst bei Ihnen. Wir werden uns spuden so viel wir können, den ein jeder wünscht sich wieder nach Europa."[8]). Connecting a variety of people who had left their homes for varying reasons, heading toward an uncertain future in new worlds, to their regions of origin, and vice versa, their letters seem rather cursory. Despite the constant threat of the next war to shake the (trans)colonial world or even during factual wartime, most letters are no more than brief notes, composed of standard phrasings, asking for money. Reports from these new – or at least other – worlds appear rather limited. On the contrary, letters seem to concentrate on the (re)establishment of a shared space to (re)enact and negotiate personal relations somewhere in between and aim at intertwining the old world and the new, creating a space referred to in research as the "epistolary space," established by more or less frequent correspondence.[9] This space, then, "[...] defines the boundaries, either imagined or actual, of [a culture's] communicative space."[10] These boundaries, I would suppose, not only refer to a divide of people with or without access to this communicative space, but they also limit what is speakable and unspeakable within this space. The narrative dimensions of the unfamiliar would then be determined by the underlying meanings and needs of the shared "epistolary space."

Considering the material and physical space letters provided, it was obviously limited to one or maybe a couple of folios[11]; the time span between writing and delivery varied from a couple of weeks to some years, constantly facing the threat of miscarriage, altogether a rather precarious "time-space" to act "familiar" and to practice a (family) life *in words* which otherwise relied on a shared and contested framework of names, fortunes, believes, and participation in, as well as mutual observation of, quarrel, care, business affairs, and even bodily expressions – in other words, daily practices and routines carried out in co-presence.[12] Bearing that in mind, it remains puzzling how interlocutors in such insecure and threatened settings managed to substitute the experience of daily life and community in conversations, more so, conversations restrained to the written word – pen and paper – even when one is to follow the understanding of letters and correspondence as "epistolary conversations."[13] Eventually, epistolary conversations in substitution for daily encounters necessitated what Ester Milne points out in her study on *Technologies of Presence*:

> The physical absence of one's epistolary partner provides both the impetus and the 'material' for a range of techniques, language uses and technological functioned aimed at creating an imagined sense of presence.[14]

It is the exploration of such techniques in eighteenth-century transmaritime correspondence between family members that forms one part of the theme running throughout this paper[15] – the manifestation of emotions and the part they had within such letters forms another. In contemporary debates – in general and in letter-writing manuals in particular – expressions of emotions and emotional behavior were evaluated according to their adequacy to individual status and appropriateness in (familiar) relations and considered to mark either authenticity or artificiality.[16] The question may then arise how expressions of emotions and emotional behavior in media of long-distance communication, predominantly in writing, worked on techniques of obtaining and retaining remote relationships. In this context, the use of language needs to be taken into account. As has been pointed out elsewhere, letters

> [...] grew in popularity at a time when qualities of 'spontaneity', 'authenticity' and 'self-expression' were highly valued: Because of the prevailing belief that letters expressed the natural 'inner' man – the 18th century found in the letter the most congenial form for what was human. In short, the letter offers the 18th century the promise to uncover the true nature of mankind by providing a privileged perspective from which man appeared at his most unaffected, and thus at his most authentic.[17]

Certainly, such understandings and perceptions of letters can be followed and will be recognized in the sources on which this article is based. However, a close case study of John Morris' love letter to Nancy from 1756 provides insights in how plagiarism – which could be read as lacking self-expression par excellence – may also be interpreted as courteous endeavor to build on traditional conventions and follow accustomed rules of courting rather than deny authenticity of feeling or ascribe it to lack of effort.

Morris' letter is one of a diverse set of correspondence stemming from the collection of the Prize Papers[18] – a collection of letters surviving only because they were sent across the ocean(s) separating Europe from the diverse overseas dominions. The common denominator of the sources showcased in the chapter was the author's long-term absence from a community she would consider and address as "family and friends."[19] However, duration and motivation for people to leave home and family differed and may well have influenced the position from which they were writing and engaging with the people they had left behind. In most cases, the writers were hoping for a return sooner or later in life, expecting only temporary absence from home. Yet, they were all facing an insecurity of when to return, with a fair chance not to return at all. For seamen like William Hodgeon, John Morris, and George Brown, but also indentured servants like Elizabeth Spriggs, their undertaking included to leave home without a distinct and certain idea if and when they were to return at all, and also without a distinct place of destination within the colonial world.

A little less uncertain of a reunion were people traveling for business reasons. However, business reasons, and in consequence types of travel, varied – merchants might settle down in the colonies temporarily to set up and run their own businesses like Graham Frank or Anne Butler in Virginia, 1756, or they would leave wife and children for shorter business obligations. Finally, enterprises might turn into permanent establishment as in the case of Sarah Rise in 1756, I.E. Roepete, né Paravincini, Edward Watts, and others, postponing a reunion to sometime "[…] in this World or the Next […]."[20]

J.C. Metzendorff seems to have been on an educational travel throughout the eighteenth-century transmaritime world when he wrote to his parents. Resembling the idea of the "grand tour,"[21] Metzendorff left his home in Hamburg to explore the world, most likely with his family's intention for him to return home matured, fit to take his place in the home business, society, and family.

Sarah Buckley's situation differed from the other examples chosen in my collection. She was well established at Newport during the American War of Independence; Sarah had a versatile record with mobility and migration. As wife of a seaman, she was familiar with long periods of separation; the community she lived in was composed of people of (different) European descent, and at the time of writing to her husband, she was facing the threat of evacuation due to acts of war.

Despite these different backgrounds, the authors of all letters had in common that they were facing unfamiliar encounters on a daily basis, at least in the framework of their correspondence with family and friends they had left behind. The letters in my study therefore constitute a space characterized by two worlds of daily experience separated from one another, written with the intention to connect them both. In the following, the techniques employed in this endeavor will be analyzed, with a particular interest on focusing on the integration of established family and relational practices and meanings with correspondence matters, particular techniques of appresentation,[22] implementation of emotions and emotional language therein,[23] and the dimension to which anything unfamiliar had a share within this epistolary space.

Bridging distances by techniques of appresentation

Sarah Buckley was separated from her husband in 1777 when the king's troops had taken over her hometown of Newport during the American War of Independence. By the time of her writing, her husband John Buckley, documented in different sources as having served as captain on several business missions,[24] had been away for almost one year and a half. The letter is addressed to a business woman in London to pass it over to John.[25] Sarah's few lines cover only one page, but include all matters of interest – in thematic as well as relational scope:

> My Paper and Time is Short but my Love is great. It is now 17 Months since I saw or heard from you, tho I saw a Gentlemen sometime ago, that saw you in April last and said you were well then, I wish I were so happy as to see you again tho this troublesome War makes me think I [moved hell] This Town was taken by the Kings Troups th 7th Day of December last, and there is nothing here now but Marshall Law [...] Mr Lopez is moved to Connecticut, This Town is Torne almost allto [poor] by the Kinds Troops Wood and provisions are very scarce and Dear hear, your Dear Mother Died last Spring. Your Little Daughter is Well mother and Sister send their Love
>
> Love to you, I hope you'll write to me as Soon as you Can and let me hear when I may be so happy as to see you again, I am my Dear Husband Your Pour loving and Obedient Wife.[26]

Her opening line, "My paper and time is Short but my Love is great," somehow puts the relational situation Sarah experiences into a nutshell. Paper and time available to her for writing are antithetical to the distance and time of absence separating her from her husband. But this deficiency is marked as being exactly contrary to the state of Sarah's emotions toward John. By pointing that out, her letter draws on, simultaneously reinsures, and gives materialized proof of the lasting and durable connection of love between husband and wife.[27] In its materiality, the letter works as token, explicitly and implicitly reflecting and covering perturbations in distance (the spatial aspect represented by the scarce paper in the process of writing, and the space between Newport and somewhere else, eventually London, which she seeks to cover with her "short paper") and time (little that she has at the time of writing, yet investing it to cover 17 months of absence).

Furthermore, her letter manages to convey all important news – the eyewitness report of an encounter between her husband and somebody she knows, the exile of the known businessman Aaron Lopez,[28] the king's troops invasion,[29] the death of her husband's mother, the well-being of daughter, sister, and mother-in-law – also as briefly as possible. While all of these news seem to be related in an arbitrary manner, Sarah's style of writing is based on two important matters: one, she lets her husband partake in her line of thoughts, writing as it comes to her mind, in a style considered to be "natural," authentic, and proving intimacy;[30] second, it is the intimacy and security within an already established (and confirmed) relationship between husband and wife that Sarah refers to and draws on. In this regard, the following letters of Rosette illustrate an exactly opposite situation and, in consequence, the status of a relationship influencing an author's writing. Rosette, an unknown woman writing in 1793 to her "cher pouble," is quite obviously insecure in their relationship, and therefore emphasizes her great affections, as well as her suffering.

> This last act will bring me death, how you, my love, want me not to be angry with you, the one I have loved so much. For you have acted like you did not want to live with me anymore. You wanted to punish me. At this point I ask nothing else than to see you [...] if you really loved me you have to have pity with me, have mercy for my sorrows. Goodby my lovely Pouble, if you want to prevail my healh, come tonight. I don't demand anything else, in God's name don't refuse to let me into your arms tonight. Your loving Rosette.[31]

In addition to feeling insecure, Rosette lacks the opportunity to draw and rely on her partner's obligations and responsibilities toward her.[32] Instead, it is her strong and vibrant emotions she must build on while promising not to put forward any expectations or liability. The agony Rosette expressed in this first letter did not fall on deaf ears (or blind eyes), since she must have received an answer. However, even in reaction to this answer, her affection itself needs to be elaborated and proved to be resilient and lasting. Rosette underscores the significance of the ongoing correspondence bringing "peace to her love," concurrently accentuating her emotion's honesty and endurance:

> You cannot imagine, my dear Pouble, the pleasure your charming letter caused to me. It brought peace to my love, for you told me to keep it safe for you. My sentiments remain, do not doubt me for an instant, for my love is lasting as never a man has been loved before.[33]

Obviously, Rosette's relationship with "Pouble" is young and fragile, and we do not know more about either him or her to judge the influence of their backgrounds on the use of affection in the negotiation of partnership, but one can see how Rosette expects her feelings to provoke reaction, rather than drawing on mutual responsibilities. Still, although Rosette overtly emphasizes her not demanding any obligations, by designing herself to be in an emotionally dependent position, she operates on notions of liability as they were traditionally ascribed to husband and wife – or men and women – but now extending from the level of physical well-being to affectionate and emotional integrity.[34] With regard to my initial questions, the letters by Sarah Buckley and Rosette give a first impression of how established meanings of relationships impacted a writer's potential to act – and act out emotions. It may seem surprising how little Sarah emphasizes her affection for her husband in contrast to Rosette's expressiveness toward a person she most likely was not too severely involved with. Considering contemporary understandings of love and devotion, as well as conventions of behavior, Sarah is acting on grounds of her established marriage. Rosette, on the other hand, may have tried to appeal to a chivalry and gallantry otherwise heavily debated already at her time.[35]

In consequence, as much as her love and affection for "Pouble" are in need of demonstration, Rosette also needs to point out how he is always present in her thoughts taking a position of her councilor and spouse:

> [...] your charming image is always in my eyes; I always talk about and to you whenever it seems approriate [...]. [36]

Rosette's relation of "Pouble's" continuous, yet imagined, presence is in varying ways strategically employed by many authors to create a sense of connectedness, or even to enact a shared experience, as in the case of Frederich Roux and his older sister "H." who are mutually addressing their brother Albert in a letter sent from Bordeaux in 1778. At first, Frederic sets out to tell his brother about the reason for writing, explaining that it was about time for him to decide

> For which profession should I fall? I have three to choose from, commerce, the navy, and plantations or sugar refineries. Certainly, I don't have much devotion for the first, for intellectual work kills me; the second, the navy, I like better, for one is to work more with the body than with the mind. [...][37]

After going on about his future plans, Frederich also brings up how others perceive him having grown; he asks Albert for advice, and even to set him up somewhere:

> My dear Albert, if you know which place suits me best? If it's at sea, or at land? I trust you will not forget your brother when an opportunity for a position occurs to you. [...][38]

After Frederich finishes, he literally passes the pen on to the sister, who then continues, and points out to the absent brother how well "little Frederich" behaves and has grown.

> My sister desires to write you a few lines as well, so I will leave the space for her to say what she has to say. Your good and affectionate brother Frederich Roux 1778
>
> [... change of hands – handing over of the pen – for the remaining 3 pages of the letter...]
>
> You can tell from Frederich's letter, my very dear brother, he behaves very well. He is grown very much, and he is honest – as you would favor him to be. [...][39]

As in the very first example of Sarah Buckley, the letter here works as material evidence of connection, but more than that, it provides a materially shared space (of writing) resulting in an opportunity for the absent brother to partake in and witness Frederic's development – the mutual sister accentuating and lending her eyes, or at least offering her eye-witness report, to Albert to observe what he cannot see from his brother's writing itself. Albert is thereby present – or apresented, that is, made present – in the situation, moment, and space of writing. Simultaneously (but asynchronically), Albert can imagine his own presence and observation of his brother behaving and writing based on his sister's report once he receives the letter.

The relational importance of such techniques and practices of apresentaion becomes obvious in Sarah Buckley's letter. Her already mentioned encounter with "[…] a Gentlemen sometime ago, that saw you in April last and said you were well then [….]" can also be read as technique of appresentation. Despite the shortness of her letter, it is of interest to Sarah to share this encounter with her husband – it not only lets him partake in her experience of relief and joy she most likely experienced during the encounter because she heard about his well-being, but the encounter also illustrates their worlds as belonging to one sphere of experience connected by people crossing boundaries between their absence and presence. Furthermore, in an era when relationship and community were not only an act of performance but also of being observable and observed by others, encounters like the one Sarah relates gave proof, formed part of, and even constituted being in a recognizable relationship.[40]

This entanglement or even union of spheres of experience through observation by others is vital in the correspondence of Graham Frank and Anne Butler. Reading their letters, we get a fine view of emotions at work in the negotiation of relationships, and vice versa. In the collection of letters, one is drawn into a family quarrel carried out via correspondence between York in Virginia, and Kirklington in Yorkshire and London. Writing protagonists are on the American side of the Atlantic: Anne Butler, Graham Frank – her former brother-in-law, and Anne Frank – Graham Frank's new wife. The letters are addressed to brother and sister (by Anne Butler), a cousin, a friend, the mother, and the Bishop of London (by Graham Frank), and the mother-in-law (by Anne Frank, Graham's new wife). In this plurivocal epistolary conversation, a quarrel over financial assets unfolds – within which the emotion of anger is quite vividly employed to negotiate relationships and interest – within the family.[41]

Anne Butler's letters to her brother and her sister introduce the situation:

> [...] F [Frank] says he was courted by my Father & sister to come into our Famaly that he has lost considerably by it & that he was obliged to take my Sisters Fortune & what he had of mine in mean good for nothing [...] yet for such scandeaolous Lies F is favoured with you while we are intirely neglected & cant obtain so much as a Linde from any Body. [...][42]

From what we learn, Graham Frank had been married to Anne Butler's sister. Upon this marriage, the couple had received a dowry of 100 L. After the death of his wife, Frank continued his correspondence and business relations with his former father-in-law, Anne Butler's father.

In the meantime, Anne had been married to some Mr. Butler – obviously without asking for or awaiting her father's consent. She blames Graham Frank for talking her into marrying without awaiting her father's and friends' approval due to the long distance between them. However, in a letter to her brother, Anne points out

> I am so unhappy as to write Letter after Letter yet cant obtain the least Favour From Hirklington. The Reason I don't know but I find it to no purpose to beg or [intreat] for an answer. That I have long done on vain. Tho I find not withstanding Fs behavior he still keeps up his correspondence with my Father & has Letters from him Freaquantly its not a Fortnight since I wrote to [Karklington] Give me lieve to Argue with you a little on this Subject. I marry'd without the consent of my Freinds ets true I confess.
>
> I was to blame in so doing. But I have not undervalued my Famaly or my self by what I have done in any respect. There was more than aprobability when every thing was Fairly represented to my Father he wou'd consent to it.

Though she does admit having violated familiar customs, she is self-confident enough to accuse her family of not entertaining further correspondence with her and her new husband, even demanding for her father's alliance and support:

> [...] After the Death of my Poor Sister [...] I should have thought his Alliance to our Famaly [...] in great measure removed & as my Father had a child [that would be herself, C.B.] living that was in the Country surely it would not be unreasonable for the Person She was married so to expect at least as much Favour as the other [...].[43]

Her argument is based on Frank's vile behavior. Both letters Anne drafts depict Frank as a

> "vile Fellow" who "[...]by his mean Arts & Hipocretical Lies has Robed me of my Friends"; a "deceitful monster [making] every person belonging to my Famaly flight & despise me."[44]

She appeals to her siblings' feeling for justice, when she

> [...] insists that you send me coppies of Fs Letters to my Father your self or any of my Brothers or Sisters.[45]

In her account of the events and circumstances, Anne seeks to put her own misbehavior of marrying without consent into perspective by emphasizing Frank's despicable character, and blames him of tarnishing her family's reputation:

> [...] He say ours is a mean Low lifed Famaly that no person in it was ever worth any thing [...] it was said in Publick Company the animal he has married was as good as his first Whife [...].[46]

In the entire dispute, Anne Butler seeks to employ her anger, justified by a claim of Frank's disloyalty, in order to discredit him, and consequently enhance her own position. Indispensable in this undertaking is the notion of honor on the one hand, and the momentum – or practice – of community within which gossip is spread. Considering the time it took letters to travel from Virginia to Europe, it is striking how effectively the spreading of gossip worked. In a letter to his mother, Graham Frank feels urged to refer to Anne Butler's letter, because he suggested that it had been taken notice of on both sides of the Atlantic. That means, it was passed around, or at least talked about its contents, prior to being sent. This "gossiping" within the realm of his remote world on the American side of the Atlantic was pressuring enough for Frank to make him feel the need to justify his choice of spouse[47]:

> For whilst I was courting her, I was informed by various People in Town, who had seen the Letter, that Mrs Butler had wrote to her Father that I was going to be married to Mr Nelson's Chamber Maid, without Beauty, Wit, Fortune, or any other Qualification to recommend her.[48]

The "people in town" who informed Frank of Anne Butler's letter are the most explicit mentioning of the new or other community Frank was part of. Frank taking notice and even feeling compelled to react to these rumors, to his mother on the other side of the Atlantic, illustrate, on the one hand, how communities were intertwined despite the distance between them. The absence of further narrations – which would have been at hand as Frank's letter to the Bishop of London indicates[49] – shows, on the other hand, the dethematization of anything *not* relating to community issues. This dethematization is not due to lack of time or space for writing, for Frank does take time and space to reply to Anne Butler's accusations:

> [...] I agree with Mrs Butler that she is not a Beaty, but yet, she is agreeable, & has Every useful Qualification to make the married State happy & as to the ornamental Part, you'll see into that by the Inclosed Letter wich she sends you.

and finally

> Where, as to Birth, she Equals Mrs Butler, & as to Fortune, she just doubles her. & I believe she's pretty near a Match for her in Every Endowment, both of Body & Mind.

On the other hand, the entire case illustrates the predicament families separated by long distance faced. Conventions and practices to entertain family (relations) necessitated the involvement of different members of different communities and of the family. Techniques to involve observers and commentators – to apresent them – were necessary and powerful tools in the negotiation of interests and relations. For Anne Butler, her conscious or unconscious ignorance of her family and friends as stake holders in her wedding plans quite obviously led to a weak position within the texture of family. Graham Frank, on the other hand, seeks to introduce his new wife into his family of origin despite the likelihood they would never actually meet.

The rules seemed to be different for men and women, as the case demonstrates. Anne Butler's "antagonist" in this feud, Graham Frank, obviously was in a comparable position to her. He had also taken a wife without his family's or friends' consent. But it is not clear whether it is the gender that makes the difference or the position from which Anne Butler and Graham Frank were arguing in the first place: while Anne Butler seems to be in the miserable situation of being in need of her family's support, blaming "that villain" Graham Frank for her miserable situation,[50] Frank is capable to almost ignore the issue entirely, mentioning the quarrel with Anne Butler only in the letter to his mother Ellen, as quoted earlier, and in the letter to his cousin Easter. He focuses on styling himself and his presence in America as a successful business matter, in which his marriage takes an essential part:

> On the breaking out of the War, I began to think that [...]; if I cou'd make my Life tolerably comfortable here; & I cou'd see no way so likely as getting a Wife. But that I might not be deprived of the greatest Happines I expect to Enjoy on this Side the Grave, I pict on One that has no Ties upon her to this Country, more than that it being her Native Place; & I believe will be as ready as my self to Embark for England, when all Circumstances Amits.[51]

And:

> But on the breaking out of the War, As I could not quit the Country Entirely, I then betook my self to a Wife. And that I might not be deprived of the Happiness at some Period of my Life, I have chosen one without any Attachments to this Country; & in the mean Time I hope I shall live in a more Eligible Manner than I have done since I parted with my Friends on your side of the Atlantic. [...][52]

In the very same context of people on both sides of the Atlantic, Graham Frank managed much better than Anne Butler to integrate his "new life" and "new wife" with the life, family, and friends whom he had left. Frank's letters do not show a comparable level of disconcertment as Anne Butler's letters, quite the contrary. In the aforementioned passage of the letter to his mother Ellen, despite the reference to the fact that he was anticipating Anne Butler's writings,

Graham concentrates on the advantages he gained by taking a new wife, blaming the circumstances, as well as emphasizing her nonexistent "Attachments to this Country." Proclaiming his intention of coming home before his death ("on this side of the Grave"), and demonstrating his knowledge of what was going on in the family, Frank emphasizes his active participation in his home community, additionally translating practices of common behavior into epistolary equivalents.

This translation of common practice into epistolary equivalents becomes most obvious in Frank's way of introducing his wife to family and friends. In the epistolary encounter with his mother, he does so by emphasizing Anne Frank's solid and dignified background and leaving it up to his mother to judge his wife's "ornamental part" from her own appearance and voice based on the content of the letter – "[…] the Inclosed Ltr wch she sends you. […]" – which he mentions in his letter. The letter was obviously crafted by Anne Frank, interacting with her mother-in-law "Mrs. Frank" for the first time:

> Hond. Madam. I make bold to write you a Letter which I hope will meet with a kind Acceptance tho from an Utter Stranger – For as I have Incread'd my Happiness by Marying your Worthy Son, I shall always think it my Duty to write to you & Likewise to serve you in any thing That lies in my Power […].[53]

The letter itself and the context provided by Graham Frank give a fine example of eighteenth-century letter writing, when manuals promoted letters as representing, or even impersonating, their authors.[54] Furthermore, the phrase "in my power" – as well as Anne's reference to her duty of writing to her mother-in-law – illustrates the empowering moment enabled by the medium of correspondence despite great distances.[55] Letters, it seems, allowed continuing familial practices, such as an introduction of a fiancée by bringing her home for the first time. Only in this setting, it is the letter as written "avatar"[56] taken home (led and directed by one's own "hand" in handwriting), put forward to be examined. In terms of emotionality, Anne Frank's case appears limited to conventions, and reserved. Still, Anne Frank makes use of expressions of emotions and emotional arousal. The letter follows the idea that the familial relations, or at least the relation between a daughter and mother-in-law was to be emotional, even when the addressee of such emotionality was an unknown, yet personally, related lady. Anne Frank is eager to reference to her marriage as a step taken to "increase her happiness," she "should be very Proud of having the happiness óf Seeing" her mother-in-law, and meanwhile "of keeping up a Particular Corespondence with" her; furthermore, Anne "shall be glad of having a correspondence with them [Frank's relations] til I have the Pleasure of Seeing them […]."

Inspecting Anne's letter, it becomes rather obvious that she is not a trained writer. Her handwriting is bold and square-cut, with the text covered with signs of editing. Bearing that in mind, the utterances Anne employs appear even more owed to a conventional, and even formulaic rhetoric of letter writing, disguising any "real" or "natural" emotions, an argument, which shall be discussed in more detail. Nonetheless, or even just because of this argument, to see how "happiness" – or an "increase of happiness" – rather than rational reasons or economic interest is regarded as legitimate motivation and justification to enter an "utter stranger's" personal sphere and family underscores the meaning and importance of emotionality within family relations. Furthermore, Anne preserves and addresses conventional patterns and mechanisms of dependence and duty of care on the superior female's side, when she hopes for her mother-in-law to "accept of my Duty sent with the Greatest Regard."

Anne's letter was obviously drafted and sent to present her to Graham Frank's mother, and also to his friends and family; the emotions put on display are meant to illustrate Anne's "ornamental part," marking "emotionality" as part of an expected social behavior rather than limiting "emotions" to a private and more intimate sphere. "Intimacy," though, played a crucial part to grade eighteenth-century interpersonal relations and found various ways of expression.[57] In the letter to his cousin Easter, Graham Frank is very straightforward about this:

> Dear Cousin, I received your long & very agreeable Letter of the 28th March. & am highly obliged to you for the Particulars you send me – Indeed you are now become my principal correspondent & the only one I have to depend on […].[58]

In the following, Frank styles himself as very well-informed and taking active part in all family affairs – commenting on some cousin's aspirations of marriage, or a nephew's as well as neighbors' (unacceptable) behaviors – familiar "chit chat." The intimacy between himself and his cousin Easter is not only explicitly exposed but also practically demonstrated, when Frank includes a particular letter for Easter to forward:

> "You'll be surpized […]" Frank explains in a post scriptum "[…] at seeing one of the inclosed Ltrs & think I want to become a Clergyman; but its no such Matter & I desire you'll put it into the Post Office without mentioning it to any Creature […]."

The letter in question is addressed to "The Right Rev.d Father in God Thomas Lord Bishop of London,"[59] which itself is decidedly "unfamiliar," elaborating on the state of the church in the colony of Virginia.

In our context, the letter is of interest in two regards: For one, in this letter, Frank gives detailed description of his perception of the state of the church in the colony. The observations he makes are not at all of interest to any purpose of his other letters, thereby underscoring the assumption how the "unfamiliar" of a new world could remain dethematized in family correspondence.

On the other hand, the fact that Frank chose to send the letter enclosed in his letter addressed to his cousin points to his effort trying to produce a notion of intimacy and connectedness with his cousin Easter – sending her the letter to be forwarded attests his faith and trust in her; it sets their relationship apart from other family relation, materially creating an epistolary niche of intimacy closing the mere geographical distance in between.

There are further examples and varying implementations of practices materially evoking notions of intimacy, closeness, and familiarity, creating niches and hide-outs. I.E. Paravincini's letter to her parents illustrates another strategy demonstrating the need for and the ability to create those intimate niches by switching the language used:

> Now let me talk to you about my little one. He is doing really well but he has been sick, the poor child. He is a big consolation for me because my husband is still gone almost every single day on the plantation to learn all about planting. I am so concerned – not without reason do I think *dat hy grote lefhebbery heef in de planterij* for he at 5 o'clock in the morning he is already at the plantation […].[60]

Though change in language use may rather catch attention than create a hide-out for it interrupts the flow of reading, it still limits the circle of potential readers to those who are capable to understand one or the other language used. Thus, the switching of language may emphasize secrecy. In case of Paravincini's letter, the painfulness of what she is about to relate – her husband's untruthfulness to her – suggests this reading; considering that she is writing to her parents, the use of Dutch also meant to switch from a more formal to an intimate code.[61] It underscores Paravincini's attempt to disclose what she is going to relate only to her parents – an epistolary strategy eventually imitating a careful whisper which can only be heard in physical proximity.

These two instances illustrate practices of crossing distances in time and space crucial to maintain notions of familiarity. And it falls to Graham Frank's said letter to the bishop of London to accentuate these crossings as "familiar" and "intimate" as opposed to an explicitly unfamiliar and not intimate verbal crossing of spatio-temporal distance: In Frank's letter to the bishop of London, he pays respect to existing hierarchies – not only by styling himself as the unknown stranger to his well-known addressee but also by designing his current place of activity as being inferior to his correspondent's whereabouts in England:

> My Lord, You will be greatly surprised at an Address from so obscure a Person as I am, in so distant a part of the World; but the great Satisfaction & real Benefit U have received by reading your Lordship's Works, particularly your late Volumns of incomparable Discourses, constrain me to offer violence to the natural Modesty & Bashfulness of our Nature, when we approach great Personages & give you the Pleasure of knowing that your Labours hath been of the greatest advantage to one, even in this

remote part of the Earth, tho the meanest of the Servants of that God & Saviour you have so long & faithfully served: & may He for the Good of his Church, preserve your Life, in the highest Felicity, to the latest Person that humanity can possibly reach: & when, for our sins, & your unspeakable Advantage, he is pleased to deprive us of you; may that Church you have, on so many Occasions, approved your self a faithful Pastor, never want such a Leader to the End of Time.

Now that I have presumed to approach your Lordship's Presence, permit me to say something of the State of the Church in this Colony. [...][62]

In the continuation of his letter, Graham lays out the dramatic situation the church and clergy are facing in Virginia and its neighboring colonies. His descriptions cover several pages, not only emphasizing the poor situation of potential clergymen as well as the deprivation in morals, but also sketching a catholic thread by the customs of his fellow countrymen to employ Scottish tutors for their children – a decidedly programmatic approach to family issues, and quite contrasting the personal details Frank discusses in his letter with Easter.

These instances portrayed epistolary practices of covering distances in time and space in their different qualities as further techniques of appresentations. Despite the need to "enter the presence" of an interlocutor, this was not to be confused with a need and want of intimacy, closeness, or connectedness. The space established by correspondence also consisted of niches, hide-outs, and separate rooms, allowing to enact families and community. It remains to be of interest to further studies to determine who was able and allowed to establish and enter niches and hide-outs, and where, when, and on which grounds.

With regard to my initial questions, the examples so far mentioned served to investigate the influence of meanings of relationships and gender, as established in common family and relational practices, on how people interacted, covered distance in time and space, and made use of emotions. An established intimate relation might serve as foundation and point of reference in communication (i.e. Sarah Buckley, Graham, and even Anne Frank), and in emotions of devotion and love; however, anger and disappointment also could be instrumentalized to call for relational engagement of the other (i.e. Rosette and Anne Butler). While the Butler-Frank family feud suggested that gender played an important part in how an actor was able to activate and play out (family) emotions, their examples already hinted at what the following two examples give proof of, that is, the question of (in)dependence seemed to have outweighed the gender aspect. Sarah Rise and Richard Tuggett are both addressing their parents – both do not seem to be in (desperate) need of support but both are interested to keep up their family relations. Sarah sends a letter home to her mother in London reporting the death of her first husband 17 years ago, as well as her having taken a new husband, "a very sober good sort of man named Robert Rise." Compared to Anne Butler, who demands her father's and family's acceptance of her husband to be the representative and trustee of the family fortune on her side of the Atlantic, Sarah Rise is not in need of such recognition. For her first marriage had left her

> "[…] very well heated upon a Plantation of my Own […]" with "[…] a son about fourteen Years of age who will be Possessor of it after my Decease […]."[63]

In her entire letter, Sarah Rise demonstrates keen interest in her family's business and fortune back home in England, but is obviously well set and independent without any need of her family's approval or support. Being needy or in want of family support, however, did not imperatively postulate strict compliance with conventional practices of family, as Richard Tuggett's letter from Annapolis to his parents in Surrey demonstrates. After explaining that he is now in the service of "Honorable Colonel Tasker" as footman, Richard complains of not having received any letter from them, ponders about his parents' well-being, breaks the news of his marriage, and asks for support in an instant:

> Honerd Father and mother, I like this opertinewtey of riting to you to lett you know that i am in maryland and a footman to the Honorable Colnatt Tasker and i am in a Good [Klue] and i am much surp[?] i never Recevd a letter from you I have sent 2 too you I live as well as any one can but to be so long fron hering or see ing from you i thank you are Ded I shall be Glad to heer from you but as i have sent 2 Letters to you and never Receved an Answer i [prospect] you are Ded I live as well as aney one Can in the world. I am marred since i cam heer and I hope to be in England in a bout 12 mounths and I shall bring my wife with me and Pray send to me som knives som buckl and Buting and Aney thing you think Proper for i can make God of money heer. I have gott a bout two hundred pound in money since I have been heer […].

In a postscriptum, Richard repeats what seems to be his greatest concern:

> PS: I have marred as [sweet] a gall a ever weef known Shee Is as trew to me as the verell sun and i shall bring her to England will me plees god i Live pray send me a Letter to me by the first ships a coms for i Long to heer from you Pray excuse the bad vriting to you for you knon i am a bad letter you doutbut sun Richard Tuggett.[64]

Richard's letter illustrates well how family members tried to translate and balance the needs of family practice in absence of each other. The interlacing of his world and his family's whereabouts is pronounced and performed by the explicit reference of Richard missing the accustomed space of familial relation – that of personal contact and eyewitness ("being so long from hearing or seeing from you").[65] Even though Richard stresses his well-being ("I live as well as anyone can in the world"), he avoids suggesting the impression that he might want to stay where he is even though he took a wife (quite resembling Graham Frank): Immediately after breaking the news of his marriage, Richard emphasizes that he shall be back in England within the year. Obviously, Richard tries to balance the need to express his own worries about his family, while intending to ease their anticipated anxiety by pointing out his good position with Colonel Tacker, and his proper installation with a "sweet girl." By this, Richard walks the line between performing independence and having to rely on or straining his familial relations too hard, and yet expressing his interest in needing their support ("Pray send to me some knives and buckl"). But in contrast to Anne Butler's interest – which could also be identified as demand – of her family supporting and accepting her husband as representative of her family's affairs in the colony, Richard Tugget embeds his request for support in a story of personal success (being footman to Colonel Tasker and having earned 200 pounds since his arrival), turning it into an offer to increase the family fortune by his activities. Noticeably, the space of his current affairs does not take place in its own rights. It is designed as space of opportunity for personal as well as communal development and benefit – but also as a place to be left as soon as possible and fit.[66]

In all of the letters showcased, it is remarkable how "home" remains to be that place of origin where people and their families originated from, despite them settling down and seeking economic well-being elsewhere: In a letter to his brother in 1756, Edward Watts breaks it down to "the Reason of my Troubling you is to Informe you that the way to Live appeasable Life is to Live at home"[67] – a conclusion with which Elizabeth Spriggs, writing in that same year, would certainly agree with. Elizabeth had come to Maryland serving as an indentured servant. In her moanful and touching letter to her father, she gives an account of her situation

> toiling almost Day and Night, [...] then tied up & whipp'd to that Degree that you'd not serve an animal [...] Nay, many Neagros are better used [...].[68]

As many further letters of indentured servants or unlucky sailors, Elizabeth craves for her father's support, asking him to send "some Relief. Clothing [being] the principal thing wanting [...]." To achieve her goal, she appeals to his parental duty, not justifying but excusing and regretting her own misbehavior to the utmost degree:[69]

> [...][any] long silence has been purely by owing to my undutifullness to you and well knowing I had offended in the highest Degree, put a tie to my tongue and pen, for fear I should be [extinet] from your good graces and add a further Trouble to you, but too well knowing your care and tenderness for me so long as I retained [any] Duty to you, induced me once again to endeavour if possible, to kindle up that flame again, O Dear

Father, belive what I am going to relate the words of truth and sincerity, and Ballance my former bad Conduct [to] my sufferings here, and then I am sure you'll pitty your Disress[ed] Daughter.

In her emotional expressivity, Elizabeth's letter resonates with Anne Butler's voicing and use of anger to pressure her father to support her; likewise, both women promise to keep silent if they do not receive any response – as Rosette does, when she pleas for her lover's attention.

As can be seen in these last examples, dependence – economic or emotional – and misfortune both serve as reference points to call for and demand somebody else's responsibility to act and support, drawing on traditional and customary reliabilities between husband and wife, men and women, or further relations within familial constellations.

Deciphering the sufferings and emotions expressed in the letters as common motifs in transmaritime family correspondence, eventually representing a specific feature of a genre, may be extended to an examination of the authenticity and originality of emotional expressions.

In focus: originality and plagiarism – the authenticity of emotional expressions

With regard to the question of authenticity and originality of emotion, the letter by sailor John Morris, serving in 1756 on a ship on the shores of Northern America, is rather intriguing:

"My dear Nancy [...]" he writes "[...] the wonders of your face made me their captive as soon as I saw them and that rare grace of yours which makes you excel all others retained me your prisoner. [...]"[70]

Morris' choice of words appears astonishing – even though his writing is easily identified as plagiarism. Who would expect a common sailor – a simpleton – to quote Ovid's "The Story of Picus and Canens" – a text well known to an eighteenth-century readership, where it reads

"[b]y those fair Eyes, she cries, and ev'ry Grace / That finish all the Wonders of your Face [...]"?

As proven plagiarism, Morris' lines might have been devalued as unnatural and inauthentic in educated circles of the time. The idea – still prevalent today – rests on a specific understanding of (emotional) authenticity, which emerged in the age of sensitivity: while innumerable letter writing manuals had offered instructions on how to write "proper" letters in accordance to conduct, occasion, and addressee by offering standardized phrasing, a new kind of manuals developed, promoting an expression in the most "natural" manner.[71]

This naturalness of written expression was to be based on natural and oral conversation. This observation appears to be of importance to me. While the development of the bourgeois and natural style of letter-writing contrasted with an aristocratic and artificial style of writing, there was no need to emphasize this demarcation in face-to-face communication. This, then, may either point to the fact that there was not much of imitation of aristocratic artificiality expected in face-to-face situations, or that people felt competent enough to demask any artificiality in direct encounters.

Following the latter line of argument, the relevance of body and expressions of the body come into play: while in written discourse, interlocutors have to rely on what is conveyed in language, in a real conversation, the body, gestures, and prosody, to name but a few characteristics, contribute to what is being said – body and voice offer a contextualization and provide an additional significancy charge.[72]

However, following my earlier reading of I.E. Paravincini's emulation of whispering by her use of foreign language, I would like to investigate further techniques in written communication which served similar purposes. But first, coming back to Morris' letter, I need to demask the complete fraud of his plagiarism, as he did not only draw on the ancient bard Ovid, but copied from another text even more substantially.

In *Pearls of Eloquence, or The School of Complements, Wherein is Shewed a Brief Description of Beauty, Vertue, Love, and Eloquence*, published in London in 1698, it reads:

> Upon his Face.
> The wonders of your face made me their captive as soons as I saw them, and that rare grace of yours, which makes you excel all others, retained me your prisoner and servant.

Though it is clear that Morris copied the entire section, the conclusion that he was not expressing his true feelings neglects two important issues: on the one hand, Morris may have tried to express himself as particularly emotional and intelligible, by charging his lines with the emotions cultivated within a manual designed for

> [...] the good and benefit of those young Ladyes, Gentlewomen, and Scholars, who are desirous to adorn their speech with gentile Ceremonies, Complemental, amorous, and high Expressions of Speaking or Writing.[73]

In this understanding, Morris' writing may be understood as a dispersed practice of intertextuality within the expression of emotion, drawing on an artifact that was part of an industry "[...] dedicated to improving 'emotional intelligence' [...]," as identified by Monique Scheer as actors within the emotional practice of naming – or signifying – emotions.[74] Drawing on a book designed for ladies in that instance might either be accidental, or it might have been for making himself understood by a member of a female emotional community as specified by the author of the book.

On the other hand, the very idea of emotions being cultivated also hints at what Scheer coins as practice of mobilizing emotions:[75] Morris was only *able to feel* the way he felt for Nancy as books like the "Pearls [...]" offered a framework and context for this perception.

A closer look at the context of Morris' declaration of affection supports my argument of epistolary techniques to emulate face-to-face encounters as mentioned earlier, for example, as Morris had his letter delivered within another letter addressed to one "Mr. Robert."[76]

Comparing Morris' letter for Nancy with the "Pearl," and then with the note addressed to Mr. Robert, the letter to Nancy is exposed as hardly original at all. Yet, by this comparison, it can be learned what *is* original. John stresses to Nancy, that once he will have returned to London, he

> [...] hopes not to go to sea no more [...]

and that she is "[...]all ways in my thoughts" – while in the accompanying letter, Morris writes, his "[...] heart is all ways with her.[...]."

One may now speculate what is more intimate – having his thoughts always occupied by Nancy, taking her with him wherever he is, or assuring his heart and feelings will always be with her. One way or the other, Morris' use of the idiom "love" indicates a notion of "love" significantly deviating from a romantic understanding as it might be attributed today, for it only occurs in four instances – and only in the accompanying letter:

> [...] give my love to Nancy [...]
> [...] give my love to Nancy [...]
> "[...] For I am very well be loved by all [...]" and signing
> [...] From your loving friend

– while styling himself as *"your humble servant"* in the letter to Nancy.

In the two letters, the manner of their composition – materially and by the mediality of originality – attests to a translation of early modern courting practices from face-to-face settings to writing: By fashioning himself as humble servant, whose thoughts are always with her, and giving way to his hopes of not having to go to sea anymore, Morris depicts himself as a courteous potential spouse. Additionally, the courting is done within the view of family and friends – acknowledging contemporary customs – not only by sending the letter to Nancy within another letter, but also by voicing his intentions already in the accompanying letter – a practice already encountered in the Frank correspondence.

Summarizing the findings with reference to the initial question of "authenticity" and "originality" of emotional expression, Morris' letters and use of emotions would support the scholarly view expressed by Barbara Rosenwein:

> [Historians of emotion] should not worry about whether an emotion is authentic unless the particular emotional community that we are studying is itself concerned about authenticity. [...] If an emotion is the standard response of a particular group in certain instances, the question should not be whether it betrays real feeling but rather why one norm obtains over another.[77]

Morris was not original in his expression of feelings, but his reference to a manual may accentuate the importance the matter had to him, trying to avoid any irritation or even insult, and aiming at being as intelligible and adequate as possible – to his Nancy and to her family.

Concluding remarks

I set out to explore how families of the eighteenth century, separated in time and space, lacking a shared daily experience, would constitute an "epistolary space" to connect their (seemingly) disconnected worlds.

The case studies of Rosette, Anne Frank, and Elizabeth Spriggs have shown how emotions were employed to create a situation of dependence from and responsibility of the remote family. Though these correspondences do not copy from writing manuals or examples, they still rely on the familiar rather than giving way to narratives of anything unknown or extraordinary. The new and unfamiliar environment serves as background narration – negatively perceived as threat and harmful – to accentuate the personal position within familial structures and responsibilities. While the unfamiliar did hardly receive an elaborate attention in the letters of Sarah Rise, Graham Frank, or Richard Tuggett, its contextualizing function shifts from threatening to a more positively judged space of potential. Nonetheless, the spatio-temporal localization of the self and the other within the epistolary space as one frame of reference was essential, forming almost always the beginning and end of a letter, when an author reported last notes received from a correspondent or gave details on how she could best be reached.[78] A diverse set of techniques of appresentation was in the hands of early modern authors to create the epistolary space as space for imagined experience, as Rosette's, I.E. Paravincini's, or Frederich's letters illustrate. But as much as the letters gave *de facto* evidence of connectedness, they also co-constructed the divide in space and time, between home and places of activity, exactly by focusing on and containing techniques and approaches of translating accustomed practices within family life to a new, and (to many writers) unfamiliar medium in correspondence, adopting to its limitations and necessities as well as potentials and advantages.

Observing Sarah Buckley as a settled, married woman, but also Rosette in quite the opposite position, it becomes obvious how the status of a relationship influenced techniques of relating to the addressee by connecting the spheres of experience on the one hand, and the invocation of emotionality on the other. The Butler-Frank correspondence illustrates well the different positions women and men took, and shows how anger could be voiced and instrumentalized despite acting from a dependent position. The examples of Sarah Rise, Richard Tugget, and Elizabeth Spriggs put these findings into perspective: The position within the grid of family and community relations – or rather writing techniques and narratives at hands – did not depend only on the duration of absence or disconnection, or on the gender of interlocutors but also on the purpose they followed, (economic in)dependence heavily impacting the need and potential to demand for family responsibility. What really is absent to a large extent in these family correspondences is the "unfamiliar" and "exotic," or encounters with the unknown *per se*. I would argue that family correspondence forms a genre marked by techniques of appresentation, recollections, addressing of family responsibilities, approaching and integrating a plurality of participants in communities at both ends of the communicative channel, and a familiar language, even relying on copying from manuals as the case study of John Morris has shown. Furthermore, the intention, meaning, and purpose of this genre were not to relate or make sense of anything new and unfamiliar. They are rather concerned with the need for familiarity, which, in turn, creates narratives of the unfamiliar either as disturbances or economic potencies, or not of interest to family and communities connected by this type of correspondence at all. In short, as long as the unfamiliar remained a cause to itself – or eventually an irritation to the individual – it had no or only a marginalized place within the space of family communication and was consequently excluded.

Notes

1 Letter from In. Kello, Virginia, to Josh Kello, London, Oct. 8th 1755; in the collection of the High Court of Admiralty (HCA) Series 30 (Admiralty Miscellanea) Piece 258, in the following HCA 30/258.
2 Kello himself appears to act as merchant ordering his brother to send him some goods he can sell in the colony. However, he is to be addressed as "Richard Kello," and he mentions another "[...] fine boy [...] now living named Richard [...]." In Lloyd DeWitt Bockstruck, *Virgina's Colonial Soldiers* (Baltimore, MD: Genealogical Pub. Co, 1988), 33, a Richard Kello is listed among the County Militia Rosters of Southampton County, Sept 12, 1754; for Virginia and the French Indian War in general, see William M. Fowler Jr., *Empires at War: The French and Indian War and the Struggle for North America, 1754–1763* (New York: Walker Books, 2005); Matthew C. Ward, *Breaking the Backcountry: Seven Years War in Virginia and Pennsylvania 1754–1765* (Pittsburgh, PA: University of Pittsburgh Press, 2004).
3 For the sixteenth and seventeenth centuries, Michael T. Ryan – in continuation of scholars such as Lucien Febvre, J.H. Elliott, or Donald Lach – explains the absence of narrations of new world encounters in letters of explorers like Columbus or Magellan by suggesting that "[...] The bewildering variety of people and diversity of cultures

did not bowl over a Europe which had cause to appreciate that variety was a fact of life [...]." Ryan ponders – just like me now:

> Why did the new worlds in Asia, Africa, and America make so little difference to contemporaries? Was there simply too much to digest over a period of two centuries? Did the diffusion of information occur at such slow pace – even by early modern standards – that the new worlds had to be rediscovered by each generation? [...]

Michael T. Ryan, "Assimilating New Worlds in the Sixteenth and Seventeenth Centuries," *Comparative Studies in Society and History* 23, no. 4 (1981), 520–521.

4 "There are no poisonous mists or rains under the Line [the equator], as some deceptive travel writers will have us believe, at least I haven't encountered any." J.C. Metzendorff to his parents and friends in Hamburg, May 30th 1778, HCA 30/727.
5 "I have now seen thousands of beautiful things: the Orkney Islands, the island of Madeira, the Pico of Tenerife and Palma, Gonera and Ferro. Bonitos and albacores, flying fish, sharks, whales, sea cows, tropical birds, and what is more of it. I've now passed the both tropical circles and the Line; I'm now at the Cape of Good Hope, I will climb the Table Mountain, with the great Indian sea [the Indian Ocean] to my left and the Ocean [the Atlantic] to my right – isn't that enviable?" J.C. Metzendorff to his parents and friends in Hamburg, May 30, 1778, HCA 30/727.
6 William Hodgeon in Maryland to his wife Ann in London, Sept. 21th 1756, HCA 30/528.
7 George Brown on Rhode Island to his parents in Berwick, Northumberland, Feb. 28, 1774, HCA 30/272.
8 "As it may please the Lord, I shall be home with you in two years' time from now. We will make haste as much as we can, for we all wish to be home in Europe." J.C. Metzendorff to his parents and friends in Hamburg, May 30th 1778; HCA 30/727.
9 The term was introduced by James How, *Epistolary Spaces: English Letter Writing from the Foundation of the Post Office to Richardson's Clarissa* (Aldershot: Ashgate Pub., 2003):

> [Epistolary spaces] are spaces of connection, providing permanent and seemingly unbreakable links between people and places. [...] epistolary spaces are 'public' spaces within which supposedly 'private' writings travel – at once imaginary and real: imaginary, because you can't really inhabit them as you can other social spaces – all meetings and incidents there are only metaphorical; real, because they were they were policed by a government ever more keen to monitor the letters that passed along the national postal routes.

"Real," I will argue, because they affected people's daily life.

10 Jahyun Kim Haboush, "Introduction. The Epistolary Genre and the Scriptural Economy of the Choson," in *Epistolary Korea: Letters in the Communicative Space of the Choson, 1392–1910*, ed. Jahyun Kim Haboush (New York: Columbia University Press, 2009), 2.
11 Folios being the format of paper for letter-writing. See James Daybell, *The Material Letter in Early Modern England: Manuscript Letters and the Culture and Practices of Letter-Writing, 1512–1635* (Basingstoke: Palgrave Macmillan, 2012); Susan Whyman, *The Pen and the People: English Letter Writers 1660–1800* (New York: Oxford University Press, 2009); Eve Tavor Bannet, *Empire of Letters: Letter Manuals and Transatlantic Correspondence, 1680–1820* (Cambridge: Cambridge University Press, 2005).
12 How shared experiences and observation of daily practices added to the social construction of an extended family (and neighborhood) has been convincingly argued and explored in Joachim Eibach, "Das offene Haus. Kommunikative Praxis im sozialen Nahraum der europäischen Frühen Neuzeit," *Zeitschrift für Historische Forschung* 38 (2011), 621–664.

13 In German: "Schriftliche Gespräche," Robert Vellusig, *Schriftliche Gespräche. Briefkultur im 18. Jahrhundert* (Köln, Weimar and Wien: Böhlau Verlag Wien, 2001); Lucas Haasis, „"„Noch bleibt mir ein Augenblick Zeit um mich mit Euch zu unterhalten." Praxeologische Einsichten zu kaufmännischen Briefschaften des 18. Jahrhunderts," in *Diskurse-Körper-Artefakte. Historische Praxeologie in der Frühneuzeitforschung*, ed. Dagmar Freist (Bielefeld: DeGruyter Transcript Verlag, 2015), 87–113.

14 Esther Milne, *Letters, Postcards, Email: Technologies of Presence* (London: Routledge, 2010), 14.

15 Studies like Sarah Pearsall's *Atlantic Families. Lives and Letters in the Later Eighteenth Century* (Oxford: Oxford University Press, 2008), emphasize "[…] many similarities [of families from the eighteenth century] to families today." However, the concept of "family" was undergoing severe changes during the early modern period – and certainly in research on this period it would need further investigation exceeding the scope of this paper. See, for example, Naomi Tadmore, "The Concept of the Household-Family in Eighteenth-Century England," *Past & Present* 151 (May 1996), 111–140; on representations: Ludmilla Jordanova, "The Representation of the Family in the Eighteenth Century: A Challenge for Cultural History," in *Interpretation and Cultural History*, ed. Joan H. Pittock, Andre Wear and Anthony Grafton (Palgrave: St. Martin's Press, 1991), 109–134; and with regard to empire and race: Daniel Livesay, *Children of Uncertain Fortune: Mixed-Race Jamaicans in Britain and the Atlantic Family, 1733–1833* (Chapel Hill: The University of North Carolina Press, 2018).

16 See in general on letter-writing: Rebecca Earle, ed., *Epistolary Selves: Letters and Letter-Writers, 1600–1945* (Aldershot: Routledge, 1999); Carol Poster and Linda C. Mitchel, ed., *Letter-Writing Manuals and Instruction from Antiquity to the Present: Historical and Bibliographical Studies*, Studies in Rhetoric/Communication (Columbia: University of South Carolina Press, 2007).

17 John W. Howland, *The Letter Form and the French Enlightenment: The Epistolary Paradox* (New York: Peter Lang, 1991), 43.

18 The Prize Papers is a collection of records of the British High Court of Admiralty. See Amanda Bevan and Randolph Cook, "The High Court of Admirality Prize Papers, 1652–1815: Challenges in Improving Access to older Records," *Archives* LIII, no. 137 (2018), 34–58.

19 Long-term absence is a matter of definition hardly ever given – even by contemporaries. As Benoît Grenier and Catherine Ferland point out in their study on women acting as proxies for their husbands:

> Considering the time necessary for transatlantic travel even for travel to the interior, journeys that justified appointing a proxy were often very long. The duration was only rarely specified in the documents, but whenever it was mentioned, it was always a matter of several months or even several years.

Benoît Grenier and Catherine Ferland, ""As Long as the Absence Shall Last": Proxy Agreements and Women's Power in Eighteenth-Century Quebec City," *Clio Women, Gender, History* 37 (2013), 12.

20 Anne Butler in Virginia to her Brother in Kirklington, North Yorkshire, Nov. 13th 1756, HCA 30/528.

21 Jeremy Black, *The British Abroad: The Grand Tour in the Eighteenth Century* (Cheltenham: The History Press, 2003); Rosemary Sweet, Gerrit Verhoeven, and Sarah Goldsmith, ed., *Beyond the Grand Tour: Northern Metropolises and Early Modern Travel Behaviour* (London and New York: Routledge, 2017); Hermann Bausinger et al., ed., *Reisekultur: Von der Pilgerfahrt zum modernen Tourismus* (München: C.H. Beck, 1991).

22 Joachim Renn, "Appresentation and Simultaneity: Alfred Schutz on Communication between Philosophy and Pragmatics," *Human Studies* 29, no. 1 (2006), 1–19. See also Hans Gumbrecht, *Production of Presence: What Meaning Cannot Convey* (Stanford, CA: Stanford University Press, 2004). Gumbrecht applies his concept of "presentification"

to present uses of and approaches to history (and the writing of history); as "[...] techniques that produce the impression (or, rather, the illusion) that worlds of the past can become tangible again [...]" (94). Techniques of "appresentation" in the letters denote techniques going in three temporal directions: making present the future reader during the process of writing, making then past author present in the moment of reading, and finally ensuring a simultaneous and permanent imagined presence of the absent person.

23 Literature on emotions and the study thereof is vast. For a discussion of the term in research, see Thomas Dixon, ""Emotions": The History of a Keyword in Crisis," *Emotion Review* 4, no. 4 (2012), 338–344; Andrew Lynch, Susan Broomhall, and Jane Davidson, ed., *A Cultural History of the Emotions* (London: Bloomsbury Academic, 2019); Jan Plamper, *The History of Emotions: An Introduction* (Oxford: Oxford University Press, 2015).

24 A ship called "Diana" with a Master Buckley sailed for Lopez from Newport to Jamaica and London; see: Guide to the Papers of Aaron Lopez (1731–1782), 1752–1794, 1846, 1852, 1953, P-11, Processed by Holly Snyder, accessed January 21, 2019, http://findingaids.cjh.org/AaronLopez.html.

25 The letter is addressed to "W or Ms Hailey," the famous London business woman Marry Hailey. Judith Jennings, *Gender, Religion, and Radicalism in the Long Eighteenth Century: The "Ingenious Quaker" and Her Connections* (Aldershot: Ashgate Pub., 2006).

26 Sarah Buckley, Newport to her husband at sea, Feb. 23rd 1777, HCA 30/272.

27 Marianna Georgievna Muravyeva, ""A King in His Own Household": Domestic Discipline and Family Violence in Early Modern Europe Reconsidered," *The History of the Family* 18, no. 3 (2013), 227–237; Pavla Miller, *Transformations of Patriarchy in the West, 1500–1900* (Bloomington: Indiana University Press, 1998); Lyndal Roper, *The Holy Household: Women and Morals in Reformation Augsburg* (Oxford: Oxford University Press, 1989).

28 Guide to the Papers of Aaron Lopez (1731–1782), 1752–1794, 1846, 1852, 1953, P-11, Processed by Holly Snyder, accessed January 21, 2019, http://findingaids.cjh.org/AaronLopez.html; Michael Feldberg, ed., *"Aaron Lopez's Struggle for Citizenship." Blessings of Freedom: Chapters in American Jewish History* (New York: KTAV, 2002); Marilyn Kaplan, "The Jewish Merchants of Newport, 1749–1790," in *The Jews of Rhode Island*, ed. George M. Goodwin and Ellen Smith (Waltham, MA: Brandeis University Press, 2004).

29 Christian M. Mcburney, *The Rhode Island Campaign: The First French and American Operation in the Revolutionary War* (Yardley: Westholme, 2011).

30 Daniele Clarke, ""Formed into Words by Your Divided Lips": Women, Rhetoric and the Ovidian Tradition," in *This Double Voice: Gendered Writing in Early Modern England*, ed. Daniele Clarke and Elizabeth Clarke (Houndsmill: Palgrave Macmillan, 2000), 61–87; Katherine Ann Jensen, *Writing Love: Letters, Women, and the Novel in France, 1605–1776* (Carbondale: Southern Illinois University Press, 1995); Susan Broomhall, ""The Ambition in My Love": The Theatre of Gendered Courtly Conduct in All's Well that Ends Well," in *The Palgrave Handbook of Shakespeare's Queens*, ed. Kavita Mudan Finn and Valerie Schutte (Basingstoke: Palgrave Macmillan, 2018), 355–372.

31 Letter by Rosette to "Pouble," written in Bordeaux March 1793; original in French; HCA 30/388. At the time of this first letter, Pouble must still have been at Bordeaux. However, the letter was later confiscated aboard a ship passing the Atlantic. Most likely, Pouble was a seaman or businessman carrying Rosette's letters with his belongings.

32 Lawrence Stone, *"The Companionate Marriage." The Family, Sex and Marriage in England 1500–1800* (New York: Harper & Row, 1977); Christine Peters, "Gender, Sacrament and Ritual: The Making and Meaning of Marriage in Late Medieval and Early Modern England," *Past & Present* 169 (2000), 63–96; Katherine Crawford, *European*

Sexualities, 1400–1800 (New York: Cambridge University Press, 2007); Sarah Hanley, "Family and State in Early Modern France: the Marriage Pact," in *Connecting Spheres: Women in the Western World, 1500–Present*, ed. Marilyn J. Boxer and Jean H. Quataert (New York: Oxford University Press, 1987), 53–63.

33 Second letter by Rosette to Pouble, March 21st 1793, original in French, HCA 30/388.
34 See footnote above and Ukinka Rublack, ed., *Gender in Early Modern German History* (Cambridge: Cambridge University Press, 2002).
35 Michèle Cohen, "'Manners' Make the Man: Politeness, Chivalry, and the Construction of Masculinity, 1750–1830," *Journal of British Studies* 44 (2005), 312–329.
36 Second letter by Rosette to Pouble, March 21st 1793, original in French, HCA 30/388.
37 Frederich Roux and his sister writing to their brother from Bordeaux to New York in 1778; HCA 32/492.
38 Frederich Roux and his sister writing to their brother from Bordeaux to New York in 1778; HCA 32/492.
39 Frederich Roux and his sister writing to their brother from Bordeaux to New York in 1778; HCA 32/492.
40 On the importance of the observation of relations by others, see Eibach, "Das offene Haus," 621–664; Naomi Tadmore, *Family and Friends in Eighteenth-Century England: Household, Kinship and Patronage* (Cambridge: Cambridge University Press, 2004).
41 See Linda Pollock, "Anger and the Negotiation of Relationships in Early Modern England," *The Historical Journal* 47, no. 3 (September 2004), 567–590.
42 Anne Butler, York, Virginia, to her sister in Kirklington, Yorkshire, Nov. 19th 1756, HCA 30/258.
43 Anne Butler, York, Virginia to her brother in Kirklington, Yorkshire, Nov. 13th, 1756, HCA 30/258.
44 Anne Butler, York, Virginia to her brother in Kirklington, Yorkshire, Nov. 13th, 1756, HCA 30/258.
45 Anne Butler, York, Virginia to her brother in Kirklington, Yorkshire, Nov. 13th, 1756, HCA 30/258.
46 Anne Butler, York, Virginia, to her sister in Kirklington, Yorkshire, Nov. 19th 1756, HCA 30/258.
47 Whom he had married without asking for consent either, to mark a gender difference here.
48 Graham Frank, York, Virginia to Ellen Frank, Yorkshire, Nov. 10th, 1756, HCA 30/258.
49 Graham Frank's letter to the bishop of London gives, on four folios, elaborate impressions and details of the colonial situation he encounters. Graham Frank, Virginia, to the Lord Bishop of London, Nov. 11th 1756, HCA 30/ 258.
50 Anne's correspondence serves an additional purpose, as Katie Barclay ("Marginal Households and Their Emotions. The 'Kept Mistress' in Enlightenment Edinburg," in *Spaces for Feeling: Emotions and Sociabilities in Britain, 1650–1850*, ed. Susan Broomhall (London and New York: Routledge, 2015), 100) argues

> For women [...], home was not simply about emotional connection within the nuclear family or with a spouse, but about being embedded within a local and known community, one which provided the sustenance of friendship and support and reinforced a person's sense of self through acknowledgement of their status and role in the community. In this, sociability within a wider community of family, friends, and neighbours was essential to a person's emotional wellbeing and selfhood, weaving together family, community, social status, and household into personal identity.

51 Graham Frank, York, Virginia, to his mother Ellen in Yokrshire, Nov. 10th 1756, HCA 30/258.

52 Graham Frank York, Virginia, to "Mrs. Casley" on Nov. 8th 1756, HCA 30/258.
53 Anne Frank to Ellen Frank, Nov. 11th 1756, HCA 30/258.
54 The power of a letter to represent its author has been elaborated by Konstantin Dierks: "[…] the emergence of the familiar letter as the dominant mode of letter writing in the eighteenth century meant that every single letter, no matter how seemingly trivial, would serve to construct and symbolise a person's social status." (Konstantin Dierks, "The Familiar Letter and Social Refinement in America, 1750–1800," in *Letter Writing as a Social Practice*, ed. David Barton and Nigal Hall (Amsterdam and Philadelphia: 1999), 38.)
55 Konstantin Dierks, *In My Power: Letter Writing and Communications in Early America* (Philadelphia: University of Pennsylvania Press, 2009).
56 While an "avatar" refers to a virtual representation in a virtual environment, the letter as avatar is a physical artifact standing in for an absent person. However, just like an avatar, the person who is represented by the letter drafts the letter according to his ideas on how he or she would like to be perceived. Robert Vellusig identifies the letter accordingly as "anwesendes Substrat des abwesenden Gesprächspartners" ("present substratum of the absent interlocutor", Vellusig, *Schiftliche Gespräche*, 26–27.
57 See Vellusig, *Schriftliche Gespräche*.
58 Graham Frank to Easter Metcalfe, Nov. 9th, 1756, HCA 30/258.
59 Graham Frank to Thomas Lord Bishop of London, Nov. 11th 1756, HCA 30/258.
60 Original in French; the Dutch part reads: "[…] that he has a great love affair at the plantation […]", I.E. Paravincini writing from Surinam to her parents in the Netherlands, HCA 30/374.
61 In this interpretation, I follow Annika Raapke, *"Dieses Verfluchte Land" Europäische Körper in Brieferzählungen aus der Karibik, 1744–1826* (Bielefeld: DeGruyter Transcript Verlag, 2019).
62 Graham Frank, Virginia, to the Lord Bishop of London, Nov. 11th 1756, HCA 30/258.
63 Sarah Rise to her mother Sarah Scribner in Stanstead in Essex, Dec. 27th 1755, HCA 30/258.
64 Richard Tuggett, Annapolis, Virginia, to his parents in Love Tweting in Surrey, Nov. 2nd 1756, HCA 30/258.
65 This can also be observed in Sarah Rise's letter to her mother, which she begins "[…] I heartily rejoice to hear of you being alive […]." In doing so, she reproduces the situation of her learning of her mother's well-being in an act of communication which is experienced quite synesthetically: by choosing expressions like the emotionally charged "heartily" and "rejoice," but also to refer to herself as "rejoicing" and "hearing," Sarah enables the reader (her mother) to picture and almost listen to her exulting the moment she hears of her mother's welfare.
66 This economic advantage gained by families through migration has let Simon Teuscher to argue for patrician families before 1500 that the "rootedness of entire families would not have been possible without a considerable mobility on the part of some individual family members […]," identifying "Mobility as a collective endeavor [where] being gone was not a position outside, but inside the family," Simon Teuscher, "Property Regimes and Migration of Patrician Families in Western Europe around 1500," in *Transregional and Transnational Families in Europe and Beyond. Experiences Since the Middle Ages*, ed. Christopher H. Johnson, David Warren Sabean, Simon Teuscher and Francesca Trivellato (New York and Oxford: Berghahn Books, 2011), 75–92.
67 Edward Watts to his brother Harry, Oct. 24th 1756, HCA 30/258.
68 Elizabeth Spriggs from Mayland to her father in London, Sept. 22nd 1756, HCA 30/258.
69 For a discussion on different views of fatherhood in historical research, see Philip Grace, *Affectionate Authorities: Fathers and Fatherly Roles in Late Medieval Basel* (Franham: Ashgate Pub., 2015).

70 John Morris in Virginia to Nancy in Tall Mage, Nov. 30th 1756, HCA 30/258.
71 See Whyman, *The Pen and the People,* 211 has pointed out: "[…] the epistolary balance between self-expression and controlled use of norms tipped towards more freedom."; Linda C. Mitchel, "Letter-Writing Instruction Manuals in Seventeenth- and Eighteenth-Century England," in *Letter-Writing Manuals and Instruction from Antiquity to the Present,* ed. Carol Poster and Linda Mitchell (Columbia: University of South Carolina Press, 2007), 178–199.
72 See on the influence of nonverbal communication Axel Hüber, *The Nonverbal Shift in Early Modern English Conversation* (Amsterdam and Philadelphia: John Benjamins Publishing Company, 2007); Peter K. Andersson, *Silent History: Body Language and Nonverbal Identity, 1860–1914* (McGill: McGill-Queen's University Press, 2018); Barbara Korte, *Body Language in Literature* (Toronto, Buffalo, NY and London: University of Toronto Press, 1997).
73 *Pearls of Eloquence, or, the School of Complements, wherein is shewed a brief description of Beauty, Vertue, Love, and Eloquence. Composed for the good and benefit of those young Ladyes, Gentlewomen, and Scholars, who are desirous to adorn their speech with gentile Ceremonies, Complemental, amorous, and high Expressions of Speaking or Writing* (London 1658).
74 Monique Scheer, "Are Emotions a Kind of Practice (and Is That What Makes Them Have a History)? A Bourdieuian Approach to Understanding Emotion," *History and Theory* 51 (May 2012), 213.
75 Scheer, "Are Emotions a kind of practice?," 209.
76 John Morris in Virginia to Steven Robert in London, Nov. 30th 1756, HCA 30/258.
77 Barbara Rosenwein, "Problems and Methods in the History of Emotions," *Passion in Context* I, no. 1 (2010), 21.
78 Dierks, *In My Power.*

Bibliography

Andersson, Peter K. *Silent History: Body Language and Nonverbal Identity, 1860–1914.* Montreal: McGill-Queen's University Press, 2018.

Barclay, Katie. "Marginal Households and Their Emotions. The 'Kept Mistress' in Enlightenment Edinburg." In *Spaces for Feeling: Emotions and Sociabilities in Britain, 1650–1850,* edited by Susan Broomhall, 95–111. London and New York: Routledge, 2015.

Bausinger, Hermann, and Klaus Beyrer, ed. *Reisekultur: Von der Pilgerfahrt zum modernen Tourismus.* München: C.H. Beck, 1991.

Bevan, Amanda, and Randolph Cook. "The High Court of Admirality Prize Papers, 1652–1815: Challenges in Improving Access to Older Records." *Archives* LIII, no. 137 (2018): 34–58.

Black, Jeremy. *The British Abroad: The Grand Tour in the Eighteenth Century.* Gloucestershire: Sutton Pub, 2003.

Broomhall, Susan. "'The Ambition in My Love': The Theatre of Gendered Courtly Conduct in All's Well that Ends Well." In *The Palgrave Handbook of Shakespeare's Queens,* edited by Kavita Mudan Finn and Valerie Schutte, 355–372. London: Palgrave Macmillan, 2018.

Clarke, Daniele. "'Formed into Words by Your Divided Lips': Women, Rhetoric and the Ovidian Tradition." In *This Double Voice: Gendered Writing in Early Modern England,* edited by Daniele Clarke and Elizabeth Clarke, 61–87. Houndmills: Macmillan, 2000.

Crawford, Katherine. *European Sexualities, 1400–1800.* Cambridge: Cambridge University Press, 2007.

Cohen, Michèle. "Manners Make the Man: Politeness, Chivalry, and the Construction of Masculinity, 1750–1830." *Journal of British Studies* 44 (2005): 312–329.

DeWitt Bockstruck, Lloyd. *Virgina's Colonial Soldiers*. Baltimore, MD: Genealogical Pub. Co, 1988.

Dierks, Konstantin. "The Familiar Letter and Social Refinement in America, 1750–1800." In *Letter Writing as a Social Practice*, edited by David Barton and Nigal Hall, 31–41. Amsterdam and Philadelphia, PA: John Benjamins, 1999.

Dierks, Konstantin. *In My Power: Letter Writing and Communications in Early America*. Philadelphia: University of Pennsylvania Press, 2009.

Dixon, Thomas. "Emotions: The History of a Keyword in Crisis." *Emotion Review* 4, no. 4 (2012): 338–344.

Earle, Rebecca, ed. *Epistolary Selves: Letters and Letter-Writers, 1600–1945*. Aldershot: Ashgate Pub., 1999.

Eibach, Joachim. "Das offene Haus. Kommunikative Praxis im sozialen Nahraum der europäischen Frühen Neuzeit." *Zeitschrift für Historische Forschung* 38 (2011): 621–664.

Feldberg, Michael, ed. *"Aaron Lopez's Struggle for Citizenship."* Blessings of Freedom: Chapters in American Jewish History. New York: KTAV, 2002.

Fowler Jr., William M. *Empires at War: The French and Indian War and the Struggle for North America, 1754–1763*. New York: Walker Books, 2005.

Grace, Philip. *Affectionate Authorities: Fathers and Fatherly Roles in Late Medieval Basel*. Farnham: Ashgate, 2015.

Grenier, Benoît, and Chaterine Ferland. "'As Long as the Absence Shall Last': Proxy Agreements and Women's Power in Eighteenth-Century Quebec City." *Clio Women, Gender, History* 37 (2013). http://journals.openedition.org/cliowgh/421.

Gumbrecht, Hans. *Production of Presence: What Meaning Cannot Convey*. Stanford, CA: Stanford University Press, 2004.

Haasis, Lucas. „'Noch bleibt mir ein Augenblick Zeit um mich mit Euch zu unterhalten.' Praxeologische Einsichten zu kaufmännischen Briefschaften des 18. Jahrhunderts." In *Diskurse-Körper-Artefakte. Historische Praxeologie in der Frühneuzeitforschung*, edited by Dagmar Freist, 87–113. Bielefeld: DeGruyter Transcript Verlag, 2015.

Haboush, Jahyun Kim. "Introduction. The Epistolary Genre and the Scriptural Economy of the Choson." In *Epistolary Korea: Letters in the Communicative Space of the Choson, 1392–1910*, edited by Jahyun Kim Haboush, 1–13. New York: Columbia University Press, 2009.

Hanley, Sarah. "Family and State in Early Modern France: The Marriage Pact." In *Connecting Spheres: Women in the Western World: 1500–Present*, edited by Marilyn J. Boxer and Jean H. Quataert, 53–63. Oxford: Oxford University Press, 1987.

How, James. *Epistolary Spaces: English Letter Writing from the Foundation of the Post Office to Richardson's Clarissa*. Aldershot: Ashgate Pub., 2003.

Howland, John W. *The Letter Form and the French Enlightenment: The Epistolary Paradox*. New York: Peter Lang, 1991.

Hüber, Axel. *The Nonverbal Shift in Early Modern English Conversation*. Amsterdam and Philadelphia, PA: John Benjamins, 2007.

Jennings, Judith. *Gender, Religion, and Radicalism in the Long Eighteenth Century: The "Ingenious Quaker" and Her Connections*. Aldershot: Ashgate Pub., 2006.

Jensen, Katherine Ann. *Writing Love: Letters, Women, and the Novel in France, 1605–1776*. Carbondale: Southern Illinois University Press, 1995.

Jordanova, Ludmilla. "The Representation of the Family in the Eighteenth Century: A Challenge for Cultural History." In *Interpretation and Cultural History*, edited by Joan H. Pittock, Andre Wear and Anthony Grafton, 109–134. London: Palgrave Macmillan, 1991.

Kaplan, Marilyn. "The Jewish Merchants of Newport, 1749–1790." In *The Jews of Rhode Island*, edited by George M. Goodwin and Ellen Smith, 13–27. Waltham, MA: Brandeis University Press, 2004.

Korte, Barbara. *Body Language in Literature*. Toronto, Buffalo, NY and London: University of Toronto Press, 1997.

Livesay, Daniel. *Children of Uncertain Fortune: Mixed-Race Jamaicans in Britain and the Atlantic Family, 1733–1833*. Chapel Hill: University of North Carolina Press, 2018.

Lynch, Andrew, Susan Broomhall, and Janes Davidson, ed. *A Cultural History of the Emotions*. London: Bloomsbury Academic, 2019.

McBurney, Christian M. *The Rhode Island Campaign: The First French and American Operation in the Revolutionary War*. Yardley: Westholme Publishing, 2011.

Miller, Pavla. *Transformations of Patriarchy in the West, 1500–1900*. Bloomington: Indiana University Press, 1998.

Milne, Esther. *Letters, Postcards, Email: Technologies of Presence*. London: Routledge, 2010.

Mitchel, Linda C. "Letter-Writing Instruction Manuals in Seventeenth- and Eighteenth-Century England." In *Letter-Writing Manuals and Instruction from Antiquity to the Present*, edited by Carol Poster and Linda C. Mitchell, 178–199. Columbia: The University of South Carolina Press, 2007.

Muravyeva, Marianna Georgievna. "'A King in His Own Household': Domestic Discipline and Family Violence in Early Modern: Europe Reconsidered." *History of the Family* 18, no. 3 (2013): 227–237.

Peters, Christine. "Gender, Sacrament and Ritual: The Making and Meaning of Marriage in Late Medieval and Early Modern England." *Past & Present* 169 (2000): 63–96.

Plamper, Jan. *The History of Emotions: An Introduction*. Oxford: Oxford University Press, 2015.

Pollock, Linda. "Anger and the Negotiation of Relationships in Early Modern England." *The Historical Journal* 47, no. 3 (2004): 567–590.

Poster, Carol, and Linda C. Mitchell, ed. *Letter-Writing Manuals and Instruction from Antiquity to the Present. Historical and Bibliographic Studies (Studies in Rhetoric/Communication)*. Columbia: The University of South Carolina Press, 2007.

Raapke, Annika. *"Dieses Verfluchte Land": Europäische Körper in Briefenerzählungen aus der Karibik, 1744–1826*. Bielefeld: DeGruyter Transcript Verlag, 2019.

Renn, Joachim. "Appresentation and Simultaneity: Alfred Schutz on Communication between Philosophy and Pragmatics." *Human Studies* 29, no. 1 (2006): 1–19.

Roper, Lyndal. *The Holy Household: Women and Morals in Reformation Augsburg*. Oxford: Clarendon Press, 1989.

Rosenwein, Barbara. "Problems and Methods in the History of Emotions." *Passion in Context* I, no. 1 (2010). https://www.passionsincontext.de/uploads/media/01_Rosenwein.pdf

Rublack, Ulinka, ed. *Gender in Early Modern History*. Cambridge: Cambridge University Press, 2002.

Ryan, Michael T. "Assimilating New Worlds in the Sixteenth and Seventeenth Centuries." *Comparative Studies in Society and History* 23, no 4. (1981): 519–538.

Scheer, Monique. "Are Emotions a Kind of Practice (and Is That What Makes Them Have a History)? A Bourdieuian Approach to Understanding Emotion." *History and Theory* 51 (2012): 193–230.

Stone, Lawrence. *"The Companionate Marriage." The Family, Sex and Marriage in England 1500–1800*. New York: Harper & Row, 1977.

Sweet, Rosemary, Gerrit Verhoeven, and Sarah Goldsmith, ed. *Beyond the Grand Tour: Northern Metropolises and Early Modern Travel Behaviour.* London and New York: Routledge, 2017.
Tadmore, Naomi. "The Concept of the Household-Family in Eighteenth-Century England." *Past & Present* 151, no. 1 (1996): 111–140.
Tadmore, Naomi. *Family and Friends in Eighteenth-Century England: Household, Kinship and Patronage.* Cambridge: Cambridge University Press, 2004.
Teuscher, Simon. "Property Regimes and Migration of Patrician Families in Western Europe around 1500." In *Transregional and Transnational Families in Europe and Beyond. Experiences since the Middle Ages,* edited by Christopher H. Johnson, David Warren Sabean, Simon Teuscher and Francesca Trivellato, 75–92. New York and Oxford: Berghahn Books, 2011.
Vellusig, Robert. *Schriftliche Gespräche. Briefkultur im 18. Jahrhundert.* Köln, Weimar and Wien: Böhlau, 2001.
Ward, Matthew C. *Breaking the Backcountry: Seven Years War in Virginia and Pennsylvania 1754–1765.* Pittsburgh, PA: University of Pittsburgh Press, 2004.
Whyman, Susan. *The Pen and the People: English Letter Writers 1660–1800.* New York: Oxford University Press, 2009.

3

AN EMOTIONAL COMPANY

Mobility, community, and control in the records of the English East India Company

Mark Williams

On 23 December 1674, Major William Puckle – an agent of the English East India Company – was issued a commission and extensive instructions from Company House in London for travel aboard the ship *Bombay Merchant* heading to Fort St. George in the Bay of Bengal. Upon arrival and consultation with the Company's agents there, Puckle was to immediately travel down the coast to the Company's factory at Machilipatnam on the Coromandel Coast. There, the instructions noted, Puckle was to be received as the third in the governing council at the Fort and given absolute and free access to 'all our bookes, consultations, & other papers, or any persons' for the expressed purpose of discovering 'abuses and miscarriages, [so] that those that have dealt unjustly may be discovered, & such that have dealt faithfully may be approved …'. In particular, the London Council wished to know 'whether our orders for religious duties are followed'; to know of 'refractory persons … that are idle, and debauched'; those trading privately without the Company's consent; those who had 'entred into ye Moors service'; those whom they should see 'discountenanced … & sen[t] for England'; and all those English 'not in our service' along with their purpose in India. To these ends, Puckle was instructed to keep 'a full narrative of [his] whole proceedings' in the form of a diary, which was to be given to the Council on his return, to inform subsequent reforms.[1]

The completed diary, which spans January 1674/1675 to January1676, represents more than a simple audit of the Company's material and financial affairs in India. It is also an inquisition into the moral state of the Company's presence in South Asia. I do not employ the term 'inquisition' here lightly: as I will show, the diary fits many of the normal tropes of the inquisitorial process familiar to historians of the church.[2] The diary attests to the diverse range of people with whom Puckle consulted and the evidence he gathered in producing a broader narrative, incorporating depositions taken from Company agents at the factory, accounts of sermons given, conversations undertaken, crimes enacted, and transcriptions of correspondence with those within and beyond the factory's walls. As his written commission suggests, Puckle's task was, in essence, to root out a sort of corporate heresy in terms grounded in the lexicon of Company prosperity: not only in religious misconduct, but also financial mismanagement, personal misbehaviour, and the unpermitted crossing of cultural boundaries (which, as I will show, were often understood within these wider matrices of Company profit). While lacking the formal legal apparatus which has shaped much of the academic discourse around inquisitorial records (especially questions of narrative and subjectivity around depositional material), the diary nevertheless reveals an intense concern for recording and reflecting the 'heresies' within the Company's remit.[3] Such 'finding out' of 'abuses and miscarriages' relied heavily upon the assessment, substantiation, and confirmation of information – the 'truth of all such informacions', as Puckle's instructions had termed it – acquired by (or extracted from) those associated with the Company across Machilipatnam's social strata. The text which Puckle subsequently produced is, like other inquisitorial material, one which speaks at multiple registers: it incorporates the narrative imposed by its creator, the experiences of the factory and those surrounding it, and the priorities of the East India Company itself as distilled through Puckle's assessments. The diary, and the broader discourses surrounding it, are therefore shaped by many of the same questions of subjectivity and multivocality highlighted by John Arnold and Lyndal Roper – 'veils' created by the institutional gaze and populated by the disembodied voices within.[4] The East India Company, as I will show, was no less concerned with the creation of an institutional line of enquiry, employing specific 'language and process' to both comprehend and report on its global activities.[5] Engaging with sources like Puckle's diary therefore demands focusing not only on the embedded narrative which Puckle has created, but also seeking out the 'voices' which might be gleaned from the wider emotional discourses surrounding Mechilipatnam and the East India Company's gaze more broadly.

A close analysis of Puckle's diary within these wider discourses surrounding East India Company legitimacy and authority necessarily demands reading the document as an emotionally laden text with specific emotive purposes. The act of observing and subsequently documenting life in Machilipatnam and the practices of Company servants within the factory there were emotional balancing acts in the production of this text. As I will show, Puckle's descriptions required projecting a sense of disconnect from what was seen and done there while also deploying emotive language to register disapproval and prompt action from those superiors to whom he ultimately answered. Affective language here takes on a distinctly transnational gloss: Puckle's diary is at once a highly localised representation of the emotional rhythms of the factory and its surrounds on a quotidian level, and also a document created in order to first travel and then project and solicit particular responses in readers as far away as Fort St. George and London. The remit of Puckle's task required that the diary also projects, where necessary, a sense of anxiety capable of spurring action while also befitting the balanced assessment of a Company servant able to read the situation 'on the ground'.[6] As I will show, this was fundamentally shaped, not only by the Company's own affairs but also by interactions beyond the factory walls. Relationships with local merchants, neighbouring towns, and the dominant empires of the region are incorporated into the diary and narrated for the prospective readership as part of the wider, anxious project. In this sense, Puckle's diary can be seen to embody Barbara Rosenwein's 'emotional community' in its most geographically expansive form. The description of a location remote from the prospective readership demanded a common lexicon of value, harm, threat, and approval in assessing Mechilipatnam within the Company's global concerns, variously articulating causes of anxiety while also attempting to ease anxieties in its prospective reader.[7] It represents an early example of what Ann Laura Stoler has described as the 'epistemic anxieties' which 'stir[red] affective tremors' in the later colonial endeavour, embodied in the 'pulse of the archive and the forms of governance that it belies'. Such documents are perhaps formulaic, but for a reason: they document, as Stoler argues, 'what could, should, and need not be done or said' within these 'never-stable' enterprises.[8] Through this, we are afforded a window into a community – both the Company and those framing it – struggling to respond to the implications of its own global enterprise, seeing – and feeling – what concerned it and building an affective language capable of spanning its expansive geography to the end of shaping and controlling its engagement with the world.

The 'abuses and miscarriages' related by Puckle to the Company at large also help to bring to life an institution primarily spoken of as a precursor to empire, as a facilitator of material change in Europe, or as an embodiment of early-modern statecraft.[9] Change both within and around the Company has been explained through its growing monopoly on violence, its shifting aggression in territorial terms, and its management of diplomacy. This seems, to me, to be a field which has, in many ways, anticipated and understood the importance of emotion within historical change, but largely as a lower-level concern: processes of change laden with affective resonances in the course of encounter and distance, but hidden beneath more dominant historiographical glosses.[10] Susan Broomhall's recent work has been suggestive in this regard in discussing the missionary endeavours of the *Vereenigde Oostindische Compagnie* (VOC), or (Dutch) United East India Company, emphasising the role of affective motifs in Company correspondence for driving 'continued engagement and exploration'. Broomhall sees these motifs 'articulated, rehearsed, and reproduced through [the Company's] documentation', compelling missionary activity through appeals to divine obligation and national pride.[11] Attention paid to emotional response and documentation within the wider processes of encounter, engagement, and (later) conquest can help to make sense of decision-making processes and the cohesion (or otherwise) of these communities across vast distances and in light of near-constant movement not only among Company agents but also among the material elements which connected it.[12] While important work by Miles Ogborn, Adrien Delmas, and others has helped to shift scholarly focus towards understanding the daily practices of writing and knowledge-gathering/circulation within these trading companies, focusing on affective language and its application(s) helps to combine such considerations of the negotiation of space and time within the wider 'globalising process' with a more precise consideration of the bonds and boundaries it created.[13] Comprehending what Philip Stern has recently termed the 'root spatial dilemma' of authority within the East India Company's structures, and understanding the 'systems and strategies produced by the Company's ever-present institutional anxieties' therefore demand closer attention to these manipulations and expressions embedded in the texts such dilemmas produced.[14] In short, we have to find a way to comprehend how the Company learned to feel.

In texts such as Puckle's diary, we can see this sort of regulation in motion, both literally and figuratively. The affective discourses in this text as part of the vast, self-writing institutional records of the EIC connect these many different strands of historiographical interpretation while also complicating understandings of this crucial institution and the people who both created and challenged it.[15] The essay will be divided into three parts. First, I will look at what Puckle 'saw' while recording the 'abuses' in Machilipatnam, focusing on the particular elements of daily life in the factory which were reported and the affective language with which Puckle describes them. This will draw attention to the particular 'anxieties' which shaped the diary and, by extension, Puckle's inquisition as a Company representative. Here, I draw on Joanna Bourke's understanding of 'anxiety' as a social state dependant on the gathering of information and the exercise of power over a perceived threat.[16] In Puckle's case, the naming and interrogation of the source(s) of these anxieties and the restitution of normal, hierarchical power over them are shown to be central to the Company priorities and the stabilisation of its emotional rhythms. I will then consider the 'silences' in Puckle's diary by examining the apparent commonplace and rhythms of Company life in Machilipatnam which clearly inform the text but are not described in comparable affective language – Stoler's 'skittish' imperial gaze.[17] Finally, I will look at the subsequent reception of Puckle's report within the wider structures of the East India Company. This will be accomplished in the first instance by tracing the reading of the diary before the Council of Fort St. George in February 1676 and the resolutions set forth in the process. A dissonant reading of Puckle's interpretation will also be provided through the analysis of the responses given at the Council by Walter Clavell, who served as the representative of the Machilipatnam factory at the hearing. This will shed light not only on the ways in which the Company responded institutionally to the appeals made through such affective language but also the ways in which it permitted or silenced alternate voices in the process of acquiring, exerting, and questioning its own global power.

I

The emotional topography of Puckle's diary is remarkable from the outset, with the landscape of its entries elevated and flattened in accordance with its author's priorities. The voyage, and the experience of travel generally, appear unremarkable within Puckle's account, contributing little to the wider narrative of the diary. From his commission, we are told that he travelled in relative comfort, having had the 'great cabben' of the *Bombay Merchant* set aside for him.[18] We learn from his own relation that the *Bombay Merchant* departed the Downs on 20 January 1674/1675 in the company of four other ships bound for the Coromandel Coast, arriving 'through good providence and the blessing of God' at Fort St. George on 24 June.[19] The days which followed at Fort St. George are related with the appearance of ritual and duty rather than descriptions of the exotic or the new: on disembarking, Puckle delivered letters to the Council and his commission was read; on 25 June, Puckle notes 'this day spent in reading letters' and that he had received the respects of the Company there, including a welcome through the firing of guns, 'it being too late last night when I landed to do it'.[20] Fusing the banal and the routine may remove any sense of drama in the voyage, but it also suggests a calming passage for a prospective Company reader into the world Puckle was beginning to describe.

Meetings conducted with local merchants elicited slightly stronger responses. Conversations with wealthy entrepreneurs such as Kasi Viranna – at that point the Company's 'chief agent for purchasing goods in Southern India' and servant of the King of Golkonda – and his account of the 'true state' of trade there brought information but also pity for the 'pore workemen' under the 'dayly oppression of Governours who seize their goods'.[21] This latter observation regarding the 'tyrannical' governments of South Asia was a common trope among Europeans in the region, and would later become part of the intellectual and emotional framework for imperial rule.[22] The neighbouring city of St Thomas (or São Tomé), visited by Puckle at the suggestion of the Company agent at Fort St. George, proved 'a curious delightful Citty' for its 'straight streets with houses well built according to ye Portugall manner without doors windows or inhabitants except vermin'. The climate of St Thomas was sufficiently 'fruitfull [and] healthfull' that Puckle's improving eye saw an opportunity, noting that it would be 'great Advantage' to the Company if 'either St Thomas were brought to Fort St George or that Fort St George were carried to St Thomas'.[23] The performance of order mingled with the prospect of further improvement here, ranging from the spaces the Company occupied (or might have) to the maintenance of Company bodies.[24]

Puckle's departure for Machilipatnam on 10 July brings about a noticeable change in the tone of his diary and the affective language incorporated into the narrative. From the moment of his arrival in the harbour's road, Puckle describes a space which is not only less ordered but also pervaded by external influence: he makes note, for instance, of the 'otherness' of the ships surrounding him, observing '11 sayle of shipps' within view. Three of these, Puckle records, belonged to the King of Golkonda (Abul Hasan Qutb Shah); two belonged to the King of Siam (Ramathibodi III); the rest, to Puckle's eyes, appeared to be 'Moores and Portugalls and Danes'. Puckle's recording of this detail cannot have been an incidental curiosity: it may well have been intended to suggest the relative weakness of the Company's presence in the region, surveying a space which might have been dominated by their own traders but which he found filled with foreign bodies. The ship which drew his greatest attention, however, belonged to another Englishman, Richard Mohun, chief of the factory, whose 'great vessel ab[ou]t 300 tuns ... lately from Persia' suggested a more direct corruption than the internationality of the harbour.[25]

Mohun's ship, and its recent journey, immediately signified the excesses with which he had come to be associated within the East India Company, and the first of the 'heresies' investigated by Puckle on behalf of the Company: private trade. This, as Philip Stern has established, was a concern born of the Company's expanding interest in maintaining a corporate monopoly on all trade conducted by Crown subjects east of the Cape of Good Hope. The institutional insecurities which this subsequently engendered brought with it – at least at this stage – as much or more violence directed towards private traders as any others.[26] In the course of reforming and controlling Company activity across such vast spaces, private trade conducted by individual servants otherwise professedly loyal to the Company would eventually be relaxed, ensuring that some – for instance, Elihu Yale or Joseph Collett – could become immensely wealthy on a personal level while still applying themselves to Company profit.[27] At the time of Puckle's visitation, however, private trade occupied a liminal moral space in the Company's anxieties. What was termed 'private trade', at its most severe, could lead to the rise of 'interlopers': comparable to smugglers but, in their perceived capacity to sow dissent through their unmitigated pursuit of personal wealth and rejection of Company authority, presenting an immediate threat. Interlopers were, in themselves, held by Company officials to be operating on the margins of both social acceptability and emotional constancy, described as 'unstable minds [and] ungovernable persons'.[28]

Puckle's characterisation of Mohun, and the affective language employed in the diary, are best understood against these wider anxieties and institutional discourses around private trade. At the time of Puckle's arrival, Mohun had been confined to his quarters on the Council's orders. Anticipating potential offence in his absence, Mohun evidently wrote to Puckle personally: meeting other members of the factory's Council aboard the *Unity*, Puckle had a letter 'put into my hands'. Puckle promptly copied the letter into his diary as part of the larger reconstruction of his arrival. Here, Mohun lamented his state and asked that Puckle 'take not unkindly [to his absence] since it springs neither from neglect or disrespect'.[29] This set the wider tone for Mohun's defence of his actions as well as his submission to Company authority: apparently contrite but also insistent upon explaining the iniquities of his position. Upon meeting with Puckle shortly thereafter in his own quarters, Mohun 'discoursed of his unhappiness as to his present condition [and] how ill he had been treated' but assured Puckle that he would submit to the Company's authority.[30] Both men apparently agreed that Puckle would treat the matter dispassionately. Puckle wrote that

> I proposed (to prevent passions) to give him his charge in writing & desired his answer in the same manner ... To wch he agreed & for examining witnesses I should to the best of my skill do impartially in taking & wording theire testimonies.[31]

The conscious exercise of restraint and the subsequent recording (or perhaps performance) of it in the diary were central to the prospect of resolution and the restoration of calm, profitable order.

Much of the remainder of Puckle's visit centred upon assembling a record of Mohun's conduct through both the testimony of his fellow agents and the material record of his activity. When Puckle confronted Mohun after being invited into the latter's private quarters, Mohun argued that he had been 'necessitated to keep up a grandeur both in Habit, Entertainment, and also in attendance' or he would 'gitt nothing by living in this Country'. Foreshadowing similar responses to charges of corruption against Warren Hastings more than a century later, Mohun put forward an argument for the incompatibility of a supposedly orthodox Company morality with the trading cultures and social habits of South Asia: for Mohun, it was a plea for sympathy grounded on the notion that his actions and affectations required new boundaries within these unfamiliar spaces.[32] Puckle, however, carried on with the assembling of evidence in the matter. Letters exchanged between agents within the factory from before Puckle's arrival were transcribed within the diary in order to establish the history of Mohun's abuses. Puckle documented conversations held with fellow agents who had observed Mohun's activities and confirmed suspicions that Mohun had personally profited from outgoing trade while his fellow agents and the Company had not. Visiting the factory sites for which Mohun had provided oversight, Puckle marvelled at the excesses, being told that Mohun must have been 'distracted' during their construction. While consulting inventories, Puckle found that Mohun had personally sent Persian wine to the Mughal governor of the territory without licence from the Company and traded on his own terms in painted cloth and salampore (painted cloth) without permission.[33] When finally tried before the Council on 12 July 1675, however, Mohun was replaced and made to wait for the next ship back to England, for which he would have to wait until January the following year.[34]

While Mohun was certainly the foremost individual concern of Puckle's larger inquisitorial visit, recording the wider rhythms of the factory also demanded a careful balancing of affective language. The state of the factory in devotional terms – observing 'whether our orders for religious duties are followed', as his instructions had required – was of immediate concern on Puckle's arrival.[35] Noting his attendance of church on the Sabbath, Puckle recorded having heard the 'padre' (as he termed him) Mr Thomas Whitehead preach on John 16 condemning 'Pride Drunkenness Swearing & Uncleannness' among those in attendance, with Puckle adding that while in the afternoon 'he onely reads prayers'. Moving from the general to the particular, Whitehead told the congregation – and Puckle recorded – that 'though Mars had some years been in the field yet he feared that more have been slain in the Courts of Venus then [sic] in the Fielde of Mars'.[36] A clear warning against the consequences of promiscuity and sexual debauchery among the factors at Machilipatnam, this was an articulation of fear regarding the consequences of crossing the cultural and racial boundaries of the factory: the perceived and real threat of spreading sexual diseases and the mixing of allegiances in the process.[37] Whitehead subsequently took it upon himself to notify Puckle that the young men of the factory had neglected to come to prayers, naming those who had not been in attendance and working with Puckle to ensure their reprimand. On 7 October, for instance, Puckle received 'information … that severall of the young men kept disorders in their chambers', drinking beyond 'the bounds of soberity'; pursuing this, Puckle noted they were 'convicted partly by proofe & ply by confession' and admonished by 'the Padre', who subsequently preached on the subject on the Sabbath following.[38]

Whitehead himself was not beyond the suspicion of Puckle or, by extension, the Company whom he was meant to embody. As Haig Smith has recently pointed out, Company chaplains were not only invested with significant moral duties in spaces where licentiousness was thought to be rife, but also frequently found themselves criticised for proving inadequate in the policing of cultural and religious boundaries.[39] The supremacy of Whitehead as chaplain within the factory was initially reasserted through Puckle's intervention; on 23 July 1675, not long after Puckle's arrival, Whitehead is noted as having complained that he had not been given due status at the dinner table and in the rest of the factory, arguing that he should be treated as second in council after the chief. Whitehead's argument for this was one of education and pedigree, 'he being a Minister and Master of Art of the University of Oxford'.[40] Puckle duly brought the issue before the Council at the next meeting on 2 August, but not without recording his reservations about the potential imbalances this would create in the factory's humours: he noted with caution 'What this little sparke may kindle, especially should it break out in ye Pulpit I cannot foresee further then [sic] the inflaming of ye dyning Roome which sometimes is made almost intollerable [sic] hot …'.[41] The language of disorder, and in particular the implicit reference to humoral imbalance, is notable in Puckle's choice of words on recording this entry: while the Company's dining halls were closely moderated spaces intended to enforce hierarchy (for instance, through separating married and single men in order to control conversation), Puckle's anxieties over possible excess reinforce a wider narrative of imbalance.[42] Puckle's examination of Whitehead's influence and moral fortitude also extended to more material manifestations. On 6 October, Puckle inspected Whitehead's library, producing in his diary 'a catalogue of the books belonging to the Honourable Company'. Divided into folio, quarto, and octavo formats, these included theological works by Henry Hammond, John Calvin, Peter Martyr, Thomas Aquinas, numerous Bibles, and a Book of Common Prayer.[43] While East India Company libraries leave little material trace, comparable lists suggest that the preponderance of Calvin's works, editions of Bibles (in English, but also in Greek, Hebrew, and indigenous languages such as Malay), and works of Anglican divines in Whitehead's library were relatively orthodox.[44] The notable absence of interposition by Puckle in producing this list – without note of remarkable inclusions, gaps, or anything that might have been thought anathema to Company aims – again reinforces this insofar as the diary itself can suggest.

With these assessments and rectifications of the mercantile and devotional orthodoxies of the factory came a broader effort to rein in excesses through the assertion of order. This endeavour, as Puckle's diary relates it, saw the disentanglement of excess and emotional indiscipline from the reasoned governance of mercantile activity. For instance, when Thomas Whitehead alerted Puckle to the widespread drunkenness and gambling among the younger men of the factory after having attended the 'punch houses' outside of its walls, Puckle promptly recorded that he personally interviewed the (largely English) owners of these punch houses, issuing licences to some on condition of ensuring moderation, and sending others back to England. The case of Thomas Davis, for instance, is instructive here: on 20 October, Thomas Whitehead informed Puckle that Davis – 'an Englishman' – kept a 'punch house' outside the factory, where he 'suffereth great disorders to be in his house not onely in ye weekedays' but also on the Sabbath. Mohun, too, confirmed these disruptions, telling Puckle that, he lived nearby and was frequently 'disturbed in his devotions' by 'ye noyse of fidlers cursing, swearing, whooping …' in Davis's house.[45] Davis was promptly brought before Puckle and the Council 'upon ye 2d message', where he was 'examined confessed & subscribed his name to ye sd examination'. This examination established not only Davis' actions as an owner of the punch house in question but also his history and wider place in the Company's control: Davis is noted as having lived around Machilipatnam 'ab[ou]t 12 years', having left England in 1661 aboard the *Royal Charles* as a cooper before taking up another position aboard the *Royal James* under one Morris Blackman. Davis, however, found himself stranded when the ship cast away from Balasore, giving him cause to revert to keeping 'an house of entertainment … most of ye time he hath lived here'. Maintaining that he only permitted gambling as a *passo tempo* and 'never knew any of ye Company's servants drunk but sometimes they would be merry in drink' and had never 'lodg[ed] strangers' while running the house, Davis signed his testimonial.[46] Testimonials from others within the Company undermined Davis, however: the physician, Thomas Morris, maintained that Davis 'kept a very disorderly house', having nearly killed two of the Company's dyers through plying excess drink; Whitehead himself claimed that Davis had so insulted the chief of the neighbouring Dutch East India Company factory that 'he would have laid Davis in irons but that he is of another nation'.[47] The following day, Davis' immoderation was punished, but not without the prospect of reform: he was 'secured in the factory' until he could be transported to Fort St. George, where, if he could prove against these 'informations' against him and that he would maintain 'good sober & peaceable behaviour', he could have his liberty.[48]

Others escaped with noticeably less severe punishment. When, for instance, two young men were found 'wanting from ye Factory' and discovered at the punch house of Andrew Gill, the latter was summoned before the Commissioners. Gill, confessing that, being an 'old man', he had no commission or licence to keep a drinking house, nevertheless appealed to the sympathies of his examiners. Gill petitioned the Commissioners for a licence against considerations that he 'hath lived 15 years in this towne in good reputation' and being 'abt 70 years of age past labour unable to returne for England' could not make a living otherwise. Producing attestations of being 'of good life & conversation' from Whitehead and others, Gill was given permission for one year to sell wine under an obligation of 1,000 pagodas (Southern Indian currency) on grounds that he keep to a strict moral code: no fighting or excessive drinking in his house; no drinking after 9 o'clock on any day, not for more than an hour, and not on the Sabbath; and no 'singing whooping hallowing musicke' to avoid 'disquiet' for 'ye neighbourhood'.[49] This suggests that mitigating factors such as age, incapacity, or attestations of good character could shift the normal mobilities through which punishment and order might have operated within the Company. In both instances, the regulation of not only homosocial space but also the activities of those individuals no longer under the direct control of the Company and operating beyond the bounds of the factory walls was paramount.[50]

The potential consequences of not governing these activities properly were exposed in vivid detail in November 1675, when the social practice of drinking outside the factory's walls produced an outbreak of violence between Company servants. On 16 November, Puckle recorded the signed testimonies of three men – Henry Colborne (a steward), Timothy Harris, and Thomas Mayo (both writers for the Company) – in the wake of a late-night disturbance, which ended with Harris arriving in the factory at midnight crying 'murder'.[51] Harris, according to the recorded examination, had been drinking with Colborne at Andrew Gill's punch-house when they heard the curfew bell ring, calling for the shutting of the factory's gates 'from 9 till ½ an hour after', whereby they removed themselves to the rooms of George Chamberlain (a member of the Council). There they found Mayo who told Harris that he knew 'Mr Harry his Unkle, yt is a stage player' back in London, but had 'kept compa[ny] with better men'. Passions flared, with Harris admitting 'he was merry in drink but not drunk', and a fight ensued during which Mayo 'thrust his thumb into one of Harris his eyes'. Fearing the loss of his eye, Harris stumbled out into the factory, and 'should have dyed [sic] thereupon' but 'cryed out Murther' and was heard by the wife of one Samuel White, an Englishman living near the factory. The chirurgeon, John Heathfield, confirmed the eye was bloodshot.[52] Mayo, in his own account of the event, recalled having been with Harris and Colborne at Gill's punch-house until they collectively moved to Mr Chamberlain's, where the insults were hurled. Mayo recalled vividly the names Harris levelled at him, including 'shabby rogue, puppy, &c.'; the ensuing fight witnessed Harris 'bit[e] a hole in Mayos leg' (shown to the Commissioners) and Mayo accidentally 'run[ning] his finger in Harris['s] eye' while attempting to seize his hair. To Mayo, however, Harris had not only appeared drunk but had drawn his sword at Gill's punch-house to taunt his company.[53] Colborne's examination confirmed that the three had met at Gill's 'by accident' before leaving at 9 o'clock and walking 'round abt ye towne for ye walks sake' before arriving at Chamberlain's house, where Harris was 'disgusted' by Mayo knowing his uncle. Colborne claimed to have intervened to break up the fight but suffered a bloody nose for it before Harris departed and screamed murder.[54]

All three accounts, as Puckle records them, bring common issues to light: the association between immoderate drinking and a rise in the passions of the three men; the straining of masculine bonds between these men as reputations were questioned and reasserted (in this case, spanning London and Machilipatnam in its geographical scope); and the consequences of Company servants moving across and outside proscribed spaces, beyond the accepted rhythms of Company life as Puckle would have it. By recording these alongside a larger narrative of emotional immoderation, indulgence, and the breakdown of discipline within the factory, Puckle was able to project for his prospective audiences a community blurred at the margins and collapsed at the centre, in desperate need of Company enforcement to restore a profitable balance.

II

Nevertheless, to read Puckle's diary as a straightforward process of the 'uncovering' of abuses, their documentation, and subsequent remedy (to the best of Puckle and the Council's abilities) risks treating the anxieties of the 'inquisitor' as the dominant influence in shaping the Company's emotional record. Puckle's diary might be read, as mentioned earlier, as an effort in easing larger institutional anxieties through the hounding out of unregulated practices and reinforcement of spaces intended to be segregated.[55] Yet, there are already slippages evident in Puckle's record and silences which speak to larger tensions. As I have already established, Puckle was acutely aware on his arrival that Machilipatnam was a space not just permeated on all sides by other powers and cultures – the ships on the horizon – but also a heterogeneous cultural space only loosely obedient to Company strictures. Closer analysis of the ways in which Puckle's narrative of regulated emotion and the controlled rhythms of profit appear broken up or intruded upon by broader cultural exchange and interaction is instructive here. This will help in situating the diary within the Company's wider anxieties beyond the narrative permitted to us by its author.

In keeping with his instructions, Puckle made a point of acquiring information about Crown subjects living beyond the Company's administration; however, hearing of these Company 'heresies' relied heavily upon the rumour, hearsay, and reportage of those who, unlike Puckle, had moved freely throughout these regions and could speak to those outside the Company's normal gaze. For instance, in January 1676, one Mr Ives, identified as the 'Son of Mr Ives of Thames Street' in the diary, appeared at the factory apparently fleeing for his life from the army of the King of Golkonda. According to Puckle's account, Ives' arrival at the factory was in pursuit of refuge from 'his French comrades' in the Golkondan army.[56] Puckle immediately plied Ives for information about his comrades there, noting their reputed character since crossing these boundaries. For instance, Puckle took note of one Mr Hull, described as having 'marryed a

Portugall woman yt proved unfaithfull to his bed', abandoning her at Madras when she sought divorce, 'not being able to bear ye reproach & affronts'; or 'one O'Brian an Irishman came forth a souldier to ye Fort' but fell out with a lieutenant and abandoned his post to join the Golkondan army; John Brawse, who had apparently been in India 'abt 10 or 12 years travaling [sic] about ye Mogulls country & most parts of India', but now joined the Mughal armies; and one 'Joseph Taylor' who sailed out in the *Bombay* only to leave his ship and go to Golkonda, where he married.[57] Of Ives himself, Puckle noted that he had served out his time in the Company '(as he said) then hearing [Machilipatnam] was a better place to live in', was persuaded by a friend to stay there, where he married the 'natural' daughter of that friend for an (as yet undelivered) 'sum of Money'.[58] In another conversation with a Mr Mallet from Bombay, Puckle was notified of some 20 English soldiers in the service of the Golkondan King alongside 'abt 60 French', as the King 'took great pleasure in his Europeans'. Puckle immediately recorded that he had been assured 'none of them ... had turned M[o]ores'.[59]

The essential contradiction for Puckle in producing these sorts of accounts therefore became the need to acquire information regarding those thought to be beyond the Company's authority (and approbation by extension) through the cooperation of those who did not themselves embody (or even acknowledge) it. This demanded, in effect, temporary extension of the wider 'emotional community' which the diary circumscribed to achieve the larger inquisitorial end of the investigation, permitting otherwise suspicious testimony into the framing of what was seen and understood to give shape to the image provided.[60] The prompts which shaped Company anxieties must also be considered as fundamentally hybrid: both drawing on and responding through the actions and language of those who crossed these boundaries.[61] In gaining intelligence about Spanish activities in the Philippines, for instance, Puckle was willing to consult an anonymous Englishman 'yt had left the King of Bantam's service after 14 or 15 years spent in ye South Seas & parts of India'. From this (curiously) anonymous individual, Puckle was able to gain information about the goods traded in Manila and the potential for spurring insurrection there against the 'Spaniards Tirany', building upon the informant's sense that Spanish subjects there 'refuse to till ye land because of oppression'. Nevertheless, these remained the insights of a man long since severed from the affairs of the Company and England at large.[62] Puckle's investment of trust and his willingness to incorporate it into the diary as a report on the present state of tensions in the Philippines necessarily required a willingness to believe that the informant had reliably consulted with local sources in the Philippines (either in their own language or through intermediaries there) as to their feelings of oppression and willingness to resist Spanish rule, that he had left the King of Bantam's service on honourable terms, and that he had arrived in Machilipatnam in a spirit of camaraderie; moreover, it required that Puckle's superiors would be willing to suspend their distrust of such a 'cosmopolitan go-between' whose divided loyalties might normally have prompted suspicion.[63]

As many of these examples have suggested, anxieties about the consequences of mobility and the spatial limits of Company control intersected with concurrent concerns about the gendered, racial, and hierarchical bounds of the factory. In the easing of many of the anxieties swirling around Machilipatnam and the Company itself, masculine emotion predominated, with the presence of women and non-European agents largely incorporated only as a source or salve for male emotional regulation. In much of the Company's records, women tend to appear only as wives to Company servants (in India or as embodiments of luxury at home) or, more often, as sources of temptation across cultural boundaries.[64] The aforementioned wife of Samuel White was among the witnesses to the screams of the temporarily cyclopean Thomas Harris, but her name is not given; Puckle does, however, later record that White, having arrived in India aboard the *Loyal Subject* escorting women to Fort St. George, had courted the then Ms Povey when she was intended for a Mr Jersey (or Jearsy). When Povey rejected Jersey and 'return'd him his tokens', she and White were married by the 'French padre' in Madras when the minister at the Fort refused to do so.[65] The example of Mr Hull marrying a Portuguese woman (again, unnamed) is in keeping with a broader tendency in the institutional record to reduce 'foreign' women to agents of male anxiety: as early as 1624, one Captain Greene was brought before the Company courts for keeping '2 Portugall women ... in his cabbin a yeare togeather', giving them 'costly apparell' and making them part of the 'shipps companye'.[66] Such desires – emotional, sexual, physical – were, as Julia Schelck has pointed out, often noted as obstacles to the 'productive capacities' of Company servants.[67] Other women – clearly part of the fabric of everyday life, but at the periphery of Puckle's institutional gaze – are permitted only a glance in the record: one 'Mrs Mingham' is noted as among the English families in neighbouring towns, but only a widow whose husband was 'cannonier to ye King of Golkonda'; another woman, listed only as a 'peon', is noted as working to 'cleanse ye [Factory] house at ½ pago[da] a month'.[68] As Amrita Sen has noted, however, the presence of such women in texts such as Puckle's diary is indicative of the ways in which women shaped, and often pushed at the confessional, cultural, and gendered boundaries of Company life even while those boundaries were in the process of being monitored and forced upon them.[69]

The capacity of not only subaltern groups such as the unnamed 'peons' who populate Puckle's diary but also the indigenous merchants and translators to shape the emotional rhythms of life in the factory can also be traced through closer attention to such small, often inadvertent, acts of inclusion in the text. Reliance on 'peons' – that is, South Asian labourers, orderlies, and servants working under the Company's remit – for the enforcement of boundaries and provision of stability in the factory is evident throughout Puckle's diary.[70] As Amrita Sen has recently argued, these incorporations of 'ordinary Indians' into Company routine were 'essential to its survival', facilitating cooperation across cultures and shaping much of the daily function of Company trade.[71] Puckle's diary confirms this dependence. For instance, on 4 September 1675, in a bout of 'd[e]lirium',

Nathaniel Cholmley, an English diamond merchant living in Machilipatnam with the Company's permission, attempted suicide by 'leaning his breast on the point of a sword', producing '5 wounds'; while Cholmley was recovering, Matthew Mainwaring (a council member) 'put peons into the house that nothing might be removed or imbezeiled [sic]'.[72] Peons could be both witnesses to disorder and agents of it: when, on 6 January 1675, a 'great brick batt' was thrown at the house of Matthew Mainwaring, three peons affirmed it to have been thrown by Samuel Wales – described as 'one of ye young men' by Puckle – which they 'affirmed to his face', only to be dismissed by Wales on grounds that 'they were black men & their testimonyes not to be taken'. Wales blasphemed 'with passion', before leaving 'in a huffing manner' once reproved.[73] When Company servants were retrieved from punch houses or made to observe curfew, peons tended to undertake the labour required which subsequently underpinned the projected calm of Puckle's diary.[74]

Such marginalised individuals and groups could also be targets of suspicion when order broke down. Not only was violence against 'peons' commonplace – to the extent that Puckle later advised that a penalty should be imposed against any found guilty of 'drubbing' them – but their ubiquity within factory life tended to leave them implicated in crimes as passive participants or manipulated accomplices.[75] Noted instances of trade, whether seemingly frictionless or recorded in a tone of frustration by Puckle, relied upon the translations and intermediation of those – including peons and brahmins – able to work between Company polarities of profit and violence.[76] Reminders of the Company's (for now) position of weakness in South Asia were frequent enough: towards the end of December 1675, the factory was evacuated to facilitate its inspection by the King of Golkonda, sending 'all ye English women to Madapollam' and the men to a tent beyond the town, with doors left open in the factory 'yt ye King may go into any house he shall please'.[77] The affective language embedded within Puckle's descriptions of South Asian society may, therefore, not have always assigned significant agency to those with whom he interacted, but the gravity of their influence on the text itself is clearly evident. This, as Susan Broomhall has suggested in relation to the VOC, was a fundamental creative (and destructive) component of the wider Company psyche; for Puckle, it was an essential – if not always conscious – element of the story being told.[78]

III

These interactions advanced in Puckle a desire to control how the Company and its agents located themselves along these mercantile and cultural boundaries. The diary concludes with a series of recommendations meant to respond to the problems of the factory. Many of these are unsurprising given the problems initially articulated by Puckle. For instance, Puckle argued for the reinforcement of strict hierarchy within the factory to ensure 'settling differences amongst the commissioners', thereby avoiding conflict. This would help to counter the perceived 'idleness' of its young men. If they were not to be 'conformed to the Rules of Government', Puckle suggested the Company adopt the Dutch example of sending 'all young men as will not be regulated to Batavia' as soldiers.[79] But Puckle was also careful to advocate a clearer, moderated engagement along the cultural boundaries of the factory. He lamented the linguistic inabilities of many within the factory – again, the young in particular – noting that only a few spoke Dutch or Portuguese and only one or two 'ye Countrey languages'. To this end, Puckle advocated daily, one-hour lessons in Portuguese and 'the Moores language' (likely Persian) after dinner each day, with the caveat that non-attendance would come at a personal cost to help pay for the tutors.[80] This would have helped to facilitate fluency in what were, by that time, the *lingua francas* of the South Asian seaboard as well as the main language of communication with the Mughal elite, likely with the aim of cutting out native intermediaries.[81] Nevertheless, such advocations on Puckle's part should not be read as a case for unadulterated cosmopolitan engagement with these same South Asian societies. The spatial terms in which these cultures were to be encountered was to be strictly controlled, especially where profit suffered. For instance, travel of 'Moors, Gentues & Persians' on Company ships was to be prevented according to Puckle, on grounds that 'it doth give them such insight into trade as may in tyme spoile the English'.[82] This was a careful management of the space of the factory to not only rectify the 'abuses' Puckle witnessed there but also to set the terms of cultural engagement in a way which would affect measured, controlled cosmopolitan trade.

Puckle's diary ostensibly worked as an affective device, prompting swift actions from the wider Company grounded on his authoritative account. The Council at Fort St. George, with the approval of Company House in London, produced a four-page set of proposals with the aim of remedying the problems the diary had exposed in Machilipatnam.[83] In many of these, the connection between managing the emotional rhythms of the factory and its day-to-day operations is evident, bringing Puckle's recommendations into almost direct effect. For instance, Company agents were instructed to pass any complaints between agents and commissioners upwards rather than settle disputes locally, fearing that otherwise 'the parties will [never] become one piece againe' in either private terms or 'in the Honourable Company's service' if hierarchy remained unenforced and unobserved.[84] The 'tyrannical' practice of private trade – here clearly echoing Mohun's case – was condemned on grounds that such practices 'justifyed the Heathen whom in words they condemn'.[85] The young men whom Puckle so often criticised were to be subject to strict moral monitoring: fines were introduced for being found drunk, for cursing, or for unlawful gaming; for being out of their chambers 'after 10 of the clock at night'; and for beating ('drubbing') Company servants or 'peons'.[86] Such strictures set into place a proposed system of moderation which would ensure calm, order, and, of course, stable conditions for trade. Puckle's language reforms were implemented for both Portuguese and Persian ('the Moors language') and to be woven into factory life. A tutor for each language was to be hired for six months, reading to the Company servants for an hour each day after dinner 'whilst they are together'. Non-attendance and incompetence in the languages were to be met with penalties: three further months could be provided at the end of six if they were not yet 'perfect'; however, speaking English during lessons would be met with forfeiture of money to help pay the tutor.[87] While linguistic ability was, as Samuli Kaislaniemi has pointed out, already entrenched in Company activity through a larger 'community of practice', such formalised lessons and the clear attempt to invest in full competence through a common lexicon must also be read as an enforcement of order and a response to the anxieties of cultural fluidity and co-dependence.[88] In extreme circumstances, those who refused to be 'conformed to Rules' were to be 'sent to the Fort [St George] and kept there', severing them from factory life entirely. That the Dutch 'send all such young men … to Batavia, & make them serve for souldyers till their time expire' was cited as a justification for this approach, as Puckle had done in his own recommendations.[89]

Curiously, however, the same document through which the proposals were issued in Council also contained a dissenting voice: that of Richard Mohun's representative, Walter Clavell, who was invited to answer for Mohun and comment on the proposals at Fort St. George.[90] Clavell's responses, which are recorded in a second column next to the original proposals in a different hand, speak directly to the tensions between the regulating impulses of the Company authorities and the realities of life in the factory. While the format of the document leaves Clavell's direct penning of the responses uncertain, the preamble to the document notes that Clavell 'will Answer for himselfe', suggesting, at the very least, transcription by a clerk at hand.[91] The responses given offer a notably dissenting voice from that of the proposals themselves. For instance, the mediation of the Company in divisions among agents is noted as having 'long been desyred', but never properly acted upon by the Company, and so 'discountenancing the transgressor at home' had been the only remedy.[92] Stricter observance of Company orders and hierarchy is responded to bitterly and with a clear tone of frustration, saying 'this were better addressed to our employers' whom Clavell noted had too easily found fault in their agents.[93] Puckle's suggestion of sending young agents to the Company fort at Batavia to gain discipline as soldiers, while agreeable in principle, is given the warning that 'a garrison is a sorry schoole of morality', and thus unlikely to provide any longer-term issues with the character of the Company's servants.[94] Lastly, Clavell replied to the charge that the carrying of 'Moors and Gentues' had 'spoiled the English' in those regions, noting that this passage was very often enforced by local governors, and therefore beyond the control of any but the highest ranking Companymen; moreover, Clavell noted, cooperation with these groups – whom he lists as 'Armenians, Indostans, Bengallers, Viziapores, Moors, Gentues, Mallabars … Javas, Chinese, Mallayes, Syamers …' – was made necessary by their 'free & uncontrolled' movement in those waters.[95] Trade made movement a reality; the Company could only restrict its own servants. To do so in the hope of spurring further reform, however, would be 'to take the[ir] bread & give it unto strangers', not only hindering trade but denying servants the capacity to survive in a cosmopolitan environment (as yet) beyond the Company's fashioning.[96] Such recommendations lay at the core of Clavell's responses to the Company's attempts at regulation and control, connecting the local and the transnational alike but suggestive of the emotional fraying which could occur in the process of regulation. Clavell's responses should, however, be read alongside a wider institutional endeavour to respond to the anxieties which Puckle's report was designed to 'expose'; while an attempt to invite a measured and informed local response to Puckle's rendering of life in Machilipatnam, Clavell's dissenting viewpoint, like the interjections of factory servants and 'silent' voices of the factory, remains veiled by the Company's own anxious self-interest.[97]

As Guido van Meersbergen has recently suggested, attention to the sort of anxieties evident in records such as these are instructive for their capacity to dissolve easy characterisations of the East India Company and the cultures with which it engaged.[98] Puckle's diary must be located at the nexus of a multitude of anxieties: its author's desire to both find and constructively respond to known disorders, uncontrolled exchanges, and interests divergent from those of the Company; the tensions between Puckle as both individual agent in his own narrative and as a performing Company servant being acted upon by that institution's influence; and finally, the intrusion – active or passive – of voices outside the Company into that narrative. Attention to affective language is not only central to understanding these constructions, it has also permitted insights into the ways in which East India Company servants strained to operate between the aspirations of the abstract entity for which they worked and the practicalities of putting them into practice across immense distances. Puckle's diary suggests overlapping and even disputed boundaries which could extend across time and space (through reports, instructions, and regulatory structures) while struggling to comprehend more localised geographies where ambition and practicality often diverged when confronted with temptation, fear, or questions of survival.[99] These were the tensions born out of the process of globalisation which the East India Company has so often embodied in historical discussion: the simultaneous creation of vast distances between individuals and communities alongside a direct need to maintain essential emotional connections for the sake of function and a sense of common purpose. In trying to resolve these anxieties and exposing others, both Puckle and his diary reveal the crucial interplay and tension between the external and internal in the shaping of Company life and the wider world of which it was – wilfully or otherwise – increasingly a part.

Notes

1. British Library India Office Records [hereafter IOR], E/3/88 Letter Book 5, 1672–1678, 79r–80v, 'Commission & Instructions to Mr Wm Puckle, 23 December 1674'.
2. On inquisition, see Christine Caldwell Ames, "Does Inquisition Belong to Religious History?" *The American Historical Review* 110, no. 1 (February 2005): 11–37.
3. Most recently Chris Sparks, *Heresy, Inquisition, and Life Cycle in Medieval Languedoc* (York: York Medieval Press, 2014); John Arnold, *Inquisition and Power: Catharism and the Confessing Subject in Medieval Languedoc* (Philadelphia, PA: University of Philadelphia Press, 2001).

4 John Arnold, "The Historian as Inquisitor: The Ethics of Interrogating Subaltern Voices," *Rethinking History* 2, no. 3 (1998): 379–386; Lyndal Roper, *Oedipus and the Devil: Witchcraft, Sexuality, and Religion in Early Modern Europe* (London: Routledge, 1994): 2–3.
 5 Arnold, "Historian as Inquisitor," 381.
 6 On anxiety, see William J. Bouwsma, *A Useable Past: Essays in European Cultural History* (Oxford: University of California Press, 1990), Ch. 6; Laurence Johnson, "'Nobler in the Mind': The Emergence of Early Modern Anxiety," *Aumla* (December 2009): 141–156; Joanna Bourke, "Fear and Anxiety: Writing about Emotion in Modern History," *History Workshop Journal* 55 (Spring 2003): 111–133.
 7 Barbara H. Rosenwein, "Problems and Methods in the History of Emotions," *Passions in Context: Journal of the History and Philosophy of the Emotions* 1, no. 1 (2010): 2–32, https://www.passionsincontext.de/uploads/media/01_Rosenwein.pdf; last accessed 26/4/2019; Barbara H. Rosenwein, *Emotional Communities in the Early Middle Ages* (Ithaca, NY: Cornell University Press, 2006).
 8 Ann Laura Stoler, *Along the Archival Grain: Epistemic Anxieties and Colonial Common Sense* (Oxford: Oxford University Press, 2009): 19–20.
 9 Philip J. Stern, *The Company-State: Corporate Sovereignty and the Early Modern Foundations of the British Empire in India* (Oxford: Oxford University Press, 2011). Also see: Maxine Berg, Felicia Gottman, Hanna Hodacs and Chris Nierstrasz, ed., *Goods from the East, 1600–1800: Trading Eurasia* (Basingstoke: Palgrave Macmillan, 2015); Kirti N. Chaudhuri, *The English East India Company: The Study of an Early Joint-Stock Company 1600–40* (London: Routledge, 1999); Philip Lawson, *The East India Company: A History* (London: Longman, 1993); David Veevers, "'The Company as Their Lords and the Deputy as a Great Rajah': Imperial Expansion and the English East India Company on the West Coast of Sumatra, 1685–1730," *The Journal of Imperial and Commonwealth History* 41, no. 5 (2013): 687–709.
10 More recent forays into subjectivity and emotion in early-modern travel writing look to offset this. For instance, Nandini Das, "Richard Hakluyt's Two Indias: Textual *sparagmos* and Editorial Practice," in *Richard Hakluyt and Travel Writing in Early Modern Europe*, ed. Daniel Carey and Claire Jowitt (Farnham: Ashgate, 2012), 119–128; Eva Johanna Holmberg, "Writing the Travelling Self: Travel and Life-Writing in Peter Mundy's (1597–1667) *Itinerarium Mundii*," *Renaissance Studies* 31, no. 4 (2017): 608–625.
11 Susan Broomhall, "'Quite Indifferent to These Things': The Role of Emotions and Conversion in the Dutch East India Company's Interactions with the South Lands," *Journal of Religious History* 39, no. 4 (2015): 524–544.
12 Susan Broomhall, "Emotional Encounters: Indigenous Peoples in the Dutch East India Company's Interactions with the South Lands," *Australian Historical Studies* 45, no. 3 (2014): 352–353.
13 Miles Ogborn, *Indian Ink: Script and Print in the Making of the English East India Company* (London: University of Chicago Press, 2007); Adrien Delmas, "From Travelling to History: An Outline of the VOC Writing System During the 17th Century," in *Written Culture in a Colonial Context: Africa and the Americas 1500–1900*, ed. Adrien Delmas and Nigel Penn (London: Brill, 2012), 97–126; Anna Winterbottom, *Hybrid Knowledge in the Early East India Company World* (Basingstoke: Palgrave MacMillan, 2015).
14 Philip J. Stern, "Response: Seeing (and Not Seeing) Like a Company-State: Hybridity, Heterotopia, Historiography," *Journal for Early Modern Cultural Studies* 17, no. 3 (Summer 2017): 110.
15 The Dutch VOC has received significantly more attention in the study of its 'self-archiving' process and forms of documentation: see Adrien Delmas, *Les Voyages de l'écrit: Culture écrite et expansion européenne à l'époque moderne; essais sur la Compagnie Hollandaise des Indes Orientales* (Paris: Honoré Champion, 2013); Remco Raben, ed., *De archieven van de Vereinigde Oostindische Compagnie (1602–1795)* (Den Haag: SDU, 1992).

16 Bourke, "Fear and Anxiety," 126–133.
17 Rosenwein, "Problems and Methods," 17; Stoler, *Along the Archival Grain*, 255.
18 IOR/E/3/88.
19 IOR/G/26/12 'Diary of William Puckle, while at Masulipatam and Fort St. George' [hereafter 'Diary'].
20 IOR/G/26/12 Diary, fo. 1.
21 Stern, *Company-State*, 95; IOR/G/26/12, 29; 30 June 1675. For Viranna in wider context, see Radhika Seshan, "Intersections: Peoples, Ports and Trade in Seventeenth-Century Surat and Madras," *International Journal of Maritime History* 29, no. 1 (2017): 119–120.
22 Sanjay Subrahmanyam, *Europe's India: Words, People, Empires, 1500–1800* (Cambridge: Cambridge University Press, 2017).
23 IOR/G/26/12 Diary, 3 July 1675.
24 While often commented upon at the time, the climates around the Indian Ocean and the bodily experience of them have received little scholarly attention. See, for instance, Huntington Library MS83394 Sir James Houblon's Notebook, fos. 18v-20r. For 19th-century commentary, see George C. D. Adamson, "'The Languor of the Hot Weather': Everyday Perspectives on Weather and Climate in Colonial Bombay, 1819–1828," *Journal of Historical Geography* 38 (2012): 143–154.
25 IOR/G/26/12 Diary, 10 July 1675.
26 Stern, *Company State*, 44–60; Miles Ogborn, "Streynsham Master's Office: Accounting for Collectivity, Order and Authority in 17th-century India," *Cultural Geographies* 13 (2006): 127–155.
27 Yale is thought to have amassed a fortune of £200,000 while in India; Collet, as governor of Madras from 1717, was rumoured to be making upwards of £10,000 per year. See Om Prakash, "The English East India Company and India," in *The Worlds of the East India Company*, ed. Huw V. Bowen, Margarette Lincoln, Nigel Rigby (Woodbridge: Boydell and Brewer, 2002), 4; "Introduction," in *The Private Letter Books of Joseph Collet*, ed. Henry H. Dodwell (London: Longman, Greens and Co., 1933), xix.
28 Stern, *Company State*, 44.
29 IOR/G/26/12 Diary, 10 July 1675.
30 IOR/G/26/12 Diary, 10 July 1675.
31 IOR/G/26/12 Diary,12 July 1675.
32 IOR/G/26/12 Diary,12 July 1675; For Hastings, see Andrew Rudd, "Space, Sympathy, and Empire: Edmund Burke and the Trial of Warren Hastings," in *The Uses of Space in Early Modern History*, ed. Paul Stock (Basingstoke: Palgrave Macmillan, 2015), 173–196.
33 IOR/G/26/12 Diary, *passim*, but esp. 31 July; 10 August; 22 September.
34 IOR/G/26/12 Diary, 16 January 1675/6.
35 E/3/88 Letter Book 5, 1672–1678, 79r–80v.
36 IOR/G/26/12 Diary, 11 July 1675.
37 Requests for medicines in other factories suggest that sexually transmitted diseases were not uncommon: see IOR/G/14/1 [Cuddalore and Porto Novo], Davis and Ord to Fort St George, 15 November 1683.
38 IOR/G/26/12 Diary, 7 October 1675; 23 October 1675.
39 Haig Z. Smith, "Risky Business: The Seventeenth Century English Company Chaplain, and Policing Interaction and Knowledge Exchange," *Journal of Church and State* 60, no. 2 (2017): 226–247.
40 IOR/G/26/12 Diary, 23 July 1675.
41 IOR/G/26/12 Diary, 23 July; 28 July. 2 August 1675.
42 For dining practices see, for instance, IOR/G/14/1 [Cuddalore and Porto Novo] Thursday 1 November 1683.
43 IOR/G/26/12 Diary, 6 October 1675.

44 For comparison, see IOR/E/3/43 [Hugli] 'A List of the Hon:bl Compas: bookes packed up in ye Chest, wrote upon Library Bantam' [Dated February 1684 in catalogue with '*Success* pacquet recd 16 Augst 1684', but most likely compiled after the loss of Bantam to the Dutch in 1682].
45 IOR/G/26/12 Diary, 20 October 1675.
46 IOR/G/26/12 Diary, 20 October 1675.
47 IOR/G/26/12 Diary, 20 October 1675.
48 IOR/G/26/12 Diary, 21 October 1675.
49 IOR/G/26/12 Diary, 22 October 1675; 26 October 1675; Stern, *Company-State*, 286.
50 On intoxication practices in this period, see Phil Withington, "Intoxicants and Society in Early Modern England," *The Historical Journal* 54, no. 3 (2011): 631–657.
51 IOR/G/26/12 Diary, 16 November 1675
52 IOR/G/26/12 Diary, 16 November 1675: Examination of Timothy Harris.
53 IOR/G/26/12 Diary, 16 November 1675: Examination of Thomas Mayo.
54 IOR/G/26/12 Diary, 16 November 1675: Examination of Henry Colborne.
55 Stern, "Response: Seeing (and Not Seeing) Like a Company-State," 112–113.
56 IOR/G/26/12 Diary, 3 January 1675/6.
57 IOR/G/26/12 Diary, 3 January 1675/6.
58 IOR/G/26/12 Diary, 3 January 1675/6.
59 IOR/G/26/12 Diary, 7 December 1675.
60 Rosenwein, "Problems and Methods," *passim*.
61 Winterbottom, *Hybrid Knowledge,* esp. 'Introduction'.
62 IOR/G/26/12 Diary, [1] September 1675.
63 Winterbottom, *Hybrid Knowledge*, 215–216.
64 Tillman W. Nechtman, "Nabobinas: Luxury, Gender, and the Sexual Politics of British Imperialism in India in the Late Eighteenth Century," *Journal of Women's History* 18, no. 4 (Winter 2006): 9–10.
65 IOR/G/26/12 Diary, 3 January 1675/6.
66 IOR/H/29/1r Extracts out of the East India Company Court Books concerning misdemeanours, December 17 [1624].
67 Julia Schelck, "The Marital Problems of the East India Company," *Journal for Early Modern Cultural Studies* 17, no. 3 (Summer 2017): 98.
68 IOR/G/26/12 Diary, 22 September 1675.
69 Amrita Sen, "Traveling Companions: Women, Trade, and the Early East India Company," *Genre: Forms of Discourse and Culture* 48, no. 2 (2015): 193–214.
70 For peon see definition in Henry Yule and Arthur C. Burnell, *Hobson-Jobson: The Definitive Glossary of British India* (Oxford: Oxford's World Classics, 2013), 410–411.
71 Amrita Sen, "Searching for the Indian in the English East India Company Archives: The Case of Jadow the Broker and Early Seventeenth-Century Anglo-Mughal Trade," *Journal for Early Modern Cultural Studies* 17, no. 3 (Summer 2017): 38–40.
72 IOR/G/26/12 Diary, 4 September 1675; 3 January 1675/6.
73 IOR/G/26/12 Diary, 6 January 1675/6.
74 For instance, IOR/G/26/12 Diary, 21 October 1675.
75 IOR/G/26/12 Diary [fo. 68], 'Proposals'; 17 November 1675.
76 IOR/G/26/12 Diary, 24 July; 4 August; 27 August.
77 IOR/G/26/12 Diary, 26 December; 28 December.
78 Broomhall, "Emotional Encounters," 351–353.
79 IOR/G/26/12 Diary [fo. 68], 'Proposals'.
80 IOR/G/26/12 Diary [fo. 68], 'Proposals'.
81 Samuli Kaislaniemi, "The Linguistic World of the Early English East India Company: A Study of the English Factory in Japan, 1621–1623," *Journal for Early Modern Cultural Studies* 17, no. 3 (Summer 2017): 40.
82 IOR/G/26/12 Diary [fo. 69], 'Proposals'.

83 IOR/E/3/36, 'Replies … to various proposals and questions by Major William Puckle', Fort St George the 16th February 1675/6.
84 IOR/E/3/36, fo. 181v.
85 IOR/E/3/36, fo. 182r.
86 IOR/E/3/36, fo. 182r.
87 IOR/E/3/36, fo. 182r.
88 Samuli Kaislaniemi, "The Early English East India Company as a Community of Practice: Evidence of Multilingualism," in *Merchants of Innovation: The Languages of Traders*, ed. Esther-Miriam Wagner, Bettina Beinhoff, and Ben Outhwaite (Berlin/New York: De Gruyter Mouton, 2017), 132–157.
89 IOR/E/3/36, fo. 182v.
90 Clavell, later a factory chief, died of plague in 1677. See IOR Eur 387A [Lawrence Papers], *passim*.
91 IOR/E/3/36, fo. 181r.
92 IOR/E/3/36, fo. 181v.
93 IOR/E/3/36, fo. 182r.
94 IOR/E/3/36, fo. 182r.
95 Reliance on the Armenian 'trade diaspora' would be partly formalised soon after these incidents in a 1688 treaty. See Sebouh Aslanian, "Trade Diaspora versus Colonial State: Armenian Merchants, the English East India Company, and the High Court of Admiralty in London, 1748–1752," *Diaspora: A Journal of Transnational Studies* 13, no. 1 (2004): 46.
96 IOR/E/3/36, fo. 181r.
97 Arnold, "The Historian as Inquisitor," 383–384.
98 Guido van Meersbergen, "Writing East India Company History after the Cultural Turn: Interdisciplinary Perspectives on the Seventeenth-Century East India Company and Verenigde Oostindische Compagnie," *Journal for Early Modern Cultural Studies* 17, no. 3 (Summer 2017): 18–19.
99 Similar questions have been raised recently in Jan Plamper, *The History of Emotions: An Introduction* (Oxford: Oxford University Press, 2012), 68–71.

Bibliography

Adamson, George C. D. "'The Languor of the Hot Weather': Everyday Perspectives on Weather and Climate in Colonial Bombay, 1819–1828." *Journal of Historical Geography* 38 (2012): 143–154.

Ames, Christine Caldwell. "Does Inquisition Belong to Religious History?" *The American Historical Review* 110, no. 1 (February 2005): 11–37.

Arnold, John. "The Historian as Inquisitor: The Ethics of Interrogating Subaltern Voices." *Rethinking History* 2, no. 3 (1998): 379–386.

Arnold, John. *Inquisition and Power: Catharism and the Confessing Subject in Medieval Languedoc*. Philadelphia, PA: University of Philadelphia Press, 2001.

Aslanian, Sebouh. "Trade Diaspora versus Colonial State: Armenian Merchants, the English East India Company, and the High Court of Admiralty in London, 1748–1752." *Diaspora: A Journal of Transnational Studies* 13, no. 1 (2004): 37–100.

Berg, Maxine, Felicia Gottman, Hanna Hodacs, and Chris Nierstrasz, ed. *Goods from the East, 1600–1800: Trading Eurasia*. Basingstoke: Palgrave Macmillan, 2015.

Bourke, Joanna. "Fear and Anxiety: Writing about Emotion in Modern History." *History Workshop Journal* 55 (Spring 2003): 111–133.

Bouwsma, William J. *A Useable Past: Essays in European Cultural History*. Oxford: University of California Press, 1990.

Broomhall, Susan. "Emotional Encounters: Indigenous Peoples in the Dutch East India Company's Interactions with the South Lands." *Australian Historical Studies* 45, no. 3 (2014): 350–367.

Broomhall, Susan. "'Quite Indifferent to These Things': The Role of Emotions and Conversion in the Dutch East India Company's Interactions with the South Lands." *Journal of Religious History* 39, no. 4 (2015): 524–544.

Chaudhuri, Kirti N. *The English East India Company: The Study of an Early Joint-Stock Company 1600–40*. London: Routledge, 1999.

Das, Nandini. "Richard Hakluyt's Two Indias: Textual *sparagmos* and Editorial Practice." In *Richard Hakluyt and Travel Writing in Early Modern Europe*, edited by Daniel Carey and Claire Jowitt, 119–128. Farnham: Ashgate, 2012.

Delmas, Adrien. "From Travelling to History: An Outline of the VOC Writing System during the 17th Century." In *Written Culture in a Colonial Context: Africa and the Americas 1500–1900*, edited by Adrien Delmas and Nigel Penn, 97–126. London: Brill, 2012.

Delmas, Adrien. *Les Voyages de l'écrit: Culture écrite et expansion européenne à l'époque moderne; essais sur la Compagnie Hollandaise des Indes Orientales*. Paris: Honoré Champion, 2013.

Dodwell, Henry H. ed. *The Private Letter Books of Joseph Collet*. London: Longman, Greens and Co., 1933.

Holmberg, Eva Johanna. "Writing the Travelling Self: Travel and Life-Writing in Peter Mundy's (1597–1667) *Itinerarium Mundii*." *Renaissance Studies* 31, no. 4 (2017): 608–625.

Johnson, Laurence. "'Nobler in the Mind': The Emergence of Early Modern Anxiety." *Aumla* (December 2009): 141–156.

Kaislaniemi, Samuli. "The Early English East India Company as a Community of Practice: Evidence of Multilingualism." In *Merchants of Innovation: The Languages of Traders*, edited by Esther-Miriam Wagner, Bettina Beinhoff, and Ben Outhwaite, 132–157. Berlin/New York: De Gruyter Mouton, 2017.

Kaislaniemi, Samuli. "The Linguistic World of the Early English East India Company: A Study of the English Factory in Japan, 1621–1623." *Journal for Early Modern Cultural Studies* 17, no. 3 (Summer 2017): 59–82.

Lawson, Philip. *The East India Company: A History*. London: Longman, 1993.

Nechtman, Tillman W. "Nabobinas: Luxury, Gender, and the Sexual Politics of British Imperialism in India in the Late Eighteenth Century." *Journal of Women's History* 18, no. 4 (Winter 2006): 8–30.

Ogborn, Miles. *Indian Ink: Script and Print in the Making of the English East India Company*. London: University of Chicago Press, 2007.

Ogborn, Miles. "Streynsham Master's Office: Accounting for Collectivity, Order and Authority in 17th-Century India." *Cultural Geographies* 13 (2006): 127–155.

Plamper, Jan. *The History of Emotions: An Introduction*. Oxford: Oxford University Press, 2012.

Prakash, Om. "The English East India Company and India." In *The World of the East India Company*, edited by Huw V. Bowen, Margarette Lincoln, and Nigel Rigby, 1–18. Woodbridge: Boydell and Brewer, 2002.

Raben, Remco ed. *De archieven van de Verenigde Oostindische Compagnie (1602–1795)*. Den Haag: SDU, 1992.

Roper, Lyndal. *Oedipus and the Devil: Witchcraft, Sexuality, and Religion in Early Modern Europe*. London: Routledge, 1994.

Rosenwein, Barbara H. *Emotional Communities in the Early Middle Ages*. Ithaca, NY: Cornell University Press, 2006.

Rosenwein, Barbara H. "Problems and Methods in the History of Emotions." *Passions in Context: Journal of the History and Philosophy of the Emotions* 1, no. 1 (2010): 2–32. https://www.passionsincontext.de/uploads/media/01_Rosenwein.pdf; last accessed 26/4/2019.

Rudd, Andrew. "Space, Sympathy, and Empire: Edmund Burke and the Trial of Warren Hastings." In *The Uses of Space in Early Modern History*, edited by Paul Stock, 173–196. Basingstoke: Palgrave Macmillan, 2015.

Schelck, Julia. "The Marital Problems of the East India Company." *Journal for Early Modern Cultural Studies* 17, no. 3 (Summer 2017): 83–104.

Sen, Amrita. "Searching for the Indian in the English East India Company Archives: The Case of Jadow the Broker and Early Seventeenth-Century Anglo-Mughal Trade." *Journal for Early Modern Cultural Studies* 17, no. 3 (Summer 2017): 37–58.

Sen, Amrita. "Traveling Companions: Women, Trade, and the Early East India Company." *Genre: Forms of Discourse and Culture* 48, no. 2 (2015): 193–214.

Seshan, Radhika. "Intersections: Peoples, Ports and Trade in Seventeenth-Century Surat and Madras." *International Journal of Maritime History* 29, no. 1 (2017): 111–122.

Smith, Haig Z. "Risky Business: The Seventeenth Century English Company Chaplain, and Policing Interaction and Knowledge Exchange." *Journal of Church and State* 60, no. 2 (2017): 226–247.

Sparks, Chris. *Heresy, Inquisition, and Life Cycle in Medieval Languedoc*. York: York Medieval Press, 2014.

Stern, Philip J. "Response: Seeing (and Not Seeing) Like a Company-State: Hybridity, Heterotopia, Historiography." *Journal for Early Modern Cultural Studies* 17, no. 3 (Summer 2017): 105–120.

Stern, Philip J. *The Company-State: Corporate Sovereignty and the Early Modern Foundations of the British Empire in India*. Oxford: Oxford University Press, 2011.

Stoler, Ann Laura. *Along the Archival Grain: Epistemic Anxieties and Colonial Common Sense*. Oxford: Oxford University Press, 2009.

Subrahmanyam, Sanjay. *Europe's India: Words, People, Empires, 1500–1800*. Cambridge: Cambridge University Press, 2017.

Van Meersbergen, Guido. "Writing East India Company History after the Cultural Turn: Interdisciplinary Perspectives on the Seventeenth-Century East India Company and Verenigde Oostindische Compagnie." *Journal for Early Modern Cultural Studies* 17, no. 3 (Summer 2017): 10–36.

Veevers, David. "'The Company as Their Lords and the Deputy as a Great Rajah': Imperial Expansion and the English East India Company on the West Coast of Sumatra, 1685–1730." *The Journal of Imperial and Commonwealth History* 41, no. 5 (2013): 687–709.

Winterbottom, Anna. *Hybrid Knowledge in the Early East India Company World*. Basingstoke: Palgrave MacMillan, 2015.

Withington, Phil. "Intoxicants and Society in Early Modern England." *The Historical Journal* 54, no. 3 (2011): 631–657.

Yule, Henry, and Arthur C. Burnell. *Hobson-Jobson: The Definitive Glossary of British India*. Oxford: Oxford's World Classics, 2013.

PART II
Images

4

LUST, LOVE AND CURIOSITY

The emotional threads in the Dutch encounter with an exotic East

Natsuko Akagawa

This chapter examines the manifestation and representations of emotion in the encounter of East and West that took place between Dutch and Japanese individuals during the period of Japan's seclusion. This is generally understood to be from around 1639 when the Portuguese were expelled from Dejima, to 31 March 1853 when the *Convention of Peace and Amity between the United States of America and the Empire of Japan* (in Japanese *Nichibei Washin Joyaku*) was signed in Yokohama, Japan.[1] The encounter with the 'West' before the reopening of Japan took place mainly on the artificial island of Dejima in Nagasaki city to which representatives of the Dutch East India Company, the only Europeans permitted into Japan, were confined. Here, and during occasional officially sanctioned journeys beyond these boundaries, a small number of Dutch[2] merchants, seamen and medical officers interacted with a range of Japanese traders, imperial officials and designated 'ladies of pleasure'. Over time, the Dejima connection facilitated interactions between a growing group of Japanese scholars and Dutch men of science, but it was also the cause of painful separations of part-Japanese children evicted from their homeland. Through the personal interactions and emotive engagements that this narrow conduit allowed would flow mutually transformative cultural influences that, in time, came to manifest themselves in the artistic, intellectual and technological spheres of both societies.

The chapter focuses, firstly, on representative Japanese artistic and associated literary images of the West as a primary source for reading emotion in this East-West encounter. Lust, love and curiosity are all emotions that are potentially attributable to scenes of sexual intimacy that took place in Dejima, which were portrayed in a Japanese art form, *shunga*. In this chapter, I contextualise these visual representations of purported emotion by examining their Dutch and Japanese cultural settings, and the artistic traditions of this genre. Secondly, the chapter then extends to briefly consider other emotional threads – love and curiosity – that are discernible as arising from this narrow 'node of contact' that contributed to the two-way flows of mutually desired information. Finally, it considers how far the limited emotive contact afforded by the Dutch presence in Dejima contributed to promoting intercultural understanding and transforming knowledge between East and West in this early modern era.

'Europeans' in Japan

European contact with Japan and the Japanese initially began with the arrival of the Portuguese in Japan in 1543. However, after the suppression of Catholicism in 1612, the Portuguese in Japan were gathered and confined in Dejima in 1636 and later expelled from Japan in 1639.[3] After the Portuguese left, the Dutch trading post in Hirado was closed, and it was relocated to Dejima in 1641. It consisted of employees of the Amsterdam registered *Vereenigde Oostindische Companie* (herein after VOC), the Dutch East India Company.[4] Thereafter, in what is known as *sakoku*, the more than two-centuries-long seclusion, entry of foreigners to Japan was limited to predominantly Dutch and Chinese men.[5] The VOC, a consortium of 17 mercantile companies, was governed by the Gentlemen Seventeen headquartered in Amsterdam. The Asian trading activities of the VOC, however, were directed from its major trading port, Batavia, on the island of Java (now Indonesia). Conscious of the distinct commercial advantage its monopolistic position in Japan had given it over its European competitors, the VOC readily agreed to the restrictions Japanese authorities imposed. They were prohibited from proselytising or bringing female companions with them, and were to be confined to the 15,000 square metre artificial island of Dejima in the port of Nagasaki. They were also obliged to continue to pay annual homage to the Shogun, a ritual that had started in 1609. This so-called *Hofreise,* or Dutch tribute mission, necessitated a long and expensive journey through the western half of the Japanese main islands to the court of the Shogun in Edo to perform *Edo Sanpu* that included the offering of expensive gifts.[6] The accounts of such journeys included in reports to the VOC in the Netherlands formed the basis of the first Dutch accounts of Japan.

It was this more than two-centuries-long exclusive Dutch presence, limited as it was to the island of Dejima, that provided the framework for a gradually expanding East-West encounter. While trading by the Dutch continued under strict conditions, over time, restrictions on movement were, to some extent, relaxed, opening opportunities for some broader interaction beyond Dejima. As will be discussed later, this notably included the importation of Dutch scientific and medical knowledge into Japan and a growing fascination in the West with Japanese porcelain, lacquer, and bronze objects and ethnographic information.

At the beginning of the seventeenth century, neither society knew much about the other. The first European account of Japan is generally considered to be a treatise titled *Historia do Japam* [*História do Japão*] by the Portuguese

Jesuit missionary Luis Frois. It consists of three parts: part one covers the period 1549–1578; part two, 1578–1582; part three, 1592 to 1593.[7] Frois arrived in Japan in 1563 when Europeans were unrestricted in their movements, and the treatise, intended as a guide to Japanese customs for fellow Jesuits coming to Japan,[8] was 'based almost entirely on first-hand observation'.[9] Luis Frois died in Nagasaki in 1597, and his writings remain an important source for understanding Japan at that time and are therefore equally appreciated by Japanese historians to this day.

Following the suppression of Catholicism and the eviction of the Portuguese in 1639, contact with and reportage on Japan were limited to the officials of the VOC. Since 1641, Company records (*Dagregisters*) had reported on Japanese practices in as far as these provided information specific to the needs of the VOC.[10] The first popular Dutch account of Japan, however, appeared in 1669. This is believed to have been based on eye-witness observations by Dutch officials during the official annual journey to Edo in 1626.[11] The 618-page book titled *Gedenkwaerdige Gesantschappen der OostIndische Maetschappij aen de Kaiseren van Japan* (Memorable Embassies of the East Indies Company to the Emperors of Japan) was published in 1669 by a Dutch explorer, Arnoldus Montanus.[12] It offered readers an eclectic mix of historical, natural, cultural and social accounts of this new and potentially profitable trading partner. The account included impressionistic images of an exotic landscape, as well as insights into the governance of the country. In emphasising the 'strange and exotic', readers were treated to descriptions of beautiful Japanese ladies, the peculiarities of their dress and customs, descriptions of musical entertainments 'unpleasant to the European ear', strange medical practices, laborious tea ceremonies and political intrigues.[13]

Japanese had been able to view Europeans in Japan after the first Portuguese landing in 1543, but the first well-known Japanese eye-witness account of Europe was published in 1590.[14] This was based on a set of notes made by *Tensho Kenou Shonen Shisetsu (Embaixada Tensho)* or the Tensho Embassy. The Embassy consisted of four young teenage boys who were sent to Europe in 1582 on an eight-year-long journey that began in Macau and continued to Lisbon, Portugal and the Vatican in Rome, with instructions to take notes of all they observed. After arriving back in Japan on July 21, 1590, their notes were used as the basis for *De Missione Legatorum Iaponensium ad Romanam Curiam* (The Mission of the Japanese Legates to the Roman Curia)[15] written by a Macau-based Jesuit Duarte de Sande and published later that year. In the course of the sixteenth century, the Catholic religion brought by the Portuguese had given rise to a form of Japanese religious art and items of Japanese woodcraft, including decorated folding room screens (*nanban byobu*) that depicted European-inspired religious figures.[16] One of the important objects brought back to Japan by the Tensho Embassy was a Gothenburg printing machine with the intention to disseminate Christian literature. Subsequently, the machine was considered as posing a threat to the integrity of the nation and was banned.

'Romping' in Dejima

Confined to the small artificial island of Dejima that had been specifically constructed in 1634 to control the activities of the foreigners, initially the Portuguese between 1636 and 1639 and thereafter exclusively the Dutch, there was little to do for the traders waiting for the appropriate monsoon winds to return south to Batavia but arrange the sale and purchase of goods. Since these men were not permitted to bring female partners with them to Japan and as Japanese were prohibited from living on the island, their sexual needs were met by the local 'public ladies' specifically designated and trained for this purpose.[17] These ladies were initially limited to nightly visits to the island, but, over time, these restrictions were less strictly enforced, and by the end of the eighteenth century, a 'five-day rule' had become common.[18]

The officially authorised supply of Japanese prostitutes to the exclusively male-centric foreign society on the island of Dejima appeared to have been generous. One Japanese account from the late eighteenth century reveals:

> Every day seventy prostitutes (yujo) leave [Maruyama], thirty-five of them for the Chinese establishment, the others to the Dutch. Although the rules required that they change clothes [between clients] […] they have no time to do so, so they just smooth down the [wrinkled] clothes a bit.[19]

The women lived in Maruyama, a specially designated brothel district of the Nagasaki city. These women were referred to differently based on the clients – those assigned to serve Dutch clients were referred to officially as *oranda-yuki*, women who served Chinese clients were termed *kara-yuki* and those that served Japanese clients were called *nihon-yuki*. Dutch sources commonly referred to them as '*keesjes*', a term derived from a Japanese word for prostitute, *keisei*,[20] although the more common term was *yujo*. In general, the *oranda-yuki* were considered the lowest category, next were the *kara-yuki* and the highest category were those called *nihon-yuki*.[21] As these were the only women the foreigners had contact with away from home, it was generally known amongst the *yujo* who entertained the Dutch and Chinese men that, beyond their fees, they would also benefit from receiving luxury gifts, kimonos and meals.[22] According to reports of the time, there were 74 brothels operating in Maruyama accommodating 766 young women in 1680, including 127 ladies of highest category, or *tayu*; in 1692, there was a total of '1443 ladies of pleasure'.[23] In addition to providing other non-sexual domestic services in Dejima, these women were also used as couriers by the Dutch to smuggle and sell goods in Nagasaki for private profit. Criminal records of the time reported the increasing numbers of *yujo* being prosecuted for offences such as smuggling. It indicated that this was not only not an uncommon practice but also that the links Dutch traders maintained with their *yujo* formed an important aspect of their existence on Dejima.[24]

Japanese accounts from the early nineteenth century explicitly confirm how Dutch *opperhoofden*, the alternating governors of the Dutch VOC trading community on the island, and their subordinates took great pleasure from such distractions during the long months between monsoon-linked shipping arrivals and departures. Although in the East Indies, cohabitation was frowned upon by VOC authorities and condemned by Protestant ministers as undermining public morality, in the Dejima settlement, it had become a universal practice. By the nineteenth century, it had become broadly condoned. It was specifically rationalised by a Dutch *opperhoofd* in Dejima in the late 1820s in the following, carefully crafted terms:

> Although ... no Japanese may live on the island of Dejima, the Japanese government does allow these women, [...] to hire themselves out to Dutch men, and they are permitted to stay on the island day and night, on condition, however, they report their presence to the Banjoos on duty at the entry gate. I am far from wanting to deny that this freedom to take these women in to service, often if not always, leads to a domestic relationship which, according to European precepts, is not moral or respectable. But, on the other hand, it is also true, that these persons are hard to exclude entirely because they provide useful domestic work such as boiling water for tea since male servants were required to leave at sun down [...] to do without which, would be too great a hardship through these long cold winter evenings.[25]

Shunga and the portrayal of European men 'at play'

Visual images of European men engaged with Japanese prostitutes became a popular subject for a traditional Japanese form of *ukiyo-e* woodblock art that evolved during the seventeenth century. Referred to as *shunga*, this genre originally developed within print literature to provide informative 'sex education', intended for both men and women. At the height of the Edo era in mid-eighteenth century, these illustrations had evolved as an independent art form. Typically, it depicted Japanese men and women engaged in sexual activities. With most of their bodies normally fully clothed, males are shown with huge phalluses in the act of uncovering, exploring or penetrating the equally prominently displayed vulva and vaginas of their female companions. The women were shown to be similarly in admiration of their male companions' grotesque appendages. Presented in a highly stylised form, these beautifully executed and colourful images documented the intimate high life of urban Japan.

It was into this *shunga* art tradition that artists inserted images of European men engaged in similar activities. In their representation of European men, *shunga* artists referenced the stereotypical images of Westerners that had become common in Edo Japan. They emphasised their foreignness by what differentiated them physically from Japanese: 'their body size, eye color, hair color and general hairiness'.[26] What was generally considered to be the Europeans' red hair was prominently featured, although sometimes also as grey to indicate age, together with a very prominent beard. To further emphasise their foreign culture, this 'hairiness' was usually presented in what for Japanese was considered to be an unacceptable state of untidiness.[27] As *shunga* figures were normally not entirely naked, to provide a more titillating effect, these images also gave attention to European attire such as shoes, stockings and the 'Dutch cloak [and], breeches'.[28] Where room settings were shown, 'Europeanness' was further often suggested by the inclusion of European furnishings such as a couch[29] or by architectural features indicating the colonial or hybrid Asian-European structures common in Dejima. This architectural style is now presented in a reconstruction of the Dejima settlement that has become a popular heritage tourist place in Nagasaki city.

As Leupp reminds us, reciprocal love is a modern conception,[30] and the term 'emotion' in its modern meaning had not yet entered the Western lexicon until the sixteenth century.[31] Nevertheless, one would expect that the feelings of pleasure that indulgence in these sexual activities gave rise would be reflected in the *shunga* representations of faces 'wearing expressions of sexual ecstasy'.[32] But, the highly stylised form of *shunga* art tends to obscure this emotion for the Western viewer. For the connoisseur of the *shunga* form, however, it is apparent that European male faces are less stylised than images of Japanese men in similar sexually explicit situations. They were also aware that these images of European men lacked a certain bodily ambience, specifically associated with sophisticated Japanese aesthetics.[33] To emphasise the emotionality of the Europeans, within the stylistic restraints of the genre, Japanese artists paid specific attention to the ruddy complexions and the thick sensuous red lips of the Dutch men. They emphasised the piercing intensity in the gaze of their large blue/green eyes directed at their female partner. This visual imagery reflected the literary images of Dutch men 'as animalistic'[34] and as 'green-eyed goblins',[35] both stereotypes reflecting a general Japanese opinion that Europeans were inferior beings. Emotion here was equated with this 'animalistic' nature.

The stylistic characteristics of the *shunga* images, in particular the exaggerated genitalia, Harris argues, derive not from an exaggerated pornographic intent, but from the limitations originally imposed on such illustrations by the small format of the books in which they first appeared.[36] Adding to the greater visibility thus provided to the sexual organs was also the fact that figures in these publications were normally otherwise fully clothed, thereby further 'draw[ing] attention to body parts that were being exposed'.[37] This did not relate to moral attitudes, as nudity as such was not perceived as 'inherently erotic', nor did sexual activity itself connote any deviant behaviour in the Edo society. Although the genre experienced some ineffectual official censorship in the early eighteenth century,[38] sex continued to be 'regarded as a natural enjoyable event and a sense of moral corruption or [...] sense of sin' did not exist.[39]

The characteristic subject matter and specific forms of the *shunga* art form, then, were determined by the constraints imposed by the context in which the *shunga* images originally appeared. Their explicitly sexual and intentionally erotic imagery evolved from their origins as illustrations in publications of erotic texts or sex manuals known as *shunpon*. Produced between 1660 and 1868, these were widely popular with the literate public of urban Edo society. The 'sexual activities' presented in these and other genres of picture books took multiple forms, responding to the diverse pursuits, interests and curiosity of consumers. This included male-male eroticism, referred to in Japanese as *nansyoku* or *dansyoku*, that was regarded in Japanese society in a way that somewhat resembles the idea of *paiderasita* (love of boys) as it was understood in ancient Greece. The texts were typically also written in a humorous style, often parodying more serious literature but claiming to be educational. They contained instructions and suggestions for maximising male and female sexual pleasure, some also including advice for male homosexual intercourse and female masturbation. Contributing to their humorous style, illustrated texts also included dialogues between sexual partners or commentary by observers of their sexual activities. The illustrations, originally monochrome line drawings, provided explicit images of sexual activities referred to.[40] Such illustrations, also called *makurae*, which was a form of art popular during the Edo era (1603–1868), are known to have evolved since the Heian era (AD 794–1185) and could take the form of paintings or woodblock prints.[41]

In the hands of its most prominent exponents, *shunga* art could attain a deep emotional dimension. Paintings by the influential print artist, Tsukioka Settei (1710–1787), for instance, who came to prominence in the latter part of the eighteenth century, came to define the best qualities of the *ukiyo-e bijin ga* (beautiful women) and *shunga* genre.[42] Through their rich colour and the 'minute attention to detail of his paintings,' Settei was able to communicate an emotional power in his prints which emphasised 'the emotional interaction between the man and the woman'.[43] Even where the sexual act itself was not featured, emotion was expressed through 'details such as the rhythmic curvature of the interlocking toes' and, for example, the pinching of the edge of a kimono or clutching on to a futon with trembling fingers.[44]

It should also be noted that the inclusion of Europeans in *shunga* art mostly 'post-dates 1790', more than a century after the arrival of the Dutch. By this time, the *shunga* art form had evolved as popular painted scrolls.[45] Master *ukiyo-e* artists, such as Hosoda Eishi (1756–1829),[46] who had their *ateliers* in the imperial capital and had never visited Nagasaki, incorporated the popular stereotypes of the foreigners in Dejima to satisfy interested Edo consumers.[47] For neither artist nor consumer was it particularly relevant whether the *shunga* image provided a realistic representation of the sexually engaged European male. What was more important was that they could recognise therein the stereotypical characteristics of the red-headed barbarians they had read about. Paintings by the Edo-era painter, Kawahara Keiga (1786–1860),[48] emphasised what Japanese found strange and uncivilised in the behaviour of the Dutch men. He showed them 'making themselves at home in Japanese houses, playing billiards, sitting on chairs or walking around on the *tatami* without taking their shoes off',[49] all of which were considered culturally offensive. By the end of the eighteenth century, the widespread image of Dutch men is reflected in the following literary image of 'Hollanders' as

> taller than other people. They are of light complexion, have large noses and stars in their eyes. By nature they are light-hearted and love to laugh. They are rarely angry – a fact that appears to relate to and suggest a character weakness. They shave their beards, cut their nails and are not dirty like Chinese. Their clothing is quite fine and decorated with gold and silver. Their eyes are just like those of a dog. Below their belt they are long of limb and the slimness of their legs reminds one of animals. When they urinate, they lift one leg like a dog. Moreover, probably because the back of their feet does not touch the ground, they attach wooden heels to their shoes, which make them look even more like dogs [...]. Because the Hollanders are devoted to erotic activity and a love of alcohol they do not live long.[50]

Many of these features and insinuations can be identified in the *shunga* images.

Dutchmen and morality at home and abroad

If the *shunga* images of Europeans are likely to have been stylised representations of imagined scenes to conform to an established Japanese art genre, they nevertheless depicted real historical events, and possibly genuine emotional states. The men who came to Dejima were almost always former residents of, or at least had departed from, the VOC headquarters in Batavia. This was a mixed, multi-Euro-Asian and multi-Asian society reflecting the cohabiting arrangements of Dutch and Eurasian men with Indonesian and African women, including slaves, that characterised such VOC outposts.[51] Thus, based on real events that took place in Dejima, *shunga* images of European men might be said to reflect, at least in a general sense, a further example of European males 'doing bad in far off places'. However, despite the widely repeated images in fictional literature and travel accounts of a morally tolerant East providing emotional 'liberation' to European men abroad,[52] VOC outposts such as Batavia and Dejima were structurally and culturally linked to the social, intellectual and moral world of the Netherlands.[53] The following question could be asked then: How might this background of what is generally perceived to have been a strict Protestant (Calvinist) society, affect the emotional state of these men when released from the moral constraints of contemporary European society?

Recent studies related to the public morality projected by the Dutch Calvinist social order point to a binary world: an active reforming state church and legislature concerned with creating a 'respectable society', and a well-utilised urban sex industry, a vibrant high-end market in literary and visual pornography and widespread drunkenness. Accounts and visual depictions of seventeenth-century Amsterdam portray the extent of this 'other world' that formed the 'dark side' of the respectable world of church-going Dutch burghers.[54]

While the Dutch Republic lacked a dominant royal or aristocratic elite, or an established church, membership of the state-supported Protestant church was 'a precondition of employment by the municipal and provincial authorities and for holding political office'.[55] The same applied to the owners and executives of the major trading house who directed the trading companies that drove the Dutch mercantile penetration of Asia. As the latter gathered in VOC chambers in Amsterdam, they would have been aware of Amsterdam's underclass, constantly added to by an influx of immigrants and itinerant workers and sailors. The corpus of Dutch paintings from the period reveals, alongside the depiction of the interiors of an idealised Dutch family life and of ecclesiastical structures, the ubiquitous presence of the Amsterdam sex trade. It had given rise to a genre of Dutch painting graphically depicting the licentious behaviour of both men and women.[56] Intended for guarded display in domestic settings, such paintings presented a variety of emotional states reflecting the bawdiness of the women, the lewdness of their male customers and the grasping nature of 'procuresses'. Unlike Japanese *shunga*, art, however, in responding to the moral contours of their society, the Dutch scenes were transformed into a puritanical, morally instructional and thus respectable public art form:[57]

> We see harlots in whorehouses, but never street-walkers. We see drunkenness, cheating, and robberies, but not fighting, police prosecution, the Spin House, or venereal diseases. We see inns and brothels, but never the famous music halls. We see musicians, but never dancing. We see young harlots, but not older ones. On the other hand, we see old and ugly procuresses, but never young bawds. For clients we see well-dressed, well-to-do youths, soldiers, even farmers, but never the sailors who formed so much of the clientele. [….] however seductive and true to life the brothel scenes may appear, they usually do not, or only partly, tell us of the reality of prostitution in the seventeenth-century.[58]

This made it possible to create a market for such paintings in an apparently church-going bourgeois world. In the meantime, reproductions of 'classical art', an innocent accompaniment to classical and Biblical scholarship at its old universities or research in private libraries, continued to afford views of the nude. As Findlen suggests, 'masturbating with the Classics' was one way in which erotic art could be secretly enjoyed within the educated middle-class society without disturbing a broader public order.[59]

Thus, although the world of the bordello and its visual depiction was not marginal to life in early modern Amsterdam, it in fact served to underscore the vociferous voice of public morality while at the same time helping to support the city's economy. At the same time, Dutch publishers in the seventeenth century were at the centre of the European production of literary pornography. Typical of this literature were the popular local titles *Het Amsterdamsche Hoerdom* (Amsterdam whores) (1681) and *De hedendaagsche Haagsche en Amsterdamse zalet-juffers* (The salon-mistresses of contemporary The Hague and Amsterdam) (1696) which went through multiple editions.[60] As well, Dutch educated classes had access to numerous French titles for which translations were not required. French erotica already had a well-known reputation by the early seventeenth century: when English managers of the East India Company came across a collection of French erotica in the early 1600s, they were reputedly so shocked that they had it burnt on the spot.[61]

In some ways, therefore, the nature and reception of sexual imagery and literary references in Europe replicates the trajectory indicated earlier for *shunga* and *shunpon* in seventeenth- and eighteenth-century Japan. As in Japan, pornography in Europe evolved together with the rise of popular literature and formed part of a wider cultural shift associated with social and political changes. In the 'West', as Lynn Hunt has argued, the emergence of a genre of specific visual and literary pornography was indicative, as well as an integral element, of the European Enlightenment.[62] Arguably comparable to the role of *shunga* and *shunpon* in Edo Japan, in France and England, at least, 'the rise in pornographic publications [...] marked the beginning of the high period of the Enlightenment as well as a period of general crisis in European society and politics'.[63]

Unlike Japan, although in the Netherlands there was an 'openness about the public discussion of sexuality [...] evident in the numerous sexual and erotic manuals published in the late seventeenth century',[64] this remained largely buried within the pages of books, many in French. This restricted it to a minority literate middle class where erotic visual representations provided by lithographs remained largely out of sight. Literary pornography appeared to lack the serious moral (libertine) or satirical political emphasis evident elsewhere in Europe, and in the course of the eighteenth century, the number and the explicit content of such publications in the Netherlands declined. As a religion-mediated middle class morality was gradually reflected in the 'bourgeoisisation' of Dutch society, prostitution was criminalised and a dedicated police force was directed to enforce a moral order.[65] Authorities removed 'all sexual references from the public sphere, whether in brothels, paintings or pornographic books.'[66] In the following century, the condemnation of immorality became increasingly vocal. In the context of the rise of a popular religious revivalist movement and a growing interest in urban reform in the Netherlands, immorality was perceived to be linked particularly to poverty and urbanisation.[67]

In Batavia, where Europeans constituted a distinct minority, a key concern of VOC officials in maintaining an appearance of moral respectability was not only to ensure social stability but also to emphasise its European identity. The Gentlemen Seventeen, the Board of the VOC that met regularly in Amsterdam, therefore, sought to emphasise the same 'moral code' of the respectable, church-going classes in the Netherlands in their correspondence with its captains and officials abroad. Upholding the Protestant maxim that wealth accumulation was a 'sign of God's grace', the VOC managers

> shared [the] spiritual rhetoric derived from Calvinism, as well as a distinct affective expression, corporate business language and orientation to Patria (the fatherland) to bind disparate individuals to Company loyalty and its mission.[68]

The public social world of Batavia centred on the Protestant church, the Dutch language and employment in the VOC.[69] In attempting to create a European-style society, various legal and cultural means were employed to assimilate the non-European associates of VOC employees. As Dutch women were prohibited to travel to the VOC outposts in view of their perceived delicacy and moral vulnerability, initially marriage with local women was promoted in an attempt to maintain the moral standards, but cohabitation was widely condoned. In a further attempt to improve public morality of the colonial settlement and bolster its 'European' population, legal arrangements were implemented for the formal registration of mixed race off-spring as European, and public orphanages were established to train and take unwanted mixed-race children out of public view.[70] Beyond the European society, the seventeenth-century colonial authorities and the Reformed Church in the East Indies showed little interest in the indigenous population other than to reconvert the converts of Portuguese Catholic missions to Protestantism and to baptise local women with whom European men produced children.[71] As in the less respectable homes of Amsterdam, however,

> within the Batavian household there could scarcely develop that family life celebrated by Dutch artists of the seventeenth century who depicted homogeneous groups of kin, soberly dressed, engaged in domestic activities in small, simply furnished chambers.[72]

Reading Japanese representation of the Southern barbarian at play

As this brief and introductory discussion of the cultural and social context of the *shunga* art form and the Europeans it represented suggests, representation of the emotions of Dutch men in Dejima is inevitably veiled by layers of cultural interventions. It is evident, firstly, that images of these foreigners were intended to conform to a particular artistic genre and are expressive of particular cultural norms of the Edo period. The *shunga* imagery was intentionally 'pornographic' in the sense that it purposefully emphasised the sexuality of the encounter. In its formative development as book illustrations, *shunga* depictions were intended to be educational; whether or not it aimed to arouse sexual and or emotional response in the viewer, as in Western pornography, these images were intended to satisfy the defined 'purpose' of this genre, and gradually to be openly enjoyed as an art form. As such, the stylised facial features of their Japanese subjects conformed to Japanese cultural precepts. Inserting the 'red barbarians' into this art form 'realism', in the sense of accurately portraying facial expressions reflecting their emotional engagement with to the attentions they received from the trained *yujo*, was secondary to meeting the demands of the genre.

Shunga depictions of Dutch men were not necessarily 'accurate' – what they illustrate are a Japanese cultural response to the presence of these Western foreigners. Representation of this response was located within a popularly understood cultural context that provided the Japanese observer with a basis for situating the foreigner in terms of known values. Characterising the Western male as a *shunga* subject contributed to normalising what was foreign, rather than representing its reality. Depictions of the imagined grotesque figures of Dutch men and their equally grotesque genitalia served to further contrast and highlight the sensuous forms and rich colouring of the Japanese textiles in which they and their partners were clothed, and which the *shunga* artworks, as art, aimed to present. As such, they contributed to articulating the widely perceived contrast between the cultures of East and West while at the same time drawing attention to a common humanity.

For a majority of the European men arriving in Dejima, 'the East' was not unknown, nor was an awareness, if not the experience, of the Amsterdam bordello, or of intimate relations with non-European women. What evidently remained different in faraway Japan was the absence of a public moral opprobrium related to such sexual activities. Nevertheless, even in Dejima, attempts were made by the Dutch *opperhoofd* to maintain public appearance, and formal restrictions were imposed by Japanese authorities on such relationships.

Knowing Japan and the West beyond Dejima

The portrayal of emotions expressive of the physical pleasure of sexual relations in which the Dutch men in Dejima engaged in formed only one emotive element in a gradually evolving mutual discovery of the other. Surviving accounts from before seclusion was imposed, and later, when restrictions began to be less strictly enforced, give evidence of personal encounters that developed in Dejima. These extended beyond feelings of desire and curiosity for some Dutch men. For Japanese, mainly women, who as a result of the restrictions imposed by Japanese authorities found themselves exiled from their homeland, essentially deported for relationships established in Dejima, the separation produced expressions of nostalgic memory and longing.

A number of Christian Japanese children of mixed parentage were expelled from Japan in the time leading up to the transition to the era of complete seclusion when Japanese Christians were persecuted and Portuguese evicted. They are remembered in Japan and the West because of letters they wrote expressing their longing for their homeland. A famous case is that of Cornelia van Nijenrode. She is featured in a 1665 painting that hangs in the Rijksmuseum in Amsterdam, together with her Dutch husband, Pieter Cnoll, who became a senior merchant in Batavia, and their two daughters.[73] In the painting, the artist, Jacob Coeman, depicted Cornelia looking determined, stiff and strong, and showing no obvious emotion. However, in a letter written in Japanese to her family in Japan (now carefully preserved in Nagasaki), her inner emotional state becomes more evident as she writes of her longing for her homeland. Another, even more famous letter, the so-called *Jyagatara bumi* (Jakarta Letter), was written by a Japanese girl of mixed race, Oharu, who was expelled to Batavia in the 1630s. This, too, expresses a memory of and longing for her Japanese homeland in deeply emotive terms. Oharu's story became known when it was recounted by the writer Nishikawa Jyoken in his book, *Nagasaki yawagusa*, published in 1720. Whether the well-written letter was actually composed by the young woman remains a matter of dispute, although, it is generally considered that the letter could be a fabrication of the author, Nishikawa Jyoken. Nevertheless, what is interesting is how writers have interpreted her circumstances as naturally entailing this longing for homeland. In both cases, it seems difficult to deny the expression of deep-felt emotion in responding to a sense of loss and separation from family, and memory of homeland, a sentiment clearly felt across cultural and national boundaries in this era.

As restrictions on the contact between Dutch men and Japanese women in Dejima were less strictly maintained, longer relationships could and evidently did develop. The most well-documented 'love relationship' on Dejima, dating from the early nineteenth century, is that of Philipp Franz Balthasar von Siebold. Siebold arrived at Dejima at the age of 27, and soon after, he met Kusumoto Taki who was 16 years of age at the time. Siebold reputedly 'fell in love' and ultimately married Taki with whom he had a daughter, Ine, who later became the first female physician in Japan. Their relationship was able to persist, with Siebold representing her to Japanese authorities as his temporary *yujo*, and in spite of the moral opprobrium of the chief VOC merchant at Dejima.[74] When the time came to return to Europe, he did so without his Japanese family, because Japanese authorities did not permit them to leave Japan. From Europe, Siebold sent her letters expressing his love for Taki and Ine. They maintained correspondence until they both married.[75] Although he later married in Europe, Siebold is believed to have continued to provide for his Japanese family, and there seems little doubt that his extant 'love letters' express genuine feelings.

In the longer term, the VOC-Japan trade link, a by-product of which was the institutionalisation of the sexual encounters in Dejima that provided the subject for representations of the West in a popular Japanese art form, also facilitated the development of other avenues of mutual information. It was the mutual curiosity of European and Japanese scientists brought into contact via Dejima that provided the basis for the more significant transfer of knowledge about 'the other'.

Understanding Siebold's individual role in the transfer of knowledge clearly also involves recognising the way broader cultural and social changes influence the 'cognitive activity, motor expression, physiological arousal, action tendencies and subjective feeing state[s]' that shape the individual's emotive response to the world around them.[76] Much early modern knowledge of the East in the West, as Lisa Roberts has emphasised, can be seen as a kind of a by-product of the expansion of trade in which what became known was transformed.[77] It was filtered via the dominant values and interests of the respective trading companies and their officials, and their practices of collection, storage and dissemination of such information.[78] In the case of Portugal, this was mediated by that state's concern to use its emerging trade networks to propagate Christian religion which, as mentioned earlier, gave rise to the earliest extensive Western account of Japan,

História do Japão, by the Portuguese Jesuit, Luís Fróis. Under these conditions, knowledge of Japan in the West, like Japanese knowledge of the West, had remained fragmentary and impressionistic. It was only much later that the intellectual and social changes in both Europe and Japan overcame the restrictive environment that persisted when confining European presence to Dutch commercial operatives to Dejima.

História do Japão was the earliest extensive non-English-language Western account of Japan, and in Japan is still considered to be one of the most reliable accounts of the country of this era. However, it was the 1727 English-language translation of the book that is generally considered to have provided the first widely consulted informative account of Japan in the West.[79] Its author, Engelbert Kaempfer (1651–1716), had been employed as a doctor between 1690 and 1692 to attend to the VOC employees in Dejima. As the subtitle of the book published subsequently would suggest, Kaempfer's scientific curiosity produced a book of encyclopaedic dimensions. It encompassed

> an account of the ancient and present state and government of that empire; of its temples, palaces, castles and other buildings; of its metals, minerals, trees, plants, animals, birds and fishes; of the chronology and succession of the emperors, ecclesiastical and secular; of the original descent, religions, customs, and manufactures of the natives, and of their trade and commerce with the Dutch and Chinese.[80]

The book became immensely popular: it ran to 12 editions and 'for over 260 years has been regarded as the most authentic eye-witness account of pre-modern Japan.'[81] However, in fact, it was not a direct reflection of the author's impressions and interpretation of what he saw and learned while in Japan. Due to a transfer of ownership of his German-language notes to England and their translation into English, Kaempfer's initial impressions were reinterpreted through the sieve of that country's contemporary politico-cultural attitudes. Moreover, apart from his textual material, Kaempfer's collection of Japanese paintings were 'smuggled out of Japan in 1692',[82] 160 of which were included in *The History of Japan*. However, virtually all were redrawn by its translator, Scheuchzer, and 'very few conform[ed] with Kaempfer's originals either in the order of layout or in artistic impression'.[83] Consequently, we can only indirectly catch a glimpse of the emotional dimensions of Kaempfer's scientifically informed curiosity.

At the same time, the imperial court of *Tokugawa Bakufu* (Shogunate), responding to the importance of the Dutch trading link, determined that it needed to gather information about the Netherlands in relation to Japan's national security.[84] In the latter half of the seventeenth century, it embarked on a policy of systematically importing books particularly of a scientific nature to 'monitor and control of foreign contacts [and] as a means of gathering information about events developing abroad'.[85] This enabled Japanese scholars to form a more nuanced impression of Western civilisation and its local representatives. By the late eighteenth century, a recognised scholarly community of Japanese experts on the West, called *rangakusha,* had founded an academic study of all things European, referred to as *rangaku,* or 'hollandology'. These studies led one leading scholar to conclude that 'in barbarian countries they know much about principle [...] there is much [in Dutch books] one can profit from [...] however, they [also] invite idle curiosity or say evil things'.[86] For this, Kaempfer had provided a useful channel for further information and consultation.

But it was not till the beginning of the nineteenth century, in a new scientific age, and following the demise of the VOC (in 1796), that Dejima, still representing the limits of European contact with Japan, became the conduit for a more significant transfer of knowledge about Japan. This has been attributed to the enthusiasm of the aforementioned Siebold who had been specifically sent to Dejima by the Dutch government to gather information about Japan. He arrived there in 1823 after being briefly appointed as physician to the Dutch colonial army in Java and given a Dutch identity to circumvent Japan's restrictions on all other nationalities entering the country.[87] At Dejima, apart from forming a relationship with Taki, he developed contacts with a range of Japanese scholars of *Rangaku* (Hollandology) with whose cooperation and assistance he was able to collect a great deal of information and material objects. Although a large proportion of his initial collection was lost as a result of a storm and subsequent confiscation by Japanese authorities, in 1828, and after subsequent visits, he succeeded in smuggling an immense collection of Japan-related material to the West. The physical, cultural and natural objects Siebold collected subsequently 'formed the nucleus of the Rijksmuseum voor Volkskunde in Leiden' and other leading academic institutions, museums and herbariums in Germany and England.[88] This was to form the basis of subsequent scholarly research on Japan in the West, for which Siebold's own multi-volume account of the government, flora and fauna of Japan published between 1832 and 1852 provided the key textual reference for the rest of the century.[89] As well, his collected objects exhibited in public museums stimulated curiosity about, and shaped popular emotional response to, the Orient in the West and the imaginary of European painters who had never visited the country.[90] It was the inspiration for what was known later as the popular nineteenth-century cultural phenomenon of *japonaise* in Europe.[91]

Reflection: transformations of knowledge of the other

As the biographies of Siebold and Kaempfer suggest, Western curiosity about Japan and the Japanese, in common with Japanese artists and early writers' representations of the West and of Westerners, was subject to significant cultural editing. Many factors intervened between the excitement of curiosity that generated their personal journey of discovery, and the processes of publication and exhibition. In the restricted circumstances of Japan's *sakoku,* it had been subject to the exigencies of collection and surveillance, of transportation and loss; in the West, of ownership and dissemination, of translation and publication, as well as of financial and institutional demands and international competition. The transformation of curiosity into 'knowledge', and its reception in the West, were ultimately framed by and viewed through the lens of layers of changing Western cultural preconceptions.

In similar ways, the *shunga* genre of *ukiyo-e* block art illustrations of European men 'caught in the act' was the product of culturally determined forms of representation, produced by artists at work in physically and socially distant locations. Within the confines of the genre, in catering for the curiosity of its Japanese viewers, it is evident that these images of Western men were presented, and read, in ways that would be meaningful only by conforming to the traditions associated with this popular art form. These images, however, derived from real interactions that took place in Dejima, where, as historical accounts indicate, within the limits allowed by the policy of *sakoku*, lust as well as love, love as well as scientific curiosity, were nurtured and 'new knowledge' was assembled.

Visual and literary representations of the West in Japan, and of Japan in the West, therefore, were not necessarily accurate. As well as being influenced by the individual emotional responses implicated in the zone of contact, knowledge about the other was inevitably shaped by prevailing cultural, national, commercial and eventually modern scientific interests. Significant questions, therefore, remain in relation to the processes involved in the 'knowledge transfer' that resulted from Japanese and Dutch encounters in the period of Japan's seclusion. The effect of such processes on the transformations of knowledge need not therefore be brushed aside, 'erase[d] or blur[red]'.[92] They are important in themselves as sources of knowledge of the history of the contact between West and East and important in revealing the cultural processes by which such interactions and transformations took place.

Notes

1 Dejima is also pronounced as Deshima. In this chapter, I use Dejima to reflect the pronunciation more frequently used in contemporary Japan. The 1853 Treaty is also known as the Kanagawa Treaty (Kanagawa Jyoyaku).
2 Not all VOC employees may have been Dutch. However, they were all collectively considered to be Dutch by Japanese officials at that time. For example, Siebold was a German but came to Dejima as a Dutch person.
3 Suppression of Christianity was enforced in late 1500s when the government started to be concerned about being colonised by the 'West'. Christianity was totally abandoned and the execution/crucifixion of 26 martyrs in Nagasaki in 1597 was one of the incidents symbolising this movement.
4 Charles Ralph Boxer, *The Christian Century in Japan, 1549–1650* (Berkeley: University of California Press, 1951), 387; Gary P. Leupp, *Interracial Intimacy in Japan: Western Men and Japanese Women 1543–1900* (London/New York: Continuum, 2003), 62.
5 Boxer, *The Christian Century,* 387.
6 Leonard Blussé, "Peeking into the Empires: Dutch Embassies to the Courts of China and Japan." *Itinerario* 37, no. 3 (2014): 13–29.
7 Luís Fróis, *Historia De Japam / Luis Frois; Edicao Anotada Por Jose Wicki*, eds. Josef Wicki and Biblioteca Nacional de Lisboa. Lisbon: Presidencia do Conselho de Ministros, Secretaria de Estado da Cultura, Direccao-Geral do Patrimonio Cultural, Biblioteca Nacional de Lisboa, 1976.

8 The first Jesuit missionary to Japan, Francisco Xavier, arrived in 1549. Luis Frois met Xavier in Goa. The account of Xavier's visit to Japan is included in James Coleridge, ed., *The Life and Letters of St. Francis Xavier*, 2nd ed., 2 vols. (London: Burns & Oates, 1890), vol. 2, 331–350, reprinted in William H. McNeil and Mitsuko Iriye, eds., *Modern Asia and Africa, Readings in World History*, vol. 9 (New York: Oxford University Press, 1971), 20–30.

9 Daniel T. Reff, "Critical Introduction: The Tratado, the Jesuits and the Governance of Souls," in *The First European Description of Japan, 1585: A Critical English-Language Edition of Striking Contrasts in the Customs of Europe and Japan by Luis Frois, S.J.*, eds. K. Richard Danford, Robin Gill and Daniel T. Reff (New York: Routledge, 2014), 6. See also Frois 1585. His book is titled *Tratado em que se contém muito sucinta e abreviadamente algumas contradições e diferenças de costumes entre gente de Europa e esta provincia de Japão* (Treatise Containing a Very Brief Description of Some Contradictions and Differences of Habits between Europe and This Province of Japan).

10 Cynthia Viallé, "Daily Life of the Dutch in Canton and Nagasaki: A Comparison Based on the VOC Dagregisters and Other Sources," *Itinerario* 37, no. 3 (2014): 153–171.

11 Blussé, "Peeking into the Empires", 19.

12 Arnoldus Montanus, *Gedenkwaerdige Gesantschappen Der Oost-Indische Maetschappy In't Vereenigde Nederland, Aen De Kaisaren Van Japan* (Amsterdam: Jacob van Meurs, 1669).

13 Blussé, "Peeking into the Empires," 14.

14 De Duarte Sande, *De Missione Legatorum Iaponensium Ad Romanam Curiam* [Dialogue Concerning the Mission of the Japanese Ambassadors to the Roman Curia]. Macau: In Macaensi portu Sinici regni: in domo Societatis Iesu, 1590, n.p.

15 Sande, *De Missione*, n.p.

16 A. H. Vlam Grace, "The Portrait of S. Francis Xavier in Kobe," *Zeitschrift für Kunstgeschichte* 42, no. 1 (1979): 54.

17 Leupp, Gary P. *Interracial Intimacy in Japan: Western Men and Japanese Women 1543–1900*. London/New York: Continuum, 2003, 107–112.

18 Fritz Vos, "*Onze Voorouders in Japan: Handel, Wetenschap En Liefde* [Our Ancestors in Japan: Trade, Science and Love]," *De Gids* 141 (1978): 220–221, 215–227; Leupp, *Interracial Intimacy*, 109.

19 Furukawa Koshōken 1980 cited in Leupp, *Interracial Intimacy*, 111.

20 Literal meaning of *keisei* means 'topple a castle'.

21 Yukiko Miyamoto, "Maruyamayujyo No Seikatsu," *Komazawashigaku* 31 (March 1984): 21–22.

22 Miyamoto, "Maruyamayujyo", 21–22.

23 Vos, *Onze Voorouders*, 219.

24 Miyamoto, "Maruyamayujyo", 21–24.

25 Opperhoofd George Felix Meylan, 1827–1830 cited in Fritz Vos, *Van Keurslijfjes en Keesjes, Bosschietes En Lijfschutten: Onze Voorouders in Japan En Korea in Het Begin Der Japanse En Koreaanse Studien in Nederland* (Leiden: Universitaire Pers, 1980), 7–8 (translated by the author).

26 Leupp, *Interracial Intimacy*, 84.

27 Timon Schreech, "Foreign Connections to Shunga," in *Shunga, Sex and Pleasure in Japanese Art*, eds. Timothy Clark, C. Andrew Gerstle, Aki Ishigami, and Akiko Yano (London: The British Museum Press, 2014), 309, 310.

28 Schreech, "Foreign Connections", 306.

29 Ibid.

30 Leupp, *Interracial Intimacy*, 81.

31 Philippa Maddern, "How Children Were Supposed to Feel: How Children Felt: England 1350–1550," in *Childhood and Emotion: Across Cultures 1450–1800*, eds. Claudia Jarzebowski and Thomas Max Safley (London/New York: Routledge, 2014), 121.

32 Frederick Harris, *Ukiyo-e: The Art Form of the Japanese Print* (Tokyo: Tuttle Publishing, 2010), 121.

33 See for example, selections of images in Screech 2003, images 1–4, pages 395–396.
34 Leupp, *Interracial Intimacy*, 84.
35 Ibid.
36 Harris, *Ukiyo-e*, 121.
37 Ibid.
38 Ellis Tinios, "Japanese Illustrated Erotic Books in the Context of Commercial Publishing 1660–1868," *Japan Review* 26 (2013): 95.
39 Harris, *Ukiyo-e*, 121.
40 Ibid.
41 Some of the artists who also created *shunga* at the time are: Hishikawa Moronobu (1618–1694), Torii Kiyonaga (1752–1815), Kitagawa Utamoro (1753?–1806).
42 Yukari Yamamoto, "Tsukioka Settei's Erotic Paintings," *Japan Review* 26 (2013): 151–167.
43 Ibid., 155.
44 Ibid.
45 Schreech, "Foreign Connections", 391.
46 Hasoda is known for his *ukiyo-e* genre of *bijin ga* (pictures of beautiful female forms) which are not necessarily erotic as were *shunga* or *makurae*.
47 Schreech, "Foreign Connections", 394.
48 One of his best-known works is Tourankanzu in the Nagasaki Museum of History and Culture, designated as Important Cultural Property. It depicts Seibold, Taki and Ine on the rooftop of their Dejima pavilion. Kawahara was also Seibold's personal painter and painted botanies and aerial views of Nagasaki and so forth. He was known to be a good observer.
49 Blussé, "Peeking into the Empires", 17.
50 Hirata Atsutane, 1813 cited in Vos, *Van Keurslijfjes en Keesjes*, 9.
51 Nicola Borchardt, "Growing Up in VOC-Batavia: Transcultural Childhood in the World of the Dutch East India Company," in *Childhood and Emotion: Across Cultures 1450–1800*, eds. Claudia Jarzebowski and Thomas Max Safley (London/New York: Routledge, 2014), 42–56; Blussé, "Peeking into the Empires".
52 Joost Coté, "Romancing the Indies: The Literary Construction of Tempo Doeloe, 1880–1930," in *Recalling the Indies: Colonial Culture & Postcolonial Identities*, eds. Joost Coté and I. Westerbeek (Amsterdam: Aksant, 2005), 133–172; Milton Osborne, "Fear and Fascination in the Tropics: A Reader's Guide to French Fiction on Indo-China," in *Asia in Western Fiction*, eds. R. Winks and J. Rush (Honolulu: University of Hawaii Press, 1990), 159–174.
53 Lewis Pyenson, "The Enlightened Image of Nature in the Dutch East Indies: Consequences of Postmodernist Doctrine for Broad Structures and Intimate Life," *Historical Studies in the Natural Sciences* 41, no. 1 (2011): 1–4; Jean Gelman Taylor, *The Social World of Batavia: Europeans and Eurasians in Colonial Indonesia* (Madison: University of Wisconsin Press, 2009), 178–180.
54 Lotte C. van der Pol, *The Burgher and the Whore: Prostitution in Early Modern Amsterdam* (Oxford: Oxford University Press, 2011); Anne-Laure van Bruaene, Sarah van Bouchaute, "Rederijkers, Kannenkijkers: Drinking and Drunkenness in the Sixteenth and Seventeenth-Century Low Countries", *Early Modern Low Countries* 1 (2007): 1–29.
55 Van de Pol, "The Burgher and the Whore", 44.
56 Lottie C. van der Pol, "The Whore, the Bawd, and the Artist: The Reality and Imagery of Seventeenth-Century Dutch Prostitution," *Journal of Historians of Netherlandish Art* 2, no. 1–2 (2010): 1–20.
57 Van de Pol, "The Whore, the Bawd, and the Artist", 13.
58 Ibid.
59 Paula Findlen, "Humanism. Politics and Pornography in Renaissance Italy," in *The Invention of Pornography: Obscenity and the Origins of Modernity, 1500–1800*, ed. Lynn Hunt (New York: Zone Books, 1993), 77–86.

60 Wijnand Mijnhardt, "Politics and Pornography in the Seventeenth and Eighteenth Century Dutch Republic," in *The Invention of Pornography: Obscenity and the Origins of Modernity, 1500–1800*, ed. L. Hunt (New York: Zone Books, 1993), 285.
61 Schreech,"Foreign Connections", 392.
62 Lynn Hunt, "Introduction: Obscenity and the Origins of Modernity," in *The Invention of Pornography: Obscenity and the Origins of Modernity, 1500–1800*, ed. Lynn Hunt (New York: Zone Books, 1993), 9–45.
63 Ibid., 33; See also Peter Wagner, *Eros Revived: Erotica of the Enlightenment in England and America* (London: Secker & Warburg, 1988).
64 Hunt, "Introduction", 33.
65 Mijnhardt, "Politics and Pornography".
66 Hunt, 33.
67 Joost Coté, "'The Sins of Their Fathers': Culturally at Risk Children and the Colonial State in Asia," *Paedagogica Historica* 45, no. 1–2 (2009): 129–142.
68 Susan Broomhall, "'Quite Indifferent to These Things': The Role of Emotions and Conversion in the Dutch East India Company's Interactions with the South Lands," *Journal of Religious History* 39, no. 4 (2015): 526.
69 Taylor, *The Social World of Batavia*, 37.
70 Ulbe Bosma and Remco Raben, *Being "Dutch" in the Indies: A History of Creolisation and Empire, 1500—1920* (Singapore: NUS Press, 2007), 37; Borchardt, "Growing Up in VOC Batavia".
71 Yusak Soleiman, *The Dutch Reformed Church in Late Eighteenth Century Java: An Eastern Adventure* (Zoetermeer: Boekencentrum, 2012).
72 Taylor, *The Social World of Batavia*, 37.
73 Leonard Blussé, *Bitters Bruid* (Amsterdam: Balans, 1997); Leonard Blussé, *Bitter Bonds: A Colonial Divorce Drama of the Seventeenth Century* (Princeton, NJ: Markus Wiener Publishers, 2002). The painting is titled: Pieter Cnoll, Senior Merchant of Batavia, his Wife Cornelia van Nieuwenrode and their Daughters Catharina (b. 1653) en Hester (b. 1659).
74 Images of Siebold, Taki and Ine are now often incorporated in visual portrayals of Nagasaki's past. His daughter, Ine, later became the first Japanese female physician to practise Western medicine in Japan.
75 James A. Compton and Gerard Thijsse, "The Remarkable P.F.B. Von Siebold, His Life in Europe and Japan," *Curtis's Botanical Magazine* 30, no. 3 (2013): 289. One of the letters from Taki to Siebold is kept at Leiden University; other letters have said to be newly found in Ehime Prefecture Japan during recent years.
76 D. Sander and K.R. Sherer, *The Oxford Companion to Emotion and the Affective Sciences* (Oxford, 2009), 92 cited in Maddern, "How Children," 123.
77 Lisa Roberts, "Re-Orienting the Transformation of Knowledge in Dutch Expansion: Nagasaki as a Centre of Accumulation and Management," in *Transformations of Knowledge in Dutch Expansion*, eds. Susanne Friedrich, Arndt Brendecke and Stefan Ehrenpreis (Berlin/Boston, MA: De Gruyter, 2015), 19–41.
78 Siegfried Huigen, Jan de Jong, and Elmer Kolfin. *The Dutch Trading Companies as Knowledge Networks* (Leiden: Brill, 2010).
79 Henk De Groot, "Engelbert Kaempfer, Imamura Gen'emon and Arai Hakuseki: An Early Exchange of Knowledge between Japan and the Netherlands," in *The Dutch Trading Companies as Knowledge Networks*, edited by Siegfried Huigen, Jan de Jong and Elmer Kolfin (Leiden: Brill, 2010), 201–209; Jayant S. Joshi and Rajesh Kumar, "The Dutch Physicians at Deijima and the Rise of Western Medicine in Japan," *Proceedings of the Indian History Congress* 63 (2002): 1062–1072.
80 Engelbert Kaempfer, *The History of Japan* (London, 1727).
81 Yu-Ying Brown, "Kaempfer's Album of Famous Sights of Seventeenth Century Japan," *The British Library Journal* 15, no. 1 (1989): 101.
82 Ibid, 90.81. Ibid, 90.
83 Ibid, 100.

84 W. J. Boot, "The Transfer of Learning: The Import of Chinese and Dutch Books in Togukawa Japan," *Itinerario* 37, no. 3 (2013): 190.
85 Ibid.
86 Ibid., 197–198.
87 See also Shozo Kure, *Shiboruto Sensei* (Tokyo: Toudou syoten, 1926).
88 Natsuko Akagawa, "Ukiyo-E in Memory," in *Ukiyo-E: Japanese Prints of the Floating World* (Perth: Vanguard Press/The University of Western Australia, 2014), 8–15.
89 Ibid.
90 Ibid.
91 Yoko Chiba, "Japonisme: East-West renaissance in the late 19th century," *Mosaic: An Interdisciplinary Journal* 2 (1998): 31; Natsuko Akagawa, *Heritage Conservation and Japan's Cultural Diplomacy: Heritage, National Identity and National Interest* (London/New York: Routledge, 2015); Akagawa, "Ukiyo-E in Memory."
92 Arndt Brendecke and Susanne Friedrich, "Introduction," in *Transformations of Knowledge in Dutch Expansion*, eds. Susanne Friedrich, Arndt Brendecke and Stefan Ehrenpreis (Berlin/Boston, MA: De Gruyter, 2015), 1–18.

Bibliography

Akagawa, Natsuko. *Heritage Conservation and Japan's Cultural Diplomacy: Heritage, National Identity and National Interest*. London/New York: Routledge, 2015.
Akagawa, Natsuko. "Ukiyo-E in Memory." In *Ukiyo-E: Japanese Prints of the Floating World*, 8–15. Perth: Vanguard Press/The University of Western Australia, 2014.
Blussé, Leonard. *Bitter Bonds: A Colonial Divorce Drama of the Seventeenth Century*. Princeton, NJ: Markus Wiener Publishers, 2002.
Blussé, Leonard. *Bitters Bruid*. Amsterdam: Balans, 1997.
Blussé, Leonard. "Peeking into the Empires: Dutch Embassies to the Courts of China and Japan." *Itinerario* 37, no. 3 (2014): 13–29.
Boot, W. J. "The Transfer of Learning: The Import of Chinese and Dutch Books in Togukawa Japan." *Itinerario* 37, no. 3 (2013): 188–206.
Borchardt, Nicola. "Growing Up in VOC-Batavia: Transcultural Childhood in the World of the Dutch East India Company." In *Childhood and Emotion: Across Cultures 1450–1800*, edited by Claudia Jarzebowski and Thomas Max Safley, 42–56. London/New York: Routledge, 2014.
Bosma, Ulbe, and Remco Raben. *Being "Dutch" in the Indies: A History of Creolisation and Empire, 1500—1920*. Singapore: NUS Press, 2007.
Boxer, Charles Ralph. *The Christian Century in Japan, 1549–1650*. Berkeley: University of California Press, 1951.
Brendecke, Arndt, and Susanne Friedrich. "Introduction." In *Transformations of Knowledge in Dutch Expansion*, edited by Susanne Friedrich, Arndt Brendecke and Stefan Ehrenpreis. Series: Pluralisierung & Autorität 44, 1–18. Berlin/Boston, MA: De Gruyter, 2015.
Broomhall, Susan. "'Quite Indifferent to These Things': The Role of Emotions and Conversion in the Dutch East India Company's Interactions with the South Lands." *Journal of Religious History* 39, no. 4 (2015): 524–544.
Brown, Yu-Ying. "Kaempfer's Album of Famous Sights of Seventeenth Century Japan." *The British Library Journal* 15, no. 1 (1989): 90–103.
Bruaene, Anne-Laure van and Sarah van Bouchaute. "Rederijkers, Kannenkijkers: Drinking and Drunkenness in the Sixteenth and Seventeenth-Century Low Countries." *Early Modern Low Countries* 1 (2007): 1–29.
Chiba, Yoko. "Japonisme: East-West Renaissance in the Late 19th Century." *Mosaic: An Interdisciplinary Journal* 31, no. 2 (1998): 1–20.

Clark, Timothy, C. Andrew Gerstle, Aki Ishigami, and Akiko Yano. *Shunga, Sex and Pleasure in Japanese Art*. London: British Museum Press, 2013.
Compton, James A. and Gerard Thijsse. "The Remarkable P.F.B. Von Siebold, His Life in Europe and Japan." *Curtis's Botanical Magazine* 30, no. 3 (2013): 275–314.
Coté, Joost. "Romancing the Indies: The Literary Construction of Tempo Doeloe, 1880–1930." In *Recalling the Indies: Colonial Culture & Postcolonial Identities*, edited by Joost Coté and I. Westerbeek, 133–172. Amsterdam: Aksant, 2005.
Coté, Joost. "'The Sins of Their Fathers': Culturally at Risk Children and the Colonial State in Asia." *Paedagogica Historica* 45, no. 1–2 (2009): 129–142.
De Groot, Henk. "Engelbert Kaempfer, Imamura Gen'emon and Arai Hakuseki: An Early Exchange of Knowledge between Japan and the Netherlands." In *The Dutch Trading Companies as Knowledge Networks*, edited by Siegfried Huigen, Jan de Jong and Elmer Kolfin, 201–209. Leiden: Brill, 2010.
Findlen, Paula. "Humanism. Politics and Pornography in Renaissance Italy." In *The Invention of Pornography: Obscenity and the Origins of Modernity, 1500–1800*, edited by Lynn Hunt, 77–86. New York: Zone Books, 1993.
Fróis, Luís. *Historia De Japam / Luis Frois; Edicao Anotada Por Jose Wicki*. Edited by Josef Wicki and Biblioteca Nacional de Lisboa. Lisbon: Presidencia do Conselho de Ministros, Secretaria de Estado da Cultura, Direccao-Geral do Patrimonio Cultural, Biblioteca Nacional de Lisboa, 1976.
Gerstle, C. Andrew. "Analyzing the Outrageous: Takehara Shunchosai's Shunga Book Makura Doji Nukisashi Manben Tamaguki (Pillow Book for the Young, 1776)." *Japan Review* 26 (2013): 169–193.
Hayakawa, Monta. "Who Were the Audiences for Shunga?" *Japan Review* 26 (2013): 17–36.
Huigen, Siegfried, Jan de Jong, and Elmer Kolfin. *The Dutch Trading Companies as Knowledge Networks*. Leiden: Brill, 2010.
Hunt, Lynn. "Introduction: Obscenity and the Origins of Modernity." In *The Invention of Pornography: Obscenity and the Origins of Modernity, 1500–1800*, edited by Lynn Hunt, 9–45. New York: Zone Books, 1993.
Jarzebowski, Claudia and Thomas Max Safley, eds. *Childhood and Emotion: Across Cultures 1450–1800*. London/New York: Routledge, 2013.
Joshi, Jayant S. and Rajesh Kumar. "The Dutch Physicians at Deijima and the Rise of Western Medicine in Japan." *Proceedings of the Indian History Congress* 63 (2002): 1062–1072.
Kaempfer, Engelbert. *The History of Japan*. London, 1727.
Kure, Shozo. *Shiboruto Sensei*. Tokyo: Tooudou syoten, 1926.
Leupp, Gary P. *Interracial Intimacy in Japan: Western Men and Japanese Women 1543–1900*. London/New York: Continuum, 2003.
Maddern, Philippa. "How Children Were Supposed to Feel, How Children Felt: England 1350–1550." In *Childhood and Emotion: Across Cultures 1450–1800*, edited by Claudia Jarzebowski and Thomas Max Safley, 121–140. London/New York: Routledge, 2014.
McNeil, William H. and Mitsuko Iriye, eds. *Modern Asia and Africa, Readings in World History*, Vol. 9. New York: Oxford University Press, 1971.
Mijnhardt, Wijnand. "Politics and Pornography in the Seventeenth and Eighteenth Century Dutch Republic." In *The Invention of Pornography: Obscenity and the Origins of Modernity, 1500–1800*, edited by L. Hunt, 283–300. New York: Zone Books, 1993.
Miyamoto, Yukiko. "Maruyamayujyo No Seikatsu." *Komazawashigaku* 31 (1984): 19–46.
Montanus, Arnoldus. *Gedenkwaerdige Gesantschappen Der Oost-Indische Maetschappy In't Vereenigde Nederland, Aen De Kaisaren Van Japan*. Amsterdam: Jacob van Meurs, 1669.

Osborne, Milton. "Fear and Fascination in the Tropics: A Reader's Guide to French Fiction on Indo-China." In *Asia in Western Fiction*, edited by R. Winks and J. Rush, 159–174. Honolulu: University of Hawaii Press, 1990.

Pyenson, Lewis. "The Enlightened Image of Nature in the Dutch East Indies: Consequences of Postmodernist Doctrine for Broad Structures and Intimate Life." *Historical Studies in the Natural Sciences* 41, no. 1 (2011): 1–40.

Reff, Daniel T. "Critical Introduction: The Tratado, the Jesuits and the Governance of Souls." In *The First European Description of Japan, 1585: A Critical English-Language Edition of Striking Contrasts in the Customs of Europe and Japan by Luis Frois, S.J.*, edited by K. Richard Danford, Robin Gill and Daniel T. Reff, 1–30. New York: Routledge, 2014.

Roberts, Lisa. "Re-Orienting the Transformation of Knowledge in Dutch Expansion: Nagasaki as a Centre of Accumulation and Management." In *Transformations of Knowledge in Dutch Expansion*, edited by Susanne Friedrich, Arndt Brendecke and Stefan Ehrenpreis, 19–41. Berlin/Boston, MA: De Gruyter, 2015.

Sande, de Duarte. *De Missione Legatorum Iaponensium Ad Romanam Curiam* [Dialogue Concerning the Mission of the Japanese Ambassadors to the Roman Curia]. Macau: In Macaensi portu Sinici regni: in domo Societatis Iesu, 1590.

Schreech, Timon. "Foreign Connections to Shunga." In *Shunga, Sex and Pleasure in Japanese Art*, edited by Timothy Clark, Andrew Gerstle, Aki Ishigami and Akiko Yano, 390–403. London: The British Museum Press, 2013.

Soleiman, Yusak. *The Dutch Reformed Church in Late Eighteenth Century Java: An Eastern Adventure*. Zoetermeer: Boekencentrum, 2012.

Taylor, Jean Gelman. *The Social World of Batavia: Europeans and Eurasians in Colonial Indonesia*. Madison: University of Wisconsin Press, 2009.

Tinios, Ellis. "Japanese Illustrated Erotic Books in the Context of Commercial Publishing 1660–1868." *Japan Review* 26 (2013): 83–96.

van der Pol, Lotte C. *The Burgher and the Whore: Prostitution in Early Modern Amsterdam*. Oxford: Oxford University Press, 2011.

van der Pol, Lotte C. "The Whore, the Bawd, and the Artist: The Reality and Imagery of Seventeenth-Century Dutch Prostitution." *Journal of Historians of Netherlandish Art* 2, no. 1–2 (2010): 1–20.

Viallé, Cynthia. "Daily Life of the Dutch in Canton and Nagasaki: A Comparison Based on the Voc Dagregisters and Other Sources." *Itinerario* 37, no. 3 (2014): 153–71.

Vlam, Grace A. H. "The Portrait of S. Francis Xavier in Kobe." *Zeitschrift für Kunstgeschichte* 42, no. 1 (1979): 48–60.

Vos, Fritz. "Forgotten Foibles: Love and the Dutch at Deishima (1641–1854)." *East Asian History* 39 (2014): 139–152.

Vos, Fritz. "*Onze Voorouders in Japan: Handel, Wetenschap En Liefde* [Our Ancestors in Japan: Trade, Science and Love]." *De Gids. Jaargang* 141 (1978): 215–227.

Vos, Fritz. *Van Keurslijfjes En Keesjes, Bosschietes En Lijfschutten: Onze Voorouders in Japan En Korea En Het Begin Der Japanse En Koreaanse Studien in Nederland*. Leiden: Universitaire Pers, 1980.

Wagner, Peter. *Eros Revived: Erotica of the Enlightenment in England and America*. London: Secker & Warburg, 1988.

Yamamoto, Yukari. "Tsukioka Settei's Erotic Paintings." *Japan Review* 26 (2013): 151–167.

5
SANTIAGO MATAMOROS/ MATAINDIOS

Adopting an Old World battlefield apparition as a New World representation of triumph

Heather Dalton

This chapter evolved from my research on how Northern European merchants experienced the Inquisition in Spain's first settlements in America.[1] As I was looking through the work of indigenous artists for their reactions to the Inquisition, and the spectacle of the Auto Fe, I noted in particular the evolving reception and interpretation of Christian images, especially Santiago Matamoros – St James the Greater, slayer of Moors. While in Northern Europe, images of Saint James the Greater depict the saint as a pilgrim with staff, prayer book and brimmed hat decorated with a scallop shell, on the Iberian Peninsula, the saint is often portrayed wielding a sword and astride a rearing white steed trampling cowering Moors underfoot. The source of this latter image is from a battle said to have occurred between Christians and Muslims at Clavijo in 834. Saint James miraculously appeared above the battlefield, galloping ahead and leading the outnumbered Christians to victory. This violent image became seared into the national psyche with the *Reconquista* and conquest of the Americas and Philippines, and it still has a strong resonance on the Iberian Peninsula and in the Philippines as well as in America. Within years of the first American conquests, the Moor under the hooves of the triumphant Saint James was often portrayed as an indigenous American. Although it is often assumed that these depictions represent an unfeeling celebration of Iberian victory, the reality is more complex.

Although Santiago Matamoros (Saint James slayer of Moors) and Santiago Mataindios (Saint James slayer of Indians) have been the focus of several studies, these have tended to focus on a specific era or locality.[2] My aim is to look at Santiago Matamoros through a wider lens; to understand how emotional practices creating, recreating, perpetuating and reacting to the image have ensured the survival of an early medieval Iberian battlefield apparition as a potent symbol in emphasising difference and maintaining fury. Amy Buono points out that we need to go beyond considering cultural exchange in terms of 'things - in - motion' to look more closely at 'the very nature of the objects' and 'their perceptual environments'. Considering the colonial Americas in particular, she asks, 'how do we contend with things that were produced and used in cultures that did not necessarily valorize the same visual and material phenomena as did early-modern Europeans?'[3] In the case of images of Santiago, I aim to understand how cultural exchange and evolving emotional responses to conversion and colonisation led to reinventions of the warlike saint. Firstly, I look at how Santiago Matamoros was created, evolved and celebrated in medieval Spain. Secondly, I explore how the saint was transported to the New World, and how those the Spanish considered to be outsiders responded to this hero of the *Reconquista*. I am particularly interested in how both Iberian and indigenous artists drew, painted or quite literally carved victory out of defeat when it came to creating images, eventually making Santiago Mataindios their own. Thirdly, I return to the present, to look at the consequences of Iberia's attachment to martial myths and current and future transformations and evocations of Santiago Matamoros into the twenty-first century.

Saint James the Apostle in medieval Spain

Saint James the Greater, known in the Spanish-speaking world as *Santiago*, was fishing in the Sea of Galilee with his brother John, and friends Peter and Andrew, when the four were called to be apostles. The brothers James and John, sons of Zebedee, are referred to in the Gospel of Mark as '*boanerges*' or 'sons of thunder' because of their zeal.[4] There are two versions of the story of how James came to be connected to Spain. One is that his zeal brought him as far west as Spain where he evangelised the people, before returning to the Holy Land. There, he became the first apostle to be martyred after Herod ordered his decapitation. James' body was then returned to Spain by his disciples in a rudderless boat that left the sea at Finisterre and finally docked in a little inland port now known as Padrón, downriver from what was to become Compostela. The other version relates how James, post martyrdom, was miraculously transported to Spain by angels where he proceeded to evangelise the Spanish people. In both versions, the body of James disappeared for 800 years until 813 when Pelayo, a hermit, was guided to his tomb by a bright star shining above what is now Santiago de Compostela in Galacia, in what is now northwestern Spain. The name Compostela means 'field of the star' (*campo de la estrella*).[5] At this time on the Iberian Peninsula, Santiago Peregrino was celebrated as the ultimate pilgrim, with staff, prayer book and brimmed hat. However, he was soon to be portrayed as a warrior saint. The inspiration behind this change in image was an apparition. In 834, 20 years after James' body was rediscovered, the saint appeared to King Ramirez of León in the thick of a battle between Christians and the Muslim Umayyads at Clavijo. Although it is now accepted that a battle never took place and that aspects of the 859 Battle of Monte Laturce were incorporated into the legend, it endured. While Alfonso II had a small chapel built over the site where Santiago's body was found, it was Alfonso III who gifted gold and land and built the 24-meter basilica at Santiago de Compostela. Alfonso was attempting to build up a cult around Santiago that would unite the emerging and divided Christian north – and he succeeded.[6] The basilica became a major pilgrim destination, and the Camiño de Santiago became a major pilgrim road. Vikings, known locally as *Lordomanes*, were enough of a threat along the nearby coastline for fortifications to be built on the Ría de Arousa to prevent raids on Santiago de Compostela, the remains of which are now known as the Towers of Catoira.[7] However, despite this very real threat from the north, it was the threat from the south that galvinised the followers of the saint. Although the Moors never exerted any real control over Galicia, Santiago's miraculous appearance, galloping ahead and encouraging the outnumbered Christians to victory against the infidel, became seared into the Iberian psyche with the *Reconquista*. The *Reconquista*, or reconquest, refers to the series of campaigns, which took place between 718 and 1492, in which the Christian kingdoms gradually conquered more and more of the Muslim Moorish states of Al-Andalus until Granada fell on 2 January 1492. As the Catholic Monarchs entered Granada, the herald declared:

> Santiago, Santiago, Santiago, Castile, Castile, Castile, Grenada, Grenada, Grenada, for those very exalted and powerful lords Don Ferdinand and Doña Isabel, king and queen of Spain, who have won from the infidel Moors this city of Granada and all its realm, with the aid of God and of the glorious Virgin, his mother, and of the blessed apostle Santiago, and with the aid of the most holy pope.[8]

The earliest artistic representation of Santiago on horseback that has survived is the Tympanum of Clavijo, c. 1238–1266, located on the western wall of the south transept of the Cathedral of Compostela.[9] The relief in the stone semicircular decoration above the doorway portrays the saint as a bareheaded horseman wielding a sword and a banner. To the front and rear of his horse are six praying men. Above are ten angels in a semicircle below a border of shells. Although this Santiago is portrayed as an inspirational leader of warriors, he is not involved in the violence of battle – he is above it with the angels as he was in the reported apparition. However, on a pendant made in 1501 (nine years after the fall of Granada), in Zamoranos, about 76 kilometres from Córdoba, the sword-wielding saint is down on the battlefield, galloping over the severed head and hand of a Moor. On what is known as the Pendóndelos Zamorano, the shells are still there, gesturing towards pilgrimage, but the emphasis is on Santiago the warrior, slayer of Moors: Santiago Matamoros.

From the beginning of the sixteenth century, when the Pendóndelos Zamorano was made, depictions of Santiago steadily became more graphically violent. Paintings, carvings and statues of Santiago Matamoros were a familiar sight in churches across Spain. For example, the altarpiece panel by Paolo da San Leocadio in the Iglesia Arciprestal de San Jaime Vila-Real, painted between 1513 and 1519, depicts Santiago Matamoros with a shell badge pinned to his black felt pilgrim's hat, galloping through a sea of dead and dying Moors with his sharpened pike raised; the brightly painted statue of Santiago Matamoros in San Giacomo Maggiore, Burgos, wears a plumed pilgrim's hat featuring two pilgrims badges, yet the armour under his cloak, his raised sword and the three felled Moors raising their arms against both blade and horses hooves gesture towards the evolution of the saint from pilgrim to inspirational warrior to conquistador. The placement of a statue of Santiago Matamoros in the Catedral de Nuestra Señora de la Asunción in Córdoba is particularly confronting. The construction of the building, commonly referred to as the Mesquita-Cateral, or Mosque-Cathedral, began in 784, resulting in what is considered to be one of the most beautiful and accomplished examples of Moorish architecture. After Córdoba returned to Christian rule in 1236, the Great Mosque, which was still being added to, was converted to a Christian church. A cathedral nave was planted right in the middle of what was and still is architecturally a mosque on the orders of Charles V. The statue of Santiago to the side of the altar is barefoot and wears his pilgrim hat, yet his raised sword and the fact that his steed's front hoofs are crushing the scull of a dying Moor symbolise the violent defeat and humiliation of invasion (Figure 5.1).

This combination of the wandering pilgrim and Muslim- slaying warrior may seem contradictory today, but it fitted perfectly with the rhetoric of the Crusades and thus to the *Reconquista* in Spain.[10] The Order of Santiago had been founded

FIGURE 5.1 Statue of Santiago Matamoros, Catedral de Nuestra Señora de la Asunción, Cordoba, Spain, photograph, 2016 (© Heather Dalton).

in the twelfth century, probably by the Augustinian canons regular, and its initial objective was to protect the pilgrims walking the Camino de Santiago (Path of St James) and to defend Christendom. The Order's insignia was and is a red cross resembling a sword, with arms and hilt ending in *fleurs de lys* or forked *cross moline*, as illustrated on the outside wall of the Church of Santiago Apóstol in Málaga (Figure 5.2).

The Church of Santiago Apóstol is the oldest Christian building in Málaga. It was built in 1490 on the ruins of an old mosque, and so dedicating it to Santiago Matamoros was very much a symbolic act of triumph. A plaque featuring Santiago's sword, flanked by scallop shells, was inserted on the mosque's surviving wall above the original Mudéjar-style central door, which is now blocked. In 1493, the Catholic Monarchs incorporated the Order of Santiago into the Spanish Crown. The knights of the Order of Santiago wore the cross on the royal standard and white cape, which can be seen on the effigy of Don García de Osorio (Figure 5.3). Don García, a knight of the Order of Santiago, was buried alongside his wife in the Church of San Pedro in Toledo. His effigy, produced between 1499 and 1505, is dressed as a knight, with his chain mail showing around his neck and a sword clasped to his chest. Yet, he wears the pilgrim's hat with the scallop shell badge pinned to the front, thus demonstrating the dual nature of the order.[11] In 1523, Pope Adrian VI united the office of Grandmaster of Santiago to the Monarchy. In the Real Armería in Madrid is a breastplate

FIGURE 5.2 Cross of the Order of Santiago with scallop shells, Santiago Apóstol, Málaga, Spain, photograph, 2016 (© Heather Dalton).

FIGURE 5.3   Effigy, alabaster, of Don García de Osorio, in the tradition of the work of Gil de Siloe, Spanish (Castilian), perhaps Toledo, c. 1499–1505 (© Victoria and Albert Museum, London).

made for Charles V by Desiderius Helmschmid of Augsburg (1513–1579). The breastplate is engraved with a large image of Santiago Matamoros on horseback trampling a Moor. In an allegorical portrait celebrating Charles V's victory over Barbarossa at Tunis in 1535, Charles V is portrayed on horseback, forcing the capitulation of an elderly bearded Muslim man.[12] The painting, in the Worcester Art Museum in Massachusetts, is catalogued under the title 'King Sapor' and is similar in composition to Durer's 1513 'Knight and the Devil'. The image mimics representations of Santiago Matamoros: the king wears armour, striking a pose typical of Santiago as the elderly man cowers beneath the hooves of his white steed. Charles V was not the only figure to undergo what Lauren Beck calls the 'Matamoros Effect'. In 1512, El Cid, a legendary character loosely based on the conquistador Rodrigo Díaz de Vivar (1043–1099), was portrayed in an edition of *Crónica* 'within the same narrative frame that readers would quickly identify as belonging to Santiago de Matamoros'.[13]

Santiago Matamoros in the Americas

The Crown of Castile regarded the conquest of the Americas as a continuation of the reconquest of Spain from the Moors. Indeed, Hieronymites friars regularly referred to the indigenous inhabitants of Hispaniola as 'Moors'.[14] In the first letter Cortez sent to Charles V from Mexico, he referred to the temples he saw in Veracruz as 'mosques'. Later, on entering Tenochtitlán, the great Aztec city that was to become Mexico City, he referred to the largest Aztec temple as the 'great mosque'.[15] Within a short time of the conquests, images of Santiago Matamoros appeared in the Americas. In 1506, a year after the colony of Havana was founded, Cuba was granted a coat of arms as a result of a request from Don Pánfilo de Narváez to the Royal Council of Castilla. The arms included the Virgin Mary ascending to heaven on a cloud (aided by four cherubs), Santiago galloping through the sky with his raised sword and flag (featuring his cross) and the emblem of the Order of the Fleece pending from a ribbon. Santiago also featured in the first arms granted to Antigua Guatemala. The capital was founded on the site of a Kaqchikel-Maya city, now called Iximche, on 25 July 1524, the feast day of Saint James, and thus named 'Ciudad de Santiago de los Caballeros de Goathemalan'. These arms depicted Santiago holding a flag and sword, galloping towards the cringing enemy, surrounded by scallop shells and above three volcanoes. One of these is erupting, gesturing towards the unpredictability of the region. Santiago continued to gallop across the arms of the capital of Guatemala until 1773 when the city was largely destroyed by an earthquake.[16]

Santiago may have resonated across the Iberian colonies, but it was in Mexico and Peru that he achieved the most traction. As well as the aforementioned coats of arms, the first depictions of Santiago to arrive in the Americas would have been paintings, small carvings and folding altarpieces – brought from places like Seville by Christian missionaries, led by the Franciscan who arrived in Mexico in 1522. Depictions of Santiago de Matamoros also occurred in books, for Juan Cromberger (the son of the Seville-based publisher, Jacome Cromberger) used an ornamental title band featuring Santiago. The saint is easily identifiable with a scallop shell on his hat, a sword in his hand and trampled foes beneath his horse's hooves. This ornamental band was used in the frontispieces of several books, including Quinto Curcio's *De los hechos del Magno Alexandre* (Seville 1534), Alonso de Palencia's translation of Flavius Josephus' *De Bello Judaico* (Seville 1536) and Gonzalo Fernández de Oviedo's *Historia General de Indias* (Seville 1535). In 1540, Juan Cromberger became the first publisher of books in the New World after he was invited to open a press in Mexico City. The *Historia*, with the ornamental band at the top of the frontispiece (Figure 5.4), was a particularly apt vehicle for the image of Santiago Matamoros leading the Spanish in their conquest of the New World. At the beginning of the next century, the ornamental band was used to illustrate Jerónimo Valera's *Comentarii ac quaestiones in universam Aristotelis*, published by Francisco del Canto in Lima in 1610.[17] Valera was a Franciscan, and this book was the first philosophical work printed in South America.[18]

Artists and craftsmen followed the Franciscan, moving to both Mexico and then to Peru. For example, Simón Pereyns, who was born in Flanders around 1530, sailed to New Spain with the viceroy Gastón de Peralta in 1566 after practising his craft in Italy, Portugal and Madrid. As a painter condemned by

FIGURE 5.4 Upper title band, Monogramist S.M.D., woodcut, 1534. Frontispiece, published by Juan Cromberger, Seville, Spain, 1535 (Courtesy of the John Carter Brown Library at Brown University).

the Inquisition, he redeemed himself by producing a number of large artworks including *Virgen del Perdón* for the cathedral of Mexico City and a series of ten paintings for one of the two sixteenth-century altarpieces to survive in Mexico – the altar of the Franciscan church of Huejotzingo (1584–1586). His 'mannerist' style was to influence religious art in Mexico for over a century.[19] Another influential artist in Spain's American colonies was Matteo Pérez de Alessio (1547–1616/1628), an Italian who worked in Seville before moving to Peru in 1588. Alessio's Santiago Matamoros at Clavijo in the Iglesia de Santiago in Seville is dressed like an apostle – bareheaded and in a billowing white gown featuring a large red cross.[20] However, he is behaving like a warrior, his sword aloft and his steed's hooves trampling the enemy into the soil. Although there are no surviving images of Santiago by Alessio in churches in Lima, he worked there for over 30 years and, like Pereyns in Mexico, had a strong influence on emerging New World artists.

By the end of the sixteenth century, paintings and statues of Christian saints populated Mexican and Andean churches. Local craftsmen began to copy these and produce paintings too.[21] Between 1604 and 1610, a Mexican indigenous artist, Miguel Mauricio, working under the guidance of the Franciscan, Fray Juan de Torquemada, carved the richly gilded central panel for the altar of a church built from the stone of Aztec temples destroyed in 1521 by Cortez. Santiago Tlatelolco still stands surrounded by the ruins of Aztec temples, and Mauricio's panel is the only surviving piece of the altarpiece.[22] It is carved in high relief and heavily gilded, featuring swathes of fabric, curling masses of human and horsehair and dismembered limbs. As it can be hard to determine details in a photograph taken in the gloom of the church, the simplified sketch in Figure 5.5 highlights the graphic details.

Mauricio's gilded Santiago is very different from the images found in Spain. He wears an outfit, which is half Spanish conquistador and half Roman general, and rather than slashing at the fallen beneath the feet of his horse, he is simply pointing down at them. The badge on the saint's plumed hat features a sun motif with a face rather than a shell. However, the greatest difference is that the dismembered men under the hooves of his horse are Aztecs – Jaguar warriors to be precise—rather than Moors. This is not Santiago Matamoros; this is Santiago Mataindios (Saint James, slayer of Indians). This image was intended to have a very brutal message: we have won and Our God is victorious. This message is emphasised by the fact that the Jaguar warrior falling under the front hoofs of Santiago's horse wears a feathered helmet in the shape of a bird's head, thus symbolising the defeat of the Aztec eagle. The gilded scrolls above the saint symbolise rolling clouds of thunder.

In the Spanish Philippines, Santiago was only ever portrayed as a slayer of Moors, yet in the Americas, he was portrayed as both Matamoros and Mataindios.[23] The rolling clouds in the aforementioned altarpiece provide a key, for while James and his brother are referred to in the Gospel of Mark as

104 Heather Dalton

FIGURE 5.5   Miguel Mauricio, painted carved panel, Iglesia de Santiago Tlatelolco, Mexico, 1604–1610. Ink and pencil sketch, 2018 (© Heather Dalton).

'*boanerges*' (sons of thunder), in the Americas, Santiago was associated with the pre-Columbian divinity of thunder and lightning who served the Sun God.[24] This association can be linked to sightings of the warrior saint at crucial points in the Spanish colonisation of the Americas, especially in Mexico and Peru. At this point, it should be pointed out that the Spanish used the term 'conquest' and terms like 'colonial Mexico' or 'colonial Peru' early on in their campaigns when the conquest was far from complete. In reality, the Crown of Castile and then the Hapsburgs conquered only certain regions. For example, when the Hapsburgs established a government in Mexico City, it linked only with certain urban areas associated generally with mining or seafaring. Beyond these areas and their outlying military forts, vast regions continued to be ruled to varying degrees by local indigenous elites.[25] This meant that in the period of flux and adaptation after those first early battles between the Spanish and local indigenous groups, stories evolved that responded to and made sense of the conflict and subsequent defeat.

For example, Bernal Díaz del Catillo, who claimed to be fighting with Cortés when the Spanish and their allies were driven out of Tenochtitlan on 8 July 1520, reported that the Virgin Mary appeared. When compiling his *True History of the Conquest of New Spain* at least 40 years later, he reported that Mary had aided the Spanish by casting sand or earth into the eyes of the pursuing Aztecs. According to Oviedo, Díaz, Gómara and Salazar, men who also wrote about the battle decades after it occurred, Santiago was at the Virgin's side – his sword, horse's hooves and mouth inflicting as much damage as the flung sand. The flinging of sand was significant because the Aztecs raked sand out in patterns before their temples. Until the late sixteenth century, a painting of Santiago and the Virgin coming to the conquistadors' aid hung in the same church as the aforementioned altarpiece panel – the Iglesia de Santiago at Tlatelolco.[26]

Between 1584 and 1615, Felipe Guaman Poma de Ayala, an indigenous Quechua nobleman in Peru, produced a 1,200-page manuscript with 400 illustrations known as 'The Nueva coronica y buen gobierno' (The new chronicle and good government). This work is, in effect, a letter to Spain's Hapsburg King Philip III, denouncing the Spanish conquest of Peru and proposing the reorganisation of colonial society in the Andes.[27] Many of the images make pointed observation about the brutal behaviour of the Spanish towards their West African slaves and Peruvians, especially those related to the conquest itself. For example, drawing 157 (page 394) shows the conquistador 'capitán Ávalos de Ayala' riding his horse over the prone Inca general 'Quizu Yupanqui', while stabbing him in the heart with his spear.[28] Drawing 163 (page 406) shows a similar battle scene, with a conquistador holding his sword and banner aloft while riding his horse over a dead or dying Inca. However, this image is not concerned with the brutality of a particular conquistador for the text reads: 'A Conquest: Miracle of St James the Great, Apostle of Christ, at Cuzco' (Figure 5.6).[29]

This image is not simply an adaption of Santiago in action at Clavijo, but it records another miraculous sighting in the New World when Santiago and the Virgin also interceded in 1536 during the siege of Cuzco. From May 1536 to March 1537, Manco Inca Yupanqui besieged the garrison of Spanish conquistadors and indigenous auxiliaries at Cuzco in the Peruvian Andes. Cuzco had been the capital of the Inca Empire until Francisco Pizarro took control in 1533. The aim of Manco Inca Yupanqui, leader of the Sapa Inca, was to restore the Inca Empire. Depending on the source, he had between 100,000 and 400,000 Incas under his command, outnumbering the 200 Spaniards and the unknown number of Inca deserters as well as ethnic groups, such as the Cañari and Chachapoyas, who supported them.[30] Poma's image of Santiago appearing at Cuzco is based on accounts written 20 years after the siege. According to these, apparitions of both Santiago and the Virgin Mary appeared at critical points. Santiago appeared during the day on the battleground, throwing thunderbolts at the enemies of Spain, while the Virgin appeared holding the baby Jesus, and flinging sand, as the Spanish made their final assault as night fell. Poma's drawing 162 (page 404) shows this – the miracle of Santa María de Peña de Francia – with the Virgin

FIGURE 5.6 Felipe Guaman Poma de Ayala, 'El primer Nueva coronica y buen gobierno' (Peru, 1584–1615), drawing 163: 404 [406], 'A Conquest: Miracle of St James the Great, Apostle of Christ, at Cuzco' (© The Royal Danish Library, GKS 2232 kvart).

Mary standing on a winged angel's head, surrounded by storm clouds, scattering sand into the eyes of the cringing Inca soldiers. The fact that Poma's avenging Virgin is not carrying Jesus is testament to the fact that no sightings of Santiago or the Virgin were recorded in the first 20 years after the battle. Once descriptions began to be recorded, the details varied, depending on the identity of the commentator. For example, some commentators reported that it was the spirit of Francisco Pizzaro who accompanied the Virgin, for Pizzaro was ensconced in the relative safety of Lima at the time. The spirit of Pizzaro's horse is described as kicking up so much dust that he blinds the Inca warriors, allowing the Spanish to gain victory.[31] Flinging or kicking up of sand or dust resonated with the Incas, just as it had for the Aztecs in Tenochtitlan, for the central sacred plaza of Cuzco was covered with sand transported overland from the sea to this high city.[32]

Although these apparitions may have been initially described by the Spanish, scholars have pointed out that the fact that they attributed victory to a religious intervention, rather the skill and/or bravery of the Spanish, meant they were palatable to all – the conquistadors, the indigenous peoples and the Spanish authorities. Other scholars disagree, suggesting that such stories were used and manipulated by the clergy to appeal to indigenous understandings of magic at the same time as promoting the idea of a medieval crusade across the Atlantic and into the future.[33] Amnon Nir considers that both are true in that 'such miraculous phenomena are characteristic of Iberian medieval culture as well as of Indigenous Andean culture'.[34] The Virgin is identified with the spirit of the mountains and Mother Earth, and Santiago is linked with the God of Thunder.[35] Illapa was the pre-Columbian divinity of thunder and lightning who served the Sun God. It appears that because the brothers James and John are referred to in the Gospel as *'boanerges'* or 'sons of thunder', James in his guise as Santiago Mataindios was increasingly identified with Illapa.[36] In drawing 131 (page 335), Poma depicts the eleventh Inca, Guayna Capac, standing on his litter and swinging a sling to throw gold projectiles, representing the lightning bolts of the Lord of Thunder. It was such rituals rather than military hardware and battlefield prowess that were thought to matter.[37] Amnon Nir explains that although stories of military miracles at Cuzco included European symbols such as halos and red crosses on chests and white horses, 'the logic which gave meaning to the images and their function in the story is entirely Andean, and foreign to Spanish thought'.[38] This is backed up by the mestizo chronicler Inca Garcilaso who spent the first 20 years of his life in Cuzco before emigrating to Spain in 1560. He reported 'the Indians were terrified at the sight of this new knight', asking 'who is the Viracocha with the *illapa* in his hand?' Garcilaso related this story as proof that his fellow Incas were open to receiving such Christian revelations because of their understanding of natural law. He described Francisco Pizarro, the leader of the Spanish, as a man consumed by pride who was far from an exemplary Christian. Garcilaso saw the interventions of Santiago and the Virgin Mary on behalf of the Spanish as evidence of God's mercy towards them.[39] Poma appears to have considered the Spanish as similarly flawed and seen Christian apparitions in a comparable light. He makes it very clear that the Incas were defeated not because of the skill or bravery of the Spanish but because of the intervention of both the Virgin Mary and Santiago.[40] In the text, Poma likens St James to the pre-Columbian divinity, Illapa.

> Lord Santiago descended with a very loud thunder, like lightning he fell from the sky on the Inca's fortress called Sacsa Guaman, which is the stronghold of the Incas above San Crist.bal. And when he fell on the ground the Indians were frightened and said that illap'a had fallen, thunder and lightning from the sky, q'accha of the Christians, Christian's grace. And this is how Lord Santiago descended to defend the Christians [...] the Indians were frightened from the great noise which the saint caused.[41]

If Poma had not labelled drawing 163 as Santiago, many would have assumed that it featured Pizarro. Indeed, in Poma's image, Pizzaro and Santiago have become one.[42] This is because Poma not only mimics the iconography of Santiago Matamoros but also depicts him as a conquistador.[43] This cross-referencing of images occurred across the Americas as indigenous images-makers began to record the ongoing conquest. A depiction of Cortés from the Mexican codex *Historia de Tlaxcala*, produced in 1585 by the *mestizo* Diego Muñoz Camargo, titled 'Alegoria de Cortez conquistador', suggests that Cortés could be Santiago.[44] Of course, as the conquest of the Americas was seen as a continuation of the *Reconquista*, it can also be argued that both Pizzaro and Cortés saw themselves as an extension of Santiago and fashioned themselves as such. Inga Clendinnen has suggested that there was such a huge admiration for the courage of horses in Mexico that this may have added to the awe in which Mesoamericans held Santiago. The *Historia de Tlaxcala* deals with the social, political, military, religious and cultural history of the Province of Tlaxcala.[45] Many of the folios depict battle scenes. As the Tlaxcaltecas were enemies of the Aztecs, and subsequently became loyal allies of the Spanish, these scenes rarely show Spaniards against Mesoamericans, but Spaniards and Tlaxcaltecas against Aztecs and the allies of Aztecs. Yet, in the majority of these images, a single conquistador on a light-coloured horse takes centre stage, raising his sword or lance as his steed tramples dismembered bodies. In some, such as the image of the battle of Nochtian on folio 316r, the conquistador is in a plumed hat and doublet; while in others, such as the one on folio 282, he is fully armoured. Folio 291 (Figure 5.7) shows Pedro de Alvarado, with sword aloft, riding down indigenous warriors in Guatemala, an area of Mexico now known as Chimaltenango.

While in the Philippines, Christian apparitions, including the Virgin Mary and Santiago, did manifest, they were never reported as physically interceding, as they did in Mexico and Peru. While the Spanish may have first alluded to battlefield apparitions in the New World in order to reinforce their own power

Santiago Matamoros/Mataindios **109**

FIGURE 5.7 Diego Muñoz Camargo, *Historia de Tlaxcala* (Mexico, 1585), MS Hunter 242 (U.3.15), folio 291, 'Battle of Guatemala' (University of Glasgow Library, Archives & Special Collections).

and that of Santiago Matamoros, the stories obviously resonated with indigenous Mexicans and Peruvians. This may have been because the Spanish deliberately linked these apparitions to local belief systems.[46] However, even if this was so, local people developed and adapted the idea of Santiago, eventually making him theirs in countless small acts of adaptation and resistance.

From the early seventeenth-century onwards, depictions of Santiago in both Mexico and Peru embraced both Santiago Matamoros and Santiago Mataindios.[47] Although other saints were portrayed trampling devils and Moors in the Americas, Santiago was very much the saint of choice when it came to such depictions of triumph.[48] He continued to be depicted as Santiago Matamoros. For example, in the mid-1600s, Simón de Barrientos carved an image of Santiago Matamoros on the lateral portal at the Church of La Compania in Arequipa, Peru.[49] Around this time, from the mid-seventeenth century, folk artists who had begun to see themselves as Peruvian, Mexican or Columbian – rather than Spanish, Inca, Aztec or any other group – began to create colourful, highly decorated images of Santiago Mataindios and sometimes Santiago Matamoros. The most spectacular of these images, generally referred to as folk or naive art, are the paintings created in Peru. In these, Santiago is generally dressed in colourful, richly embroidered flowing clothes and a plumed hat. With his sword held aloft, he gallops against a piercingly blue sky on his white charger. Sometimes there are rolling thunderclouds in the distance, alluding to Illapa, the God of Thunder. A single Amerindian or Moor lies prone beneath Santiago's horse, showing no obvious signs of injury. There are no piles of bodies or dismembered limbs, and nature in all its beauty has entered the equation. As in Figure 5.8, colourful birds and/or

FIGURE 5.8 Santiago Mataindios, Cuzco School, Peru, oil on canvas, 1690–1720.
Source: File:Santiago Mataindios.jpg (Wikimedia Commons, the free media repository).

butterflies fly around the saint, the verdant flowers and the framing trees. Images like these hung in small churches across the Andes, and in some homes too, for, although Santiago remained a religious symbol, by this time he had taken on the trappings of a Hispanic/Amerindian folk hero.

At the same time as these highly decorative folk images were produced, other artists continued to produce images of Santiago Mataindios that reinforced a way of remembering history in a particular region. Just as the artists of the sixteenth-century *Historia de Tlaxcala* did not reflect the binary of Spaniards against Mesoamericans, later artists, who identified with the Tlaxcaltecas, continued to emphasise that Santiago was on their side. A pair of eighteenth-century paintings hang in the Museo de las Culturas de Oaxaca in Mexico, titled 'Spaniards and Mesoamericans with Santiago Matamoros presiding'. While one scene shows Santiago Matamoros in action at Clavijo, trampling dead and dying Moors beneath his horse, the other, unusually, shows a still Santiago seated on his horse, standing with the Tlaxcaltecas and the Spanish, in a show of strength against the Aztecs and their supporters.

In the Viceroyalty of Peru, where Santiago was associated with the God of Thunder, Spanish authorities became increasingly concerned that indigenous children were not only calling the saint 'Illapa' but were calling on him to make them stronger so they could beat the Spanish when they grew up. In 1649, the archbishop of Lima denounced this adaptation of the saint, ruling that the only diminutive the saint could be known by was 'Diego'.[50] It was a losing battle. In Cuzco, the eve and saint's day of St James –25th July – became infused with multiple meanings and an increasingly important event for the remnants of the city's Inca nobility. Religious festivals, such as this, and the Corpus Christi Procession, in which the Christian saint or symbol was associated with a pre-Columbian divinity, were opportunities to come together and celebrate both their Christian and, perhaps more importantly, their ethnic identities.[51] From the 1760s, the indigenous nobility's group identity was increasingly under threat under the impact of the Bourbon reforms. For the first time since the conquest, many noble Inca families found themselves subject to tribute payments and legally liable for forced labour service.[52] This was an assault upon their honour as well as their status, and they turned to *their* saint – Santiago – to lead them in their fight to retain their livelihoods and their ethnic identity. When the Peruvians rose up against the Spanish in the nineteenth century, they formally transformed the saint that had become an established part of their religious culture into Santiago 'Mataespañois' Santiago, Slayer of Spaniards. Cuzco, considered by Crown officials and policy-makers to be the military and political key to the whole of Spanish South America, became the nucleus of subversive politics in the last half-century of colonial rule (from around 1770 to 1825). A silver statuette in the Museum of Pilgrimages, Santiago de Compostela, depicts Santiago, sword in hand, galloping after a fleeing Spaniard.[53]

Today, across South and Central America, Santiago represents both the 'sagrado y profano' (sacred and profane) – on the one hand a Christian saint, and on the other a pagan symbol. In the Andes, the saint is called upon to intervene when it comes to the well-being of pets and livestock, regulation of the weather and even to promote fertility. As the centre of festivities, he often embodies a playful ritual, subverting his original role. There were agricultural festivals, with their roots in rural areas prior to the arrival of Europeans, which have recently been adopted by those living in urban areas, including in Lima. In this setting, they may have become increasingly commercialised, but the dances celebrating Santiago continue to bind.[54] In Mexico, Santiago Matamoros became a particularly significant figure in the Bajo Bravo area, especially for the rancheros responsible for defending isolated frontier settlements.[55] This is reflected in the names of towns, such as Heroica Matamoros in the north east of Mexico (in Tamaulipas), which was fortified during the Texan Revolution. Today, festivals celebrating Santiago take place across Mexico on 25 July. In the mountain town of Concepción de Buenos Aires in the state of Jalisco in central western Mexico, a statue of Santiago Matamoros, brandishing a sword and wearing a cowboy hat, is carried through the streets on a palanquin. The bearers are dressed as monsters, symbolising the defeat of the indigenous warriors of Tonalá, who were transformed into hideous monsters in 1530 for opposing the conquistador Nuño de Guzman.

The Franciscans built the stone church of San Bartolomé Apóstol in Cocucho in the state of Michoacán in the late 1500s. Today, the spectacular mural on the underchoir attracts a constant stream of tourists. It was painted circa 1760 when the church was remodelled. The large central panel features Santiago trampling Moors, surrounded by Spanish soldiers praying or firing muskets. Above the saint is a depiction of God the Father, with the Virgin Mary on his right and Christ on his left. All the figures are dressed in eighteenth-century Spanish Mexican fashions.[56] Images of Santiago Matamoros appear in many of the mission churches in this state.[57] It has been suggested that the fact that missions and monasteries continued to be built in a fortress-like style long after the threat of indigenous rebellion in New Spain subsided, reflects the fact that Islam, chiefly characterised by the Ottoman Other, continued to be perceived as a threat to Europe in the eighteenth century. Indeed, guidelines were put in place for seeking out Moslem heretics across the New World, although they were rarely utilised.[58] As in Spain, many of the fortress-like religious institutions housing images of Santiago Matamoros also feature Mudéjar-inspired decorative elements, attesting to the process of transculturation occurring within the Iberian Peninsula and beyond to the Americas.[59]

Today, the saint's day is celebrated by processions and 'a dance in two parts': the first part depicts the encounter of Muslims and Christians and the defeat of the Moors; and the second, the conversion of the Moors. However, generally only the second half is celebrated now. Both men and women dress as Moors in colourful costumes and fantastical headdresses.[60] In an influential essay published in 1984, Richard Trexler explained that these rituals, and the mock battles in particular, constituted a 'military theatre of humiliation'.[61] While Trexler saw the indigenous performers as taking on the identity of the Moors and thus 'exhibiting their own defeat', others – this author included – see the situation as more complex – a joyous subversion of defeat.

Consequences of Spain's attachment to a warlike and racist Santiago

While in Peru and Mexico, Santiago – as the focus of an emotional journey – can be seen as epitomising religious, cultural and even racial interaction and exchange, in El Salvador and Spain in the 1930s he became an anti-communist figurehead. In Tepecoya, 'San Esteban' appeared on a huge white horse and halted the insurrectionary forces. In Nahuilingo, a similar apparition appeared which many assumed was Santiago. The saint's appearances meant that in March 1932, the archbishop of San Salvador named the warrior on a white horse as a defender against communism.[62] In Spain, Franco not only associated Santiago with the expulsion of the Other – in this case, the communists – but also with the idea of racial purity and supreme masculinity. Since 1627, Teresa of Avila had been celebrated in Madrid as co-patron saint of Spain, alongside Santiago. This had caused dissent, especially in Castile, and so after the Civil War, Franco reinstated Santiago as Spain's only patron saint. He focused on Santiago Matamoros, as embodying both the religious and masculine attributes that personified *Hispanidad* or Spanish selfhood.[63]

In 1954, Franco visited Santiago Compostela, lauding Spain's 'great crusading spirit on behalf of the Church in the great days of her Empire and in the recent Civil War'. Later, when he sent his only Moroccan general, Mohamed ben Miziam, there to make the offering on 25 July, officials covered the base of José Gambino's particularly bloodthirsty eighteenth-century statue with a cloth to hide the decapitated heads and dismembered bodies. In the 1990s, some Spaniards refused to walk the Camino de Santiago, considering that Franco had effectively transformed it into a fascist route. This put the spotlight on Santiago Matamoros, encouraging a national discussion on this image of the saint.[64] However, in 2004, in the wake of the Madrid train bombings, furious public reaction forced officials of the Cathedral of Santiago Compostela to abort their plans to replace Gambino's statue of Santiago Matamoros with one of Santiago Peregrino.[65] This shows that, as the patron saint of the Spanish people and their symbolic defender against the infidel, Santiago Matamoros still evokes strong loyalties. While articles in newspapers and blogspots, such as Luís Afonso Assumpção's 'Swimming Against the Red Tide', have reacted with anger to recent attempts at making the statue less offensive by covering Santiago's victims with flowers, others do not think the flowers go far enough in mitigating the statue's horror.[66] For example, a journalist for *The Irish Times* was emotional in her description of 'this portrait of a murder' 'hidden behind a joyless arrangement of plastic white daisies, the sculptured head of a man stares back, open mouthed in pain, blood flowing from his neck, his eyes seemingly resigned to death'.[67]

In his 2008 article, 'James the Greater: Interpreting the Interstices of Santiago as Peregrino and Matamoros', John Moore states that while the pilgrim saint 'challenges hierarchy as a democratic symbol of Everyman's travails', the image of *Matamoros* 'promotes a rigid social structure as an icon of rank and violence and of the Church's prominence in the reconquest enterprise'. Although this statement does not sum up the situation in South America where Santiago's multilayered adaptations are embedded in folklore and still evolving in carnival rituals, it is still relevant to Spain. When Spanish troops were sent to Iraq in July 2003, the red cross of Santiago Matamoros adorned the soldiers' uniforms.[68] The Order of Santiago remains under the protection of the Spanish crown. As of 2014, there were 35 knights and 30 novices in the Spanish Order of Santiago, which is only open to practising Catholics who can prove legitimacy going back four generations, 200 years of confirmed nobility and that their lineage is free from non-Christian contamination. And they must pledge to defend the Immaculate Conception of Mary.[69] In the wake of 9/11, further terrorist attacks (real and imagined), and the influx of refugees from the Middle East, a growing number of European and North American right-wing and Islamophobic groups, such as 'The White Knights', are resurrecting the iconography of Santiago Matamoros.[70] One group sells T-shirts online featuring the Cross of St James, a sketch of Santiago Matamoros and 'Kaffir' in Arabic script. The garment description explains that 'Infidel' is translated into the Arabic 'Kaffir' so there 'will be no miscommunication when you wear it… or when the IS inspired savages see it'.[71] Suarez International, an organisation hosting 'warriortalk' forums, selling firearms and running courses in using them, sells the 'Saint James Crusader Logo Shirt' for US$17.99. This is a black T-shirt featuring the cross of Santiago superimposed over a line drawing of St James on his horse, above the words: 'Protecting Christendom Since 842 A.D'.[72]

On 6 September 2017, the Basque newspaper *Deia* (The Call) published an article in which they suggested that those who slandered ETA in the press were also guilty of stirring up hatred against Muslims: '*Islamofobia y Santiago Matamoros*'. The author points out that in the demonstrations on the streets of Barcelona on 26 August 2017, the majority of placards declared 'no' to the arms trade, the next highest number declared 'no' to Islamophobia and then came the placards supporting Catalonian independence. The author points out that Islamic fanaticism today is a reflection of the Christian fanaticism of previous centuries and that '*históricamente los musulmanes fueron mucho más tolerantes con las ideas y las prácticas religiosas que los cristianos*' (historically, Muslims were much more tolerant of religious ideas and practices than Christians). After pointing out that the state has never really apologised to the Muslims and Jews for the expulsions and ill-treatment of the past, the author declares that as long as Santiago is the patron saint and images of him on his white horse remain, then the will of the majority – that Islamophobia will be erased – will never come about. While the focus of this article is on supporting '*la gran nación europea que es Catalunya*' (the great European nation that is Catalonia), Santiago is evoked to make the point that not only does he still exist in image and form in countless locations, but that since September 11, Spanish politicians intent on suppressing regional aspirations are often those who evoke him and take advantage of Islamophobia to further their ends – 'Al vent del último franquismo' (the last vent of Francoism).[73]

Conclusion

Depictions of Saint James the Greater are some of the most diversified in Christian iconography. In Spain, James, the martyred apostle, was transformed by the communication of a powerful myth from peregrinating pilgrim saint to ultimate warrior saint – Santiago Matamoros. Unlike Saint George, his foe was not a single mythical beast but a group of people – Muslim Umayyads. Despite the fact that the apparition of the saint appeared to King Ramirez of León during a ninth-century battle that never took place, the legend endured, fuelled by the *Reconquista* between 718 and 1492. Taken to America by the Spanish, Santiago Matamoros came to stand for very different things as Amerindians responded to and interpreted images of the saint as not only the slayer of Muslims but also as Santiago Mataindios, their conqueror. While the emotional impact of Santiago Mataindios as a symbol of conquest must have initially evoked horror and fear, this martial image was, over time, appropriated, inverted and made theirs. As Monique Scheer has pointed out, 'Emotions change over time not only because norms, expectations, words, and concepts that shape experience are modified, but also because the practices in which they are embodied, and bodies themselves, undergo transformation'.[74] Although in Spain Santiago Matamoros maintains his association with the idea of pure blood and is still a potent rallying symbol for opposing 'The Other', in South and Central America, Santiago the folk hero stands as the poster boy of the polyglot – a symbol of putting on a brave face and carving a strong community out of defeat.

Notes

1 Heather Dalton, ""Suffering Rewarded": An English Merchant, Marriage and the Inquisition in the Post-Reformation Iberian Atlantic," in *Keeping Family in an Age of Long Distance Trade, Imperial Expansion and Exile, 1550–1850*, ed. Heather Dalton (Amsterdam: University of Amsterdam Press, 2020).

2 For example: Nicolás Cabrillana Ciézar, *Santiago Matamoros: historia e imagen* (Málaga: Servicio de Publicaciones, Diputación de Málaga, 1999); Craig H. Roell, *Matamoros and the Texas Revolution* (Denton: Texas State Historical Association, 2013); Anna Sulai Capponi, "El culto de Santiago entre las comunidades indígenas de Hispanoamérica: símbolo de comprensión, reinterpretación compenetración de una nuevarealidad espiritual," *Imaginário* 12, no. 13 (2006): 249–277; Javier D. García, "Santiago Mataindios: la continuación de un discurso medieval en la Nueva España," *Nueva Revista de Filología Hispánica* 54, no. 1 (2006): 33–56; Max Harris, *Aztecs, Moors and Christians: Festivals of Reconquest in Mexico and Spain* (Austin: University of Texas Press, 2000); David Cahill, *The Inca and Corpus Christi: The Feast of Santiago in Colonial Cuzco* (Amsterdam: CEDLA, 1999).

3 Amy Buono, "Early Modern "Non-Objects"," in *Reframing the Renaissance for the 21st Century. An RSA Roundtable Commemorating the 20th Anniversary of Reframing the*

Renaissance, ed. Claire Farago (Boston, April 2, 2016). Although Buono focuses on the cultural traditions and artistic practices of Pre-Columbian and colonial Brazil, her question is valid across the board.
4 (Mark 3:17), from Galilean dialectal corruption of Hebrew bene reghesh (sons of rage), interpreted in Greek as 'sons of thunder'.
5 See, for example: Richard A. Fletcher, *Saint James's Catapult: The Life and Times of Diego Gelmírez of Santiago de Compostela* (New York: Oxford University Press, 1984); Sophia Deboick, "The Enigma of Saint James," *Guardian*, July 24, 2010.
6 Fletcher, *Saint James's Catapult*, 70–72, 176.
7 See Ann Christys, *Vikings in the South: Voyages to Iberia and the Mediterranean* (London: Bloomsbury Academic, 2015).
8 Amy G. Remensnyder, *La Conquistadora: The Virgin Mary at War and Peace in the Old and New Worlds* (New York: Oxford University Press, 2014), 89.
9 John K. Moore, Jr., "James the Greater: Interpreting the Interstices of Santiago as Peregrino and Matamoros," *La corónica* 36, no. 2 (2008): 313–344.
10 Moore, "James the Greater," 315; Fletcher, *Saint James's Catapult*, 297–299; Stephen B. Raulston, "The Harmony of Staff and Sword: How Medieval Thinkers Saw Santiago Peregrino and Matamoros," *La Corónica: A Journal of Medieval Hispanic Languages, Literatures, and Cultures* 36, no. 2 (2008): 358.
11 Peter Linehan, *Spain: A Partible Inheritance, 1157–1300* (Oxford: Blackwell Publishing Ltd., 2011), 10.
12 Netherlandish, 1525–1535. See: Jan van Herwaarden, "The Emperor Charles V as Santiago Matamoros," *Peregrinations: Journal of Medieval Art & Architecture* 3, no. 3 (2012): 83–106.
13 Lauren Beck, "Visualising the Cid and His Enemies in Print: The Matamoros Effect," *Image & Narrative* 17, no. 1 (2016): 8.
14 The island in the Antilles now divided into Haiti and the Dominican Republic.
15 Luis Weckham, *The Medieval Heritage of Mexico*, trans. Francis M. Lopez-Morillas (New York: Fordham University Press, 1992), 182.
16 For examples of the coats of arms of Antigua Guatemala and the city of Cuba, see woodcuts by Gil González Dávila in *Teatro eclesiastico de la primitiva iglesia de las Indias occidentales*, vol. 1 (Madrid: Diego de la Carrera, 1649).
17 See "Cromberger, Juan, d. 1540," Primeros Libros de las Américas, accessed December 2, 2018, http://primeroslibros.org/about_printers.html?lang=en&by=cromberger and https://dl.wdl.org/13745/service/13745.pdf. Accessed December 2, 2018.
18 For further information see Roberto Hofmeister Pich, "The Account of Transcendental Concepts by Jerónimo Valera (1568–1625) in His Summulae dialecticae (1610)," *Quaestio: Journal of the History of Metaphysics* 14 (2014): 299–314.
19 Clara Bargellini, "The Renaissance at Huejotzingo," in *Reframing the Renaissance for the 21st Century. An RSA Roundtable Commemorating the 20th Anniversary of Reframing the Renaissance*, ed. Claire Farago (Boston, April 2, 2016).
20 Also known as Matteo da Lecce, *Santiago matamoros en la Batalla de Clavijo*.
21 Maya Stanfield-Mazzi, *Object and Apparition: Envisioning the Christian Divine in the Colonial Andes* (Tucson: University of Arizona Press, 2013), 29; Claudia Brosseder, *The Power of Huacas: Change and Resistance in the Andean World of Colonial Peru* (Tucson: University of Arizona Press, 2014), 258.
22 Donna Pierce, "At the Crossroads: Cultural Confluence and Daily Life in Mexico, 1521–1821," in *Painting a New World: Mexican Art and Life, 1521–1821*, eds. Donna Pierce, Rogelio Ruiz Gomar and Clara Bargellini (Colorado: Denver Art Museum, 2004), 30; José Guadalupe Victoria, "Noticias sobre la destrucción del retablo del Tlatelolco," *Anales del Instituto de Investigaciones Estéticas* 16, no. 61 (1990): 73–80.
23 Ethan P. Hawkley, "Reviving the Reconquista in Southeast Asia: Moros and the Making of the Philippines, 1565–1662," *Journal of World History* 25, no. 2–3 (2014): 285–310; Christina H. Lee, "The Chinese Problem in the Early Modern Missionary

Project of the Spanish Philippines," *Laberinto* 9 (2016): 5. In the Philippines the Archangel Michael had the role of suppressing the Chinese devil. For representation of St Michael in the Americas, see Escardiel González Estévez1, "La iconografía de los Siete Arcángeles en el retablo hispanoamericano. Heterodoxia, censura y devoción publica," in *O Retábulo no Espaço Ibero-Americano: Forma, função e iconografia*, ed. Ana Celeste Glória (Lisboa: Instituto de História da Arte da Faculdade de Ciências Sociais e Humanas / NOVA, 2013), 79–90.
24 (Mark 3:17), from Galilean dialectal corruption of Hebrew bene reghesh (sons of rage), interpreted in Greek as 'sons of thunder'.
25 Tatiana Seijas, "Social Order and Mobility in 16th- and 17th-Century Central Mexico," in *The Oxford Research Encyclopedia of Latin American History* (Oxford University Press USA, 2016), Available at latinamericanhistory.oxfordre.com (OUP-USA Mirror, 31 August 2018).
26 Remensnyder, *La Conquistadora*, 297–299.
27 Julio Ortega, "Representation and Appropriation in Guamán Poma de Ayala," trans. Philip Debenshire, *Journal of Global Initiatives* 7, no. 2 Pervuvian Trajectories of Sociocultural Transformation (2012): 15.
28 Guaman Poma, *Nueva corónica y buen gobierno* (1615), drawing 157: Captain Luis de Ávalos de Ayala kills Quizo Yupanqui Inka in the conquest of Lima. Det Kongelige Bibliotek, accessed November 4, 2019, http://www.kb.dk/permalink/2006/poma/394/en/text/?open=idp363664.
29 Poma, *Nueva corónica*, drawing 163: 'A Conquest: Miracle of St James the Great, Apostle of Christ, at Cuzco. The entire manuscript is available on The Royal Danish Library website at: Det Kongelige Bibliotek, accessed November 4, 2019, http://www.kb.dk/permalink/2006/poma/info/en/frontpage.htm.
30 Amnon Nir, "The "Military Miracles" in the 1536 Siege of Cuzco," in *Unlocking the Doors to the Worlds of Guaman Poma and His Nueva Corónica*, eds. Rolena Adorno and Ivan Boserup (Copenhagen: Royal Library, Museum Tusculanum Press, 2015), 286.
31 Nir, "Military Miracles," 273–275.
32 Remensnyder, *La Conquistadora*, 299.
33 Stanfield-Mazzi, *Object and Apparition*, 29; Sabine MacCormack, "History, Historical Record, and Ceremonial Action: Incas and Spaniards in Cuzco," *Comparative Studies in Society and History* 43, no. 2 (2001): 329–363; Nir, "Military Miracles," 270; Nir, "Military Miracles," 272–275; Remensnyder, *La Conquistadora*, 269–290, at 269.
34 Nir, "Military Miracles," 270.
35 Nir, "Military Miracles," 272–275; Remensnyder, *La Conquistadora*, 299.
36 Walter Starkie, *The Road to Santiago: Pilgrims of St. James* (Berkeley and Los Angeles: University of California Press, 1965), 13; Ortega, "Representation and Appropriation," 11–21.
37 Nir, "Military Miracles," 275.
38 Nir, "Military Miracles," 280.
39 Garcilaso de la Vega "1966/2, book 1, chapt. 1, 634 and book 2, chapt. 24, 802,", in *Garcilaso Inca de la Vega: An American Humanist, A Tribute to José Durand*, ed. José Anadón (Notre Dame: University of Notre Dame Press, 1998); Garcilaso de la Vega 2009 [1617]/2, book 2, chapt. 25, 178 in Nir, "Military Miracles," 286–287.
40 Poma, *Nueva corónica*, drawing 163. Captain Luis de Ávalos de Ayala kills Quizo Yupanqui Inka in the conquest of Lima. GKS 2232 4°. The miracle of Santa María de Peña de Francia: Inka soldiers are frightened in battle by the miraculous apparition and flee. Det Kongelige Bibliotek, accessed November 4, 2019, http://www.kb.dk/permalink/2006/poma/404/en/image/ and Det Kongelige Bibliotek, accessed November 4, 2019, http://www.kb.dk/permalink/2006/poma/406/en/text/.
41 Translation of page 407 in Nir, "Military Miracles," 285.
42 Nir, "Military Miracles," 284.
43 Stanfield-Mazzi, *Object and Apparition*, 29.

44 Inga Clendinnen, *Aztecs: An Interpretation* (New York: Cambridge University Press, 1991), 82–83; Diego Muñoz Camargo, *Historia de Tlaxcala* (Mexico, 1585), University of Glasgow Library, MS Hunter 242 (U.3.15). eleanor.lib.gla.ac.uk/record=b1160328. Also see: Frederico Navarrete, "Beheadings and Massacres: Andean and Mesoamerican Representations of the Spanish Conquest," *Anthropology and Aesthetics* 53, no. 54 (2008): 64.
45 For The *Historia de Tlaxcala* see: Glasgow University Library, accessed November 4, 2019, http://special.lib.gla.ac.uk/exhibns/month/jan2003.html.
46 Remensnyder, *La Conquistadora*, 299.
47 See Javier Dominguez Rodriguez, *De Apostol Matamoros a Yllapa Mataindios: Dogmas e Ideologias Medievales en el (Des)cubrimiento de America* (Salamanca: Ediciones Universidad Salamanca, 2008).
48 Vivian Marcela Carrión Barrero, "Pintura colonial y la educación de la mirada. Conformación de identidades y de la otredad," *Tabula Rasa* 4 (2006): 241–265.
49 Luis Enrique Tord, *Arequipa artística y monumental* (Lima-Arequipa: Banco del Sur del Perú, 1987); Antonio San Cristóbal, *Arquitectura planiforme y textilográfica virreinal de Arequipa* (Lima-Arequipa: Universidad Nacional de San Agustín, 1997).
50 Reinhild Margarete von Brunn, "Metamorfosis y Desaparición del Vencido:desde la subalternidad a la complementariedad en la imagen de santiago ecuestre en Perú y Bolivia" (unpublished thesis, University of Chile), 2009.
51 See Carolyn Dean, *Inka Bodies and the Body of Christ: Corpus Christi in Colonial Cuzco, Peru* (Durham: Duke University Press, 1999); Carolyn Dean and Dana Leibsohn, "Hybridity and Its Discontents: Considering Visual Culture in Colonial Spanish America," *Colonial Latin American Review* 12, no. 1 (2003): 5–35.
52 Cahill, *The Inca and Corpus Christi*, 1–58.
53 This work can be viewed on the Museos de Galicia website, accessed March 25, 2019, http://museos.xunta.gal/es/peregrinacions.
54 Juan José García Miranda, "Las fiestas agroganaderas y santiago apóstol," *Runa Yachachiy, Revista electrónica virtual* (2011): 2, 17. Available at Runa Yachachiy 2019, accessed March, 27, 2019, http://www.alberdi.de/coleccion2011.html.
55 See Roell, *Matamoros and the Texas Revolution*.
56 See photographs of the underchoir at: colonialmexico, accessed March 25, 2019, http://colonialmexico.blogspot.com/2014/09/missions-of-michoacan-san-bartolome.html.
57 For example: Santiago Charapan, Tupataro, Angahuan and Nurio.
58 Thomas DaCosta Kaufmann, "Islam, Art, and Architecture in the Americas: Some Considerations of Colonial Latin America," *Anthropology and Aesthetics* 43 (2003): 46–47.
59 Kaufmann, "Islam, Art and Architecture," 50.
60 Harris, *Aztecs, Moors, and Christians*; Susanna Rostas, *Carrying the Word: The Concheros Dance of Mexico City* (Boulder: University Press of Colorado, 2009); Max Harris, *Carnival and Other Christian Festivals: Folk Theology and Folk Performance* (Austin: University of Texas Press, 2003).
61 Richard Trexler, "We Think, They Act: Clerical Readings of Missionary Theatre in 16th Century New Spain," in *Understanding Popular Culture: Europe from the Middle Ages to the Nineteenth Century*, ed. Steven L. Kaplan (Berlin and New York: Mouton, 1984), 189–227; Harris, *Aztecs*, 2.
62 Jeffrey L. Gould and Aldo A. Lauria-Santiago, *To Rise in Darkness: Revolution, Repression, and Memory in El Salvador, 1920–1932* (Durham and London: Duke University Press, 2008), 249.
63 Donn James Tilson, "Devotional-Promotional Communication and Santiago: A Thousand-Year Public Relations Campaign for Saint James and Spain," in *Public Relations: Critical Debates and Contemporary Practice*, eds. Jacquie L'Etang and Magda Pieczka (Mahwah and London: LEA Publishers, 2006), 176. A painting, commissioned by Franco, depicting Santiago flying over his head hangs in the Military Archives in Madrid.

64 Nicole Rasch, "The Camino de Santiago as Global Narrative: Literary Representations and Identity Creation," in *The Camino de Santiago in the 21st Century: Interdisciplinary Perspectives and Global Views*, eds. Samuel Sánchez y Sánchez and Annie Hesp (New York: Routledge, 2015), 194–211.
65 This was reported in newspapers across Europe. See for example: Isambard Wilkinson, "Public Outcry Forces Church to Keep Moor Slayer's Statue," *The Daily Telegraph*, July 22, 2004.
66 Luís Afonso, "Saint-James from Compostela: The "Moor Slayer" and the Politically Correct," swimming against the red tide, February 17, 2008, accessed March 21, 2019, http://againstred.blogspot.com/2008/02/saint-james-from-compostela-slayer-and.html. See also: "Santiago And The Moors Are At It Again," Infidel Blooger's Alliance, November 5, 2006, accessed March 21, 2019, http://ibloga.blogspot.com.au/2006/11/santiago-and-moors-are-at-it-again.html.
67 Mary Boland, "Opportunistic Cult of the Moor-Slayer at Camino's End," *The Irish Times*, November 5, 2010, accessed March 22, 2019, https://www.irishtimes.com/news/opportunistic-cult-of-the-moor-slayer-at-camino-s-end-1.672768.
68 Moore, "James the Greater," 313–344.
69 Rebecca C. Quinn, "Santiago as Matamoros: Race, Class, and *Limpieza de Sangre* in A Sixteenth-Century Spanish Manuscript," *The Larrie and Bobbi Weil Undergraduate Research Award Documents (2011)*, Paper 1, http://digitalrepository.smu.edu/weil_ura/1.
70 See, for example, Arzu Merali and Massoud Shadjareh, *Islamophobia – The New Crusade* (London: Islamic Human Rights Commission, 2002).
71 T-shirt available from: SuarezInternational, accessed May 14, 2016, http://www.onesourcetactical.com/st-james-infidel-t-shirt---tan-1.aspx.
72 T-shirt available from: SuarezInternational, accessed December 23, 2018, https://suarezinternational.com/saint-james-crusader-logo-shirt/.
73 Patxi Zabaleta, "Islamofobia y Santiago Matamoros," *Deia*, September 6, 2017, accessed March 27, 2019, https://www.deia.eus/2017/09/06/opinion/tribuna-abierta/islamofobia-y-santiago-matamoros.
74 Monique Scheer, "Are Emotions a Kind of Practice (and Is That What Makes Them Have a History)? A Bourdieuian Approach to Understanding Emotion," *History and Theory* 51 (May 2012): 193–220.

Bibliography

"Santiago And The Moors Are At It Again." Infidel Blooger's Alliance, November 5, 2006. Accessed March 21, 2019. http://ibloga.blogspot.com.au/2006/11/santiago-and-moors-are-at-it-again.html.
Afonso, Luís. "Saint-James from Compostela: The "Moor Slayer" and the Politically Correct." swimming against the red tide, February 17, 2008. Accessed March 21, 2019. http://againstred.blogspot.com/2008/02/saint-james-from-compostela-slayer-and.html.
Anadón, José, ed. *Garcilaso Inca de la Vega: An American Humanist, A Tribute to José Durand*. Notre Dame: University of Notre Dame Press, 1998.
Barrero, Vivian Marcela Carrión. "Pintura colonial y la educación de la mirada. Conformación de identidades y de la otredad." *Tabula Rasa* 4 (2006): 241–265.
Beck, Lauren. "Visualising the Cid and His Enemies in Print: The Matamoros Effect." *Image & Narrative* 17, no. 1 (2016): 5–14.
Boland, Mary. "Opportunistic Cult of the Moor-Slayer at Camino's End." *The Irish Times*, November 5, 2010. https://www.irishtimes.com/news/opportunistic-cult-of-the-moor-slayer-at-camino-s-end-1.672768.
Brosseder, Claudia. *The Power of Huacas: Change and Resistance in the Andean World of Colonial Peru*. Tucson: University of Arizona Press, 2014.

Brunn, Reinhild Margarete von. "Metamorfosis y Desaparición del Vencido: desde la subalternidad a la complementariedad en la imagen de santiago ecuestre en Perú y Bolivia." Unpublished thesis, University of Chile, 2009.

Buono, Amy. "Early Modern "Non-Objects"." In *Reframing the Renaissance for the 21st Century. An RSA Roundtable Commemorating the 20th Anniversary of Reframing the Renaissance*, edited by Claire Farago. Boston, April 2, 2016.

Cahill, David. *The Inca and Corpus Christi: The Feast of Santiago in Colonial Cuzco*. Amsterdam: CEDLA, 1999.

Capponi, Anna Sulai. "El culto de Santiago entre las comunidades indígenas de Hispanoamérica: símbolo de comprensión, reinterpretación compenetración de una nuevarealidad espiritual." *Imaginário* 12, no. 13 (2006): 249–277.

Christys, Ann. *Vikings in the South: Voyages to Iberia and the Mediterranean*. London: Bloomsbury Academic, 2015.

Ciézar, Nicolás Cabrillana. *Santiago Matamoros: historia e imagen*. Málaga: Servicio de Publicaciones, Diputación de Málaga, 1999.

DaCosta Kaufmann, Thomas. "Islam, Art, and Architecture in the Americas: Some Considerations of Colonial Latin America." *Anthropology and Aesthetics* 43 (2003): 42–50.

Dalton, Heather. "'Suffering Rewarded': An English Merchant, Marriage and the Inquisition in the Post-Reformation Iberian Atlantic." In *Keeping Family in an Age of Long Distance Trade, Imperial Expansion and Exile, 1550–1850*, edited by Heather Dalton. Amsterdam: University Of Amsterdam Press, 2020.

Dean, Carolyn, and Dana Leibsohn. "Hybridity and Its Discontents: Considering Visual Culture in Colonial Spanish America." *Colonial Latin American Review* 12, no. 1 (2003): 5–35.

Dean, Carolyn. *Inka Bodies and the Body of Christ: Corpus Christi in Colonial Cuzco, Peru*. Durham: Duke University Press, 1999.

Deboick, Sophia. "The Enigma of Saint James." *Guardian*, July 24, 2010.

Estévez, 1Escardiel González. "La iconografía de los Siete Arcángeles en el retablo hispanoamericano. Heterodoxia, censura y devoción publica." In *O Retábulo no Espaço Ibero-Americano: Forma, função e iconografia*, edited by Ana Celeste Glória, 79–90. Lisboa: Instituto de História da Arte da Faculdade de Ciências Sociais e Humanas / NOVA, 2013.

Fletcher, Richard A. *Saint James's Catapult: The Life and Times of Diego Gelmírez of Santiago de Compostela*. New York: Oxford University Press, 1984.

García, Javier D. "Santiago Mataindios: la continuación de un discurso medieval en la Nueva España." *Nueva Revista de Filología Hispánica* 54, no. 1 (2006): 33–56.

Gould, Jeffrey L., and Aldo A. Lauria-Santiago. *To Rise in Darkness: Revolution, Repression, and Memory in El Salvador, 1920–1932*. Durham and London: Duke University Press, 2008.

Harris, Max. *Aztecs, Moors and Christians: Festivals of Reconquest in Mexico and Spain*. Austin: University of Texas Press, 2000.

Harris, Max. *Carnival and Other Christian Festivals: Folk Theology and Folk Performance*. Austin: University of Texas Press, 2003.

Hawkley, Ethan P. "Reviving the Reconquista in Southeast Asia: Moros and the Making of the Philippines, 1565–1662." *Journal of World History* 25, no. 2–3 (2014): 285–310.

Herwaarden, Jan van. "The Emperor Charles V as Santiago Matamoros." *Peregrinations: Journal of Medieval Art & Architecture* 3, no. 3 (2012): 83–106.

Lee, Christina H. "The Chinese Problem in the Early Modern Missionary Project of the Spanish Philippines." *Laberinto* 9 (2016): 5–32.

Linehan, Peter. *Spain: A Partible Inheritance, 1157–1300*. Oxford: Blackwell Publishing Ltd., 2011.

MacCormack, Sabine. "History, Historical Record, and Ceremonial Action: Incas and Spaniards in Cuzco." *Comparative Studies in Society and History* 43, no. 2 (2001): 329–363.

Merali, Arzu and Massoud Shadjareh. *Islamophobia – The New Crusade*. London: Islamic Human Rights Commission, 2002.

Miranda, Juan José García. "Las fiestas agroganaderas y santiago apóstol." *Runa Yachachiy, Revista electrónica virtual* (2011): 1–23. http://www.alberdi.de/coleccion2011.html.

Moore, Jr, John K. "James the Greater: Interpreting the Interstices of Santiago as Peregrino and Matamoros." *La corónica*, 36, no. 2 (2008): 313–344.

Navarrete, Frederico. "Beheadings and Massacres: Andean and Mesoamerican Representations of the Spanish Conquest." *Anthropology and Aesthetics* 53, no. 54 (2008): 59–78.

Nir, Amnon. "The "Military Miracles" in the 1536 Siege of Cuzco." In *Unlocking the Doors to the Worlds of Guaman Poma and His Nueva Corónica*, edited by Rolena Adorno and Ivan Boserup, 269–290. Copenhagen: Royal Library, Museum Tusculanum Press, 2015.

Ortega, Julio. "Representation and Appropriation in Guamán Poma de Ayala." Translated by Philip Debenshire. *Journal of Global Initiatives* 7, no. 2 Pervuvian Trajectories of Sociocultural Transformation (2012): 11–21.

Pich, Roberto Hofmeister. "The Account of Transcendental Concepts by Jerónimo Valera (1568–1625) in His Summulae dialecticae (1610)." *Quaestio: Journal of the History of Metaphysics* 14 (2014): 299–314.

Pierce, Donna. "At the Crossroads: Cultural Confluence and Daily Life in Mexico, 1521–1821." In *Painting a New World: Mexican Art and Life, 1521–1821*, edited by Donna Pierce, Rogelio Ruiz Gomar and Clara Bargellini, 25–47. Colorado: Denver Art Museum, 2004.

Poma, Guaman. *Nueva corónica y buen gobierno*. 1615.

Quinn, Rebecca C. "Santiago as Matamoros: Race, Class, and *Limpieza de Sangre* in A Sixteenth-Century Spanish Manuscript." *The Larrie and Bobbi Weil Undergraduate Research Award Documents (2011)*, Paper 1. http://digitalrepository.smu.edu/weil_ura/1.

Rasch, Nicole. "The Camino de Santiago as Global Narrative: Literary Representations and Identity Creation." In *The Camino de Santiago in the 21st Century: Interdisciplinary Perspectives and Global Views*, edited by Samuel Sánchez y Sánchez and Annie Hesp, 194–211. New York: Routledge, 2015.

Raulston, Stephen B. "The Harmony of Staff and Sword: How Medieval Thinkers Saw Santiago Peregrino and Matamoros." *La Corónica: A Journal of Medieval Hispanic Languages, Literatures, and Cultures* 36, no. 2 (2008): 345–367.

Remensnyder, Amy G. *La Conquistadora: The Virgin Mary at War and Peace in the Old and New Worlds*. New York: Oxford University Press, 2014.

Rodriguez, Javier Dominguez. *De Apostol Matamoros a Yllapa Mataindios: Dogmas e Ideologias Medievales en el (Des)cubrimiento de America*. Salamanca: Ediciones Universidad Salamanca, 2008.

Roell, Craig H. *Matamoros and the Texas Revolution*. Denton: Texas State Historical Association, 2013.

Rostas, Susanna. *Carrying the Word: The Concheros Dance of Mexico City*. Boulder: University Press of Colorado, 2009.

San Cristóbal, Antonio. *Arquitectura planiforme y textilográfica virreinal de Arequipa*. Lima-Arequipa: Universidad Nacional de San Agustín, 1997.

Scheer, Monique. "Are Emotions a Kind of Practice (and Is That What Makes Them Have a History)? A Bourdieuian Approach to Understanding Emotion." *History and Theory* 51 (May 2012): 193–220.

Seijas, Tatiana. "Social Order and Mobility in 16th- and 17th-Century Central Mexico." In *The Oxford Research Encyclopedia of Latin American History*. Oxford University Press USA, 2016. Available at latinamericanhistory.oxfordre.com (OUP-USA Mirror, 31 August 2018).

Stanfield-Mazzi, Maya. *Object and Apparition: Envisioning the Christian Divine in the Colonial Andes*. Tucson: University of Arizona Press, 2013.

Starkie, Walter. *The Road to Santiago: Pilgrims of St. James*. Berkeley and Los Angeles: University of California Press, 1965.

Tilson, Donn James. "Devotional-Promotional Communication and Santiago: A Thousand-Year Public Relations Campaign for Saint James and Spain." In *Public Relations: Critical Debates and Contemporary Practice*, edited by Jacquie L'Etang and Magda Pieczka, 167–186. Mahwah and London: LEA Publishers, 2006.

Tord, Luis Enrique. *Arequipa artística y monumental*. Lima-Arequipa: Banco del Sur del Perú, 1987.

Trexler, Richard. "We Think, They Act: Clerical Readings of Missionary Theatre in 16th Century New Spain." In *Understanding Popular Culture: Europe from the Middle Ages to the Nineteenth Century*, edited by Steven L. Kaplan, 189–227. Berlin and New York: Mouton, 1984.

Victoria, José Guadalupe. "Noticias sobre la destrucción del retablo del Tlatelolco." *Anales del Instituto de Investigaciones Estéticas* 16, no. 61 (1990): 73–80.

Weckham, Luis. *The Medieval Heritage of Mexico*. Translated by Francis M. Lopez-Morillas. New York: Fordham University Press, 1992.

Wilkinson, Isambard. "Public Outcry Forces Church to Keep Moor Slayer's Statue." *The Daily Telegraph*, July 22, 2004. http://www.telegraph.co.uk/news/worldnews/europe/spain/1467621/Public-outcry-forces-church-to-keep-Moor-Slayers-statue.html.

Zabaleta, Patxi. "Islamofobia y Santiago Matamoros." *Deia*, September 6, 2017. Accessed March 27, 2019. https://www.deia.eus/2017/09/06/opinion/tribuna-abierta/islamofobia-y-santiago-matamoros.

6

RIDING THE JUGGERNAUT

Embodied emotions and 'Indian' ritual processions through European eyes, c. 1300–1600

Jennifer Spinks

A striking late sixteenth-century engraving depicts the so-called Indian 'juggernaut' (Figure 6.1). Elephants draw a wagon supporting a grotesque deity accompanied by female musicians. Men throw themselves beneath the rolling wheels, and another slashes his leg with a knife. This scene unfolds in the Indian kingdom of Narsinga, the accompanying text tells us. And – although the word is not used in the text – the scene depicts a type of procession that would become well known as the juggernaut.

This image was first produced in the late sixteenth century to accompany Jan Huygen van Linschoten's account of his travels in India and widely disseminated in the well-known De Bry printed *Voyages* from the end of the sixteenth century.[1] The juggernaut, a form of religious procession in which the bodies of ecstatic Hindu worshippers were supposedly crushed under the wheels of wagons bearing statues of Hindu gods, is most often associated with the city of Puri in the state Odissa. The ritual is connected to the eleventh- or twelfth-century Hindu Jagannath temple, with three carved deities annually carried in procession, and worshippers pulling ropes to move the vehicles.[2] Jagannath therefore likely provides the etymological basis of the word juggernaut – although it was not used in late medieval or early modern European descriptions.[3]

This chapter aims to unpack some of the emotional dynamics of the 'Indian' juggernaut viewed through the prism of early modern northern European religious anxieties. It first examines the textual and visual forms through which Europeans created the juggernaut (c. 1300–1600), and then examines the European sources that likely also helped to shape it. It does not aim to provide Indian perspectives on these encounters, which lie outside the scope of this study. Rather, the chapter seeks to open up questions about what Europeans saw, misunderstood and polemically conveyed to domestic audiences back in Europe.[4] It also aims to examine how useful this type of imagery is for thinking about the expression of

FIGURE 6.1 Johann Theodor de Bry, image of the 'juggernaut', engraving, *India Orientalis, Teil II* (Jan Huygen van Linschoten), 1598–1628, fig. xxii. Basel University Library, EUU I 70–71: 1.

emotion in visual forms that rely on sound and movement.[5] The juggernaut has received very little attention in studies of European views of Asia, despite its dramatic imagery and significant analogies with European processions and religious experiences, examined below.[6]

In one of the most widely circulated and influential European descriptions of the juggernaut, armchair traveller John Mandeville described how 'some [pilgrims] fall down in front of the chariot and let it ride over them, and so some die and others have their arms or legs broken, and they do this out of love for their idol'.[7] Love and violence are here entwined, revealing an anxious fascination with the performance of religious ecstasy in foreign contexts.[8] But they also recognisably tap into domestic traditions of political and religious public processions in early modern Europe. In important comparative ways, this reflected the performative roles of bodies, images and objects in European sacred spaces and processions. The juggernaut surely also recalled for Europeans the frenzied Bacchic processions that they understood as having quite literally originated in India. The fusion of movement and of dramatic bodies tapped into new trends in mannerist art, and Europeans saw much that was familiar in constructing their image of the idolatrous, ecstatic, Indian 'other'.

Despite the relative neglect of the juggernaut, recent work by David R.M. Irving gives festival processions and their control a pivotal place in the intersection between Western colonisers and indigenous peoples in South East Asia.[9] European visual culture of the sixteenth century is likewise saturated with the iconography of triumphs and processions. These include religious processions such as those for Corpus Christi and by flagellants, Petrarchan triumphs, militarised processions that look back to the tradition of the Triumph of Caesar, images of the Four Horsemen of the Apocalypse, royal entries into cities and parodic processions such as those attached to carnival, especially in Reformation print culture.[10] The sixteenth century also saw the inclusion of non-European themes in royal and other civic entries connected with cities, in which people, animals and objects were used to represent the East, or other parts of the globe beyond Europe's borders.[11]

European reports of worshippers self-harming in juggernaut-style processions were initially fed through Mediterranean channels. However, the juggernaut seems to have gained particular polemical and visual traction in Northern European printed visual and textual representations. Travel narratives – some illustrated – that reported religious processions constitute the source base for this study. The juggernaut forms a vivid moment within these narratives. While religion is central in each case, the authors wrote from varying perspectives. Some were missionaries, others travelled in a secular capacity and one – perhaps the most important, John Mandeville – was an armchair traveller with an uncertain biography. As Nandini Das wrote recently in relation to English views of Japan in the sixteenth century: 'Much of this fragmentary knowledge was evidently secondhand, borrowed, or translated; some was misconstrued or mistransposed. Yet collectively, they form a part of the encounter as much as the actual momentous meeting of the traveller and the host nation'.[12] The sources in this article similarly provide vivid textual and visual glimpses of the ways that Europeans understood the so-called juggernaut in religious and emotional terms, and how it became a new trope in the period c. 1300–1600. Europeans developed stereotypes about Indian religion as emotionally driven in ways that were based upon frenzied movement, sound and violence. In doing so, these sources othered Indian worshippers but also meaningfully communicated with Europeans.

*****

European ideas about the juggernaut seem to have emerged through medieval travel narratives that reported on 'Indian' (likely varieties of Hindu) religious practices. Texts by the Dominican missionary Jordan of Catalonia (c. 1329), and especially by the Franciscan missionary Odorico da Pordenone (c. 1330),[13] established tropes that were developed in works by merchant Niccolò Conti (as reported to Spanish diplomat Pero Tafur in 1438 and to Italian humanist Poggio Bracciolino in 1441), and – most significantly, for the visual tradition and wider sixteenth-century diffusion – by armchair traveller John Mandeville (c. 1356).[14] While this article cannot comprehensively survey all reports of the juggernaut (let alone the many variants in manuscript and print editions), these authors demonstrate how the concept of the juggernaut became widely circulated in textual form across Europe in complex ways that were evidently intended to trigger European emotions.

Jordan of Catalonia and Odorico of Pordenone described physical sacrifice linked to religious rituals in southern India. Both had spent time in China and in India as missionaries, and their ideas therefore reached Europe via channels that were particularly concerned with the place of Christianity in India. Each wrote travel narratives intended to convey the successes of their overseas missionary activities to date and to stress the urgent need for further support. These were also narratives that contained useful and diverting stories, and they found audiences beyond fellow missionaries and ecclesiastics. Multiple manuscript editions testify to a wider reach, particularly of Odorico's text, which would be very widely diffused.[15]

Jordan of Catalonia's travel narrative, the *Mirabilia*, was geographically organised across regions including Armenia, Arabia, the lands of the 'Great Tartar', and with several chapter given to different regions in India. Jordan, the first bishop of Kollam on the Malabar Coast of India, paid as much attention to flora, fauna and social customs as to religious structures and rites. His descriptions of the latter included an intense scene of religious self-harm. He recounted how grateful male worshippers, helped by deities in times of trouble, would soon after participate in processions, where they would '... go with singing and playing before the idol when it is carried through the land (like the image of the Virgin Mary here among us at the Rogation tides)'. These men would carry a sword, and at the climax of the procession would 'cut off their own heads before the idol'.[16]

Odorico's travel narrative covered similar geographical terrain, and he regaled his readers with descriptions of courts, of commodities, of animals and plants and even with practical information for travellers about the likely availability of accommodation. The everyday life of local people was most often treated through religious scenes, reflecting his missionary activities and desire to promote the need for those activities to European readers. One of the most intense scenes recounted an event that recognisably depicted what would later become known as the juggernaut. This report firmly laid the foundations for the European stereotype of the juggernaut, with worshippers dying under the wheels of a processional wagon. Odorico described, in a passage that demands quoting at length, how:

> ...annually on the recurrence of the day when that idol was made, the folk of the country come and take it down, and put it on a fine chariot; and then the king and queen and all the pilgrims, and the whole body of the people, join together and draw it forth from the church with loud singing of songs and all kinds of music; and many maidens go before it two by two chaunting in a marvellous manner. And many pilgrims who have come to the feast cast themselves under the chariot, so that its wheels may go over them, saying that they desire to die for their God. And the car passes over them, and crushes and cuts them in sunder, and so they perish on the spot. And after this fashion they drag the idol to a certain customary place, and they drag him back to where he was formerly, with singing and playing as before. And thus not a year passes but there perish more than five hundred men in this manner; and their bodies they burn, declaring that they are holy, having thus devoted themselves to death for their God.[17]

The 'idol', a central figure of these scenes, was inherently negative for Europeans.[18] Nonetheless, Europeans framed the idol in terms that at times had positive and familiar associations. Like Jordan referencing rogation, Odorico used Christian comparisons when identifying the idol, writing that:

> It is as big as St. Christopher is commonly represented by the painters, and it is entirely of gold, seated on a great throne, which is also of gold. And round its neck it hath a collar of gems of immense value. And the church of this idol is of pure gold, roof (and walls) and pavement. People come to say their prayers to the idol from great distances, just as Christian folk go from far on pilgrimage to St. Peter's.[19]

The magnificence of the idol reveals its falseness, Odorico seemed to suggest, but there were also positive points in his text about magnificence, understood through Christian analogies. Odorico also described other examples of religious self-harm, including pilgrims with knives stuck in their arms, worshippers who cut off chunks of their flesh in temples before deities and even suicide, after which 'they take his body and burn it, for they look on him as a saint, having thus slain himself for his idol'.[20]

Odorico situates his description of the 'idol' immediately after a passage on Thomasians (or Nestorians, adherents of an Eastern Syriac form of Christianity) in the 'kingdom of Mobar', on the southeast coast of India. In this realm, he writes, 'laid the body of the blessed Thomas the Apostle'.[21] Odorico specifically describes this group as 'Christians, but vile and pestilential heretics', and the two stories cluster in a group, but specifically distinguish between and indeed implicitly compare the 'bad' Christians and the sincere (if idolatrous) Hindu worshippers of the idol. Their physical sincerity is partly expressed through emotional, devout, sincere, but frighteningly frenzied bodily movement and music.

Armchair traveller John Mandeville's *Travels*, which circulated from c. 1356, brought the juggernaut material directly into a northern European context through a transmission process that certainly drew upon Odorico and likewise located the juggernaut in the Ma'bar (Malabar) region of India, in the city of Calamy, in the south.[22] Mandeville's famous text, which begins with a journey to the Holy Land, would circulate very widely in both manuscript and printed form, despite the unknown origins of the author. What Mandeville lacked in the eyewitnessing credentials of an Odorico or a Jordan (or indeed a Marco Polo), he would make up for with a vivid and compelling narrative. The early section of the book focused intensely on the Holy Land and the wonders found there, before branching out to the further corners of the world. The Christian framework underpinned the book's reports of wondrous objects, landscapes, plants and peoples, and Mandeville's attention to devotional practices and the emotional gestures of Indian worshippers. Mandeville described a juggernaut-like event in vividly emotional terms that stressed the joyfulness of this self-harming form of worship:

> All the local virgins go in front of the chariot at the head of the procession, in pairs; then all the pilgrims follow, some of whom fall down in front of the chariot and let it ride over them, and so some die and others have their arms or legs broken, and they do this out of love for their idol. They believe that the more pain they suffer for their idol's sake, the more pleasure they'll have in the next world. ... Immediately in front of the chariot are countless local minstrels, making many different melodies.[23]

Mandeville added that 'One can find few Christians who are willing to suffer so great a penance for Our Lord's sake as these people do for their idol'.[24] He was similarly non-judgemental when describing associated ritual suicides, which he identified as honourable and indeed comparable to sainthood. 'Here', he wrote, 'friends of the dead burn their bodies and take the issues and keep them as relics, and they say that this is a holy thing'.[25]

By dwelling upon Christian analogies of movement and devotion, Mandeville intensified an approach developed by Odorico, developing explicit comparisons to western Christian faith and rituals. Joy and fear, music and movement, violence and ecstasy run through these descriptions. He differs from Odorico by spatially co-locating this group with Thomasians, and actually situating the deity (which was 'finely and expensively crafted with precious gems and with pearls, of a false god') within the 'Church of St Thomas'.[26] Mandeville therefore presents an overlapping vision of Thomasians and Hindus.

The European stereotype of the juggernaut was firmly embedded by the time Italian merchant Niccolò Conti's stories of his travels were recorded by Spanish diplomat Pero Tafur in 1438 and Italian humanist Poggio Bracciolino in 1441.[27] Conti had spent some years in the Indies as a merchant, and had converted to Islam for pragmatic reasons during his travels. His account – put into writing by others upon his return to Europe – covered similar ground to earlier travel books and was shaped by Christian imperatives, because Conti hoped to receive absolution from the Pope for his temporary conversion.[28] Tafur had travelled with Conti in the near East, and his status as a diplomat shows the appeal of the text in political contexts hungry for news about distant lands. Humanist and papal secretary Bracciolini's version would secure a wider diffusion of Conti's narrative. This text paid less attention than those by previous authors to parallel modes of worship, although it did note that 'Gods are worshipped throughout all India, for whom they erect temples very similar to our own'.[29] The juggernaut is situated in 'Bizenegalia' (Viyanagar, in southern India), and he recorded how:

> Many, carried away by the fervour of their faith, cast themselves on the ground before the wheels, in order that they may be crushed to death – a mode of death which they say is very acceptable to their god. Others, making an incision in their side, and inserting a rope thus through their body, hang themselves to the chariot by way of ornament, and thus suspended and half dead accompany their idol. This kind of sacrifice they consider to be the best and most acceptable of all.[30]

The text evidently drew upon a well-circulated tradition by this point, although the reference to 'half-dead' hanging bodies added a new dimension. Conti's travels would be transmitted widely in textual terms through their inclusion in Chapter 4 of Poggio Bracciolini's *De varietate fortuna*.[31] But it is surely Mandeville's publishing sensation, his *Travels*, that provides us with the best snapshot of the juggernaut at the close of the medieval period – not least because it is the text that would launch a visual tradition. Medieval manuscripts of these texts do not seem to include illustrations of juggernaut-type processions, despite the vivid descriptions available to artists.[32] The closest may well be a scene from John of Mandeville in a luxurious fifteenth-century manuscript which depicts a worshipper self-harming before a deity on a column outside the tomb of St Thomas.[33]

★★★★★

130 Jennifer Spinks

The visual tradition of the juggernaut can be much more firmly linked to the rise of print. The first known European depiction of the juggernaut seems to have been produced in Augsburg in 1481, in an edition of Mandeville's *Travels*. Despite the sense of sound, movement, collective worship and dramatic, violent action integral to the texts described above, the image is disappointingly simple and static (Figure 6.2).[34] The Mandeville visual tradition did not

FIGURE 6.2 Anonymous artist, depiction of the tomb of Saint Thomas and of the 'juggernaut', woodcut, in John Mandeville, *Das buch des ritters herr hannsen von monte villa aus dem Franz. Übers. Von Michael Velser* (Augsburg, 1481), fol. 54 v. Bayerische Staatsbibliothek München, 2 In.c.a. 1083, fol. 54v.

Riding the juggernaut 131

begin by replicating the lively, dynamic, processional dimensions of his text. Instead, the falseness of the deity was stressed in a visually awkward depiction of a cart with its idol, and a single worshipper on his knees. This worshipper wears a hat that could be read as either Jewish or Arabic in style, and a curving sword that is certainly meant to read as the marker of an Islamic figure, and which also alluded to some aspects of the violent self-harm described by Mandeville, although not the frenzied bodies under rolling wheels.[35] Despite the temptation to read the scene through a biblical lens, this was not a stray, repurposed printer's woodblock illustrating Elijah in his cart and about to ascend to the heavens. Instead, it seems to have been created specifically for this Augsburg edition of Mandeville, and then to have been copied elsewhere, notably in the English Wykyn de Worde edition of 1499. However, the majority of printed editions of Mandeville were not illustrated or did not include this scene.[36]

One additional fascinating image merits noting (Figure 6.3). This image appeared in a sixteenth-century manuscript (Codex 1889) now held in the Casanatense library in Rome. It was likely prepared by an Indian artist with links to the Portuguese community in Goa in the first half of the sixteenth century.[37] While it depicts bodies graphically dismembered, and several figures who seem to leap in the air on the wagon itself, the majority of the participants are more sedately

FIGURE 6.3   Anonymous artist, depiction of the 'juggernaut', manuscript, *Album di disegni, illustranti usi e costumi dei popoli d'Asia e d'Africa con brevi dichiarazioni in lingua portoghese*, Codex Casantense 1889, fig. c. 78. Biblioteca Casantense, Ms.1889 c.78.

seated, with none of the music-making and surging crowds reported by Odorico and Mandeville. It brings the drama of broken bodies (missing in Mandeville) to the scene, although the deity is less prominent. Access to this fascinating image would have been limited, and its influence on the wider discourse about the 'juggernaut' is difficult to assess. Instead, it would be several printed sources that put visual depictions of the juggernaut into wider circulation, providing visual form to earlier description's fusions of embodied emotion, sound and movement. While the first, stilted European illustration did not achieve this, two later illustrated publications – one French, and one from the Low Countries – used imagery to ratchet up the emotional impact of these scenes for Europeans and to express emotion in an embodied way.

In his 1575 *Cosmographie universelle*, French Franciscan André Thevet located a description and illustration of the juggernaut on the island of Elephanta (Figure 6.4).[38] A cosmographer, and from 1562 guardian of the royal cabinet of curiosities at Fontainebleau, Thevet is best known for his writing on Brazil.[39] But he also prepared this global cosmography, drawing upon other authors and in particular recasting, Gallicanising and Catholicising German Protestant Sebastian Münster's earlier *Cosmographei*.[40] Thevet described the well-known temples and sculptures of Elephanta, as well as a processional deity, or 'beautiful doll' ('belle poupee'), which he characterised as central to the island's religious life. He described how:

> It is carried along once a year on a chariot with eight wheels, drawn by the elders of the land. Amongst them (as you are able to see in the illustration), there are a good number of girls holding branches in their hands, who sing of the miracles of their idol.[41]

Thevet described how people had come from far away to participate but were in the process 'mistreated' ('abusé'), as 'many of them threw themselves under the wheels of the chariot'.[42] In the accompanying image by an anonymous artist, a musician blows a conch shell-like instrument at the front of the wagon, and the worshippers in the lower half perform acts of ecstatic worship and self-harm.[43] They are matched by the dancing males and – especially – females in the upper half, including a vast number of people processing either to or from the cave temple. From the large wheels to the music-making to the bodies moving around the landscape, this is a scene that stresses sensory and ecstatic activity.[44] Like Jordan of Catalonia centuries earlier, Thevet used his discussion of local religious rites to write disparagingly about 'Turcs, Mores &Arabes'. He compared the scene to those who travel to Medina 'to see the tomb of the imposter Arab' ('de voir le to[m]beau de l'imposterur Arabe', that is, the tomb of Muhammad, located in Medina).[45] By focusing on harm to crowds, Thevet may have been conflating Medina with reports of pilgrimage to Mecca, or he may have been referring to Medina as one of the busiest sites of Islamic pilgrimage. It is clear that the intended parallel was negative, with a crush of many bodies caught up in a scene of

De A. Theuet. Liure XI. 384

autres, qui sont tous garnis autour de figures. Quant à l'Idole qui est posée au bout dudit temple, elle est de la haulteur d'vn homme. Elle est conduite vne fois l'an sur vn Chariot à huict rouës, & trainée par les plus anciens du païs: dans lequel (comme vous pouuez voir par ceste presente figure) y a vn bon nōbre de filles, tenās des rameaux en leurs mains, & qui chantent les miracles, qu'ils disent auoir esté faits par leur Idole. Et fault icy penser, que de plus de cent lieuës le peuple vient, pour assister à la procession de ceste belle-poupee: de laquelle ce pauure peuple est si abusé, que lors qu'elle passe parmy la rue, plusieurs d'eux se precipitent dessoubz les rouës du Chariot, & pensent faire aussi bien, que quelques Turcs, Mores & Arabes, lors qu'ils se iettent au parfond de la mer Rouge, allans à Medine, ou se creuent les yeux, pource qu'ils ne sont dignes, disent-ils, de voir le tōbeau de l'imposteur Arabe, ainsi qu'ailleurs ie vous ay deduit.

Idole conduire par les tusaires.

Autres idolatres Indiens, aussi courageux que les premiers, couppent auec leur cousteau vn morceau de chair de leur iambe, cuisse, ou bras: & deuant qu'estre surprins de ceste grand' douleur, par l'incision fraischement faite sur leur membre, mettet ce morceau de chair au bout de leur flesche, & auec leur arc ruent la flesche en l'air, & ceux qui meurent sur le champ, sont conduits & portez par leurs Prestres au sommet de la montaigne. Voyla que ie vous ay voulu dire en passant de ceste isle fertile & abondāte en tous biens. Là où sont des plus belles fontaines que l'on sçauroit trouuer. Elle est faicte & tributaire au grand Roy de Cambaia, qui n'est point si petit compagnon, qu'il n'ait, lors qu'il marche en bataille, soixante mille cheuaux, trois cens Elephans pour conduire les munitions, & cent mille hommes à pied. Vray est qu'ils ne sont adextres aux armes, veu que vingt mille hommes des nostres romproient la teste à tout cela. Ce Roy a quatre Gouuerneurs, qui s'appellent, l'vn *Milagobin*, & le second *Camallo-mal-*

tt ij

FIGURE 6.4 Anonymous artist, image of the 'juggernaut', engraving, André Thevet, *La cosmographie universelle*, 2 vols (Paris: Pierre d'Huilier, 1575), sig. 47.P.29 (vol. 2), fol. 384 recto. ÖNB Vienna: 47.P.29. (Vol.1), pag. 384r.

physically dangerous emotional intensity. This passage as a whole belongs to the tradition of seeing aspects of Hinduism in partly positive terms, especially when implicitly compared, as here, to Islam. Sincere Hindu worship expressed through the body and intense emotions had a positive value, despite the worship of an 'idol', and it was the rushing crowds from beyond the core group of worshippers who caused a problem.

The final representation considered in this article is the one that opened it, from Jan Huygen van Linschoten's *Itinerario*. The lavishly illustrated *Itinerario* first appeared in 1595/96 and featured a series of engravings.[46] In 1598, it was republished in the second part of Johann Theodor de Bry's *Indiae orientalis* (German edition), and in 1599 in the *Indiae orientalis* (Latin edition) with engravings by Johannes van Doetecum and sons Baptista and Joannes. It was in these De Bry editions that the Linschoten's processional scene of the juggernaut was first illustrated. These publication dates also map onto the years of the first formal Dutch expedition in the East Indies, which concluded in 1597. Linschoten's *Itinerario* takes us to the period when the Dutch were on the verge of beginning their domination of colonial activity in Asia.

The Linschoten image stressed music-making, with several sorts of drums and wind instruments being played by the 'Königs Wiber' (wives of the king) in the wagon. This was a new element for both the text and image. On the left-hand side, the surging bodies of the worshippers at the head of the procession, leading the elephants, lend the image a festive air. The almost naked bodies of the worshippers in the foreground, cutting their flesh and being crushed underneath the wheels of the wagon, add movement and intensity to the scene and likely reflected the popularity of mannerist art in the Netherlands in the later sixteenth century.[47] Linschoten repeated the links between self-harm and martyrdom – 'Several throw themselves under the wheels of the wagon and let the wheels roll over them, and their broken bodies remain lying there' – that we have seen in other reports, although his own views were not directly expressed.[48] The scene depicted the Hindu worshipper in the extremities of deep emotion – from joyful music-making to ecstatic self-mortification – and the dynamic sense of travel makes this one of the most lively images in the De Bry sequence. Lack has suggested that, as for the Casanatense manuscript from earlier in the sixteenth century, the original drawings may reflect some kind of collaboration or association between indigenous and European artists. This must remain a speculative point – not least as this particular image was one of a handful of new scenes from Linschoten's text newly depicted in the De Bry editions.[49] Linschoten wrote about his five years in the employment of a Portuguese archbishop in India (from 1583), and thus this text emerged from a Catholic context. However, this is complicated by the fact that Linschoten later converted to Calvinism, and his work appeared with presses that we associate more with Protestantism, and circulated most widely in northern Europe, in Protestant regions or areas that saw significant conflicts over religion.[50]

The actions of the worshippers were evidently in some senses intended to be read as shockingly alien to European audiences. Yet we should not forget that comparable statues of the saints and Christ and the Virgin Mary, encountered in ritualised but also passionate processions, were very familiar to Europeans. By the end of the sixteenth century, they were often rejected in Protestant communities and vigorously celebrated – or contested – in Catholic environments undergoing the renewal of the Catholic Reformation. European descriptions of the juggernaut had developed over several hundred years – and as argued later, should be set in the context of a range of cultural and religious domestic developments in Europe – but it was these two later sixteenth-century images that pulled together the focus on movement, self-harm, religious ecstasy and emotion in a dramatic new visual way. They remind us of the etymological and profound link between motion and emotion.[51] When examining the juggernaut through European eyes, we need to pay attention to European religious practices across the later medieval and early modern periods, and also take into account that some practices changed, intensified or became more contested across the period in which this textual and visual trope developed.

*****

The juggernaut was, of course, a European fabrication that tells us about European fears, fascinations and desires. It may have originated in and been sustained by some form of eyewitness reporting of worship in India. It was reshaped into a stereotypical format that (in both positive and negative terms) stressed self-harm, faith and emotionally expressive behaviours that struck a chord with Europeans. But what specific European sources and ideas did it reflect? There were a range of parallel and conceptually related European developments that stressed the same nexus of processional motion, emotion and religious fervour, and that account for the presence of self-harming violence as well as music and dancing. For while Europeans may have been shocked by the otherness of various Indian religious rituals, they often looked for points of similarity and analogy, creating domestic meaning from scenes that at first glance seemed entirely foreign.[52]

Specific parallels between the juggernaut and European religious rituals were drawn by some of the authors, as we have seen earlier – from rogation days to relics. We can also look more broadly to European culture for evidence that the juggernaut's movement, sound, violence and emotions resonated with specific religious developments in Europe. In particular, the rise of flagellant movements and of Corpus Christi traditions surely provides an important context for the development of imagery of the juggernaut. Flagellant movements gained in popularity from the thirteenth century and were especially active during periods of social crisis. These public processions, in which bodies were visibly injured in demonstrations of ecstasy and faith, knitted together pain, worship and movement. Flagellants were contentious figures (condemned by Clement VI in a bull of 1349, with similar condemnations to follow), who were often less than welcome in communities. In the sixteenth century, flagellant groups experienced a revival and spread to the Spanish Americas. For some, they became strongly linked to a physical, embodied way of being Catholic in the century of Reformation. As Barnes reminds us, they gained traction again in the context of the French Wars of Religion, during a setting of polemical reports of violence and indeed massacres.[53] Religion often became entwined with violence in this period, in ways that stressed ritual action.[54] These processions did not, however, include carriages or indeed deities.[55]

Another religious ritual less bound up with violence than flagellation, but deeply concerned with bodies in motion and rites of sacrifice, also had an important history across the period in which the juggernaut came to the attention of Europeans: the summer festival of Corpus Christi. Missionary Jordan of Catalonia in his c. 1329 *Mirabilia Descripta* had described how '[they] go with singing and playing before the idol when it is carried through the land (like the image of the Virgin Mary here among us at the Rogation tides)', that is, on days of fasting and prayer observed with processions. Protective processions in Europe, especially in times of agricultural or other crises, involved the wider community in physically vigorous, emotionally intense rituals. They could involve processions to the boundaries of parishes and villages, often carrying statues of the saints or the Virgin Mary, to ward off disaster and foster good fortune.[56] Other forms of processional ritual also developed in significance across the period examined in this chapter.[57] Corpus Christi became prominent in the Christian calendar in the later middle ages, and in the fourteenth and fifteenth centuries became increasingly strongly associated with the act of ritual procession, and in some regions incorporated music and dance.[58] Corpus Christi's celebration of the Eucharist, of the blood and body of Christ, meant that it was a church ritual in which the wholeness and partition of a sacred body in motion was paramount. As such, it had conceptual parallels with the juggernaut – or more properly, for Europeans acculturated to the new feast of Corpus Christi, events like Corpus Christi processions must have formed a reference point for Christians 'reading' the juggernaut. Corpus Christi processions, as Charles Zika has suggested, helped to change the focus in the fifteenth century away from sanctioned pilgrimage and towards processional rituals that demarcated local spaces through movement and events that stressed the local.[59] Perhaps the juggernaut, in echoing forms of protective procession and Corpus Christi rituals, forms part in a different way of this changing view of space, borders, identity and religion – and one that would become more, rather than less, significant as Reformation and Counter-Reformation changes swept across Europe, and public processions became an important and visible marker of changing religious identities.[60]

The civil conflicts of the second half of the sixteenth century saw notable attention to reports of violence. The French Wars of Religion saw a new attention to forms of interpersonal violence, notably massacres, committed in the context of civil war. The Dutch Revolt was marked by atrocities that mocked and attacked bodies in sadistic ways. These were accompanied by a rise in print culture depicting graphic forms of violence.[61] The changes of the Reformation and Counter-Reformation meant that religious rituals like Corpus Christi or the actions of flagellants were rejected by Protestant communities. Counter-Reformation Catholic communities could take one of two paths: an increase in expressive devotional forms, or a policing of 'uncontrolled' activities that did not fit into the measured new world of Counter-Reformation piety, which stressed conformity as well as renewal. These religious changes unfolded alongside increasing travel beyond Europe's borders in the wake of the expansion of the late fifteenth century. The vigorous visual images of a juggernaut-style procession in Thevet (1575) and Linschoten (from 1598) reflected a European world shaped by new religious and global forces. It is also no accident that these were visual images. The sixteenth-century visual attention to muscular, naked bodies in dramatic motion – one hallmark of the new Italian mannerist style, which took on prominence in France and then in the Low Countries as the century progressed – was ideally suited to the extremity of the juggernaut as a theme.[62] While the contested Christian ritual activities described above form one context, we must also turn to visual traditions rooted in classical imagery to more fully understand how Europeans 'saw' the juggernaut.

Intensely physical processional scenes with extreme emotional dimensions took on new form in this period through a revival of the tradition of the triumph. Petrarch's *I Trionfi* and its visual representations also therefore form an underpinning for the European imagery of the juggernaut, and one that particularly stressed violence in imagery of the triumph of death, with unforgettable scenes of bodies brutally crushed under wheels. Maarten van Heemskerck's sixteenth-century figure of Death is shrill and grinning, presiding over a nightmarish, apocalyptically chaotic landscape (Figure 6.5).[63] This and similar European images developed from the Roman tradition of the processional triumph in which the spoils of victory – including the bodies of the captured – were processed through the city, in a view of victory which was decisively about appropriating the non-Roman 'other'.[64]

One sixteenth-century tapestry depicts Fame trumpeting her status to the four corners of the world (Figure 6.6).[65] Her wagon tramples upon the very concept of death, depicted as women identified as the Three Fates.[66] This noisy scene of fame triumphing over death brought together similar themes to the juggernaut, and ones that became very familiar in Europe. One of the accompanying figures in some variants has been identified as Alexander the Great, the 'conquerer' of India.[67] The chariot is pulled by elephants, associated with India (as well as with military triumphal processions in Rome), and heralding the elephants in the Linschoten juggernaut scene which would, like this tapestry, be produced in the southern Netherlands. The iconography of Fortune, her elephants, Alexander and the three deaths circulated across the century, appearing in the late sixteenth-century French print cycle *Le vray miroir de la vie humaine*, a contemporary of the Linschoten imagery.[68]

FIGURE 6.5 Philips Galle, after a drawing by Maarten van Heemskerck, 'The Triumph of Death', engraving, plate 3 from the series 'The Triumphs of Petrarch', c. 1565. Museum no. 1937,0915.271. © The Trustees of the British Museum.

FIGURE 6.6 Anonymous artist, 'Triumph of Fame over Death', tapestry, c. 1500–1530. Bequest of George D. Pratt, 1935, accession number 41.167.2. Open access image, The Metropolitan Museum of Art, New York.

The juggernaut was, above all, likely to have recalled for Europeans the frenzied Bacchic processions which Europeans understood as having quite literally originated in India – from where Bacchus travelled. These representations tapped into non-Christian religious practices seen through a longer, pagan time frame.[69] They remind us that 'othered' bodies in sixteenth-century Europe need to be set in a long history of global encounters looking back well before the rounding of the Cape of Good Hope or the travels of medieval merchants and missionaries. While some Bacchic (or Dionysian) scenes depicted slothful drunkenness, it was active and ecstatic movement – the *furor* of the ancient world – that was much more often emphasised.[70] At the close of the fifteenth century, humanist Polydore Vergil did not repeat the long-established connection between Bacchus and India in his chapter on Bacchanalian rites in his 1499 *On Discovery*. But he did stress the nexus between violence, music and ecstatic experience:

> Slaughter and debauchery so abounded that anyone slow to fornicate or intolerant of vice (eventually they admitted no one older than twenty) was murdered. …. no voice of complaint could be made out above the moaning and the banging of timbrels and cymbals … Their religion reached its apex when men made demented prophecies and contorted their bodies in a frenzy, while married women dressed as Bacchae ran about with hair disheveled….[71]

Maarten van Heemskerck's painting of 1536/37 (Figure 6.7) grew out of an extraordinarily rich range of approaches to the theme of Bacchus in fifteenth-century art and humanist thought.[72]

This sits alongside the stress on movement and music in the most famous textual interpretation of Bacchus in Book 4 of Ovid's *Metamorphoses*, here in a sixteenth-century translation:

> Thou with bittes the sturdy neckes doste bend
> Of spotted Lynxes: throngs of Frowes and Satyres on thee tend,
> And that olde Hag that with a staffe his staggering limmes doth stay
> Scarce able on his Asse to sit for reeling every way.
> Thou commest not in any place but that is hearde the noyse
> Of gagling womens tatling tongues and showting out of boyes,
> With sound of Timbrels, Tabors, Pipes, and Brazen pannes and pots
> Confusedly among the rout that in thine Orgies trots.[73]

Bacchus was a figure who offered an entertaining vision of a drunken pagan God, but who also embodied a creative, generative and intellectually rich life force.[74] In a discussion of Aby Warburg's concept of the *Pathosformel* with its 'images of life in motion' in which gestures and poses from antiquity were borrowed and reused to create new (and often newly moralised and sometimes specifically

FIGURE 6.7   Maerten van Heemskerck, 'Triumph of Bacchus', oil on wood, c. 1536/1537, Kunsthistorisches Museum Vienna. ©KHM-Museumsverband.

Christianised) imagery that had emotional as well as artistic energy. Heather McStay O'Leary recently observed that 'what the Bacchic figures gave especially was a visual form for extreme emotion'.[75] She further notes that 'Warburg saw in the revival of the fluttering exteriors of antique art a deeper renewal of the inner passions and emotions of ancient beings. … For Warburg, *Pathos* meant movement, intense emotion, and vital energy'.[76] The textual and visual imagery of Bacchus, revived and reinvented, helps us to understand the appealing and multilayered interaction of movement, sound and emotion in the juggernaut. Both the Thevet and Linschoten images should be understood in this context, and also in the context of the rise of mannerist art in the sixteenth century, with its attention to muscular bodies, movement and exaggerated postures. These were themes that the De Bry family developed with particular skill throughout their illustrated *Voyages*, and the juggernaut scene (Figure 6.1) forms a particularly vivid example and apt closing point.

★★★★★

Sculptures of deities were mobile objects in Hindu India of the sixteenth century, just as they were (and remain) in many different religious contexts. They were carried in processions and as part of boundary rituals well beyond the confines of temples.[77] These actions could form focus points of Hindu resistance to early modern Portuguese colonial and missionary activity.[78] Deities like the goddess Baghvati were relocated secretly outside areas of Portuguese dominance in the sixteenth century; Baghvati became part of an annual 15-day procession that involved travel to various households.[79] Relocated temple sites strengthened the power of deities. Their new locations outside Portuguese control were increasingly ornately decorated, and their processional journeys became ever more meaningful. Paul Axelrod and Michelle A. Fuerch observe that this was a 'testimony to a process of Hindu thinking which connects persons in complex, substantive ways to their deities, and in turn, persons and deities to the soil'.[80] Royal decrees in partly Christianised Goa in the late sixteenth and the seventeenth centuries repeatedly forbade Hindu temples, idols and festivals – a sure sign that they remained a visible presence. While the European viewpoint is explicitly the focus of this article, the continuing role of Hindu processions and deities reminds us that they were a crucial part of two-way encounters.[81]

The sources about the so-called juggernaut described in this article tell us about Europeans, of course, and not about what 'really happened' in Indian religious processions (or indeed what local people thought of the Europeans encountering and circulating reports about these events). The deeply felt emotions engendered by ritual religious acts belong first to the depicted participants (here, the local Hindu people) but they also – and more substantially – belong to the European eyewitness observers, the European authors of travel narratives of varying degrees of accuracy and the European audiences for new scenes of India. Europeans did not directly articulate how the juggernaut made them feel, but rather used expressive and dramatic gestures to shape a complex and ultimately negative stereotype. Visual and textual European representations of the juggernaut seem to have explicitly sought to trigger sensory and emotional responses to the depicted bodies and rituals by setting them in motion. These descriptions and images of a juggernaut reflect a European fascination with and growing anxieties about the performative roles of ecstatic bodies. European representations of non-European religious and ritualised practices and objects in the sixteenth-century were undoubtedly constructed through the paradigm of 'otherness'. Vanita Seth has recently argued that 'otherness' in the early modern period needs to be problematised because of the particularly fragmented nature of European identity at that time.[82] We can overstate the extent to which Europeans were trying to construct horrifying 'religious others' through difference. Similarities and shared ways of expressing emotion through the body were also part of how European made sense of what they saw. Marianne O'Doherty has recently stressed the existence of two coexisting traditions across this period, in which

> a vision emerges of the Indies as not only a space of marvellous and monstrous extremes but also a site of places on earth that seem to bear the touch of the divine or promise access to a transcendent reality.[83]

This twin view was also reflected in conflicted – or at least complex – ways of writing about and depicting the juggernaut.

The later sixteenth-century images discussed above appeared – not coincidentally – in the fractious and often violent environment of post-Reformation France and the Low Countries. Images and objects in European sacred spaces and processions, such as those for Corpus Christi and especially by flagellants, were also key contextual points of reference, but so too were ongoing European interests in extra-Christian legends and themes concerning Bacchus, the Triumph of Death and the non-Christian 'other' across time as well as space. The juggernaut acted as a form of entertainment, but also spoke to very real anxieties and social, cultural and especially religious preoccupations as Europeans recast their relationship with India, and with themselves, in a changing religious and global world. Emotions expressed through the body, through reported sound and movement, and designed to trigger strong responses in the European reader or viewer were one part of this changing worldview.

Notes

1 Ernst van den Boogaart, *Civil and Corrupt Asia: Image and Text in the* Itinerario *and the* Icones *of Jan Huygen van Linschoten* (Chicago: University of Chicago Press, 2003); Michiel van Groesen, *The Representations of the Overseas World in the De Bry Collection of Voyages (1590–1634)* (Leiden: Brill, 2008). I am grateful to the editors and to Charles Zika for help with aspects of this essay.
2 For a recent description of the ritual procession today, and its origins, see "The Festival and Tales of the Juggernaut," *The Telegraph India*, (6 July 2016), https://www.telegraphindia.com/states/odisha/the-festival-and-tales-of-the-juggernaut/cid/1506691.
3 The processions and religious acts described and depicted in this article are almost entirely located by European authors in southern India, where Europeans had most contact, and extending no further north than Elephanta, close to modern-day Mumbai. None are near Puri, in eastern India.
4 For an overview of important discussions of the complexities of European views in a precolonial period, adapting and to some extent critiquing Edward Said's orientalism thesis, see Kim Phillips, *Before Orientalism: Asian Peoples and Cultures in European Travel Writing, 1245–1510* (Philadelphia: University of Pennsylvania Press, 2014), 15–27. See also Meera Juncu, *India in the Italian Renaissance: Visions of a Contemporary Pagan World 1300–1600* (London: Routledge, 2016), 7–10.
5 On emotions and 'others', see Giovanni Tarantino and Charles Zika, ed. *Feeling Exclusion: Religious Conflict, Exile and Emotions in Early Modern Europe* (Abingdon: Routledge, 2019). On visual sources and the generation as well as depiction of emotion, with a particular focus on human bodies, see Patricia Simons and Charles Zika, "The Visual Arts," in *A Cultural History of the Emotions in the Late Medieval, Reformation and Renaissance Age*, eds. Andrew Lynch and Susan Broomhall (London: Bloomsbury Academic, 2019), 85–106. On early modern European dance and its emotional valences see Denis Collins and Jennifer Neville, "Music and Dance," in *A Cultural History of the Emotions in the Late Medieval, Reformation and Renaissance Age*, eds. Andrew Lynch and Susan Broomhall (London: Bloomsbury Academic, 2019), 49–67, especially 57–67. On the combination of dancing and 'othering' in a European setting, using visual and textual sources, see Charles Zika, "Towards an Alien Community of Dancing Witches in Early Seventeenth-Century Europe," in *Feeling Exclusion*, eds. Tarantino and Zika. Related issues are examined in a modern context in Axel Michaels and Christoph Wulf, ed. *Emotions in Rituals and Performances: South Asian and European Perspectives on Rituals and Performativity* (New Delhi/Abingdon: Routledge, 2012).

6 See brief discussions of religious violence, including some material that is discussed in this chapter, in Marianne O'Doherty, *The Indies in the Medieval West* (Turnhout: Brepols, 2013); Joan-Pau Rubiés, *Travel and Ethnology in the Renaissance: South India through European Eyes, 1250–1625* (Cambridge: Cambridge University Press, 2000), 109, 116, Juncu, *India in the Italian Renaissance*, 67–68 (on Odorico), 113–114, and van Groesen, *The Representations of the Overseas World in the De Bry Collection of Voyages*, 163–164.
7 John Mandeville, *The Book of Marvels and Travels*, trans. and ed. Anthony Bale (Oxford: Oxford University Press, 2012), 78.
8 A parallel activity which has received more attention is the act of suttee, or 'widow-burning'. Juncu, *India in the Italian Renaissance*, 104–109 and 182–184, and Stephanie Leitch, *Mapping Ethnography in Early Modern Germany: New Worlds in Print Culture* (New York: Palgrave Macmillan, 2010), 128–129.
9 David R.M. Irving, *Colonial Counterpoint: Music in Early Modern Manila* (Oxford: Oxford University Press, 2010), 212–213.
10 Larry Silver, "Triumphs and Travesties: Printed Processions of the Sixteenth Century," in *Grand Scale: Monumental Prints in the Age of Dürer and Titian*, eds. Larry Silver and Elizabeth Wyckoff (New Haven: Yale University Press, 2008), 15–32; Lyndal Roper and Jennifer Spinks, "Karlstadt's *Wagen*: The First Visual Propaganda for the Reformation," *Art History* 40, no. 2 (2017): 256–285.
11 Donald F. Lack, *Asia in the Making of Europe*, 3 vols, *Vol. II: A Century of Wonder*, book one (Chicago: University of Chicago Press, 1965–1993), 93.
12 Nandini Das, "Encounter as Process: England and Japan in the late Sixteenth Century," *Renaissance Quarterly* 69, no. 4 (2016): 1343–1368, see 1345.
13 O'Doherty, *The Indies in the Medieval West*, 57; Juncu, *India in the Italian Renaissance*, 63–77.
14 Well-known travel narratives by Giovanni de' Marignolli and Marco Polo, or the Prester John letter, do not include juggernaut-style processions.
15 See O'Doherty, *The Indies in the Medieval West*, 306. In particular, Odorico's text would influence John Mandeville's *Travels*. Odorico would later also be included in Ramusio's important sixteenth-century collection of travel writing.
16 Friar Jordanus, *The Wonders of the East*, trans. Henry Yule (London: Hakluyt Society, 1893), 33. On this material see O'Doherty, *The Indies in the Medieval West*, especially 81.
17 Odoric of Pordenone, *Cathay and the Way Thither: Being a Collection of Medieval Notices of China. Vol II: Odoric of Pordenone*, ed. Henry Cordier, new edition (Farnham: Hakluyt edition, reprinted Ashgate, 2010), 144–145.
18 On foreign 'idols' through European eyes see Joan-Pau Rubiés, "Theology, Ethnography, and the Historicization of Idolatry," *Journal of the History of Ideas* 67, no. 4 (2006): 571–596; Rubiés, *Travel and Ethnology in the Renaissance*, especially 108–109 and 213 on idolatry and violence, Partha Mitter, *Much Maligned Monsters: A History of European Reactions to Indian Art*, second edition (Chicago: University of Chicago Press, 1992); Maria Effinger et al., ed. *Götterbilder und Götzendiener in der Frühen Neuzeit. Europas Blick auf fremde Religionen*, exhibition catalogue (Heidelberg: Universitäts Verlag Winter, 2012); Jennifer Spinks, "The Southern Indian 'Devil in Calicut' in Early Modern Northern Europe: Images, Texts and Objects in Motion," *Journal of Early Modern History* 18, no. 1–2 (2014): 15–48; Suzanne Conklin Akbari, *Idols in the East: European Representations of Islam and the Orient, 1100–1450* (Ithaca: Cornell University Press, 2009); Juncu, *India in the Italian Renaissance*, especially 49–52, 65–69, 115–118 and 177–182; van Groesen, *The Representations of the Overseas World in the De Bry Collection of Voyages*, 219–247.
19 Odoric of Pordenone, *Cathay and the Way Thither*, 142–143.
20 Odoric of Pordenone, *Cathay and the Way Thither*, 145. There is a similar passage in the late thirteenth-century *Travels* of Marco Polo, though it is set in a framework concerning legal punishment for crime. Marco Polo, *The Travels*, translation and introduction by Ronald Latham (London: Penguin, 1958), 264. He does not, however, include a juggernaut-like procession with an idol.

21 Odoric of Pordenone, *Cathay and the Way Thither*, 142. O'Doherty, *The Indies in the Medieval West*, stresses the importance of Thomas, see especially 34–36 and 76–80. She makes a brief connection to the juggernaut but does not develop the material, 79–80. On the renewed significance in the sixteenth century of locations associated with Thomas, see Ines G. Zupanov, *Missionary Tropics: The Catholic Frontier in India (16th–17th Centuries)* (Ann Arbor: University of Michigan Press, 2005), 87–110.
22 O'Doherty, *The Indies in the Medieval West*, 212.
23 Mandeville, *The Book of Marvels and Travels*, 78.
24 Mandeville, *The Book of Marvels and Travels*, 78.
25 Mandeville, *The Book of Marvels and* Travels, 78. Variations across editions should be noted. The 1481 Augsburg edition discussed below adds child sacrifice by parents to the list of activities. John Mandeville, *Das buch des ritters herr hannsen von monte villa*, trans. Michael Velser (Augsburg: Anton Sorg, 1481), fol. 55 recto. O'Doherty notes that one particular Medieval Latin tradition of Mandeville took on negative tones in discussing religious rites. See O'Doherty, *The Indies in the Medieval West*, 217, for Mandeville texts with positive readings, and 230–237 for a more negative (Latin) version of the text towards pagan worship. Contemporary annotations on manuscripts reveal that readers saw Indian religion in both positive and negative terms. See O'Doherty's fascinating analysis of extant annotations, 183–191.
26 Mandeville, *The Book of Marvels and Travels*, 77.
27 On Conti see O'Doherty, *The Indies in the Medieval West*, 58–59. See also Juncu, *India in the Italian Renaissance*, 92–118 (on Poggio Bracciolino).
28 O'Doherty, *The Indies in the Medieval West*, 58.
29 Niccolò Conti, "Travels," edition by Poggio Bracciolini, in *India in the Fifteenth Century*, ed. and trans. R.H. Major (London: Hakluyt Society, 1857), 1–39, see 27.
30 Conti, "Travels," 28.
31 The text circulated on its own in an earlier edition.
32 See O'Doherty, *The Indies in the Medieval West*, for an analysis of the visual traditions of key authors discussed in this article. See especially her discussion of BnF, MS fr. 2810 (which includes texts by Marco Polo, Odorico da Pordenone, and John Mandeville), 119, and Odoric in BAV, MS Urbinati latini 1013, see especially 157. She also notes the BL, MS Royal 19 D.i 'which has images but ones with a military, Saracen focus that are "bland and generic"' (122, 123). The modern edition of BAV, MS Urbinati latini 1013 in the Odorico da Pordenone, *Memoriale Toscano. Viaggio in India e Cina (1318–1330)*, ed. Lucio Monaco (Torino: Edizioni dell'Orso, 1990) indicates that the relevant passage of the text (104–106) is not illustrated. On the paucity of European medieval manuscript images of Indians, see Juncu, *India in the Italian Renaissance*, 11–12.
33 BnF, MS fr. 2810, fol. 186 verso [https://gallica.bnf.fr/ark:/12148/btv1b52000858n/f376.image]. The Mandeville image comes from the second, later section of the manuscript (c. 1470–1475, illuminated by Evrard d'Espinques).
34 John Mandeville, *Das buch des ritters herr hannsen von monte villa aus dem Franz*, trans. Michael Velser (Augsburg: Anton Sorg, 1481), fol. 54 verso.
35 Ruth Mellinkoff, *Outcasts: Signs of Otherness in Northern European Art of the Late Middle Ages* (Berkeley: University of California Press, 1993), 2 vols, ch. 3 (59–94, and accompanying plate in vol. 2); Debra Higgs Strickland, *Saracens, Demons and Jews: Making Monsters in Medieval Art* (Princeton: Princeton University Press, 2003), ch. 4 (157–210).
36 This is evident through a survey of available digitised editions. The competing German edition of 1481, published in Basel and based on the translation by Otto van Diemeringen, did not include the passage on the juggernaut in the text. John Mandeville, *Reise ins Heilige Land*, trans. Otto von Diemeringen (Basel: Bernhard Richel, 1481?). For an argument that the Basel 1481 edition was the basis for a French edition, and that it, in turn, was the basis for the English edition, see Josephine Waters Bennett,

"The Woodcut Illustrations in the English Editions of 'Mandeville's Travels'," *The Papers of the Bibliographical Society of America* 47, no. 1 (1953): 59–69. However, the Wynken de Worde edition does include the juggernaut scene.

37 For reproductions and an analysis, see Luise de Matos, *Imagos do Oriente no século XVI: Reprodução do Códice português da Biblioteca Casanatatense* (Lisbon: Imprensa Nacional Casa da Moeda, 1985). On the stylistic aspects of the works and for an argument that the images are by an Indian artist who trained in a Sultanate setting and worked in Goa, see J.P. Losty, "Identifying the Artist of Codex Casanatense 1889," *Anais de História de Além-Mar* XIII (2012): 13–40.

38 André Thevet, *La cosmographie universelle* (Paris: Guillaume Chaudiere, 1575), For the image see fol. 384 recto (book XI, chapter XI).

39 Based on some first-hand experience. See Frank Lestringant, *André Thevet* (Genève: Librairie Droz, 1991).

40 Although Münster had not described a juggernaut.

41 'Elle est conduite vne fois l'an sur vn Chariot à huict rouës, & trainee par les anciens du païs: dans lequel (comme vous pouuez voir par ceste presente figure) y a vn bon no[m]bre de filles, tena[n]s des rameaux en en leurs mains, & qui chantent les miracles, qu'ils disent auoir esté faits par leur Idole.'

42 'plusieurs d'eux se precipitent dessoubz les rouës Du Chariot'. Thevet, *La cosmographie universelle*, fol. 384 recto.

43 Partha Matter writes about Elephanta through European eyes in visual culture, and discusses another image from Thevet's chapter, but not the processional scene. See Mitter, *Much Maligned Monsters*, 37.

44 Montaigne has a rather more dour report of a juggernaut in his essay "A Custom on the Island of Cea," describing it as a 'solemn procession', and not mentioning music or dancing. Michel de Montaigne, *The Complete Essays*, trans. and ed. M.A. Screech (Harmondsworth: Penguin, 1991), 405. The passage forms part of a larger discussions of suicide, zeal and sacrifice in battle. It is from the late [C] version of the essay, written after Montaigne's increased exposure to reports about Asia from the late 1580s. On Montaigne and Asia see Lack, *Asia in the Making of Europe, Vol. II, A Century of Wonder*, book one, 296–297.

45 Thevet, *La cosmographie universelle*, fol. 384 recto.

46 van den Boogaart, *Civil and Corrupt Asia*. He suggests that Karel van Mander may have been involved in the creation of the images, 34–36.

47 See discussion below on mannerism, and note 67.

48 'Etliche legen sich unter die Räder des Wagens und lassen ihn über sich fahren, und sie bleiben also, ganz zerknitscht, tot liegen.' I use the German text which accompanies the new juggernaut illustration in the De Bry edition: Jan Huygen van Linschoten, *Ander Theil der Orientalischen Indien / Von allen Vo[e]lckern / Insulen / Meerporten / fliessenden Wassern und anderen Orten / so von Portugal auß / lengst dem Gestaden Affrica / biß in Ort Indien vnd zu dem Land China / sampt anderen Insulen zu sehen seind …* (Frankfurt am Main: Johan Saur, 1598), plate XXII. See also Friedemann Berger, ed. *De Bry. India Orientalis. Erster Teil* (Leipzig and Weimer: Gustav Kiepenheuer Verlag, 1979), plate 36. See the commentary and extended quotation from this section of van Linschoten's book 198–210. There are overlaps in the text here with Thevet's *Cosmographie universelle*, possibly suggesting that van Linschoten may have utilised Thevet or shared a common third source.

49 Lack, *Asia in the Making of Europe, Vol. II: A Century of Wonder*, book one, 66.

50 Although Michiel van Groesen cautions that the De Bry family, for commercial reasons, did not want to lose Catholic markets. Michiel van Groesen, *The De Bry collection of Voyages*, especially 249–279.

51 For an overview of the etymology of the word emotion and its early modern usage – including its link to body language – see Patricia Simons, "Emotion," in *Early Modern Emotions: An Introduction*, ed. Susan Broomhall (London: Routledge, 2017), 36–39.

52 On this point, see also Grégoire Holtz, "Démonologues et voyageurs: le demon de l'analogie'," in *Voyager avec le diable: Voyages reels, votyages imaginaires et discours démonologiques* (VXe-XVIIe siècles), eds. Grégoire Holtz and Thibaut Maus de Rolley (Paris: Presses de l'Université Paris-Sorbonne, 2008), 165–181, Leitch, *Mapping Ethnography*, 127–131, and Spinks, " Devil in Calicut."
53 A.E. Barnes, "Religious Anxiety and Devotional Change in Sixteenth Century French Penitential Confraternities," *Sixteenth Century Journal* 19 (1988): 389–405, see 392.
54 See the classic Natalie Zemon Davis essay "Rites of Violence: Religious Violence in Sixteenth-Century France," *Past and Present* 59 (May 1973): 51–91, and also the recent edited collection of work done in response to that famous essay. Neil Cox and Mark Greengrass, "Painting Power: Antoine Caron's Massacres of the Triumvirate," in *Ritual and Violence: Natalie Zemon Davis and Early Modern France*, eds. Graeme Murdock, Penny Roberts and Andrew Spicer (Oxford: Oxford University Press, 2012), 241–274.
55 Norman Cohn, *The Pursuit of the Millennium: Revolutionary Millenarians and Mystical Anarchists of the Middle Ages*, revised edition (London: Pimlico, 2004), 127–147, Barnes, "Religious Anxiety and Devotional Change."
56 See, for example, the sometimes contentious processions in Cologne from the sixteenth century, and similar examples in Augsburg which expressed renewed Catholic confidence. Bridget Heal, *The Cult of the Virgin Mary in Early Modern Germany: Protestant and Catholic Piety, 1500–1648* (Cambridge: Cambridge University Press, 2007), 226–229 (Cologne) and 154–155 (Augsburg).
57 In his examination of the Holy Blood procession in Bruges (celebrating the Holy Blood relic on 3rd May from the thirteenth century onwards), Andrew Brown offers a detailed analysis of the different civic and religious identities at stake in these sorts of processions. Andrew Brown, *Civic Ceremony and Religion in Medieval Bruges c. 1300–1520* (Cambridge: Cambridge University Press, 2011), 37–72.
58 See Miri Rubin, *Corpus Christi: The Eucharist in Late Medieval Culture* (Cambridge: Cambridge University Press, 1991); Charles Zika, "Hosts, Processions and Pilgrimages: Controlling the Sacred in Fifteenth-Century Germany," *Past and Present* 118 (February 1998): 25–64, see especially 37–48. For the use of the Corpus Christi in a Bavarian Counter Reformation environment, see Nadja Irmgard Pentzlin, "The Cult of Corpus Christi in Early Modern Bavaria: Pilgrimages, Processions, and Confraternities between 1550 and 1750" (PhD diss., University of St Andrews, 2014), Chapter 3.
59 Zika, "Hosts, Processions and Pilgrimages," see 63.
60 Pentzlin notes how in some areas, like Catholic Munich under the Wittelsbach dukes, "Corpus Christi processions had increased enormously by the end of the sixteenth century." Pentzlin, "The Cult of Corpus Christi in Early Modern Bavaria," 119.
61 Jennifer Spinks, "Civil War Violence, Prodigy Culture and Families in the French Wars of Religion," in *Disaster, Death and the Emotions in the Shadow of the Apocalypse, 1400–1700*, eds. Jennifer Spinks and Charles Zika (Basingstoke: Palgrave Macmillan, 2016), 113–134, see 115.
62 Linda Murray, *The High Renaissance and Mannerism: Italy, the North and Spain 1500–1600*, revised edition (London: Thames and Hudson, 1977), 125. For examples of bodies of this type in Mannerist prints, see Bruce Davis, *Mannerist Prints: International Style in the Sixteenth Century*, exhibition catalogue (Los Angeles: Los Angeles County Museum of Art 1988), and Ger Luitjen, ed. *La Bella Maniera. Druckgraphik des Manierismus aus der Sammlung Georg Baselitz* (Bern/Berlin: Verlag Gachnag & Springer, 1994).
63 For another example, see BL Harvey 2593 which depicts a grimly funereal black cart pulled by black oxen and transporting skeletal grey Death with his scythe and shroud, and trampling underfoot gorgeously dressed contemporary figures from different walks of life.
64 Mary Beard, *The Roman Triumph* (Cambridge, MA: The Belknap Press of Harvard University Press, 2007).
65 See Adolfo Salvatore Cavallo, *Medieval Tapestries in The Metropolitan Museum of Art* (New York: The Metropolitan Museum of Art / Harry N. Abrams, 1993), 463–478.

66 Cavallo, *Medieval Tapestries in the Metropolitan Museum of Art*, 467.
67 On the Alexander label, and its reuse in a later print noted below, see Cavallo, *Medieval Tapestries in The Metropolitan Museum of Art*, 466–467.
68 Published by Charles Vigoureux in Paris in the late sixteenth century [https://gallica.bnf.fr/ark:/12148/btv1b550018790/f4.item]. See Cavallo, *Medieval Tapestries in The Metropolitan Museum of Art*, 470.
69 See, for example, Juncu, *India in the Italian Renaissance*, 80, on Boccaccio's revival of this idea.
70 Michael Philipp, ed. *Dionysus: Rausch und Ekstase*, exhibition catalogue (Munich: Hirmer, 2013).
71 Bacchic rites in Polydore Vergil's 1499 *On Discovery*, ed. and trans. Brian P. Copenhaver (Cambridge, MA: Harvard I Tatti Renaissance Library, 2002), 479–481.
72 See Heather O'Leary McStay, "'Viva Bacco e viva Amore': Bacchic Imagery in the Renaissance," (PhD diss., Columbia University, 2014).
73 Ovid, *The xv. Booke of P. Ouidius Naso, entytuled Metamorphosis*, trans. Arthur Golding (London: Willyam Seres, 1567), book Iv, 84.
74 See especially McStay, "'Viva Bacco e viva Amore'," 10–11, and her discussion of Alberti and movement.
75 McStay, "'Viva Bacco e viva Amore'," 59–60. On *Pathosformel* in relation to sixteenth-century northern European print culture, see Edward H. Wouk, "From Lambert Lombard to Aby Warburg: *Pathosformel* as grammar," *Nederlands Kunsthistorisch Jaarboek / Netherlands Yearbook for the History of Art*, 68, no.1 (2019): 100–135. More generally, see Philippe-Alain Michaud, *Aby Warburg and the Image in Motion*, trans. Sophie Hawkes (New York: Zone Books, 2004).
76 McStay, "'Viva Bacco e viva Amore'," 65–66. See also 9.
77 Spinks, "Devil in Calicut," 36–37. For the emotional dimensions of pilgrimage 'near and far' and an overview of its historical roots in Hindu culture, see Vasudha Dalmia, "Pilgrimage, Fairs and the Secularisation of Space in Modern Hindi Narrative Discourse," in *Patronage and Popularisation, Pilgrimage and Procession: Channels of Transcultural Translation and Transmission in Early Modern South Asia*, ed. Heidi Rika Maria Pauwels (Wiesbaden: Harrassowitz Verlag, 2009), 117–133, see 117–118. Paramasivan notes the 'wave of emotional devotionalism (*bhakti*) that became characteristic of popular religious experience in North India around the fifteenth century', Vasudha Paramasivan, "Yah Ayodhyā Vah Ayodhyā: Earthly and Cosmic Journeys in the *Ānand-laharī*," in *Patronage and Popularisation, Pilgrimage and Procession*, ed. Pauwels, 101–115, see 103.
78 Paul Axelrod and Michelle A. Fuerch, "Flight of the Deities: Hindu resistance in Portuguese Goa," *Modern Asian Studies* 30, no. 2 (1996): 387–421.
79 Axelrod and Fuerch, "Flight of the Deities," 393–394. This is one of a number of similar examples.
80 Axelrod and Fuerch, "Flight of the Deities," 395.
81 Axelrod and Fuerch, "Flight of the Deities," especially 411–416.
82 Vanita Seth, *Europe's Indians: Producing Racial Difference* (Durham, NC: Duke University Press, 2010).
83 O'Doherty, *The Indies in the Medieval West*, 42.

Bibliography

Akbari, Suzanne Conklin. *Idols in the East: European Representations of Islam and the Orient, 1100–1450*. Ithaca: Cornell University Press, 2009.

Axelrod, Paul, and Michelle A. Fuerch. "Flight of the Deities: Hindu Resistance in Portuguese Goa." *Modern Asian Studies* 30, no. 2 (1996): 387–421.

Barnes, A.E. "Religious Anxiety and Devotional Change in Sixteenth Century French Penitential Confraternities." *Sixteenth Century Journal* 19 (1988): 389–405.

Beard, Mary. *The Roman Triumph*. Cambridge, MA: The Belknap Press of Harvard University Press, 2007.
Bennett, Josephine Waters. "The Woodcut Illustrations in the English Editions of 'Mandeville's Travels'." *The Papers of the Bibliographical Society of America* 47, no. 1 (1953): 59–69.
Berger, Fridemann, ed. *De Bry. India Orientalis. Erster Teil*. Leipzig and Weimer: Gustav Kiepenheuer Verlag, 1979.
Brown, Andrew. *Civic Ceremony and Religion in Medieval Bruges c. 1300–1520*. Cambridge: Cambridge University Press, 2011.
Cavallo, Adolfo Salvatore. *Medieval Tapestries in the Metropolitan Museum of Art*. New York: The Metropolitan Museum of Art / Harry N. Abrams, 1993.
Cohn, Norman. *The Pursuit of the Millennium: Revolutionary Millenarians and Mystical Anarchists of the Middle Ages*. Revised edition. London: Pimlico, 2004.
Collins, Denis, and Jennifer Neville. "Music and Dance." In *A Cultural History of the Emotions in the Late Medieval, Reformation and Renaissance Age*, edited by Andrew Lynch and Susan Broomhall, 49–67. London: Bloomsbury Academic, 2019.
Conti, Niccolò. "Travels," edition by Poggio Bracciolini. In *India in the Fifteenth Century*, edited and translated by R.H. Major, 1–39. London: Hakluyt Society, 1857.
Cox, Neil, and Mark Greengrass. "Painting Power: Antoine Caron's Massacres of the Triumvirate." In *Ritual and Violence: Natalie Zemon Davis and Early Modern France*, edited by Graeme Murdock, Penny Roberts and Andrew Spicer, 241–274. Oxford: Oxford University Press, 2012.
Dalmia, Vasudha. "Pilgrimage, Fairs and the Secularisation of Space in Modern Hindi Narrative Discourse." In *Patronage and Popularisation, Pilgrimage and Procession: Channels of Transcultural Translation and Transmission in Early Modern South Asia*, edited by Heidi Rika Maria Pauwels, 117–133. Wiesbaden: Harrassowitz Verlag, 2009.
Das, Nandini. "Encounter as Process: England and Japan in the late Sixteenth Century." *Renaissance Quarterly* 69, no. 4 (2016): 1343–1368.
Davis, Bruce. *Mannerist Prints: International Style in the Sixteenth Century*, exhibition catalogue. Los Angeles: Los Angeles County Museum of Art, 1988.
Davis, Natalie Zemon. "Rites of Violence: Religious Violence in Sixteenth-Century France." *Past and Present* 59 (May 1973): 51–91.
de Matos, Luise. *Imagos do Oriente no século XVI: Reprodução do Códice português da Biblioteca Casanatatense*. Lisbon: Imprensa Nacional Casa da Moeda, 1985.
de Montaigne, Michel. *The Complete Essays*. Translated and edited by M.A. Screech. Harmondsworth: Penguin, 1991.
Effinger, Maria, Cornelia Logemann, Ulrich Pfisterer, and Margit Krenn, ed. *Götterbilder und Götzendiener in der Frühen Neuzeit. Europas Blick auf fremde Religionen*, exhibition catalogue. Heidelberg: Universitäts Verlag Winter, 2012.
Heal, Bridget. *The Cult of the Virgin Mary in Early Modern Germany: Protestant and Catholic Piety, 1500–1648*. Cambridge: Cambridge University Press, 2007.
Holtz, Grégoire. "Démonologues et voyageurs: le demon de l'analogie'." In *Voyager avec le diable: Voyages reels, votyages imaginaires et discours démonologiques* (VXe-XVIIe siècles), edited by Grégoire Holtz and Thibaut Maus de Rolley, 165–181. Paris: Presses de l'Université Paris-Sorbonne, 2008.
Irving, David R.M. *Colonial Counterpoint: Music in Early Modern Manila*. Oxford: Oxford University Press, 2010.
Jordanus, Friar. *The Wonders of the East*. Translated by Henry Yule. London: Hakluyt Society, 1893.

Juncu, Meera. *India in the Italian Renaissance: Visions of a Contemporary Pagan World 1300–1600*. London: Routledge, 2016.

Lack, Donald F. *Asia in the Making of Europe*, 3 vols, *Vol. II: A Century of Wonder*, book one. Chicago: University of Chicago Press, 1965–1993.

Leitch, Stephanie. *Mapping Ethnography in Early Modern Germany: New Worlds in Print Culture*. New York: Palgrave Macmillan, 2010.

Lestringant, Frank. *André Thevet*. Genève: Librairie Droz, 1991.

Losty, J.P. "Identifying the Artist of Codex Casanatense 1889." *Anais de História de Além-Mar* XIII (2012): 13–40.

Luitjen, Ger, ed. *La Bella Maniera. Druckgraphik des Manierismus aus der Sammlung Georg Baselitz*. Bern/Berlin: Verlag Gachnag & Springer, 1994.

Mandeville, John. *Das buch des ritters herr hannsen von monte villa*. Translated by Michael Velser. Augsburg: Anton Sorg, 1481.

Mandeville, John. *Reise ins Heilige Land*. Translated by Otto von Diemeringen. Basel: Bernhard Richel, 1481?

Mandeville, John. *The Book of Marvels and Travels*. Translated and edited by Anthony Bale. Oxford: Oxford University Press, 2012.

McStay, Heather O'Leary. "'Viva Bacco e viva Amore': Bacchic Imagery in the Renaissance." PhD diss., Columbia University, 2014.

Mellinkoff, Ruth. *Outcasts: Signs of Otherness in Northern European Art of the Late Middle Ages*. 2 vols. Berkeley: University of California Press, 1993.

Michaels, Axel and Christoph Wulf, ed. *Emotions in Rituals and Performances: South Asian and European Perspectives on Rituals and Performativity*. New Delhi/Abingdon: Routledge, 2012.

Michaud, Philippe-Alain. *Aby Warburg and the Image in Motion*, trans. Sophie Hawkes. New York: Zone Books, 2004.

Mitter, Partha. *Much Maligned Monsters: A History of European Reactions to Indian Art*, second edition. Chicago: University of Chicago Press, 1992.

Murray, Linda. *The High Renaissance and Mannerism: Italy, the North and Spain 1500–1600*, revised edition. London: Thames and Hudson, 1977.

O'Doherty, Marianne. *The Indies in the Medieval West*. Turnhout: Brepols, 2013.

Odoric of Pordenone. *Cathay and the Way Thither: Being a Collection of Medieval Notices of China. Vol II: Odoric of Pordenone*. Edited by Henry Cordier, new edition. Farnham: Hakluyt edition, reprinted Ashgate, 2010.

Odorico da Pordenone. *Memoriale Toscano. Viaggio in India e Cina (1318–1330)*. Edited by Lucio Monaco. Torino: Edizioni dell'Orso, 1990.

Ovid. *Metamorphoses* IV 17–32. Verse translatd by Allen Mandelbaum. New York: Harcourt, 1993.

Paramasivan, Vasudha. "Yah Ayodhyā Vah Ayodhyā: Earthly and Cosmic Journeys in the *Ānand-laharī*." In *Patronage and Popularisation, Pilgrimage and Procession: Channels of Transcultural Translation and Transmission in Early Modern South Asia*, edited by Heidi Rika Maria Pauwels, 101–115. Wiesbaden: Harrassowitz Verlag, 2009.

Pentzlin, Nadja Irmgard. "The Cult of Corpus Christi in Early Modern Bavaria: Pilgrimages, Processions, and Confraternities between 1550 and 1750." PhD diss., University of St Andrews, 2014.

Phillips, Kim. *Before Orientalism: Asian Peoples and Cultures in European Travel Writing, 1245–1510*. Philadelphia: University of Pennsylvania Press, 2014.

Philipp, Michael, ed. *Dionysus: Rausch und Ekstase*, exhibition catalogue. Munich: Hirmer, 2013.

Polo, Marco. *The Travels.* Translation and introduction by Ronald Latham. London: Penguin, 1958.
Roper, Lyndal, and Jennifer Spinks, "Karlstadt's *Wagen*: The First Visual Propaganda for the Reformation." *Art History* 40, no. 2 (2017): 256–285.
Rubiés, Joan-Pau. "Theology, Ethnography, and the Historicization of Idolatry." *Journal of the History of Ideas* 67, no. 4 (2006): 571–596.
Rubiés, Joan-Pau. *Travel and Ethnology in the Renaissance: South India through European Eyes, 1250–1625.* Cambridge: Cambridge University Press, 2000.
Rubin, Miri. *Corpus Christi: The Eucharist in Late Medieval Culture.* Cambridge: Cambridge University Press, 1991.
Seth, Vanita. *Europe's Indians: Producing Racial Difference.* Durham, NC: Duke University Press, 2010.
Silver, Larry. "Triumphs and Travesties: Printed Processions of the Sixteenth Century." In *Grand Scale: Monumental Prints in the Age of Dürer and Titian*, edited by Larry Silver and Elizabeth Wyckoff, 15–32. New Haven: Yale University Press, 2008.
Simons, Patricia. "Emotion." In *Early Modern Emotions: An Introduction*, edited by Susan Broomhall, 36–39. London: Routledge, 2017.
Simons, Patricia, and Charles Zika. "The Visual Arts." In *A Cultural History of the Emotions in the Late Medieval, Reformation and Renaissance Age*, edited by Andrew Lynch and Susan Broomhall, 85–106. London: Bloomsbury Academic, 2019.
Spinks, Jennifer. "Civil War Violence, Prodigy Culture and Families in the French Wars of Religion." In *Disaster, Death and the Emotions in the Shadow of the Apocalypse, 1400–1700*, edited by Jennifer Spinks and Charles Zika, 113–134. Basingstoke: Palgrave Macmillan, 2016.
Spinks, Jennifer. "The Southern Indian 'Devil in Calicut' in Early Modern Northern Europe: Images, Texts and Objects in Motion." In *Journal of Early Modern History* 18, no. 1–2 (2014): 15–48.
Strickland, Debra Higgs. *Saracens, Demons and Jews: Making Monsters in Medieval Art.* Princeton: Princeton University Press, 2003.
Tarantino, Giovanni, and Charles Zika, ed. *Feeling Exclusion: Religious Conflict, Exile and Emotions in Early Modern Europe.* Abingdon: Routledge, 2019.
Thevet, André. *La cosmographie universelle.* Paris: Guillaume Chaudiere, 1575.
Van den Boogaart, Ernst. *Civil and Corrupt Asia: Image and Text in the* Itinerario *and the* Icones *of Jan Huygen van Linschoten.* Chicago: University of Chicago Press, 2003.
Van Groesen, Michiel. *The Representations of the Overseas World in the De Bry Collection of Voyages (1590–1634).* Leiden: Brill, 2008.
Van Linschoten, Jan Huygen. *Ander Theil der Orientalischen Indien / Von allen Vo[e]lckern / Insulen / Meerporten / fliessenden Wassern und anderen Orten / so von Portugal auß / lengst dem Gestaden Affrica / biß in Ort Indien vnd zu dem Land China / sampt anderen Insulen zu sehen seind ...* Frankfurt am Main: Johan Saur, 1598.
Vergil, Polydore. *On Discovery.* Edited and translated by Brian P. Copenhaver. Cambridge, MA: Harvard I Tatti Renaissance Library, 2002.
Wouk, Edward H. "From Lambert Lombard to Aby Warburg: *Pathosformel* as Grammar." In *Nederlands Kunsthistorisch Jaarboek / Dutch Yearbook for the History of Art* 68 (2019): 100–135.
Zika, Charles. "Hosts, Processions and Pilgrimages: Controlling the Sacred in Fifteenth-Century Germany." *Past and Present* 118 (February 1998): 25–64.
Zupanov, Ines G. *Missionary Tropics: The Catholic Frontier in India (16th–17th Centuries).* Ann Arbor: University of Michigan Press, 2005.

PART III
Materials

7

ROBBING THE GRAVE

Stealing the remains of the blessed John of Matha from the church of S. Tommaso in Formis in 1655

Lisa Beaven

On the evening of the 18 March 1655, two lay friars of the Spanish Discalced Trinitarian Order, Fray Gonzales di Medina and Fray José Vidal, left their monastery in Rome and made their way under cover of darkness to the church of S. Tommaso in Formis on the Caelian Hill, where they stole the remains of the founder of their Order, the Blessed John of Matha. This chapter draws on an unpublished deposition describing a meeting in Madrid in 1657 when the men involved relinquished the remains into the care of the papal nuncio, Camillo Massimo.[1] My aim is to examine this theft from multiple points of view: the religious emotion that impelled it, the political context and the diplomatic cross-cultural ramifications it had for Italy and Spain. The interaction between religious materiality and emotion that was the consequence of the theft of relics from a church is closely paralleled in medieval accounts of holy thefts, revealing the continuity between medieval and early modern Catholic materiality. Conversely, the lack of a local cult of John of Matha, and the affective ties that linked his remains with a foreign order, are characteristic of the Catholic reform, when the cult of saints became a transnational phenomenon.

The Order of the Most Holy Trinity for the Redemption of Captives

St. John of Matha was the founder of the Order of the Most Holy Trinity for the Redemption of Captives, which was approved by Pope Innocent III in 1198.[2] As the name suggests, the Order's purpose was to redeem Christian captives from Muslim territories, within the framework of the devotion to the Trinity.[3] Members wore a large red and blue cross on their habits, echoing crusading orders such as the Knights Templar and the Order of the Knights of St. John (Figure 7.1). The Trinitarian rule stated that a third of the Order's income was to

154 Lisa Beaven

FIGURE 7.1 Anonymous illustration of a Trinitarian habit, opp. 225, in M.A.R. Tuker and Hope Malleson's *Handbook to Christian and Ecclesiastical Rome*, (London: Adam and Charles Black, 1900). Out of copyright. Reproduced with the kind permission of the British School at Rome Library (Photo: author).

go towards the ransoming of slaves,[4] which in subsequent centuries would prove problematic, as the Order struggled to maintain the economic means to carry out its primary mission.[5]

Very little is known about John of Matha, who died in 1213 in Rome. After his death, his body was displayed to the public for four days, before being buried with great ceremony in the church of S. Tommaso in Formis in an ornate marble sarcophagus.[6] His tomb rapidly became the site of pilgrimage and veneration, and according to his biographer Don Antonio Francesco Tarizzo, a pure liquid with the sweetness of celestial fragrance oozed out from his tomb that was able to cure bodies stricken by malign fevers.[7] The convent and church of S. Tommaso in Formis, which had been given to the Order during the lifetime of John, was united with the chapter of St. Peter's in 1387 after a steep economic decline of the Trinitarian Order in the fourteenth century which culminated in their abandonment of the property in 1382.[8] After 1575, the church, by now almost derelict, was repaired by the Vatican chapter and rented out to a hermit, who functioned as a caretaker. The alienation of the Order from the burial site of its founder was to prove a decisive factor in subsequent events.

By the time of the theft, the Counter-Reformation and its broad programme of reform had given rise to a number of movements for reform among established orders, especially in Spain. There the general chapter of the Order of the Trinitarians determined that in each region, two or three houses were to be reformed according to the original rule of the Order.[9] When these proved reluctant to enforce the primitive rule, John the Baptist of the Conception in 1597 founded a monastery for reformed Trinitarians in Valdepeñas that did so, known as the Discalced Trinitarians.[10] In 1599, he secured permission from Pope Clement VIII to take oversight of the Discalced Trinitarian congregations. But, as Butler in his *Lives of the Saints* stated, Pope Clement VIII also granted to the Discalced Carmelites and Franciscan observants 'oversight of the reform of the [Trinitarian] order'.[11] The resulting fragmentation meant that the Order consisted of a reformed congregation, the Discalced Trinitarians, the majority of whom were Spanish, and the unreformed Trinitarian Order, whose members were predominantly French, although some unreformed convents also existed in Spain.[12] Neither reformed nor unreformed congregations had full control over the order, and neither controlled the church that housed the tomb of their founder.

At the time of the death of John Baptist of the Annunciation in 1613, there were 34 reformed convents in Spain. It was at this time that the reformed order began to make their presence felt in Rome. Fra Gabriel dell'Assunta, together with two fellow monks, bought the first house for the Order on 4 September 1610 at the Quattro Fontane, on the site that would become S. Carlo alle Quattro Fontane and the Trinitarian monastery.[13] The reformed Trinitarians also exerted influence at the Spanish court, with the Duke of Lerma being a major patron; also, a number of celebrated Trinitarian preachers were on intimate terms with the Spanish royal family.[14] The Spanish Discalced Trinitarians actively commissioned paintings and prints emphasising the life, miracles and visions associated with John of Matha as part of a campaign for his canonisation. For example, as early as 1632, Vicencio Carducho was contracted by the Discalced Trinitarians in Madrid to paint a cycle of paintings for their church that depicted the lives of John of Matha and Felix of Valois, for which he was paid 800 ducats.[15] Another important work was the painting commissioned from Juan Carreño de Miranda in 1665 to adorn the high altar of the Trinitarian church at Pamplona in Navarre.[16] The size of this painting and its focus on his most famous vision suggest it formed part of a campaign to promote the cause for his canonisation.

A central part of any campaign for the canonisation of a holy figure was the creation of a shrine around his or her burial place. Shrines were places of pilgrimage: sites to be ornamented and celebrated where a saint's connectivity to a community could be felt. It was through the decoration and development of cult spaces through pilgrimage, ephemeral spectacles, processions and potential miracles that arguments could be put forward in support of canonisation. Such sites linked place and advocacy through intimacy with the bodily remains of the cult figure. In the seventeenth century, cults associated with figures that were not yet canonised were becoming subject to increased scrutiny. Ditchfield cites the example of Camillo de Lellis, who died in 1614. Like Matha, he was the founder of an order, the Ministers of the Sick, and in 1620, the Order's request to display a portrait of their founder over his tomb was refused by the Holy Office, which was trying to assert its control over grass-roots movements for canonisation.[17] Hence, lack of access to the burial site of their founder of the order was a significant obstacle for the Discalced Trinitarians. Although John of Matha was not yet a saint, the Trinitarians viewed his remains as relics, although the extent to which the remains of a *beato* or those of a holy person could be considered as relics and venerated was a matter of controversy.[18] As Alexandra Walsham has stated:

> A relic is ontologically different from a representation or image: it is not a mere symbol or indicator of divine presence, it is an actual physical embodiment of it, each particle encapsulating the essence of the departed person, pars pro toto, in its entirety.[19]

Saints were thought to jealously guard their bodily remains, and communicated through them. In this way, saints had agency and were desirous of being appropriately honoured. As Panciroli put it:

> That joy and great contentment that the saints receive from the honour and esteem produced by the reliquaries that we make for them on earth, is such that when reliquaries are hidden and deprived of the reverence owed to them, the saints themselves have revealed their whereabouts to certain people in order that the reliquaries should be transferred elsewhere to more greatly honour them[20]

For the Trinitarians, honouring the bodily remains of their founder was not possible. They had limited access to the site, and the chapter of St Peter, who had control of the site, had been excavating in the area around the church and selling the antiquities discovered to Marchese Girolamo Mattei who owned the adjoining villa. In 1634, the chapter rented the church to Marchese Girolamo Mattei, whose intention was to incorporate the church and an adjoining building that had been a hospital into his villa.[21] Although the rental agreement stipulated that a priest had to celebrate mass in the church every Sunday, it was not considered by the Order to be a functioning church.

The Spanish in Rome

The actions of the two lay brothers need also to be seen in the context of the broader influence of the Spanish in Rome. By the seventeenth century Rome witnessed the establishment of permanent extra-territorial embassies in the city, in the form of the Spanish palace near Trinità dei Monti, the Florentine embassy near Piazza Navona and the French embassy in the Farnese palace. Spain and

France, as traditional enemies, exerted enormous influence in the city via cardinals, factions, national churches and communities. In what John Marino has described as the 'face-to-face culture of early modern European towns', the urban landscape of Rome was increasingly politicised by conflicts and skirmishes between representatives of these two countries.[22] Dandelet has demonstrated that the numbers of Spanish living in Rome were considerable, with one estimate in 1582 stating that the Spanish community in Rome numbered approximately 30,000, or 30% of the city's total population.[23] The Spanish, like the French, were vigilant at enforcing their sovereignty over the streets surrounding their embassy and national church. A flashpoint was the Piazza di Spagna, where the Spanish occupied their embassy below the area that is now the 'Spanish Steps' and the French Minims occupied the church of SS. Trinità dei Monti above.

While *sbirri* (the papal police), Roman nobles and the civic magistrates of the *popolo Romano* all contributed to the exercise of power in the city, it was the unenviable task of the governor of Rome to keep the peace. This task became more difficult as clashes between those affiliated with one or the other country became more common. For example, on the last day of July in 1635, a certain Cavalier Sforza, in the early hours of the morning on his way to the house of a courtesan, Anna Cantatrice, was ambushed by Frenchmen. In the ensuing gunfight involving arquebuses,[24] a French footman of the French Ambassador was killed. Hearing of this, Cardinal Antonio Barberini, the cardinal nephew of Pope Urban VIII and a loyal supporter of the French, proceeded from his palace with a personal guard of papal cavalry and made his way in his carriage down the Corso, where he met Marchese di Castel Rodrigo, the Ambassador of Spain, who was accompanying Sforza to his house. Sforza got out of the carriage and apologised for the incident, pleading self-defence (Later that night, Sforza would flee his lodgings to seek refuge in the Spanish embassy). For Giovanni Battista Spada, governor of Rome, who recorded this incident in his diary, the entire episode was alarming. Sforza was aligned with Contestabile Colonna, a representative of the most powerful noble family in Rome, who was at odds with Cardinal Richelieu, whom he felt did not treat him with the dignity appropriate to his position when he had visited him upon his arrival in Rome.[25] Spada wrote that there was

> a serious danger of lighting a great fire between the [ambassador], who would draw to his side all of his nation as well as the French factions in Rome, and the Contestabile Colonna, who could rely on all the Roman nobility to take his part.[26]

All of this, he feared, could result in '*qualche gran disordine*' (some great disorder).

The *sede vacante*

If order was maintained with difficulty in normal circumstances, it broke down completely on the death of the Pope. The period of the conclave was known as the *sede vacante*, 'the vacant seat', and was characterised by the absence of papal rule and a fragmented civic order. All heads of the departments of the Curia ceased to exercise their offices during this time and the prisons released their prisoners. The *sede vacante* was so notorious for its lawlessness and violence that many noble families bought in protection in the form of armed guards. John M. Hunt has demonstrated the extent to which the citizens of Rome took advantage of the situation to settle scores: violent acts increased from about 1.8 a day under papal rule to about 8 a day during the *sede vacante*.[27]

The theft of the body of John of Matha

The *sede vacante* between the death of Pope Innocent X on 7 January 1655 and the election of Pope Alexander VII on 7 April was unusually long, lasting for three months. It appears that the two lay brothers who carried out the theft, Fray Gonzales di Medina and José Vidal, took advantage of the situation to carry out their plan. According to the deposition of the two brothers, at dusk on 18 March, they made their way to the church of S. Tommaso in Formis carrying a candle and an iron bar.[28] Arriving at the garden of the Mattei and finding the gate locked, they climbed over the wall.[29] Finding the door of the church also to be locked, they borrowed a ladder from the garden and climbed up to a window in the church. They manoeuvred the ladder through the window and climbed down into the interior. They lit the candle they had brought with them and two others on the altar when they heard three voices. They blew out two of the candles and waited, frightened and alert. Hearing nothing more, they climbed back up the ladder to check that there was no one outside. Reassured, they approached the tomb, and after saying their prayers to John of Matha, pried open the stone lid of the sepulchre and found the remains of three bodies inside. Based on the prayer at the head, they identified the founder of the Order, noting that his bones were whiter than those of the two other bodies which were positioned in the corners of the tomb (later to be identified as the second and third generals of the Order); they took only John's remains and left.

It is not precisely clear what route they took on their return. Their account states that on passing the monastery of the Discalced Trinitarians, which may have been their own monastery, the bell in the campanile rang out once without any human intervention, which they took to be a miraculous sign of divine approval for their actions.

Their motivation as described in the deposition was '*buon zelo*'. The deposition reads 'these two last [the brothers], without advice or participation of others, but only moved by good zeal' removed the body.[30] Florio's 1611 Italian-English dictionary translates '*zelo*' as 'earnest affection, jealous love or emulation, or a jealous care'. Jealously was a term widely used in the early modern period when it was understood as having a multiplicity of meanings that overlapped with 'vigilance' and 'scrutiny', and, in some contexts, was understood to be a form of 'envy'. 'Zeal' functioned as 'compound passion composed of antithetical elements', although in Robert Burton's eyes, it was so vehement that he viewed it as a 'species apart'.[31] It was also closely associated with religion. An English pocket dictionary of 1765, for example, defined it as '[a]n earnest passion, or fervor of soul, especially when employed about the interest of religion'.[32] Some understood zeal to be a particular emotion, as in the case of Florio's description of it as 'jealous love', while others viewed it as composite of love and anger. In the medieval period, it was often linked to vengeance, particularly in a crusading context,[33] but the consensus was that zeal was 'a high strain of all of the affections'.[34] As Fenner put it: 'zeal is the transportation of the soul out of it self. When a man is zealous in a passion, he is transported out of himself, the passion hath command of him, and not he of his passion'.[35]

The implication of the use of the term 'zelo' in the deposition, then, is that the two brothers were so inflamed with devotion that their religious fervour drove them to remove the body. The Discalced Trinitarians, like many other Spanish reformed orders, demonstrated an intense religious fervour, particularly through a range of high-profile preachers such as Fray Hortensio Felix de Paravicini. While useful in a preacher, demonstrations of religious fervour were regarded as dangerous by the authorities, as many in Spain believed in the power of intercession that could be exerted by holy people. The Spanish Inquisition regarded individual demonstrations of extreme religious emotion and extreme devotional regimens with suspicion, particularly in female penitents and visionaries, regarding them as possible examples of false or feigned sanctity. In the ecclesiastical literature of the period, religious fervour was also regarded with ambivalence. Ignatius of Loyola warned specifically against what he called 'excessive fervor' in a letter to the Fathers and scholastics at Coimbra, arguing it could turn 'good into evil and virtue into vice'.[36] Whether or not religious fevour or zeal would have been considered a justifiable reason for such an action, in and of itself, is highly dubious. Even in the more turbulent medieval period, it seems that removing relics in the dead of night from a church would have been regarded as the wrong way to go about claiming a saint, and if the thieves were caught, they would have been required to return the relics.[37]

Geary's research on medieval thefts of relics has neatly summarised the arguments concerning the moral justifications of such actions, among which was the fact that saints were living powerful individuals, so that stealing their relics against their will was not conceivable.[38] In fact, thefts of relics were really a form of 'ritual kidnapping by which the saint was passed from one community to another'.[39] The social and cultural justification of such thefts in subsequent narratives was critical to the development of the cult around the relic in its new context.

In many particulars, the account of the two Spanish monks conforms closely to the hagiographical tradition of the accounts of sacred thefts in medieval Europe. First, it was committed by two monks, which was the norm with monastic thefts. Second was the fact that, from the point of view of the thieves, the saint (or *beato*) was not being properly venerated. His church was not owned by the

Order; moreover, it was 'half ruined' and the saint was alone 'amidst the city'. The poor state of churches in which relics were kept was a common justification for removing them in the medieval period.[40] Third, it was claimed that the theft was associated with a miracle (the pealing of the bell), albeit a weak one in this case, with the bell understood as a sign of the approval of the move by the saint.

However, the account of the Spanish monks differs in one important respect from the examples cited by Geary in that it occurred at a time when identifying and legitimating relics was becoming increasingly important. The institution that oversaw the Catholic response to Protestant criticisms with respect to saints' relics and their cults was the Sacred Congregation of Rites and Ceremonies. This was founded in 1588, the year that also witnessed the publication of the first volume of Cesare Baronio's *Annales ecclesiastici,* when the Catholic Church was attempting to position the cult of the saints within a stronger historical framework. Part of this process involved greater scrutiny of existing relics, and Simon Ditchfield and others have shown that in the seventeenth century, the authentication, translation and display of relics became subject to unprecedented regulation.[41] Regional churches were required to submit their local saints' offices to Rome for approval, and if evidence could not be found for the authenticity of relics, they were removed and their shrines demolished. The rediscovery of the catacombs, as Olds noted, created identification dilemmas on an unprecedented scale for the church, as it was often impossible to distinguish between the bones of martyrs and those of ordinary Christians or pagans.[42]

The situation was further complicated by the body of evidence suggesting that in spite of the best efforts of the Church, an illicit trade in objects and body parts from the catacombs continued throughout the seventeenth century. The repeated issuing of edicts forbidding entry into cemeteries and catacombs where saints' relics were located is testament to this. One of these edicts, issued on 25 September 1599, forbade anyone from entering into the catacombs for the purpose of extracting relics, and for those defying the edict the punishment was permanent exile in the galleys.[43] In 1603, Clement VIII issued an edict prohibiting the unlicensed removal of material from the catacombs. Another issued on the 15 October 1605 by Girolamo Pamphilij forbade entry into the cemeteries and catacombs in the Roman Campagna and ordered owners of such property in the Campagna to block access to them.[44] Some years later, on 12 August 1613, Paul V issued another edict forbidding entry to any catacomb inside or outside Rome for the purposes of extracting relics, which states specifically that many have defied previous edicts.[45] It is addressed to the owners of vineyards and territory on the periphery of Rome; it instructs them to block all entrances to caves and catacombs on their land within ten days, and commands all landowners who discover a cemetery on their land to notify the authorities. Another was issued in the following year on 16 May 1614, forbidding the extraction of relics of saints from churches, pious places, cemeteries and grottos both inside and outside Rome, as well as forbidding notaries to witness such extractions.[46] The reference to notaries in this last edict suggests that bones and body parts extracted from the catacombs were being sold on a market where evidence of their origin mattered. The frequent issuing of such edicts also suggests they were ineffective. Harris has recently shed light on some of the intermediaries operating in the relic trade in Rome, as well as highlighting Spanish involvement in extracting relics from the catacombs.[47]

The actions of the Trinitarian monks stand apart from this more organised trade in looting by relic-hunters. Their theft was highly targeted and directed at a specific body in a specific church, rather than raiding catacombs to see what turned up. It was primarily motivated by their frustration at lack of access to the tomb of the founder of the Order. At a time when church authorities were seeking to legitimate relics by means of written evidence and careful identification of remains in the form of labels, the monks' illicit actions in removing some of the bones and not others risked breaking the bond between John of Matha and his bodily remains, directly imperilling his identity.

Back in their monastery, Fra José Vidal kept the remains of John of Matha in his cell. Given the numinous power of relics, his proximity to the bones in the confines of his cell would have had a powerful effect on him emotionally. The theft was discovered when Fra Gonzales confessed to Don Diego de Solis, his confessor, who refused to absolve him until he put the remains back where he found them. It is at this point that events took an unexpected turn. When Don Diego de Solis reported the events to his superior, Fra Pietro Arrias Portocarrero, Procurator of the Province of Castile, the latter, instead of endorsing Don Diego's actions, directed the two monks to return to the church and steal the remains of the second and third generals of the Order from the tomb as well. This time they left a note describing their actions.

Unlike the first theft, this one speaks to the ambitions of Portocarrero, and to the tensions both within the Trinitarian Order, and between the nation-states of France and Spain. The French Trinitarians were promoting the canonisation of the supposed co-founder of the Trinitarian Order, Felix of Valois, official proceedings to acknowledge his cult having begun in the 1630s.[48] After the intervention of the French king, the Congregation of Rites approved his cult as immemorial in 1666, in spite of a lack of historical proof or a burial place.[49] The theft, therefore, can also be viewed as a manifestation of national ambitions within the Trinitarian Order, with the reformed Spanish Order championing the cause of John of Matha, while the French promoted the cult of Felix of Valois. Portocarrero's decision may have been motivated both by faith and by the rivalry between the two nations. Zeal's close relationship with jealousy is relevant in this context, as '*zeloso*' is translated in Florio's dictionary as 'fearing lest the thing that he loveth should be common to another'. As a word, it conveys the possessive nature of the emotion that gives us an insight into what prompted Portocarrero's actions. His overriding desire was to obtain the relics of the founder of the Order for the Discalced Spanish Trinitarians and ensure this event was publicised. Eventually the remains of all three men were smuggled out of Rome to Naples, and leaving the other two bodies with the Duke of Terranova in Naples, the

Discalced Trinitarians moved the remains of John of Matha to Spain. In 1657, they relinquished them into the care of the papal nuncio in Madrid, Camillo Massimo.

This episode was a problem for the Church, which was facing strong condemnation and criticism from the Protestants about false relics and the illicit trade in relics.[50] The theft of the founder of a religious order from within a church, rather than a cemetery or catacomb, suggested a lack of discipline and oversight, and smacked of illicit trade. On the other hand, demanding the remains be returned was also fraught with difficulty. The Discalced Trinitarians were well established as ransoming agents for Italy and the Hapsburg lands, whose governments had increased need for them as the Hapsburg-Ottoman conflict escalated.

In the end, the papacy procrastinated. When Camillo Massimo left his post as papal nuncio in Madrid to return to Rome, he passed the remains of John of Matha to his successor Carlo Bonelli, who passed them, in turn, to his successor Vitaliano Visconti.[51] The chest containing them remained in the chapel of the palace of the papal nuncio in Madrid. Part of the deposition, apparently written by Visconti, recommends the remains be relinquished into the care of the Discalced Trinitarians in Madrid, where they can be properly venerated, so the devout can be consoled by them.[52] According to this view, Matha's remains were not so much stolen as moved away from a place without a community to be part

FIGURE 7.2 Relic of the scapula of St. John of Matha, Church of S. Crisogono, Rome (Photo: author).

of the community that revered him the most, the Discalced Trinitarian Order. However, it was not until 1721 that the *Sacra Congregazione dei Riti* officially recognised the relics, and at that time they were installed in the Trinitarian convent in Madrid. In 1835, they were moved again to the convent of the Trinitarian nuns of Lope de Vega in Madrid. In 1966, the relics were moved again, this time to the convent of the Trinitarians in Salamanca, where they remain.

John of Matha was never officially canonised; instead he was given what is known as an 'equivalent canonization', according to which the Pope enjoins the church to observe the veneration of a saint by inserting his feast into the *liturgical* calendar of the universal church.[53] Whether the theft was part of an official tactic of the Discalced Trinitarians or an impulsive act impelled by religious fervour as the deposition suggests, as a saint-making strategy it proved to be a disastrous one, condemning the founder of the Trinitarian Order to obscurity.[54] In Rome today, all that remains of John of Matha is the relic of his scapula (Figure 7.2) in the church of San Crisogono, apparently left behind by Gonzales di Medina and Vidal in their haste.

Appendix

Biblioteca Angelica, Rome
Ms 1659
This volume consists of a number of miscellaneous personal papers pertaining to Cardinal Camillo Massimo, and was purchased by the Angelica Library, together with some other manuscripts with a provenance to Massimo, in the nineteenth century. The deposition is described in the index to the volume as *Informatio emin.mi di.ni Nuncii hispaniarum fol. 270–271*.

[fol. 270r.]
'Furono essaminati in questo tribunale l'anno 1657 à 14 di Giugno d'ordine di Monsig.r Massimi fra Pietro Arrias Porto Carrero Spagnolo Trinitario Calzato già Procuratore Generale nella Corte di Roma, fra Gonzalvo di Medina suo compagno, e fra Gioseppe Vitale dell'istesso Ordine sopra l'estrattione del Corpo del B. Giovanni de Matha dalla Chiesa di S. Tomasso de formis, nella quale si ritrovava collocato, dalle depositioni de quali resulta, che li due ultimi senza consiglio, aviso [sic] ò participatione d'altri, mà solamente mossi da buon zelo, perchè il Beato ricevette la dovuta Veneratione, parendo loro, che questa non se li prestasse per star la Chiesa fuori di Roma celebrandovesi la Messa solamente nelli giorni di Domenica, e nella festa del Santo Titolare, determinorno di pigliare il detto Corpo, e collocarlo nella Chiesa del loro Convento nell'istessa Città di Roma; Onde li 18 di Marzo 1655 alle cinq[ue] della notte s'inviorno verso S. Tomasso, portando seco un palo di ferro, una candela, et il foule per accenderla; Et arrivati, al Giardino de Matthei, in cui per essere la Porta serrata, salirno per la Muraglia; E perchè la porta della Chiesa stava anch'essa serrata, si valsero d'una scala, che ritrovorno nel Giardino, mediante la quale salirno ad una finestra della Chiesa, e mettendola poi per le parti di dentro, vi discesero, et accendendo la

candela che havevano portata, e due altre, che stavano nell'Altar Maggiore; si avvicinarono al Sepolcro, e sentendo tre voci, restarono spaventati e smorzorono due delle trè candele accese, conservandone una sotto l'Altare, osservando se si sentiva altro rumore, e non sentendolo, salirono per la stessa scala per scoprire, se nel Giardino vi era gente; Mà non vedendo alcuno, assicurati discesero nuovamente nella Chiesa, e dopò haver fatto Oratione al Santo, alzorno col palo di ferro le pietre del Sepolcro, e trovorno trè corpi divisi, cioè nella parte superiore, quello del B. Giovanni, in cima della cui testa vi era un'Oratione, e nelli due angoli li corpi del 2.o, e 3.o Generale dell'Ordine sudetto con alcune cedole, che lo dichiaravano, e le ossa di questi si differenziavano da quelle

[fol. 270v.]
del B. Giovanni, apparendo le prime in giallite, e quelle del B. Giovanni assai bianche, pigliorno il Corpo del Beato, lasciando l'altri due, si partirno alla volta del loro Convento; E mentre passavano avanti quello de Trinitarij Scalzi, sentirono sonare una Campana, ancorche fussero le otto della Notte, nel qual tempo non soleva toccarsi, e perciò lo tennero per Miracolo, attribuendolo à causa di trarre seco il Corpo del Beato, il quale conservorno nelle Cella di detto frà Gioseppe, nè ciò pervenne à notitia di alcuno fin tanto che frà Gonzalvo si andò à confessare in compagnia di D. Diego de Solis; E non havendo voluto il Confessore assolverlo, se prima non restituiva il detto corpo al suo luogo, il medesimo Don Diego riparando in ciò, lo interrogò poi della causa, la quale fù à lui palesata con promessa di secretezza, mà questa non ostante egli la communicò al detto Procurator frà Pietro Arrias, il quale fece instanza à frà Gonzalvo, e frà Gioseppe sudetti, che li consignassero il Corpo, e ricessandoessi d'acconsentirvi, frà Pietro fece tali dimostrationi, che si cominciò à publicare, e così stimarono bene di consignarglelo, ponendolo nella Cassa, nella quale hora si ritrova; E perchè dubitarno, che per esser restati nel Sepolcro li due altri corpi, non si sarebbe creduto, che mancasse l'altro del B. Giovanni, penserno di tornar alla Chiesa di S. Tomasso à fine di pigliarli, come fecero la Notte de 6 Aprile di detto anno, portando scritto una Cedola con alcuni segni di Croce, e cassature, nella quale si dichiarava ch'essi havevano estratto il Corpo del B. Giovanni nella Notte della festa di S. Gioseppe e che alli 6 d'Aprile parimente di Notte, erano tornasi à pigliare li due altri, e dove si trovasse altra cedola con i medesimi segni, ivi stava il corpo del Beato giuntamente, al quale ne misero un'altra simile; Et arrivati alla detta Chiesa, aprirno il Sepolcro, e levorno li due Corpi, che con lasciarvi la detta Cedola, lo servorno

[fol. 271r.]
tornandosene al loro Convento; E perchè si cominciò à publicare il caso, temendo il castigo, si partirno per Spagna con di detti trè Corpi, e portando seco à Madrid il Corpo del Beato Giovanni, lasciorno l'altri due al Duca di Terranova in Napoli, e poi lo consegnorno in una Cassa Serrata, e sigillata al detto Mons.r Massimi in deposito, il quale partendosi, lo lasciò al Sig.re Card: Bonelli, e da S. E. fù consegnato à me; Onde mi pare molto conveniente al Servitio di Dio, che si collochi nella Chiesa de Padri Trinitarij Scalzi di Madrid, la quale è assai conspicua,

et honorificamente ornata acciochè si dia al Beato ogni più decente Veneratione, e le persone divote ricevano delle consolationi spirituali, che sogliono conseguire con simili Venerationi tanto più che ad instanza, e spesa della detta Religione si sono prese informationi, e fatte diligenze in questo Tribunale in tempo del Sig. re Card. Bonelli sopra il culto, et honore dato per il passato al detto Beato, nè per parte della Religione de Trinitarij Calzati, n'è stata fatta instanza alcuna per la consegna di detto corpo, rimettendomi sempre à quello, che saprà meglio disporre la somma prudenza di S. Santità, che è quanto mi occorre dire à V. Em.za sopra il contenuto dell'ingionto Memoriale pervenutomi con sua benig.ma adi primo Marzo prossimo passato.'

Notes

1 This was apparently written by Vitaliano Visconti (Borromeo), who was apostolic nuncio to Spain from 1664 to 1668.
2 John of Matha was born in 1154 in France, and died in 1213 in Rome. In several histories of the Order, Felix of Valois is described as the co-founder of the order, but in 1969, the Trinitarians acknowledged John of Matha as their sole founder. See James W. Brodman, *Charity and Religion in Medieval Europe*, (Washington, DC: Catholic University of America Press, 2009), 152.
3 Scholars have noted the distinction between "slave" and "captive" in all languages around the Mediterranean rim. Miguel Cervantes, for example, was a captive, taken prisoner while on a voyage and valued for his ability to be exchanged for a ransom price. See Michel Fontenay, "Esclaves et/ou Captifs. Préciser les concepts," in *Le commerce des captifs. Les intermédiaries dans l'échange et le rachat des prisonniers en Méditerranée, XVe–XVIIIe siècle*, ed. Wolfgang Kaiser (Rome: École Française de Rome, 2008), 15–24.
4 The rules stated:

> Omnes res, undecumque licite veniant, in tres partes dividant equales; et in quantum due partes sufficient, exequantur ex illis opera misericordie, cum sui, ipsorum et eis necessario famulantium moderata sustentatione. Tercia vero pars reservetur ad redemptionem captivorum, qui sunt incarcerati pro fide Christi a paganis: vel dato precio rationabili pro redemptione ipsorum vel pro redemptione paganorum captivorum, ut postea rationabili commutatione et bona fide redimatur christianus pro pagano secundum merita et statum personarum.

Die Register Innocenz' III, 1. Pontifikatsjahr, 1198/1199, (Graz and Cologne, 1964), 703–704.
5 For more on this see Luciano Palermo, "Gestione economica e contabilità negli enti assistenziali medievali," *Reti Medievali Rivista*, 17:1 (2016): 120–121.
6 Entry on St. John of Malta in *Biblioteca Sanctorum* (Rome: Della Pontificia Universita Lateranese, 1965), 6, 827.
7 D. Antonio Francesco Tarizzo, *Compendio del Gloriosissimo Patriarca S. Giovanni di Matha* (Turin: Per Domenico Paulino, 1698), 107.
8 La chiesa e l'ospedale fra il XII e il XIV secolo. L'insediamento dell'ordine dei Trinitari nel 1209', in *Caelius I*, ed. Alia Englen, (Rome: L'Erma di Bretscheider, 2003), 403–404. See also Ottavio Panciroli, *I tesori nascosti nell'alma città di Roma* (Rome: appresso Luigi Zannetti, 1600), 780, where he states that Pope Gregory XIII conceded the church of S. Stefano in the Piazza di Pietra to the Trinitarian Order.
9 Alban Butler, *Butler's Lives of the Saints*, revised by John Cumming (Minnesota: The Liturgical Press, 1998), 154.
10 Ibid.
11 Ibid.

12 The hostility between the two congregations is exemplified by an incident cited by Butler in which members of the unreformed Trinitarians came to Valdepeñas and assaulted John Baptist, throwing him into a ditch (*Butler's Lives of the Saints*, 154). The history of the Order is complicated due to an earlier attempt at reform in the sixteenth century which saw some Trinitarians choosing strict observance of the rule, but allowing other monks who declined to follow this rule to stay on in the monasteries. This is what prompted John Baptist of the Conception to found separate discalced monasteries. There were also discalced Trinitarian nuns, who followed the leadership of Angela della Concepcion. A third order attached to the discalced Congregation was established at Marseille in 1845. See M.A.R. Tuker and Hope Malleson, *Handbook to Christian and Ecclesiastical Rome*, II and III (London: Adam and Charles Black, 1900), 221–225.

13 Juan María Montijano García, "Introduction," in *San Carlo alle Quattro Fontane di Francesco Borromini nella 'Relatione della fabrica' di fra Juan de San Buenaventura*, ed. Juan María Montijano García (Milan: Edizioni il Polifilo, 1999), 27. The discalced friars had early support from Cardinal Bandini who granted them some land there. According to Tuker and Malleson, the discalced Trinitarians had the following houses: S. Crisogono, S. Carlo alle Quattro Fontane, S. Stefano degli Abissini and Santa Maria alle Fornaci, while the calced friars were based at the church of the Holy Trinity in Condotti until the end of the nineteenth century. See Tuker and Malleson, *Handbook to Christian and Ecclesiastical Rome*, 224–225.

14 Ronald Cueto, "Fervor / Fanatismo or Entorno / Enfoque: The Problem of the Female Visionary in the Catholic Monarchy," in *Faith and Fanaticism: Religious Fervour in Early Modern Spain*, eds. Lesley K. Twomey and Robert Hooworth-Smith (Aldershot: Ashgate, 1997), 13.

15 This cycle included nine paintings depicting events from the life of John of Matha, Mary Crawford Volk, *Vicencio Carducho and Seventeenth Century Castilian Painting*, reprint of author's thesis from Yale, 1977 (New York and London: Garland Publishing, 1977), 242.

16 Juan Carreño de Miranda, "The Mass of the Foundation of the Order of the Trinitarians," 5 × 3.15 m., Louvre Museum, Paris. This illustrates the moment when John of Matha officiated at his first mass, and as he elevated the host, he saw an angel with its hands placed on the heads of two slaves kneeling and bound at its feet. It was then he determined to found an order dedicated to freeing Christian slaves in Muslim lands.

17 Simon Ditchfield, "Thinking with Saints: Sanctity and Society in the Early Modern World," *Critical Inquiry*, 35:3 (2009): 579.

18 Simon Ditchfield discusses this issue at some length in relation to Antonio Galliano's attempts to gather information about local saints' cults by requesting information from various churches, the resulting material constituting what Ditchfield describes as "something not far short of a census of saints and their relics from the Italian peninsula and beyond"; Simon Ditchfield, *Liturgy, Sanctity and History in Tridentine Italy* (New York: Cambridge University Press, 1995), 48. Galliano established a set of criteria for establishing whether or not a holy person who had not yet been canonised could be legitimately honoured and revered, which included issues such as precedent, continuity of cult practices and decoration of tombs. See ibid., 47–52.

19 Alexandra Walsham, "Introduction: Relics and Remains," *Past and Present*, 206: Supplement 5 (2010): 12.

20 This is a relatively free translation of the original statement in Italian:

> quell'allegrezza, e contento grande, che ricevono dall'honore, e stima, che delle Reliquie loro facciamo in terra, talmente che stano alle volte nascoste, e prive della debita riverenza, loro stessi l'hanno rivelate ad alcuni, acciò si trasferessero altrove, perche fossero maggiormente honorate …
>
> (author's translation)

Panciroli, *I tesori nascosti*, 835.

21 Apart from mass on Sundays, the church was opened once a year to celebrate the feast day of the founder. See Floriana Svizzeretto, "La chiesa e l'ospedale fra il XII e il XIV secolo. L'insediamento dell'ordine dei Trinitari nel 1209," in *Caelius I*, ed. Alia Englen (Rome: L'Erma di Bretschneider, 2003), 406.
22 John Marino, "The Zodiac in the Streets: Inscribing 'Buon Governo' in Baroque Naples," in *Embodiments of Power: Building Baroque Cities in Europe*, eds. Gary B. Cohen and Franz A. J. Szabo (New York and Oxford: Berghahn Books, 2008), 203.
23 Thomas Dandelet, "Searching for the New Constantine: Early Modern Rome as a Spanish Imperial City," in *Embodiments of Power: Building Baroque Cities in Europe*, eds. Gary B. Cohen and Franz A.J. Szabo (New York and Oxford Berghahn Books, 2008), 193.
24 BAV, Barb. Lat. 4975, *Racconto delle Cose più considerabili che sono occorse nel Governo di Roma* (Diary of Giovanni Battista Spada. f. 14v.–15v.). An arquebus was a long gun that appeared in Europe in the fifteenth century. I have worked from the manuscript in the Vatican, but the diary has also been published. For the published version, see Giovanni Battista Spada, *Racconto delle Cose più considerabili che sono occorse nel Governo di Roma*, ed. Maria Teresa Bonadonna Russo (Roma: Presso la Società alla Biblioteca Vallicelliana, 2004), 16–17.
25 Cardinal Richelieu had not accompanied the Contestabile Colonna to his carriage after his courtesy visit, and thus, from Colonna's point of view, did not afford him sufficient respect. As Russo explains it, citing Ms. Urb Lat 1647, f. 210v. and Ms. Urb. Lat 1648, f. 254 (Biblioteca Apostolica Vaticana):

> Alla morte del suo nipote ex-fratre Marc'Antonio IV, nel 1611, Filippo Colonna (1578?–1639) era divenuto capo della famiglia e Gran Contestabile del Regno di Napoli [...]. Per questo, e per la sua parentela coi Barberini [...] non credeva di dover cedere la precedenza a chicchessia, mentre il Richelieu, forte della sua doppia veste di Cardinale e Ambasciatore, e dell'appoggio del Card. Antonio, nemico dei Colonna, riteneva di poter accampare diritti in proposito.

26 BAV, Barb. Lat. 4975, *Racconto*, f. 15r.:

> Maggior pericolo d'accendere un gran fuoco hebbe à cagionare quello, che segui trà il Sig.r Cardinale di Lione, et il Sig.r Contestabile Colonna, poiche tirando il Sig.r Cardinale dalla sua parte tutta la Natione, e fattione Francese, il Sig.r Contestabile all'incontro tutta la Nobiltà Romana avezza à correre à quella casa in simili accidenti, poteva succedere qualche gran disordine.

Spada was worried because Colonna had summoned armed men to Rome. See Spada, *Racconto delle Cose più considerabili*, 138, n. 120, where Russo quotes the *Avviso* of 28 July 1635, Cappon, 21, f. 229: "Havendo il sig. Cotestabile Colonna fatto venire a Roma una gran quantità de suoi vassali armati li tiene nel suo palazzo alla grotte di Nerone."
27 John M. Hunt, *Violence and Disorder in the Sede Vacante of Early Modern Rome 1559–1655* (PhD diss., Ohio State University, 2009), 129. These figures are based on the mandatory reporting from doctors and barbers of suspicious wounds found.
28 Biblioteca Angelica Rome, Ms. 1659, f. 270: "Onde li 18 di Marzo 1655 alle cinq[ue] della notte s'inviorno verso S. Tomasso, portando seco un palo di ferro, una candela, et il foule per accenderla."
29 This wall today is too high to scale without equipment. It appears to be the original wall of the villa.
30 Biblioteca Angelica Rome, Ms. 1659, f. 270r.:

> Furono essaminati in questo Tribunale l'anno 1657 à 14 di Giugno d'ordine di Monsig.r Massimi fra Pietro Arrias Porto Carrero Spagnolo Trinitario Calzato già Procuratore Generale nella Corte di Roma, fra Gonzalvo di Medina suo Compagno, e fra Giuseppe Vitale dell'istesso Ordine sopra l'estrattione del Corpo del B. Giovanni de Matha dalla Chiesa di S. Tomasso de Formis, nella quale

si ritrovava collocato, dalle depositioni de quali resulta, che li due ultimi senza consiglio, aviso [sic] ò participatione d'altri, mà solamente mossi da buon zelo, perchè il Beato ricevette la dovuta Veneratione, parendo loro, che questa non se li prestasse per star la Chiesa fuori di Roma celebrandovesi la Messa solamente nelli giorni di Domenica, e nella festa del Santo Titolare, determinorno di pigliare il detto Corpo, e collocarlo nella Chiesa del loro Convento nell'istessa Città di Roma.

31 Steven Wagschal, *The Literature of Jealousy in the Age of Cervantes* (Columbia and London: University of Missouri Press, 2006), 7.
32 *A Pocket Dictionary; or Complete English Expositor Shewing Readily the Part of Speech to Which Each Word Belongs...* (London, 1765), 453.
33 See Susanna A. Throop, "Zeal, Anger and Vengeance: The Emotional Rhetoric of Crusading," in *Vengeance in the Middle Ages: Emotion, Religion and Feud*, eds. Susanna A. Throop and Paul R. Hyams (Aldershot: Ashgate, 2010), 182.
34 W. Fenner, *A Treatise of the Affections: Or, the Soules Pulse* (London, 1642), 118.
35 Even allowing for the important differences in meaning between Protestant and Catholic accounts of zeal, this comment speaks to the contemporary belief that zeal is an intensification of all emotions, rather than a separate emotion. See Fenner, *A Treatise of the Affections*, 139.
36 Ignatius de Loyola, *Powers of Imagining*, trans. Antonio T. De Nicolas (New York: State University of New York Press, 1986). Letter to the Fathers and Scholastics at Coimbra, Portugal. Known as the 'Letter of Perfection', 329–337. This quote is from the section warning against indiscreet fervour, 334:

> It is thus, as St. Bernard says, that the enemy has no more successful trick for depriving the heart of real charity than to get her to act rashly and not in keeping with spiritual reasonableness. "Nothing in Excess", said the philosopher. And this principle should be our guide even in a matter pertaining to justice itself, as we read in Ecclesiastes, "Be not over just" (Eccles. 7:17). If one fails to observe this moderation, he will find that good is turned into evil and virtue into vice.

37 Patrick J. Geary, *Sacra Furta: Thefts of Relics in the Central Middle Ages* (Princeton: Princeton University Press, 1978), 136.
38 Ibid., 133.
39 Ibid., xi.
40 Ibid., 138.
41 Simon Ditchfield, "Tridentine Worship and the Cult of Saints," in *The Cambridge History of Christianity*, vol. 6: Reform and expansion 1500–1660, ed. Ronnie Po-Chia Hsia (Cambridge: Cambridge University Press, 2007), 205–206.
42 Katrina Olds, "The Ambiguities of the Holy: Authenticating Relics in Seventeenth-Century Spain," *Renaissance Quarterly*, 65:1 (2012): 140.
43 25 September 1599, Rome, edict issued by Cardinal Vicario Generale Girolamo Rusticucci forbidding entry into the catacombs for the purpose of extracting relics, with the penalty for such an offence being life in the papal galleys. Summary published in *Regesti di Bandi, Editti, Notificazioni e provvedimenti diversi, relativi alla città di Roma ed allo Stato Pontificio*, 1 (Rome, 1930), 137.
44 15 October 15 1605, edict by Cardinal Girolamo Pamphilij, forbidding entry into cemeteries and catacombs in the Roman Campagna, and instructing landowners to block all access points. Summarised in *Regesti di Bandi*, 11.
45 *Editti e Bandi*, Biblioteca Casanatense, Per. Est 18/1-210, 4, 394. Edict issued by Cardinal Millini and dated 12 August 1613, titled "Che non si possi entrare nei Cimiteri, Grotte, & Catacombe che sono dentro, e fuori di Roma, ne estrarre qualsivoglia minima particella di Reliquie". The section indicating these edicts were consistently ignored reads:

Se bene con altri Editti del nostro Tribunale da i nostri Predecessori altre volte è stato prohibiti, che non si potesse da alcuna persona entrare nelle Giotte, e Cimiteri di questa Città di Roma, e da quelli estrarre Reliquie; nondimeno vedendosi per esperienza, che molti contravengono alla sudette proibitioni, et volendo noi hora opportunamente provedere à questo inconveniente.

46 16 May 1614, edict issued by the Cardinal Vicario Giovanni Garzia Milini, prohibiting the extraction of relics of saints from churches, sacred places, cemeteries and grottos inside and outside Rome, and prohibiting notaries to witness such extractions, Arch. Stato, *Bandi*, vol. 11. *Regesti di Bandi, Editti, Notificazioni*, 159.
47 K.A. Harris, "Gift, Sale, and Theft: Juan di Ribera and the Sacred Economy of Relics in the Early Modern Mediterranean," *Journal of Early Modern History*, 18 (2014): 1–34. See also Gianvittorio Signorotto, "Cercatori di Reliquie," *Rivista di storia e letteratura religiosa*, 31 (1985): 383–418.
48 Ditchfield, "Thinking with Saints," 581.
49 Ibid.
50 Calvin was particularly scathing about relics and the failure to diligently authenticate them. See J. Calvin, *Traité des reliques* (Geneva, 1543) and J. Calvin, *Tracts Relating to the Reformation*, trans. Henry Beverage, 3 vols. (Edinburgh, 1844–51). See also J. Calvin, *Institutes of the Christian Religion*, trans. Henry Beveridge (Grand Rapids, 1989).
51 BAV, Ms. 1659, f. 271 r.:

E perchè si cominciò à publicare il caso, temendo il castigo, si partirno per Spagna con di detti trè Corpi, e portando seco à Madrid il Corpo del Beato Giovanni, lasciorno l'altri due al Duca di Terranova in Napoli, e poi lo consegnorno in una Cassa Serrata, e sigillata al detto Mons.r Massimi in deposito, il quale partendosi, lo lasciò al Sig.re Card: Bonelli, e da S. E. fù consegnato à me.

52 Vitaliano Visconti was apostolic nuncio to Spain from 1664 to 1668. He was elected Cardinal in 1667.
53 His feast day is 8 February. According to Tuker and Malleson, writing in 1900, the 'cause' for the canonisation of John of Matha was before the Congregation of Rites. See Tuker and Malleson, *Handbook to Christian and Ecclesiastical Rome*, 222.
54 I have borrowed the term "saint making" from Simon Ditchfield's article "Thinking with Saints."

Bibliography

A Pocket Dictionary; or Complete English Expositor Shewing Readily the Part of Speech to Which Each Word Belongs... London, 1765.
Biblioteca Sanctorum, vol. 6. Rome: Della Pontificia Universita Lateranese, 1965.
Brodman, James W. *Charity and Religion in Medieval Europe*. Washington, DC: Catholic University of America Press, 2009.
Butler, Alban. *Butler's Lives of the Saints*, revised by John Cumming. Minnesota: The Liturgical Press, 1998.
Calvin, Jean. *Institutes of the Christian Religion*, translated by Henry Beveridge. Grand Rapids: Eerdmans: 1989.
Calvin, Jean. *Tracts Relating to the Reformation,* translated by Henry Beverage, 3 vols. Edinburgh, 1844–51.
Calvin, Jean. *Traité des reliques*. Geneva, 1543.
Cueto, Ronald. "*Fervor / Fanatismo* or *Entorno / Enfoque*: The Problem of the Female Visionary in the Catholic Monarchy." In *Faith and Fanaticism: Religious Fervour in*

Early Modern Spain, edited by Lesley K. Twomey and Robert Hooworth-Smith, 7–21. Aldershot: Ashgate, 1997.

Dandelet, Thomas. "Searching for the New Constantine: Early Modern Rome as a Spanish Imperial City." In *Embodiments of Power: Building Baroque Cities in Europe*, edited by Gary B. Cohen and Franz A. J. Szabo, 191–202. New York/Oxford: Berghahn Books, 2008.

Die Register Innocenz' III, 1. Pontifikatsjahr, 1198/1199 edited by O. Hageneder and A. Haidacher. Graz/Cologne: Böhlau, 1964.

Ditchfield, Simon. *Liturgy, Sanctity and History in Tridentine Italy: Pietro Maria Campi and the Preservation of the Particular*. New York Cambridge University Press, 1995.

Ditchfield, Simon. "Thinking with Saints: Sanctity and Society in the Early Modern World." *Critical Inquiry*, 35, no. 3 (2009), 552–584.

Ditchfield, Simon. "Tridentine Worship and the Cult of Saints." In *The Cambridge History of Christianity*, vol. 6: Reform and expansion 1500–1660, edited by Ronnie Po-Chia Hsia, 201–224. Cambridge: Cambridge University Press, 2007.

Englen, Alia, ed. *Caelius I. Santa Maria in Domnica, San Tommaso in Formis e il Clivus Scauri*. Rome: L'Erma di Bretschneider, 2003.

Fenner, W. *A Treatise of the Affections: Or, the Soules Pulse*. London, 1642.

Fontenay, Michel. "Esclaves et/ou Captifs. Préciser les concepts. " In *Le commerce des captifs. Les intermédiaries dans l'échange et le rachat des prisonniers en Méditerranée, XVe-XVIIIe siècle*, edited by Wolfgang Kaiser, 15–24. Rome: École Française de Rome, 2008.

Geary, Patrick J. *Sacra Furta: Thefts of Relics in the Central Middle Ages*. Princeton: Princeton University Press, 1978.

Harris, K.A. "Gift, Sale, and Theft: Juan di Ribera and the Sacred Economy of Relics in the Early Modern Mediterranean." *Journal of Early Modern History*, 18 (2014), 1–34.

Hunt, John M. "Violence and Disorder in the Sede Vacante of Early Modern Rome 1559–1655." PhD diss., Ohio State University, 2009.

Loyola, Ignatius of. *Powers of Imagining*, translated by Antonio T. De Nicolas. New York: State University of New York Press, 1986.

Marino, John. "The Zodiac in the Streets: Inscribing 'Buon Governo' in Baroque Naples." In *Embodiments of Power: Building Baroque Cities in Europe*, edited by Gary B. Cohen and Franz A. J. Szabo, 203–229. New York/Oxford: Berghahn Books, 2008.

Montijano García, Juan María. "Introduction." In *San Carlo alle Quattro Fontane di Francesco Borromini nella 'Relatione della fabrica' di fra Juan de San Buenaventura*, edited by Juan María Montijano García. Milan: Edizioni il Polifilo, 1999.

Olds, Katrina. "The Ambiguities of the Holy: Authenticating Relics in Seventeenth-Century Spain." *Renaissance Quarterly*, 65, no. 1 (2012), 135–184.

Palermo, Luciano. "Gestione economica e contabilità negli enti assistenziali medievali." *Reti Medievali Rivista*, 17, no. 1 (2016), 113–132.

Panciroli, Ottavio. *I tesori nascosti nell'alma città di Roma*. Rome, 1600.

Regesti di Bandi, Editti, Notificazioni e provvedimenti diversi, relativi alla città di Roma ed allo Stato Pontificio, vol. 1. Rome, 1930.

Signorotto, Gianvittorio. "Cercatori di Reliquie." *Rivista di storia e letteratura religiosa*, 31 (1985), 383–418.

Spada, Giovanni Battista. *Racconto delle Cose più considerabili che sono occorse nel Governo di Roma*, edited by Maria Teresa Bonadonna Russo. Rome: Presso la Società alla Biblioteca Vallicelliana, 2004.

Svizzeretto, Floriana. "La chiesa e l'ospedale fra il XII e il XIV secolo. L'insediamento dell'ordine dei Trinitari nel 1209." In *Caelius I*, edited by Alia Englen, 395–405. Rome: L'Erma di Bretschneider, 2003.

Tarizzo, D. Antonio Francesco. *Compendio del Gloriosissimo Patriarca S. Giovanni di Matha*. Turin, 1698.
Throop, Susanna A. "Zeal, Anger and Vengeance: The Emotional Rhetoric of Crusading." In *Vengeance in the Middle Ages: Emotion, Religion and Feud*, edited by Susanna A. Throop and Paul R. Hyams, 177–201. Aldershot: Ashgate, 2010.
Tuker, M.A.R., and Hope Malleson. *Handbook to Christian and Ecclesiastical Rome*. London: Adam and Charles Black, 1900.
Volk, Mary Crawford. *Vicencio Carducho and Seventeenth Century Castilian Painting*. New York/London: Garland Publishing, 1977.
Wagschal, Steven. *The Literature of Jealousy in the Age of Cervantes*. Columbia/London: University of Missouri Press, 2006.
Walsham, Alexandra. "Introduction: Relics and Remains." *Past and Present*, 206, Supplement 5 (2010), 9–36.

8

DAYS OF WRATH, DAYS OF FRIENDSHIPS

The materiality of anger and love in early modern Denmark

Jette Linaa

This chapter aims to investigate the role of emotions in the negotiation and performance of cultural encounters. Specifically, the aim is to shed light on how cultural encounters illuminate different emotional regimes, how materiality is embedded in such regimes and, finally, analyse how performances of emotions contribute to the construction of identity in an ethnically divided town. The chapter takes as its starting point two case studies: first, a cultural encounter of a highly volatile nature centred on one kind of materiality, and, second, meetings between friends and family centred on materiality of a very different kind. Both case studies provide significant information on the role of emotions in the negotiation of identities within an ethnically divided town. This chapter is rooted in the tradition of historical archaeology, and, as such, the secondary aim is to investigate the role of materiality in such cultural encounters. How were emotions embedded in and negotiated through materiality? Since archaeology focuses on the study of the relationship between humans and materiality, this paper will investigate how materiality was linked to emotions in the early modern world, and how such emotions were managed by means of social practices. However, since emotions are highly dependent on context, the paper will take care to contextualise the particular cultural encounter in focus here.[1] The case on which this paper is constructed concerns consumption studies in the broadest sense, which relate not to food and drink in the sense of resources, ingredients and recipes, but to the way in which communities are created and recreated through consumption and through the social practices in which consumption is embedded. In this paper, attention is directed towards the performances of emotions in encounters between two cultural groups: Danes and immigrants. As we will see, these encounters were orchestrated around opposing emotions, and therefore provide insights into how people dealt with emotional binaries such as trust and fear, delight and loathing, approval and shame and love and fear. The aim here is to study on a fundamental level the role of materiality in the creation and negotiation of such emotions as well as how such emotions functioned in cultural encounters in an unstable time.

The case study treated in this paper takes place in the Danish city of Elsinore, a town that housed the largest migrant community of any Scandinavian city in the years around 1600 (Figure 8.1). Elsinore, the seat of the Sound Toll from 1426 onwards, was the second largest Danish town after Copenhagen, and it was undoubtedly the most cosmopolitical of any city in the Twin Kingdoms of Denmark-Norway. The town flourished in the middle of the Dutch Golden Age as hundreds, even thousands, of ships setting out from ports in the Netherlands heading for the Baltic anchored in the town every year and had to pay the Sound Toll. The business opportunities offered by this traffic meant that the city grew into the largest hub for shipping and maritime trade in Scandinavia. The growth of the city was partly a result of a deliberate effort on the part of King Frederik II (1556–1588) and his son Christian IV (1588–1648) to modernise Denmark from being a medieval kingdom to becoming an empire of the North. The king grasped the opportunities afforded by the stream of wealthy and resourceful refugees from the Dutch wars of independence that reached the North, and he permitted many of them to settle in Elsinore on favourable terms. This migration meant that the town grew from c. 4,500 inhabitants in 1560 to c. 7,000 in 1600, a third of whom were migrants or of migrant descent.[2]

Many of the migrants in the city became immensely wealthy from shipping and trading with the many Dutch ships, and the Dutch neighbourhood in Elsinore still bears witness to that wealth. The Dutchmen settled in a newly constructed neighbourhood between the castle and the town centre. Much of this neighbourhood was destroyed when war hit the city in 1658, but the remaining houses by Dutch architects for Dutch citizens are among the finest examples of Dutch renaissance architecture in Denmark. Charles Ogier (1594–1656), secretary of the French ambassador at the court of King Christian IV, describes the Dutch part of the city in 1634 and remarks on its beauty and neatness:

> The streets are fairly broad and straight; the houses of considerable size and almost all built from bricks. Light falls through windows of the purest glass, polished every week…..The men are tall and well-built, the women neat and beautifully built, with blue eyes and blonde hair, white-skinned and rosy-cheeked like children. They are tall and stately, and as they cover their bosoms with their scarfs and do not seek the attention of men, they remind me of our nuns.[3]

Ogier also remarks on the splendid equipment in the Dutch homes:

> We entered the living room, which was very neat with five windows facing the sea. The walls were covered in paintings from floor to ceiling, and benches covered in cushions and blankets lined the walls.

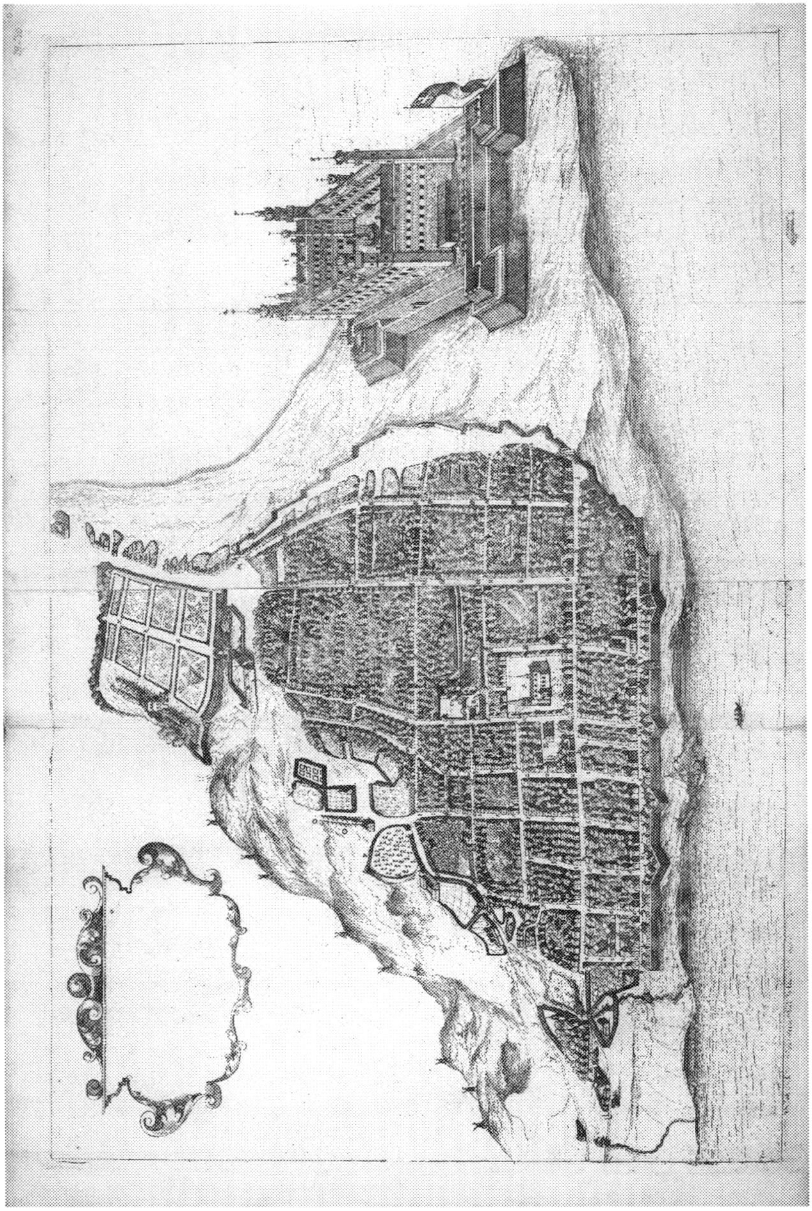

FIGURE 8.1 *Helsingör med sine Gader og Stræder, Cronborg Slot ved Siden, Peder Hansen Resen, 1677* © Det Kongelige Bibliotek, Copenhagen.

He goes on:

> Two tables were covered with the finest cloth. A jug and basin basis were placed on one, and on the other stood two silver jugs containing water and wine.[4]

Ogier's host during his stay in the city was the director of the Sound Toll, Willum Rosenvinge, the richest man in town, who lodged visitors of high rank in one of his mansions in the central part of the Dutch neighbourhood; this was a mansion previously inhabited by the well-known Danish-Dutch painter Pieter Isaacsz (1569–1625), court-painter to Christian IV. Pieter Isaacsz and his brother, the historian Isaac Pontanus, were sons of the merchant Isaac Pieters from Amsterdam, Dutch agent in Elsinore from 1569 to 1594.[5] The role of the agent was to take care of the interests of the Netherlands in the city – a position that included many negotiations with the directors of the Sound Toll when disputes over payment arose and, on a few occasions, with the king himself. The agents were highly respected men who acted as unofficial leaders of the town's migrant community. In 1634, Carel van Cracow was the Dutch agent, later ambassador, of Elsinore, a position he held from 1628 until his death in 1646.[6] For many years, van Cracow lived in the Dutch part of town with his wife and daughters, and he was buried in Elsinore's St. Mary's Church, where his tomb in the nave can still be seen. Ogier describes van Cracow as a well-informed man, very experienced in diplomacy from having held posts at several princely houses, as well as at the court of the Spanish king, and he was highly respected by the French ambassador.[7] His daughter Birgitta married a Swedish nobleman residing in town, Magnus Durrell, while his other daughter Maria married Johan van Galen, who was Commodore of the Netherlands. Cracow was indeed highly respected among his peers: His daughters were very frequently asked to be godmothers at baptisms in the city.[8] Since the baptismal records of Elsinore are only preserved from 1637 onwards, the social position of Isaac Pieters cannot be measured by the same means. However, as we shall see, Pieters does appear to have taken on the role of chief negotiator for the migrants when conflicts with the Danes threatened the peace in the city.

Research history

The archives of the city of Elsinore contain the richest body of historical sources from the early modern period. Unpublished probate inventories, tax records, citizen rolls and court records that hold a wealth of information on migrants in the city are available in the Danish National Archives. Several historical works analysing migration have used those sources, the most comprehensive of which is a volume on the foreign inhabitants and citizens of Elsinore between 1550 and 1600 written by the historian Allan Tønnesen.[9] This book presents detailed biographical information on hundreds of migrants and links them to specific ethnic groups by their names and descent. The biographies include information on financial circumstances, origin, year of migration, kinship, business relations and sometimes material possessions. Other pieces of information, mostly relating to topographic details and legal issues from the fifteenth to the eighteenth century, can be found in the cultural-historical work *Helsingør i Sundtoldstiden 1426–1887*, I–II, by Laurids Pedersen.[10] Biographical information on civil servants of the city, some of whom were of migrant origin, can be found in *Helsingørs Embeds- og Bestillingsmænd*.[11] The probate inventories, which are preserved from 1571 onwards, are an essential source on the materiality of both Danes and migrants. The probate inventories for the years 1571–1582 have been published in their entirety,[12] while a selected inventory from 1571 to 1620 was published in 1903.[13] Relevant information on the cultural horizon of the migrants is presented by means of an analysis of their possessions of paintings and books by Poul Eller and Charlotte Appel.[14] Both studies are based on the unpublished probate inventories in the Danish National Archives. Data on specific migrants, as well as many Danes, are found in *Dansk Biografisk Leksikon*.[15] Further information specifically on the influence of Dutch migrants on cultural connections in fields such as art and architecture is available in the volumes *Holland-Danmark*, I–II,[16] and in Badeloch Noldus' works on cultural connections between the Netherlands and the North,[17] while Thomas Riis (1988) has discussed Scottish connections in *Should Old Acquaintance be Forgot… Scottish-Danish Relations c. 1450–1700*.[18] Although much has been published, the substantial part of this material remains unpublished, and a good portion of that unstudied, too. This means that discoveries can be made every day, and one such discovery is the court case at the heart of this study.

The materiality of anger

The materiality of anger comes forth through a court case. The court case concerned imparts significant information on the role of emotions within the negotiation of identities in the ethnically divided town of Elsinore. The conflict was rooted in the fact that the migrant community had no defined legal recognition in the town: It lacked formalised institutions and was not represented in the town council – an entirely different situation from the one in Sweden where migrants were secured a representative in the town councils.[19] In the absence of a formal institution, the migrant community looked to informal leaders such as the Dutch agent, who seem to have been the spokesperson for the migrant community in times of crises. Even so, the legal position of the agent was no different from that of the ordinary citizens, just as the legal position of the migrant citizens was no different from that of their Danish neighbours. The customary position of the agent is nonetheless visible in several court cases centring on conflicts between Danes and migrants, and it is among these we find this specific case. The conflict evolved around what seemed to be minor disagreements between Danes and migrants. However, the root of the dispute lay in the discrepancy between the formal and the informal legal position of the migrants. Formally, the migrants and Danes had equal constitutional rights and were subject to the same laws and regulations; Danes and migrants alike were obliged to act in accordance with the town privileges. The aim of these was to regulate how trade was conducted in the city to ensure that all citizens had equal opportunities for business and commerce.[20] Yet, several complaints made by Danish citizens to the municipality document that the Danes of the city thought that the citizens of migrant descent acted unneighbourly and unfairly by disrespecting these privileges.[21] For example, they traded on Sundays and in the countryside, and they sailed out to the ships in the sound to trade with them before the Danish merchants had a chance to meet the shipmasters: all illegal practices. The court was unable to put a stop to such transgressions, but, at the same time, any violations on the part of the Danes were severely punished. Moreover, the economically and socially superior position of the migrants, which was partly achieved by methods the Danes perceived as unfair, provoked the resentment of the Danes.

The Danes complained repeatedly to the king throughout the 1580s, stating that the migrants monopolised the lucrative trade with the Dutch ships, an action that was illegal according to town privileges, and that the Danes were becoming destitute as a result.[22] However, the king supported the migrants because their ties to the Netherlands were economically crucial to Denmark, and so the complaints had no effect. The result of this on life in the city was profound, because the migrants now saw no reason to integrate with the Danes or even respect the town privileges; instead, they segregated completely by strengthening their economic ties with each other, choosing other migrants as godparents to their children and the majority marrying people of similar descent. This segregation was aided by the fact that the migrants were given their own church in 1577, where Lutheran sermons were held in German. This church developed into an important hub for the social life of the migrants.[23] The household was the only scene where migrants and Danes met on a daily basis, but since the migrant families employed Danish servants, the asymmetric power relations did little to ease the tensions. There is little doubt that the Danes of the city, as well as the municipalities, perceived the migrants as one coherent community: they were frequently addressed as 'westerners' or 'Dutchmen' in official documents, such as decrees and court records. Furthermore, bynames indicating origin, for example, Berent Hollænder (Berent from Holland), whom we are going to meet shortly, are very common in written records and reflect the forms of address among the townsmen, for example, in the lists of creditors and debtors in the probate records and in witness statements in court. This indicates that descent was a crucial signifier in the eyes of the Danes.[24]

Since the migrants' violations of the town privileges went unpunished, although the Danes had just cause, the Danes found no outlet for their anger and resentment through the formal legal system. Instead, they found an outlet through the local legal system: the town assembly. This was the civil court of the town where inhabitants of the city could be accused, tried and sentenced under the watchful eye of the public. The procedures varied but were based on a unity of legislative, juridical and executive powers. Sometimes the president of the court, the mayor and the councillors assembled a formal jury, while at other times they asked the spectators present to voice their opinion and then sentenced in accordance with that. The court treated a wide range of offences, from theft to homicide and adultery, but it was also able to judge in matters that went unspecified in the written laws, but were against the unwritten laws and common decency. The court was able to deny prospective citizens the right to remain in town if the neighbours testified that they had acted against common decency, such as had been incolved in fighting and had housed people with bad reputations.[25] Since the town bailiff, the mayor and the councillors were all of Danish descent, as were the majority of the townspeople, the power to decide what was unlawful or indecent was in the hands of the Danes, and this power gave the Danes of the city significant leverage. The court became an instrument for managing and controlling the anger and resentment of the Danes. The migrants were an economically strong community in the town and were, moreover, under royal protection, but they were still a minority and could not expect to be treated as mildly by the local court as by the king. In practice, by giving a voice to the Danish community of Elsinore, the court became an essential outlet as well as a moderating factor. This moderating function of the court may be the reason why the Danish anger does not seem to have given rise to random or organised acts of violence targeting migrants, although violence frequently did occur in the city. Charles Ogier witnesses a violent fight between two sailors and describes with shock and awe how they wounded each other with knives, while at the same time comparing the courage of duelling French noblemen unfavourably to the courage of these two sailors: Ogier's description of his travels is very much a morality tale.[26] The Danes were no more peaceful than the migrants, and they could have found a vent for their emotions by assaulting random migrants but for the fact that such actions would have been punished according to the laws of the city.

Furthermore, given the level of royal protection enjoyed by the migrants, violent attacks could have led to severe repercussions from King Frederik II. Instead, the town assembly became an arena where anger at the migrants could flow freely with few, if any, implications for the Danes, while the mayor and councillors at the same time sought to moderate this anger. This role as moderators was emphasised by the fact that mayors and councillors were the only Danes in the city to have close business relations with the migrant community. The list of debtors and creditors in the probate inventories of the city reveals as much.[27] They had gained the trust of both parties, and both parties were dependent on them in turn; this dual position allowed them to take on the role of negotiators of the relationship between the separate groups within the city, including the resentment and envy felt by the Danes.

No written sources tell of the emotions harboured by the migrants in these times of conflict, as no diaries or letters from their hand have been identified. However, when conflicts were brought to the town assembly, words of fear and bewilderment fill the records, as we will see, and it is likely that the Dutchman felt the resentment of the Danes, although we cannot tell whether they understood its causes. The effects appear to be visible in the written sources that shed light on the strength of the ties between the migrants in town: They enmeshed themselves in close business networks with each other, but only rarely did they trade with the Danes (Figure 8.2). No matter the cause, the negative emotions felt – and shown – by the Danes may have been a factor that made the migrants stick together, just as the resentment of the Danes may have provided a more profound sense of unity and commitment to one another within this group.

However, occasionally the anger of the Danes rose to new levels, and extraordinary measures needed to be taken in order to keep the peace. Such an occasion took place on 14 July 1583 when a man called Berent Hollænder (Berent Dutchman) was confronted by his Danish neighbours. The case is found in the court records in the town bailiff's archives at the Danish National Archives.[28] The court assembled in the town hall in the presence of some citizens. The later events make it very clear that these were Danes. As usual, the court consisted of the councillors and was presided over by Mayor Jørgen Mahr. Mahr was, besides being a mayor, an immensely wealthy merchant of Scottish descent, who was a long-time inhabitant of the town. He was experienced in the administration in the city, had been a councillor since 1566 and a mayor since 1578 and his Scottish ancestry – his father was a Scottish migrant – allowed him to take on a role of informal mediator between the two communities in town.[29] The councillors were all merchants – being a merchant was a prerequisite for being elected to council: Anders Sachs, Mads Lauridsen, Frederik Lyall, Hans Nielsen, Oluf Pedersen and Anders Hess. All these men were members of the urban elite and had been born in the city as sons of mayors or councillors. All of them seem to have been of Danish descent, except for Frederik Lyall, who was the son of the Scottish-born former mayor Alexander Lyall. This was regular practice. No migrant was elected mayor or councillor between 1560 and 1660, although nothing prohibited the inclusion of migrants in the town government.[30] The town councils were largely self-supplementing, not democratic, institutions, and the exclusion of most migrants from such posts indicates that these people were not members of the social networks that linked the urban elite. However, the few migrants that did become members of the council, such as Alexander Lyall, had married daughters of mayors and councillors and had become very closely tied to the Danish Urban elite in that way.

On this summer's day, the court proceedings were noted down by the town scribe, the Danish-born Morten Nielsen. The headlines state the time and date as well as the persons present; the notes then continue (my translation):

> The citizens spoke among themselves and asked the mayor and council about the case of the impurity [urenlighed] that Berent Hollander has raked himself and removed from his houses, which the raker had not done. Mayor Jørgen Mahr replied that Berent came to his door and asked him

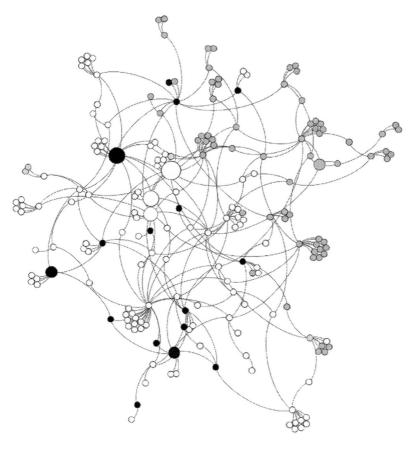

FIGURE 8.2 Results of network analysis based on the debts registered in 48 probate inventories in Elsinore 1590–1600. The origin of creditors and debtors is marked. White: Dutch-born: Grey: Danish-born. Black marks ownership of the specific cultural goods in question here: Dutch paintings and books, coconut cups, porcelain and stoneware mugs. This analysis demonstrates that communities within the town were primarily segregated and that the owners of such cultural goods were predominately members of the city's immigrant community. Source: Elsinore Town Bailiff, Probate Records 1590–1600, The Danish National Archives.

why the townsmen had told him that he could not live here. Then Jørgen told him [that the] citizens would not tolerate that he had done the raker's job. Then Berent replied: "The citizens complain about me, and that is only the job of mayor and council. If I cannot live here, then I want to be told the reason why."[31]

The case was obviously a matter of great concern in town and focused on Berent Hollænder, who had himself done the job that should be done by the raker. The raker was a civil servant with particular duties centring on emptying the latrines of the townsmen, so it seems likely that Berent had emptied his latrine himself. Word of Berent's action came out, and some townsmen had told Berent that he must leave town. However, Berent had refused being banished by the citizens and had confronted the mayor, who had told him than the townsmen would not tolerate that he had done the raker's job. However, Berent seems to have become angry and told the mayor that banishments were a matter for the mayor and council to decide on, not the citizens, and that he, were he not allowed to stay in town, demanded an explanation. Berent seems to have thought that his banishment went against town legislation, and he was right. No written law forbade people to empty their own latrines, and deportation was usually a matter to be treated by the town assembly, not the public. The source continues:

> And since the Berent in question was present, the citizens were asked whether they would allow him to remain a citizen of the town. The common citizens answered that they would by no means agree to have him as their fellow citizen because he had done the raker's job and made a raker of himself. Then he was told by the mayor and council to leave town and if he wanted to know the reason why they would happily tell him.[32]

Occasionally witness statements are written down precisely as spoken, but that is not the case here. Still, the Danish words used in this court case are remarkable, because they are loaded with emotion. The written statement is neutral in its descriptions until the last sentence, where the emotions burst through. The Danish words used when Berent is told to leave town: 'packe sig ud af byen', carry strongly negative connotations: The German and Dutch word 'pack' was used as a derogative term for people who were held in contempt. Furthermore, the words that the mayor and council use to address the Dutchman: '*If he wanted to know the reason why they would happily tell him*', just after he had been exposed to the very public humiliation of being identified with the raker and rejected by the townspeople, are negative in the context, maybe even spiteful, even though the words themselves are neutral. They threaten to deepen the public humiliation and rejection by repeating the words of the citizens.

It seems that Berent was confronted on this day with negative emotions on several levels. He was publicly rejected and humiliated by the townspeople at the town assembly. Furthermore, he was rejected and humiliated by the mayor in public, by the very man whom he had privately asked for help. And still nobody had explained to him why he was being expelled in this highly irregular manner. Berent seems to have offended the Danes in the city as well as the mayor. He had offended the Danes by doing the raker's job in the first place. Furthermore, by refusing to leave quietly, but confront the mayor instead, claiming that the banishment was unlawful – which, strictly speaking, it was – he had deepened the conflict by trying to force the mayor to reprimand the townspeople, which the mayor seems to have been very reluctant to do. All the while, nobody had told Berent what he had done that was so terrible – they had explained that his actions had associated him with the raker, but not why this was an offence so severe that is was to be punished with banishment. The reason Berent did not understand this was because the raker was associated with negative emotions in Denmark, but not in the Netherlands – Berent's homeland. The origin of the Danish perception of his action was that the raker – the emptier of cesspits – was a social outcast. The raker as a civil servant was introduced in Christian IV's town law of 1524.[33] However, even though the raker was a civil servant, he was a social outcast. The raker in Elsinore lived outside of town in an isolated location, and his house had a reputation for assembling the social outcasts of the town: the hangman and criminals of the lowest order who had been banished from town.[34] The obligations of the raker were diverse. Among his responsibilities was helping the hangman, emptying latrines and cesspits, removing putrefying animals from the streets, sweeping chimneys and killing stray dogs. The fact that the raker and his family were social outcasts, lodged in the most negative emotions of disgust and contempt, reveals the darker sides of early modern mentality. The status as a social outcast prevented the raker from socialising with anyone but his kind. Pedersen describes how the raker, even in the late eighteenth century, was banished from most inns in the city. In those where he was permitted access, he had a mug of his own and he emptied it standing: nobody would share a bench, eat a meal or have a drink with him.[35] The negative emotions directed towards the rakers by the Danes in Elsinore did not differ significantly from the emotions directed towards rakers in other cities. The social banishment of rakers was common in many Danish towns.[36]

As suggested, the attitude towards renovation workers was very different in Berent's homeland. Renovation workers in Amsterdam were not surrounded by negative emotions but were respected civil servants.[37] This is why the harsh Danish attitude towards anyone who was associated with the raker may have come as an unpleasant surprise to Berent Hollænder. The clash between two social perceptions surrounding cesspits – one of regulations and hygiene on the part of the Dutchmen, and one of taboo on the part of the Danes – was profound. However, as Berent Hollænder experienced, rationality and hygiene had no place in the worldview of the Danes. Theirs was a world where even the slightest association with the raker was enough to be contaminated and become an outcast. It seems that the very association with the materiality handled by the raker, in this case the contents of a cesspit, was enough to transfer the negative emotions that clung to this materiality, and in turn to the rakers, to the unknowing Berent. The fact that the raker was shunned in inns and had to take his beer standing from a mug of his own indicate that his status was transferred by touching anything he touched. The bench would be contaminated from touching the raker's body, and the next body that touched the bench would be contaminated as well. According to this perception, the emotions of anger, fear and contempt that clung to the raker's body and were transferred to the materiality he handled were infectious through touch, and, as such, all social practices must exclude the raker and any materiality associated with him. This is why Berent Hollænder had to be removed, or the negative emotions that clung to him would spread to anyone who socialised with him in the neighbourhood and the city. So he had to be expelled from the town, just as the materiality he had touched had to be removed. The outcast status of the raker was not a cultural perception limited to the Danes alone; such perceptions existed in Germany as well, but not in the Netherlands.[38]

Berent seems to have been oblivious to the lurking danger of doing the raker's job. He repeatedly asks for an explanation why his neighbours forbade him to stay in the city, and why they were allowed to do so when the formal power to decide on such matters was in the hands of the mayor and council. Berent neither knew the principle of transferral of negative emotions through association with the raker nor understood or respected the fact that the two legal systems crossed in the town assemblage: a formal legal system based on written law and an informal legal system based on the unwritten perceptions of norms and neighbourly behaviour. The formal judicial system was in the hands of mayor and councillors, but within the informal legal system, legislative, executive as well as judiciary power was in the hands of the Danes – and the Danes passed sentence in accordance with their specific cultural perceptions, only some of which were shared by the migrants. Furthermore, by telling the mayor that it was his job to judge, Berent had put his finger on a sore point. The power relation between the formal and the informal legal system was under constant negotiation, and on this occasion in favour of the townsmen. Objectively, Berent was right: The formal power to expel was in the hands of the mayor and council. However, this mattered little when the mayor was unable to support him. Had the mayor not supported the informal court's sentence – that Berent must leave – then he would de facto have sentenced his townsmen to be outcasts themselves. Such a ruling would very likely have multiplied the anger of the townsmen, and both Berent and the mayor would have felt the executive power of the town's Danish inhabitants. As mentioned, Berent could have left the city quietly after his private conversation with the mayor. The fact that he attended the court assembly, although he was not formally summoned, put the mayor in a problematic situation. If he sentenced in favour of Berent he would put himself at risk, and if he sentenced in favour of the Danes, he would risk provoking the migrants in town into action. The fact that the mayor threatened to humiliate Berent further by repeating the sentence passed by the townsmen is easily interpreted as an outburst of negative emotions towards Berent for putting the mayor at risk. We can only speculate whether the mayor would have humiliated Berent like this if he had had the support of the migrant community in Elsinore.

Sadly, the court records do not describe the reaction of the migrant community to the banishment of Berent. The documents do not mention any other Dutchmen being present that day in court, so if any were there to support Berent, they did not voice their support. We can probably assume that the migrant community did not support Berent for fear that the negative emotions towards him would spread to other members of their community. In refusing to support Berent, they may thus have acknowledged that his case was lost, even though he was formally in the right; they recognised the strength of the Danish cultural perceptions and accepted the fact that the formal legal system was unable or unwilling to protect anyone from the anger of the Danes. They may even have recognised that they had to respect the social rules of the Danes, no matter how unfair or illogical they might seem to them.

Both Danes and migrants of the town may well have remembered a similar case that took place 14 years earlier. This was a conflict that had threatened to release the wrath of the Danes on all the migrants in the city. That case has been unfolded previously, and it is sufficient here to repeat that the case centred on a Dutch sailor who, in their eyes, had insulted the Danish community in the worst possible way: He had relieved himself in public, stating that he would gift that to the Danes in Elsinore to eat.[39] This conflict was only resolved through determined action on the part of both communities.[40] Many of the people who took part in the conflict resolution in 1569 were also involved in 1583. Jørgen Mahr and four of the council members who presided over the court, Anders Sachs, Mads Lauridsen, Frederik Lyall and Hans Nielsen, were members of the court on that day in 1569. The very influential Dutch agent in town, Isaac Pieters, was among the most active Dutchmen in the previous case, and he was still present in town in 1583. Pieters may well have played a moderating role, telling his countrymen that his experience was that sacrificing a troublemaker was preferable to risking the wrath of the Danes. The lessons learnt from that previous court case may explain why no one from the migrant community seems to have supported Berent. The fact that mayor and councillors at the previous trial acted with great diplomacy leaves little doubt that their harsh treatment of Berent was a deliberate choice. The migrants no doubt felt the anger and resentment of the Danes in cases like this. That a migrant could be expelled for acting according to the laws of hygiene and order may well have contributed to the identity formation of the migrants. On the other hand, the triumph of the Danes on this day very much played into the identity formation of this group by handing them one of their few victories.

The probate inventories: tokens of love and longing

The case of Berent Hollænder has revealed the materiality of fear and how emotions such as fear figured as part of the identity of the Danes. To investigate the materiality of other emotions, we have to leave the court records that centre on negative emotions and turn to the inventories that describe the contents of various townspeople's homes in great details. The probate inventories of Elsinore are preserved from 1572 onwards in the National State Archives. The process was highly regulated: The contents of the homes, the real estate and the outstanding debt and credit relations were registered and evaluated shortly after the death of the householder under the supervision of the town bailiff and two councillors. This valuation formed the basis for the settlement of debts and the distribution of the remaining assets to the heirs. The largest part of the probate records remains unpublished, but approximately 1,500 probate records from the period 1572–1650 have been transcribed and quantified in the course of the urban diaspora project.[41] Among those are the probate records of some Dutchmen dating from the sixteenth century, and these will constitute the kernel of the following analysis. As stated earlier, the probate inventories from Denmark have not been the subject of large-scale research. Dutch historical archaeology, however, is rich with analysis based entirely or partly on probate inventories, and only a few of the many volumes and papers that draw upon this material can be addressed in this short chapter. This paper focuses on objects included in what is usually called luxuries, such as cups of sea shells or coconuts mounted in silver or gold, and porcelain. The primary source of inspiration is Rengenier C. Rittersma's edited volume *Luxury in the Low Countries*, which focuses on a discussion of Netherlandish material culture that includes considerations on the exchange of luxury as well as considerations on the social practices surrounding its use. Especially the introduction by Rittersma on the link between the display of luxury and social status, the contributions of Hester Dibbits on display practices in the Dutch homes and of Florike Egmond on the practices surrounding the use and exchange of *Naturalia* have been very helpful in the writing of this chapter.[42] Also Anne Gerritsen's paper on the use of global material culture in the early modern Netherlands and her thoughts on global connectivity have been of great value.[43] Likewise, Anne McCant's analysis of how far exotic goods, such as coffee, tea, silk and other eastern commodities, spread in the middle classes in the late seventeenth and eighteenth centuries is based on inventories from Britain and the Netherlands.[44] Moreover, Irma Thoen's volume *Strategic Affection* on gift exchange in the seventeenth-century Netherlands has been especially important.[45] The published diary of the Dutch schoolmaster David Beck 'Spiegel van Mijn Leven' for the year 1624 is also a rich source for the study of the social practices surrounding hospitality and gift exchange. Finally, Ilana Krausman Ben-Amos' volume on the many practices surrounding gift-giving in early modern England has been invaluable in the analysis of exchange in Elsinore.[46]

The probate inventories of the migrants in Elsinore between 1571 and 1600 reveal that the homes contained an almost overwhelming number of items, and, in that regard, they did not differ from the equally well-equipped homes of wealthy and middle-class people in Amsterdam.[47] The kitchens of houses in Elsinore were bursting at the seams with pewter pots and pans and iron kettles. Mirrors in guilt or ebony frames, portraits, religious or landscape paintings as well as prints adorned every wall in the hallways and living rooms, while candlesticks and chandeliers of brass secured ample lighting. Tables and chairs, beds and benches, with numerous duvets and cushions, filled every room. Bibles and religious books in Dutch and German were stored on special shelves, occasionally accompanied by writings by Philippe Melanchthon and Luther's Catechism in Danish. An astonishing amount of linen, tablecloths and towels were stored in chests and laid out on beds and benches, just as clothing items such as capes and shirts, skirts, hats and shoes, stockings and trousers were present in vast, almost unbelievable, quantities in many homes. A good deal of these objects had their parallel in the homes of the Danes, but the Dutchmen in Elsinore possessed concrete material object that was rarely found in the homes of the Danes: paintings and prints, described as 'Dutch', depicting landscapes, towns and princes. A good example is Jacob Gotsloff, who owned a painting of Brussels, a picture of a lion hunt, a landscape depicting Northern Holland and his own portrait.[48] The probate inventories reveal an interest in culture and history among the migrants, with Dutch Bibles, psalm books and history books being present in many homes. The pictures and books of Elsinore have been the subject of a significant amount of research.[49] However, many items relating to communal meals – for instance, coconut cups mounted in silver or pewter, bowls and cups of porcelain and stoneware mugs and jugs – are also found; these are things that are very rarely, if ever, seen in Danish homes. The location of these objects speaks a language of appreciation: they adorned the heart of the homes. Never placed in the kitchen or the scullery, the pictures are hung on the walls in halls and private chambers, the Bibles are placed in the living rooms as well and the tableware is kept in bedchambers and the most important assemblage rooms: in short, places where the Danish servants rarely entered.[50]

The possession of such cultural goods among the Danes and migrants of Elsinore can be analysed using Gephi, a visualisation programme for network analysis, and such a study yields a distribution of the origin of the people who owned the cultural goods described earlier as well as the economic ties they had to each other and to the Danes in the city (Figure 8.2). This is important because other written records that shed light on the community formation among the migrants are only preserved from the early seventeenthh-century onwards. The figure is based on the 40 inventories in which creditors are listed, listing a total of 254 debtors and creditors, who have been registered according to their known origin from biographical sources. The figure, first and foremost, demonstrates that the migrant and Danish communities were largely segregated: Few people had business relations to both Danes and migrants. Furthermore, migrants of Dutch and German descent seem to have been entangled in shared networks that only rarely included Danes.

The figure furthermore demonstrates that these specific types of cultural goods were owned by migrants at this time and only very rarely found in Danish ownership. It is fair to say that the cultural goods circulated among the migrants without reaching the Danes. The probate inventories also suggest how the items came to Elsinore. They are primarily found in the ownership of shipmasters and merchants. One of these was Jacob Meurs, a shipmaster born in Hoorn and married to Diuffe; when his wife died in 1596, he was in possession of a stone jug for wine.[51] Meurs' name occurs several times in the Sound Toll books, passing through the sound of Øresund on his way from Amsterdam to ports in the Baltic with cargoes of spices, salt and stone mugs; this shows that this shipmaster may well be among the suppliers of such items to the city.[52] The only Dane to own this type of cultural goods at this time is Ellen Kelsdatter, employed by Jacob Meurs, who left a stone mug behind at her death in 1592.[53] The mug may well be second-hand goods left to her by her employer since no other servants in the city had such assets. Some of the migrants who left behind cultural products are well-known figures: Among them was the shipmaster Stefan Hennicke, a refugee from the religious wars in the Netherlands who received special permission from King Frederik II to settle in Elsinore in 1576.[54] Hennicke left behind a large crucifix and several books in Dutch and Latin.[55] Another was the shipmaster Willum Heinrichs and his wife Ryken Dirichs – Willum was, like Isaacs Pieters, one of the informal leaders of the migrant community in town and held illegal Calvinist services in his home. He left behind a pulpit, a Dutch prayer book and several stone mugs.[56] Precisely where in the home these cultural goods were kept is revealed in the inventory of the shipmaster Albert von Hoff and his wife Nylchen Cornelisdatter, who stored a *Spanish stone dish* in the living room.[57]

Unfortunately, no letters or diaries from these people have been preserved, so we have no direct knowledge of when and how they used these cultural goods. We do know that the ties between the Dutch community in town and the shipmasters on the Dutch ships passing through the sound of Øresund were close. Several Danish merchants complained about the frequent hospitality offered by the migrants to the shipmasters who were waiting to pay the Sound Toll.[58] It is possible that such items represented gifts from these shipmasters to their hosts within the town, transported on Dutch ships carrying spices and salt to the Baltic. Furthermore, the very placement of such items in the halls and the chambers points towards an appreciation of them for their decorative qualities rather than for their functional ones. The smooth surfaces of the jugs and vessels offered very different tactile experiences than the rough surfaces of wooden plates or the heaviness of pewter jugs. The bright colours and elegant lines of plates and pitchers also contrasted with the dull greyish pewter and the greying of much-used wooden items. Given these locations, they may well have been activated during communal meals in the homes and in connection with the exchange of hospitality between friends, neighbours, relatives and business relations within the community. Such a transfer of hospitality may not have deviated much from the frequency and character of the one documented in the diary of the Dutch schoolmaster David Beck 'Spiegel van Mijn Leven' for the year 1624.[59] In this diary, the sharing of meals and drink in the homes is a daily occurrence which includes family and friends, friends of friends and people who were business associates. Such an exchange of hospitality in a small city like Elsinore would secure that the cultural goods were seen by many and activated on

188 Jette Linaa

FIGURE 8.3 This table scene depicting a Dutch family at mealtime represents the inventories rather well. The meal is taken from pewter plates and jugs, while a porcelain bowl points towards ties to the wider world. Prosperous Calvinist family. Anonymous, 1627 ©Rijksmuseum Amsterdam.

many occasions during the year. Since they were used during communal meals among the migrants, these objects were embedded in these people's friendships and shared culture, strengthened by the fact that the items were manufactured in or traded from the Netherlands. All of the different sorts of goods in question here were very frequently found in the homes of people living in Amsterdam – among the friends and relatives of the exiles in Elsinore.[60] The fact that the migrants acquired similar objects as their relatives in their homeland, and used them according to the same social practices, indicates that they lived within the same cultural sphere, recreating a little bit of their ancestral home in the North (Figure 8.3).

The cultural goods were not particularly valuable economically, compared to silver jugs and gilt glasses, but they played a very different role and were probably appreciated for their intangible qualities: their design, fashion and novelty as much as their links to the home and the wider world.[61] They may therefore be seen as carriers of love and friendship and as linked to the very core of the identity of the Dutchmen, just as they were the centre of attention during the communal meal, which constituted the social glue in the early modern period. The items had a very different meaning for the Danes. In the 1640s, when the items show up in the Danish homes, they are kept in the kitchen, never displayed in the hall.[62]

Conclusion

This paper revolves around two cases, and both of them serve to demonstrate how the negotiation and performance of emotions contributed to the construction of identities within an ethnically divided town. One of the cases concerns anger; the other love. In the first case, the anger of the Danes was ignited by an unwitting migrant, who in his own eyes had handled a specific kind of materiality appropriately, but inappropriately in the eyes of his Danish neighbours. Therefore, this case is a window onto the ways in which performances of emotions that centred on particular social practices contributed to the construction of identities among the Danes and also among the migrants of the town. It is also an example of how a Danish mayor succeeded in managing the emotions of his countrymen: By persuading the migrants to sacrifice one of their own, he was able to disarm an ethnic conflict threatening the town. As such, the town council became a scene for elaborate, almost theatrical, negotiations of the emotions of the common man who witnessed the trials. The actions of mayor and court, as well as those of leading Danes and migrants, indicate that they were very aware of the fact that the court served dual functions: one was to pass judgement in cases involving crimes, the other was to avert a constantly lurking ethnic conflict through careful managements of anger and fear.

The second case revolves around love and friendship and shows how materiality linked to performances of love and friendship circulated among the migrants of the town for a number of decades before this particular materiality showed up among the Danes. And when this materiality did show up among the Danes, it was not invested with the same degree of respect – rather the opposite, in fact. Both cases show how materiality embedded in different social practices negotiated the emotions of the participants, calling upon the strongest emotions of love and friendships in one case, and upon the strongest emotion of anger and disgust in another. In this study, the negative emotions of disgust and anger are ascribed to the Danes who target a migrant, while the positive emotions of love and friendship are attributed to migrants interacting with each other. This paper does not claim to show the full nuances of the relationship between Danes and migrants or the complete picture of how emotions were involved in the construction of identities. The fact that the negative version of identity formation is analysed here by means of consulting court records pertaining to a case against a migrant, while the positive version is investigated with a starting point within migrant homes, practically guarantees that they will come across as friendly and peaceful, while the Danes come out looking like aggressors. If we examined the migrants on the basis of the many violations of town regulations, they would come across as callous and devious, while the Danes would look fearful and pressured. However, court records showing a migrant in the role of direct aggressor, confronting a Dane, are nowhere to be found, and the friendship and love of the Danes were not expressed through any particular materiality that we can identify in the probate inventories. That is, of course, not to say that negative emotions such as anger and hatred played a more significant role in the negotiations of the identity of the Danes than did friendship and trust, just as friendship and love did not constitute an inherent characteristic of the migrants – Ogier's description of the violent fight between two sailors serves to prove that point. However, there is little doubt that, within the segregated town, the migrants perceived their Danish neighbours negatively, as envious and angry, and the eviction of our migrant must have done little to settle the fear of the Dutch. This fear may have lent their tokens of home, friendship and love an extra dimension as well as fed into their perception of being different. The Danish disgust of the contents of the cesspit as well as their treatment of the raker may have seemed very strange to the Dutchmen, and the migrants' emotional attachment to fragile items of no monetary value may have seemed odd to the Danes. Danes and migrants may have behaved strangely in the eyes of each other, but the fact that materiality had the ability to embed, negotiate and transfer emotions was something they had in common. Even so, the point is that their emotional attitudes to the materiality at the heart of this study were very different: what was disgusting to the Danes was not so to the migrants, and what was treasured by the migrants was trash in the eyes of the Danes. However, learning to respect the emotions of the other, while at the same time discussing their strange habits, may have been a key factor in the survival of the migrant community of the city.

Notes

1. Linaa, "Negotiating Ethnic Identities"; Tarlow, "Emotion in Archaeology", 722.
2. Degn, *Sound Toll*; Grinder-Hansen, *Frederik 2*; Heiberg, *Christian IV*; Tønnesen, *Helsingørs Udenlandske Borgere*.
3. Ogier, *Det Store Bilager i København*, 5–6.
4. Ibid., 4.
5. Tønnesen, *Helsingørs Udenlandske Borgere*, 123.
6. Pedersen and Bobé, *Helsingør Sundtoldstiden*.
7. Ogier, *Det Store Bilager*, 11.
8. Parish Registers, St. Mary's Church, The Danish National Archives.
9. Tønnesen, *Helsingørs Udenlandske Borgere*.
10. Pedersen and Bobé, *Helsingør Sundtoldstiden*.
11. Hostrup Schultz, *Helsingørs Embeds- Og Bestillingsmænd*.
12. Dupont, *Helsingør Skifteprotokol 1571–1582*.
13. Olrik, *Borgerlige Hjem i Helsingør*.
14. Appel, *Læsning Og Bogmarked*; Eller, *Borgerne Og Billedkunsten*.
15. Cedergreen-Bech, *Dansk biografisk leksikon*.
16. Fabricius et al., *Holland-Danmark*.
17. Noldus, *Trade in Good Taste*.
18. Riis, *Should Auld Acquaintance Be Forgot*.
19. Andersson, Fritz, and Olsson, *Göteborgs Historia*; Dalhede, "Foreign Merchants".
20. Tønnesen, *Helsingørs Udenlandske Borgere*, 51–54.
21. Ibid., 46–47.
22. Ibid., 44–49.
23. Linaa, *Urban Diaspora*.
24. Tønnesen, *Helsingørs Udenlandske Borgere*, 38.
25. Pedersen and Bobé, *Helsingør Sundtoldstiden*, 152–162; Tamm, *Dansk Retshistorie*.
26. Ogier, *Det Store Bilager*, 11–12.
27. Linaa, "Negotiating Ethnic Identities".
28. Court Records X, 1583–1586, p. 8a.
29. Hostrup Schultz, *Helsingørs Embeds- Og Bestillingsmænd*, 4; Tønnesen, *Helsingørs Udenlandske Borgere*, 103.
30. Hostrup Schultz, *Helsingørs Embeds- Og Bestillingsmænd*.
31. Danish National Archives, Elsinore Town Bailiff's Archives, Court Records X, 1583–1586, p. 8a.
32. Ibid.
33. Linaa, *Urban Consumption*; Lysbjerg Mogensen, *Idealstat Og Lov*.
34. Pedersen and Bobé, *Helsingør Sundtoldstiden*, 112–116.
35. Pedersen and Bobé, *Helsingør Sundtoldstiden*, 285.
36. Hübertz, *Aktstykker Vedkommende Staden*.
37. Oosten, *De Stad*; Sosna and Brunclíková, *Archaeologies of Waste*.
38. Schulz, „Keramik".
39. Linaa, "Negotiating Ethnic Identities".
40. Linaa, "Negotiating Ethnic Identities"; Tønnesen, *Helsingørs Udenlandske Borgere*, 58.
41. Linaa, "Urban Experiment"; Linaa, *Urban Diaspora*; Linaa, "Negotiating Ethnic Identities".
42. Rittersma, "Putting Social Status and Social Aspirations on Display"; Egmond, "Precious Nature"; Dibbits, "Pronken as Practice".
43. Gerritsen et al., *Global Lives of Things*.
44. McCants, "After-Death Inventories".
45. Thoen, *Strategic Affection*.
46. Beck and Veldhuijzen, *Spiegel*; Ben-Amos, *Culture of Giving*.
47. Schama, *Embarrassment of Riches*.

48 Probate Inventories 08.12.1601.
49 Appel, *Læsning Og Bogmarked*; Eller, *Borgerne Og Billedkunsten*.
50 Linaa, *Urban Diaspora*.
51 Probate Inventories 07.12.1596.
52 www.Soundtoll.nl.
53 Probate Inventories 27.04.1592.
54 Bricka et al., *Kancelliets Brevbøger Vedrørende Danmarks*, 15.
55 Probate Inventories 08.09.1597.
56 Probate Inventories 21.05.1599.
57 Probate Inventories 07.07.1598.
58 Tønnesen, *Helsingørs Udenlandske Borgere*, 46–47.
59 Beck and Veldhuijzen, *Spiegel*.
60 Loughman, *Public and Private Spaces*, 71–72; McCants, "After-Death Inventories".
61 Rasterhoff, "Markets for Art", 259.
62 Probate Inventories 21.05.1647.

Bibliography

Unpublished sources

The Danish National Archives, Probate Inventories II–V, Elsinore Town Bailiff's Archive.
The Danish National Archives, Court Records X, 1583–1586, Elsinore Town Bailiff's Archive.
The Danish National Archives, The Sound Toll Books, Øresunds Toldkammer (www.soundtoll.nl).

Secondary Sources

Andersson, Bertil, Martin Fritz, and Kent Olsson. *Göteborgs Historia: Näringsliv Och Samhällsutveckling*. Stockholm: Nerenius & Santérus, 1996.
Appel, Charlotte. *Læsning Og Bogmarked I 1600-Tallets Danmark*. Copenhagen: Museum Tusculanum, 2001.
Beck, David and Sven E. Veldhuijzen. *David Beck: Spiegel Van Mijn Leven: Een Haags Dagboek Uit 1624*. Hilversum: Verloren, 1993.
Ben-Amos, Ilana Krausman. *The Culture of Giving: Informal Support and Gift-Exchange in Early Modern England*. Cambridge: Cambridge University Press, 2008.
Bricka, C. F., L. Laursen, E. Marquard, G. Olsen, J. Jørgensen, J. Holmgaard, and O. Degn. *Kancelliets Brevbøger Vedrørende Danmarks Indre Forhold: I Uddrag*. Copenhagen, 1885.
Cedergreen-Bech, S. *Dansk biografisk leksikon*. Copenhagen: Gyldendal, 1979.
Dalhede, Christina. "Foreign Merchants in Early Modern Sweden: A Case of Intermarriage, Trade and Migration." In *Facing Otherness in Early Modern Sweden: Travel, Migration and Material Transformations, 1500–1800*, edited by Magdalena Naum and Fredrik Ekengren, 145–168. Woodbridge: Boydell & Brewer, 2018.
Danmarks Kirker: Frederiksborg Amt (Ii), vol. II. Copenhagen: Nationalmuseet, 1964.
Degn, Ole. *The Sound Toll at Elsinore: Politics, Shipping and the Collection of Duties 1429–1857*. Copenhagen: Museum Tusculanum Press, 2017.
Dibbits, H.C. "Pronken as Practice. Material Culture in the Netherlands, 1650–1800". In *Luxury in the Low Countries: Miscellaneous Reflections on Netherlandish Material Culture, 1500 to the Present*, edited by R.C. Rittersma, 135–158. Brussels: Faro 2010.
Dupont, Michael. *Helsingør Skifteprotokol 1571–1582*. Copenhagen: Selskabet for Udgivelse af Kilder til Dansk Historie, 2014.

Egmond, F. "Precious Nature. Rare Naturalia as Collectors' items and Gifts in Early Modern Europe". In *Luxury in the Low Countries: Miscellaneous Reflections on Netherlandish Material Culture, 1500 to the Present*, 47–66, edited by R.C. Rittersma. Brussels: Faro, 2010.

Eller, Povl. *Borgerne Og Billedkunsten På Christian Den Fjerdes Tid: Uddrag Af Helsingørs Skifteprotokoller 1621–1660*. Frederiksborg Amts Historiske Samfund, 1975.

Fabricius, K., L.L. Hammerich, and V. Lorenzen. *Holland-Danmark: Forbindelserne mellem de to Lande gennem Tiderne I-11*. Copenhagen: Jespersen og Pio, 1945.

Gerritsen, Anne and Georgio Riello. *The Global Lives of Things: The Material Culture of Connections in the Early Modern World*. London: Routledge, 2016.

Grinder-Hansen, Poul. *Frederik 2: Danmarks Renæssancekonge*. Copenhagen: Gyldendal, 2013.

Heiberg, Steffen. *Christian IV: Monarken, mennesket, myten*. Viborg: Gyldendal, 1988.

Hostrup Schultz, V. *Helsingørs Embeds- Og Bestillingsmænd: Genealogiske Efterretninger*. Copenhagen: Schultz, 1906.

Hübertz, J. R. *Aktstykker Vedkommende Staden Og Stiftet Aarhus*. Copenhagen, 1845.

Krogh, Tyge. "Bødlens Og Natmandens Uærlighed." *Historisk tidsskrift* 94, no. 1 (1994): 30–57.

Larrington, Carolyne. "Diet, Defecation and the Devil: Disgust and the Pagan Past." In *Medieval Obscenities*, edited by Nicola McDonald, 138–155. Woodbridge: York Medieval Press, 2006.

Linaa, Jette. "Danish Is as Danish Does: Negotiating Ethnic Identities in Early Modern Elsinore, Denmark." *International Journal of Historical Archaeology* 2019, no. 1 (2019): 1–34.

Linaa, Jette. "Den Monstrøse Materialitet. Om Placeringen Af 16 Middelalderlige Latriner Fra Aarhus." *Kulturstudier* 7, no. 2 (2016): 23–40.

Linaa, Jette. *Urban Consumption: Tracing Urbanity in the Archaeological Record of Aarhus C. Ad 800–1800*. Højbjerg: Jutland Archaeological Society, 2016.

Linaa, Jette, ed. *Urban Diaspora: The Materiality of Immigrant Communities in Early Modern Denmark*. Aarhus: Aarhus University Press/Archaeological Society of Jutland, 2019 (forth).

Linaa, Jette. "The Urban Experiment. Assimilation, Integration and Segregation in Early Modern Elsinore." In *Urban Variation: Utopia, Planning and Practice*, edited by Per Cornell, Lars Ersgård, and Andrine Nilsson, 305–328. Gothenburg: Lulu, 2018.

Loughman, John Montias and John Michael. *Public and Private Spaces: Works of Art in Seventeenth-Century Dutch Houses*. Zwolle: Waanders, 2000.

Lysbjerg Mogensen, Christina. *Idealstat Og Lov: En Analyse Af Embedsmandsstaben I Christian Ii's Land- Og Bylov (1522)*. Aarhus: Christina Lysbjerg Mogensen, 2016.

McCants, A. "After-Death Inventories as a Source for the Study of Material Culture, Economic Well-Being, and Household Formation among the Poor of Eighteenth-Century Amsterdam." *Historical Methods: A Journal of Quantitative and Interdisciplinary History* 39, no. 1 (2006): 10–23.

Noldus, Badeloch. *Trade in Good Taste: Relations in Architecture and Culture between the Dutch Republic and the Baltic World in the Seventeenth Century*. Turnhout: Brepols, 2004.

Ogier, Charles. *Det Store Bilager I Kjøbenhavn 1634* [Ephemerides sive Iter Danicum, Svecicum, Polonicum]. Memoirer Og Breve; 20. Fotografisk optryk ed.: August Bang, 1969.

Olrik, Jørgen. *Borgerlige Hjem i Helsingør for 300 Aar siden*. Copenhagen: Gad, 1906.

Oosten, Roos van. *De Stad, Het Vuil En De Beerput: De Opkomst, Verbreiding En Neergang Van De Beerput in Stedelijke Context*. Leiden: Sidestone Press, 2015.

Pedersen, Laurits and Louis Bobé. *Helsingør Sundtoldstiden 1426–1857*, vol. 2. Copenhagen: Nyt Nordisk Forlag, 1926.

Rasterhoff, C. "The Markets for Art, Books, and Luxury Goods". In *The Cambridge Companion to the Dutch Golden Age. Cambridge Companions to Culture*, edited by G.H. Janssen and H.J. Helmers, 249–267. Cambridge: Cambridge University Press, 2018.

Riis, Thomas. *Should Auld Acquaintance Be Forgot…: Scottish-Danish Relations c. 1450–1707*. Odense: Odense University Press, 1988.

Rittersma, R.C. "Putting Social Status and Social Aspirations on Display: A Panoramic Study on Manifestations of Luxury in the Low Countries, 1500 to the Present". In *Luxury in the Low Countries: Miscellaneous Reflections on Netherlandish Material Culture, 1500 to the Present*, edited by R.C. Rittersma, 10–24. Brussels: Faro, 2010.

Schama, Simon. *The Embarrassment of Riches: An Interpretation of Dutch Culture in the Golden Age*. London: Collins, 1987.

Schulz, C. "Keramik des 14. bis 16. Jahrhunderts aus der Fronerei in Lübeck." *Lübecker Schriften zur Archäologie und Kulturgeschichte* 19 (1990): 163–203.

Sosna, Daniel and Lenka Brunclíková. *Archaeologies of Waste: Encounters with the Unwanted*. Oxford: Oxbow Books, 2017.

Tamm, Ditlev. *Dansk Retshistorie. 2*, expanded ed. Copenhagen: Jurist-og Økonomforbundet, 1996.

Tarlow, Sarah. "Emotion in Archaeology." *Current Anthropology* 41, no. 5 (2000): 713–746.

Thoen, Irma. *Strategic Affection: Gift Exchange in Seventeenth-Century Holland*. Amsterdam: Amsterdam University Press, 2007.

Tønnesen, Allan. *Helsingørs Udenlandske Borgere Og Indbyggere Ca. 1550–1600*. Ringe: Misteltenen, 1985.

PART IV
Travel writing

9

"A COUNTRY WHERE REASON DOES NOT RULE THE HEART"

Spanish exuberance and the traveller's gaze

Thomas C. Devaney

In 1603 and 1604, Barthélemy Joly, a lawyer and self-styled "almoner and counsellor to the king of France," visited Spain in the company of the Abbot General of Cîteaux, most likely Edmond de la Croix, in order to inspect the various Cistercian houses in Aragón and Catalonia and reunite a fractured order.[1] The journey lasted for several months, and Joly devoted a good bit of his time to maintaining a detailed journal. In some ways, this journal reads like a litany of complaints, perhaps reflecting the contemporary state of Franco-Spanish relations and the fact that the Abbot's mission was unsuccessful (he, in fact, died in Barcelona before the journey could be completed). Joly expressed his disdain for the food, the wine, the quality of the inns. He was annoyed by the beggars, who were not only persistent but insisted on being addressed as "Señor." He suggested that artisans took no pride in their work and that Spanish notions of honour were leading the country into ruin. But despite this generally negative portrayal of Spain, Joly could also, at least occasionally, acknowledge that not everything about the country was terrible. Thus, he admitted that the elegance of Barcelona was the equal of (nearly) any city in France and that the craftsmen of Aragón were happy and prosperous. Similarly, his comments about Spain's internal politics, while often coloured by preference for his native France, sometimes demonstrated care and insight.

Given the nature of his mission, it is not surprising that Joly had much to say about Spanish religious practices. And here, the contrast between Joly the disgruntled traveller and Joly the fair-minded observer is most apparent. He acknowledged the beauty of the churches but credited "the splendour of this nation" to its obsession with "outward appearance."[2] He admired the Inquisition, but warned fellow travellers to take care with what they said, for its agents could be overzealous at times. His account of an auto-da-fé held in Valladolid described it as "the judgment of God" while also expressing sympathy for the condemned. Joly was most struck, however, by the intense emotional character of Spanish religious observances, a theme to which he returned again and again and about which he expressed the same ambivalence. When writing of the clergy, for instance, he commented that,

> In their preaching, they make use of a very great vehemence, as was pointed out by one of them, in one of his printed sermons: 'This gravity and composure, this moderation in speech is what pleases me, and I confess that I disapprove of vociferous preachers who make provocative gestures or wriggle about for a laugh, preachers who cry and think they imitate Christ, he who so gently opened his mouth and taught all.' Two things therefore disturb me about the Spanish sermons: the extreme, almost turbulent, vehemence of the preacher and the continual sighs of the women, so loud and forceful that they completely disrupt one's attention.[3]

But Joly was not always able to maintain such critical detachment and could not always consider himself immune to the passions of the crowd. In Valladolid, witnessing what he called a "doleful procession of penitents," he observed that "they whip themselves outrageously and they pass in procession through the night, so sad that no heart is so hard as not to be moved." "A large black cross preceded them," he went on,

> and a man also in black, dripping with tears. Then, by the sombre light of the stars and a few torches, there passed a silent crowd in black, all covered except for their eyes and their shoulders, upon which these determined soldiers dealt their blows. They were animated in this gloomy combat by the lugubrious notes of a trumpeter in black, which sound fit well with the rattle of the scourges and the weeping of the women and the people, who sympathized with their pain. This makes a music so doleful that the sighs entering the ear move one's soul with a sense of having offended God that is no less than that of the flagellants, so that each person tries to imitate them, with the same or some other kind of visible penance.[4]

✶✶✶✶✶✶✶✶

Spain is different. Such at least was the consensus in early modern Europe. And the mostly negative images of Spain promulgated during the sixteenth and seventeenth centuries—either the Black Legend of Inquisition, repression, and backwardness, or a more dismissive picture of a country peripheral to general European developments—continued to be influential well into the twentieth century. As Joly's diary indicates, that sense of difference extended to understandings of how Spaniards expressed emotion. In the pages that follow, I explore how travellers from various European countries responded to public displays of religious emotions in Spain. These were the emotional experiences about which travellers tended most often to comment, in part because religious practices of all kinds were of great interest and in part because they were visible. The perceived effusiveness with which Spaniards expressed religious emotions was not only a point of difference but also a proxy for all the ways in which Spaniards were both unlike and inferior to the observer. Scholarship on Reformation-era emotions often emphasizes confessional differences. Yet both Catholic and Protestant observers depicted Spain as exceptional; emotions were thus markers of not only religious but also national identity.

In the Middle Ages, northern Europeans mostly knew of Spain either as a battleground against Islam, a place where aspiring crusaders could fight for God without travelling so far as the Holy Land, or as the endpoint of the Camino del Santiago, one of the most popular pilgrim routes. It was, in other words, a foreign place to which one went to fulfil vows. But Spain bore no predominantly negative connotations at that time.[5] This changed, dramatically, in the sixteenth century. As several modern scholars have argued—including J.N. Hillgarth in his *Mirror of Spain* or Henry Kamen in *Imagining Spain*—the origins of anti-Spanish discourse have much to do with Reformation-era religious divides and with the Habsburg Empire's hegemony during its brief but brilliant heyday.[6] Early modern Spain was a military, political, economic, and cultural force that could not be ignored, but which was also poorly understood. On one level, outsiders tended to view Spain with the combination of envy and fear that every superpower must face. In Protestant lands, however, this was buttressed by Spain's role in Europe's wars of religion as self-proclaimed defender of Catholic orthodoxy. Thus, for many Protestants, Spain was the "personification of evil, superstition, and oppression."[7]

One effect of these religious and political rifts was that they impeded travel between Spain and the rest of Europe. And so the accounts of individual travellers had outsized influence in the development of this imagined Spain. Unable or unwilling to visit themselves, readers in, for instance, England relied on travellers' reports for knowledge about Spain to a far greater degree than they did for France or even Italy. Those travellers found much that was unfamiliar, and, as travellers always do, they interpreted novelties through the prism of their existing experiences and biases. Few people, then as now, could honestly agree with Montaigne, who claimed to consider "all men my fellow citizens" and argued that he did not particularly favour "the sweetness of my native soil."[8] In the early modern period, however, this general aversion to the unfamiliar combined with political and religious disputes to foster a particular vision of Spain. And so, when these travellers wrote of outlandish, "Moorish" customs or extravagant honour or the horrors of the Inquisition, they helped to establish Spain as strange, difficult to understand, and somehow not fully European.

The Reformations imposed radical changes on believers throughout Europe, forcing them to rethink their rituals, social patterns and even the traditional ordering of the annual calendar. Emotional practices were not neglected. A close study of the different approaches that the Catholic, Lutherans and Calvinists adopted towards the late-medieval legacy of affective devotions has opened new avenues for historians to explore efforts to direct believers towards new lifestyles and forms of piety. Susan Karant-Nunn, for instance, has used early modern German sermons to show how emotions were at the heart of debates over proper Christian behaviour. What emerges is hardly a stereotypical picture of dour Protestants and effusive Catholics. Yet Karant-Nunn does point to the ways in which Protestants developed an idealized image of male self-control while constantly denigrating Catholic affective practices as vague, disordered, and feminine.[9] Other scholars have considered the creation of what we might refer to as "emotional communities" or "emotional regimes." Drawing on the theoretical frameworks of Barbara Rosenwein and William Reddy, Francois Soyer argues that the organizers of public baptisms of Muslims in early modern Iberia aimed to create a sense of communal identity, binding the spectators together through their collective emotional response to specific symbols.[10] Another strand of inquiry explores spiritual thinkers—such as Teresa de Ávila or Ignatius Loyola—in order to better understand how early modern people conceptualized religious emotions.[11] And still other scholars have pointed to the power of public media in helping people to reconcile themselves to the traumatic breaks with the past that the Reformations had entailed. By arguing for drama as an "affective technology," to give one example, Steven Mullaney shows how particular representations of the past established a "felt history" that offered solace while establishing new, post-Reformation, collective identities.[12]

This is far from a comprehensive summary of scholarship on Reformation-era emotions, but it does suggest some of the main themes of that body of work. There are two nexuses which unite most (but quite definitely not all) of these perspectives. The first is an emphasis on prescriptive evidence, on the kinds of sources meant to instil emotional rules and norms. Printed sermons and plays or accounts of the staging of autos-da-fé tell us much about the aims of religious reformers or playwrights, but much less about how their messages were received. Did viewers or listeners accept these messages or act on them? Even studies that examine individual emotional responses are typically limited to materials penned by clerics or well-educated laypeople, materials that nearly always reflect the attitudes of a narrow slice of society. And many of these sources, including Teresa de Ávila's *Vida* or Francisco de Osuna's *Abecedario espiritual*, were themselves didactic. The second unifying feature of this body of scholarship is an emphasis on the public performance of emotion. In some cases—as with sermons or plays—this was literal performance. But the significance of expressing emotions in public settings, often in conventional ways, is clear. This is not to say that such expressions were insincere; as Monique Scheer has argued, the idea of a dichotomy between interior, sincere feeling and outward expression is a modern one.[13] Rather, the communal expression of emotions was critical to their meaning. When people collectively wept while appealing to God for relief from collective afflictions, such as drought, plague, or military defeat, the purpose was, as William Christian points out, to ensure that "the hearts of the entire community had been moved."[14]

Any study of travellers' accounts of Spanish emotions must address similar themes. Most travellers were unable to speak Spanish; they based their impressions on what they could see. And, since foreigners only rarely had intimate access to Spaniards' private lives, what they could see was limited to the public sphere. Many offered a kind of wordscape, a verbal collage of visual impressions meant to give readers a sense of what Spain looked like: the view from the road, urban architecture, changing fashions, the pomp of official ceremonies, and so on. Most travellers endeavoured to define the Spanish national character to show readers what Spaniards were like. But such attempts were necessarily limited in their scope; travellers could (and did) comment on the significance of what they saw, but these interpretations came from a consciously external perspective. At religious events, however, they might view intense and public displays of emotion. At such moments, travellers could imagine that, despite their status as outsiders, they had glimpsed the *real* Spain. Thus, we have often detailed reports of street sermons, of pilgrimages to shrines, occasionally of Masses, and most often of processions—ranging from penitential flagellants to the elaborate events conducted on Corpus Christi or during Holy Week.

Many of those who penned descriptions of Spain in the sixteenth or seventeenth century were envoys or at least associated with diplomatic enterprises. Some were of noble families; others were connected to ecclesiastic missions. Nearly all were well educated.[15] These privileges come through in their accounts. Visitors from Protestant countries, unsurprisingly, often viewed Spanish affective piety through the prism of confessional identity, disparaging what they considered to be blind, gullible devotion inspired by profane theatrics. Their accounts taught through negative examples, implicitly warning readers to avoid the errors of the emotionally exuberant Spaniards. In so doing, travellers clarified their own views on the "proper" expression of religious emotion.

The very vividness of their accounts served this didactic purpose. Mullaney has suggested that theatrical depictions of improper passions (he uses the example of revenge) are effective means of establishing emotional norms. As he puts it, "the audience's affective reactions are often catalyzed—induced, felt, and experienced as emotions—most effectively when they are alienated from the emotions expressed or represented on stage."[16] Such a process may well have been at work in reform-minded travellers who, when scrutinizing a fervent sermon or a flagellant procession, found their affective sensibilities confirmed (or even newly discovered) through a Spanish antimodel, and then attempted to replicate that experience by evoking similar feelings of disgust or contempt in readers. From this perspective, travelogues are themselves affective documents on multiple levels.

It is too simple, however, to view the situation from a purely confessional point of view. Protestant observers could find much to admire in Spanish piety, while visiting Catholics might be as harsh in their condemnations as any reformist firebrand. Indeed, Catholic travellers often presented Spanish piety as different, as something particularly Spanish. The issue, then, is not necessarily one of Protestant versus Catholic emotional regimes, but of attempts to categorize national identities in terms of emotional norms. In whichever case, Spain was the theatre in which travellers staged visions of outlandish emotions and worked to shape readers' opinions about their otherness.

★★★★★★★★

The earliest traveller's account I have considered was published in 1556 and the latest in 1691, but the majority date from the central decades of the seventeenth century. And, although English and French voices are overrepresented, I have included authors from across Europe. Each of them wrote for specific audiences, with particular agendas, and under individual circumstances. This study thus encompasses a wide range of cultural, political, and religious perspectives and must necessarily be impressionistic. My goal is neither to present a comprehensive account of all traveller's reports about Spain nor to closely examine the particular circumstances of individual reports. Rather, I aim to demonstrate the prevalence of several trends; whatever the purpose of an individual author, there were certain ways of writing about Spain, tropes that built with each new travel account and which contributed to a generalized notion of "Spanish" character.

Most visitors, for instance, agreed that Spaniards brought immense energy to their devotions. In terms that echoed those of Joly, Marie-Catherine Le Jumel de Barneville, baroness d'Aulnoy, commented that

> there are only a few great preachers; there are some who are rather dramatic: but whether their sermons are good or bad, the Spaniards who hear them beat their chests from time to time with an extraordinary fervour, interrupting the preacher with the dolorous cries that emerge from their troubled consciences.[17]

On another occasion, d'Aulnoy recounted the story of Don Fernán de Toledo who, while visiting an ill aunt, found himself mistaken for a local holy man, the "Saint of Galicia," who was known for performing miracles. Don Fernán was quickly besieged by supplicants who would not let him leave until he had bestowed a blessing. D'Aulnoy went on:

> There was no point in speaking to them, the noise and the press of the crowd were so great that no one could hear him. They brought their rosaries to touch him, and those that were further away threw their beads at his head, along with hundreds of holy medallions. The most zealous began to cut his cloak and his clothes. It was then that his fear began to be very great lest, in order to multiply his relics, they should cut him to pieces.[18]

The veracity of this and other events in her *Relation du voyage d'Espagne* has been challenged; at the least, she certainly tended to embellish the truth. D'Aulnoy was best known for her collection of fairy tales; indeed, she perhaps coined the term with her *Les Contes des Fées*, and her stories of Spain may fall into the same category. One modern editor has suggested that she never visited Spain at all, instead composing her account through a combination of imagination and borrowings from earlier reports. It is more likely, however, that she spent at least some time in Spain. In any event, her *Relation*, presented as a series of 15 letters to a cousin living in France, was immensely popular and deeply influenced perceptions of Spain for more than a century.

It would be no exaggeration to call it the most famous of all early modern accounts of travel to Spain. By 1782, the *Relation* had appeared in 11 French editions, as well as 15 English, 1 Dutch, and 3 German editions. Notably, it was not translated into Spanish until the late nineteenth century.[19] D'Aulnoy's letters were popular not only for their vivid style and comic accounts of the foibles of the nobility but also for a particular, and negative, vision of Spaniards that accorded with her readers' expectations and resonated in several countries. Implicit in that representation was the suggestion that Spanish piety was based on false beliefs and that the enthusiastic devotion of the people was a sign of their gullibility. It was not only that, in their excitement, the people had mobbed the wrong person; she also scoffed at the very notion of the "Saint of Galicia," someone who had performed miracles "as it is pretended."[20]

The notion that public displays of religious emotion signified naïveté or even superstition was common and predated d'Aulnoy. Sir Charles Cornwallis was, from 1605 to 1609, the first English ambassador resident in Spain in nearly half a century. In addition to questioning the sincerity of nobles "knocking upon their breasts" in devotion to the Virgen de Atocha, he contended that "Spaniards universally are much inclined to religion and devotion but that with such immeasurable superstition and aptness to believe false miracles and fayned fables of the sanctity of any person whatsoever."[21] Similarly, Sir Richard Wynne toured Spain in 1623 while accompanying Prince Charles of Wales during the Prince's ultimately futile attempt to marry Maria Anna, Infanta of Spain. Wynne noted with disdain that,

> upon holydays all these people do but go from one cross to another shrine, with their beads in their hands, praying in a language they do not understand, and adoring of dumb images. So much zeal joined with blind devotion I never saw afore.[22]

Lewis Owen went further in his 1626 *Running Registre*, an account of English colleges and seminaries in foreign countries. Though Owen had lived in Spain as a Catholic exile (and perhaps had been ordained as a Jesuit), he had by this time developed an intensely anti-Catholic outlook. "These poore blinde people," he complained, "they will upon their knees howl and cry (like Baal's priests) unto the blessed Virgin Mary and the saints, and never call or pray to God for help."[23] Still later, Lady Ann Fanshawe was in Spain from 1664 to 1666 when she accompanied her husband, Richard Fanshawe, the English ambassador. Unlike many other travellers, she combined a generally positive view of the country with knowledge of the language. She nevertheless concluded that "the nation is most superstitiously devout in the Roman Catholic religion."[24] Thus, Madame D'Aulnoy, who published her letters slightly later and might have drawn on these or other accounts, would have surprised few when she lamented that Spain had so much wealth but is "a country where reason does not rule the heart."[25]

Some travellers found overt displays of emotion to be unbecoming, even profane. The Dutch Protestant Antoine de Brunel, whose commentary elsewhere was often rather biting, seemed more baffled than offended by the dances, the elaborate costumes of fantastical creatures, and the general laughter and drunkenness, than he encountered during the 1655 Corpus Christi celebrations in Madrid.[26] But Wynne, after watching a procession in Madrid to celebrate the canonization of San Isidro Labrador, noted that, among the friars and crosses,

> were Morris-dancers, pageants, trumpeters, and a number of other light things, far unfit to be mixed with anything that had a show of religion. At the sight of these things most of the people as they passed by, fell on their knees.[27]

There is a perhaps intentional ambiguity in Wynne's account as to whether the spectators knelt in response to the religious or the secular elements in the procession. When he saw Franciscan friars enter midnight Mass at Christmas dressed as shepherds while laughing and jumping, Jean Muret, a chaplain at the French embassy in the 1660s, grumbled that

> it seems to me that they could be content with that interior joy which is only seen by God alone and which has nothing to do with buffoonish rites of paganism; or, if they wish to show their joy by some external mark, it seems to me that the procession which they made a quarter of an hour later, and which was really as edifying as the rest had been scandalous, would be enough.[28]

But were these intense emotions even sincere? Many travellers expressed incredulity, contending that emotions so dramatic could only be bogus. The flagellants, for instance, that had so impressed Joly with their sombre procession, struck others as exhibitionist. In 1623, the English ambassador Walter Aston commented snidely on their "divers new inventions for martyrizing themselves."[29] The vigour of Holy Week flagellants in Madrid shocked Muret, who

> found, almost everywhere, men dressed in white, their shoulders bare and all bloody, and giving themselves such blows that they echoed from the vaults and sometimes splashed drops of blood on the faces of their helpers. In truth, I have never felt more sick at heart then when seeing such things.[30]

There was, he suggested, at least some exhibitionism in their efforts. Two Italian visitors in 1614 noted wryly that noble flagellants seemed to whip themselves only when they were near carriages bearing ladies, an opinion repeated by Madame de Villars later in the century.[31] Even Joly was not certain about the sincerity of noble penitents, for

> besides these companies of flagellants [the ones whom he admired] can be seen many others of quality, preceded by pages with torches, in Valladolid and most everywhere in Spain; even the seigneurs don't spare themselves any less than the others, and they are carried home bloody and half dead. Others carry even bigger and heavier crosses. It would be happy indeed if the devil, who is subtle, can be kept out of this display of vanity. What makes me wonder is that the pages and lackeys can identify [their masters], even though their clothes are covered.[32]

Accusations of hypocrisy extended far beyond the practice of flagellation. Madame d'Aulnoy recounted, with a bit of relish, that "the women who leave their homes to go to Mass hear a dozen of them, and are so distracted that one can easily see that they are focused on something other than their prayers." But,

> whenever the Host is raised, the women and the men each give themselves twenty blows of the fists on their chests. This makes such a racket that, the first time I heard it, I had a great fright and thought they were pounding each other.[33]

Despite their disapproval, many travellers expected such insincerity. Elsewhere, d'Aulnoy recounted a conversation she had had with the gentleman Don Frederic de Cardonne, who summarized the Spanish character. Among other qualities, he said, "they are prudent, jealous beyond measure, disinterested, poor economists, discrete, superstitious, zealous Catholics, at least in appearance."[34]

John Bradforth, a self-styled "serving man" who spent time in both the Spanish Netherlands and Spain itself, did not hesitate to accuse all Spaniards of hypocrisy, describing in derisive terms

> how they carry their beads openly to be seen by all people; how they pray in every corner of the streets so that every man may hear them; how they kneel at every man's door, before images knocking, crossing, sobbing, sighing, wringing their hands, wagging their heads, with such other unseemly manners, so that all men may perceive their repentance.[35]

A century later, in 1660, an anonymous English pamphlet, titled *The Character of Spain*, dismissed Spanish affective piety as "pretended zeal to Religion... a meer ceremony among them." The emphasis on ceremony, its author continued, had quite eroded the underlying beliefs, so that "Bible, Alchoran, Talmud, or Golden

Legion, all's one."[36] A Venetian ambassador summarized the opinions of many when he reported in 1683 that, despite the grandeur of the churches in Spain, the gifts of the faithful, and the great number of monks, it remained that the fervour "of the nobles and the magnates is mere hypocrisy, that of the fools and the vulgar is simple superstition."[37]

Even sincere attempts to inspire religious emotions might fall flat. Brunel condemned the sinfulness of the women who worked in public brothels, but acknowledged that "there is a day dedicated to exhorting them to penitence; it is a Friday in Lent." But the prostitutes' displays of emotion at this penitential service, according to Brunel, were either false and thus essentially meaningless, or else they resulted in permanent enclosure. As he described it, such interventions generally failed:

> they are conducted by one or two Alguacils [judges or officials] in the Church of las Recogidas… There, they are pushed over to the pulpit of the preacher, who does his best to touch their hearts, but only rarely with success. After he has exhorted them in vain for a long while to reform themselves, he descends from the pulpit and presents to them the crucifix, saying to them, 'Embrace our Lord,' and, if any of them do embrace him, they are taken and shut up in the Convent of the Repentant. But often most of them lower their gaze and shed tears, without raising a hand to what is presented, and with such a grimace continue their debauched lives. The story of the Magdalene, which is constantly told to them, does not make them want to imitate her.[38]

The prostitutes in Brunel's account wept. But they were the wrong sort of tears, shed from sorrow at their own situations rather than out of love for Christ.

****

I have focused thus far on negative reactions, but certainly there were travellers who were impressed by the emotionality of Spanish devotions. The Polish noble Jacob Sobieski complained during his 1611 visit to the shrine at Santiago de Compostela about the "superstition" of the pilgrims, while still acknowledging that he was impressed by depth of their devotion. Alfonso Ragona of Vicenza was impressed by the feast dedicating the new cathedral of Segovia in which he saw "men and women holding hands… running, running, dancing, jumping with different gestures and movements behind and in front of the processions… In sum, I took great pleasure and consolation."[39] Some travellers found themselves drawn in by the beauty of the religious art or by the solemnity of the rites they witnessed. A pair of German Protestants from Leipzig, Jakob (Diego) Cuelbis and Joel Koris, who travelled through much of Iberia in 1599–1600, experienced sympathetic emotional responses, much as did Joly during the flagellant procession. Describing the revered crucifix at the Convent of San Agustín in Burgos, Cuelbis noted that this object was usually kept in a shadowed niche, but "the people burst out crying in devout contemplation every time they are shown it, and one cannot see it without falling to their knees."[40] Similarly, the Dutchman Henri Cock, who settled in Spain after the excesses of the Calvinists in his native Gorkum, wrote of a crucifix at Balaguer in Catalonia. It was, he said, "much visited by pilgrims and citizens… it makes one shed tears and sigh if one really looks at it."[41]

Such reactions could be disconcerting for some visitors. Another Protestant, Robert Bargrave, was certainly no admirer of Spanish Catholicism but, when he visited the Capuchine convent of Santo Christo in Madrid in 1654, he was struck by the way in which the "truly devout Friers" unveiled an image of Christ. "It," he went on, "struck such a lively apprehension into my hart of *Christs* passion that I know not when I prayed with a more fervent devotion, though void of all Superstition, to the Image itself."[42] A lack of "superstition" was not, it seems, sufficient to prevent affective reactions to this ceremony. Don Frederic de Cardonne, in telling Madame d'Aulnoy of some of Spain's holiest places, was careful to distance himself from the beliefs upon which the Shrines of Montserrat or Pilar had been founded; "one pretends" that the Virgin Mary had appeared there or that the images are miraculous. Even so, he adds, there are many truly devout people in these places and "everywhere a certain air of solitude and devotion that touches those who visit there."[43] Here, as elsewhere, d'Aulnoy's account summarized the impressions of previous travellers: though the Spanish might be misled in their beliefs, the sensory experience of their solemn rites could be moving indeed.

****

Several trends should now be apparent. Most travellers agreed on the intense emotional energy that Spanish people brought to religious events. And they frequently questioned the validity of those emotions, attempting to find some way to deny their significance. Some contended that they were the product of superstition— usually exploited by friars who riled the people with fiery sermons or tall tales of miracles in order to open their wallets. Others viewed the passion of Spanish devotional practices as hypocrisy, a theatrical show of piety without substance. In both cases, there is the implication that the behaviours were suspect, that proper people would not, in the normal course of things, experience or express emotions in these ways. The former issue, of superstition, links intense emotion and irrationality. Although entirely at odds with contemporary Spanish understandings of religious emotions, this reflects ideas that were starting to emerge in some regions of Europe regarding reason, self-moderation, and emotion that would much later be described by Norbert Elias as part of what he called the "civilizing process."[44]

But it was not simply that the Spanish were passionate in their devotions. Rather, many travellers could not credit them with sincerity. Perhaps they felt compelled to reject what they saw, to dismiss it as mere artifice. For if they acknowledged that these emotions were real, it would mean that the Spanish must feel and display emotions completely alien to the observer, to the "European." Or else they simply could not understand how the sight of a crucifix could inspire overwhelming passion or were unable to comprehend the ensemble of passions that might lead one to whip oneself bloody in service of faith. But we might also consider the note of envy or even defensiveness in many visitors' reports. Early modern Spanish authors interpreted the open expression of religious emotions as evidence that one had opened his or her heart to god. When faced with the certainty, the fervour, the immersion in a communal identity that devout Spaniards displayed with their tears, sighs, and joy, travellers had to either acknowledge that validity of these devotions—as Bargrave, for one, was (perhaps reluctantly) able to do—or find a way to dismiss them in order to defend their own ideas of proper piety.

Some travellers sought to resolve this apparent paradox by commenting on the sensory environments. Consider again how Joly described the penitential procession, or the German students' surprise at how "the people burst out crying," or Ragona's pleasure in the noise of the crowd. In each case, there was an interplay of light and sound: the dark clothes of the flagellants, the sombre notes of the trumpet, the strident tones of a preacher, or the manner in which a holy effigy was drawn from shadow into light. Madame d'Aulnoy was not alone in commenting more than once on the opulent lighting in Spanish shrines, in apparent contrast to her expectations. The result was "a certain air" that affected visitors and created circumstances in which, they suggested, *anyone* might have an emotional response. Still, in all cases, there was an effort to explain what would, apparently, not have been immediately comprehensible to their readers.

Many Protestant travellers, of course, represented Spanish affective piety as evidence of the spiritual and intellectual barrenness of Catholicism. As such, their comments were part of larger efforts to discredit Catholicism and could be directed at Catholics anywhere. In fact, Protestant travellers to other Catholic countries found no lack of religious practices to which they objected. They sometimes shared Bargrave's concern about falling under the "spell" of Catholic superstition. In one case, at least, visiting Protestants signalled their resistance through inappropriate emotional gestures. Sir Thomas Browne complained, "At a solemn prosession I have wept abundantly while my consorts, blind with opposition and prejudice, have fallen into an accesse of scorne and laughter."[45] Browne did not specify where this had happened, but it is likely to have been Italy or France. One might then discuss the accounts of Protestant travellers in Spain as simply other manifestations of such "opposition and prejudice" or surmise that they wrote of Spanish practices in formulaic terms that confirmed what was already well known.

Still, these reports indicate that emotional practices were one of the ways in which Protestants and Catholics distinguished themselves from each other. Protestants not only saw Catholics as superstitious or suggested that their supposed piety was a sham but also understood stereotypically Catholic emotional responses as somehow making mockery of the serious business of religion. One effect of all this was a feminization of Spanish religious practices. This is explicit, of course, in complaints about the loud sighs of female worshippers. But the contrast between the ways in which Protestant visitors described Spanish affective devotion and their implicit expectation that faith be defined by reason, restraint, and prudence—qualities typically coded as male—characterized that devotion as irrational, unseemly, and exhibitionist, and thus as feminine.

Yet it is not sufficient to note only that Protestants drew sharp contrasts between their ideals of proper emotional norms and those of Spain and thus that emotions were a key means of differentiating between Catholicism and Protestant practices. Catholic visitors, like Jean Muret, also described Spanish religious practices in terms that raised questions about their sincerity or their appropriateness. Even those accounts that praised Spanish devotions or expressed the travellers' own emotional reactions, such as Joly's awestruck impressions of the flagellant procession, served to represent Spain as different, even otherworldly. Although political tensions underlay much of this, the connotations of all these opinions about Spanish religious emotions complemented other generally accepted ideas about Spain, and thus acted to intensify them. Like the "Black Legend" of Spain's backwardness and intolerance, the stereotype of a particular kind of Spanish affective piety has endured for centuries. As such, these travel accounts contributed to what we might think of as an externally imposed emotional regime, an attempt to define and judge a society's character through its perceived emotional norms. This had little direct impact on most Spaniards who, of course, did not read these accounts. But foreign ridicule did embarrass the government which, in the late seventeenth and especially the eighteenth century, took steps to moderate aspects of religious practice that were now seen as indecorous, especially during major processions. Travellers' accounts, therefore, make clear that the sixteenth and seventeenth centuries were a period during which emotional norms not only became confessional markers but also national ones.

Notes

1 Barthélemy Joly, "Voyage de Barthélemy Joly en Espagne (1603–1604)," ed. Lucien Barrau Dihigo. *Revue hispanique* 20 (1909), 460–618. The manuscript bears the title: *Voyage faict par M. Barthelemy Joly, conseller et ausmonier du roy, en Espagne, avec M. Boucherat, abbe et general de l'ordre de Cisteaux.* Yet Nicholas II Boucherat was not elected Abbot until October 1604; as José García Mercadal points out, the title is a later addition to the manuscript. See Mercadal, "Bartolome Joly. Viaje por España," in *Viajes de extrangeros por Espana y Portugal* (Madrid: Aguilar, 1959), 46. I am here following Marc Dalmau Vinyal's suggestion that Joly travelled with Edmond de la Croix; see Dalmau Vinyals, "El viatge de Barthelemy Joly amb l'abat Edmond de la Croix als monestirs cistercencs de la Corona d'Aragó a inicis del segle XVII," *Revista de Catalunya* 289 (2015): 11–21.
2 Joly, "Voyage," 553: "le faste de ceste nation, toute confite au dehors et es apparences exterieures."
3 Joly, "Voyage," 554:

En leurs predications, ilz usent d'une vehemence trop grande, au dire mesme d'un entre eux, en une de ses predications imprimees. Esta gravedad y compostura, esta moderacion en el decir es la que me contenta y appruevo, y confiesso que soy del parecer que reprueva predicadores vocingleros que hazen gestos y meneos provacativos a risa, que lloran y piensan que imitan a Christo, que con tanta suavidad abriava su boca y enseñava a todos. C'est pourquoy deux choses me troubloient aux sermons d'Espagne, ceste vehemence extreme, presque turbulente, du predicateur et les soupirs continuelz des femmes, si grans et vehemens qu'ilz perturboient toute l'attention.

4 Joly, "Voyage," 556:

Mais la dolente procession des penitens, que vont par la ville, attiroient asses nostre vue pour lors eslognee de toute vanité. Ilz se fouetent outrageusement et passent en procession sur la nuict, composee de tant de tristesse qu'il n'est cœur si dur qui ne s'en esmeuve. Une grande croix noire precede, et un quidam aussy noir, semé de larmes; suit à la sombre lueur de quelques torches et des astres flambeaux, une muette trouppe noire et toute couverte, hormis les yeulx et les espaules, sur lesquelles ces soldats determinés menent englantement les mains, animés à ce triste combat par le son d'une lugubre trompette noire, dont le tarrare s'accorde avec les cliquetis des escorgés et les helas des femmes et populace, qui compatit à la douleur, faict une musique trop dolente, dont les souspirs penetrans par l'oreille touchent au vif et mattent d'attrition d'avoir tant offensé Dieu, non moings que ces battus, que chacun se propose d'imiter en pareille ou autre sorte de sensible penitence…

5 On medieval travel to Spain, see *Viajes y viajeros en la España medieval: actas del V Curso de Cultura Medieval, celebrado en Aguilar de Campóo (Palencia) del 20 al 23 de septiembre de 1993*, ed. José Luis Hernando, Miguel Ángel García Guinea, and Pedro Luis Huerta Huerta (Madrid: Fundación Santa María la Real, Centro de Estudios del Románico, 1997).

6 For discussions of Spanish difference in early modern thought, see J.N. Hillgarth, *The Mirror of Spain, 1500–1700: The Formation of a Myth* (Ann Arbor: University of Michigan Press, 2000); Henry Kamen, *Imagining Spain: Historical Myth and National Identity* (New Haven, CT: Yale University Press, 2008); and Barbara Fuchs, *Exotic Nation: Maurophilia and the Construction of Early Modern Spain* (Philadelphia: University of Pennsylvania Press, 2009). On the "Black Legend" in particular, see Sverker Arnoldsson, *La Leyenda Negra: Estudios Sobre Sus Orígines* (Göteborg: Elander, 1960); William S. Maltby, *The Black Legend in England* (Durham, NC: Duke University Press, 1971); Joseph Pérez, *La leyenda negra* (Madrid: Gadir, 2009); and Ricardo García Cárcel, "Reflexiones sobre la leyenda negra," in *Las vecindades de las monarquías ibéricas*, ed. José Javier Ruiz Ibáñez (Madrid: Fondo de Cultura Económica, 2013), 43–80.

7 Hillgarth, *Mirror of Spain*, viii.

8 Michel de Montaigne, *The Complete Essays*, trans. M.A. Screech (London: Penguin, 2003), III:9, 1100.

9 Susan Karant-Nunn, *The Reformation of Feeling: Shaping the Religious Emotions in Early Modern Germany* (Oxford: Oxford University Press, 2010). See also her "'Christians' Mourning and Lament Should not Be Like the Heathens': The Suppression of Religious Emotion in the Reformation," in *Confessionalization in Europe, 1555–1700*, ed. John M. Headley, Hans J. Hillerbrand, and Anthony J. Papalas (Aldershot: Ashgate, 2004), 107–129; and "Catholic Intensity in Post-Reformation Germany: Preaching on the Passion and Catholic Identity in the Sixteenth and Seventeenth Centuries," in *Politics and Reformations: Studies in Honor of Thomas A. Brady, Jr.*, ed. Christopher Ocker, Michael Printy, Peter Starenko, and Peter Wallace (Leiden: Brill, 2007), 373–396.

10 Francois Soyer, "The Public Baptism of Muslims in Early Modern Spain and Portugal: Forging Communal Identity through Collective Emotional Display," *Journal of*

Religious History 39 (2015): 506–523. See also see Barbara H. Rosenwein, *Emotional Communities in the Early Middle Ages* (Ithaca, NY: Cornell University Press, 2006); and William M. Reddy, *The Navigation of Feeling: A Framework for the History of Emotions* (Cambridge: Cambridge University Press, 2001).

11 For instance, Elena Carrera, "The Emotions in Sixteenth-Century Spanish Spirituality," *Journal of Religious History* 31 (2007): 235–252; and eadem, "*Pasión* and *afección* in Teresa of Avila and Francisco de Osuna," *Bulletin of Spanish Studies* 84 (2007): 175–191.
12 Steven Mullaney, *The Reformation of Emotions in the Age of Shakespeare* (Chicago, IL: University of Chicago Press, 2015).
13 Monique Scheer, "Are Emotions a Kind of Practice (and Is That What Makes Them Have a History)?," *History and Theory* 51, no. 2 (2012): 215.
14 William A. Christian, Jr., "Provoked Religious Weeping in Early Modern Spain," in *Religion and Emotion: Approaches and Interpretations*, ed. John Corrigan (Oxford: Oxford University Press, 2004), 34.
15 For an extensive, nearly comprehensive, list of travel accounts, see Raymond Foulché-Delbosc, *Bibliographie des voyages en Espagne et en Portugal* (Paris: H. Welter, 1896).
16 Mullaney, *The Reformation of Emotions*, 49.
17 Marie-Catherine d'Aulnoy, *Relation du voyage d'Espagne*, 3 vols. (Paris: Claude Barbin, 1691), 3:349:

> Il y a peu de grands Predicateurs: il s'en trouve quelques-uns qui sont assez pathetiques; mais soit que ces Sermons soient bons ou mauvais, les Espagnols qui s'y trouvent s'y frappent la poitrine de tems en tems, avec une ferveur extraordinaire, interrompant le Predicateur par des cris douloureux de componction.

18 D'Aulnoy, *Relation*, 3:226–227:

> Il n'estoit point au fait; il avoit beau parler, on ne l'écoutoit pas tant le bruit & la presse estoit grande; on lui faisoit toucher des chapelets, & celles qui estoient éloignées les lui jettoient à la teste avec des centaines de médailles. Les plus zelées commencerent à lui couper son manteau & son habit. Ce fut alors qu'il eut la peur entiere, que pour multiplier ses reliques on ne le taillast par morceaux.

19 See Raymond Foulché-Delbosc's introduction to a reprinting of the 1692 English translation of the *Relation*: Marie-Catherine d'Aulnoy, *Travels into Spain*, ed. Raymond Foulché-Delbosc (London: Routledge, 2014 [1930]), i–lxxiv; Hillgarth, *Mirror of Spain*, 60–62. On fairy tales, see Marie-Catherine d'Aulnoy, *Les Contes des fées*, 4 vols. (Paris: Claude Barbin, 1697–8).
20 D'Aulnoy, *Relation*, 3:225: "C'est un Saint qui àce que l'on prétend a fait des miracles."
21 Sir Charles Cornwallis, in British Library MS Harley 7007, ff. 255r–v, and MS Cotton Vesp. C.X., ff. 10v–11, as cited in Hillgarth, *Mirror of Spain*, 131.
22 Sir Simonds d'Ewes, *Autobiography and Correspondence*, ed. J.O. Halliwell-Phillips (London: Richard Bentley, 1845), 2:417. On Wynne's mission, see Glyn Redworth, *The Prince and the Infanta: The Cultural Politics of the Spanish Match* (New Haven, CT: Yale University Press, 2003).
23 Lewis Owen, *The Running Registre: Recording a True Relation of the State of the English Colledges, Seminaries and Cloysters in all forraine Parts* (London: Robert Milbourne, 1626), 68.
24 Ann Fanshawe, *The Memoirs of Lady Fanshawe, Wife of Sir Richard Fanshawe, bart., Written by Herself* (London: Henry Colburn and Richard Bentley, 1830), 210.
25 D'Aulnoy, *Relation*, 3:226–227: "un païs où la raison n'a guére d'empire sur le cœur."
26 Antoine de Brunel, *Voyage d'Espagne, curieux, historique et politique, fait en l'année 1655…* (Paris: Robert de Ninville, 1666), 110–114.
27 D'Ewes, *Autobiography and Correspondence*, 451.
28 Jean Muret, *Lettres écrites de Madrid en 1666 et 1667*, ed. Alfred Morel-Fatio (Paris: Bonnedame et fils, 1879), 47:

il me semble qu'ils pourroient se contenter de cette joye interieure qui n'est veüe que de Dieu seul et qui ne tient point des solemnitez boufonnes du paganisme; ou bien, s'ils veulent montrer leur joye par quelque marque exterieure, il me semble que ce seroit assez d'une procession qu'ils firent un quart d'heure aprez et qui fust veritablement aussi edificative que le reste avoit esté scandaleus.

29 Walter Aston, BL, MS Additional 36,449, f. 45., as cited in Hillgarth, *Mirror of Spain*, 138, n. 45.
30 Muret, *Lettres*, 65:

je trouvay presque partout des hommes revetus de blanc, les epaules nues et toutes sanglantes, et se donnant de si grand coups, qu'outre que la voute en retentissoit, ils faisoient quelquefois eclabousser les goutes sur le visage des assistant. En verité, je n'ai jamais en plus mal au cœur que voyant ces choses.

31 Hillgarth, *Mirror of Spain*, 138–139. Madame de Villars was the wife of Pierre de Villars, French ambassador to Spain at various points between the 1660s and 1680s. As Hillgarth notes, Spanish flagellents were a source of both disgust and fascination for many visitors.
32 Joly, "Voyage," 556–557:

Outre ces compagnies de battus se voyent plusieurs autres de qualité, precedez de pages avec flambeaux, à Valladolid et ainsy par toute l'Espagne; mesme ces seigneurs ne s'espargnent rien moings que les autres, jusque à estre remenés par dessoubs les bras, senglans et à demy mortz; d'autres portent des croix plus grosses et pesantes qu'eux; bien hureux si le diable, qui est subtil, n'y mesle point la vanité: ce qui me le faict croire, est ces pages et laquais qui les descouvrent, contraire à la couverture de leur habit.

33 D'Aulnoy, *Relation*, 3:291:

Les femmes qui vont à la Messe, hors de chez elles, en entendent une douzaine, & marquent tans de distraction, que l'on voit bien qu'elles sont, occupées d'autre chose que de leurs Prieres… Lorsqu'on leve Nôtre Seigneur, les Femmes & les Hommes se donnent chacun une vingtaine de coups de poing dan la poutrine; ce qui fait un tel bruit, que le premiere fois que je l'entendis, j'ûs une grande frayeur, & je crûs que l'on se battoit.

34 D'Aulnoy, *Relation*, 1:184: "ils sont prudens, jaloux sans mesure, des-interessez, peu œconomes, cachez, superstitieux, fort Catholiques, du moins en apparence."
35 John Bradforth, *The copye of a letter, sent by Iohn Bradforth to the right honorable lordes the Erles of Arundel, Darbie, Shrewsburye, and Penbroke, declaring the nature of the Spaniardes…* (Wesel?: J. Lambrecht?, 1556?), n.p.:

how thei carie their beades openly, to be sene of all people: how they praye in euerye corner of the streates, that euery man maye heare them: how they knele at euery mans dore, before Imags knockinge, crossinge, Sobbinge, syghinge wringinge their handes, waggynge their heades, with suche other vnsemelye maners, that all menne maye perceiue their repentaunce.

36 *The Character of Spain or, an Epitome of Their Virtues and Vices* (London: Nath. Brooke, 1660), 78–79.
37 Nicolò Barrozzi and Guglielmo Berchet, *Relazioni degli stati europei lette al Senato degli ambasciatori veneti nel secolo demimosettimo*, Series 1, Spagna, 2 vols. (Venice: Pietro Naratovich, 1856–60), 2:479: "Tutto ciò non toglie che penetrandosi nella midolla, non si discerna essere il credere ne'grandi e ne'principali una mera ipocrisia; negl'idioti e nel volgo una semplice superstizione."
38 Brunel, *Voyage*, 134–135:

qu'il y air pourtant un iour dedié à les exhorter à la repentance; c'est un Vendredy de Caresme, qu'elles sont conduites par un ou deux Alguazils à l'Eglise de las Recogidas... Là on les met au pied de la Chaire du Predicateur, qui fait son mieux pour leur toucher le cœur, mais il en vient rarement à bout, apres les avoir assez long temps exhortées en vain, à s'amander, il descend de la Chaire, & leur presenre le Crucifix, en disant, levoicy, le Seigneurm embrassez-le, & si alors il y en a quelqu'une qui l'embrasse, on la prend & on l'enferme dans le Convent des Repenties. Mais le plus souvent elles ne sont que baisser la veuë & ietter des larmes, sans porter la main à ce qu'on leur presente, & avec cette grimace continuent leur vie débordée, & l'Histoire de la Magdelaine qu'on leur prosne tout au long, ne les touche pas tant qu'elles vueillent l'imiter.

39 Alfonso Ragona, "El viaje a España del noble vincentino Alfonso Ragona (1557–1561)," ed. Gabriel Llompart, in *Gesammelte Aufsätze zur Kulturgeschichte Spaniens* 27 (Münster Westfalen: Aschendorff, 1973), 406: "huomini et donne, quali si tenevano per mano... correndo, ballando, saltando con diversi gesti et movimenti in dietro et inanzi delle processioni... In somma: hebbi gradissimo spasso et consolation."

40 Diego Cuelbis, *Thesoro Chorographico de las Espannas*, Biblioteca nacional de España MSS 18472 (nineteenth-century copy of BL Harley MS 3822 by Pascual de Gayangos), ff. 18r–v: "gente llora por la debota contemplacion cada vez quando lo muestran y no se puede ver sin caer a las rodillas." See also Salvador Raya Retamero, *Andalucía en 1599 vista por Diego Cuelbis* (Benálmadena: Caligrama, 2002). Henri Cock also mentions this crucifix, but only briefly, *Description de l'Espagne par Jehan Lhermite et Henri Cock*, ed. Jérôme-P. Devos (Paris: S.E.V.P.E.N., 1969), 112.

41 Hillgarth, *Mirror of Spain*, 144–145.

42 *The Travel Diary of Robert Bargrave, Levant Merchant, 1647–1656*, ed. Michael G. Brennan (London: Hakluyt Society, 1999), 202–204 (emphasis in original).

43 D'Aulnoy, *Relation*, 1: 160: "par tout un certain air de solitude & de devotion qui touche ceux qui s'y rendent... L'on pretend."

44 Norbert Elias, *The Civilizing Process* (Oxford: Blackwell, 1994).

45 Thomas Browne, *Religio Medici* (London: Andrew Crooke, 1645), 5–6; Hillgarth, *Mirror of Spain*, 133.

Bibliography

Arnoldsson, Sverker. *La Leyenda Negra: Estudios Sobre Sus Orígines*. Göteborg: Elander, 1960.

Barrozzi, Nicolò and Guglielmo Berchet. *Relazioni degli stati europei lette al Senato degli ambasciatori veneti nel secolo demimosettimo*, Series 1, Spagna, 2 vols. Venice: Pietro Naratovich, 1856–60.

Bradforth, John. *The Copye of a Letter, Sent by Iohn Bradforth to the Right Honorable Lordes the Erles of Arundel, Darbie, Shrewsburye, and Penbroke, Declaring the Nature of the Spaniardes...* Wesel?: J. Lambrecht?, 1556?.

Brennan, Michael G., ed. *The Travel Diary of Robert Bargrave, Levant Merchant, 1647–1656*. London: Hakluyt Society, 1999.

Browne, Thomas. *Religio Medici*. London: Andrew Crooke, 1645.

Brunel, Antoine de. *Voyage d'Espagne, curieux, historique et politique, fait en l'année 1655...* Paris: Robert de Ninville, 1666.

Carrera, Elena. "The Emotions in Sixteenth-Century Spanish Spirituality," *Journal of Religious History* 31 (2007): 235–252.

Carrera, Elena. "*Pasión* and *afección* in Teresa of Avila and Francisco de Osuna," *Bulletin of Spanish Studies* 84 (2007): 175–191.Christian, William A., Jr. "Provoked Religious

Weeping in Early Modern Spain," in *Religion and Emotion: Approaches and Interpretations*, ed. John Corrigan, 33–49.Oxford: Oxford University Press, 2004.

The Character of Spain or, an Epitome of Their Virtues and Vices. London: Nath. Brooke, 1660.

Cock, Henri. *Description de l'Espagne par Jehan Lhermite et Henri Cock*, ed. Jérôme-P. Devos. Paris: S.E.V.P.E.N., 1969.

d'Aulnoy, Marie-Catherine. *Les Contes des fées*, 4 vols. Paris: Claude Barbin, 1697–8.

d'Aulnoy, Marie-Catherine. *Relation du voyage d'Espagne*, 3 vols. Paris: Claude Barbin, 1691.

d'Aulnoy, Marie-Catherine. *Travels into Spain*, ed. Raymond Foulché-Delbosc. London: Routledge, 2014 [1930].

d'Ewes, Simonds. *Autobiography and Correspondence*, ed. J.O. Halliwell-Phillips. London: Richard Bentley, 1845.

Elias, Norbert. *The Civilizing Process*. Oxford: Blackwell, 1994.

Fanshawe, Ann. *The Memoirs of Lady Fanshawe, Wife of Sir Richard Fanshawe, bart., Written by Herself*. London: Henry Colburn and Richard Bentley, 1830.

Foulché-Delbosc, Raymond. *Bibliographie des voyages en Espagne et en Portugal*. Paris: H. Welter, 1896.

Fuchs, Barbara. *Exotic Nation: Maurophilia and the Construction of Early Modern Spain*. Philadelphia: University of Pennsylvania Press, 2009.

García Cárcel, Ricardo. "Reflexiones sobre la leyenda negra," in *Las vecindades de las monarquías ibéricas*, ed. José Javier Ruiz Ibáñez, 43–80. Madrid: Fondo de Cultura Económica, 2013.

Hernando, José Luis, Miguel Ángel García Guinea, and Pedro Luis Huerta Huerta, eds. *Viajes y viajeros en la España medieval: actas del V Curso de Cultura Medieval, celebrado en Aguilar de Campóo (Palencia) del 20 al 23 de septiembre de 1993*. Madrid: Fundación Santa María la Real, Centro de Estudios del Románico, 1997.

Hillgarth, J.N. *The Mirror of Spain, 1500–1700: The Formation of a Myth*. Ann Arbor: University of Michigan Press, 2000.

Joly, Barthélemy. "Voyage de Barthélemy Joly en Espagne (1603–1604)," ed. Lucien Barrau Dihigo. *Revue hispanique* 20 (1909): 460–618.

Kamen, Henry. *Imagining Spain: Historical Myth and National Identity*. New Haven, CT: Yale University Press, 2008.

Karant-Nunn, Susan. "Catholic Intensity in Post-Reformation Germany: Preaching on the Passion and Catholic Identity in the Sixteenth and Seventeenth Centuries," in *Politics and Reformations: Studies in Honor of Thomas A. Brady, Jr.*, ed. Christopher Ocker, Michael Printy, Peter Starenko, and Peter Wallace, 373–396. Leiden: Brill, 2007.

Karant-Nunn, Susan. "'Christians' Mourning and Lament Should Not Be like the Heathens': The Suppression of Religious Emotion in the Reformation," in *Confessionalization in Europe, 1555–1700*, ed. John M. Headley, Hans J. Hillerbrand, and Anthony J. Papalas, 107–129. Aldershot: Ashgate, 2004.

Karant-Nunn, Susan. *The Reformation of Feeling: Shaping the Religious Emotions in Early Modern Germany*. Oxford: Oxford University Press, 2010.

Maltby, William S. *The Black Legend in England*. Durham, NC: Duke University Press, 1971.

Mercadal, José García. "Bartolome Joly. Viaje por España," in *Viajes de extrangeros por Espana y Portugal*, ed. José García Mercadal, 46–125. Madrid: Aguilar, 1959.

Montaigne, Michel de. *The Complete Essays*, trans. M.A. Screech. London: Penguin, 2003.

Mullaney, Steven. *The Reformation of Emotions in the Age of Shakespeare*. Chicago, IL: University of Chicago Press, 2015.

Muret, Jean. *Lettres écrites de Madrid en 1666 et 1667*, ed. Alfred Morel-Fatio. Paris: Bonnedame et fils, 1879.

Owen, Lewis. *The Running Registre: Recording a True Relation of the State of the English Colledges, Seminaries and Cloysters in all forraine Parts*. London: Robert Milbourne, 1626.

Pérez, Joseph. *La leyenda negra*. Madrid: Gadir, 2009.

Ragona, Alfonso. "El viaje a España del noble vincentino Alfonso Ragona (1557–1561)," in *Gesammelte Aufsätze zur Kulturgeschichte Spaniens* 27, ed. Gabriel Llompart, 397–418. Münster Westfalen: Aschendorff, 1973.

Reddy, William M. *The Navigation of Feeling: A Framework for the History of Emotions*. Cambridge: Cambridge University Press, 2001.

Redworth, Glyn. *The Prince and the Infanta: The Cultural Politics of the Spanish Match*. New Haven, CT: Yale University Press, 2003.

Retamero, Raya. *Andalucía en 1599 vista por Diego Cuelbis*. Benálmadena: Caligrama, 2002.

Rosenwein, Barbara H. *Emotional Communities in the Early Middle Ages*. Ithaca, NY: Cornell University Press, 2006.

Scheer, Monique. "Are Emotions a Kind of Practice (and Is That What Makes Them Have a History)?," *History and Theory* 51, no. 2 (2012): 193–220.

Soyer, Francois. "The Public Baptism of Muslims in Early Modern Spain and Portugal: Forging Communal Identity through Collective Emotional Display," *Journal of Religious History* 39 (2015): 506–523.

Vinyals, Marc Dalmau. "El viatge de Barthelemy Joly amb l'abat Edmond de la Croix als monestirs cistercencs de la Corona d'Aragó a inicis del segle XVII," *Revista de Catalunya* 289 (2015): 11–21.

10

SENSIBLE DISTANCES

The colonial projections of Therese Huber and E. G. Wakefield

Lisa O'Connell

1

During the eighteenth century, the South Pacific became available to European expansion, and specifically to British exploration, trade and penal settlement. Recent scholarship has shown that this expansion occurred without agreement as to its function and benefits. As Jonathan Lamb has argued, the establishment of Britain's Pacific dominions was characterised less by deliberate policy than by confusion in the face of the unknown.[1] In this sense, the 'enlightened' engagement with the Pacific looks back to the tropes of wonder and curiosity that organised early modern speculations about the austral unknown as much as it looks forward to the increasingly systematised conceptions of empire that came to organise modern settler colonial projects. First-wave Pacific voyage literature typically emphasised the ties of fellow-feeling and decency which bound Europeans to the inhabitants of the newly chartered regions, drawing upon universalist concepts of enlightenment and civilised advancement on the one hand, and conventional literary tropes of sentiment, friendship, sympathetic exchange, on the other. Erasmus Darwin's allegorical poem, *The Temple of Nature; or, the Origin of Society* (1803), figured civilisation's advancement as a steady global march of 'Reason, Sympathy and Hymen', for instance, while Johann Reinhold Forster memorably wrote of his encounter with native Tahitians on Cook's second voyage as an engagement that evoked the *sensus communis* of all mankind. 'Their hearts', he wrote, 'are capable of the warmest attachment, of the most generous friendship, and of the most tender connexions...[W]hat a great and venerable blessing benevolence is...when...it connect[s] all mankind...into one family...'.[2]

For all its immediacy and emotion, however, the early Pacific colonialism of sensibility, as we might call it, barely lasted into the nineteenth century. In the wake of the establishment of the Botany Bay penal colony, and in the aftermath of 1789, the Pacific was increasingly figured as a place of settlement (understood in Australia's case as an occupation of *terra nullius*). The South Seas became a site of a new kind of imaginary—one dedicated, in part, to the post-revolutionary reconstitution of social order. Drawing on two very different early-settler colonial fictions, this paper explores an unlikely connection between literary sensibility and the fantastic forms of colonial projection it enabled, on the one hand, and the social policies of benevolent improvement that marked the Australasian colonies from their beginnings, on the other. Therese Huber's *Abentheuer auf einer Reise nach Neu-Holland* [Adventures on a Voyage to New Holland], the first novel set in the new Australian penal colony, used a language of sentimental progressivism to figure the redemptive power of love and family in the wake of Revolutionary failure, placing women at the centre of a complex and equivocal settler vision. Edward Gibbon Wakefield's *Letter from Sydney* (1829), by contrast, was an early statement of 'systematic colonization', a conservative model of politically free, self-governing colonial society that Wakefield first conceived as a trenchant critique of Britain's sentimental mismanagement of the penal colony. Neither Wakefield nor Huber ever visited Australia. Yet even as their fictional projections onto colonial space expressed very different political wills and desires, they revealed an unexpected set of emotional confluences underpinning the post-revolutionary settler imaginary.

Therese Huber was very much a woman of her time. Born in 1764, and raised as the highly educated daughter of the Göttingen classical philologist Christian Gottlob Heyne, she was remembered by Wilhelm von Humbolt as the most outstanding woman he ever met.[3] In her youth, she married Georg Forster, the German-born, English-educated naturalist and revolutionary who, as a young man, had accompanied his father, Johann Reinhold Forster, on Cook's second voyage. After the younger Forster's early death in 1793 left her in debt, Huber turned to journalism and fiction writing, producing 6 novels and more than 60 stories, including a revolutionary novel, *Die Familie Seldorf* (1795–1796), which remains her most remembered work.[4] Well known to German literary historians, Huber's fiction is strikingly under-read in the broader scholarship of British and European romanticism and colonialism. The existing anglophone commentary on the *Abentheuer*, mostly generated by Australian-based Germanists and Forster scholars, has had little or no uptake in discussions of early Australian settler fiction, for instance.[5] This situation stands in need of correction even if, unlike the *Abentheuer* itself which was first translated in 1966, most of Huber's work remains unavailable in English translation.[6]

As a prolific female writer of the 1790s well-versed in anglophone thought and writing of the day, Huber stands as a compelling European counterpart to progressive English writers such as Mary Wollstonecraft, Mary Robinson and Elizabeth Inchbald, whom she read, and whose commitment both to the fiction of sensibility and to a burgeoning concept of women's rights she uniquely extended to the South Seas.[7] The *Abentheuer*, an epistolary novel published under her second husband Ludwig Huber's name and serialised in the German women's magazine *Flora* in 1793–1794, was her first effort at fiction.[8] It ventriloquised Georg Forster's voice so as to recast his tragic demise in global terms. Drawing heavily on his letters and travel writing, it returned him to a fictional New Holland that was now in part transformed by a distinctly feminised settler ethic.

Georg Forster was, of course, a towering figure of enlightened progressivism. At a young age, he had published his own account of Cook's second voyage, *A Voyage Round the World* (1777), widely celebrated for its freshness and modernity.[9] Prominent in German intellectual circles (debating with Kant and others), Forster was an outspoken critic of the French *ancien régime*, writing a preface to the German edition of Thomas Paine's *Rights of Man* (1792), and mixing with Paine, Wollstonecraft and other radicals in France.[10] Historian Reinhart Koselleck argues in his essay on the emergence of the modern concept of emancipation that Forster was the first person to 'subsume the Kantian philosophy of history' into a project of general human emancipation.[11] We can add that for Forster the project of liberation was global. In 'Cook der Entdecker', published in 1787, just a year after his endorsement of the proposal to establish a new British penal colony at Botany Bay, Forster celebrated Cook's voyages as the dawn of a new age for 'the…advance of our whole kind towards a certain goal of perfection', giving South Seas utopianism a newly radical inflection.[12]

In the immediate aftermath of the French revolution, Forster and his circle enacted emancipation in their everyday lives. After Huber and Forster's troubled marriage had come undone, they lived openly in a ménage à trois with her then husband-to-be, journalist Ludwig Huber. In progressive terms, their lives were widely regarded as being located at a cutting edge where the politics of liberation, the ethics of sensibility and advanced secular knowledge intersected. After France's victory over the German army in 1792, Therese and Ludwig fled to Switzerland with her children, and Forster became one of the Rhineland's revolutionary leaders. He arrived in Paris during the Terror, to represent the Republic of Mainz at the capital of liberation. Following the Prussian reclamation of the territory, however, he was condemned by the Jacobins and denounced as a traitor in Germany. Forsaken by his former allies and cut adrift from his family, Forster died a pauper's death in Paris in January 1794.

Taking Forster's end-of-life isolation and disgrace as its point of departure, Huber's *Abentheuer* tells the story of Rudolph, an erstwhile revolutionary in flight from the Terror, who, in his political disappointment, travels to the Botany Bay colony en route to China and India. His opening letter, addressed to Reinette and Berthold (the fictional Therese and Ludwig Huber), his only remaining 'friends in Germany', explains his departure:

> No, my friends, I repeat: your tender sensibilities lead you astray if you number this journey among my misfortunes. The opportunity to leave ★ ★ ★ is a proof that Fortune is smiling on me once more; the first step towards restoring me to all of you and to myself is to flee from the Europe that

now rejects me and to seek security and peace in a pure and youthful land where Nature shall redeem the dregs of degenerate race. Misled by false theorising what incredible actions did I not perform in the cause of Freedom: heedless of the scenes of misery, hatred and baseness which sprang up around me and which I myself helped to create I marched on bravely and steadfastly towards a future that was to improve and reward mankind.[13]

Misled by 'false theorising' (and equally wary of 'tender sensibilities'), Rudolph wishes to be restored to 'Nature' and 'reconcile[d] ... to mankind once more', as he later puts it (33). Posed in these melancholic terms, his act of *Weltflucht* retains little of the expansive optimism of the two Forsters' earlier Pacific adventures. While perhaps traces of the elder Forster's sentimental colonialism are apparent, nothing remains of the younger Forster's overweening conception of 'the general enlightenment of all civilized peoples'.[14]

That Huber's text belongs to quite another historical moment is clear when Rudolph figures himself as an abject outsider, a 'citizen of the world, rejected by every well-ordered community' (37). Undertaking his journey on a convict ship, he poses as a poor English free-settler, remarking ironically on his secret kinship with the prisoners: 'I cannot but laugh to think that I am being most readily conveyed for money to a place whither, were I but known, I would perhaps be transported *gratis*, and most rudely into the bargain' (23). On board the ship, the truth of European society is revealed as a story of systemic injustice, criminalisation and oppression. It is nonetheless a society whose transportation to the antipodean *terra nullius* offers some possibility of social redemption, if not the salvation of Rudolph himself.

That possibility unfolds as an inset story about a young English widow, Frances Belton, whom Rudolph befriends, and who has been convicted for theft and implicated in the murder of an abusive fellow servant. At the novel's beginning, she is held beneath the deck in the transport ship with her young daughter, Betty, before acting heroically to save an unwanted newborn (later named Clara) from the murderous intentions of its mother, a 'wretched prostitute' (33). The child's rescue and subsequent care under Frances's guardianship is one of a series of sentimental tableaux that structure the *Abenthueur* as a narrative of global sensibility. Each 'touching moment', which 'overwhelm[s]' Rudolph with 'emotion' (22), works incrementally to rouse him from despair. In this way, his journey unfolds as a staged itinerary of emotion as stirred by his recollection of a delicate rose bush by the Rhine (22–23), by the moving sight of an 'honest Hottentot' family on the South African Cape (36–37) and, finally, by the happy reunion of Frances with her husband, Henry Belton, on Norfolk Island (65).

Upon arrival at Sydney Cove, however, Rudolph observes that the penal colony, once a 'natural paradise', is now disfigured by 'a lamentable race of men' with 'no motive for virtue'(49). These remarks amount a pointed rebuttal of Forster's own expectation of its capacity for rehabilitation and renewal, as Judith Wilson has observed.[15] Huber's narrative suggests, rather, that it is only upon their release that a handful of 'the best' felons (including Frances's husband separated from her after leading a failed coalminers' rebellion in Wales) are able to redeem themselves through active labour and land ownership (49). This is precisely the kind of argument for civilisation and settlement that will later be developed by colonial theorists such as E. G. Wakefield. In the culmination of Frances's story, however, Huber tentatively imagines another kind of settler ethic which takes a distinctly female form. When Frances is reunited, quite by coincidence, with her husband on Norfolk Island, she at last fully explains her own crime as one of honourable self-defence. Freed from the shame of infamy, the ameliorative emotional effects of domestic sentiment—love, honesty, belonging, compassion and affection—take their course and her story ends in the happy reconstitution of her extended family on Norfolk Island among a community of ex-felons and free-thinkers. In this context, the rescued baby Clara emerges as a symbol of new life and hope in the fledgling colony, as aspired to, but not achieved, by still-restless Rudolph who observes that '[t]he creature looks as if she felt Love and Humanity are the only bonds that join her to society' (98).

Arguably, Frances Belton's female-convict-cum-settler story speaks not just to Huber's embrace of a reconstructed, colonial form of domestic sentimentalism but to her attempt to appeal to the new female readerships that sustained commercial women's magazines like *Flora*.[16] In this regard, Huber's attempt to fashion a post-revolutionary Pacific settler vision stands against the wave of political reaction that condemned Forster and other Revolutionary enthusiasts while also tempering the vaulting worldly (and distinctly male) ambition of the progressive cause. If Huber began her fiction-writing career ventriloquising her ex-husband, she soon found her way to embracing women's stories of family, love and affect as the basis of her own fictional trajectory which never again repeated the blend of whimsical Pacific projection and domesticity that characterised the *Abentheuer*.

It is no coincidence that the narrative's vision of a new social order based upon familial bonds and settler community unfolds not in New South Wales itself but on Norfolk Island. This is yet another way in which Huber both recalls and distances herself from Forster's ghost. Forster was present when Cook took possession of Norfolk Island in 1774, and in his *Voyage* he had singled it out as a location of particular beauty and potential.[17] Huber only equivocally reproduces his enthusiasm, however, when Rudolph writes upon his arrival:

> What strange scenes have I to witness in this distant unknown corner of the earth! Can it really be true, my dear ones? Do certain people really have second sight by which they perceive the marvellous ways of Destiny, just as our nurses claim that children born on a Sunday can see spirits?
> (50)

Rudolph's earnestness has given way to a lighter, more whimsical tone which underscores Norfolk Island's status as a magical and unreal setting. It is hard to miss Huber's irony here since the island's strangeness and distance can be understood both to amplify and cast doubt upon the feminised settler vision it offers.

By contrast, the New South Wales penal colony's core function for Huber is to provide a concrete setting for a distanced yet *passionate* moral reckoning with the aftermath of revolution from the point of view of its broken and defeated male participants. Henry Belton, like Rudolph, is figured sympathetically as a 'noble idealist' (60), now burdened with a 'mutilated' heart (114). In what amounts to a soft renunciation of rebellion, Rudolph/Forster explains to Henry the 'honourableness of error' as he puts it (63)—that their resistance to tyranny led them to commit acts of violence that were rightly punished by law in their respective homelands ('politically and historically you were in the wrong,' he says (64))—while nonetheless continuing to affirm liberation more generally (62–64; 114). Once an accommodation between 'good conscience' (61) and the rule of law is agreed between the two men as the basis of new life in the *terra nullius*, Henry can be (miraculously) reunited with Frances and a new social order can be imagined on the basis of their mutual redemption. Rudolph himself, however, continues to wander, headed towards death.

Indeed, Rudolph's fate underscores the degree to which Huber's *Abentheuer* is ordered by a revolutionary melancholy that limits its redemptive and utopian ambitions. It is as if the failure of the French revolution to reconstitute Europe has detached the ethics of sensibility from the politics of liberation or indeed any larger social project, sealing it into a remote and privatised domestic scene. The South Sea settler colony is here pictured not as a revitalised organic society, nor as a place where reason and justice reign or where sentimental relations spontaneously extend themselves; rather it is pictured as a place where the shards of a rotten society may, at least occasionally, germinate scattered familial love and solidarity under the rule of law (98). And perhaps most strikingly, Rudolph, the alienated intellectual whose romantic commitments to passion, freedom and progress have come undone, anticipates later romantic literary wanderers like Byron's Childe Harold or Shelley's Frankenstein and his creature.

To be sure, Rudolph's fictional recapitulation of Forster's *Voyage* is a global journey of despair punctuated by moments of intense sensibility. That he hovers listlessly between exile and death is confirmed by 'The Lonely Deathbed' (*Das einsame Todbett*), the 'postscript to, and explanation of' (110) *Abentheuer* that Huber completed a decade later, with a preface that confirmed the identity of her hero as Forster.[18] In this text, Rudloph/Forster again lives on, having departed the Botany Bay colony for the 'primeval world' of Asia (as Forster's own last letters to Huber, which she drew upon almost verbatim, suggest he intended) where he hopes to be bound 'once again to humanity' (115). There amongst 'simple people of the Ganges' and the 'ruins of the ancient world' (115), Rudolph's *wanderlust* finally abates after witnessing an Indian man, old and 'blind', receiving a simple meal of dates and rice from his family (122). Returning to Europe to seek out his own wife and daughter, Rudolph dies alone in Berg, unaware that his family is close by and that the doctor who attends him is his own future son-in-law.

The haunting melancholy of Huber's Pacific settler vision is largely enabled by the double narrative structure of the *Abentheuer*, which, as we have seen, presents two post-revolutionary trajectories: the Belton family's penal-cum-settler narrative framed by that of Forster/Rudolph, the world-weary, cosmopolitan wanderer in flight from the collapse of Europe's revolutions. Arguably too, the double structure allows Huber's novel to straddle two important emergent forms of fiction: the novel of sensibility and the political novel. Frances's inset narrative of transportation to the penal colony shares much with its very near anglophone contemporary, William Godwin's *Caleb Williams* (1794), which sought to amplify the message of his radical tract, *An Enquiry into Political Justice* (1793). As a servant falsely accused of theft (48), Frances is a kind of female Caleb (although she is unrepentant for the murder she has committed in defence of her virtue); on one occasion, false charges against her are dropped in a courtroom scene in which her truth-telling—her 'clear and convincing' answers (48)—has a transformative effect on the court's officials, as does Caleb's exposé of Mr Falkland's crimes in the final scene of Godwin's narrative. Henry Belton, too, shares many of Caleb's circumstances—a bright boy of poor family, selected to serve as private secretary to a local nobleman [the Duke of ★★★] who later rebels and falls foul of the world that has elevated him (59). Most strikingly, the blank finality and solitude of Caleb's anticipated death in the original manuscript ending of Godwin's novel, in which he renders himself as a 'GRAVE-STONE!—an obelisk', shares much with Rudolph's end in Huber's *The Lonely Death Bed* which tells us plainly enough, 'He sank alone into the grave' (123).[19]

Huber's and Godwin's novels foreground blighted subjectivities, which, in turn, structure their ambivalent, irreal settings: Huber's remote Pacific and Godwin's Gothicised England. Each novel ends tragically: Forster/Rudolph dies alone, while Caleb's story ends in defeat and self-hatred. Like Mary Shelley's *Frankenstein* (1818), another Caleb-inspired narrative, the *Abentheuer* uses family ties to interrupt the trajectories of male revolutionary ambition/nihilism. Arguably, Huber's challenge to those trajectories is more radical than Shelley's critique of Prometheanism, not just because it is self-consciously aware of the family's limitations, but because it places a woman—an unrepentant female convict no less—at its narrative's centre. With this move, Huber plausibly conceives of the Australian colony both as a place where figures of revolutionary failure could go to die and where victims of social injustice could experience muted forms of moral and emotional regeneration.

2

The post-revolutionary settler imaginary took another direction in Edward Gibbon Wakefield's work. His *Letter from Sydney* (1829), a polemical critique of the penal colony, was marked by a striking disjunction. Channelling the voice of a reform-minded colonist, it was composed in Newgate prison while Wakefield was serving a three-year sentence on charges of conspiracy relating to his abduction of a schoolgirl. While it passed itself off as non-fiction, *Letter from Sydney* harnessed a fictional persona of fantastic self-projection to a new, rationalised strain of colonial political economy.

Wakefield was colonisation's first systematic theorist. At a time when Bentham and other philosophic radicals viewed colonies as little more than throwbacks to the mercantilist past that limited political and economic freedom, he argued passionately for their potential benefits.[20] Extending the principles of classical economics derived from Smith, Malthus and Ricardo into a theory of imperialism that envisaged self-governing settler colonies as loyal and happy participants in a British free-trade empire, he believed that colonies could provide labour markets for Britain's 'redundant population', as well as new opportunities for capital investment and commodity markets for English manufactures without distorting the home economy. Improvement, he argued, was contingent upon wealth creation alone, not fellow-feeling. Thus, slavery 'exists, not to gratify the hearts of cruel men, but to fill the pockets of those who, without slavery, would be poor and insignificant. It will never be abolished by appeals to the hearts of slave-owners.'[21] In this spirit, Wakefield's colonial writings routinely staged fictionalised renunciations of sympathy on the part of colonial capitalists and landowners, whereby English gentlemen colonists, men of feeling at the outset of their settler ventures, become hard-headed men of utility upon their exposure to the frontier.[22] Indeed, they become figures not unlike Wakefield himself: passionate advocates for an economistic, means-end orientated colonial policy that displaces moral sense and moral argument within calculations of common good or general utility.

Wakefield's theory was first articulated precisely in relation to New South Wales.[23] It put forward an ingenious and technically sophisticated scheme for the restricted sale of colonial 'waste lands' (his term) that would fund the passage of immigrant workers from Britain so as to deploy an oversupply of labour at home to end a labour shortage in the penal settlement. The fixing of a so-called 'sufficient price' for colonial lands would achieve two related ends. First, it would regulate the numbers of labourers who could become land-owners, thereby producing the requisite balance between land under cultivation and labour supply so as to keep wages low and markets profitable for colonial capital. Second, it would concentrate the settler population (the proportion of people to territory, as Wakefield put it) in such a way so as to produce the conditions (that is, the cheap labour) upon which the accumulation of wealth, and thus, crucially, 'civilisation', was understood to depend.

Wakefield's theory was essentially a colonial adaptation of Ricardo's analysis of the relations between land, labour and capital. He believed the setting of a fixed price for land could function as a means of tweaking the three-factor economy in the colonial context where large expanses of territory otherwise threatened the supply-side advantage by inflating the value of labour and diminishing capital returns. More than other political economists of his day, however, Wakefield theorised the connection between a managed economy and social relations (or what he called 'civilised' values). He was able to do so precisely because he understood himself to be projecting sound economic principles into the apparently blank space of the colonies. His working definition of colonisation was 'the creation and increase of *everything but land*, where there is *nothing except land*' (135)—an invocation of *terra nullius* that paradoxically helped bring the social and cultural relations of colonial capital more clearly into view. For Wakefield, the 'sufficient price' mechanism was not just the means by which the chaos of the colonial wilderness could be brought to order. It was also the means by which the failures of English society—its pauperism, its criminality, its delegitimated oligarchy—could be overcome. Indeed, settler societies were otherwise at risk of lapsing into barbarism or 'newness'—the forms of cultural degeneration caused by the isolation and deprivation of the colonial frontier—of which America, even more than the penal colony in New South Wales, was Wakefield's primary exemplification.

Wakefield's interest in the social relations of capital later led Marx to acknowledge him as the leading political economist of his period. It was this aspect of his writing, too, which conversely licensed him to merge policy-orientated analysis with extravagant fantasy and rhetorical excess. Here is how the *Letter from Sydney* imagines happy colonial and metropolitan communities as by-products of a futuristic imperial economy in which labour and land have struck a perfect balance:

> …[C]olony and…mother country [will] become partners in a new trade—the creation of happy human beings; one country furnishing the raw material—that is, the land, and the dust of which man is made; the other furnishing the machinery—that is, men and women, to convert the unpeopled soil into living images of God.
>
> (168)

Wakefield radically refigures the global sympathy appealed to by eighteenth-century benevolent sentimentalists like the elder Forster as something like the industrial production of human beings. But older tropes of colonial familialism have not just been reconstructed within a Utilitarian calculus of the free-trade economy. A godly creative power is attributed to colonial economic relations, and particularly to 'sufficient price', as the single mechanism by which land, labour and capital will generate civilisations from nothingness.

It turned out that Wakefield was wrong about 'sufficient price' and most aspects of his theory.[24] By the 1840s, systematic colonisation had spawned a number of ventures in Australia and New Zealand (and later also in Brazil), but none came close to realising Wakefield's forecasts, and all demanded that he modify or abandon his principles in the face of local conditions. It took just a few years for South Australia, the very first Wakefieldian settlement established in 1836, to discredit Wakefield's claims for 'sufficient price'. In theory, a fixed price would regulate the expansion of settlement and generate proportional immigrant labour supply. In fact, it had merely enriched British investors, who failed to employ local labour and readily resold their land for huge profits that were lost to the colony. Further experiments with Wakefieldian land reform in New South Wales pointed to the impracticality of so-called 'concentrated settlement' in the colonial context. Wakefield had theorised culture as an effect of population mass, and calculated that restricted land sales would enable class and property relations to be finessed in such a way as to optimise civilised social outcomes.[25] What he had not understood was that an artificially 'concentrated' economy could only hobble development in New South Wales where ventures like sheep farming required vast amounts of acreage to be profitable.

It is perhaps unsurprising that having once been celebrated as a heroic figure—a great 'founding father' and an 'architect of the British Commonwealth'—Wakefield is now more commonly perceived as an ideologue of Anglophile settler colonialism.[26] Yet this characterisation does justice neither to the radical and utilitarian roots of systematic colonisation nor, indeed, to the distinctive style and utopian eccentricity of a text like *Letter from Sydney*. Wakefield wrote *Letter from Sydney* from Newgate prison where he was serving a 3-year sentence on charges of conspiracy relating to his abduction of Ellen Turner, a 15-year old schoolgirl and heiress to Manchester banking fortune, in March 1826.[27] With the help of his brother William, he had kidnapped Turner from her boarding school and had spirited her away to Gretna Green where she had married him, believing the union would save her father from financial ruin. The point of recalling *Letter from Sydney*'s sensational back story is to remind ourselves of the extremity of the disjunction between its authorial and fictional worlds. Narrated in the persona of a disgruntled colonial landowner, *Letter* was published in 9 anonymous instalments in the *Morning Chronicle* before being issued as a book edited under the name of Wakefield's friend and fellow radical reformer, Robert Gouger, in December 1829.[28] Yet Wakefield never left England. He arranged rather to read every available published account of the Botany Bay penal colony while in his prison cell. His *Letter* wove the descriptive detail of those texts into the analytical categories of classical economics so as to present itself deceptively, or at least fictively, as the letters of a reform-minded colonist.

All this is not to suggest that we read *Letter from Sydney*'s nascent colonial plan in narrowly biographical terms. The text is not adequately understood as an extension of the character traits that led Wakefield to abduct Ellen Turner, as some recent critics have suggested (though there is clearly an important link between the adventurism of the life and the work in his case).[29] Nor is it a simple fantasy, even if it is tinged by a certain romantic daring. Rather, *Letter from Sydney*'s significance, and indeed its *sui generis* status in the colonial archive, lie in its particular blend of utopian dreaming and utilitarian policy formulation. It imagines a new world that enjoys all the virtues and refinements of the Mother Country while being freed of evil, injustice and poverty. Even more remarkably, this is a colonial utopia anchored in policy minutiae: fixed-price land sales, land tenure, labour relations, investment returns and so on. In this regard, *Letter from Sydney* joins together two very different intellectual and political orders: that of philosophic radicals like Bentham, Ricardo and Adam Smith, on the one side, and of a certain Romantic reactionary sentimentalism (of Southey, the later Coleridge and Burke, for instance), on the other.

3

The settler colonial fictions of Therese Huber and E. G. Wakefield draw upon and transform the legacy of sentimental colonialism that marked eighteenth-century European engagements with the Pacific. Huber reimagines George Forster's South Sea voyage so as to reckon with revolutionary hope and disappointment. Wakefield, on the other hand, seeks to displace older paradigms of colonial engagement and emotion by embracing modern utilitarian forms of calculus. Each project is marked by an extraordinary disjunction between its fictional and authorial worlds which helps to fuel its colonial settler vision. As Forster's ex-wife and a first-time female author, Huber conceived of the Australian penal-settler colony as a place where revolutionary failure could go to die but also where the dynamic of familial love could exercise a certain curative power on those whose revolutionary wills had led to their victimhood. Wakefield, on the other hand, readily assuming the mantel of an English colonist (even while serving time as a felon), conceived of New South Wales as a place where cutting-edge social reasoning—that is, the reform program of philosophic radicalism—could, paradoxically, establish a traditional, hierarchical and organic society protected against revolutionary desire and upheaval. Between them, the matrix of a post-revolutionary romantic politics of settlement, bound to an affective structure which joins hope, transgression and loss, becomes apparent.

Notes

1 Jonathan Lamb, *Preserving the Self in the South Seas, 1680–1840* (Chicago, IL: Chicago University Press, 2001), 4.
2 Johann Reinhold Forster, *Observations Made during a Voyage Round the World*, ed. Nicholas Thomas, Harriet Guest, and Michael Dettelbach (Honolulu: University of Hawai'i Press, 1996), 222–223.
3 Quoted in Leslie Bodi's Preface to *Adventures on a Journey to New Holland and The Lonely Deathbed*, ed. Leslie Bodi, trans. Rodney Livingstone (Melbourne: Lansdowne Press, 1966), 17.
4 The novel's full title is *Die Familie Seldorf: Eine Erzählung aus der französischen Revolution*. Jeannine Blackwell notes that it is possibly the only contemporary novel of the French Revolution to appear in German. See "Therese Huber," in *German Writers in the Age of Goethe, 1789–1832*, ed. James Hardin and Christoph E. Schweitzer (Detroit, MI: Gale, 1989), 189. Scholarship on the novel includes Stephanie M. Hilger, "Sara's Pain: The French Revolution in Therese Huber's Die Familie Seldorf (1795–1796)," in *Contemplating Violence: Critical Studies in Modern German Culture*, ed. Stephani Engelstein and Carl Niekerk (Amsterdam: Rodophi, 2011): 35–48, and Helmut Peitsch, "Die Revolution im Familienroman: Aktuelles politisches Thema und konventionelle Romanstruktur in Therese Hubers Die Familie Seldorf," *Jahrbuch der Deutschen Schillergesellschaft* 28 (1984): 248–269.

5 Anglophone scholarship by Australian-based Germanists (after Bodi) includes: Alan Corkhill, *Antipodean Encounters: Australia and the German Literary Imagination, 1754–1918* (New York: P. Lang, 1990); Michaela Krug, "'A Huge Land without Life and without Murder': Australia in Therese Forster-Huber's *Adventures on a Journey to New Holland*," in *Modern Europe: Histories and Identities*, ed. P. Monteath and F. S. Zuckerman (Adelaide: Australian Humanities Press, 1998), 353–363; and Judith Wilson's two excellent essays, "Abjection, Subjection, Redemption: Georg Forster's and Therese Huber's Perspectives on the Penal Colony," *Georg-Forster-Studien* 14 (2009), 133–188 and "'Wen die Schande einmal gefaßt Hat …'": Therese Huber's *Abentheuer auf einer Reise nach Neu-Holland* and the Question of Guilt," in *Migration and Cultural Contact: Germany and Australia,* ed. A. Bandhauer and M. Veber (Sydney: Sydney University Press, 2009), 223–240.

6 Bodi's edition made Huber's text available to anglophone readers in 1966. The German text is available in Heuser's edited collection of Huber's works, published in 1999. "Abentheuer auf einer Reise nach Neu-Holland," in *Romane und Erzählungen* 7, ed. M. Heuser (Hildesheim, Zurich, New York: Olms, 1999), 84–253.

7 Huber grew up reading English novels in her father's house and later translated English novels in Mainz with Forster. Her friend, Dorothea Margarete Forkel, translated Inchbald's *A Simple Story* in 1792 and William Godwin's *Caleb Williams* in 1795. See Peitsch, "Die Revolution," 250 n.11.

8 The journal's full title was *Flora: Teutschlands Töchtern geweiht von Freunden und Freundinnen des schönen Geschlechts* [Flora: Germany's Daughters Dedicated by Friends of the Fair Sex]. The story was originally serialized in *Flora* 4, 1793: 241–274 and *Flora* 1, 1794: 7–43, 209–275.

9 Forster's German translation of his *Voyage*, titled *Reise um die Welt* (1778), introduced the newly discovered South Pacific to the German reading public and was acclaimed for the freshness and clarity of its prose. In his preface to the German edition, Forster emphasised the subjective nature of description in travel writing. Leading German literary figures of the day praised the text, including Alexander von Humboldt, who held it to be the first truly modern account of scientific exploration. See Graham Jefcoate, "Forster, (Johann) Georg Adam (1754–1794)," *Oxford Dictionary of National Biography* (Oxford University Press, 2004); online edn, May 2009 http://www.oxforddnb.com.ezproxy.library.uq.edu.au/view/article/9909, accessed 23 May 2020.

10 When Georg Forster visited Paris in July 1793, he met Thomas Paine, Mary Wollstonecraft and others at the house of Thomas Christie. See K. W. Cameron, ed., *Shelley and His Circle, 1773–1822* (Cambridge, MA: Harvard University Press, 1961), 1:125. Peter Marshall also notes that he transcribed extracts from the copy of Godwin's *Political Justice* which Charrelin had delivered to the National Convention. See *William Godwin* (New Haven, CT: Yale University Press, 1984), 119. On Forster's period in Paris, see also Peter Morgan, "Republicanism, Identity and the New European Order: Georg Forster's Letters from Mainz and Paris 1792–93," *Journal of European Studies* 22, no. 1 (1992): 71–100.

11 Reinhart Koselleck, "The Limits of Emancipation: A Conceptual-Historical Sketch", in *The Practice of Conceptual History: Timing History, Spacing Concepts*, trans. Todd Samuel Presner (Stanford, CA: Stanford University Press, 2002), 254: "In Paris during the Revolution, Forster was the first to subsume the Kantian philosophy of history under the new and fashionable concept of emancipation."

12 "Cook the discoverer" (1787), quoted in John Gascoigne, "The German Enlightenment and the Pacific," in *The Anthropology of the Enlightenment*, eds. Larry Wolff and Marco Cipolloni (Stanford, CA: Stanford University Press, 2007), 163. Forster's earlier (1786) essay on the Pacific is "Neuholland und die brittische Colonie in Botany-Bay," in *Georg Forsters Werke: Sämtliche Schriften, Tagebücher, Briefe*, vol. 5, ed. Academie der Wissenschaften der DDR (Berlin: Akademie-Verlag, 1985), 161–183.

13 Therese Huber, *Adventures on a Journey to New Holland and The Lonely Deathbed*, ed. Leslie Bodi, trans. Rodney Livingstone (Melbourne: Lansdowne Press, 1966), 21. All subsequent in-text citations are to this edition of the text.
14 Quoted in Gascoigne, 163.
15 Wilson, "Abjection, Subjection, Redemption", 165; "'Wen die Schande einmal gefaßt hat …'", 136–137.
16 For a more extended reading of the Frances Belton narrative and its deployment of sympathy, see Wilson "Abjection, Subjection, Redemption," 179–187; "'Wen die Schande einmal gefaßt hat …'", 232–234.
17 Once again, Judith Wilson's scholarship is instructive: on Huber's engagement with Forster's account of Norfolk Island in his *Voyage round the world*, see "Abjection, Subjection, Redemption," 174–177; "'Wen die Schande einmal gefaßt hat …'", 229–231.
18 'The Lonely Deathbed' was likely written in 1804 and published in 1810, under L. F. Huber's name, as part of his collected works. See Bodi, 127. His edition's translation of *The Lonely Death Bed* is based on the text printed in *L. F Hubers sämtliche Werke seit dem Jahre 1802* (Zweiter Theil, Tübingen, 1810), 319–349.
19 William Godwin, *Caleb Williams*, ed. Pamela Clemit (Oxford: Oxford University Press, 2009), 311.
20 The utilitarians were ardent free traders, opponents of the Corn Laws and of the existing colonial empire. Bentham's *Emancipate Your Colonies* (originally addressed to Talleyrand in 1793) was published in England 1830. See Bernard Semmel, "The Philosophic Radicals and Colonialism," *The Journal of Economic History* 21, no. 4 (1961): 513–525, and Alan Mark Thornton, *The Philosophic Radicals: Their Influence on Emigration and the Evolution of Responsible Government for the Colonies* (Claremont, CA: Pomona College, 1975), 30–32.
21 Edward Gibbon Wakefield, *The Collected Works of Edward Gibbon Wakefield*, ed. Muriel F. Lloyd Prichard (London: Collins, 1968), 113.
22 As Wakefield underscores, these examples are "[d]rawn [...] from books and verbal reports of sincere men who had passed many years in the colony" (*The Collected Works*, 102).
23 Wakefield's theory was further refined and elaborated in his *A View of the Art of Colonization… in Letters between a Statesman and a Colonist* (1849), which included an extended section on England and America. With 20 years between them, *Letters from Sydney* and *A View of the Art of Colonization* are generally considered as the bookends of Wakefield's colonial theorising/speculation. Both were fictions.
24 See Philip Temple, *A Sort of Conscience: The Wakefields* (Auckland: Auckland University Press, 2002), 133–134.
25 That is, the restriction of land sales would both protect the value of existing land holdings and prevent labouring classes from becoming property holders too readily.
26 In the words of Philip Temple, Wakefield set out "to manufacture kitset Little Englands" in the antipodes (134). As early as 1848, the socialist Labour League criticised systematic colonisation as simply a "facsimile of English society with its classifications" (quoted in Temple 132), identifying Wakefield's scheme with the "ameliorative" politics of the middle-class reform movement. The second key objection to Wakefield's work was that his understanding of colonial settlement involved the systematic erasure of indigenous cultures. His theory was premised upon the concept of terra nullius which took no account of the native peoples' prior possession of the "waste lands" it proposed to package and cultivate. Nor did it concern itself with the questions of law and sovereignty that underpinned its assumption that secure private property would form the basis of colonial settlement. Celebratory accounts of Wakefield include Paul Bloomfield, *Edward Gibbon Wakefield: Builder of the British Commonwealth* (London, 1961) and R. Garnett, *Edward Gibbon Wakefield: the Colonization of South Australia and New Zealand* (London, 1898).

27 For a full account of the abduction, see Kate M. Atkinson, *Abduction: The Story of Ellen Turner* (Stockport: Blenkins Press, 2002).
28 Temple, *A Sort of Conscience*, 134. Wakefield's adventurism was in tension with the utilitarian emphasis on prudence and steady calculation. Bertrand Russell pointed out this discrepancy in reverse: 'The intellectual conviction that pleasure is the sole good, together with the temperamental incapacity for experiencing it was characteristic of the Utilitarians.' Quoted in Thornton, *Philosophic Radicals*, 12.
29 See, for example, Ged Martin, "Wakefield's Past and Futures," in *Edward Gibbon Wakefield and the Colonial Dream: A Reconsideration*, ed. Friends of the Turnbull Library (Wellington: GP Publications, 1997), 32 and Lydia Wevers, "My Mrs Harris," in *Edward Gibbon Wakefield and the Colonial Dream: A Reconsideration*, ed. Friends of the Turnbull Library (Wellington: Friends of the Turnbull Library; GP Publications, 1997), 179–185.

Bibliography

Atkinson, Kate M. *Abduction: The Story of Ellen Turner*. Stockport: Blenkins Press, 2002.
Blackwell, Jeannine. "Therese Huber. " In *German Writers in the Age of Goethe, 1789–1832*, edited by James Hardin and Christoph E. Schweitzer, 187–192. Detroit, MI: Gale, 1989.
Bloomfield, Paul. *Edward Gibbon Wakefield: Builder of the British Commonwealth*. London: Longmans, 1961.
Cameron, K. W., ed. *Shelley and His Circle, 1773–1822*. Cambridge, MA: Harvard University Press, 1961.
Corkhill, Alan. *Antipodean Encounters: Australia and the German Literary Imagination 1754–1918*. New York: Peter Lang, 1990.
Darwin, Eramus. *The Temple of Nature; or, The Origin of Society*. 1803. Literature Online. 23 May 2020 http://lion.chadwyck.com.
Forster, Georg. "Neuholland und die brittische Colonie in Botany-Bay." 1786. In *Georg Forsters Werke: Sämtliche Schriften, Tagebücher, Briefe*, vol. 5, edited by Academie der Wissenschaften der DDR, 161–183. Berlin: Akademie-Verlag, 1985.
Forster, Georg. *A Voyage Round the World, in His Britannic Majesty's sloop, Resolution, Commanded by Capt. James Cook, during the Years 1772, 3, 4, and 5*. London, 1777.
Forster, Johann Reinhold. *Observations Made During a Voyage Round the World*, edited by Nicholas Thomas, Harriet Guest, and Michael Dettelbach. Honolulu: University of Hawai'i Press, 1996.
Garnett, R. *Edward Gibbon Wakefield: The Colonization of South Australia and New Zealand*. London, 1898.
Gascoigne, John. "The German Enlightenment and the Pacific. " In *The Anthropology of the Enlightenment*, edited by Larry Wolff and Marco Cipolloni, 142–171. Stanford, CA: Stanford University Press, 2007.
Goldstein, Jürgen. *Georg Forster: Zwischen Freiheit und Naturgewalt*. Berlin: Matthes & Seitz, 2015.
Hilger, Stephanie M. "Sara's Pain: The French Revolution in Therese Huber's Die Familie Seldorf (1795–1796)." In *Contemplating Violence: Critical Studies in Modern German Culture*, edited by Stephani Engelstein and Carl Niekerk, 35–48. Amsterdam: Rodophi, 2011.
Huber, Therese. "Abentheuer auf einer Reise nach Neu-Holland." In *Romane und Erzählungen*, vol. 7, edited by M. Heuser, 84–253. Heldesheim/Zurich/New York: Olms, 1999.

Huber, Therese. *Adventures on a Journey to New Holland and The Lonely Deathbed*, edited by Leslie Bodi, trans. by Rodney Livingstone. Melboune: Lansdowne Press, 1966.

Jefcoate, Graham. "Forster, (Johann) Georg Adam (1754–1794)." In *Oxford Dictionary of National Biography*. Oxford University Press, 2004; online edn, May 2009 http://www.oxforddnb.com.ezproxy.library.uq.edu.au/view/article/9909, accessed 23 May 2020.

Koselleck, Reinhart. *The Practice of Conceptual History: Timing History, Spacing Concepts*, trans. by Todd Samuel Presner e.a.. Stanford, CA: Stanford University Press, 2002.

Krug, Michaela. "'A Huge Land without Life and without Murder': Australia in Therse Forster-Huber's *Adventures on a Journey to New Holland*." In *Modern Europe: Histories and Identities*, edited by P. Monteath and F. S. Zuckerman, 353–363. Adelaide: Australian Humanities Press, 1998.

Lamb, Jonathan. *The Preservation of the Self in the South Seas, 1680–1840*. Chicago, IL: Chicago University Press, 2001.

Marshall, Peter H. *William Godwin*. New Haven, CT: Yale University Press, 1984.

Martin, Ged. "Wakefield's Past and Futures." In *Edward Gibbon Wakefield and the Colonial Dream: A Reconsideration*, edited by Friends of the Turnbull Library, 29–44. Wellington: GP Publications, 1997.

Peter Morgan. "Republicanism, Identity and the New European Order: Georg Forster's Letters from Mainz and Paris 1792–93." *Journal of European Studies* 22, no. 1 (1992): 71–100.

Peitsch, Helmut. "Die Revolution im Familienroman: Aktuelles politisches Thema und Konventionelle Romanstruktur in Therese Hubers *Die Familie Seldorf*." *Jahrbuch der Deutschen Schillergesellschaft* 28 (1984): 248–269.

Semmel, Bernard "The Philosophic Radicals and Colonialism." *The Journal of Economic History* 21, no. 4 (1961): 513–525.

Temple, Philip. *A Sort of Conscience: The Wakefields*. Auckland: Auckland University Press, 2002.

Thomas, Nicholas and Oliver Berghof, eds. *Forster's A Voyage Round the World*. Honolulu: University of Hawai'i Press, 2000.

Thornton, Alan Mark. *The Philosophic Radicals: Their Influence on Emigration and the Evolution of Responsible Government for the Colonies*. Claremont, CA: Pomona College, 1975.

Wakefield, Edward Gibbon. *The Collected Works of Edward Gibbon Wakefield*, edited by Muriel F. Lloyd Prichard. London: Collins, 1968.

Wevers, Lydia. "My Mrs Harris." In *Edward Gibbon Wakefield and the Colonial Dream: A Reconsideration*, edited by Friends of the Turnbull Library, 179–185. Wellington: Friends of the Turnbull Library; GP Publications, 1997.

Wilson, Judith. "Abjection, Subjection, Redemption: Georg Forster's and Therese Huber's Perspectives on the Penal Colony." *Georg-Forster-Studien* 14 (2009): 133–188.

Wilson, Judtih. "'Wen die Schande einmal gefaßt hat …': Therese Huber's *Abentheuer auf einer Reise nach Neu-Holland* and the Question of Guilt." In *Migration and Cultural Contact. Germany and Australia*, edited by A. Bandhauer and M. Veber, 223–240. Sydney: Sydney University Press, 2009.

11

ANIMALS AND EMOTIONS IN THE EARLY MODERN WORLD

Margaret R. Hunt

Human-animal interactions are a universal feature of life on planet Earth, and they are often accompanied by a good deal of emotion.[1] The first of the three questions that animate this paper is rather basic: whose emotions are we talking about? Can we reconstruct "real" animal emotions in the early modern period, or is the historian always only studying the feelings humans attributed to animals? This paper argues that we can intuit what *some* non-human animals' emotions were, though we need to do so with care. The second question revolves around what those often emotion-laden interactions between humans and non-human animals actually meant: what did they "do" in historical terms? The intersection of humans and non-human animals can be shown to have resulted historically in different behaviours for both – behaviours that are at least in part to do with emotions. It follows from this that we should rethink the explicit or implicit view that culture is only made by and for humans, something historians and other "humanists" have been slower to do than, say, anthropologists and archaeologists.[2] The third question is theoretical and methodological: what epistemological approaches work best for exploring cross-species emotional regimes and evaluating their historical impact across time and space? This essay argues that looking at emotion "interspecifically" (that is, in the context of encounters between different species) needs some especially interactive, fluid and temporally complex understandings of what emotions are and how they function in the world.

Animals, humans and emotion, past and present

For millennia, the issue of non-human animal emotions has been closely bound up with the theological and ethical problem of how to justify humans' domination over animals.[3] Confining ourselves, for the present, just to the dominant religious traditions of West Asia, North Africa and Europe –the so-called

Abrahamic religions– we see that their originary sacred writings and traditions (among them the Bible, the Qur'an and the Sunnah[4]) are all very much concerned with the question of animal-human relations. In fact, most of them pay more attention to the animal-human binary than they do to other common forms of domination.[5] In Genesis 1:28 (sacred to Jews and Christians and revered by Muslims), God issues the famous command to Adam and Eve: "Be fruitful, and multiply, and replenish the earth, and subdue it: and have dominion over the fish of the sea, and over the fowl of the air, and over every living things that moveth upon the earth."[6] Other passages in the Hebrew Bible seek to define exactly what "dominion" entails. Thus, they explicitly permit animals to be used for food, as beasts of burden and for their milk, skin and hair/fur. Moreover, the Hebrew Bible includes elaborate directions for the sacrifice of animals in the course of religious ceremonies, and there are numerous references to God's enjoyment of the pleasing aroma of burning (sacrificial) meat.[7]

Some debate surrounds the extent to which animal sacrifice – a key features of traditional Judaism – continued to be necessary for Christians, and it is usually argued that Jesus' sacrifice obviates the need for it. On the other hand, Jesus himself ate fish, and almost certainly lamb,[8] and quasi-sacrificial practices, such as killing and eating the fatted lamb on Easter, were and are to this day common in many Christian communities. The Islamic sources will be discussed in more detail later, but suffice it to say that the Qur'an and Sunnah also approve (though with a number of provisos) the use of animals to carry loads, for their milk and skin, as human food and as sacrificial offerings.[9]

Christian theologians, often taking their cue from Aristotle, have generally been hostile to the notion that animals have rational souls or the possibility of eternal life. There also tend to be relatively few discussions of animal emotion in Christian biblical or post-biblical sources, at least up until relatively recently.[10] By contrast, both the Jewish and Islamic sources generally assumed animals had feelings, and often tried to shield them from unnecessary pain and mental suffering. Rabbinic Judaism mostly endorsed the view that animals had something like a soul and that, in the words of one modern scholar, "even domestic animals live for their own sake and not just for ours."[11] It also took a dim view of hunting, perhaps because hunting was often inspired by motives other than the need for food, and it was hard to ensure that the animal died in a ritually proper manner.[12] The Islamic sources go farther: most argue that animals not only have consciousness, feelings and souls but that they are actually natural Muslims – perhaps better Muslims than people are – and that they form communities and glorify God in their own way. In conformity with this quite inclusive view of animals, the Qur'an and Sunnah pay a lot of attention to protecting animals from cruelty, overwork or a needless death, and they often do so in ways that make it clear that the animal's inner feelings are one of the main things at stake.[13] Moreover, as Housni Alkhateeb Shehada has shown, interest in the inner feelings of animals formed a significant theme in a number of philosophical and medical writings in the centuries after the Prophet Muhammed's death.[14]

It is always risky to assume that theologians speak for the whole population and still more of a problem to think that people uniformly follow religious precepts. Though many Christian churchmen and philosophers doubted that animals had souls or consciousness, both European and Middle Eastern popular cultural traditions are full of talking and deliberating animals (the parliament of birds, a literary theme in both the Middle East and Europe, is just one example among many),[15] and ordinary people clearly believed animals to possess all kinds of emotions. Not only were animals portrayed as feeling anger, vengefulness, maternal protectiveness, love, piety and so forth, but they were routinely used allegorically to indicate virtues (and their attendant emotions) that humans should emulate and vices they should avoid. Moreover, most of these allegorical usages drew their power precisely from the belief that animals actually did feel these things. The snake, the archetypal symbol of malevolence towards humans, is a case in point, but there are many others. Ants and bees really were thought to be industrious, lions were imagined to be brave and (in a perhaps less familiar association) the hoopoe bird was assumed to exhibit an especially strong form of family love.[16] All this suggests that there was little or no unanimity on the question of whether animals could think and feel emotion, which is still the case in the present day.

Agency and its alternatives

The question of non-human animal emotion tends to be linked closely to problems of agency. The claim that at least some animals have or have had both individuality (which includes feelings and cognition) and agency is an important rallying point for animal rights activists. It has also influenced writing on the history of animals, a field that has followed a somewhat parallel trajectory in this respect to scholarship on the history of women, minorities, enslaved persons, peasants, the industrial working class and colonial subalterns.[17] And yet, it is also the case that, over time, many historians have gotten less and less comfortable with the notion of agency. Walter Johnson, a historian of American slavery, has argued that the preoccupation with uncovering agency "smuggles a notion of the universality of a liberal notion of selfhood, with its emphasis on independence and choice" into the study of highly oppressive institutions like slavery. According to Johnson, the obsession with agency flattens out profound social differences (which often revolved around limiting the choices of some groups while enhancing those of others) and diverts attention from the actual lives of subject peoples. It is, he argues, more about historians congratulating themselves on their own choices than it is about real people in the past.[18] If "agency," and particularly its assumption that the agent possesses a self-reflexive capacity to change his or her life-situation, is a problem for thinking about enslaved humans, how much more of a problem is it for animals, who live so far outside the conventions of liberal agency that they can be killed, cooked and eaten? At the same time, how is it possible to think about individuals or groups leaving a mark on history – even if it is a small one – without crediting them with some kind of agency?

Erica Fudge, an animal studies theorist and historian, has suggested one solution to this conundrum. She argues that when we consider the past, we need to put aside the conceit of self-reflexive intentionality, and ask instead what difference animals (and "animal-made-objects" – that is, animal products, such as leather or meat) made in what she likes to refer to as "the so-called human world." That means thinking about agency less in terms of the transcendent intentionality either of individual animals or individual humans, and more in terms of polytemporal networks of people, animals and things – networks that form culture, generate change over time and frequently challenge human intent.[19] This approach is indebted to the study of material culture, especially thing theory as it has developed under the influence of Arjun Appadurai, Bill Brown and others, and it also owes a good deal to Bruno Latour et al.'s actor-network theory.[20] These and similar approaches stress the interdependence of humans both with other species and with "inanimate," but nevertheless potentially powerful objects and technologies, and they tend to de-emphasise both individual and collective human agency. In Latour's words:

> There is no model of (human) actor in ANT [Actor-Network Theory] nor any basic list of competences that have to be set at the beginning, because the human, the self and the social actor of traditional social theory is not on the agenda.[21]

In the present essay, actor-network theory is used rather freely, though also flexibly. For one thing, the "social actor" continues to be on *my* agenda, but perhaps not in a traditional fashion. Moreover, I do not assume, as ANT (actor-network theory) sometimes does, that there is nothing outside the network. Sandra Harding and others have taken Latour, in particular, to task for the way he neglects the prior power relations and "Big Systems" (colonialism, gender hierarchy, chattel slavery, etc.) that often define the contours of networks, as well as the degree of effectiveness any given agent or group of agents, animate or not, has within a given network.[22] That having been said, the notion of networked emotion holds promise, and this essay explores several cases in which interspecific encounters between non-human animals and people illuminate a complex world of emotion and interactive agency, though of a highly situated, networked and polytemporal kind.

The claim that emotions are about much more than "individual feelings" is not new. Both the "interpersonal" and "social" nature of emotions are important features of the history of emotion as it has emerged in the last two decades or so.[23] Thus, we hear of "emotional regimes" and especially "emotives" (William Reddy), "emotional communities" and "communities of feeling" (Barbara Rosenwein), "interpersonal" versus "social" emotions (Peter Dixon), along with a good deal of interesting speculation about how emotions actually move individuals, groups and communities.[24] What is proposed here is simply a different version of the notion that emotion is more than individual, one that tries out the notion of an emotional actor-network in which animals, people and things all have a role.

Several scholars have tried explicitly to link the fields of the history of emotions and animal studies. One of the most important of these is Pascal Eitler, whose essay in the volume *Emotional Lexicons*, a volume that originates in the History of Emotions Research Center of the Max Planck Institute, does an excellent job of laying out the commonalities. His work is, however, focused somewhat more on the modern than the early modern period.[25] For the early modern period, two different bodies of work hold promise for thinking about animals and emotions. The first is the work of Erica Fudge, including both her writing on early modern English animals and people, and her conceptually linked writing about animals and humans in the modern day.[26] The second, perhaps less known to anglophone scholarship, is a long and fruitful tradition of writing on animal/human interaction in various parts of the Islamic world, one that pays attention both to emotion and to the medieval and early modern periods. Much of this is available only in Arabic and Turkish. However, a recent edited collection by Suraiya Faroqhi, which contains a number of articles translated into English, gives some sense of the richness of this historiography.[27] The next section of this essay is heavily indebted to writings in this tradition and especially to the Faroqhi volume.

Mohammed's cat

The Prophet Muhammed certainly believed that animals had emotions. A hadith, found with minor variations in several collections, reads

> We were with the Apostle of Allah (pbuh) during a journey. He went to ease himself. We saw a bird with her two young ones and we captured her young ones. The bird came and began to spread its wings. The Apostle of Allah (pbuh) came and said: Who grieved this bird [i.e., who made this bird grieve] for its young ones? Return its young ones to it.[28]

The Prophet also concerned himself with the welfare of a number of other kinds of animals, including insects (in the same hadith, the Prophet condemned people who set ant colonies on fire),[29] frogs, hoopoes, cats, camels and dogs, though he was fairly ambivalent about the latter species. Cruelty to animals (e.g., branding them on the face, cutting off body parts, slaughtering them in a way that caused them unnecessary pain or mental distress, taking away their offspring in a callous manner) were all condemned. Moreover, it was forbidden to kill animals merely for recreation: "If someone kills a small bird for no reason," the Prophet is reputed to have said, "it will beseech Allah on the Day of Resurrection saying: Oh Lord, so and so killed me for no reason, and he did not kill me for any beneficial purpose."[30] The Prophet also several times implied that charity to animals was as meritorious as charity to people.[31] Kindness to animals was part of an array of other forms of compassion that were central to the message of the Qur'an and Sunnah, including compassion towards new-born children (especially the famous condemnations of infanticide, particularly of girls), orphans, wives, slaves and the poor.[32]

In the modern day, the early Muslim community and the Prophet himself have acquired a strong retrospective reputation for caring about cats. The evidence for this is, however, rather scant. One of the Companions of the Prophet (those men and women who embraced Islam during the Prophet's lifetime) was affectionately nicknamed Abu Hurayrah "Father of the Kitten," apparently because of his love of cats.[33] A hadith repeated with variations in several of the early hadith collections concerns a woman who went to hell because she starved her cat to death.[34] And there are a number of ahadith that address the question of whether or not cats are ritually clean animals (the general conclusion was and is that they are).[35] However, it is important to note that cats were just one of many species included in early Islamic injunctions about kindness to animals, and by no means the most common one. In fact, the bulk of the references to cats in the ahadith are repetitions of or variations on the story of the woman who starved her cat to death.

Whatever the relative importance of cats might have been for the Prophet and the early Muslim community, over time, the association between Islam and cats took on a life of its own. Probably the most popular story told about the early Muslim community and cats comes from quite a bit later and initially had nothing to do with the Prophet. As Housni Alkhateeb Shehada shows, the earliest known version of what later turned into a tale about the Prophet Muhammed and his cat is found in a fourteenth-century compilation of biographies of significant men and women in the history of Islam, penned by the Damascene historian Shams al-Dīn al-Dhahabī (1274–1348). The story goes that a cat was sleeping on the sleeve of the influential twelfth-century Sufi sheik, Abū al-'Abbās al-Rifā'i. When the sheik needed to go out, he was unwilling to disturb the sleeping cat, so he cut or tore off the sleeve of the robe.[36] In the later fifteenth century, a version of this story, or perhaps a parallel popular tale, was taken up by a Flemish traveller named Josse van Ghistele as part of an explanation for why Damascus (then still part of the Mamluk Sultanate) maintained a refuge for ancient cats – something he found quite novel. Van Ghistele tells a somewhat similar story to that of al-Dhahabī. However, now the pious man has been transformed into the Prophet Muhammed himself, and the emotional stakes are higher, because the cat is said to have actually given birth to kittens on (the Dutch actually reads "under") the Prophet's sleeve. The part about cutting off the sleeve so as not to disturb the cat remains the same, after which van Ghistele has the Prophet remark that "it would have been a great sin had he disturbed an animal that came to him for help and support in her time of greatest need."[37] About three quarters of a century later, the story was retold by the diplomat Ogier Ghiselin de Busbecq, who was in Istanbul from 1554 to 1562, though this time it featured a sleeping cat (essentially al-Dhahabī's version but attributed to the Prophet). According to Busbeq,

> Mahomet, their Law-giver...was so much in love with a Cat, that, when one of them fell asleep upon his Sleeve, as he was reading at a Table, and

the time of his Devotion drew near, he caused his Sleeve to be cut off, that he might not awake the Cat by his going to the Mosque.[38]

Minor variations on this tale would turn up for at least the next two and half centuries in European accounts of travel to the Ottoman Empire, usually (as with both van Ghisele and de Busbecq) as part of an explanation for why Muslims were so solicitous towards animals, and cats in particular.[39] Whether the story ever was a genuine Islamic tradition – at least as a story about the Prophet – is lost to history, but what is clear is that, by the early twentieth century or earlier, it had been adopted into Turkish-language sources, and today it is repeated more or less uncritically in many Islamic contexts (and widely on the Internet in a number of languages) as proof of the Prophet Muhammad's abiding love of and compassion towards cats.

It is tempting to read this story (in both al-Dhahabī's version and its later incarnations) against modern-day experiences with cats: tempting but not without its risks.[40] It is certainly the case that many modern house-cats like a warm place to sleep, and they spend a lot of the day napping. They also tend to like to find a textile to lie on. And many domesticated cats like close body contact with humans and other warm species. Cats curl up to sleep in a way that many humans find particularly appealing, and they appear absorbed in their sleep, so much so that the length people will go to avoid disturbing a sleeping cat has become something of an in-joke. These modern-day experiences make it easy to identify with, even, in a sense, to relive, the story of the cat sleeping on the sleeve of Muhammed, and the tale's very familiarity undoubtedly helps explain its popularity in the present day. The problem for the historian is whether the behaviours described earlier, which, it is important to note, involve choices on the part of both cats and people, are actually universal or transhistorical. Probably scepticism is in order, at least with respect to whether cats and humans actually behaved this way during the lifetime of the Prophet Muhammed. Probably we will never know, but it seems perfectly possible that the majority of cats in the Arabian Desert oases of the early seventh century, where the Prophet Muhammed first disseminated his message, were seen more in terms of their contribution to pest control than as a species people cuddled up against, or allowed to sleep undisturbed on expensive textiles. The tradition that Abu Hurayrah earned the nickname "Father of the Kitten" because of his love of cats actually militates against the view that closeness to cats was the norm among the Companions, since nicknames are usually based on something that makes a person stand out from the crowd.

Still, at least from the first half of the fourteenth century, when al-Dhahabī wrote his famous biographical dictionary, one can probably more confidently use this story to think about the emotions of both humans and cats. We might note that both al-Dhahabī and, later, van Ghisele were based in Damascus, and de Busbecq in Constantinople, meaning that the cats they were describing (or at least the ideal cat they had in mind when they told their respective versions of the cat-on-the-sleeve story) were probably not patrolling desert grain-stores for prey, but were urban house-cats, who, no doubt, occasionally hunted vermin, but who also had a clear companionate status. The main point the European Christian retailers of the cat-on-the-sleeve story were trying to get across was that, at least by the late Medieval Period, Muslims seemed more fond of animals (cats in particular) and more attentive to their welfare than most Christian Europeans were, and there is no good reason to doubt them. Thus, van Ghiselin claims that after the cat episode, the Prophet Muhammed "blessed all those who would do good unto those animals [cats] and damned them who would do them evil."[41] De Busbecq told the cat-on-the-sleeve story as the prelude to a discussion of the Islamic love of cats, and the popular Turkish antipathy to people who would torture animals.[42] Joseph Pitton de Tournefort, a French naturalist who travelled about the Ottoman Empire from 1700 to 1702, refers to the cat story (de Busbecq's version) as part of a quite well-informed and sympathetic discussion of Islamic beliefs about animals. He also describes the organised feeding of street dogs, including charitable endowments "settled in form by Will, for maintaining a certain number of Dogs and Cats so many Days in the Week," people who paid for animals' veterinary care as an act of charity and people buying caged birds so as to free them.[43] Charles-Sigisbert Sonnini de Manoncourt, another Frenchman, living and travelling in the Ottoman Empire between 1777 and 1780, told the cat-on-the-sleeve story in the context of observing, with some surprise, that cats could be found "in all the houses of Egypt" and that "[y]ou see some of them, in the mansions of the rich, partaking of the cushions ...[while] their masters...take pleasure in stroking them with the hand and in lavishing caresses on them..."[44]

Exactly what emotions and what sorts of animal and human intentionality are implied in the story of the cat on (or under) the sleeve? Let me mention several. First, the cat must decide where it is safe and pleasant to sleep, or, as the case may be, to give birth: which humans, in short, to trust. The human must decide whether or not to let the cat sleep on the expensive textile (one's sleeve, rugs, bed-covering, etc.) and whether to disturb it if it does. And there is emotion too, in this case emotions that are both simple and complex to parse. At the heart of the matter is something like restful contentment, both on the part of the cat and on the part of the person she trusts enough to sleep near or on. But a good part of that trust and contentment seems either to be transferred from one species to another or to be in some way mutually reinforcing. This is a networked emotion, and it is also one in which both animals and humans participate, at least to some degree on their own terms.

The cat is still a favoured animal in many predominantly Muslim contexts, and especially in the Middle East. However, it is unclear whether that is because the Prophet Muhammed approved of having cats, but not dogs, in the house; the result of later, mostly non-canonical stories about the Prophet's or other pious persons' special affection for cats (like the cat-on-the-sleeve story); or some other reason. Believing Muslims today tend to follow Muhammed in considering cats to be ritually clean animals.[45] This also means that in some parts of the Muslim world today, it is rather common to find cats in mosques. A cat that drinks from the water with which a Muslim performs his or her ritual ablutions before prayer does not thereby make the water unclean.[46] Moreover, cats are reputed to be especially drawn to people who are praying, which, to some people, shows how spiritually evolved cats are; the more sceptical may wonder if cats are not attracted to prayer rugs and to the wall-to-wall carpeting in many mosques, the body-heat of the people who frequent them and the fact that feeding programmes for street cats often take place in the vicinity of mosques. There is also a theory that cats scrupulously avoid stepping on (and thus defiling) the Holy Qur'an. Moreover, the meme of cats in holy places is in wide circulation on the Internet. There is a whole genre of short videos of imams and cats, cats in mosques, cats settling near people at prayer, people feeding cats near mosques and the cats of Mecca.[47]

The emotions in the tale that precipitated this whole discussion – the almost certainly apocryphal story of the cat on or under the sleeve of the Prophet Muhammed's robe – speak less to the feelings of individual people and animals than to emotional interactions at the species level – centuries of (probably urban) cats seeking warm, safe places to sleep and bear their young, and of humans feeling warm about themselves for not disturbing them. But the popularity of this polytemporal tale today comes, surely, from its familiarity to anyone who has ever lived closely with a cat. And in the Muslim context, the story (or stories) take on added power because they intersect with a set of ethical precepts (do not torture cats; animals have feelings too), religious beliefs (cats are ritually clean; animals glorify God in their own way) and institutions (refuges for old cats, bequests to feed street animals, etc.) that, over the centuries, generated a distinctive mode of living with cats.[48] This mode can truly be said to have been created historically by both people and animals – and, with a nod to Latour, perhaps with some contribution from textiles as well.

A man, a boy and four horses

On September 2, 1680, in the county of Berkshire in England, one John Sawyer, "a man of good repute among his Neighbours, that lived Soberly and Honestly," and his 13-year-old son, Richard were ploughing a field with four horses. Though the day started fair, by about 11:00 am, "the sky began to lower, the Clouds grew thick, and soon it Lightned and Thundred, and some showers of Rain fell." Two other plough-teams were at work in the same field at the same time, but "their Cattel being affrighted and unruly," they stopped work and went home. A few hours later, when the weather had cleared again, a passer-by was shocked to come upon John and Richard Sawyer and all four horses lying stone dead upon the ground in the middle of their field, the victims, apparently, of a lightning strike. They too had decided to call it a day, but they had left it too late. The verdict of the coroner's inquest was that the tragedy "was the immediate providence of Almighty God."[49] But a more down-to-earth reading of the pamphlet in which this story appeared suggests that John Sawyer's fatal mistake lay in the fact that he had not listened to his animals soon enough. The other two plough-teams were saved because their handlers paid attention when their animals showed fear and refused to cooperate. Unfortunately for Sawyer, his son and the horses, he failed to read the signs of danger, and so he and his entire team paid with their lives.

This may qualify as a case of animal agency. The cattle pulling the plough felt fear when they encountered thunder and lightning; they communicated that fear to their handlers with their body language and "unruliness," and they and the ploughmen survived. It could also be that the cattle, who tend, as a species, to be more fearful of sudden noises than most horses, sounded the alarm while the horses did not[50] (among other things, this story illustrates the eclecticism with which humans utilised large four-footed animals in farm work). However, one should be a bit sceptical about the sequence of events in this particular case (animals show fear, humans heed them –or not – and are then saved – or not) simply because the anthropocentric trope of animals who sense danger earlier than humans do was and still is so conventional. It does not mean such things never happened; just that they may not have happened in this case. This conventional explanatory sequence owed a lot to the role of animals in human settlements. Many human-animal interactions sought to capitalise on abilities, sensitivities or, indeed, emotional states that particular species of animals possessed and that differed from those of humans. Humans exploited the hunting dog's enthusiasm for the chase, watchdogs' acute sense of hearing and tendency to bark fearfully at strangers, the horse's ability to run and pull relatively heavy loads and so forth. So humans had no difficulty grasping and accepting that animals had abilities they lacked. Situations where animals "saved" or "warned" humans also flattered humans' belief that their servant-animals loved them and wished them well, and reassured them that the whole system of hierarchy was working as it should – for the benefit of humans. But that also meant that there was a widespread cultural belief that it was important to try to figure out what individual animals were trying to "say," especially in potentially dangerous situations.

While this sad little story follows certain conventions, it does demonstrate a key feature of interspecific relations: the idea that one part of the job of animals is to "tell" or otherwise convey to humans when to be afraid. It is also notable that animal-human communication is part of the mix and that both sides are expected to work to understand. This was not new. As the Neo-Platonist Porphyry had argued centuries earlier, farmers, herdsmen, huntsmen and so on do understand the language of animals and the animals understand them, at least at the level of daily tasks. To Porphyry, this suggested "a similarity of intellect, by which they [humans and animals] mutually operate upon and move each other."[51] Like Porphyry, seventeenth-century people had no doubt that animals could communicate about important matters. Moreover, when they broke their routine, and showed fear or even disobeyed, humans were wise to listen. Once again, though, these things apparently operated cross- or polytemporally. Despite the very concrete information as to the place and the time claimed by this pamphlet ("the Parish of Cookham in the County of Berks[hire], Sept. 2, 1680"), the story told here is only peripherally about an event that happened in a particular parish on a particular day. Rather, it speaks to a larger genre of prescriptions and warnings (many of them oral) about how human-animal interactions should ideally work and of the perils that await if either side fails to understand.

The joys of killing like an animal

A fundamental feature of upper-class cultures in many early modern societies was hunting prey with the help of other non-human animals (most often horses, hounds or birds, the latter usually from the orders *accipitriformes* (hawks and so on) and *falconiformes* (falcons)).[52] The helper animals had various roles. In the iconic British fox hunt, brought to its highest pitch of development in the eighteenth and early nineteenth centuries, unarmed men on horseback rode in the wake of a pack of baying hounds who chased a fox up hill and down dale until such time as they were able to catch it – which they frequently failed to do. If they did catch it, the hounds tore it to pieces and ate it, ideally within sight of the human "hunters" following close behind, so that the latter could participate vicariously in the climactic moment of the kill. Stag-hunting essentially involved dogs chasing a stag while the humans followed on horses. When the stag finally dropped from exhaustion, either the dogs killed it or (more ideally) a human hunter stepped in at the last minute and delivered the *coup de grâce* with a sword or a gun. Falconry, practised across Europe and the Middle East, involved training birds of prey to hunt and catch smaller birds in the sky or various small mammals or birds on the ground and then return with them to the handler's wrist.

Hunting with helper animals, particularly at the sophisticated level that characterised early modern elite hunting, was very much about humans harnessing the non-human abilities of the helper animal – the speed of horses; the tracking and chasing ability, doggedness and blood lust of a pack of hounds; the ability to fly, sharp eyesight and aerial pursuit capability of a hawk or falcon – so as to enhance the emotional kick of chasing after and killing prey. The human hunter experienced these better-than-human traits by virtue of his or her (usually his) proximity to and identification with the helper animals, and the chase and especially the kill – represented as positively orgasmic in some manuals –[53] sealed the bond. As one modern falconer has remarked, "falconry allows me to step into [the bird's] world for a time and be an active part of the natural order in a way that very few people ever get to experience."[54] In a kind of cross-species virtual reality, the hunter adopted or co-opted the animal's superhuman abilities whilst retaining his or her humanness.

Here we see another human-animal connection around, in this case, a very particular emotion: the joy of the chase and killing, but in an enhanced state where one temporarily acquired – or felt one acquired – some non-human abilities, and perhaps a non-human lack of inhibitions as well. Once again the emotions were not just individual; in fact, they gained intensity from the fact that they were transferred between and among animals and people. Moreover, these powerfully networked emotions had implications that went well beyond the hunt itself. Hunting with helper animals offered an opportunity to bond, in a highly charged context, both with certain prestige animals and with other hunters. The experience of hunting together was, in turn, closely tied, across Europe, the Middle East, and beyond, to the preservation of human hierarchies, particularly those of class and gender.[55] The elite character of hunting with helper animals stemmed partly from the staggering expense involved in the acquisition and upkeep of falcons, top-quality hunting dogs, horses and so forth, but it was further buttressed by prohibitions on commoners hunting (and especially hunting with animal help) and by numerous gender taboos.[56] What this meant in practice was that, across Europe and the Middle East, the joy of killing like an animal was almost always an emotional and sensory experience confined to very rich and politically well-connected men. This is a good example of an actor network that cannot be understood separately from larger systems of power. It also reminds us that, although particular human-animal networks may be hard to pin down in terms of time and place, that does not mean they do not change over time. The central role that hunting with animals once played in upper-class male culture has almost entirely disappeared today, and the notions of masculinity and status it produced and enshrined have been replaced with very different cultural styles and preoccupations, new actor networks of people, animals and things, new hierarchies and, presumably, new emotions.[57]

Love, guilt and history

The intellectual parameters of humans' dominion over nature began to shift in Christian Europe in the early modern period, and by the later eighteenth century, the issue of the treatment of animals had grown quite heated in some circles. One contributing factor was the growing impact of new emotional styles, such as sentimentalism, which increasingly rubbed up against the functionalist attitude towards animals endorsed both by Scripture and, ironically, by some scientists.[58] Another factor was the increasing realisation by some Europeans that other parts of the world exhibited quite different attitudes towards animals than those to which they were accustomed. As we have seen, European travellers to Muslim lands soon grasped the fact that Islamic notions about animals were quite unlike those of most Christians. Benjamin Arbel has provided an excellent, though not exhaustive, account of some of the many Western writers, from well-known philosophers like Michel de Montaigne and Jeremy Bentham, to more obscure writers on ethics and morality, who cited Muslim precedent as part of larger discussions of the treatment of animals.[59] Often, as Arbel shows, their information about Islamic ethics was drawn from the same travellers' writings we have been discussing in this essay. The increasingly frequent encounters between European Christians and Hindu Brahmins, mostly in South Asia, also offered food for thought. So, for example, European travellers, many of them employees of one or another of the European East India Companies, encountered a good deal of anger from some Hindus at Europeans openly killing cattle for food, and at times this caused quite serious logistical headaches especially for the English, who were accustomed to getting a good deal of their protein in the form of salted beef.[60]

Because it upset their plans, most Europeans met Brahmins' scruples against torturing, killing and eating sentient beings with non-comprehension, and even ridicule.[61] However, like earlier travellers, who wondered at the cat shelters and street-feeding of dogs in medieval Damascus and other Islamic cities, early modern European travellers to India were intrigued by the animal hospitals set up by pious Hindus and Jains in places like seventeenth-century Surat, as well as by charitable people who would buy old or sick animals from their owners so that they would not be slaughtered.[62] And ridicule was not the universal response. It is notable that John Oswald, the author of one of the most impassioned late eighteenth-century attacks in English on meat-eating, vivisection and other crimes against animals (*The Cry of Nature: or, an Appeal to Mercy and to Justice, on behalf of the Persecuted Animals,* of 1791), was converted to vegetarianism and reverence for sentient life through encounters with Brahmin intellectuals while he was stationed in India in the service of the British East India Company.[63] Perhaps appropriately, he grounds his argument primarily in emotion, both that of people and of animals:

> The dumb creatures...were sent by God into the world, to exercise our charity; and by calling forth our affections to contribute to our happiness. We [Oswald is here ventriloquizing upper-caste Hindus] consider them [non-human animals] as mute brethren, whose wants it becomes us to interpret, whose defects it is our duty to supply. The benevolence which on them we bestow, is amply repaid by the benefits which they bring; and the pleasing return for our kindness is, that endearing gratitude which renders the care of providing for them rather a pleasing occupation than a painful task.[64]

Oswald's tract is at least as indebted to late eighteenth-century sentimentalism as it is to Indian Brahmins, and it is saturated with anthropomorphic condescension as well. But surely he is not wrong to think that emotions, both pleasing and (to modern eyes) repugnant, suffuse animal/human relations almost wherever we look.

But what did these emotions actually do? Did they play any role in history? And, once again, who felt them? On the human side, one emotion that probably played a role in rethinking animal-human relations was guilt, and some of this was surely of long-standing. One does not need origin stories, religious permissions and detailed regulations if the practices in question are essentially unproblematic.[65] Part of the problem was that although humans dominated and exploited animals, they also loved some animals, and, at times, felt themselves loved in return. Still in play, however, were the following questions: What animals could one love? How could one love them? Could they really love you back? And what difference did affectionate relationships between animals and humans really make?

Let us close with one final story, this one very much about love, but, as I will argue, a mediated, contextual and even networked love, and one that probably did make some small difference in the larger scheme of things. The French naturalist Charles-Sigisbert Sonnini, whom we have already encountered, was a confirmed dog-lover, and he spent several pages in his *Travels in Upper and Lower Egypt* (1799) excoriating Egyptians for the barbaric way that they treated dogs, those "symbol[s] of an unalterable fidelity and attachment [to man]."[66] Sonnini, who spent more than two years in Egypt, was quite troubled by the way Egyptians lavished love and care on cats (which he considered to be a treacherous, superficial and generally insignificant species) while shunning the touch of "creatures possessed of infinitely more sensibility," that is, dogs. Still, he was forced to acknowledge that, as a result of the indulgent treatment they received, Egyptian cats were unusually amiable and trusting. In fact, he made a point of contrasting them to the abused, desperate, half-feral cats he had been accustomed to in France.[67] But he also thought that Egyptians' preference for cats over dogs was a sign of cultural inferiority. According to Sonnini, a nation where "[the] seductive exterior of the cat appear[s] preferable to the docility, to the exquisite instinct, to the sagacious fidelity of the dog" is "a nation, for which physical objects are all in all, and morals next to nothing…."[68] In short, Sonnini had no trouble reconciling Egyptians' singular pet preferences with standard Orientalist discourses of difference.

And then Sonnini fell in love with a Turkish Angora cat. Perhaps because it was hard for him to imagine himself becoming so attached to a cat, he spends a good deal of time describing their relationship and praising the cat's extraordinary physical beauty, goodness, gentleness and affection for him: "In my solitary moments, she adhered to my side, interrupted me frequently in the midst of my labours or my meditations, by little caresses extremely affecting: she likewise followed me in my walks." They travelled together: "On a journey, she reposed tranquilly on your knees, there was no occasion to confine her." When they were apart, "she sought and called for me incessantly with the utmost inquietude," and when he returned, she recognised his voice, and "seemed to find me again, each time, with increased satisfaction." He calls her "my principal amusement for several years," claims that the cat's love for him showed on her face and says that "her tender caresses made me forget my troubles, and consoled me in my misfortunes." Moreover, far from being treacherous and superficial (as he had previously assumed cats to be), she was truer to him than many of the human beings he knew. He ends his account with an affecting description of her final illness:

> [M]y beautiful and interesting companion perished. After several days of suffering, during which I never forsook her, her eyes, constantly fixed on me, were at length extinguished….My tears flowed….They flow at this moment…Feeling hearts will pardon me this digression of sorrow and of gratitude.[69]

It seems that one of the gentle, familiar and trusting cats of the Ottoman lands had won the heart of a foreigner with a very different set of experiences and assumptions when it came to cats.[70]

Again, we may debate whether or not this was a case of animal agency. I think the record is clear that the Angora was attached to Sonnini in her own way. But this story had a whole series of people, animals, cultural tendencies, religious precepts and daily examples of close cat/human contact behind it, some of which were discussed earlier in this essay. It had, in short, a history, as Sonnini was well aware. This complex was what made it possible for Sonnini, while living in Ottoman Egypt, to love and be loved by an animal he could not have imagined being close to in his home country (he did think the cats of Paris less brutalised, degraded and unlovable than cats in his own part of northeast France). At the same time, not all of this was distinctively Egyptian, or even Muslim. The very way Sonnini tells the story reveals some of his own preoccupations (loyalty and trust being key ones), and his confident use of the fashionable language of sensibility ("My tears flowed…They flow at this moment…" etc.) indicates a willingness to commit himself emotionally, though the cross-species nature of this love was a little unusual, and he was quite clear that the strangest thing of all was that this was a cat and not a dog.[71] And last but surely not least, there was the cat herself, of whom we cannot say much, but we can say that she had a significant impact on Sonnini and found a comfortable and happy home for herself until death struck her down. Was the connection they had world-changing? It certainly was for him. If we want to know about the ways interactive and networked animal and human emotions help to form culture, generate change and challenge human assumptions and intent (in Sonnini's case, a prejudice both against cats and against those "nations" that harbored too great a fondness for them), we must surely take such stories seriously.

Conclusion

This essay has been an attempt to look both at some of the historical evidence for interspecies emotion and at some of the theoretical frames that may help us to think more productively about emotion in a world unlikely to have been made solely for the benefit of humans. The approach has deliberately been both geographically dispersed and temporally complex. In the story of Muhammed's cat, we traced the connections between historically demonstrable ethical and religious positions on animals (including cats) expressed in the Qur'an and numerous ahadith, a much later story about a particular sheik and a cat, and the reluctance many people feel, and apparently have long felt, about disturbing a sleeping cat, even if it is sleeping on an expensive textile. Over time, as we saw, the tale of the cat on the sleeve of the sheik was transformed into a story about the Prophet Muhammed, and widely diffused by European travellers as part of an effort to explain differences between Christian and Muslim treatment of some animals. Today, the story has been reappropriated by Muslims and forms one of several justifications for welcoming cats into a number of religious settings. It also forms the basis for a vibrant Internet genre that celebrates the connection between pious Muslims and cats.

The seventeenth-century account of an English plough-team struck by lightning focuses on several issues to do with animal emotion and agency. On the one hand, it explores long-standing claims about the ability of working animals and working humans to communicate over shared tasks. On the other hand, it seeks to show that, in the eyes of seventeenth-century people, failure to grasp what one's animals were saying or "feeling" could have serious, even deadly, consequences. We should be wary of assuming that this story actually unfolded in the way it is presented, largely because the narrative fits too neatly into a long tradition of stories in which animals "save" humans and, in so doing, confirm their willingness to serve them. This story is more akin to a parable than to a true description of a real event. However, the more general phenomenon of four-legged beasts of burden conveying their concern and fear – in short, their emotions – through their body-language and "unruliness" surely stems from real observations of farm animals. The argument here is that by looking at episodes in which animals try to influence events, whether or not they succeed, we can discover some of the networked intersections between the agency of animals and that of humans.

In the modern day, elite hunting with helper animals has largely disappeared along with the intense emotions that accompanied it. In this section, the argument was made that hunting offered access to a kind of "cross-species virtual reality" in which the hunter "used" various animals' great-than-human abilities to enhance the kick of pursuing and killing prey. This favourite activity of nobles and monarchs, across both Europe and the Middle East (and indeed, beyond), was very much a networked one. The helper animals, the people and even the prey participated in a blizzard of emotions: the excitement of the chase, the desperation of being chased, the joy (or, for the prey, the fear and pain) of the final kill, the exhilaration of performing masculine tasks in front of other men and the feeling of connection between and among horses, birds of prey, dogs and people. And the rewards, at least for the hunters, both animal and human, were great. It was not uncommon, we are told, for noblemen to feed and house their horses and their hunting dogs better than their human servants.[72]

Much has changed since the early modern period. Aristocratic influence and prestige have largely vanished; most people today care far more about pop music stars. Large hunts involving significant numbers of helper animals are rare, elite men perform both status and masculinity in alternative ways (though still often in ways linked to sport) and their relationships to animals, and presumably their emotions, are also different from what they were. This is a clear case where the maintenance of hierarchies relied upon the networked emotions both of animals and people, but, over time, almost everything has been rearranged.

In the final section, we looked at another kind of change – having to do with ideas about "the other," whether human or animal. Early modern Europeans' encounter with foreign climes and non-Christian cultural systems was only one of the forces that encouraged a rethinking of attitudes towards animals, but it was an important one. However, it is difficult to know exactly how that change of mind occurred. Was it really the impact of travel narratives, and the philosophers and ethicists they influenced? In point of fact, there are many historical examples of people changing their views as a result of something they read. However, in this section, I wanted to explore a somewhat different avenue of causality. The purpose of telling the story of Sonnini and the Angora cat is to show how a highly emotional relationship between a person and an animal could have the effect of upending, at least temporarily, many of the things the human assumed to be true about the world – including, in this case, a whole series of yoked beliefs about both cats and Muslims. In the end, emotions can and do make a difference in the world; both animals and humans experience them, and people, animals, things and feelings form parts of larger networks that construct and connect multiple past and present times.

Notes

1 The binary animal/human is an unsatisfactory one, but also, at present, not easily dispensed with. This essay at times refers to "non-human animals" and at times to humans and animals, trusting the reader to realise that humans are also members of the Kingdom Animalia. My thanks to the members of the Högreseminariet, Uppsala University History Department, to Sebastian Kühn and to Claudia Jarzebowski for comments on earlier versions of this paper.
2 See, for instance: Brian Boyd, "Archaeology and Human–Animal Relations: Thinking through Anthropocentrism," *Annual Review of Anthropology* 46 (2017): 299–316; Jeffrey Bussolini, "Recent French, Belgian and Italian Work in the Cognitive Science of Animals: Dominique Lestel, Vinciane Despret, Roberto Marchesini and Giorgio Celli," *Social Science Information* 52, no. 2 (June 1, 2013): 187–209.
3 Keith Thomas, *Man and the Natural World: Changing Attitudes in England, 1500–1800* (New York: Oxford University Press, 1996) outlines the debate in the early modern period.
4 For purposes of this essay, "Sunnah" is understood to mean "whatever the Prophet was reported to have said, did, or permitted others to do." Quotation from http://www.newmuslim.net/quran-sunnah/definition-sunnah/ accessed 21 March 2019. The major way to know this, though not the only one, is through the evidence of ahadith (singular: hadith), which were oral reports about the Prophet's words and deeds recounted by his Companions, passed down to subsequent generations through a more or less authoritative chain and later put into written form.
5 This issue is dealt with in more detail in Margaret R. Hunt, "Relations of Domination and Subordination in Early Modern Europe and the Middle East," *Gender & History* 30, no. 2 (2018): 366–376.
6 King James Version of 1611.
7 Genesis 8:20, Exodus 29:18 and more than a score of other references.
8 Luke 24:42, Matthew 26:17–23.
9 Qur'an 5:1–5 (human can kill and eat livestock and some other animals); 5:96 (permission to engage in fish-eating); 6:142 (animals can be used for load-carrying); 16:66 (humans can take the milk of certain animals); 16:80 (humans can use animal skins).
10 A brief outline of Christian (scholastic) claims about animals' lack of a rational soul can be found in Benjamin Arbel, "The Attitude of Muslims to Animals: Renaissance Perceptions and Beyond," in *Animals and People in the Ottoman Empire*, ed.

Suraiya Faroqhi (Istanbul: Eren, 2010), 57–74 here 59–60. See also Gary A. Kowalski, *The Souls of Animals* (Novato, CA: New World Library, 2007); Lloyd Strickland, "God's Creatures? Divine Nature and the Status of Animals in the Early Modern Beast-Machine Controversy," *International Journal of Philosophy and Theology* 74 (2013): 291–309. On the other hand, there have been a number of religious orders and Christian sects who have practised vegetarianism or pescatarianism, most often for ascetic reasons. For a defense of Christian ideas about animals see Rod Preece, "Darwinism, Christianity, and the Great Vivisection Debate," *Journal of the History of Ideas* 64, no. 3 (2003): 399–419.

11 David Mevorach Seidenberg, "Animal Rights in the Jewish Tradition," in *The Animal Ethics Reader*, ed. Susan J. Armstrong and Richard G. Botzler (New York: Routledge, 2016), 289–293, quotation 289.

12 Seidenberg, "Animal Rights in the Jewish Tradition," 290.

13 Relevant Qur'anic passages include 6:38; 16:69; 17:44. There is a fairly significant secondary literature on this subject, to which Suraiya Faroqhi's edited volume *Animals and People in the Ottoman Empire* forms a good introduction (see above footnote 10). In this volume, see especially Arbel, "Attitude of Muslims to Animals."

14 Housni Alkhateeb Shehada, "Arabic Veterinary Medicine and the 'Golden Rules' for Veterinarians According to a Sixteenth-Century Medical Treatise," in *Animals and People in the Ottoman Empire*, ed. Suraiya Faroqhi (Istanbul: Eren, 2010), 315–331; See also Housni Alkhateeb Shehada, *Mamluks and Animals: Veterinary Medicine in Medieval Islam* (Leiden: Brill, 2012). A somewhat more ambiguous picture is presented in Peter Adamson, "The Ethical Treatment of Animals," in *The Routledge Companion to Islamic Philosophy*, ed. Richard C. Taylor and Luis Xavier López-Farjeat (London: Routledge, 2015), 371–382.

15 See especially Farid Ud-Din Attar, *Mantiq-uṭ-Ṭayr, The Conference of the Birds* (twelfth century), the title of which is drawn from the Qur'an 27:16. Geoffrey Chaucer's Parliament of Birds (ca. 1383) bears many similarities to Attar's work, though apparently these are fortuitous. See Maryam Khoshbakht, Moussa Ahmadian and Shahrukh Hekmat, "A Comparative Study of Chaucer's The Canterbury Tales and Attar's the Conference of the Birds," *International Journal of Applied Linguistics and English Literature* 2, no. 1 (2013): 90–97.

16 Dean Sakel, "The Ottoman-Era Physiologus," in *Animals and People in the Ottoman Empire*, ed. Suraiya Faroqhi (Istanbul: Eren, 2010), 129–150 here 143. The association of the hoopoe with family love presumably derives from the fact that the male feeds the female during courtship and incubation of the eggs.

17 A useful overview can be found in *Inquiry: An Interdisciplinary Journal of Philosophy*, Volume 52, 2009 – Issue 3 (2009): special issue on Human and Non-Human Animal Agency.

18 Walter Johnson, "On Agency," *Journal of Social History* 37, no. 1 (September 5, 2003): 113–124, quotation 115. Similar doubts about the motives of researchers are aired in Saba Mahmood, *Politics of Piety: The Islamic Revival and the Feminist Subject* (Princeton, NJ: Princeton University Press, 2004) and Lynn M. Thomas, "Historicising Agency," *Gender & History* 28, no. 2 (August, 2016): 324–339.

19 Erica Fudge, "Renaissance Animal Things," *New Formations* 76, no. 76 (2012): 86–100.

20 Arjun Appadurai, ed., *The Social Life of Things: Commodities in Cultural Perspective* (Cambridge: Cambridge University Press, 1986); Bill Brown, "Thing Theory," *Critical Inquiry* 28, no. 1 (2001): 1–21; Bruno Latour, *Reassembling the Social: An Introduction to Actor-Network-Theory* (Oxford University Press, 2005); Bruno Latour and Couze Venn, "Morality and Technology," *Theory, Culture & Society* 19, no. 5–6 (2002): 247–260; and Edwin M. Sayes, "Actor-Network Theory and Methodology: Just What Does It Mean to Say That Nonhumans Have Agency?" *Social Studies of Science* 44, no. 1 (2014): 134–149.

21 Bruno Latour, "On Actor-Network Theory: A Few Clarifications," *Soziale Welt* 47, no. 4 (1996): 369–381 here 373.
22 Sandra Harding, *Sciences from Below: Feminisms, Postcolonialities, and Modernities* (Durham, NC: Duke University Press, 2008), 42–46.
23 A useful overview is Nicole Eustace et al., "'AHR' Conversation: The Historical Study of Emotions," *The American Historical Review* 117, no. 5 (2012): 1486–1531.
24 Barbara H. Rosenwein, "Worrying about Emotions in History," *The American Historical Review* 107, no. 3 (2002): 821–845 has perhaps the most influential formulation:

> [Emotional communities] are precisely the same as social communities-families, neighborhoods, parliaments, guilds, monasteries, parish church memberships-but the researcher looking at them seeks above all to uncover systems of feeling: what these communities (and the individuals within them) define and assess as valuable or harmful to them; the evaluations that they make about others' emotions; the nature of the affective bonds between people that they recognize; and the modes of emotional expression that they expect, encourage, tolerate, and deplore. (842)

See also Jan Plamper et al., "The History of Emotions: An Interview with William Reddy, Barbara Rosenwein, and Peter Stearns," *History and Theory* 49, no. 2 (2010): 237–265, and Thomas Dixon, "Social Emotions," in *Emotional Lexicons: Continuity and Change in the Vocabulary of Feeling 1700–2000*, ed. Ute Frevert and Thomas Dixon (Oxford: Oxford University Press, 2014), 203–229. For a particularly subtle discussion of emotions as a historical force see Margrit Pernau, "Feeling Communities: Introduction," *The Indian Economic & Social History Review* 54, no. 1 (January 1, 2017): 1–20.

25 Pascal Eitler, "The Origin of Emotions: Sensitive Humans, Sensitive Animals," in *Emotional Lexicons: Continuity and Change in the Vocabulary of Feeling 1700–2000*, ed. Ute Frevert and Thomas Dixon (Oxford: Oxford University Press, 2014), 91–117. Eitler does, in fact, deal with several eighteenth-century philosophers, but the centre of gravity of the paper is clearly in the nineteenth and twentieth centuries. See also Jopi Nyman and Nora Schuurman, *Affect, Space and Animals* (Routledge, 2015) mainly focused on the nineteenth to twenty-first centuries.

26 Erica Fudge, *Perceiving Animals: Humans and Beasts in Early Modern English Culture* (Champaign: University of Illinois Press, 2002); Erica Fudge, *Animal* (London: Reaktion Books, 2004); Erica Fudge, *Brutal Reasoning: Animals, Rationality, and Humanity in Early Modern England* (Ithaca, NY: Cornell University Press, 2006); and Erica Fudge, *Pets* (London: Routledge, 2014).

27 Faroqhi, ed., *Animals and People in the Ottoman Empire*. See also Alkhateeb Shehada, *Mamluks and Animals;* and Alan Mikhail, *The Animal in Ottoman Egypt* (Oxford: Oxford University Press, 2013).

28 *Sunan Abu Dawud*, trans. Ahmad Hasan, 3 vols (Lahore: Sh. M. Ashraf, 1984), Vol. 2, 740, haddith 2669.

29 *English Translation of Sunan An-Nasâ'i*, trans. Nâsiruddin Khattâb, 6 vols (Riyadh: Darussalam, 2007), Vol. 5, 210, hadith 4363 (narrated by Abu Hurayrah) "An ant bit one of the prophets, and he ordered that the ant nest be burned. Then Allah revealed to him: 'One ant bit you, and you destroyed one of the nations that glorify Allah.'"

30 Sunan an-Nasa'i Vol. 5, 251, hadith 4451.

31 See e.g., Sahih al-Bukhari ahadith 557 and 2320 (Sunnah.com, accessed 6 August 2020).

32 On female infanticide see especially Avner Giladi, "Some Observations on Infanticide in Medieval Muslim Society," *International Journal of Middle East Studies* 22, no. 2 (May 1990): 185–200. The literature on slaves, orphans, wives and so forth in Islamic religious context and Islamic legal practice is vast. For an influential, though now somewhat dated, introduction to the issues, see Joseph Schacht, *An Introduction to Islamic Law*, vol. 71 (New York: Oxford New York Press, 1964).

33 Cyril Glassé, *The New Encyclopedia of Islam* (Altamira: Rowman, 2003), 102.
34 Sahih al-Bukhari ahadith 745, 2365, 3318, 3482. The Prophet also disapproved of selling dogs and cats: Sahih Muslim, hadith 743 (Sunnah.com accessed 6 August 2020).
35 A number of ahadith and jurisprudential discussions deal with the ritual cleanliness of cats. See e.g., Fiqh-us-Sunnah, fiqh 1.6; Sunan of Abu-Dawud, ahadith 43 and 44; Muwatta Imam Malik, Book 2, Number 2.3.13; Sunan ibn Majah, ahadith 367, 368 and 369 (Sunnah.com, accessed 6 August 2020).
36 The original tale is told in al-Dhahabī, *Siyar aʿlām al-nubalā'* (The Lives of Noble Figures), biography 28, cited in Alkhateeb Shehada, *Mamluks and Animals*, 77–78 and 78n.
37 Alkhateeb Shehada, *Mamluks and Animals*, 77–78; Joos Van Ghistele, *Tvoyage van Mher Joos van Ghistele, oft Anders... in den Landen van Sclauonien, Griecken, Turckien, Candien, Rhodes en[de] Cypers. Voords ooc in den Lande van Beloften, Assirien, Arabien, Egypten, Ethyopien, Barbarie[n], etc.* (Ghent: Henric van den Keere, 1557), 240–241. My thanks to Susanna Erlandsson and Sander Kollaard for helping me with the sixteenth-century Dutch. Van Ghistele visited Damascus sometime between 1481 and 1485.
38 Ogier Ghiselin de Busbecq, *Travels into Turkey: Containing the Most Accurate Account of the Turks, and Neighbouring Nations, etc. ... translated from the Latin* (London, 1744), 140. De Busbecq had been sent as ambassador to the Sublime Porte by Ferdinand I (Austrian Emperor and later also Holy Roman Emperor).
39 Arbel, "Attitude of Muslims to Animals," 65–70 discusses a number of these travellers.
40 The study of animal emotion has relied heavily on the evidence of modern-day experiences with animals. Influential accounts of animals (and especially animal emotion) often include this kind of reportage. See, for example, Temple Grandin, *Thinking in Pictures* (New York: Vintage Books, 1996), Elizabeth Marshall Thomas, *The Hidden Life of Dogs* (Boston, MA: HMH, 2010); and Elizabeth Marshall Thomas, *The Tribe of Tiger* (New York: Simon and Schuster, 2001). The benefits and risks of using such evidence in the context both of "sensory history" and of networked understanding of people, animals and things are outlined in Erica Fudge, "Renaissance Animal Things," *New Formations* 76, no. 76 (2012): 86–100; and Erica Fudge, *Pets* (London: Routledge, 2014). See also Mikhail, *Animals in Ottoman Eqypt*, 11–12.
41 Van Ghistele, *Tvoyage*, 241.
42 De Busbecq, *Travels into Turkey*, 140–141.
43 Joseph Pitton de Tournefort, *A Voyage into the Levant: Perform'd by Command of the Late French King*, 2 vols (London, 1718), vol. 2, 62–63.
44 Charles-Sigisbert Sonnini, *Travels in Upper and Lower Egypt: Undertaken by Order of the Old Government of France...*, trans. Henry Hunter, 3 vols (London: Printed for John Stockdale, 1799), Vol. I, 286–290, quotation 288.
45 See above note 35.
46 Muwatta Imam Malik, Book 2, Number 2.3.13.
47 There are dozens of these videos, and often they are accompanied by comments testifying to the natural piety of cats. See e.g., https://www.youtube.com/watch?v=MF7pTSCP4UM, accessed 13 March 2019 and https://www.youtube.com/watch?v=JHGfiwQYu6U&t=62s, accessed 26 March 2019.
48 I do not wish to imply that this is an unchanging tradition. In the nineteenth and twentieth centuries, in the interests of modernisation, many cities in the Middle East violently rid themselves of street dogs, and there were efforts to suppress *waqfs* (charitable trusts) devoted to charity to animals. On this issue, see Catherine Pinguet, "Istanbul's Street Dogs at the End of the Ottoman Empire," in *Animals and People in the Ottoman Empire*, ed. Suraiya Faroqhi (Istanbul: Eren, 2010), 353–371, and Alan Mikhail, *The Animal in Ottoman Egypt* (Oxford: Oxford University Press. 2013).
49 Anon. *A Full and True Relation of the Death and Slaughter of a Man and His Son at Plough, Together with Four Horses, in the Parish of Cookham in the County of Berks, Sept. 2, 1680 Slain by the Thunder and Lightning That Then and There Happened, as May Fully Be*

Testified by Credible Persons Whose Names are Hereunto Adjoyned... (London: Printed for John Harding, 1680).
50 For useful remarks on some of the species characteristics of early modern English cattle, see Erica Fudge, "Milking Other Men's Beasts," *History and Theory* 52, no. 4 (2013): 13–28.
51 Porphyry, *On Abstinence from Animal Food*. The translation of the passage is from the late eighteenth century and drawn from John Oswald, *The Cry of Nature, or an Appeal to Mercy and Justice, on Behalf of the Persecuted Animals* (London: J. Johnson, 1791), 121. For more on Oswald see below.
52 A large literature surrounds elite hunting. A useful introduction for Britain is Mike Huggins, "Sport and the British Upper Classes c.1500–2000: A Historiographic Overview," *Sport in History* 28, no. 3 (September 1, 2008): 364–388. For the European Continent see: Marcello Fantoni et al., *The Princely Courts of Europe: Ritual, Politics and Culture under the Ancien Régime, 1500–1750* (London: Weidenfeld & Nicolson, 1999). For the Ottoman Empire see Elisabetta Borromeo, "The Ottomans and Hunting According to Julien Bordier (1604–1612)," in *Animals and People in the Ottoman Empire*, ed. Suraiya Faroqhi (Istanbul: Eren, 2010), 219–233; and Gilles Veinstein, "Falconry in the Mid-Sixteenth Century Ottoman Empire," in *Animals and People in the Ottoman Empire*, ed. Suraiya Faroqhi (Istanbul: Eren, 2010), 205–218.
53 See e.g., Peter Beckford, *Thoughts on Hunting, in a Series of Familiar Letters to a Friend* (London, 1798), 168–169. The element of sexual release in hunting is stressed in Norbert Elias and Eric Dunning, *Quest for Excitement: Sport and Leisure in the Civilising Process*. (Dublin: University College Dublin Press, 2008), an iconic work in the sociology of sport.
54 http://www.cracked.com/personal-experiences-2356-the-badass-life-modern-day-falconer.html, accessed 30 April 2018.
55 For a good account of the hunt as a vehicle for elite male bonding and especially as a tool of diplomacy, see Elisabetta Borromeo, "The Ottomans and Hunting According to Julien Bordier (1604–1612)," in *Animals and People in the Ottoman Empire*, ed. Suraiya Faroqhi (Istanbul: Eren, 2010), 219–233 especially 229–231. For the expense see Veinstein, "Falconry in the Mid-Sixteenth century Ottoman Empire." On prestige animals and their role in upper-class life (including in relation to hunting) and in the display and preservation of hierarchy see Marcy Norton, "Going to the Birds: Animals as Things and Beings in Early Modernity," in *Early Modern Things: Objects and Their Histories, 1500–1800*, ed. Paula Findlen (New York: Routledge, 2013), 58–83.
56 A classic account is Edward P. Thompson, *Whigs and Hunters: The Origins of the Black Act* (New York: Pantheon, 1973). On gender see Callum Mckenzie, "'Sadly Neglected' – Hunting and Gendered Identities: A Study in Gender Construction," *The International Journal of the History of Sport* 22, no. 4 (July 1, 2005): 545–562.
57 On the gradual infiltration of the hunt by non-nobles and by some women, especially in the later nineteenth and twentieth centuries, see, inter alia, Bernadette Bucher, "Rites et Stratégies d'Adaptation: La Chasse à Courre en Bocage Vendéen," *Études Rurales*, no. 87/88 (1982): 269–286, and David C. Itzkowitz, *Peculiar Privilege: A Social History of English Foxhunting 1753–1885* (Brighton: Edward Everett Root Publishers, 2016). There is also a significant literature on the dwindling popularity of hunting in much of Europe and the Middle East in the modern era, as a result of the decline of the traditional nobility, growing opposition to the hunt on sentimental, ethical and (sometimes) religious grounds, the destruction of wild animal habitats and other factors.
58 On shifting attitudes, see especially Thomas, *Man and the Natural World*, 143–190.
59 Arbel, "Attitude of Muslims to Animals" see especially 59–61.
60 Much of the literature on cow protection campaigns deals with the later nineteenth century, but it was an issue, especially for the British, from considerably earlier. See e.g., Philip Anderson, *The English in Western India; Being the Early History of the Factory*

at Surat, of Bombay, and the Subordinate Factories on the Western Coast. From the Earliest Period until the Commencement of the Eighteenth Century (Bombay: Smith and Taylor, 1854), 107–108. The issue of vegetarianism and Hinduism (and especially controversies about the killing and eating of cows) is a complicated one. Though ancient Hindu writings are quite mixed on the issue of vegetarianism (and cows), and some, usually lower-caste Hindus, have traditionally eaten beef, in the last century or so, "cow protection" has become a major justifications for violent attacks –up to and including lynching– by Hindus on Muslims and lower-caste people. There is a growing literature on this phenomenon, for which Juli L. Gittinger, "The Rhetoric of Violence, Religion, and Purity in India's Cow Protection Movement," *Journal of Religion and Violence* 2, no. 5 (2017): 131–149. serves as a good introduction.
61 Thomas, *Man and the Natural World*, 21. There were far fewer close encounters with Buddhists, at least during the early modern period, and into the nineteenth century, many Europeans considered Buddhism to be a branch of Hinduism. On this, see Audrius Beinorius, "Buddhism in the Early European Imagination: A Historical Perspective," *Acta Orientalia Vilnensia* 6, no. 2 (2005): 7–22. Similarly, some of the practices Europeans were encountering were probably Jainist, but for most Europeans, Jainism did not register as a separate faith before the nineteenth century. On this, see Mitch Numark, "The Scottish 'Discovery' of Jainism in Nineteenth-Century Bombay," *Journal of Scottish Historical Studies* 33, no. 1 (April, 2013): 20–51.
62 John Ovington, *A Voyage to Suratt in the Year 1689* (London: Tonson, 1696), 300.
63 John Oswald, *The Cry of Nature, or an Appeal to Mercy and Justice, on Behalf of the Persecuted Animals.* (London: J. Johnson, 1791). For Oswald's life see T. Henderson, "Oswald, John (c. 1760–1793), Journalist and Poet," *Oxford Dictionary of National Biography*. Retrieved 30 Apr. 2018.
64 Oswald, *Cry of Nature*, 8–9.
65 A provocative discussion of psycho-social conflicts over animals in the early Islamic community is Mohammed Hocine Benkheira, Catherine Mayeur-Jaouen, and Jacqueline Sublet, *L'animal en Islam* (Paris: Les Indes savantes/Archive ouverte en Sciences de l'Homme et de la Société, 2005).
66 Sonnini, *Travels in Upper and Lower Egypt*, Vol. I, 288.
67 Sonnini, *Travels in Upper and Lower Egypt*, Vol. I, 289–290. He grew up in the Duchy of Lorraine, annexed by France in 1766.
68 Sonnini, *Travels in Upper and Lower Egypt*, Vol. I, 288.
69 Sonnini, *Travels in Upper and Lower Egypt* Vol. I, 290–292. Ellipses in the original.
70 Cats of the Angora breed are, even today, sometimes said to act more like dogs than cats. Sonnini actually claims, as part of trying to explain how he could love a cat, that this Angora "possessed the nature of the most amiable dog, beneath the brilliant fur of a cat" (291).
71 There is a large literature on weeping and the cult of sensibility. See Anne Coudreuse, *Le Goût des Larmes au XVIIIe Siècle* (Paris: FeniXX, 1999); and Marco Menin, "'Who Will Write the History of Tears?' History of Ideas and History of Emotions from Eighteenth-Century France to the Present," *History of European Ideas* 40, no. 4 (2014): 516–532.
72 Norton, "Going to the Birds"

Bibliography

Adamson, Peter. "The Ethical Treatment of Animals." In *The Routledge Companion to Islamic Philosophy*, ed. Richard C. Taylor and Luis Xavier López-Farjeat. London: Routledge, 2015, 371–382.

Alkhateeb Shehada, Housni. "Arabic Veterinary Medicine and the 'Golden Rules' for Veterinarians According to a Sixteenth-Century Medical Treatise." In *Animals and People in the Ottoman Empire*, ed. Suraiya Faroqhi. Istanbul: Eren, 2010, 315–331.

Alkhateeb Shehada, Housni. *Mamluks and Animals: Veterinary Medicine in Medieval Islam*. Leiden: Brill, 2012.

Anderson, Philip. *The English in Western India; Being the Early History of the Factory at Surat, of Bombay, and the Subordinate Factories on the Western Coast. From the Earliest Period until the Commencement of the Eighteenth Century*. Bombay: Smith and Taylor, 1854.

Anon. *A Full and True Relation of the Death and Slaughter of a Man and His Son at Plough, Together with Four Horses, in the Parish of Cookham in the County of Berks, Sept. 2, 1680 Slain by the Thunder and Lightning That Then and There Happened, as May Fully Be Testified by Credible Persons Whose Names Are Hereunto Adjoyned...* London: Printed for John Harding, 1680.

Appadurai, Arjun, ed. *The Social Life of Things: Commodities in Cultural Perspective*. Cambridge: Cambridge University Press, 1986.

Arbel, Benjamin. "The Attitude of Muslims to Animals: Renaissance Perceptions and Beyond." In *Animals and People in the Ottoman Empire*, ed. Suraiya Faroqhi. Istanbul: Eren, 2010, 57–74.

Beckford, Peter. *Thoughts on Hunting, in a Series of Familiar Letters to a Friend*. London, 1798.

Beinorius, Audrius. "Buddhism in the Early European Imagination: A Historical Perspective." *Acta Orientalia Vilnensia* 6, no. 2 (2005): 7–22.

Borromeo, Elisabetta. "The Ottomans and Hunting According to Julien Bordier (1604–1612)." In *Animals and People in the Ottoman Empire*, ed. Suraiya Faroqhi. Istanbul: Eren, 2010, 219–233.

Boyd, Brian. "Archaeology and Human–Animal Relations: Thinking through Anthropocentrism." *Annual Review of Anthropology* 46 (2017): 299–316.

Brown, Bill. "Thing Theory." *Critical Inquiry* 28, no. 1 (2001): 1–21.

Bucher, Bernadette. "Rites et Stratégies d'Adaptation: La Chasse à Courre en Bocage Vendéen." *Études Rurales* 87/88 (1982): 269–86.

Bussolini, Jeffrey. "Recent French, Belgian and Italian Work in the Cognitive Science of Animals: Dominique Lestel, Vinciane Despret, Roberto Marchesini and Giorgio Celli." *Social Science Information* 52, no. 2 (June 1, 2013): 187–209.

Coudreuse, Anne. *Le Goût des Larmes au XVIIIe Siècle* (Paris: FeniXX, 1999).

Dixon, Thomas. "Social Emotions." In *Emotional Lexicons: Continuity and Change in the Vocabulary of Feeling 1700–2000*, ed. Ute Frevert and Thomas Dixon. Oxford: Oxford University Press, 2014, 203–229.

Eitler, Pascal. "The Origin of Emotions: Sensitive Humans, Sensitive Animals." In *Emotional Lexicons: Continuity and Change in the Vocabulary of Feeling 1700–2000*, ed. Ute Frevert and Thomas Dixon. Oxford: Oxford University Press, 2014, 91–117.

Elias, Norbert and Eric Dunning, *Quest for Excitement: Sport and Leisure in the Civilising Process*. Dublin: University College Dublin Press, 2008.

Eustace, Nicole et al. "'AHR' Conversation: The Historical Study of Emotions." *The American Historical Review* 117, no. 5 (2012): 1486–1531.

Fantoni, Marcello et al. *The Princely Courts of Europe: Ritual, Politics and Culture under the Ancien Régime, 1500–1750*. London: Weidenfeld & Nicolson, 1999.

Fudge, Erica. *Animal*. London: Reaktion Books, 2004.

Fudge, Erica. *Brutal Reasoning: Animals, Rationality, and Humanity in Early Modern England*. Ithaca, NY: Cornell University Press, 2006.

Fudge, Erica. "Milking Other Men's Beasts." *History and Theory* 52, no. 4 (2013): 13–28.

Fudge, Erica. *Perceiving Animals: Humans and Beasts in Early Modern English Culture*. Champaign: University of Illinois Press, 2002.

Fudge, Erica. *Pets*. London: Routledge, 2014.

Fudge, Erica. "Renaissance Animal Things." *New Formations* 76, no. 76 (2012): 86–100.

Ghiselin de Busbecq, Ogier. *Travels into Turkey: Containing the Most Accurate Account of the Turks, and Neighbouring Nations, etc.... Translated from the Latin*. London, 1744.

Ghistele, Joos Van. *Tvoyage van Mher Joos van Ghistele, oft Anders... in den Landen van Sclauonien, Griecken, Turckien, Candien, Rhodes en[de] Cypers. Voords ooc in den Lande van Beloften, Assirien, Arabien, Egypten, Ethyopien, Barbarie[n], etc*. Ghent: Henric van den Keere, 1557.

Giladi, Avner. "Some Observations on Infanticide in Medieval Muslim Society." *International Journal of Middle East Studies* 22, no. 2 (May 1990): 185–200.

Gittinger, Juli L. "The Rhetoric of Violence, Religion, and Purity in India's Cow Protection Movement." *Journal of Religion and Violence* 2, no. 5 (2017): 131–149.

Glassé, Cyril. *The New Encyclopedia of Islam*. Altamira: Rowman, 2003.

Grandin, Temple. *Thinking in Pictures*. New York: Vintage Books, 1996.

Harding, Sandra. *Sciences from Below: Feminisms, Postcolonialities, and Modernities*. Durham, NC: Duke University Press, 2008, 42–46.

Henderson, T. "Oswald, John (c. 1760–1793), Journalist and Poet." *Oxford Dictionary of National Biography*. Retrieved 30 Apr. 2018. doi: 10.1093/ref:odnb/20922

Hocine Benkheira, Mohammed, Catherine Mayeur-Jaouen, and Jacqueline Sublet. *L'animal en Islam*. Paris: Les Indes savantes/Archive ouverte en Sciences de l'Homme et de la Société, 2005.

Huggins, Mike. "Sport and the British Upper Classes c.1500–2000: A Historiographic Overview." *Sport in History* 28, no. 3 (September 1, 2008): 364–388.

Hunt, Margaret R. "Relations of Domination and Subordination in Early Modern Europe and the Middle East." *Gender & History* 30, no. 2 (2018): 366–376.

Itzkowitz, David C. *Peculiar Privilege: A Social History of English Foxhunting 1753–1885*. Brighton: Edward Everett Root Publishers, 2016.

Johnson, Walter. "On Agency." *Journal of Social History* 37, no. 1 (September 5, 2003): 113–124.

Khoshbakht, Maryam, Moussa Ahmadian, and Shahrukh Hekmat. "A Comparative Study of Chaucer's The Canterbury Tales and Attar's The Conference of the Birds." *International Journal of Applied Linguistics and English Literature* 2, no. 1 (2013): 90–97.

Kowalski, Gary A. *The Souls of Animals*. Novato, CA: New World Library, 2007.

Latour, Bruno. "On Actor-Network Theory: A Few Clarifications." *Soziale Welt* 47, no. 4 (1996): 369–381.

Latour, Bruno. *Reassembling the Social: An Introduction to Actor-Network-Theory*. Oxford: Oxford University Press, 2005.

Latour, Bruno and Couze Venn. "Morality and Technology." *Theory, Culture & Society* 19, no. 5–6 (2002): 247–260.

Mahmood, Saba. *Politics of Piety: The Islamic Revival and the Feminist Subject*. Princeton, NJ: Princeton University Press, 2004.

Marshall Thomas, Elizabeth. *The Hidden Life of Dogs*. Boston, MA: HMH, 2010.

Marshall Thomas, Elizabeth. *The Tribe of Tiger*. New York: Simon and Schuster, 2001.

Mckenzie, Callum. "'Sadly Neglected' – Hunting and Gendered Identities: A Study in Gender Construction." *The International Journal of the History of Sport* 22, no. 4 (July 1, 2005): 545–562.

Menin, Marco. "'Who Will Write the History of Tears?' History of Ideas and History of Emotions from Eighteenth-Century France to the Present." *History of European Ideas* 40, no. 4 (2014): 516–532.

Mikhail, Alan. *The Animal in Ottoman Egypt*. Oxford: Oxford University Press, 2013.

Norton, Marcy. "Going to the Birds: Animals as Things and Beings in Early Modernity." In *Early Modern Things: Objects and Their Histories, 1500–1800*, ed. Paula Findlen. New York: Routledge, 2013, 58–83.

Numark, Mitch. "The Scottish 'Discovery' of Jainism in Nineteenth-Century Bombay." *Journal of Scottish Historical Studies* 33, no. 1 (April, 2013): 20–51.

Nyman, Jopi and Nora Schuurman. *Affect, Space and Animals*. New York: Routledge, 2015.

Oswald, John. *The Cry of Nature, or an Appeal to Mercy and Justice, on Behalf of the Persecuted Animals*. London: J. Johnson, 1791.

Ovington, John. *A Voyage to Suratt in the Year 1689*. London: Tonson, 1696.

Pernau, Margrit. "Feeling Communities: Introduction." *The Indian Economic & Social History Review* 54, no. 1 (January 1, 2017): 1–20.

Pinguet, Catherine. "Istanbul's Street Dogs at the End of the Ottoman Empire." In *Animals and People in the Ottoman Empire*, ed. Suraiya Faroqhi. Istanbul: Eren, 2010, 353–371.

Pitton de Tournefort, Joseph. *A Voyage into the Levant: Perform'd by Command of the Late French King*. 2 vols. London, 1718.

Plamper, Jan et al. "The History of Emotions: An Interview with William Reddy, Barbara Rosenwein, and Peter Stearns." *History and Theory* 49, no. 2 (2010): 237–265.

Preece, Rod. "Darwinism, Christianity, and the Great Vivisection Debate." *Journal of the History of Ideas* 64, no. 3 (2003): 399–419.

Rosenwein, Barbara H. "Worrying about Emotions in History." *The American Historical Review* 107, no. 3 (2002): 821–845.

Sakel, Dean. "The Ottoman-Era Physiologus." In *Animals and People in the Ottoman Empire*, ed. Suraiya Faroqhi. Istanbul: Eren, 2010, 129–150.

Sayes, Edwin M. "Actor-Network Theory and Methodology: Just What Does It Mean to Say That Nonhumans Have Agency?" *Social Studies of Science* 44, no. 1 (2014): 134–149.

Schacht, Joseph. *An Introduction to Islamic Law*, vol. 71. New York: Oxford University Press, 1964.

Seidenberg, David Mevorach. "Animal Rights in the Jewish Tradition." In *The Animal Ethics Reader*, ed. Susan J. Armstrong and Richard G. Botzler. New York: Routledge, 2016, 289–293.

Sonnini, Charles-Sigisbert. *Travels in Upper and Lower Egypt: Undertaken by Order of the Old Government of France...*, trans. Henry Hunter, 3 vols. London: Printed for John Stockdale, 1799.

Strickland, Lloyd. 'God's Creatures? Divine Nature and the Status of Animals in the Early Modern Beast-Machine Controversy'. *International Journal of Philosophy and Theology*, 74 (2013), 291–309.

Thomas, Keith. *Man and the Natural World: Changing Attitudes in England, 1500–1800*. New York: Oxford University Press, 1996.

Thomas, Lynn M. "Historicising Agency." *Gender & History* 28, no. 2 (August, 2016): 324–339.

Thompson, Edward P. *Whigs and Hunters: The Origins of the Black Act*. New York: Pantheon, 1973.

Ud-Din Attar, Farid. *Mantiq-uṭ-Ṭayr, The Conference of the Birds*. Twelfth century.

Veinstein, Gilles. "Falconry in the Mid-Sixteenth Century Ottoman Empire." In *Animals and People in the Ottoman Empire*, ed. Suraiya Faroqhi. Istanbul: Eren, 2010, 205–218.

PART V
Literary accounts

12

TRAVEL, EMOTIONS AND TIMELESSNESS

On otherworldly encounters in medieval narratives

Jutta Eming

The distinction between historical or external time and psychological time can be considered one of the fundamental insights of Western philosophy and literature.[1] It traces back (at least) to Augustine's thesis that the individual's mind is not well attuned to historical time but does have the potential to reflect Divine eternity.[2] Literary history offers an excellent field of research into the relations of such varying levels of time, and their interconnectivity. Narratology, and especially Gérard Genette, have maintained[3] that the back-and-forth manipulation of time is one of the most basic narrative techniques, and throughout time, poets have used a wide range of tools for organising time and storytelling. Nonetheless, scholarship holds that it is predominantly the literature of modernism that reveals an "almost obsessive concern" with time, its concepts, representations and psychology.[4]

In the following, I wish to show that premodern literature has indeed developed its own, very specific ways of reflecting time. However, I will not link concepts of time to psychology or subjectivity in general but use the much more differentiated categories of emotions instead. In this regard, temporality is also an especially important aspect in defining an emotion. For instance, emotions are generally classified according to intensity and duration. Some emotions have specific temporal indexes, such as hope and fear, which are directed towards the future.[5] Something similar may be said of trust. Remorse or contrition, in contrast, is the emotional state that is directed towards one's past, or even the irreversibility of one's past. Possibly, the most obvious example in this respect is melancholy, which has been intrinsically linked to the planet-god Saturn. He represents the Roman equivalent of Chronos, the Greek god of time who devoured his own children. Accordingly, melancholy may be referred to as an emotional state which contemplates the passing of time.[6]

How might this configuration between time and emotion be used in order to highlight aspects of cultural encounters? Studies of premodern travel narratives reveal that emotionality and temporality are, in fact, curiously interrelated. In many medieval and early modern romances, travelling to and in foreign countries and experiencing new cultures are reflected in modes of feeling and an awareness—or unawareness—of time. In other words, specific experiences of emotionality and time can serve as signifiers for cultural alterity. In accordance with differing conventions of literary genres and topoi, medieval romances are creative in developing different views on how experiences of time and emotion are intertwined, even dependent on each other. In the following, I wish to show that ultimately, emotionality and temporality can be decisive with regard to the question as to whether these experiences can be integrated into a protagonist's cultural horizon or not.

Alexander and the loss of the flower-maidens

The first of two examples I would like to discuss are from literary traditions of the marvellous; more precisely, they are descriptions of other worlds. The first example comes from the narratives of Alexander the Great and his travels through India, although they only appear in a few of its numerous literary adaptations.[7] I will be primarily concerned with the *Straßburger Alexander* which is believed to have been written as early as 1187. Contrary to Annette Volfing's view, it shows that the medieval Orient takes on the features of a "mythical otherworld".[8] Fundamentally, the episode exemplifies the purposes of Alexander's oriental travels, according to Volfing as, "exploring the nature and limits of humanity".[9] It belongs to the literary, mythical and folkloric tradition of the "other world", which has been analysed in a classic study by Howard Patch.[10] Among the general features of other worlds, Patch lists "the abnormal passage of time–short or long–during the visit".[11] The protagonists might spend a year somewhere, for instance, but have the impression that their stay was only for three months. Further notable similarities are (1) difficult access, for example, over a water barrier, a river or the sea, which may mean that the other world is located on an island, and (2) that the landscape consists of or contains a garden, often with (3) "conspicuous" fruit-laden trees, singing birds and/or music.[12] Possible sources are Arabic natural history[13] and tales of the so-called Celtic maiden lands.[14] During his travels, Alexander is intentionally seeking the marvellous. This is how he encounters the wooded area where the flower-maidens live:[15]

Dô wir fûren bî dem mere,	When we have arrived over the ocean
dô reit ih ûzer dem here	I left my troops behind and rode further
mit drîn dûsint mannen.	with three thousand of my men.
Dô hûbe wir unsih dannen	We set us on the path
und wolden wundir besehen.	and wanted to see marvels.
Dô sâhe wir verre dannen stên	Then we saw in the distance a
einen hêrlîchen walt.	beautiful forest.[16]

Travel, emotions and timelessness **261**

Upon arrival, the forest reveals itself as a perfect *locus amoenus* with associations to the earthly paradise.[17] There are beautiful trees, flowers, grass and many kinds of herbs, and it is surrounded by water. As Alexander and his men approach, they hear the sounds of lyres and harps and the sweetest imaginable music ([...] *den sûzesten sanc / der von menschen ie wart gedâht*).[18] Then they see hundreds and thousands of young girls making music and dancing on the green grass. Alexander and his men are absolutely enthralled, but also moved:

Dâ vergaz ih angist unde leit	Then my men and I forgot all our fear
unde mîn gesinde,	and pain
unde swaz uns von kinde	and whatever sorrow we may have
ie leides gescach	experienced from childhood to this
biz an den selben tach.	very day.
Mir dûhte an der stunt,	At this point I felt as if
ih ne wurde niemer ungesunt,	I would never be miserable again
ob ih dâr imer mûste wesen,	that if I stayed there forever
sô wâre ih garwe genesen	that I would completely get rid of
von aller angistlîcher nôt	anything that frightened me
und ne forhte niwit den tôt.[19]	and would not be afraid of death anymore.

The passage highlights one of the most important potentials of the marvellous, that is, to touch the emotions in unprecedented ways. Except for its clearly erotic undertones, here, the marvellous offers an emotional state that is almost completely stripped of earthly references and shows similarities to narratives about medieval encounters with fairies.[20] Remarkably, the difficult emotions that the men are freed from are named quite precisely: they lose their fear, sorrow and potential for misery, all of which are replaced by feelings of sufficiency, in fact, total satisfaction. At the same time, these emotions are indistinguishably linked with experiences of cultural alterity and, to a degree, natural alterity. The maidens were not born of humans but grew out of large red and white flowers and are in danger of dying if exposed to the sun.[21] In this world, Alexander encounters a different order in nature, which is also identifiable by cultural codes. The girls know how to play musical instruments, are 12 years old at the time of their "blossoming" and are exceptionally beautiful, with clothes that grow onto their bodies. Aside from their exceptional singing, they also speak Alexander's language. He describes them in a letter to his mother as "courtly" and writes that their behaviour is exactly what one expects from courtly maidens.[22] On the other hand, they do not live in hierarchical structures. Unlike the amazons, who were ruled by a queen, their lifestyle bears the utopic element of true equality.[23] Therefore, they also represent a completely alternative society.[24]

Obviously, Alexander and his men are drawn to this strange world. They are welcomed by the friendly flower-maidens and are encouraged to pitch their tents in the forest:

Dô lâge wir dâr mit scalle	We were lying there amidst the sound
und froweten unsih alle	and we all took pleasure from the presence
der seltsênen brûte.	of the strange brides.
ih und mîne lûte,	I and my man,
wir wolten dâr blîven	we wanted to stay there
unde nâmen si ze wîben	and took them as wives
und hatten mêr wunnen	and we were more in bliss
dan wir ie gewunnen,	than ever
sint daz wir worden geborn.[25]	since we were born.

It is only after they have left the forest that Alexander can tell the exact time period of 3 months and 12 days that were spent there.[26] While still with the girls, his mode of experience was to lose himself in momentary delight and be forgetful of the past. So timelessness highlights emotion, emotion highlights timelessness and through their interconnectivity they mark a cultural alterity which ultimately cannot be easily integrated into Alexander's life. He either stays and relinquishes his identity, or he must leave. Eventually, he does leave, but only as a consequence of the alternative order of nature he was so attracted to. When the seasons change and fall transforms the forest, the girls fade like flowers and die. Alexander is filled with sympathy and deep sorrow, and finally leaves.[27]

Ultimately, the experience cannot be integrated into Alexander's European feudal identity and leaves behind no other impression but a memory. All the same, one fact must not be underestimated—Alexander and his men were recipients of knowledge. They gained insights into a different cosmological and natural order, about a different way to organise society and finally a unique way of experiencing love. Nonetheless, this form of cultural contact did not lead to a true cultural exchange. Despite the fact that Alexander and his men where perfectly happy while staying with the flower-maidens and were ready to leave everything behind and forget the past, they did not. In the end, they were forced to helplessly witness the death of their lovers and return to their previous lives. The culture of origin and the foreign culture of the other world remained mutually exclusive.

Generic timelessness in *Apollonius of Tyrland*

My second example concerns the poetics of timelessness with regard to emotion, but within an entire subgenre of romance as opposed to a particular text. In the so-called love-and-adventure novel, the absence of any experience of time has been famously conceptualised by Mikhail Bakhtin as a central characteristic.[28] The genre tells of the formation of a conflict-charged "love", with partners from different cultures, religions and (apparently) different classes who must fight against external threats to their happiness. The difficulties within their surroundings finally lead to an extended separation, and during this separation to "adventures". Typically, the hero is forced to search for his beloved on a long journey, because she has been sold as a slave in the Near East. In extreme cases, to achieve his goal, he must circumnavigate the entire Mediterranean. Bakhtin holds that through their adventures, the protagonists often become acquainted with very exotic lands, but do so without becoming permanently marked by their exposure to foreignness. In Bakhtin's view, the literary spaces do not stand in conjunction with special social or cultural characteristics of the areas encountered. Everything is equally and abstractly "foreign",[29] and the adventures themselves seem transferable. An event in Babylon could just as easily take place in Egypt or Byzantium, or *vice versa*.[30] In other words, Bakhtin holds that the authors of love-and-adventure novels fail to emphasise cultural contexts. As Lawrence Kim notes:

> For Bakhtin, this is the whole point of the romance – the couple's love for each other never changes, despite near-deaths, kidnappings and other suitors. The novels are thus organised around a series of ordeals designed to test the characters' faith in each other and to reaffirm what had already existed from the beginning – their love.[31]

So again, an apparent timelessness while travelling is related to emotionality; only this time, it works the other way around. The experience of love remains untouched by the timelessness of adventure and travelling.

Bakhtin has often been critised for his view, and scholarship has given numerous examples of instances when time indeed does matter in this particular genre. In the text I wish to examine more closely, both tendencies can be observed: timelessness and attempts to overcome it. The text represents one of the German versions of the narratives about *Apollonius, King of Tyre*, which was "extremely popular throughout the Middle Ages and into the Renaissance".[32] The version in question shares the plot line with many other European renditions. It begins "with a tyrannical and incestuous father", and through structural and motivic analogies, gives the impression throughout that the "shadow of incest" is hanging "over the story till the end".[33] Something similar can be said about Apollonius. He loses his wife during a journey overseas after she has given birth to their daughter. He then leaves his daughter as an infant with foster parents, promising to return one day. Additionally, he vows not to cut his hair and nails until they are reunited. While this decision is undoubtedly modelled after religious practices and is meant to symbolise the strong attachment to his daughter as well as his longing for her, it is also an attempt to fight the timelessness of travel through body memory. Even though Apollonius and his wife are finally reunited again, the female character who drives the genre conventions and motivates the protagonist's urge to reunite is neither his lover nor his wife, but his daughter. This is reflected, among other things, in the fact that the hero's adventures are intertwined on different levels with questions of just rule and appropriate behaviour toward one's children. This also holds for the version I wish to examine more closely in the following—Heinrich von Neustadt's *Apollonius von Tyrland*, written around 1300.

In this case, travelling is pushed to an extreme. Heinrich von Neustadt's Apollonius journeys extensively from the Mediterranean to the Middle East, to the Far East, and also westward (Spain), spending many years in exotic and marvellous lands. The romance's topography is partly idealised, and at least partially based on real and identifiable locations. For instance, the land of Chrysa is believed to represent India.[34] Many of these dominions are then incorporated into Apollonius's own realms, which leads to extended relationships and sometimes marriage with several women. This reveals family and governance to be the core themes of the story. Many of these areas, however, have also been usurped by monstrous creatures with which Apollonius must do battle. All in all, the romance offers a true "monster-show", arguably the most extensive and detailed in medieval German literature.

Related to a specific geography, the descriptions of monstrous races have Greek origins and are laid out in the works of Herodotus, Megasthenes and Ktesias. Greek natural history conceptualises monstrous races as being inhabitants of Ethiopia and, most importantly, of India. As Rudolf Wittkover has famously coined, they were "marvels of the East".[35] The adaptations of these marvels in literary texts of the Middle Ages potentially demonstrate "that colonial discourse has its roots in classical and medieval literature".[36]

Since antiquity and up through the Middle Ages and the early modern period, conventional taxonomy has always considered monsters to be people and not animals. Consequently, in natural histories, such as those by Pliny the Elder and Isidor of Seville, monsters have been discussed in chapters about human beings. However, in literary texts from the Middle Ages and later, the most obvious feature of monstrosity is its similarity to animals. Even though monsters can sometimes resemble plants or machines, more often than not man is thought to look like a monster if he has animal features. In fact, due to the Christian religion's belief in the fallen nature of man, the corruption of the clear hierarchy between humans and animals in Paradise was a continuing source of concern that stimulated theological, political and literary debates.[37] My subsequent analysis will show that the comparison to animals is particularly adept in regarding monstrosity, and how to deal with it hermeneutically. I will discuss examples of monsters as well as monstrous or imaginary animals, and I will make the point that their interpretation is highly contingent upon their respective literary contexts and different aestheticising strategies.

As Jeffrey Jerome Cohen notes with regard to crossovers between men and dogs:

> Human and canine affects freely play across its species-mingling flesh, marking it as alien. Miscegenation made corporeal, he has no secure place in a Christian identity structure generated around a technology of exclusion. A category of violence, the monster must be marginalized to keep the system pure.[38]

This marginalisation of monsters, however, has a flip side to it. This is because as much as monstrous encounters reaffirm identities, they also challenge them.

Monstrosity can also designate and reflect certain aspects of the hero's personality. The specific meanings they reveal stand in specific relation to the literary protagonist who encounters them, and to the overall plot lines and themes of the texts. In the following example, this means that the monstrous creatures he confronts are also characterised by family relations.

Contrasting families counterbalancing time: the encounter with Flata

The extended episode of the gigantic monster Kolkan and his mother Flata uses gender stereotypes. They are intended to underline Flata's malevolence:

Flata ist des tievels weib:	Flata is the devil's spouse:
Verflucht sey poser leib!	Cursed shall be her awful body!
Si ist zwayer manne langk.	She is as tall as two men.
Unmassen schnell ist ir gangk,	Terribly quick is her walk,
Ir lauff ist schnell unmaßleich.	she runs extremely fast.
Ir antlitz ist fraßlich.	Her face is dreadful.
Geleich ainer wilden katzen	Long like a wild cat's
Lanck sind ir dy tatzen,	are her paws,
Die haben span lange kla.	which have very long claws.
Schwartz, langk sind ir di pra.	Long and black are her eyebrows.
Ir pruste gend ir auff den pauch.	Her breasts hang down to her belly.
Si ist allenthalben rauch.	She is covered everywhere with fur.
Viltzet ist ir lock.	Her hair is matted.
Ir ars ist sinewel als ain stock.	Her ass is as round as a stick.
Sy hicklet recht als ain pock.	She hobbles like a goat.
Di naßlocher sind ir weyt:	Her nostrils are wide:
Ain rotzel ir da vor leyt,	slime hangs out of them,
Das ist langk als ain wurst;	long as a sausage;
Ich gewan nie so grossen durst	I've never been thirsty enough
Das ich mit ir wolte trincken.	to even consider taking a drink with her.
Lanck, durr sind ir di schincken.	Long, skinny are her shanks.
Sy hatt dracken fusse.[39]	She has feet like a dragon's.

The description of Flata continues and is exceptionally long. The passage cited is of special interest because of its comparisons to animals. On the whole, the description is more hybrid but still extremely misogynistic. These animal comparisons are precisely meant to ridicule the femininity of Flata's body. With their animal-like appearance, all of these body parts collectively become a grotesque parody of the kind of feminine physique that might be considered worthy of a man's desire. Even the repugnant slime hanging from her nose is associated by the narrator with forms of consumable fluids, which in certain contexts might be indirectly associated with a woman. In this case, "taking a drink with her" would be part of a strategy of seduction. The Flata character is an interesting and uncommon example of a medieval literary depiction that is clearly intended to provoke the emotion of disgust. Further, the source of revulsion is a woman whose body is abhorrent to legitimate male expectations. In her own way, Flata contributes to a discourse on evoked and subsequently dismissed erotic attraction that is a central focus of *Apollonius*. This is best represented by the plot's core theme of the father-daughter relationship.[40]

So the romance's concern with transgressive erotic behaviour is embedded in the larger scheme of the plot that emphasises the ideal of a harmonious, caring family.[41] Aside from her appalling appearance and complete undesirability, Flata is also part of an extended family of monsters. Her relationship to her son Kolkan, whom she fiercely protects, mirrors the hero Apollonius's dedication to his long lost daughter. One could say that by implementing encounters with such reflecting characters within the world of adventure, the romance counterbalances the generic feature of timelessness.

In fact, throughout Apollonius's adventures, there are numerous, paradoxically intertwined episodes when the awareness of time is lost and regained. In the paradise-like land of Chrysa, for instance, he enters a fountain of youth, loses his beard and lives for a time as a much younger man. This lasts only until his wife sees him with a new lover through the magic of a mirrored column. For some time, he travels "undercover" and takes on a different name, "Lonius", which is only a moderate departure from his real name. As the end of his journeys approaches, Apollonius and his followers come across two old men, Henoch and Elias. They tell them that no other humans had arrived in that place during the last thousand years. Apollonius and his company react with the emotions of curiosity and wonder:

Das nam di leute wunder.	That amazed them.
Sy fragten sy pesunder:	They asked specifically:
'Durch Got, herre, ir sult uns sagen:	for God's sake, Sir, you should tell us
Seyt ir so alt von den tagen?	are you that old?
Und was ditz wunder mayne	And what about the wonder
Das ir hie seyt allaine.'[42]	that you have been here completely alone.

The old men then explain that they are waiting for the return of Jesus Christ on Judgement Day and inquire if Apollonius has heard anything about him. Surprisingly, the pagan Apollonius is not only aware of Christ and his worldly life, he can also recount the story of the crucifixion and resurrection of ten years before. At this point, as Wolfgang Achnitz notes, it is suddenly possible for the reader to calculate the year of Apollonius's travels as A.D. 44, the time he has spent since leaving his daughter as 14 years, as well as all other time periods and relationships he has experienced since.[43]

Of course, exact dates and numbers are of lesser interest here. What stands out is the fact that the romance attempts to negotiate different levels of time with regard to travelling, cultural alterity and emotion. In the case just discussed, we can observe the Augustinian differentiation between individual time spent by the protagonist and historical time. The emotions of curiosity and wonder help Apollonius to identify his place in sacred time. Throughout the romance, many more instances occur where different levels of time are related to cultural encounters and emotional experience. At this point, there are too many to comprehensively discuss, and they are also too differentiated to summarise. Instead, I will give one last, but outstanding, example.

Milgot: the friendship of a lifetime

On an island that Apollonius and his men reach after a shipwreck, they encounter an animal named Milgot.

Do sach er das gegen im gie	Then he realised that
Ain tier, das was herleich:	a gorgeous animal approached him:
Sein varbe di was wunderleich.	its colour was marvellous.
Senft leich was sein gangk.	It walked smoothly
Es was wol ains speres langk.	and was about as long as a speer.
Sein haut was grun als der chle,	Its skin was as green as clover,
Sein pauch weiß als der schne.	its belly as white as snow.
Stumpfat was im der munt	The mouth was truncated
Und murrat als ain vogelhunt.	like a bird dog.
Mer dan tausent lay var	There were more than a thousand
Was das tier her und dar.	colours on the animal.
Sein haupt trug es schon enpar,	Its head was held high,
Auff seinem hirne da vor	on the front of its head
Ain krone von ir selber art:	was a crown:
So schone nie gemachet ward	none was ever crafted so beautifully
Von goltschmides henden.	by any goldsmith.
Do gedauchte den ellenden	It made the suffering man think
So schone creature	that such a beautiful creature
War nicht ungehewre.	could not be monstrous.
Doch vorcht er es ain tail.[44]	Nonetheless, he feared it a little.

While corporeal hybridity is one of the most distinctive characteristics of monsters, it is rarely an element in descriptions of animals. The *Physiologus* gives a few examples, for instance, when describing the hyena.[45] In the *Apollonius* romance, we are supposed to imagine this creature as beautiful, mostly because of its intense colours, its graceful movements and the precious crown on his head. It appears to be a crossover between a dog and a cat. Like the marvellous dog Petitcreiu from Gottfried von Straßburg's *Tristan* romance, it seems to be a completely imaginary animal. However, its invention does not actually make it seem less "real" within the context of the story.

Boria Sax suggests that such delineations depend on historical taxonomies:

> An imaginary animal is a creature that seems to belong to a realm fundamentally different from, yet somehow allied with, our own. Its most basic characteristic is the combination of relatively familiar features with heightened alterity.[46]

According to this line of reasoning, monsters, on the other hand, stand in "radical alterity" to humans and "dramatise some aspect of the human condition".[47] What's more, monsters, "by providing the sharpest possible contrast, help us to define our humanity".[48] The episode with Flata has already revealed these poetics of contrast. In spite of her hideous features, Flata serves as the positive model of a caring mother and alludes to Apollonius' relationship to his daughter. By comparison, an imaginary animal's relationship to humans can seem very close and often invested with affection.[49] I will return to this aspect later.

The creature in Heinrich's *Apollonius* romance is proactive with its attempts to ease Apollonius remaining fears:

Das tier nam des heren war.	The animal realised the presence of the man.
Es hett all solche gepär	It consistently acted
Als es frewnt war.	as if it were a friend.
Es kroch zu dem werden	It crawled towards the noble man
Mit dem pauch auf der erden:	with its belly on the ground:
Es spilte als ain hundelein.	it played like a little dog
'Herre Got, was mag ditz sein?'	'My God, what can this be
Sprach der helt. 'es get hie pey	the hero said. 'It behaves just as if
Recht als es frewnt sey.	it were friendly.
Ich wil warten und sehen	I will wait and see
Was an mir welle geschehen.'	just what will happen to me.'
Er stieß das messer ein wider.	He sheathed his knife.
Das tier legt sich vor im nider,	The animal lay down before him,
Sein haupt auff seine fusse.	its head upon his feet.
Sein gesmach was so susse	It had such a sweet smell about him
Das er da von ain kraft gewan.	that he gained some energy from it.
Do gedachte der werde man	So the noble man thought
'Leichte will sich Got erparmen	'Maybe God will have mercy on me
Uber mich vil armen.'	in my misery.'
Ain küneß hertz er gevieng.	He gained new confidence.
Das dier vor im enweg gieng	The animal walked ahead
Und det im mit dem haupte kunt	and signalled to him with its head
Das er im volgte an der stund.	that he should follow him now.
Er det es und gieng im nach.[50]	He did this and went along.

In a book that examines Apollonius through the lens of eschatology, Achnitz has given an extensive analysis of Milgot and his behaviour.[51] Despite the romance's predominantly vernacular content, this approach makes some degree of sense for a work of art that was created within a religious culture. Nonetheless, I am not sure if biblical hermeneutics are as applicable to an understanding of Milgot as Achnitz suggests. The associations to the Old and New Testaments he names are less obvious to me, as are the relations to comparable animals/creatures in preceding courtly romances.[52] I would agree with Achnitz to a certain extent, that when faced with a curious animal such as Milgot, readers of the story are forced to make decisions about questions of right and wrong.[53] It is not convincing, however, that a correct interpretation lies in God providing Apollonius with a specific place in eschatology.[54] To say the least, there are many other possible secular associations, for instance, the relationships between anthropological limits, transgressions and the similarities between man and animal.

Apollonius discovers that the crowned creature reigns as king over a variety of wild animals who strive to make the traveller feel as comfortable as possible. They engage in various civilising acts, for instance, digging a well to provide Apollonius with fresh water, showing him a den to sleep in and providing him with the means to cook his meals while continuing to eat their own food raw. Therefore, Christian Kiening, in an earlier study of the many transitions between the human and the animalistic in "Apollonius", has called the episode with Milgot a Robinsonade *avant la lettre*.[55] On his island, however, Robinson imposed his version of civilised life upon the wild indigenous culture that he encountered. By comparison, Milgot and his animal subjects already seem to have a clear grasp of Apollonius's civilised needs, even though they do not share them. In other words, they demonstrate an understanding and respect for otherness that is unparalleled by any of the other monstrous *and* human encounters on the island.

Because it features "a social structure which significantly differs from the social structure known to the western traveller",[56] Milgot's island kingdom represents a utopian, and especially peaceful lifestyle in concert with the other animals on the island. Not only is Milgot able to discipline even the wildest of the other animals by natural authority, his community of animals goes to great lengths to hospitably provide Apollonius with all human necessities for survival.

However, the sorcerer Archiron, who is travelling with Apollonius, knows that the animal has very special powers. Any human who eats its heart will live for 100 years. Therefore, the sorcerer tries to persuade Apollonius to kill Milgot, so that they might share the heart and both extend their lives in this extraordinary way. But Apollonius is filled with sympathy for Milgot and likewise filled with horror and disgust at the prospect of killing the friendly creature.

It is here that animal features are revealed to be especially significant and important. While monsters typically arouse emotions such as fear, horror and/or disgust (less often, pity or desire) in humans, human–animal encounters can be transformed into closer and longer-lasting relationships. These may arouse positive emotions such as trust, loyalty, fidelity and love. Because of this tradition, the relation to Milgot takes on the model of an emotionally invested friendship, and, as a consequence, leads Apollonius to acknowledge how precious the culture is that has welcomed him. He chooses to refrain from destroying the animal even at the price of not extending his own lifespan. In this respect, he is learning about human values from animals at the margins of the world. He acknowledges the preciousness of the nature-culture that had welcomed him and refrains, by emotion-invested friendship, from destroying it, even if it means bypassing the opportunity to live a longer life.

Conclusion

In conclusion, it is not too surprising that in premodern travel narratives, cultural contacts lead to emotional responses. Literary texts make full use of their potential to relate such contacts through descriptions of foreign topographies, objects and human beings. This is accomplished by using a variety of tools, including the rhetorics of extended ekphrasis, soliloquies and various topoi such as "the marvels of the east". Through these lenses, cultural encounters may appear as curious, astounding, frightening or enriching. By connecting to specific experiences of time, these travel narratives are also efficient in relating aspects of cultural contacts on different levels: identity construction, memory, experience and knowledge. In the stories of Alexander the Great and Apollonius, the protagonists are led to extremes, specifically due to experiencing forms of timelessness. In the *Straßburger Alexander*, the hero has an otherworldly encounter with flower maidens and enjoys an episode of intense delight that causes him to forget the past. In *Apollonius von Tyrland*, the protagonist acts within the generic frame of the escapist adventure novel. He undertakes years of travelling, which at first seem to have no lasting effects, either physically or with regard to his identity. Through monstrous encounters, however, he is repeatedly confronted with questions about appropriate ways of dealing with governance, family, friendship, fidelity and love. In the end, Alexander's experience with timelessness cannot be mediated with his usual identity as a conquering hegemon. In the Apollonius narrative, however, in order to return to his family, the hero must first confront a great variety of other-worldly humans and animals who conduct themselves with exemplary social behaviour. By highlighting time and emotion, and their interrelatedness, these narratives not only show that travelling is a dangerous endeavour and that cultural encounters are fundamentally interesting. More precisely, they also make the point that travelling leads to experiences that question the foundations of cultural identity: knowledge about one's self, family, love, as well as standards and values to live by.

Notes

1 Alexander Demandt, *Zeit: Eine Kulturgeschichte* (Berlin: Propyläen, 2015), 34–40. Demandt does not apply the terms of historical and psychological time, but distinguishes between subjectivity and objectivity of time instead.

2 Interestingly enough, Augustine holds that such experiences can be provided by poetry, see Uta Störmer-Caysa, *Grundstrukturen mittelalterlicher Erzählungen: Raum und Zeit im höfischen Roman* (Berlin/New York: De Gruyter, 2007), 6–13. For an extended discussion of Augustine's concept of the threefold experience of time (*Confessions*, Book XI, XXXI) and its consequences for narratology, see Paul Ricoeur, *Time and Narrative*, vol. 1, transl. Kathleen McLaughlin (Chicago, IL et al.: University of Chicago Press, 2009).
3 Gérard Genette, *Narrative Discourse: An Essay in Method*, 4th print (Ithaca, NY: Cornell University Press, 1990).
4 Edward Quinn, *A Dictionary of Literary and Thematic Terms* (New York: Checkmark Books 1999/2000), entry "time" 324–325, here: 324.
5 See Aaron Ben-Ze'ev, *The Subtlety of Emotions* (Cambridge, MA: MIT Press, 2000), 473–489; Arno Anzenbacher, "Die Phänomenologie der Angst bei Thomas von Aquin," *Das Mittelalter* 12 (2007): 85–96.
6 See in general, Raymond Klibansky, Erwin Panofsky, and Fritz Saxl, *Saturn und Melancholie: Studien zur Geschichte der Naturphilosophie und Medizin, der Religion und der Kunst* (Frankfurt am Main: Suhrkamp, 1990).
7 For recent research into the cultural entanglements of the stories about Alexander the Great, see Richard Stoneman, *The Legends of Alexander the Great* (New York: I. B. Tauris, 2011); Catherine Gaullier-Bougassas and Margaret Bridges, eds. *Les voyages d'Alexandre au paradis. Orient et Occident, regards croisés* (Turnhout: Brepols, 2013), as well as Markus Stock, ed. *Alexander the Great in the Middle Ages: Transcultural Perspectives* (Toronto: University of Toronto Press, 2016).
8 Annette Volfing, "Orientalism in the *Straßburger Alexander*," *Medium Aevum* 79, no. 2 (2010): 279.
9 Ibid., 278.
10 See Howard Patch, *The Other World: According to Descriptions in Medieval Literature* (Cambridge, MA: Harvard University Press, 1950). For a more recent study, see Judith Klinger, "Anderswelten," in *Literarische Orte in deutschsprachigen Erzählungen des Mittelalters*, eds. Tilo Renz, Monika Hanauska, and Mathias Herweg (Berlin/Boston, MA: De Gruyter, 2018), 13–39.
11 Patch, *The Other World*, 3.
12 See ibid.
13 Al-Masudi, died 956, describes Maidens growing in trees and dying when falling down like ripe fruit, see Elisabeth Lienert, "Einführung," in Pfaffe Lambrecht, *Alexanderroman. Mittelhochdeutsch / Neuhochdeutsch*, ed. Elisabeth Lienert (Stuttgart: Reclam 2007), 7–51, 18, ann. 33.
14 These are Celtic stories of realms full of beautiful women who "freely share the joys of love" (see Patch, *The Other World*, 58). Patch discusses an episode of the French *Roman d'Alexandre* which shows some similarities, see 282–283, noting that it reminds of the Celtic tales but is probably of Oriental origin.
15 As observed by Susanne Friede, *Die Wahrnehmung des Wunderbaren. Der Roman d'Alexandre im Kontext der französischen Literatur des 12. Jahrhunderts* (Tübingen: Niemeyer, 2003), 478–479. Compare this passage also for general observation on the construction of the marvellous by the narrator.
16 *Straßburger Alexander*, ed. Lienert (l. 4707–4713), my translation.
17 This holds especially for parallels to descriptions of paradise in Muslim traditions, see Catherine Gaullier-Bougassas, "Les eaux troublées de la quête d'Alexandre et les sources orientales du Roman d'Alexandre français. Fontaine de vie, fleuve de mort et Paradis terrestre," in *Les voyages d'Alexandre*, ed. Gaullier-Bougassas/Bridges, 191:

> Dans le prolongement des influences Orientales et pour la création de ce paradis sensuel des filles-fleurs, nous serions aussi tentée, sans pouvoir apporter de preuve certaine, de poser l'hypothèse de réminiscences, dissociées de tout lien avec le spirituel, de quelques traits de la vision du paradis selon l'islam, teile que le Moyen Âge la percevait.

See also the analysis of the episode in Jutta Eming, Falk Quenstedt, and Tilo Renz, "Das Wunderbare als Konfiguration des Wissens: Grundlegungen zu seiner Epistemologie," *Working Paper 12/2018 des Sonderforschungsbereichs 980 Episteme in Bewegung. Wissenstransfer von der Alten Welt bis in die Frühe Neuzeit*, (open access), 11–14.
18 *Straßburger Alexander*, l. 4720–4721.
19 Ibid., l. 4780–4790.
20 See Friede, *Die Wahrnehmung des Wunderbaren*, 53–54.
21 As hybrids between man and plant, they fall under the definition of monsters, see Friede, *Die Wahrnehmung des Wunderbaren*, 222.
22 Friede, *Die Wahrnehmung des Wunderbaren*, 51, points out that with their looks and behaviour they also resemble fairies.
23 See ibid.
24 As described by Tilo Renz, "Utopische Elemente der mittelalterlichen Reiseliteratur," *Das Mittelalter* 18 (2013): 129–152. By the same author, see also "Ferne-Utopien." In *Literarische Orte in deutschsprachigen Erzählungen des Mittelalters. Ein Handbuch,* ed. Tilo Renz, Monika Hanauska, and Mathias Herweg (Berlin/Boston, MA: De Gruyter, 2018), 129–145.
25 *Straßburger Alexander*, l. 4867–4875.
26 L. 4882–4883.
27 The connection of time and emotion in this respect does not follow any pattern of repetition. Interestingly, in the French *Roman d'Alexandre*, which is the other Alexander narration that features the flowergirl-episode, the men do not wish to stay forever; they experience fear and just leave the girls behind.
28 See Michail M. Bachtin, *Chronotopos*, transl. Michael Dewey (Frankfurt am Main: Suhrkamp, 2008); "Epos und Roman. Zur Methodologie der Romanforschung," in *Disput über den Roman. Beiträge zur Romantheorie aus der Sowjetunion 1917–1941*, ed. Michael Wegner et al. (Berlin, Weimar: Aufbau-Verlag, 1988), 490–532.
29 See Bachtin, *Chronotopos*, 25.
30 See ibid., 26.
31 Lawrence Kim, "Time", in *The Cambridge Companion to the Greek and Roman Novel*, ed. Tim Whitmarsh (Cambridge: Cambridge University Press, 2008), 151–152.
32 Elizabeth Archibald, *Incest and the Medieval Imagination* (Oxford: Clarendon Press, 2003), 95.
33 Ibid., 93.
34 See Wolfgang Achnitz, *Babylon und Jerusalem. Sinnkonstituierung im "Reinfried von Braunschweig" und im "Apollonius von Tyrland" Heinrichs von Neustadt* (Tübingen: Niemeyer, 2002), 276.
35 Rudolf Wittkower, *Allegory and the Migration of Symbols* (London: Thames and Hudson, 1977), 46.
36 Andrea Rossi-Reder, "Wonders of the Beast. India in Classical and Medieval Literature", in *Marvels, Monsters, and Miracles. Studies in the Medieval and Early Modern Imaginations*, eds. Timothy S. Jones and David A. Sprunger (Kalamazoo: Medieval Institute Publications, 2002), 66.
37 Udo Friedrich, *Menschentier und Tiermensch. Diskurse der Grenzziehung und Grenzüberschreitung im Mittelalter* (Göttingen: Vandenhoeck & Ruprecht, 2009), 39–144.
38 Jeffrey Jerome Cohen, *Of Giants: Sex, Monsters, and the Middle Ages* (Minneapolis/London: University of Minnesota Press, 1999), 134.
39 *Heinrichs von Neustadt "Apollonius von Tyrland" nach der Gothaer Handschrift, "Gottes Zukunft" und "Visio Philiberti" nach der Heidelberger Handschrift*, ed. Samuel Singer (Berlin: Weidmannsche Buchhandlung, 1906), 3–328, l. 4374–4395 (translation by author).
40 In Heinrich's version, this is also reflected prominently in the hero's love relationship with the dark-skinned Palmina, which is given a highly ambivalent treatment by the author. The model is probably Wolfram's von Eschenbach *Parzival*, more specifically the hero's father Gahmuret's relationship with Belakane.

41 Christian Kiening, *Unheilige Familien: Sinnmuster mittelalterlichen Erzählens* (Würzburg: Königshausen & Neumann, 2009), 37–41.
42 *Apollonius von Tyrland*, l. 14818–14823.
43 Achnitz, *Babylon und Jerusalem*, 334–335.
44 *Apollonius von Tyrland*, l. 6618–6637.
45 See Physiologus, transl. and ed. by Otto Schönberger, 40–41.
46 Boria Sax, *Imaginary Animals: The Monstrous, the Wondrous and the Human* (London: Reaktion Books, 2013), 47.
47 Ibid., 95.
48 Ibid.
49 See the most recent discussion from Rosmarie Thee Morewedge, "Magical Gifts in Gottfried von Strassburg's Tristan and Isolde and the Rejection of Magic", in *Magic and Magicians in the Middle Ages and the Early Modern Time. The Occult in Pre-Modern Sciences, Medicine, Literature, Religion, and Astrology*, ed. Albrecht Classen (Berlin/New York: de Gruyter, 2017), 322–31.
50 *Apollonius von Tyrland*, l. 6652–6675.
51 See Achnitz, *Babylon und Jerusalem*, 285–300.
52 Achnitz names a creature described in one of Ijob's dialogues with God (Ijob 40, 6–41, 26) (Achnitz, *Babylon und Jerusalem*, 293). In Luther's translation, it is named Leviathan, while in other translations it is referred to as a crocodile. It is called the king of animals, but it does not wear a crown, as Achnitz suggests. What's more, it is a fearsome creature with a heart of stone. As Achnitz rightly points out, the animal in *Wigalois*, which bears some resemblance to Milgot, serves as a mediator for the entrance into the other world (of death) (Achnitz, *Babylon und Jerusalem*, 291–292). However, it is not clear that the island Milgot inhabits could be considered an enchanted world, like in *Wigalois*, nor that one in fact needs a guide to enter it.
53 See Achnitz, *Babylon und Jerusalem*, 295.
54 See ibid., 295–296.
55 Christian Kiening, "Apollonius unter den Tieren", in *Literarische Leben. Rollenentwürfe in der Literatur des Hoch- und Spätmittelalters*, eds. Matthias Meyer and Hans-Joachim Schiewer (Tübingen: Niemeyer, 2002), 427.
56 Renz, "Utopische Elemente", 129 (translation by author).

Bibliography

Achnitz, Wolfgang. *Babylon und Jerusalem. Sinnkonstituierung im "Reinfried von Braunschweig" und im "Apollonius von Tyrland" Heinrichs von Neustadt*. Tübingen: Niemeyer, 2002.
Anzenbacher, Arno. "Die Phänomenologie der Angst bei Thomas von Aquin." *Das Mittelalter* 12 (2007): 85–96.
Archibald, Elizabeth. *Incest and the Medieval Imagination*. Oxford: Clarendon Press, 2003.
Bachtin, Michail M. *Chronotopos*, translated Michael Dewey. Frankfurt am Main: Suhrkamp, 2008.
Bachtin, Michail M. "Epos und Roman. Zur Methodologie der Romanforschung." In *Disput über den Roman. Beiträge zur Romantheorie aus der Sowjetunion 1917–1941*, edited by Michael Wegner et al., 490–532. Berlin/Weimar: Aufbau-Verlag, 1988.
Ben-Ze'ev, Aaron. *The Subtlety of Emotions*. Cambridge, MA: MIT Press, 2000.
Cohen, Jeffrey Jerome. *Of Giants: Sex, Monsters, and the Middle Ages*. Minneapolis/London: University of Minnesota Press, 1999.
Demandt, Alexander. *Zeit: Eine Kulturgeschichte*. Berlin: Propyläen, 2015.
Eming, Jutta, Falk Quenstedt, and Tilo Renz. "Das Wunderbare als Konfiguration des Wissens–Grundlegungen zu seiner Epistemologie," *Working Paper 12/2018 des*

Sonderforschungsbereichs 980 Episteme in Bewegung. Wissenstransfer von der Alten Welt bis in die Frühe Neuzeit, (open access), 11–14.

Friede, Susanne. *Die Wahrnehmung des Wunderbaren. Der Roman d'Alexandre im Kontext der französischen Literatur des 12. Jahrhunderts*. Tübingen: Niemeyer, 2003.

Friedrich, Udo. *Menschentier und Tiermensch. Diskurse der Grenzziehung und Grenzüberschreitung im Mittelalter*. Göttingen: Vandenhoeck & Ruprecht, 2009.

Gaullier-Bougassas, Catherine. "Les eaux troublées de la quête d'Alexandre et les sources orientales du Roman d'Alexandre français. Fontaine de vie, fleuve de mort et Paradis terrestre." In *Les voyages d'Alexandre,* edited by Gaullier-Bougassas/Bridges, 165–210. Turnhout: Brepols, 2013.

Gaullier-Bougassas, Catherine and Margaret Bridges, eds. *Les voyages d'Alexandre au paradis. Orient et Occident, regards croisés*. Turnhout: Brepols, 2013.

Genette, Gérard. *Narrative Discourse: An Essay in Method*. 4th print. Ithaca, NY: Cornell University Press, 1990.

Heinrichs von Neustadt "Apollonius von Tyrland" nach der Gothaer Handschrift, "Gottes Zukunft" und "Visio Philiberti" nach der Heidelberger Handschrift, ed. Samuel Singer. Berlin: Weidmannsche Buchhandlung, 1906.

Kiening, Christian. "Apollonius unter den Tieren." In *Literarische Leben. Rollenentwürfe in der Literatur des Hoch- und Spätmittelalters*, edited by Matthias Meyer and Hans-Joachim Schiewer, 415–431. Tübingen: Niemeyer, 2002.

Kiening, Christian. *Unheilige Familien. Sinnmuster mittelalterlichen Erzählens*. Würzburg: Königshausen & Neumann, 2009.

Kim, Lawrence. "Time." In *The Cambridge Companion to the Greek and Roman Novel,* edited by Tim Whitmarsh, 145–161. Cambridge: Cambridge University Press, 2008.

Klibansky, Raymond, Erwin Panofsky, and Fritz Saxl. *Saturn und Melancholie: Studien zur Geschichte der Naturphilosophie und Medizin, der Religion und der Kunst*. Frankfurt am Main: Suhrkamp, 1990.

Klinger, Judith. "Anderswelten." In *Literarische Orte in deutschsprachigen Erzählungen des Mittelalters*, edited by Tilo Renz, Monika Hanauska, and Mathias Herweg, 13–39. Berlin/Boston, MA: De Gruyter, 2018.

Lienert, Elisabeth. "Einführung." In Pfaffe Lambrecht, *Alexanderroman*. Mittelhochdeutsch/Neuhochdeutsch, edited by Elisabeth Lienert, 7–51. Stuttgart: Reclam, 2007).

Morewedge, Rosmarie Thee. "Magical Gifts in Gottfried von Strassburg's Tristan and Isolde and the Rejection of Magic." In *Magic and Magicians in the Middle Ages and the Early Modern Time. The Occult in Pre-Modern Sciences, Medicine, Literature, Religion, and Astrology*, edited by Albrecht Classen, 315–335. Berlin/New York: de Gruyter, 2017.

Patch, Howard. *The Other World: According to Descriptions in Medieval Literature*. Cambridge, MA: Harvard University Press, 1950.

Quinn, Edward. *A Dictionary of Literary and Thematic Terms*. New York: Checkmark Books, 1999/2000.

Renz, Tilo. "Ferne-Utopien." In *Literarische Orte in deutschsprachigen Erzählungen des Mittelalters. Ein Handbuch*, edited by Tilo Renz, Monika Hanauska, Mathias Herweg, 129–145. Berlin/Boston, MA: De Gruyter, 2018.

Renz, Tilo. "Utopische Elemente der mittelalterlichen Reiseliteratur." *Das Mittelalter* 18 (2013): 129–152.

Ricoeur, Paul. *Time and Narrative: Vol. 1,* translated by Kathleen McLaughlin. Chicago, IL et al.: University of Chicago Press, 2009.

Rossi-Reder, Andrea. "Wonders of the Beast. India in Classical and Medieval Literature." In *Marvels, Monsters, and Miracles. Studies in the Medieval and Early Modern Imaginations*, edited by Timothy S. Jones and David A. Sprunger, 53–66. Kalamazoo: Medieval Institute Publications, 2002.

Sax, Boria. *Imaginary Animals. The Monstrous, the Wondrous and the Human*. London: Reaktion Books, 2013.

Stock, Markus, ed. *Alexander the Great in the Middle Ages: Transcultural Perspectives*. Toronto: University of Toronto Press, 2016.

Stoneman, Richard. *The Legends of Alexander the Great*. New York: I. B. Tauris, 2011.

Störmer-Caysa, Uta. *Grundstrukturen mittelalterlicher Erzählungen: Raum und Zeit im höfischen Roman*. Berlin/New York: De Gruyter, 2007.

Volfing, Annette. "Orientalism in the *Straßburger Alexander*." *Medium Aevum* 79, no. 2 (2010): 278–299.

Wittkower, Rudolf. *Allegory and the Migration of Symbols*. London: Thames and Hudson, 1977.

13

"ALWAYS FLEEING AWAY"

Emotion, exile and rest in the Old English *Life of St Mary of Egypt*

Andrew Lynch

The legend of St Mary of Egypt, first appearing in sixth-century Byzantine Middle Eastern culture, became widely popular in medieval Latin and vernacular versions.[1] The first known version, sometimes attributed to Sophronius, Patriarch of Jerusalem, reworks an earlier tale of a holy man who finds a solitary female penitent living in a cave.[2] From the later eighth century, Mary's legend circulated in a Latin version by Paul the Deacon. With differing emphases and accounts of provenance, it has continued in multiple forms in Orthodox and Roman churches to the present day, and also found repeated expression in secular culture. There have been many artworks, including those by Quentin Matsys, Tintoretto and Emil Nolde. Mary features in the second part of Goethe's *Faust*, later adapted for Mahler's Eighth Symphony, and in a Respighi opera, the poetry of John Berryman and John Tavener's *Mary of Egypt* (1992), based on a life (1974) by the Yorkshire Abbess Thekla. A Coptic Egyptian cinema adaptation of the story also exists.[3]

Sophronius was a strong defender of the dual nature of Christ – human and divine – and so of Christ's possession of the human ability to choose. If he or a like-minded cleric is the legend's author, that may lie behind its interest in an appalling sinner's conversion by divine mercy, and its veneration of a being that late antique society considered "a sort of human vermin."[4] As Jane Stevenson shows, it was a radical extension in Christian emotional sympathy that allowed a "harlot" like Mary any social or spiritual consideration.[5] Her legend is notable as a hagiographic representation of a saintly life in exile like those of earlier desert fathers like Jerome,[6] but it is applied to a notorious female placed completely outside the bounds of religious and secular community by her former way of life. The full title of the legend is *De Transitu Mariae Ægyptiace* – her "passing," "how she completed the days of her life in the desert" (58/3–4) but also, conceivably, her "crossing" or "passage" on earth from one state to another. The central question is how this passage from rejected sinner to saint takes place. Will the story of her desert life reveal just another form of exclusion from the world or something more? In what follows, I argue that Mary's emotions, understood as a set of "bodily practices," are crucial in establishing the desert of her banishment as a powerful and positive *emotional space*.[7] The desert where she repents is an exilic location so extreme and depleted in normal terms as to be no "place" at all, but her strenuous emotional labour gradually converts it to a model of peace and plenitude. Accordingly, the "desert" of Mary's exile is not present as a fixed geographical location or a landscape but as an "emotional geography," in which the "first and foremost, most immediate and intimately *felt* geography is the body, the site of emotional experience and expression *par excellence*."[8] Mary's bodily practices in the desert instance many of the features that occur in medieval literature of exile, both in religious and secular texts. These involve isolation in a wilderness setting; loss of signs of identity, such as name and clothing; lack of food; change in appearance; lack of directed movement.[9] The nature of this emotional repertoire is, in Monique Scheer's terms, directly related to the social circumstances and cultural modes within which it is learned and practised as an "experience" and "manifested in bodily processes."[10] In identifying the desert as such an emotional space, Mary creates and communicates new understandings of her story's institutional and ideological centre – the monastery – then finally shows her own life to have been an even higher "other way to salvation."

The earliest vernacular version of Mary's life is an Old English translation of Paul the Deacon's text found in a manuscript of Ælfric's *Lives of the Saints*, though it is not by Ælfric.[11] Hugh Magennis has shown that it was inserted into BL MS Cotton Julius E. vii, "at a late stage."[12] Magennis argues that in its emphasis on eremitical contemplative life, and the prestige it gives to an uneducated, lowborn and non-virginal female, it presented "a radically alternative spiritual ideal" from Ælfric's to late Anglo-Saxon readers. It remains a challenging work today, as recent studies suggest.[13] In all versions of Mary's legend, the basic story is similar, although it is differently structured. In some, the story begins with Mary's own life. In the Old English text, following its original, Mary's spectacular account of sin and repentance is framed within the journeys of Zosimus, a monk, who finds her as a penitent in the desert beyond the Jordan, hears her life story and later gives her communion before she dies. He buries her body in the desert, and then carries the tale of her sanctity back to his fellow monks. I shall argue that rather than diminishing Mary's prestige in the tale, or the importance of her agency, this narrative frame strategy is subtly constructed to accord her a special importance.

The Old English (OE) story begins, after its prologue, with Zosimus, an exemplary monk in Palestine, in search of even greater holiness. He has lived faultlessly in the cloister since birth, and is "oppressed" (*gecnyssed*) (62/59) by thoughts that he may already have reached perfection and will not able to achieve more because there is no one better than he is to teach him. An angel reminds him that "there is no person that can show himself perfect" and tells him "go out from your land" (*far ut of þinum earde*) where he will undergo a greater "struggle" (*gewinn*) than he has ever known, "in order that you may perceive and understand how great are other paths to salvation" (*hu miccle synd oþre haelo wegas*) (62/68–75). Zosimus, dedicated to the monastery at birth, has imagined that the way to "perfection" or "completion" (*ful-fremednysse*) must be a continuing accretion of holiness like his own, "from the beginning" (*fram frymþe*), an accomplishment in "all the monastic rules" (*eallum þam munuclicum regolum*) dependent on the best professional training (61/24–39). In some respects, he is going to be very surprised. The same may be said for the reader, for whom Zosimus provides a model in his expectations and reactions.[14] As Andrew Scheil says, "the narrative constantly foregrounds the importance of the reader in the hermeneutic circle, moving back and forth between the 'known' of the reader's expectations and the 'unknown' of the text's silences."[15]

Nevertheless, this is not a story of a potentially overweening monk who needs to be humbled by seeing the superior virtues of a convertite. The OE life strongly approves of strict obedience to the rule and abnegation of the flesh through abstinence. It is precisely because of these practices, along with his psalm singing and meditation on Scripture, that Zosimus is sometimes granted "divine enlightenment through revelation from God" (*godcundan onlihtnysse þurh ateowednysse fram Gode*) (60/40–62/55). But there is a twist. Mary, not some monk or male hermit, turns out to be the superior being among those "who love the desert" (*þæra sy þe westen lufiaþ*) (62/66) and whom he has sought as a teacher. In order to achieve further enlightenment, he must learn "*other*" ways." He must "go out," leaving the monastery where he has been all his life and keep company with an uneducated sinner, a woman. Zosimus never fails in his duties as a monk, but what he receives from and through Mary is an *emotional* awakening different from his habitual hope of learning more "monastic works" (*munuclicum weorcum*), "actions" (*dædum*) and stricter "exaltation" or observance (*mærsung*) (61/40–45). The moral seems twofold: God grants Zosimus's prayer for more instruction; he is allowed to find enlightenment because he is such a good ascetic monk. Yet his foretold "struggle" is not, as we might have expected, with the practices of an even stricter monastery, although he finds such a place. Rather, its nature becomes externalised in the spontaneous and embodied emotionalism of his time in the desert with Mary, unlike his regulated and intellectualised life hitherto. The story of their relationship creates the desert as an "emotional space" for him too, in which his ascetic life is first estranged in form and concept so that it can be rediscovered and re-animated by new depths of feeling.

This process of emotional awakening begins with Zosimus's arrival at an outlying and secret monastery beside the Jordan. As the tale continues, the Jordan becomes, among other things, a symbolic boundary between communal and eremitical forms of religious life – the collective discipline of the cloister and solitary existence outside it where the rule is a matter of personal discipline. The text tells us that in their Lenten retreat in the desert, the monks deliberately kept apart "in such a way that none of them knew the conduct or deeds of another"

(68/162–164). Zosimus is prepared for his adventures in the desert by finding monks whose description introduces thematics of heat, light, love and emotional elevation that are later found strongly associated with Mary. The Jordan monks are "shining" (*scinende*) in their works and "boiling" or "burning" "in spirit" (*on gæste weallende*), in what seems to be a reference to the "welling" of vital spirits up from the heart in moments of joy. We are told they practise abstention to "show themselves the keener (*scearpran*) in the true love of God" and to be "dead in body and living in spirit" (*on lichaman dead and on gæste libbende*) (65/102–112). The narrative emphasises also the collective character of this emotional condition amongst them, in a clear difference from the concentration on Zosimus as an individual and on his desire for self-improvement, in the description of his home monastery. While he is right to seek self-improvement, as the abbot tells him (64/94–97), the story will become overall one of his emotional socialisation through what he learns to *feel* for and through Mary, matters which will eventually strengthen the whole monastery when they are revealed. After her death, he "conceal[s] nothing" "so that they all exalt… the glories of God" (118/950–954). The ending of the story echoes its beginning, which argues that no one "should keep secret the glorious works of God" (58/11–14). This emphasis may well be an apology for uncovering the sensational – and possibly hard to credit (58/18–60/22) – nature of Mary's life – but it also gives the legend a broader function as the fulfilling of a divine purpose. Beyond that, it maintains a connection with themes of silence and speech, concealment and revelation, that feature startlingly in the poem's desert narrative.

One could well take the Jordan monastery for an image of the cloister as already an ideal "desert," since it is secluded, with "the gate always shut up" (66/125–127), cares for no earthly concerns (64/108–110) and has no contact with secular society (66/130–132). What changes most for Zosimus when he finds Mary in the desert is the element of "struggle" he has been promised, which turns out to be deeply physical and emotional in nature. Nothing prepares the reader for this meeting in the account of the monks' annual Lenten desert foray, which highlights their habitual preparations, consistency of conduct, self-sufficiency and above all solitariness, each avoiding company and "remain[ing] by himself" to seek union with God. Their goal is to be *in* the desert, not to travel *through* it, and certainly not to meet anyone. Zosimus, by contrast, "desire[s] to come across some father in the desert, who might edify him" and journeys for 26 days in a straight line, "as though he were purposefully travelling to some particular person" (70/193–197). God has guided him to the Jordan monastery, as we have been told (66/132–135), but once in the desert, his own desire is made to seem the driving force, with the effect of giving this space a highly emotional character.

Desire and emotion become overt when Zosimus gets his first glimpse of Mary. At first, he fears that she is a phantom illusion, but then sees that it is "a human being" running away from him and then, more specifically, "a woman, extremely black in her body… and the hair of her head was as white as wool and no longer than down to her neck" (70/204/–72/218). That is, Zosimus identifies Mary as a human female because he sees her fully naked. What follows might seem at first glance a complete contradiction of Zosimus's vowed life of celibacy and self-mortification because the encounter opens out into a language of joyful desire and emotional arousal:

> Zosima kept gazing intently at these details (*þa wisan*), and because of the longed for loveliness (*gewilnedan swetnysse*) of that glorious sight (*þære wuldorfæstan gesihðe*) filled with joy (*fægen gefremede*), he ran speedily in the direction in which he had seen [her] hastening.
>
> *(72/219–222)*

Readers have been told enough of Zosimus's desire for a holy instructor, and know enough of the genre they are reading to realise that his joy and longing should be interpreted as chaste. His instinctive joy shows that he thinks the search for a guide to *ful-fremednysse* (completion/perfection) has found its object. As Lees and Watt say, "Mary's physical age has no meaning to him; she is a desert mother, ahead of him on the path to perfection."[16] It has been pointed out that Mary is "turned into an ideal whose figuration embraces much of what virginity covers in other texts."[17] Yet the situation has much potential for humour: we see an ageing monk run after a naked woman, one whose age and burned complexion, by conventional contemporary standards, make her an unlikely sexual attraction, and so may make him seem all the more desperate.

This encounter begins what seems a topsy-turvy situation. The desert space will abound in emotional outcomes that reverse, and even parody, Mary's and Zosimus's lives on the other side of Jordan:[18] now she flees, and the man has to chase *her*; she and Zosimus prostrate themselves together for "many hours" (74/276–76/279); the priest kneels weeping to the penitent, receives *her* instructions and goes home only to long for their next meeting (104/723–106/763); he "eagerly looks[s]" for her, like a hunter "seeing if he might be able to catch… the sweetest wild animal" (*þæt sweteste wildeor gegripan*) (114/871–875). It may well seem that "Zosimus finds himself undone by Mary,"[19] but this deliberately ambivalent language is controlled in a spiritual reading by a transference of his "great need" (*micle neod*) (74/272) to another plane, where, for those "dead in body but living in spirit," desire is attached to the search for divine grace. To make the point, carnal and spiritual apprehensions of Mary coexist in the narrative at this stage. Zosimus is still not quite sure "what kind of wild beast" (*hwæt þæt wildeora*) he might be seeing, yet addresses her as "you handmaid of God." While still knowing nothing, he intuits that she is a long-term ascetic seeking the reward of salvation (72/235–239).

Zosimus's intuition of Mary's life in the desert has no normal cognitive source. Like her knowledge of his name, rank and monastery (74/250–265; 104/723–726), it is a direct gift from God, and in each case it is manifested in bodily emotional reactions. For him, seeing the "details" of her body brings joy and tearful longing for instruction – his "great need" – because in her scorched skin and nakedness, she incarnates bodily mortification. For her, his sight brings on shame at exposing the "womanly frailty" (*wiflican tydernysse*) with which she has sinned, and so motivates her reciprocal "need" (74/268–275) for clothing. They meet on either side of "a dried up stream" symbolically "marked out" (*getacnod*) (72/242) as the "dead" body which contains the living spirit. Zosimus sees her as "made dead to the world with regard to the concerns of youth" (... *of þæm geongran dæle*) (76/289–292), but Mary's concern for her nakedness and worried demand to know why he has "toil[ed]" after her fits the text's later revelation that her peace of the body is not simply the result of age but comes after physical and emotional labour over 17 years (98/616–618) – "struggling and striving" (*winnende and wraxligende*) 675–676) – and may still be at risk through the act of confession itself, 30 years later (96/608–98/612).

Very unlike Zosimus in his confidence that he can only advance towards perfection (62/54–67), Mary sees herself still as a "sinful woman." His anxiety that she may be "a spirit" (*gaste*) "that was praying there in some sort of pretence" (... *mid hwilcere hiwunga*) (80/337) provokes a revealing response. She is *not* reducible to a *gast* (80/342) or "appearance" (*gesihþe*) (76/290) revealed to *him* – whether real or deceptive. As if to counter the critical view that sees her as "define[d]... by her position in a series of male-male exchanges,"[20] she insists that she is an autonomous female human being with a body and a history that exceeds his vision: "I am a sinful woman... and I am no spirit but dust and ashes and wholly flesh and nothing spirit-like" (80/342–345). To learn from her requires Zosimus to "struggle" and fully acknowledge both her embodiment and his own. He has to "go out from... [his] land," "desire," feel "joy," "run," "toil," "groan," "weep," "sigh," "gasp," "fear," "sweat," "tremb[le]" and "beg" to hear Mary's life story as it extends over embodied human time and space in order to know why he has been divinely moved to grant her spiritual authority. Body, time, space and all the motions and emotions connected with these make up the "other way" that is revealed to him.

Mary's account of her life is therefore given a particular value and authority by its framing within the story of Zosimus's quest. Yet, as befits a penitent sinner, Mary's own words are dominated by self-accusations and fears that her listener will despise her. It is Zosimus, holding that "grace is not recognized on grounds of rank but is accustomed to indicate itself by works of the soul" (76/294–296), who finds it "so salutary a story" (*swa halendre gerecedysse*) (86/420–421). As in his first sight of her in the desert, there is a potential for surprise and irony in this benign response to a naked revelation of sexual sin – Mary thinks her tale will "defile both you and the air itself" (85/406–7) – but it is the appropriate reading for his "need." Indeed, Mary's promise to "hide nothing" (82/355) picks up the narrative's running theme of concealment and revelation as an indication to the reader that Zosimus is now receiving the teaching he wants. Several aspects of Mary's story relate to his own: the heavenly direction that preserves Mary unknown to herself and guides her to Jerusalem on Holy Rood Day is paralleled by Zosimus's journey in the desert "as though he were travelling to find some particular person" (70/196–197), and each at a crucial life-stage has heard a voice that sends them away on a new path.

Yet for all these likenesses, and however edifying the story is in its guise as spiritual instruction for a monk, there is no denying that Mary's adventures as a sinner and penitent have an emotional appeal that surpasses anything granted to Zosimus simply in his own right. For Zosimus, life has been a long striving to be better and better. For Mary, it has been a reckless race to the bottom, until her miraculous conversion. Her sex life expands and becomes more culpable right up to the moment of her barring from the temple on Holy Rood Day: she has prostituted herself for the first time to take ship to Jerusalem, and "polluted" (*besmat*) (88/451) both foreigners and townspeople as well as fellow passengers. The narrative reveals conventional misogynistic assumptions that she is the sole source of "pollution" in these acts, personally "compel[ling]" men "to sin" (86/430–432) and "enticing" them into "the trap of perdition" (*grin forspillednysse*) (86/454). Yet in context, these hostile gender attitudes make the authority given to Mary, as a penitent, over the holy Zosimus all the more remarkable. Her story engenders greater emotional effect because it demonstrates divine patience and mercy all the more strikingly in contrast to hypocritical human condemnation, and shows God reintegrating an outcast into society on new terms. Although Mary has come as close as possible to non-being-in-the-"world," she centres a reconstitution of Christian community. Although *she* feels "shamed" by her past story and her nakedness, as the sign of her sin, Zosimus is deeply moved by her repentance and her asceticism, and her wider social significance is made clear: she quickly questions him about "how the flock of Christ's true-believing congregation are now looked after" (78/310–311) and her life offers hope to all "sinners and wrong-doers" (92/547–548).

While this is a text that famously abjects the body as an occasion of sin, it also makes bodily and affective events the means of Mary's personal reorientation towards God. The circumstances of Mary's conversion show that for her, an illiterate, religious "knowledge" is achieved through the medium of the flesh. It is not until a divine force prevents her from entering the temple and her body (*lichama*) is exhausted (*swiðe geswenced*) with repeatedly pushing against it that she begins "earnestly to think it over" (*ofer þæt georne wenan*): "Then truly knowledge of salvation touched my mind and the eyes of my heart" (88/476–90/487). Emotions, affects and gestures never mentioned before in her career – "powerful fear" (*stranglic fyrhto*), "trembling all over in excitement" (*eall byfigende gedrefed*) (92/528–529), weeping and kissing – mark the conversion. On Holy Rood Day, her body changes from an abstracted and routinised medium of "wicked lusts" (*unrihtlican lustes*) (436), lacking in emotion and any affect beyond habitual "heat" and "burning," to become newly sentient and spiritually informative.

In all versions of the story, there is the striking detail that Mary has sinned from pure inclination for sex, not from any worldly motive. Her condition is what might now be called "hypersexuality" or "sexual addiction," except that in this Christian context, it is thoroughly moralised. She is "on fire with the passion of desire for sin" *(mid þære hatheortnysse þæs synlustes)* (82/376–377), "the passion of my lusting for pleasure" *(þære þrowunge mines wynlustes)* (84/403) and the "pleasure of my body" *(mines lichaman luste)* (86/419), but for all that her compulsion for sex leads her a lonely and joyless life. The force that holds Mary back at the temple door, so that "[she] alone is thrust out" *(wæs ic ana ut ascofen)* while "they were all received inside" *(hi ealle þyder inn onfangene wæron)* (88/471–472), may illustrate a social isolation more than a special sinfulness: Magennis remarks that "the men who use Mary" are not "divinely prevented from entering the temple because of their sins."[21] She speaks of a search for "co-workers" *(emwyrhtena)* in sex but has no real social or affective ties with anyone. The "world" that she will reject has already rejected her; she embodies this as she stands "alone in a particular corner" *(ana... on summum hwome)* outside the temple (480–481). The spatial symbolism here anticipates the desert location where Mary will live alone and apart. Yet her vowed exclusion from human society is not simply a price she must pay for inclusion in grace – admission to the church, the sight of the Holy Rood and Christ's mercy. Rather, the new "glory" *(wuldor)* (92/544) revealed to her in Christ actually provides her first sense of universal human belonging. She can now identify herself as a social being – as one of "we sinful" *(we synfulle)* whose repentance Christ accepts (92/545–547). That understanding eventually permits the one emotionally meaningful earthly relationship she will ever have, and through it Zosimus, in turn, has revealed to him the "glory" *(wuldorfæstlicnesse)* that God grants to the penitent sinner (102/703–710).

For the first time, a *conscious* sinner, Mary of Egypt, finds her true vocation. She offers the reader a perfect model of repentance in this episode: complete humility yet faith in Christ's will to save her, compunction of heart, oral confession, a willingness to perform bodily penance and a firm purpose of amendment. That she has confessed fully and received absolution is shown by her reception of communion after a symbolic cleansing in the Jordan (94/577–96/582), a kind of re-baptism.[22] Her participation in the Eucharist here will be matched 48 years later in the same place when she comes back across the Jordan to receive it from Zosimus (110/824/–112/833). Her answers to his questions about the difficulties of abstinence, especially celibacy, but also abstention from rich food, wine and "lewd songs" (96/605–98/641), seem especially suited to the concerns of a monk, but Mary's reliance on her "surety" *(mundbyrdnesse)* and "covenant" *(truwan)* with the Virgin, her "guarantor" *(borhhanda)* (98/629–659), introduces a new female element into Zosimus's patriarchal world. Overall, the narrative follows a pattern in which Mary's life in the desert is represented as both an example to Zosimus of a more perfect ascetic monasticism of his own kind, and as an "*other* way," a life incomparable to his in its wonderful spiritual intensity. They share much, but by different means, being totally different in their background and education. Through psalm-singing and "the study of Holy Scriptures," he is granted "revelation from God of the holy vision" (60/40–62/55). Mary, quite uneducated, simply "sees" *(ic... geseah)* "the holy mysteries of God" *(þa halgan Godes gerynu)* in the "glory" (*wuldor*) of the Cross (902/535–536) and knows Scripture without a human intermediary: "God's word... teaches this human understanding from within" (*Godes word... innan lærende þis mennisce andgyt*) (102/697–698). Fighting temptation, she sees "a light shining everywhere about me" and feels "a secure peace" (*sum stapolfæstlic smyltnyss*) (98/639–640). This "peace" recalls the "repose" (94/556) that has been promised to Mary in the desert. The comforting "light" will develop in intensity throughout the story, as the intense moonlight when Mary crosses Jordan (110/805–807) and the "shining sun" Zosimus finds by her dead body (114/885), a sign of sanctity.

Through all this symbolism, it is made clear that sincerity of repentance, intensity of perception and fullness of belief count for more than quantity of knowledge. Mary, unlike Zosimus, does not seek to *know* more. Rather, she gains a more intimate connection with the divine by a simple willingness to do without everything extraneous to her hope of salvation. The narrative structures this difference sequentially. At first, Mary's living on almost no food is resembled to an extreme version of monastic self-mortification, as shown by her careful accounting of the man-made food she takes immediately after conversion – half a loaf (96/582–583) – then the two-and-a-half loaves she takes into the desert and slowly consumes over "some time" (*sumere hwile*) (96/591–604). Once her first 17 years in the desert are over, Mary lives randomly on the plants she finds (100/663–664). She receives no clothing, food or instruction from human or animal, only mystically from God (102/691–698). Her miraculously light footprint on land and water, witnessed by her levitation in prayer and (later) her walking over the Jordan, is a related symbolic feature.

Zosimus's role in the story, from this point of view, is not to emulate but simply to record the "other way" these wonders reveal, but that process also has separate stages. Through listening to Mary, we discover that Zosimus is wrong at first when he sees her as having obtained what he calls "the inalienable blessing of your perfection" (*þæt unbereafigendlice gebæd þinre fulfremednysse*) (76/297–298). In his "joy" and "need," he has forgotten the angel's warning that no one is perfect (62/70–71). Mary's closing reference to "all the things that were accomplished concerning me," "a wretched harlot" (100/699–702), underlines the necessary coexistence in her of two self-identifications: the sinner she remains and the glorious saved soul God can make her. Zosimus's response at the end of her story shows he has learned better: "Now I truly know that you [God] do not abandon any of those who seek you" (102/709–710). He now sees that, as Mary herself has said (86/435–438), her conversion illustrates God's wonderful, patient will to save. In the same way, the expression of Mary's emotional life is divided between penitent and recipient of grace: as a conscious sinner, she continues to weep and sigh to the end (112/856), receives her final communion "sorrowing tearfully" (110/830–831) and her last spoken words to Zosimus are "Pray for me, and protect me in my unhappiness" (*ungesælignesse*) (112/853). Yet she shines, works wonders and brings "joy" as a "holy handmaid of God." We learn both what she is to herself and what she can mean to others.

Mary is no stoic. She weeps and laments bitterly, on an emotional edge as much as a geographical and social one. This extreme of sorrow is represented not just as penitential reparation but as a necessary heuristic process: she has to suffer so much pain so that through acceptance of the suffering as heaven-sent, she can find "rest." That strenuous emotional process defines the "marked out" spot where she is eventually found by Zosimus. Yet we learn that she has no fixed place in the desert but continually moves: "I have kept apart, always fleeing away" (*ic feorrode, symle fleonde*) (96/588). Paradoxically, this continual movement comes to constitute her place of rest in God. Mary's desert existence does not present a case of "emotions connected with specific places"[23] but of the alternative that Barbara Rosenwein identifies in the work of Gregory the Great – his use of *spatium* to signal "the spaces of times" and the "spaces of life."[24] In a contrast to her earlier designation of places and journeys – Alexandria, the ship, Jerusalem, the temple, the courtyard, the church of St John the Baptist by the Jordan – once in the desert, Mary measures time only by clothing, food and her body. Her clothes rot off, her bread is consumed, she withers and blackens and she marks the years by emotions and affective reactions rather than by specific locations. What Rosenwein says of a miracle scene related by Gregory could equally apply to her: "What power the action… are emotions, feelings born of the situation itself and of the proper human responses to it."[25] So we read of the first 17 years of penitence in which she is strongly assailed by temptations, and the emotions, affects and gestures associated with her "struggle": "lusts," "desires," weeping, beating the breast, "overwhelming grief" and at last "a secure peace" (98/616–641). In this time-space, Mary's bodily and emotional suffering, rather than a location or a landscape, constitutes her desert – icy coldness, "scorching" and "burning," reduced to lying "down on the ground, almost completely without breath" (100/662–673). Zosimus does not suffer in these ways, but his emotions on meeting and listening to her, with their associated affects and gestures – fear, trembling, tears, prostration – often resemble hers. Her emotional influence brings him to share with her both a human sympathy and an enriched sense of the goodness of God. In this embodied way, Mary and he may be said to have a mutual "personal attachment."[26] The emphasis on shared affect and emotion – on "feelings" – in their relationship moderates the critical view that primarily in this text "knowledge is associated with sight, with spectacle."[27]

The ending of the story, after Mary's first conversation with Zosimus has concluded, stages her brief return into the realm of time and place before leaving this life. Details of dates and locations reoccur as Mary plans the future: she arranges for Zosimus to bring her the Eucharist in a year's time by the far bank of the Jordan on Holy Thursday evening. In doing so, she consciously returns to the memory of her communion in the Church of John the Baptist on the day of her conversion. He also brings her other food from which she symbolically consumes three lentils, matching the three loaves she bought that day. Apart from its symbolic logic, her acceptance of the redundant food is a kindness to "the old man" (*þam ealdan*) in his well-meaning but limited understanding of her condition. Though she is preparing for death that very day, as he later learns, out of sympathy for him she eats as much as will keep the soul "undefiled" (112/848–853). The emotional bond between them remains, even as her higher status and authority become increasingly apparent: "he touched her feet.... And then weeping and sighing she left him, and he did not dare to hinder her in any respect; in no respect would she be hindered" (112/854–858).

For Zosimus, who is filled with "longing," "astonishment," "joy" and "awe," there is a sense of closure to his education in "other ways to salvation." After Mary, surrounded by brightness, walks over the river, he thanks God that through seeing her he has learned to measure himself as inferior beside "the higher perfection of these others" (*þæm gemete þæra oþra fulfremodnysse*) (110/822–823). The surprising use of the plural here suggests that Mary is to be understood not only as an individual but as a type of the "purified" repentant, those whom she has called "we sinful" (545), "who first cleanse themselves" (*þe hi sylfe aer clænsiað*) and will be "like [God] himself" (110/817–823). The suggestion is that she is fully purged of sin and will ascend straight to heaven at death. On her last day, Mary repeats the sequence of compunction, confession and communion of the day she converted. Together, she and Zosimus participate in a form of the mass, throughout which her status seems to alter. Before taking communion from Zosimus, she utters the *Credo* and *Pater noster*, but then addresses God directly in the words of Simeon in Luke 2, 28–30, the *Nunc dimittis*. Mary is thus a member of the laity, reciting the prayer of the faithful and mediating her relationship with God through the sacrament administered by the priest – she has insisted that Zosimus not kneel to her (110/811–813) – but she assumes a patriarchal persona higher than his, and Zosimus himself now thinks of her as a "saint" (*halgan*) (112/864). If we can take Mary as a heightened example of the "other way to salvation" of lay penitents, then the story is strongly reiterating here Zosimus's earlier view that grace is not shown by "rank" (*medemnysse*) but "works of the soul" (*þære sawla dædum*) (76/298). The function of the male celibate priesthood is both endorsed and challenged by the potential educational message in Mary's life story. She and Zosimus need each other, but his need turns out to be greater.

The narrative account of Mary's death and burial, as discovered by Zosimus when he returns to the desert in a year, keeps her authority intact. Zosimus gives her a burial service, involving his characteristic psalm-singing, but still "wonders whether this would be pleasing to her" (114/890–891), and again struggles physically and emotionally, this time to bury her, until miraculously helped. One effect of this emphasis on his uncertainty and difficulties is to resist the notion that the full meaning of Mary's existence can be removed from the desert and appropriated for clerical use. Zosimus returns over the Jordan with her name, permission to tell her story and some orders for improving monastic "practices" (*mynsterwisan*) (120/955), but with the strange effect that the monastery sponsors a feast day based on the authority of an illiterate female sinner, whose body remains obscurely buried in the desert, just as it was first found lying there. To bring Mary's body back over the river, after her living "death in the body," would be not only to cross her wishes but to misread the special power of her exile. It would also, just possibly, threaten patriarchal and celibate dominion. Mary's prestige is great because she has been able to expiate *so much* sin of the flesh. The always virginal oblate Zosimus could never face such a challenge or have such a victory, but to emphasise that point might have dangerous consequences. Does greater sinning hold greater potential for later repentant holiness? Leaving Mary in an unmarked grave in the desert avoids the problem, and is one of several instances in the story where the dangers that might lie in exalting her above Zosimus are policed: she insists repeatedly on his rank as priest and "abbot" (e.g., 76/279–284), and rebukes him for kneeling to her while bearing the sacrament (110/811–813). The message he finds written by her corpse maintains the double nature of their relationship to the end: she humbly asks "Abbot Zosimus" to "have mercy on my body," bury it – "add dust to dust" – and "pray for her" (114/893–895), but the very fact of his receiving a written message from an illiterate shows a divine hand has been at work (116/899–901), and he knows she has gone straight to God (116/909). It is noteworthy that in this final communication with him, written after death, out of human time, she neither laments nor calls herself a sinner.

So, although this story concludes in the monastery, its heart remains in the desert. The monks' recognition of Mary as a saint celebrates the goal of ascetic life as the "rest" of union with God in heaven, as Mary understood when she "saw… the holy mysteries of God in the Holy Rood" (535–536), and "the glory which we sinful people do not see by our deserts" (544–545). God is "rest," "peace" and "glory" as the conclusion of all saints lives. But the "other way" to God in this story begins in spaces "outside" church institutions – the "corner" (*hwomme*) in the courtyard with the Virgin's image (88/481) and the desert. From there, the way to God is the "brave struggle" (*ellenlic gewinn*) that the story promises from the outset (58/2–3), maintained within the world of volatile emotions. The careers of Zosimus, told like Abraham to "go out from your land,"[28] and of Mary, told to "cross over the river Jordan," both illustrate this. As a saint, Mary's characteristic acceptance of all sorrows or joys as God's will stabilises and protects her even in the midst of continuing physical and emotional suffering. Her "suffering" (willing endurance) of this suffering transforms where she is into a space of "rest." In her desert life, "apart, always fleeing away" (96/588), Mary emulates the unchanging Providential "patience" that has led her into the wilderness and protects her there. Because to her as a saint, God is the unchanging referent of all narrative events, wherever she "rests" in God is central. As living humans – meaning in the terms of this story "we sinful people" – we can know Mary's past sinfulness and repentant suffering, because we share that kind of story with her. As Jeff Malpas writes, "[t]o have a sense of one's own past is to have a grasp of one's present and future in relation to the 'story' of one's embodied activity within the places in which one lives and with respect to the objects and persons in those places."[29] But, like the divine "mysteries" she saw in the Holy Rood, and like her unmarked grave, Mary's 30 years of "rest" in the desert remain unknowable. As earthly beings, tied to the narrative of time, place, persons and objects, readers can fully know only her "struggle." Otherwise, like Zosimus, we see her leaving us behind.

Notes

1 For a survey of the pre-Conquest growth of the legend, see Jane Stevenson, "The Holy Sinner: The Life of Mary of Egypt," in *The Legend of Mary of Egypt in Medieval Insular Hagiography*, eds. Erich Poppe and Bianca Ross (Dublin: Four Courts Press, 1996), 19–50.
2 Ibid., 20–21.
3 See "St Mary the Egyptian Trailer": https://www.youtube.com/watch?v=f0T2b-ZhoHfk. Accessed 16 January, 2019.
4 Stevenson, "The Holy Sinner," 28.
5 Ibid.
6 Hugh Magennis, ed. and trans., *The Old English Life of St Mary of Egypt* (Exeter: Exeter University Press, 2002), 4–5. Subsequent in-text references to the legend, both text and translation, are to this edition.
7 For this term, see Barbara H. Rosenwein, "Emotional Space," in *Codierungen von Emotionen im Mittelalter / Emotions and Sensibilities in the Middle Ages*, eds. C. Stephen Jaeger and Ingrid Kastin (Berlin: De Gruyter, 2003), 287–303. See also Monique Scheer, "Are Emotions a Kind of Practice (and Is That What Makes Them Have a History)? A Bourdieuan Approach to Understanding Emotion", *History and Theory* 51, no. 2 (2012): 217: "People inhabit and move around in spaces as much as in communities, and the notion of spaces emphasizes the body and its senses more than does the notion of the value system of a community."
8 Joyce Davidson and Christine Milligan, "Embodying Emotion Sensing Space: Introducing Emotional Geographies," *Social and Cultural Geography* 5, no. 4 (2004): 523.
9 See Andrew Lynch, "Malory and Emotion," in *A New Companion to Malory*, eds. Megan G. Leitch and Cory James Rushton (Cambridge: D. S. Brewer, 2019), 183–184.
10 Scheer, "Are Emotions a Kind of Practice," 205: "Like all practices, emotions are simultaneously spontaneous and conventional."
11 See Magennis, *Life*, 18–25.
12 Ibid., 19.
13 Clare A. Lees and Diane Watt, "Age and Desire in the Old English *Life of St Mary of Egypt*: A Queerer Time and Place?" in *Middle-Aged Women in the Middle Ages*, ed. Sue Niebrzydowski (Cambridge: D. S. Brewer, 2011), 53–68. Victoria Blud, *The Unspeakable, Gender and Sexuality in Medieval Literature, 1000–1400* (Cambridge: D. S. Brewer, 2017), 21–60.
14 See Lees and Watt, "Age and Desire," 50: "like Zosimus, the reader's belief is to be confirmed, or changed, in the process of spiritual reading."
15 Andrew P. Scheil, "Bodies and Boundaries in the Old English Life of St. Mary of Egypt," *Neophilologus* 84, no. 1 (2000): 138.
16 Lees and Watt, "Age and Desire," 59.
17 L. M. C. Weston, "Saintly Lives: Friendship, Kinship, Gender and Sexuality," in *The Cambridge History of Early Medieval English Literature*, ed. Clare A. Lees (Cambridge: Cambridge University Press, 2013), 399.
18 It has been pointed out also that the story of Mary's voyage to find more lovers in Jerusalem "is a sacrilegious parody of pilgrimage." See Simon Lavery, "The Story of Mary the Egyptian in Medieval England", in *The Legend of Mary of Egypt*, eds. Poppe and Ross (Dublin: Four Courts Press, 1996), 130.
19 Lees and Watt, "Age and Desire," 59.
20 Weston, "Saintly Lives," 401.

21 Magennis, *Life*, 6.
22 See ibid., 126, n. 575–576.
23 Rosenwein, "Emotional Space," 289.
24 Ibid., 293.
25 Ibid., 291.
26 See Magennis, *Life*, 6.
27 Weston, "Saintly Lives," 402.
28 Genesis 12.1.
29 Jeff Malpas, *Place and Experience: A Philosophical Topography* (Cambridge: Cambridge University Press, 2009), 185.

Bibliography

Blud, Victoria. *The Unspeakable, Gender and Sexuality in Medieval Literature, 1000–1400*. Cambridge: D. S. Brewer, 2017.
Davidson, Joyce and Christine Milligan. "Embodying Emotion Sensing Space: Introducing Emotional Geographies." *Social and Cultural Geography* 5, no. 4 (2004): 523–532.
Lavery, Simon. "The Story of Mary the Egyptian in Medieval England." In *The Legend of Mary of Egypt in Medieval Insular Hagiography*, edited by Erich Poppe and Bianca Ross, 113–148. Dublin: Four Courts Press, 1996.
Lees, Clare A. and Diane Watt. "Age and Desire in the Old English *Life of St Mary of Egypt*: A Queerer Time and Place?" In *Middle-Aged Women in the Middle Ages*, edited by Sue Niebrzydowski, 53–68. Cambridge: D. S. Brewer, 2011.
Lynch, Andrew. "Malory and Emotion." In *A New Companion to Malory*, edited by Megan G. Leitch and Cory James Rushton, 177–190. Cambridge: D. S. Brewer, 2019.
Malpas, Jeff. *Place and Experience: A Philosophical Topography*. Cambridge: Cambridge University Press, 2009.
Magennis, Hugh, ed. and trans. *The Old English Life of St Mary of Egypt*. Exeter: Exeter University Press, 2002.
Rosenwein, Barbara H. "Emotional Space." In *Codierungen von Emotionen im Mittelalter / Emotions and Sensibilities in the Middle Ages*, edited by C. Stephen Jaeger and Ingrid Kastin, 287–303. Berlin: De Gruyter, 2003.
Scheer, Monique. "Are Emotions a Kind of Practice (and Is That What Makes Them Have a History)? A Bourdieuan Approach to Understanding Emotion." *History and Theory* 51, no. 2 (2012): 193–220.
Scheil, Andrew P. "Bodies and Boundaries in the Old English Life of St. Mary of Egypt." *Neophilologus* 84, no. 1 (2000): 137–156.
"St Mary the Egyptian Trailer": https://www.youtube.com/watch?v=f0T2bZhoHfk. Accessed 16 January, 2019.
Stevenson, Jane. "The Holy Sinner: The Life of Mary of Egypt." In *The Legend of Mary of Egypt in Medieval Insular Hagiography*, edited by Erich Poppe and Bianca Ross, 19–50. Dublin: Four Courts Press, 1996.
Weston, L. M. C. "Saintly Lives: Friendship, Kinship, Gender and Sexuality." In *The Cambridge History of Early Medieval English Literature*, edited by Clare A. Lees, 381–405. Cambridge: Cambridge University Press, 2013.

14

FROM AARON TO OTHELLO

The changing emotional register of blackness in Shakespeare

Bríd Phillips

Aaron, the wicked Moor in Shakespeare's *Titus Andronicus,* and Othello, the noble Moor in *Othello*, strike very different chords when one considers how each Moorish character is portrayed.[1] Both are crafted within the *habitus* of late Elizabethan London within 10–15 years of each other. *Habitus,* following Monique Scheer, relates to "the 'schemes of perception, thought, and action' that produce individual and collective practices, which in turn reproduce the generative schemes."[2] Within this framework, there is an acknowledgement of the history contained in the body of evolution, the history of the society in which the individual is situated, and the self-history which is moulded by the emotional practices carried out on a daily basis. Both the characters, Aaron and Othello, are responses to the system of cognitive and motivating structures that governed the negotiation of cross-cultural exchanges emotionally and socially, which, in turn, led to, often almost imperceptible change in societal emotional responses. A consideration of change at this time is strengthened by work such as that of Patricia Akhimie who notes, through her exploration of conduct literature, that "early modern people had begun to think of themselves as malleable, believing they could shape their own social identities by engaging in or adopting certain customary practices."[3] Such keenness to adopt new practices points to change within the *habitus*.

    The emotional dissonance of blackness between the two plays can be considered as a moment of 'friction' between the *habitus* and a changing social environment. To quote Scheer, it is a moment when friction ensues as actors or bodies enact cultural scripts out of place,[4] in which emotions "are more fruitfully thought of as habits emerging where bodily capacities and cultural requirements meet."[5] In this schema, emotions are a form of practice that depend on four overlapping categories of emotional practice: mobilizing, naming, communicating, and regulating the passions.[6] This chapter is an exploration of the cross-cultural exchanges reflecting this friction or dissonance. By analysing the emotionality encompassing the characters of Aaron and Othello in the two plays, I point to the dialectic surrounding cross-cultural exchanges relating to the idea of the Moor in London at the time which was influenced by political and cultural events and negotiated through ideas of otherness, character-traits, and, not least, colour. Although significantly these exchanges are marked by a fluctuating chromatic register, it is the cultural and social trajectory which is the subject for exploration rather than a singular focus on ideas of race.[7]

Emotional reactions to and from the body are socially ordered in that emotions can be viewed as a practice that relates to habit. From medieval traditions, the early modern period inherited a complex set of cultural relationships and emotional practices associated with the colour black. These habits and practiced ways of thinking also incorporated the idea of black as a physical characteristic. Many medieval church wall paintings featured devils with black-coloured skin which promulgated such ideas. These images of devils were also found in illuminated manuscripts, alabaster tablets, and painted windows.[8] While this view is commonly held through the late medieval and into the early modern period, it does not reflect the evolving complexity of practices in the early modern period that blackness connoted. Richard Blunt notes that "the black character was simply a visual representation of evil" in the medieval context.[9] Blunt continues by saying that the early black character on stage "represents damnation or folly and a way of looking at good versus evil," while in the latter period, it "was a representation of a multidimensional person."[10] While he acknowledges a change in representation, Blunt does not explore in detail why this change has occurred. In Shakespeare's literature, these ideas continue, and, for example, in *Love Labour's Lost* circa 1598, he writes that "black is the badge of hell, the hue of dungeons, and the school of night," 4.3.250–251.[11] In this context, black signifies hell, captivity, and nefarious teachings which align with the attitude that we find in *Titus Andronicus*. However, in *Sonnet 127,* in terms of the lover, black is the new fair. This sonnet begins the dark lady sequence, and here the speaker claims that while "in the old age black was not counted fair" (1), "now is black beauty's successive heir" (3). While many attempts have been made, the sonnets are difficult to date with any certainty. It is likely that they were written in periods of plague when theatre work dwindled, but this is not certain.[12] What is clear is that Shakespeare was engaging with ideas of competing discourses of complexion, colouring and the duplicitous nature of a fair-coloured face. The fair face could be improved or even changed by means of artifice, but a dark complexion could not be overwritten.

During the early modern period, people in Elizabethan England began, through voyages and successful expeditions to lands in Africa, India, and the Americas, to think differently about the 'other.'[13] With each new encounter, it was necessary to redefine what that 'other' or the 'barbarian' might mean.[14] There is a debate about the extent and significance of this contact, but it is certain that it did bring about some change.[15] G. K. Hunter notes that in *The Discovery of*

Witchcraft [Reginald], Scott says "a damned soule may and dooth take the shape of a blacke moore."[16] Nevertheless, it is important to point out that the word 'Moor' had no clear racial status at this time and was much more a marker of the exotic than of colour.[17] Virginia Mason Vaughan notes that "[a]lthough in some texts early modern writers distinguished between 'tawny' Moors of northern Africa and 'blackamoors' from the sub-Saharan region, the two were often conflated in the popular mind."[18] The conclusion being that the use of the term 'blackamoor' could not be taken as a determination of exact colour or origin. As John Gillies suggests,

> [i]n Shakespeare…, the 'exotic' not only embraces the black, the tawny, the monstrous, the savage, the barbarous, the New World and the Old, but touches all with 'wonder' and treats the ancient and Renaissance versions of otherness ('cannibals' and 'anthropophagi') as interchangeable.[19]

The reaction to the term relies on patterns of understanding and emotional responses created by a shared *habitus*. 'Blackness' and the term 'blackamoor' could mean to include all those at the periphery, a pagan 'other' in opposition to a white civilized Christian.[20] Within the Christian tradition of blackness, it is even suggested that faith could wash away the staining caused by sin. The Church Father, Augustine, says that "Ethiopians… [are] black in their natural sinfulness; but they may become white in the knowledge of the Lord."[21] The explanation for dark pigmentation in this context was associated with the transgressions of Cham, son of Noah, who became dark-skinned for his sins and inhabited the liminal edges of the earth in a position of servitude. Richard Hakluyt, writing in 1589, reports that Cham had disobeyed God and had carnal relations with his wife in the Ark. As a punishment, he had a son named Chus who was "blacke and loathsome" and "of this blacke and cursed Chus came all these blacke Moores which are in Africa."[22] The natural state of blackness is both undesirable and indelible and cannot be washed away. These ideas are extended further by Ania Loomba who suggests that Renaissance thinking on blackness was led by the thought that blackness, both as a moral quality and a skin colour, was dominant and could contaminate whiteness rather than the other way around.[23] Margaux Deroux also notes the intersection of the early modern discourse on colour as both emotionally and morally related.[24] This emotional and moral relation is evident in both the plays under examination.

In early Tudor England, black people appeared on the social landscape in minor numbers: in 1501 as part of Catherine of Aragon's retinue, and as skilled labourers during the time of friendly relations between Spain and England. In the 1570s, according to Imtiaz Habib, Africans appeared as commodities in Elizabeth I's household, sparking the appearance of Africans in personal bondage to the Elizabethan ruling class.[25] In 1585, *The Barbary Company* was founded to facilitate commercial ventures between England and Morocco (although the license expired without renewal in 1597). These physical appearances in social and cultural contexts are accompanied by corresponding appearances of black characters on the English stage. Vaughan notes that

> by the 1580s blackened faces on the public stage resonated with traditional rural and urban signifying codes that had developed out of different performance traditions ... The black devil and trickster who subverted the Christian community, and the Moorish king who ruled over an exotic realm far from England's shores, were equally enduring symbols of alterity.[26]

With these ideas in mind, it is clear that there is already evidence of competing practices surrounding the figure on stage.

The physical record documented in London between 1585 and 1590 from household accounts, government proclamations, legal records, and parish entries, to name a few, shows the numbers for black people at the time *Titus Andronicus* may have been written. The terms 'blackamoor' and 'negro' are used in these records without discrimination. Sensationally in 1589, at the wedding of James VI and Anne of Denmark, a blackamoor appeared in coloured dress carrying a sword, while four naked blackamoors danced in the snow, the four later dying of pneumonia.[27] The entire record indicates their servile position with little social engagement beyond spectacle and death. Despite evidence that suggests an earlier period of professional black people in Scotland and England, black people in the later sixteenth century were arriving as commodities via expeditionary trips to Africa and the Western Atlantic.[28] In this context, they were viewed as a subhuman enslaved class. However, conflict and complexity with this view arose because, as Vaughan notes,

> for Londoners in 1594, caught in a continuing war with Spain and facing seriously for the first time the dangers of territorial expansion, anxieties about cultural exchange were very real. [*Titus Andronicus*] ... must have mirrored, to some extent, their own fears.[29]

Englishness and a sense of identity could be marked by that which it was not: 'the other.' The English stage became an important medium to probe the emotional reaction to encroaching otherness, not least through references to the blackamoor. Blunt notes that it "seems that the representation of race began playing a role somewhere around the time of Shakespeare's early plays, although how the audience interpreted a blackface in medieval drama carried over into the racial representation of Moors on stage."[30] Again, there is friction between the form blackness should take on the stage.

Titus Andronicus was written at a time when England was attempting to build New World colonies. It reflects many of the anxieties felt in England around this unavoidable contact with the dark-skinned person. In the play, this anxiety is specifically located in the character of Aaron the Moor where we find a conflation of the earlier colour-coding ideology and a germinal 'proto-racism.'[31]

Vaughan notes that at this time, "blackface functioned as a polyphonic signifier that reflected changing social contexts and helped to create expectations and attitudes about black people."[32] A contemporary illustration, the Peacham drawing, named so for its inclusion of 'Henricus Peacham' written in the margin, gives one example of the fear and otherness focused on Aaron. The dating of the drawing is unclear, and estimates range from 1595 to 1615. What is clear is that it may correlate to the dating of the play's original production. It may be that Peacham saw the play and from that viewing constructed the drawing, or that he read the play and imaginatively reconstructed the scene in his head. This gives us an idea of contemporary reception of Aaron.[33] In the drawing, there are three figures with white faces – assumed to be Titus the Roman, and two figures, possibly soldiers, situated to the left. They face a suppliant Tamora, Queen of the Goths, with Chiron and Demetrius her sons bound behind her. In the far right, behind the Goths, is Aaron the Moor, wielding a weapon, dramatically poised with black face and limbs. He is an outsider to be feared, disrupting and dominating the tableau, laden with the inherited tradition of evil and destruction. This contemporary picture gives expression to many of the emotions which could be mobilized, named, communicated, and regulated around the Aaron.

Initially, in the play, Aaron appears on stage as Tamora's silent slave, colluding with the discourse of the enslaved blackamoor.[34] Deroux states that "Aaron is only allowed to function within the framework that early modern thought provides for blackness, and thus, the only way in which he can become self-actualized is by embodying blackness to its fullest extent."[35] Within this framework, he uses language effectively when alone on stage and, perhaps in defiance of the narrow terms of self-actualization allowed to him, develops an agency which precipitates an extensive part of the action that follows. He says of Tamora that he will "mount her pitch" (1.1.513) which may be a falconry idiom, or to the audience it may also have been a sexual reference. Quite soon, he also says he will "wanton with this queen" (1.1.520). In displaying an overt sexuality, he is developing the stereotype of the highly sexualized black 'other,' but by indicating his position as Tamora's lover, he is elevating his status to align with hers, especially as she is now the emperor's wife. Dympna Callaghan notes that Aaron makes attempts to disrupt the supremacy of whiteness which can be seen in his choice of lover.[36] In this context, Tamora is the ultra-white hue of the German Goth, as Saturninus says, "A goodly lady, trust me, of the hue/ That I would choose were I to choose anew" (1.1.265–266). Her ultra-whiteness is composed in opposition to Aaron's ultra-blackness.[37] Within the Goth royal family grouping, Aaron commands respect as Tamora's sons, perhaps from a position of being the 'other' themselves, praise him saying "thy counsel, lad, smells of no cowardice" (1.1.632).

When we first see Aaron and Tamora on stage alone in act 2, Tamora indicates both her acceptance of him as a man rather than a slave and her strong and insistent love for him. This is an interesting situation, as the paleness of her complexion has been noted but she is still cast as the 'other' by many of the Romans, which develops from their general distrust of non-Romans. Tamora has no issues with the Moorish, non-Goth component of Aaron's character, addressing him as "[m]y lovely Aaron" (2.2.10) in an act which sees her naming and reinforcing her emotional position. Aaron underscores Tamora's amatory position with an offensive and dangerous blackamoor by describing himself as having

> a fleece of woolly hair that now uncurls
> Even as an adder when she doth unroll
> To do some fatal execution?
> (2.2.34–35)

When Aaron states that "blood and revenge are hammering in [his] head" (2.2.39), he is playing up to ideas of the vengeful and bloodthirsty black-faced character.

Blackness through association with Aaron begins to leech onto Tamora. Lavinia is quick to notice their relationship, by suggesting that Tamora and Aaron are in a sexual liaison. Lavinia's thoughts are more clearly articulated by Bassianus who says,

> Believe me, queen, your swart Cimmerian
> Doth make your honour of his body's hue,
> Spotted, detested and abominable.
> (2.2.72–74)

Bassianus is suggesting that Aaron hails from the furthest and darkest part of Europe which both defines and explains Aaron's origins. By calling him "barbarous Moor" (2.2.78), Bassianus labels Aaron and seals his own fate, as Aaron has no qualms about inciting and committing barbarous acts. In an interesting twist, after Lavinia has been raped and attacked and her brothers accused of the murder of her husband Bassianus, Titus does not suspect the Moor of having any hand in these acts. Aaron does not appear to Titus as the most obvious villain. Indeed, when Titus is brought false hope from Aaron that his sons might live, he refers to Aaron as "gentle Aaron" and "[g]ood Aaron" (3.1.158; 162). Perhaps this act of blindness is to underline the fact that Aaron is intrinsically untrustworthy but trustable to those who wish to see more than the stereotype.

Significantly, Shakespeare adds complexity to the black devil on stage by portraying Aaron as a highly sexual being who is proud of his desires. Aaron marks the beginning of the staging of black male characters whose sexuality is part of their persona. Aaron also continues the tradition of the medieval black devil in that he manipulates those around him in dialogue with the audience. He aligns his facial colouring with religious immorality, vowing that he "will have his soul black like his face" (3.1.206). This vow is compounded by its utterance after convincing Titus to have his own hand cut off in the mistaken belief that it will save his sons. However, as we shall see, he also has the capacity by the end of the play to confound and undermine the symbolism of blackness. The complex articulation of his black character onstage elicits various emotional responses including fear, admiration, loathing, and love. His inhumanity is implied through references which compare him to "a black ill-favoured fly" (3.2.67, lines found in the folio edition). Such associations, including comparisons to dog, raven, and snake imagery, emphasize the lack of humanity in and expressed towards Aaron. All these references serve to strengthen the emotional valence of black as evil and fearful, particularly as he is described as a "coal-black Moor" (3.2.79, folio edition). However, in a moment of curious particularity, Aaron is endowed with more intelligence and quick thinking than Chiron and Demetrius, the sons of Tamora. In a moment of crucial illumination for the Goth princes, young Lucius presents the sons with weapons wrapped in verses written by the poet Horace. Aaron understands that Titus knows about the sons' crimes against Lavinia as the verse translates as "the man of upright life and free from crime does not need the javelins and bows of the Moor."[38] It is a warning of danger that the young men do not understand or act upon. Aaron's part in not explicitly pointing out the danger can be explained by his devotion to acts of evil.

The proto-racist discourse climaxes when Tamora, queen of the Goths, produces a son by Aaron. Race, lineage, and colour are thrown into the spotlight as the nurse enters "with a blackamoor child" seeking "Aaron the Moor" (4.2.51).[39] Although the nurse addresses Aaron as "gentle Aaron" (4.2.56), she announces that God has sent a devil, reiterating the moral and religious ideology of blackness, adding that the baby is "a joyless, dismal, black and sorrowful issue," who is "as loathsome as a toad/ Amongst the fair-faced breeders of our clime" (4.2.68–70). The nurse indicates that Tamora wishes Aaron to murder the child. Aaron answers, "Zounds, ye whore, is black so base a hue?" while addressing the baby as a "beauteous blossom" (4.2.73; 74). Demetrius reacts to the news by calling Aaron a "hellish dog" and a "fiend" (4.2.79; 81). Demetrius notes that this act will bring shame on his mother, shame that is predicated on her association and procreation with the black-faced Aaron. This exchange complicates the coding of black as evil and introduces an anxious tension around miscegenation. Aaron himself, despite being a willing embodiment of the current ideology of blackness, introduces the notion that blackness can have a different emotional register other than the baseness which is the normative emotional setting.

Aaron rehearses commonplaces about the demonic quintessence of Negritude, but in the invocation of "Ye white-lim'd walls!" (4.2.100), he posits a monstrous inversion of racial identity: whiteness is merely a temporary emulsion and not intrinsic in contrast to a fast and permanent black identity. Black, says, Aaron, is better than white, because white is characteristically subject to black inscription: it can be defaced. Black, in contrast, can neither be written on, nor can it be returned to white. Aaron paraphrases an old adage saying,

> For all the water in the ocean
> Can never turn the swan's black legs to white
> Although she lave them hourly in the flood.
> (4.2.103–105)

This is an adaptation of a proverb which would have been commonplace and referred to one's inability to wash the Etiope white. In arguing for the positive specificity of Negritude, Aaron counters the dominant idea of originary whiteness.[40] In the exchange centred on the appearance of the dark-skinned newborn, most of the emotions mobilized are ones of fear, shame, and loathing. Aaron counters these emotions by revealing a strong love towards his son, championing the advantages of his dark skin, saying "Coal-black is better than another hue/ In that it scorns to bear another hue" (4.2.101–102). The startling emotional change in Aaron may be prompted by the appearance of his own flesh and blood, suggesting that concerns of lineage are equally important to someone with his Moorish background. Not only does he share the concerns of the dominant class, but he exhibits pride in the essence of his 'otherness.'

Aaron ridicules Tamora's sons for their white skin colour as a "treacherous hue, that will betray with blushing/ The close enacts and counsels of thy heart" (4.2.119–120). In this discourse, chromatically inscrutable black-pigmented skin does not publicly betray emotions by blushing. Such a closed countenance unsettles onlookers anxious to divine motivations for Aaron's evil behaviour. Thomas Wright, who wrote *The Passions of the Mind in General* originally in 1601, also comments on the apparent double reality of blushing, saying, "[w]e may also perceive the cause of blushing, for those that have committed a fault ... or at least imagine they are thought to have committed it ... they blush, because nature being afraid, lest in the face the fault be discovered, sendeth the pure blood, to be a defence and succor, the which effect, commonly, is judged to proceed from a good and virtuous nature, because no man can but allow, that is good to be ashamed of a fault."[41] In this context, it is important to feel and also to display shame for a fault which is only possible if one's complexion allows the act of blushing. In turn, it is only through such a public display that you are validated in this act of humiliation. Black-pigmented skin could not participate in this act and was distrusted for this reason. Personal improvement was also predicated on forms of 'othering' as "the pursuit of personal improvement was accomplished in part by the simultaneous stigmatization of particular kinds of difference."[42] Non-blushing was a distinct form of difference which set black skin apart from lighter skin tones.

Despite their discrepancy in colour, Aaron points out that his newborn son and Chiron and Demetrius are brothers. Such discourse points to early considerations of miscegenation, a concern that complicated cultural tensions in a changing social environment. The presence of mixed-race children points to a sophisticated anxiety around the 'othering' of black-skinned people. Vaughan notes that "[w]hile the Goths have become 'incorporate' in Rome, Aaron remains ineluctably the other. His evil behaviour and his physical features – black skin and wooly hair – have been made to signify a new sort of barbarousness."[43] His very insistence on his position as the black face of evil leads to a disruption in the discourse when he is confronted by the presence of his son. Gillies believes that

> Aaron begins by representing all the viciousness and pollutiveness of the classical barbarian writ large (he is precisely 'a craftier Tereus'). Yet the

very excess of his outrageousness – begetting of a blackamoor child' upon the Roman empress – leads to a rebirth of just those familial and civic bonds which he has so spectacularly violated.[44]

While Aaron identifies himself with evil on account of his black appearance, his resolve to save his child contradicts that position, complicating the blackness which he and others know him for. Aaron is the first instance of the Shakespearean paradox of the Moor with a redemptive quality. I would add that Aaron's capacity for trenchant language complicates the emotional response to his presence both on and off stage. We are confronted with his reactions to Tamora, the Romans, the Goths, and, of course, his own son. His actions mobilize the emotions of those around him and cause hectic communication of those very emotions.

When Aaron resolves to swap his baby with a white baby born to a Moor and his fair wife to preserve the baby's life, we are forced to acknowledge further complexity. For, as Francesca T. Royster points out

> if mothers can be bought off so easily, why didn't Aaron just buy a white baby? His insistence on obtaining a baby who looks white but is 'really' Moorish suggests allegiance to his race, a commitment to establishing a foothold of power for Moors within the very heart of Rome.[45]

As discussed earlier, ideas of lineage appear to resonate equally strongly with Aaron the Moor as with those who dominate him.

Aaron refers to the baby as a "thick-lipped slave" (4.2.177), and again when he is found by the advancing Goths, he is overheard soothing the baby with the words, "Peace, tawny slave" and "Peace, villain, peace" (5.1.27; 33). With these words, he is presenting his son as a culmination of the cultural ideology associating the black body with slavery and a subordinate position. He does not object when Lucius calls him "the incarnate devil" (5.1.40) and describes the baby as the "growing image of thy fiend-like face" (5.1.45). Instead, he tacitly acknowledges this positioning of his character by the tenor of his negotiations for his son's life. Aaron seeks to save his son and himself by saying he can describe numerous crimes which Lucius will never know the truth of if Aaron dies. Lucius turns down Aaron's exhortation to swear, as Aaron "believest no god./ That granted, how can thou believe an oath?" (5.1.71–72). Aaron, clever as he is, notes that Lucius can swear by his own god as Aaron knows this will hold Lucius to the bargain even if Aaron himself does not believe in the oath. Again, this exchange validates Aaron's position as a barbarous heathen, but it also underlines his intelligence which is a recent development for the stock character. After Aaron confesses all his machinations in the bloody deeds that have happened in Rome, a Goth states, "What, canst thou say all this and never blush?" (5.1.121). Aaron's reply is "Ay, like a black dog, as the saying is" (5.1.122). This is a reiteration of the conflict which arises when one's skin cannot reflect internal emotions.

On his entry to Rome, Lucius describes Aaron as "this barbarous Moor, / This ravenous tiger, this accursed devil" (5.3.4–5), and later "inhuman dog, unhallowed slave!" (5.3.14). Marcus in the final stages of the play describes Aaron's son as "the issue of an irreligious Moor" and Aaron as "the Chief architect and plotter of these woes" (5.3.120–121). Both of these instances promulgate the normative position of the blackamoor as the enslaved devilish character whose raison d'être is to cause barbarous destruction. Aaron's only regret as he faces death is any missed opportunities to cause harm.

After *Titus Andronicus* first came to the stage, there was a slight shift in the social and cultural appearances of black people in England. The physical record of black people across London changes slightly at this time. Where previously the record mainly noted spectacle, deaths, and servitude, now the record mentions legal cases concerning carnal relations, marriages, and also a royal proclamation deporting blackamoors from England. The reasoning behind proclamations issued by the Queen were initially contingent on political and economic issues, but they move subtly to displaying a racial tone which was seated in perceived threats to England's economy, unity, and identity.[46] The social landscape was further complicated by the presence of an elite Moor in London.

The portrait of Abd el-Ouahed ben Messaoud ben Mohammed Anoun, ambassador to Elizabeth I from Muly Hamet, shows the Moroccan ambassador, aged 42, possibly painted during the six months he spent in London during 1600/1601 while negotiating a potential alliance against Spain. The portrait shows a distinguished man dressed in flowing white robes with a white turban and a dark cloak.[47] Hanging from his side is a richly carved sword and scabbard. His face appears somewhat fair. His presence brought the regal Moor to the attention of Londoners. Bernard Harris states that the "picture represents 'ocular proof' of what Elizabethans saw as a Moor of rank."[48] It is also possible that Shakespeare's company, The Lord Chamberlain's Men, performed at court in the Christmas season of 1600–1601 before the ambassador's departure, but even if this is not the case, it can be conjectured that Shakespeare would have heard about the ambassador as he and his entourage were present there for many months. Previous concerns around 'otherness' were now complicated by the realization that the Moors were potential allies against the Spanish and could boast a nobility previously unacknowledged and unwitnessed at such close proximity. While cultural lineage and a religious tradition elevated some African groups, like the Moroccan political elites, others continued to be associated with a dearth of religion and culture.[49] In the wake of such contradictions, Shakespeare's *Othello* appears on the stage, perhaps even prompted by the ambassadorial visit.[50] There were also other influential resources available to Shakespeare at this time, such as John Pory's 1600 translation of John Leo's *A Geographical Historie of Africa*.[51] Pory's translation was also brought out coincidentally while the Moroccan entourage was in London, indicating a wide interest and capitalization on the visit. Leo, himself a Moor brought up in Barbary, wrote about his countrymen, and his description resonates with certain aspects of Othello's character.

In *Othello,* these cultural shifts are noticeable where individuals have the capacity to react with a degree of agency while working within the constraints of socialization. There is evidence of some germinal shifts, but it is confined to the overall boundaries imposed by cultural and social requirements. By the time *Othello* played, audiences, like those who had enjoyed *Titus Andronicus,* were familiar with blackface devils on stage. However, unlike Aaron, who reflects many stock characteristics such as devilry, evil, and unchristian behaviour, there is more complexity surrounding Othello's ethnicity, religion, and more fundamentally his character. *Othello* appears to be capitalizing on a moment of friction in blackamoor portrayal. Emily C. Bartel notes that plays before *Othello* did not pose ideology or performative issues "precisely because their Moors did not double as heroes."[52] Othello is figured initially as a character distancing himself from the 'other.' For example, Othello talks of "cannibals" and "Anthropophagi" (1.3.144; 145), with the wondrous 'other' far removed from both Venetian society and Othello himself. Disturbingly, in *Othello,* it is Iago the white Venetian who embodies the evil 'other.' This may have been calculated to shock an audience used to the black character embodying the evil devilish character such as Aaron did. Distinct from Aaron, who is complicit in his own construction of evil, it is Iago who painstakingly constructs an edifice of evil for and around Othello. Such contradictions conspire to allow a portrayal of Othello as someone who is derided in the street and honoured in the senate. More so than in *Titus Andronicus,* characters obfuscate and question accepted doctrine.

The opening night scene features Iago prompting a biased reaction against Othello from the outset by describing Othello to Roderigo as "loving his own pride and purposes" (1.1.11). In this one phrase, Iago has managed to suggest that Othello is excessively emotional, suffers from pride, is self-interested, and has an inflated opinion of his own worth. It is a clever instance of mobilizing Roderigo's emotions, an instance which also names and communicates the emotions while indicating the emotional style of the men's exchanges. Iago baits Brabantio, Desdemona's father, with the words, "an old black ram/ Is tupping your white ewe... the devil will make a grandsire of you" (1.1.87–88; 90). With these words, the bestial images recall the bestiality associated with characters such as Aaron. The irreligious evil implied by calling Othello a devil furthers older stereotypes, while the thoughts of offspring from the union links the conversation with germinal ideas intersecting race and lineage. Roderigo, less sophisticated but equally eager to continue the negativity around Othello, says, "[w]hat a full fortune does the thicklips owe/ If he can carry't thus" (1.1.65–66). His derogatory comment is situated in othering the physical appearance with less nuances than Iago offered. Roderigo again uses physicality to describe Othello to Brabantio, saying that Desdemona has been transported "to the gross clasps of a lascivious Moor" (1.1.124). Iago relies on the received image of the black bestial devil to generate a false opinion of Othello, while Roderigo then implies sexual incontinence. Both Iago and Roderigo avoid using Othello's name in the opening scene, dehumanizing the 'Moor' in the process. Horrified at the proposed union, Brabantio says that Desdemona is too shy and retiring "[t]o fall in love with what she feared to look on?" (1.3.99). Othello's dark complexion becomes an object of fear and dread in this transaction, made more real by naming.

Othello defies the presented notions of his character with his initial presence on stage. He aligns himself with an elevated social position, noting to Iago, "I fetch my life and being/ From men of royal siege" (1.2.21–22). Othello is engaged here with more contemporary conflictions, urging his Moorish self to be considered above the stereotype of the devilish slave. Iago urges Othello to flee the scene, but Othello replies

> Not I, I must be found,
> My parts, my title and my perfect soul
> Shall manifest me rightly.
>   (1.2.30–32)

Othello, with confidence that initially proves well-founded, behaves and also wishes to be seen behaving with dignity befitting his elevated station. In the council rooms, the Duke's greeting is "[v]aliant Othello" (1.3.49). The Duke names Othello and uses the moment to add praise and denote Othello as courageous. The scene moves quickly to a proxy trial as Othello is demanded by Brabantio and more gently by the rest of the council to explain how he wooed Desdemona. It is notable that all of those present wanted to hear the explanation, indicating that it is not self-evident. During his self-defence, Othello explains that it was his stories which enchanted Desdemona, and not any magic.

Among the tales, he tells "[o]f being taken by the insolent foe/ And sold to slavery" 1.3.138–139). This jars with his regal bearing and in some respects alludes to the stereotype of the enslaved blackamoor. It seems that there is a surface to Othello that can be scratched to reveal a fundamental commonality with the received commonplace ideas regarding the blackamoor. When Othello explains how his tales of cannibals and anthropophagi, and the men whose heads grew beneath their shoulders, enthralled Desdemona, the manifestly 'other' serves to make Othello less alien both to Desdemona and also to the wider audience. Othello, insisting that he is past carnal desires and would wish Desdemona with him only for her mind, speaks directly against the sexualized image presented by Iago. There was an association with the colour black and tangentially the blackamoor with overt sexual desires. Thomas Wright, writing in 1603, relays cultural associations with various colours, saying,

> The redde is wise,
> The browne is trustie,
> The pale peevish,
> The black lustie.[53]

Desdemona, for her part, says, "I saw Othello's visage in his mind" (1.3.253), asking the company to look beyond his skin colour and implicitly beyond the stereotype. The Duke's final words on the marriage to Brabantio, "your son-in-law is far more fair than black" (1.3.291), reverts to a chromatic discourse that acknowledges the association of black with evil but asks Brabantio to look to Othello's positive character traits.

Iago both reinforces and subverts the stereotype, reducing Othello to the standard view of Moors, "changeable in their wills" and an "erring Barbarian" (1.3.347; 357), while declaring in private, that the Moor "is of a free and open nature/ That thinks men honest that but seem to be," (1.3.398–399). Having created this tension early in the play, Iago sustains it until Desdemona's murder in the final act. Iago also reinforces and heightens emotions by repeatedly naming them; he says, "I hate the Moor" (1.3.366 and repeating the line at 1.3.385). This is part of the way emotions are both felt and experienced. Iago says the cause of his hatred is "hearted" – firmly fixing this as an emotional reaction that he can name. This naming can be used to achieve an emotional state individually, but also to induce that state in others, which Iago does to Roderigo. When Iago is persuading Roderigo of Desdemona's infidelity, he says, "[h]er eye must be fed, and what delight/ shall she have to look on the devil?" (2.1.223–224). This seemingly unsophisticated pronouncement, when examined in more detail, actually resonates with the ideas Roderigo previously expressed about Othello. Iago is managing Roderigo's emotions by exchanging ideas, which are familiar to Roderigo and thus more easily assimilated. Later Iago declares that Othello is of a "constant, loving, noble nature" (2.1.287), but paradoxically Iago also fears that Othello has a lusty nature and has had a sexual relationship with Emilia. This reinforces the tensions Iago created from the beginning regarding the character and emotional capacity of Othello.

When roused on account of a fight amongst his officers and a Venetian gentleman, Othello says, "Are we turned Turks? ... For Christian shame, put by this barbarous brawl" (2.3.167; 169). In this moment, Othello is aligning himself with the discourse that privileges Christian superiority. He uses a religious marker without the colour linkage to avoid ostracizing himself as he understands the heathen label assigned to the stereotypical blackamoor. G. K. Hunter suggests that Elizabethans tempered their construction of the foreigner through their traditional religious views,[54] which makes even more sense of Othello's utterances. Despite all his efforts, Othello begins to succumb to the black stereotype, saying,

> Now, by heaven,
> My blood begins my safer guides to rule
> And passion, having my best judgement collied,
> Assays to lead the way.
> (2.3.200–203)

Othello is becoming the emotionally incontinent blackamoor that he has actively worked against since his marriage to Desdemona, and possibly before, when he promoted Cassio above Iago.

Iago, confounding the expectations of the audience, quickly occupies the space of blackened devil himself. He aligns himself with the position using the same language he had applied to Othello:

> When devils will the blackest sins put on
> They do suggest at first with heavenly shows
> As I do now.
> (2.3.346–348)

The association of devilry and blackness in the moral sense paradoxically linked with Iago's white Venetian complexion would, I suggest, serve to unsettle the audience more than Iago's efforts to blacken Othello's moral standing. Building upon the unsettling tension, Iago suggests that Desdemona could not sustain her emotional attachment to Othello because of a germinal but growing racial point of difference, which is gaining currency within the play. He uses this argument to convince Othello of his unsuitability and potential unworthiness to couple himself with Desdemona:

> Ay, there's the point: as, to be bold with you,
> Not to affect many proposed matches
> Of her own clime, complexion and degree,
> Whereto we see, in all things, nature tends.
> (3.3.232–235)

Iago points to racial separation as normative, and so unsettles Othello who begins to consider whether it is his blackness or his age which has influenced Desdemona's treachery. Othello muses when alone,

> Haply for I am black,
> And have not those soft parts of conversation
> That chamberers have,
> (3.3.267–269)

Iago has effectively seen to it that the situation whereby Othello is viewed through his black skin colour allows Iago protection in the dominant societal group. An exclusion of some in society rewards others with inclusion. In an earlier play, *The Merchant of Venice*, worth is also linked to skin colour. In this play, the Prince of Morocco, one of Portia's suitors, has a complexion which is off-putting to the ladies. His worth is related to his complexion, and although he notes its difference, he is unable to recognize his lack of worth based on this characteristic. Portia says, "[i]f he have the condition of a saint and the complexion of a devil, I had rather he should shrive me than wive me" (1.3.124–126).[55] For him, his dark skin signals for audiences his lack of appeal for Portia.[56]

Othello, in his distress at suspecting that Desdemona is false, links her reputation with the notion of evil being black, saying, "her name, that was as fresh/ As Dian's visage, is now as begrimed and black/As mine own face" (3.3.389–391). The terminology echoes Aaron's previous words aligning his soul with his black face. As Patricia Akhimie notes,

> the multiple meanings of blackness are brought into play as characters and audiences attempt to understand to what extent Desdemona's recklessness and Othello's devolving conduct are related to his identity as a person with dark skin, as a foreign-born 'Moor', and as a mercenary and therefore untrustworthy traveler. This scrutiny, in turn, produces and stigmatizes the mark of darkness.[57]

At this point, Desdemona remains unwavering in her love and loyalty to Othello. She says,

> my noble Moor
> Is true of mine, and made of no such baseness
> As jealous creatures are.
> (3.4.26–28)

And when asked by Emilia if he is the jealous type, she replies, "I think the sun where he was born/ Drew all such humours from him" (3.4.30–31). It is significant that Desdemona is unwavering in her opinion of Othello right up until her death. Her emotional engagement with him as her lover is unchanging and unregulated by the underlying societal expectations. Even as she lies dying by Othello's hand, Desdemona still asks Emilia to "commend me to my kind lord" (5.2.123).

The contamination of Othello's character is complete when, in the company of Lodovico, a nobleman of Venice, Othello calls Desdemona a "Devil!" (4.1.239) and strikes her. Lodovico, who admires and respects Othello, cannot reconcile this presentation with his memories of the Moor, saying, "[i]s this the noble Moor whom our full senate/ Call all in all sufficient?" (4.1.264–265). Iago has been successful, and Othello has publicly become the stereotype which he has sought to confound. Desdemona's death brings the culmination of Iago's insidious reformulation of attitudes around Othello's Moorish identity. Emilia, having previously classified Othello on the same level as any other man, now addresses Othello as "the blacker devil," "dull Moor," and "cruel Moor." Othello laments, "O cursed, cursed slave!" (5.2.274), when he finds out the truth about Desdemona's innocence. It is not clear whether he is referring to himself or someone else, possibly Iago, but Lodovico positions Othello as a slave capable of evil and murder, saying,

> O thou Othello, that wert once so good,
> Fallen in the practice of a cursed slave,
> What shall we say to thee?
> (5.2.288–290)

Othello, perhaps salvaging some vestiges of his former honourable self, replies,

> Why, anything;
> An honourable Murderer, if you will,
> For nought I did in hate, but all in honour.
> (5.2.290–292)

Othello asks to be remembered as a man whose fault lies in misplaced emotion, as he "loved not wisely, but too well" (5.2.342).

In *Othello*, Shakespeare has distributed the accepted traits of the dark-skinned 'other' among many of the characters, both black and white, which questions a universal consideration of the Moor in the play. The indelible nature of his blackness is commensurate with an indelible social difference or flaw, which cannot be erased. However, the actions of Othello himself play an integral part in promulgating both the accepted discourse and an alternate more complex discourse that questions accepted orthodoxies. Iago is the inchoate racist vilifying Othello in a late Elizabethan London where Othello might not be 'the other' but part of the social fabric. I argue that by positioning Othello as part of society, audiences are prompted to explore the meaning of blackness in the context of both a literal colour and a figurative term for evil within a subtly changing *habitus*. This is a *habitus* which is stretching its boundaries and looking towards the slave trade, which gained currency in the first decades of James English reign.[58] Ultimately, Othello and those around him are manipulated by the dominant expression of emotion which causes them to change and perform an emotion that aligns the group as a whole. As the performance of emotions is dynamic and also unexpected in certain situations, then the outcomes are not always certain. As Scheer states, "emotional practices can be carried out alone, but they are frequently embedded in social settings."[59]

The learned experience of emotions, which is clear in an examination of the two plays, elicits the reactions that are evident to both Aaron and Othello from within the character himself and also externally from those around them. The emotions are a culmination of mind, body, and social experience. The body of both these characters has been shown to be capable of inducing a particular type of emotional practice in others. The expectations of the group are implicated in learned habits of feeling and stored in the *habitus*. Without mapping a change in the *habitus* too closely to a single event, I am suggesting that the change in cultural and social relations over this period may be taken as a moment in time when it is possible to evaluate change.

To conclude, as Vaughan has stated, "[m]iscegenation … becomes a marker for a variety of social problems, and *Titus Andronicus* established a pattern that would be repeated in English and American literature and culture for centuries."[60] However, there were subtle historical changes affecting the *habitus* at the turn of the century, such as the ambassador's visit and the record of Moors in servitude, getting married, and having sexual relationships, sometimes with white people. The effects of these changes can be seen in the interrogation of accepted cultural and emotional discourses in the later play, *Othello*. Ultimately, the ending of *Othello* serves to underline the strength of the shared patterns of emotional understanding created by the body and the linguistic repetition of patterned responses to the term 'blackamoor.' While there is evidence of attention to internal processes of emotional practices the outcome is predicated on the strength of the learned culturally specific emotional connotations of the 'blackamoor' body. The bodies of Aaron and Othello provided the moment in which the *habitus* may have been modified and even reshaped at a germinal level. However, the range of practices which were culturally inculcated at this moment also played an overwhelming part in the outcomes played out on the stage. Blackness as a register of emotional negativity is both questioned and compromised within a framework of cross-cultural exchanges marked by new negotiation and organization of colour references.

Notes

1 William Shakespeare, *Othello*, 3rd ed., ed. E. A. J. Honigmann (London/New York: Bloomsbury Arden Shakespeare, 2004). William Shakespeare, *Titus Andronicus*, 3rd ed., ed. Jonathan Bate (London/New York: Bloomsbury Arden Shakespeare, 2006). Jonathan Bate provides in-depth research and analysis to suggest that the play was written in late 1593 and performed in January 1594. He allows that there may be an earlier version perhaps even written by Shakespeare.
2 Monique Scheer, "Are Emotions a Kind of Practice (and Is That What Makes Them Have a History)? A Bourdieuian Approach to Understanding History," *History and Theory* 51:2 (2012): 201. In this reference Scheer is quoting from Bourdieu's theories discussed in Pierre Bourdieu, *The Logic of Practice* (Stanford, CA: Stanford University Press, 1992), 53–54.
3 Patricia Akhimie, *Shakespeare and the Cultivation of Difference: Race and Conduct in the Early Modern World* (New York/London: Routledge, 2018), 16.
4 Scheer, "Are Emotions a Kind of Practice," 204.
5 Ibid., 202.
6 Ibid., 209–217.
7 Ideas of race are touched on, and I wish to acknowledge the need to keep these ideas at the forefront of scholarship for reasons best described by Peter Erickson and Kim Hall, "'A New Scholarly Song': Rereading Early Modern Race," *Shakespeare Quarterly* 67:1 (2016): 1–13 and Ian Smith, "We Are Othello: Speaking of Race in Early Modern Studies," *Shakespeare Quarterly* 67:1 (2016): 104–124.
8 For further references, see David Bindman and Henry Louis Gates Jr, eds., *The Image of the Black in Western Art: From the Early Christian Era to the "Age" of Discovery: From the Demonic Threat to the Incarnation of Sainthood* (Cambridge, MA: Belnap Press of Harvard University Press, 2010).
9 Richard Blunt, "The Evolution of Blackface Cosmetics on the Early Modern Stage," in *The Materiality of Color: The Production, Circulation, and Application of Dyes and Pigments, 1400–1800*, eds. Andrea Feeser, Maureen Daly Goggin, and Beth Fowkes Tobin (Farnham: Ashgate, 2012), 217–234.
10 Ibid., 218.
11 William Shakespeare, *Love's Labour's Lost*, 3rd ed., ed. H. R. Woudhuysen (London/New York: Bloomsbury Arden Shakespeare, 2015). In appendix 1, Woudhuysen describes his hypothesis on the timing of this play.
12 William Shakespeare, *Shakespeare's Sonnets*, ed. Katherine Duncan-Jones (London/New York: Bloomsbury Arden Shakespeare, 2015). Duncan-Jones discusses the dating of the sonnets in detail in her introduction.

13 Kim F. Hall discusses the impact on travel narratives on early modern English thinking. *Things of Darkness: Economies of Race and Gender in Early Modern England* (Ithaca, NY/London: Cornell University Press, 1995).
14 Virginia Mason Vaughan, "The Construction of Barbarism in Titus Andronicus," in *Race, Ethnicity, and Power in the Renaissance*, ed. Joyce Green MacDonald (Cranbury, NJ: Associated University Presses, 1997), 166.
15 Margo Hendricks, "Surveying 'Race' in Shakespeare," in *Shakespeare and Race*, eds. Catherine M. S. Alexander and Stanley Wells (Cambridge: Cambridge University Press, 2001), 4.
16 G. K. Hunter, *Dramatic Identities and Cultural Tradition: Studies in Shakespeare and His Contemporaries* (Liverpool: Liverpool University Press, 1978), 34.
17 Ibid., 40. For a nuanced reflection on ambiguities which indicate racial intolerance, see Kyle Grady, "Othello, Colin Powell, and Post-Racial Anachronisms," *Shakespeare Quarterly* 67:1 (2016): 68–83.
18 Virginia Mason Vaughan, *Performing Blackness on English Stages, 1500–1800* (Cambridge: Cambridge University Press, 2005), 4–5.
19 John Gillies, *Shakespeare and the Geography of Difference* (Cambridge: Cambridge University Press, 1994), 33.
20 See Dennis Austin Britton, *Becoming Christian: Race, Reformation, and Early Modern English Romance* (New York: Fordham University Press, 2014), particularly Chapter 4 for discussion regarding Othello's Christian position.
21 St Augustine, Enarrationes in Psalmos, (P.L. xcii, col.938) found in Hunter, *Dramatic Identities and Cultural Tradition*, 48.
22 Richard Hakluyt, *The Principal Navigations Voyages Traffiques and Discoveries of the English Nation*, vol. 7 (Glasgow: James MacLehose and Sons, 1904), 264.
23 Ania Loomba, "Racial and Religious Difference," in *Shakespeare and Race*, eds. Catherine M. S. Alexander and Stanley Wells (Cambridge: Cambridge University Press, 2001), 211.
24 Margaux Deroux, "The Blackness Within: Early Modern Color-Concept, Physiology and Aaron the Moor in Shakespeare's *Titus Andronicus*," *Mediterranean Studies* 19:1 (2010): 86–101.
25 Imtiaz Habib, *Black Lives in the English Archives, 1500–1677: Imprints of the Invisible* (Aldershot: Ashgate, 2008), 74.
26 Vaughan, *Performing Blackness on English Stages, 1500–1800*, 33.
27 Habib, *Black Lives in the English Archives*.
28 Ibid., 63.
29 Vaughan, "The Construction of Barbarism in Titus Andronicus," 177.
30 Blunt, "The Evolution of Blackface Cosmetics on the Early Modern Stage," 221.
31 For further discussion on this idea see Vaughan, *Performing Blackness on English Stages, 1500–1800*, 47–48.
32 Ibid., 2.
33 Shakespeare, *Titus Andronicus*. Bate describes the dating of the painting and its provenance in the introduction to this Arden edition of the play.
34 Carolyn Sale explores the possibility that Aaron also represents a relationship with England's own history of the ancient Briton and England's relationship to Aeneid in "Black Aeneas: Race, English Literary History, and the 'Barbarous' Poetics of *Titus Andronicus*," *Shakespeare Quarterly* 62:1 (2011): 25–52.
35 Deroux, "The Blackness Within," 97.
36 Dympna Callaghan, *Shakespeare without Women Representing Gender and Race on the Renaissance Stage* (London: Routledge, 2000), 80.
37 Francesca T Royster, "White-Limed Walls: Whiteness and Gothic Extremism in Shakespeare's *Titus Andronicus*," *Shakespeare Quarterly* 51:4 (2000): 432–455.
38 Shakespeare, *Titus Andronicus*, n. 219.
39 Ayanna Thompson posits that 'Race is a social construct that classifies humans based on physical, cultural, and religious differences, but these constructs are historically,

nationally, and performatively informed.' in "Shakespeare, Race, and Performance," *Shakespeare Bulletin: A Journal of Performance Criticism and Scholarship* 27:3 (2009): 359.
40 Callaghan, *Shakespeare without Women Representing Gender and Race on the Renaissance Stage*, 80.
41 Thomas Wright, *The Passions of the Mind in General*, ed. William Webster Newbold (New York: Garland, 1986 [1603]), 1.7.106–116.
42 Akhimie, *Shakespeare and the Cultivation of Difference*, 12.
43 Vaughan, "The Construction of Barbarism in Titus Andronicus," 17.
44 Gillies, *Shakespeare and the Geography of Difference*, 112.
45 Royster, "White-Limed Walls", 453.
46 Emily C. Bartels, *Speaking of the Moor: From Alcazar to Othello* (Philadelphia: University of Pennsylvania Press, 2008), 116.
47 This portrait now hangs in The Shakespeare Institute, Stratford-upon-Avon, England.
48 Bernard Harris, "A Portrait of a Moor," in *Shakespeare and Race*, eds. Catherine M. S. Alexander and Stanley Wells (Cambridge: Cambridge University Press, 2001), 23.
49 Ania Loomba, *Shakespeare, Race, and Colonialism* (Oxford: Oxford University Press, 2002), 81.
50 Shakespeare, *Othello*, 4–5. Honigmann suggests that the ambassador could be an actual model for Othello.
51 Emily C. Bartels discusses the influence of John Pory as she digests the fashioning of the Moor on stage in her article "Making More of the Moor: Aaron, Othello, and Renaissance Refashionings of Race," *Shakespeare Quarterly* 41:4 (1990): 433–454.
52 Bartels, *Speaking of the Moor: From Alcazar to Othello*, 160.
53 Wright, *The Passions of the Mind in General*, 196.
54 G. K. Hunter, "Elizabethans and Foreigners," in *Shakespeare and Race*, eds. Catherine M. S. Alexander and Stanley Wells (Cambridge: Cambridge University Press, 2001), 51.
55 William Shakespeare, *The Merchant of Venice*, 3rd ed., ed. John Drakakis (London/New York: Bloomsbury Arden Shakespeare, 2010).
56 Akhimie, *Shakespeare and the Cultivation of Difference*, 3.
57 Ibid., 64.
58 Sujata Iyengar, *Shades of Difference: Mythologies of Skin Color in Early Modern England* (Philadelphia: University of Pennsylvania Press, 2005).
59 Scheer, "Are Emotions a Kind of Practice," 211.
60 Vaughan, *Performing Blackness on English Stages, 1500–1800*, 50.

Bibliography

Akhimie, Patricia. *Shakespeare and the Cultivation of Difference: Race and Conduct in the Early Modern World*. New York/London: Routledge, 2018.
Bartels, Emily C. "Making More of the Moor: Aaron, Othello, and Renaissance Refashionings of Race." *Shakespeare Quarterly* 41, no. 4 (1990): 433–454.
Bartels, Emily C. *Speaking of the Moor: From Alcazar to Othello*. Philadelphia: University of Pennsylvania Press, 2008.
Bindman, David and Henry Louis Gates Jr, eds. *The Image of the Black in Western Art: From the Early Christian Era to the "Age" of Discovery: From the Demonic Threat to the Incarnation of Sainthood*. Cambridge, MA: Belnap Press of Harvard University Press, 2010.
Blunt, Richard. "The Evolution of Blackface Cosmetics on the Early Modern Stage." In *The Materiality of Color: The Production, Circulation, and Application of Dyes and Pigments, 1400–1800*, edited by Andrea Feeser, Maureen Daly Goggin, and Beth Fowkes Tobin, 217–234. Farnham: Ashgate, 2012.
Bourdieu, Pierre. *The Logic of Practice*. Stanford, CA: Stanford University Press, 1992.

Britton, Dennis Austin. *Becoming Christian: Race, Reformation, and Early Modern English Romance.* New York: Fordham University Press, 2014.
Callaghan, Dympna. *Shakespeare without Women: Representing Gender and Race on the Renaissance Stage.* London: Routledge, 2000.
Deroux, Margaux. "The Blackness Within: Early Modern Color-Concept, Physiology and Aaron the Moor in Shakespeare's *Titus Andronicus*." *Mediterranean Studies* 19, no. 1 (2010): 86–101.
Erickson, Peter and Kim Hall. "'A New Scholarly Song': Rereading Early Modern Race." *Shakespeare Quarterly* 67, no. 1 (2016): 1–13.
Gillies, John. *Shakespeare and the Geography of Difference.* Cambridge: Cambridge University Press, 1994.
Grady, Kyle. "Othello, Colin Powell, and Post-Racial Anachronisms." *Shakespeare Quarterly* 67, no. 1 (2016): 68–83.
Habib, Imtiaz. *Black Lives in the English Archives, 1500–1677: Imprints of the Invisible.* Aldershot: Ashgate, 2008.
Hakluyt, Richard. *The Principal Navigations Voyages Traffiques and Discoveries of the English Nation,* vol. 7. Glasgow: James MacLehose and Sons, 1904.
Hall, Kim F. *Things of Darkness: Economies of Race and Gender in Early Modern England.* Ithaca, NY/London: Cornell University Press, 1995.
Harris, Bernard. "A Portrait of a Moor." In *Shakespeare and Race,* edited by Catherine M. S. Alexander and Stanley Wells, 23–36. Cambridge: Cambridge University Press, 2001.
Hendricks, Margo. "Surveying 'Race' in Shakespeare." In *Shakespeare and Race,* edited by Catherine M. S. Alexander and Stanley Wells, 1–22. Cambridge: Cambridge University Press, 2001.
Hunter, G. K. *Dramatic Identities and Cultural Tradition: Studies in Shakespeare and His Contemporaries.* Liverpool: Liverpool University Press, 1978.
Hunter, G. K. "Elizabethans and Foreigners." In *Shakespeare and Race,* edited by Catherine M. S. Alexander and Stanley Wells, 37–63. Cambridge: Cambridge University Press, 2001.
Iyengar, Sujata. *Shades of Difference: Mythologies of Skin Color in Early Modern England.* Philadelphia: University of Pennsylvania Press, 2005.
Loomba, Ania. "Racial and Religious Difference." In *Shakespeare and Race,* edited by Catherine M. S. Alexander and Stanley Wells, 203–224. Cambridge: Cambridge University Press, 2001.
Loomba, Ania. *Shakespeare, Race, and Colonialism.* Oxford: Oxford University Press, 2002.
Royster, Francesca T. "White-Limed Walls: Whiteness and Gothic Extremism in Shakespeare's *Titus Andronicus.*" *Shakespeare Quarterly* 51, no. 4 (2000): 432–455.
Sale, Carolyn. "Black Aeneas: Race, English Literary History, and the 'Barbarous' Poetics of *Titus Andronicus.*" *Shakespeare Quarterly* 62, no. 1 (2011): 25–52.
Scheer, Monique. "Are Emotions a Kind of Practice (and Is That What Makes Them Have a History)? A Bourdieuian Approach to Understanding History." *History and Theory* 51, no. 2 (2012): 193–220.
Shakespeare, William. *Love's Labour's Lost,* 3rd ed., edited by H. R. Woudhuysen. London/New York: Bloomsbury Arden Shakespeare, 2015.
Shakespeare, William. *Othello,* 3rd ed., edited by E. A. J. Honigmann. London/New York: Bloomsbury Arden Shakespeare, 2004.
Shakespeare, William. *Shakespeare's Sonnets,* edited by Katherine Duncan-Jones. London/New York: Bloomsbury Arden Shakespeare, 2015.

Shakespeare, William. *The Merchant of Venice*, 3rd ed., edited by John Drakakis. London/New York: Bloomsbury Arden Shakespeare, 2010.

Shakespeare, William. *Titus Andronicus*, 3rd ed., edited by Jonathan Bate. London/New York: Bloomsbury Arden Shakespeare, 2006.

Smith, Ian. "We Are Othello: Speaking of Race in Early Modern Studies." *Shakespeare Quarterly* 67, no. 1 (2016): 104–124.

Thompson, Ayanna. "Shakespeare, Race, and Performance." *Shakespeare Bulletin: A Journal of Performance Criticism and Scholarship* 27, no. 3 (2009): 359–361.

Vaughan, Virginia Mason. *Performing Blackness on English Stages, 1500–1800*. Cambridge: Cambridge University Press, 2005.

Vaughan, Virginia Mason. "The Construction of Barbarism in Titus Andronicus." In *Race, Ethnicity, and Power in the Renaissance*, edited by Joyce Green MacDonald, 165–180. Cranbury, NJ: Associated University Presses, 1997.

Wright, Thomas. *The Passions of the Mind in General*, edited by William Webster Newbold. New York: Garland, 1986 [1603].

15

EMOTIONS, IDENTITY AND PROPAGANDA

Ottoman threat and confessional divide in later sixteenth-century Germany

Hannes Ziegler

The long series of conflicts between the Ottoman Empire and the *christianitas* that were triggered by the fall of Constantinople in 1453 and that culminated in events such as the Long Turkish War (1593–1606) and the Great Turkish War (1683–1699) at the end of the seventeenth century had a heavy impact on the political culture of European reigns. This went beyond the immediate repercussions in terms of diplomacy and armed conflict. In the case of the Holy Roman Empire, the frequent clashes at the frontier regions in the kingdom of Hungary and on the Balkans came to have a lasting influence on the form and formation of the central political forum, the imperial diet and the fiscal structure of the Empire, as was demonstrated by Winfried Schulze in his seminal contribution on the Ottoman threat in the second half of the sixteenth century.[1] Also beyond the Empire, news about decisive events such as the Battle of Lepanto were eagerly received and hotly discussed throughout the entire *christianitas*.[2] Yet the real significance of this confrontation – a confrontation that was more often than not mental rather than real – may well be found on a cultural level. "The negative influence", Thomas Kaufmann has prominently argued, "of the Ottomans on the cultural identity of late medieval and early modern Europe can hardly be overestimated".[3] With the Ottoman, he contends, the linguistically, nationally, politically, culturally and religiously fragmented European Christianity found its contrastive opponent and an "extra-positional" alterity that allowed to imagine itself as a unity.[4] The construction of a distinctly Christian and European belonging was, in other words, decisively shaped by the construction of an antagonistic image of the Ottomans in Europe by way of the literally endless stream of anti-Ottoman homiletics and propaganda flooding the European market. Perhaps surprisingly, however, research also shows unanimously that there was no fundamental difference regarding this confrontation between the different Christian confessions that had started to fragment Europe in an increasingly complex patchwork of religious affiliations from the beginning of the sixteenth century.[5] Catholics, Lutherans and Calvinists all resorted to the same imageries and stereotypes in their anti-Ottoman writings.

And yet within the process of intra-Christian confessional differentiation, a similar mechanism can be observed. In the Holy Roman Empire – perhaps the exemplary place for a politically sanctioned confessional coexistence after the Augsburg Peace of 1555 – the notable rise and intensification of inter-confessional propaganda between Catholic, Lutheran and Calvinist factions before the outbreak of the Thirty Years War has long been taken to be "mirroring" simultaneously occurring processes of seclusion and consolidation of the confessions in the second half of the century.[6] Confessional identity, in this interpretation, was the result of a positive fixation of core doctrines in a codified form along with the formation of a corresponding church organisation on the level of the territorial reigns.[7] Confessional propaganda, on the other hand, was seen as the spiteful overboiling of religious emotions, the visible product and expression of difference and the futile attempt to convince the enemy of the truth in religious matters.[8] Only in recent years has it been acknowledged that confessional propaganda played an equally decisive part in establishing and forming confessional identities and confessional cultures in the Holy Roman Empire.[9] Rather than aiming to persuade the opponent, these powerful and forthright invectives were aimed at stabilising and modulating the perceptions and the identity of the writers' or preachers' own group, in order "to sow the seeds of conviction deep", as Susan Karant-Nunn has put it.[10] Once again, then, and in a similar way as in anti-Ottoman writings, the vivid negative construction of an "extra-positional" alterity in a setting of mental rather than real confrontation served to construct and stabilise identities of specific groups.

This apparently structural mechanism of polemical antagonism is not the only thing that these two settings have in common, however. Throughout the Long Turkish War between 1593 and 1606 – and thus during a time when confessional antagonisms visibly sharpened – anti-Ottoman pamphlets and confessional propaganda pieces were often authored by the very same persons and published at the very same times. Furthermore, emotions and emotional language played an essential, yet still underestimated, role in both settings. To be sure, anti-Ottoman sentiments have been understood in terms of fear and anxiety for a long time, and with Andreas Bähr's recent study of fear and fearlessness, this tradition has been commendably updated to the conceptual state of the art in the history of emotions.[11] Moreover, beyond fear in particular, a general "emotionalization" among European recipients has been described as the main purpose of the dramatised portrayal of Ottoman cruelties.[12] Mentioning of the role of emotions in confessional propaganda, on the other hand, is brief and largely superficial, despite claims that it may prove worthwhile to chart a "topography of fear" based on confessional antagonisms in the Empire.[13] This gap is even more notable, given that emotions have recently been awarded a prime place among the ways in which the confessions in sixteenth-century Germany moulded themselves into distinct and specific communities of faith. According to Susan Karant-Nunn, emotions were "a powerful index of identity" and a potent tool for preachers to set the emotional mood in members of their faith.[14] Yet while she explores the ways that different confessions understood and appealed to the emotions, thus claiming that there are differences in the ways they do so, she does not look at inter-confessional interactions and potential processes of differentiation. This particular problem surely warrants attention, therefore, but perhaps the bigger task is to recognise the astounding concurrence of emotional language in the shaping of identities in both anti-Ottoman and confessional propaganda, especially when these were written by the very same authors.

This chapter, then, is aimed at analysing the concurrence of emotional discourse as it relates to the forming of group identities in confessional and in anti-Ottoman propaganda. Its focus will be on the 1580s and 1590s, when a marked increase in confessional pamphlets coincided with a wave of anti-Ottoman writings in the wake of the outbreak of hostilities on the Ottoman border in 1593. The main protagonists will be Lucas Osiander and Georg Scherer, who – apart from being of some renown in their respective Lutheran and Jesuit communities – each published several printed sermons against the Ottomans during those years, while being, at the very same time, engaged in a confessionally motivated pamphlet war with each other. In arguing that emotions were instruments to organise and modulate the political and theological differences as well as the cultural divergence between the respective social, confessional and cultural groups, I will rely, to some extent, on Barbara Rosenwein's concept of emotional communities, exploring how the belonging to these communities was constructed and maintained.[15] It should be noted, however, that I am not suggesting that the status of emotions was purely rhetorical in these writings. Given that rhetorical invocations of emotions cannot be successful unless there is a chance to meet the recipient on an emotional level comprehensible to him or her, I will follow the methodical assumption that the importance of emotional language rests on the possibility to correspond to or even to evoke actual emotions. After all, it can be, and in fact has been, convincingly argued that the very function of emotional rhetoric – or emotives, as William Reddy has chosen to call emotion words – is to evoke, shape and direct actual emotional responses.[16]

I

The starting point for many of the prints throughout the time period in question was to attest a state of disorder in the Holy Roman Empire, emotional and otherwise. To understand why they did so, it is important to understand who the authors are. Two particular prominent proponents of both anti-Ottoman writings and confessional propaganda will serve here to illustrate mechanisms that permeate both genres. Lucas Osiander, born in Nuremberg in 1534, was the son of the famous Lutheran reformer Andreas Osiander.[17] After studying theology and moving to the duchy of Württemberg in his youth, he quickly climbed the ladder of ecclesiastical positions to eventually become court chaplain to Duke Christoph in 1567, and gained an important position at the court of Duke Ludwig, who he had helped educate. During Ludwig's reign, he was diplomatically active in the preparation of the Formula of Concord, and thus involved in the written and positive regulation of Lutheran core beliefs. At the same time, however, he was particularly active as a polemical writer and perhaps one of the leading proponents of anti-Jesuit polemics in the 1580s, which he helped transform from primarily theological controversies to arguments more immediately relevant to the political situation of the Empire.[18] During the same years, he was also engaged in the anti-Turkish pamphlet campaign.[19] Georg Scherer, on the other hand, came from modest circumstances in mid-century Austria and was able to attend the newly founded Jesuit gymnasium in Vienna on a stipend.[20] Quickly rising to a central role in the Jesuit College in Vienna, he became actively involved in Counter-Reformation measures in the Austrian Habsburg territories. His fame was such that he was able to secure the position of court chaplain at the Vienna Hofburg under Emperor Rudolf II, and he also became confessor to Rudolf's sons Ernst and Maximilian. Whereas his organisational talent in managing the Vienna Jesuit College was somewhat dubious, his real calling turned out to be the theological and political defence of the Habsburg as well as Jesuit positions in controversial writings ("Kontroverspublizistik") which he launched both at inner-Catholic developments and particularly at the writings of Lutheran preachers, prominent among which was Lucas Osiander.[21] In fact, his dispute with Osiander was such that the prints – often directly aimed at each other – can be read as a sequence of writings answering to each other, resulting in a real dialogue.[22] Much like Osiander, however, Scherer also published a number of texts against the Turks in the 1590s.[23]

Before moving to the content of the texts, something must be said about the genre. The texts under scrutiny in this chapter are either sermons or polemical pamphlets, which, though a distinct genre, possess striking similarities to sermons in terms of structure, rhetoric and authorship.[24] For the transmission of theological and social ideals to the followers of the respective churches, sermons were of major importance in this period. Through sermons, Susan Karant-Nunn argues, preachers communicated what they "most urgently wanted the common resident to hear".[25] These texts can thus serve as a prime source for the implementation of theological and social beliefs in communities, since, as Norbert Haag claims, they were not simply intended to communicate, but to influence.[26] Sabine Holtz has even argued that this was not just a top-down process, but that there was a reciprocal exchange and influence between everyday life as experienced by the religious community and those in positions of ecclesiastical authority.[27] Nonetheless, it obviously remains notoriously difficult to deduce to what extent and exactly how sermons have taken effect on the level of those addressed by them. What impact they had on their listeners thus remains almost impossible to pin down. This is further complicated by the fact that most sermons only exist in their printed form, and it is equally hard to establish if they were, in fact, ever held in the first place. Despite those caveats, however, sermons can still be used to study the intentions of the churches towards their adherents and have convincingly been employed by Susan Karant-Nunn in gaining access to the complex field of religious emotions.[28] As anti-Ottoman sentiments in particular were primarily transmitted through sermons – along with the regular prayers and church bell ringings ordered by the authorities – there is no reason why an analogous approach to the emotions intended to be invoked by these writings should be less feasible.[29] It may tell us little about how the common (wo)man felt about the Ottoman or the adherent of a different confessional group, yet it still tells us much about how they were supposed to feel and what ends these emotions served.

II

With regard to a possible confrontation with the Ottomans, the state of the Holy Roman Empire was, according to both writers, disorderly and desolate. Perhaps not altogether surprisingly given their professional profile, however, theirs was less a concern with the political constitution of the Empire, which more often attracted the attention and caused worries among more secular writers especially surrounding the imperial diets.[30] Instead, they focused on the moral or emotional constitution of its inhabitants as well as the soldiers that were supposed to confront the enemy. In this perspective, perhaps the most important concerns vis-à-vis the Ottoman threat were the disruptive and fatal effects of fear, acquiescence and internal hatred. This fear, which was occasioned by the cruelty and barbarous manner of the enemy, was such that it made the "Christian's hair stand on end" and caused them to "throw their hands up in horror", according to Lucas Osiander. In fact, to him, this was a type of fear that had never before been experienced by Christianity.[31] Osiander's resulting main objective – namely of encouraging and reassuring his listeners – was shared by Scherer and most other anti-Ottoman writers. In a 1596 sermon dedicated to the officers and common soldiers currently fighting in Hungary, Scherer aimed to encourage the soldiers to have a "brave", "unflinching and unshrinking heart", for there was no place for fear among fighting soldiers.[32] For not only did military leaders regard it as a disgrace, God himself had ordered the timid to be banned from battlefield.[33] More importantly, Scherer went on to equate fear with disorder[34] and characterised it as a feminine trait.[35] The love of country and its military defence were falling apart under the disintegrating influence of fear. Or, in the words of another catholic preacher, Michael Anisius: "The world has lost its order, it is a chaos, a jumble, a confusion, it is an outright hell, where there is no order and regularity".[36]

A second major concern, especially with regard to those farther away from the frontiers and not involved in the fighting – the peasants and artisans and princes in the various principalities of the Empire – was exactly the opposite of fear, namely, acquiescence, "false security" and resignation. One of the devil's many temptations, Scherer argued, was to make people believe Christianity was already beaten and the only thing left to do was to meekly succumb and acknowledge the Ottomans as the new rulers.[37] Many dangers, according to these writers, lay in either resigning to that belief or, as Osiander explicitly admonished, in underestimating the dangers to which the Holy Roman Empire was exposed. Those disbelievers needed to be woken up and aroused for they were so deeply in dreams of security that not even then would they feel anything if one would split wood on their backs, as a contemporary saying went.[38] False security, however, was not the only thing that weakened the Empire. According to Lucas Osiander, another major cause for concern was the lamentable decline of unity and brotherly love among the Christian subjects of the Holy Roman Emperor and the simultaneous rise of hatred as a sign and marker of discord.

> How strongly have taken the upper hand envy and hate, malevolence and thirst for revenge, when one friend starts quarrels and arguments because of a single word or (as the saying has it) because of a herring's nose?[39]

To be sure, the rise of hatred and the waning of love that Osiander referred to in this passage were perceived to be the consequences of the confessional division in the Holy Roman Empire. In many respects, dangers seen as a result of the Ottoman threat were formulated (and visibly intensified) against the backdrop of the political and confessional division, both by Osiander and Scherer as well as other writers.[40] For what was true for Osiander's and Scherer's interpretation of the military confrontation with the Ottomans was equally true for their take on the state of the Holy Roman Empire regarding the religious and political confrontation between Catholics and Protestants. Here, too, the natural, necessary and God-given order was deeply disturbed. For Scherer, it was again fear and hatred that reigned, and again these were equated with disorder. Fear and hatred were corrupting the correct order of emotions, which consisted, according to him, of "Christian love".[41] But where did fear and hatred come from? For Scherer, it was – perhaps unsurprisingly – the confessional polemics of the opposite party that gave rise to hatred, especially the writings of Lucas Osiander, who, in the eyes of Scherer, clearly followed in the footsteps of Martin Luther, the "preacher of uproar" and the "prophet of murder".[42] In the wake of these hateful writings, many authors claimed, all love must surely die. Christoph Rosenbusch, a fellow Jesuit from Augsburg and a fellow combatant of Scherer's in his attacks on Osiander, also elaborated on this point:

> Such slander does no good; it plants no love, no gentleness, no amicability, no civil and smooth cohabitation. Instead it cancels all trust, all friendship, and all political peace between the adherents of the two faiths [...] All gentleness, all friendship and all kinship is void and disrespected, and love is utterly expired.[43]

Lucas Osiander – the one explicitly attacked by Scherer and Rosenbusch – actually shared this diagnosis, but his search for the causes of this situation led – quite naturally – to a different explanation. It was the Jesuits who, according to him, lacked any sense for Christian love and who went after the Lutherans with such hatred and resentment, thus disturbing the peaceful constitution of the Holy Roman Empire.[44] If the Jesuits possessed even a "spark of the gentle spirit of Christ", he argued, they would not only stop hating and persecuting the Lutherans, but positively cherish and love them.[45] With regard to the situation in the Empire, what was in fact most disconcerting for Osiander was that he perceived the Jesuits to be destroying the bonds of trust among the confessional groups within the Empire by arguing that Catholics needed to keep no trust with heretics such as the Lutherans.[46] Naturally, Scherer denied such allegations and claimed instead that it was Osiander's hateful slander that caused suspicion and mistrust.[47] It was Osiander, wrote Rosenbusch, who spread fear and anxieties among the princes of the Empire, thereby destabilising unity and orderly proceedings.[48]

In these basic assessments of the state of the Holy Roman Empire vis-à-vis the confessional division as well as the Ottoman threat, emotions clearly possessed descriptive value for illustrating and explaining the state of affairs to the reader or listener. The two main emotions present in these writings are love and hatred, in a basic opposition of all things good and bad. Frequently, these are either explicitly or implicitly equated with political and social order or disorder, and they are understood to represent or contribute to political concord and discord, respectively. This rather basic dichotomy is, in many of the writings in both genres, frequently blurred by a wider semantic and emotional field in which the two emotions are embedded: love is accompanied by friendship and trust, while hatred is linked with fear and resentment. The narrative purpose of this dichotomy appears, at first glance, quite obvious: A once healthy state of affairs is contrasted with a rather bleak portrayal of the immediate present and future, which is attributed to the negative influence of an external force. Depending on the position of the writer, this external alterity is either identified as the Ottomans as enemies of Christianity, the Lutherans as heretics vis-à-vis the unified Catholic Church or the Jesuits as externally (namely by the Pope) sanctioned intruders in a national religious community of faith. And yet there is more to it than that. The authors generally show the Empire in disorder, because they want to do something about it. Order *is* to be restored. And while this is certainly true for a political and religious level, it is also true for the emotional level. Indeed, emotions, it can be argued, play a key role in restoring that order.

III

The prints, in fact, rarely stop at the diagnosis. Whenever the authors write about emotions, they do so with a clear judgement on what is right and what is wrong. At the same time, they are eager to encourage and instil all the right emotions while doing away with the wrong ones, thus putting the emotions in order. In other words, emotions become a matter of choice. But along what criteria must emotions be chosen and ordered? And as both writers essentially operate with the same basic emotions, can we perceive any differences regarding confessional attitudes? Throughout many of the prints it is, in fact, implicitly clear that the moral evaluation of emotions is circumstantial. What is called for in a given situation is essentially a question of appropriateness. And this appropriateness, in turn, depends on criteria such as time, place, direction and degree. A few examples will illustrate this point.

Regarding the Christian soldiers in confrontation with the Ottomans, it is evident that their hearts must be filled with bravery rather than fear. Many sermons are devoted to instilling soldierly bravery. Namely, Scherer is eager to encourage the proper soldierly spirit in the men at the border at the time of battle.[49] "Do not be fainthearted or afraid", he quotes Deuteronomy, and goes to some lengths in admonishing bravery.[50] In other prints, it is not the excess of one emotion in particular that is called for, but rather the correct modulation of a whole emotional style. The key word is *Constantia*, that is, a certain peace of mind regarding the horrors of war.[51] Thomas Sigebertus' elaborate 1595 sermon on constancy is, in fact, a deliberate reference to Justus Lipsius, the Flemish philosopher, and his ideas on *Constantia* stemming from the internal Dutch conflict of the time.[52] It is no coincidence, one should note here, that Sigebertus is himself a Protestant, for, as Susan Karant-Nunn has argued, Lutheran appeals to emotions were more open to the implicit moderating effect of constancy, whereas the "sensitive tone of Catholic homiletics is opposed to that of Neostoicism".[53] This emphasis on correct modulation rather than excessive emotion is also apparent in Osiander's sermons. Perhaps because his arguments are not solely directed towards those on the frontier, however, Lucas Osiander takes a wider perspective. In a sermon printed in 1595, Osiander addresses both the soldiers at the frontier and the ones left behind, that is the general imperial public. Interestingly, there is a rather peculiar tension between the proper emotions for each of these groups. While Christianity lives, according to Osiander, in fear of the Ottoman threat, it is essentially the soldiers and commanders that need encouragement and consolation.[54] A rather different sort of encouragement is directed towards the people at home, however, who often feel all too secure and comfortable to give a care about the dire situation at the frontier.[55] While the former feel too much – in this case fear – the latter feel too little. What is needed is the right degree of feeling according to the circumstances the respective groups find themselves in. Too much fear will make the soldiers fickle, while too little fear will make them bold and overconfident. At the same time, recklessness and insensibility will direct the ones at home towards petty emotions, strife and quarrel.[56] While Osiander is here attempting to find the appropriate degree of feeling for both the ones at home and the ones at the frontier, he is also aware that his intentions for doing so may easily be misunderstood. Osiander, in fact, goes to some lengths to guard himself against accusations that he might frighten the soldiers or reassure the careless. "God forbid that I should frighten honest Christian soldiers, because I am only warning those that are hesitant to exert themselves in this matter that concerns body and soul".[57] Orderly emotions, in other words, have a proper place, a proper time and a proper degree.

In confessional confrontation, on the other hand, the emotional question is less a matter of degree but rather a question of direction. While it is clear for most authors that in one single political body one should meet one another with friendship and kindness, it is by virtue of their Christianity that Protestants and Catholics should consort with one another in what they call Christian love. At the same time, however, confessional propaganda deliberately excludes certain groups from this community of feeling. For Lucas Osiander, Jesuits cannot and must not be trusted, for their hearts and designs are scheming and treacherous.[58] As trust is, by contemporary definition, a community of mind similar to contemporary ideas of friendship, this exclusion also works the other way round. Andreas Erstenberger for example, one of the most notorious Catholic confessionalists of the 1580s and 1590s, openly debated the possibility of trust among the members of different confessions.[59] For Scherer, accordingly, there can be neither love nor friendship with heretics, among which he counts, unsurprisingly, Osiander and his like.[60] Trust and love and friendship are thus essentially as good or bad as fear and hatred and resentment. The question is towards whom they are directed. And once again, we can find an inherent tension in these prints: While there can generally never be enough Christian love in the Holy Roman Empire, an excess of friendship and trust towards certain groups within the Empire is marked as being disorderly, dangerous and potentially fatal. It is, in one word, inappropriate. The underlying message of all of these prints therefore is that emotions need to be and, more importantly, *can* be adapted to varying situations. The question is: to what end and for what purpose?

IV

Why, then, is it so important to feel the right thing in a given situation? The remainder of this chapter will argue that emotions fulfil a number of important functions both in anti-Ottoman and in confessional propaganda.

Perhaps most importantly, emotions can be shown to have an important role in the mechanism of forming and stabilising identity described at the beginning of this chapter for both genres of propaganda. Emotions are an extremely convincing and thus very effective way to mark the difference and to stabilise the separation between different groups of people. Both in confessional propaganda and in anti-Ottoman writings, there is an often implicit assumption that there is a fundamental emotional rift between friends and enemies which serves as a visible marker of belonging. Regarding the military confrontation, fear is not something that the Ottoman soldiers *should* feel; fear *belongs* to them as much as courage naturally belongs to the Christian soldiers. If, for whatever reason, this is not the case, it is an aberration from the natural order of things and a punishment of God:

> From these many and similar examples and histories it can be sufficiently learned that the fright and pusillanimity appertain to the pagan and the

Turk not to the faithful who put their faith in the true God. Yet should it happen that Christians too get the shivers and the urge to flee, it must be considered a punishment of God for our sins.[61]

A similar dichotomy between "us" and "them" is present in confessional propaganda. If Christian love is always the natural state of affairs for the writer's own group, hatred and fear are constantly there to indicate the other and his actions. The opponent, the "other", can be singled out by his stirring of hatred and his falling away from the spirit of Christ.[62] In these and similar ways, emotions mark and stabilise the difference between different groups of people and corresponding emotional communities.[63]

One can push this argument even further. Because it is not coincidental that emotions should be of such central importance here. Most of the prints operate on the assumption that emotions are visible markers of identity and belonging. Who and what a person really is, can be outwardly discerned by that person's feelings. Lucas Osiander for his part is, for example, quite sure that it will not be hard to distinguish the malevolent within the Empire, because they do not possess Christian love, and it is Christian love in particular that characterises the righteous. This kind of love, according to Osiander, is inspired by Christ, while hatred is a product of the devil.[64] Georg Scherer operates with much the same assumption: fear and hatred are not accidental. They are outwardly visible indicators for an evil person.[65]

But what is the source of this assumption? In both cases, it is indeed based on scripture. Namely Osiander is quoting a passage from the *Gospel of John*.[66] In this passage, John has Jesus say: "A new commandment I give to you, that you love one another: just as I have loved you, you also are to love one another. By this all people will know that you are my disciples, if you have love for one another".[67] The crucial sentence here is the last one. From this passage, Osiander as much as Scherer deduce the assumption that emotions are an indicator of the inner self. All people will know who you are if they can see what you feel. To feel the right thing in a given situation is such a very important matter, because a person's identity as righteous Christian and his or her belonging to the right kind of (confessional, political, social) community depend on that person's feelings. And perhaps tellingly, this societal function of feeling is as inclusive as it is exclusive. Scherer writes at one point: "Degeneres timor arguit. Fear will determine who is unworthy".[68] From this perspective, it becomes quite clear why the adaptation to the right emotional setting is of such key importance both in confessional and in military conflict. What people feel determines who they are and to which side of a conflict they belong. Their emotions show them to be friends, but they can also mark them out as enemies.

A second function of this emotional language concerns the question of confrontation: Emotions, one can argue based on the writings discussed in this chapter, are an important tool to prepare for confrontation. For all of the authors in question, confrontation is a crucial perspective and, to some extent, the ultimate focal point of their writings. It does not matter whether this confrontation is military or theological. Every confrontation has a mental side to it, and it is, in fact, this aspect of mental confrontation that confessional writing and anti-Ottoman preaching is aimed at. This is because physically as well as emotionally every confrontation is a particularly vulnerable situation, open to opportunities as well as dangers. While the confessional confrontation, on the one hand, always promises the opportunity to convert members of opposing confessional groups, there is at the same time also the constant danger of members of the own confession to be converted. Emotional weakness is to be avoided and a firm sense of belonging and a solid emotional defence to be achieved.[69] The same is true, on the other hand, for the military confrontation: here, the opportunity for victory is closely connected with the danger of defeat. To achieve the former and to avoid the latter, soldiers as well as peasants, merchants and princes need to be in the right state of mind. Alert, but not in panic; bold, but not overconfident.[70] Emotions, in this sense, are at the very core of what these writers – theologians, for the most part – are aiming at in their audience: faith.

V

There is an abundance of both anti-Ottoman writings and confessional pamphleteering in the period in question here, namely, the 1580s and 1590s. Yet though both the material itself and the general political situation are in many ways strikingly similar to the kind of religious strife combined with anti-Ottoman sentiments discernible in the rather well-studied period of Martin Luther and his immediate contemporaries, the writings of the later sixteenth century remain, despite the richness of the material available, understudied, to say the least.[71] What this chapter has attempted to do on the basis of only a small number of authors writing in this period was to determine some of the fundamental rhetoric mechanisms of this literature as it relates to group identities and the role of emotions and emotional language. It should have become clear that, despite their being little studied in the historiography of this particular subject, emotions fulfilled important functions for both genres in that they served as visible markers and comprehensible illustrators (even, or perhaps especially, for the common man) of both differentiation to external groups and stabilisation of internal identities within certain groups. Whether they were conceived of as a mental preparation for situations of armed or religious conflict or as a way of stabilising and identifying emotional communities, emotions were often awarded a prime place in these writings. What is more, they can be shown to be at the core of performative mechanisms of exclusion and inclusion. It is not, one could sum up the argument of the aforementioned writers, that being part of a certain group will make one feel certain emotions (as opposed to other emotions that one might possibly feel); it is rather that feeling a particular set of emotions under given circumstances will make one part of a certain group of people, confessional or otherwise.

This seemingly fundamental role of emotional language notwithstanding, these findings must be regarded as preliminary on several counts. This chapter is based on a number of prominent examples from both the anti-Ottoman and the confessional genre in these decades, but more work needs to be done on these writings both in general and regarding specific sets of questions such as those deriving from emotion history. Secondly, emotions have been deliberately singled out in this chapter in order to get a better understanding of their place and rhetoric function in these writings, but if their overall importance is to be evaluated, we not only need a broader look at the genre as a whole, but emotions also need to be related to the specific contexts both within and surrounding these writings. Based on Susan Karant-Nunn's research, one way ahead would perhaps be to ask whether the emotional responses apparent in these writings conform to the emotional style of the specific confessional groups and how this relates to their respective theological stances on, for example, faith or eschatological beliefs. Obviously, such a line of inquiry would have to somehow dissolve the apparent tension between distinct emotional communities of belief, as shown by Karant-Nunn, and the apparently similar, if not identical, emotional responses of writers of different confessional groups to both Ottoman and confessional alterities, as shown earlier. Close to court as these writers usually were, there is also the political context of the writers and their patrons to be accounted for, quite obviously so in terms of the anti-Ottoman writings, but perhaps also regarding the confessional differences. Finally, the specific cultural impact of these particular decades needs to be taken into account to get a clearer idea on why and how the writers' take on emotions might differ from earlier or later periods. Does the combined impact of heightened confessional strife across Europe, the urgency of the Ottoman threat along with societal crises such as the witch hunts of this period give a specific edge to the ways emotions were referred to and conceived of in these writings? The relevance of these and other questions, as far as they relate to emotions specifically, clearly lies in their role for the stabilisation of emotional communities described earlier. For if we accept that both anti-Ottoman and confessional writings were not, as once maintained, simply an effect or a consequence of preceding processes of group formation, but were themselves highly relevant for how these processes operated in wider sections of society, then one might be well advised to examine the role of emotions and emotional languages for processes such as confessionalisation.

Notes

1 Winfried Schulze, *Reich und Türkengefahr im späten 16. Jahrhundert. Studien zu den politischen und gesellschaftlichen Auswirkungen einer äußeren Bedrohung* (München: Beck, 1978).
2 Stefan Hanss, *Lepanto als Ereignis: Dezentrierende Geschichte(n) der Seeschlacht von Lepanto (1571)* (Göttingen: V&R, 2017). See also the excellent volume by Gabriele Haug-Moritz and Ludolf Pelizäus, eds., *Repräsentationen der islamischen Welt im Europa der Frühen Neuzeit* (Münster: Aschendorff, 2010).
3 Thomas Kaufmann, *"Türckenbüchlein". Zur christlichen Wahrnehmung "türkischer Religion" in Spätmittelalter und Reformation* (Göttingen: V&R, 2008), 60.

Emotions, identity and propaganda 323

4 Ibid., 15. See also Susan R. Boettcher, "German Orientalism in the Age of Confessional Consolidation: Jacob Andreae's Thirteen Sermons on the Turk, 1568", *Comparative Studies of South Asia, Africa and the Middle East* 24 (2004): 101–115.
5 Kaufmann, *Türckenbüchlein*, 57; Schulze, *Reich und Türkengefahr*, 51; Alexander Schmidt, *Vaterlandsliebe und Religionskonflikt. Politische Diskurse im Alten Reich (1555–1648)* (Leiden/Boston: Brill, 2007), 241, 244. With somewhat different emphasis and results Norbert Haag, "'Erbfeind der Christenheit'. Türkenpredigten im 16. und 17. Jahrhundert", in *Repräsentationen der islamischen Welt im Europa der Frühen Neuzeit*, eds. Gabriele Haug-Moritz and Ludolf Pelizäus (Münster: Aschendorff, 2010), 127–149. See also Almut Höfert, "Alteritätsdiskurse: Analyseparameter historischer Antagonismusnarrative und ihre historiographischen Folgen", in *Repräsentationen der islamischen Welt im Europa der Frühen Neuzeit*, eds. Gabriele Haug-Moritz and Ludolf Pelizäus (Münster: Aschendorff, 2010), 21–40. Damaris Grimmsmann, while stressing the basic commonalities, sees some differences regarding the contents and specific arguments employed. Damaris Grimmsmann, *Krieg mit dem Wort: Türkenpredigten des 16. Jahrhunderts im Alten Reich* (Berlin/Boston: De Gruyter, 2016). Finally, for the Catholic side Martin Hille, *Providentia Dei, Reich und Kirche: Weltbild und Stimmungsprofil altgläubiger Chronisten 1517–1618* (Göttingen: V&R, 2010), 287–322.
6 Karl Lorenz, *Die kirchlich-politische Parteibildung in Deutschland vor Beginn des dreissigjähriges Krieges im Spiegel der konfessionellen Polemik* (München: Beck, 1903), 8.
7 Heinz Schilling, "Die Konfessionalisierung im Reich. Religiöser und gesellschaftlicher Wandel in Deutschland zwischen 1555 und 1620", *Historische Zeitschrift* 246 (1988): 1–45.
8 Lorenz, *Kirchlich-politische Parteibildung*; Richard Krebs, *Die politische Publizistik der Jesuiten und ihrer Gegner in den letzten Jahrzehnten vor Ausbruch des dreissigjährigen Krieges* (Halle, 1890).
9 Kai Bremer, *Religionsstreitigkeiten. Volkssprachliche Kontroversen zwischen altgläubigen und evangelischen Theologen im 16. Jahrhundert* (Tübingen: De Gruyter, 2005); Hildegard Traitler, *Konfession und Polemik. Interkonfessionelle Flugschriftenpolemik aus Süddeutschland und Österreich (1564–1612)* (Frankfurt/Main: Peter Land, 1989); Ursula Paintner, *'Des Papsts neue Creatur'. Antijesuitische Publizistik im Deutschsprachigen Raum (1555–1618)* (Amsterdam/New York: Brill, 2011); Irene Dingel, Wolf-Friedrich Schäufele, eds., *Kommunikation und Transfer im Christentum der Frühen Neuzeit* (Mainz: V&R, 2007).
10 Susan Karant-Nunn, *The Reformation of Feeling: Shaping the Religious Emotions in Early Modern Germany* (Oxford: Oxford University Press, 2010), 6.
11 Andreas Bähr, *Furcht und Furchtlosigkeit. Göttliche Gewalt und Selbstkonstitution im 17. Jahrhundert* (Göttingen: V&R, 2013). See from the older literature, Hans Joachim Kissling, "Türkenfurcht und Türkenhoffnungen im 15./16. Jahrhundert. Zur Geschichte eines 'Komplexes'", *Südost-Forschungen* 23 (1964): 1–18.
12 Almut Höfert, *Den Feind beschreiben. "Türkengefahr" und europäisches Wissen über das Osmanische Reich 1450–1600* (Frankfurt/Main: Campus, 2003), 76.
13 Thomas Kaufmann, "Protestantischer Konfessionsantagonismus im Kampf gegen die Jesuiten", *Konfessioneller Fundamentalismus. Religion als politischer Faktor im europäischen Mächtesystem um 1600*, eds. Heinz Schilling and Elisabeth Müller-Luckner (München: Oldenbourg, 2007), 103. See, however, the works by Ursula Paintner, who frequently mentions emotions as a relevant factor of polemical pamphlets, albeit only in passing: Paintner, *'Des Papsts neue Creatur'*, 375–380.
14 Karant-Nunn, *The Reformation of Feeling*, 255.
15 While Barbara Rosenwein has argued for the concept of emotional communities in the early Middle Ages, Susan Karant-Nunn has fruitfully applied this concept to the sixteenth century. See Barbara Rosenwein, *Emotional Communities in the early Middle Ages* (Ithaca: Cornell University Press, 2006). Karant-Nunn, *The Reformation of Feeling*.
16 William Reddy, *The Navigation of Feeling. A Framework for the History of Emotions* (Cambridge: Cambridge University Press, 2001).

17 Gottfried Seebaß, "Osiander, Andreas", *Neue Deutsche Biographie* 19 (1999): 608–609; Theodor Schott, "Osiander, Lucas", *Allgemeine Deutsche Biographie* 24 (1887): 493–495. For Lucas Osiander see also the detailed study by Sivert Angel, *The Confessional Homiletics of Lucas Osiander (1534–1604)* (Tübingen: Mohr Siebeck, 2014). The book does not discuss Osiander's engagement in confessional polemics.
18 Osiander is, in fact, a prime example for the process of politicisation of anti-Jesuit writings asserted by Kaufmann, in that Osiander started with attacks on the religious teachings of the Jesuits in the 1560s and moved to an attack on the political impact of their teachings as well as their presence in the Empire in the 1580s. See Kaufmann, *Konfession und Kultur*, 205–299. From Osiander's numerous publications, those especially relevant to the context of this chapter are Lucas Osiander, *Warnung/ Vor der falschen Lehr/ und Phariseischen Gleißnerey der Jesuiter* (Tübingen, 1568); Lucas Osiander, *Warnung vor der Jesuiter blutdurstigen Anschlägen unnd bösen Practicken. Durch welche sie die Christliche/ reine/ evangelische Lehr/ sampt allen denen/ so sich zu derselben offentlich bekennen/ außzutilgen/ unnd des Römischen Antichrists tyrannisch Joch der Christenheit widerumb auffzutringen understehn* (Tübingen, 1585); Lucas Osiander, *Abfertigung der vermeindten Replic/ Christophori Rosenbusches/ Jesuiters/ welche er wider Lucam Osiandrum D. newlich im Truck außgesprengt (...)* (Tübingen, 1587); Lucas Osiander, *Bericht. Vom Faßnacht Triumph/ Georgii Scherers/ eines Jesuiters* (Tübingen, 1587). Lucas Osiander, *Endtliche Abfertigung der beider Jesuiter/ Christoffen Rosenbuschen/ und Georgen Scherers. Darinnen erwisen würdt/ daß den Jesuitern nicht ungütlich beschehen/ in dem meniglich (hohes und niders Stands) vor ihnen/ als vor den Zerstörern des Religionsfridens/ unnd Anstifftern der Verfolgungen (wider die Evangelischen Christen) trewlich gewarnet werden* (Tübingen, 1589).
19 Lucas Osiander, *Christlicher/ notwendiger Bericht/ Welcher Gestalt sich die Christen darein schicken sollen/ damit sie dem Türcken ein behrarrlichen abbruch thun/ unnd ein heilsamen Sig erlangen mögen. Darauß auch zuvernemen/ waran es biß daher gefehlet/ daß dem Türcken kein glücklicher Widerstand gethon worden/ sondern sein Macht je länger je mehr zugenommen. Allen Christlichen Evangelischen Heerpredigern unnd Kriegsleuten nutzlich zu lesen* (Tübingen, 1585).
20 Vgl. Robert Pichl, "Scherer, Georg", *Neue Deutsche Biographie* 22 (2005): 689–960. See also Traitler, *Konfession und Politik*, 71–75.
21 Georg Scherer, *Rettung der Jesuiter Unschuld wider die Gifftspinnen Lucam Osiander* (Ingolstadt, 1586); Georg Scherer, *Triumph der Warheit/ wider Lucam Osiandrum* (Ingolstadt, 1587); Georg Scherer, *Fortsetzung deß Triumphs der Warheit/ wider Lucam Osiandrum* (Ingolstadt, 1588).
22 For a deeper analysis of this controversy, which involved also the Jesuit Christoph Rosenbusch, see Thomas Gloning, "The Pragmatic Form of Religious Controversies around 1600: A Case Study in the Osiander vs. Scherer & Rosenbusch Controversy", *Historical Dialogue Analysis*, eds. Andreas H. Jucker, Gerd Fritz, and Franz Lebsanft (Amsterdam: John Benjamins Publishing, 1999), 81–110.
23 Georg Scherer, *Ein Christliche Heer-Predig Allen Kriegs-Obristen/ Hauptleuthen/ Bevelchshabern und dem gantz Christlichen Kriegßvolck/ so sich der zeit in Hungern wider die Türcken gebrauchen lassen/ zu einer nachrichtung in Druck verfertigt* (Wien, 1596); Georg Scherer, *Ein trewhertzige Vermahnung/ Daß die Christen dem Türcken nicht huldigen/ sondern Ritterlich wider ihn streitten sollen. Gepredigt auff dem Küniglichen Schloß zu Preßburg in Hungern/ am ersten Sontag in der Fasten/ im wehrenden Landtag* (Dillingen, 1597).
24 Bremer, *Religionsstreitigkeiten*, 232–236.
25 Karant-Nunn, *The Reformation of Feeling*, 6.
26 Haag, *Erbfeind der Christenheit*, 129.
27 Sabine Holtz, *Theologie und Alltag: Lehre und Leben in den Predigten der Tübinger Theologen 1550–1750* (Tübingen: Mohr Siebeck, 1993).
28 Karant-Nunn, *The Reformation of Feeling*.
29 The most exhaustive study of anti-Ottoman sermons in the Holy Roman Empire is Grimmsmann, *Krieg mit dem Wort*. Emotions are not specifically covered by this otherwise excellent volume.

30 See for example Maximilian Lanzinner, *Friedenssicherung und politische Einheit des Reiches unter Kaiser Maximilian II. (1564–1576)* (Göttingen: V&R, 1993).
31 Osiander, *Christlicher/ notwendiger Bericht*, 1.
32 Scherer, *Heer-Predig*, Aii–Aiii:

> Auß diser instruction unnd fürgestecktem zill/ will ich auch nicht schreiten/ Sonder mein vorhabende Predig dahin ordnen und anstellen/ damit alle Obristen/ Haubtleuth/ Bevelchshaber/ und gemeine Kriegsknecht/ darauß ein dapffers Hertz fassen/ wider den Ertz unnd Erbfeindt deß Christlichen Namens und Glaubens wider den Türcken, dann ein unerschrocken und unverzagtes Hertz haben/ ist der fürnembsten unnd nothwendigisten stücken eins/ so zur Kriegsexpedition und Heerzug gehören.

33 Bii f.
34 Scherer, *Heer-Predig*, Biii: "Summa alle dapffere KriegsFürsten und FeldtObristen haben zu jederzeit die unordentliche forcht unnd flucht für den Feinden/ für ein grosse schandt und sonderliche straff und plag von Gott gehalten."
35 Ciii.
36 Michael Anisius, *Siben Catholische Predigen/ Bey gemeinen Processionen/ Kirch unnd Bittfahrten wider deß Christlichen Namens Erbfeind dem Türcken/ gehalten zu Bamberg/ im 4. unnd 95. Jahr* (München, 1599), 169: "Dann die Welt hat kein Ordnung mehr ist ein Chaos, ein Mißmasch / ein Verwirrung / ist ein rechte Höll / da kein Ordnung und Richtigkeit nicht ist."
37 Scherer, *Ein trewhertzige Vermahnung*, Aiii:

> Under andern Versuchungen aber ist zu disen jetzt schwebenden Kriegsläufen unnd Zeiten bey vilen/ dise/ daß nemblich der laidige Teufel vielen starck ein und fürbildet/ Es sey mit uns Christen/ deß Türcken halber schon auß/ Man soll Hertz/ Händ und Füß fallen lassen/ die Waffen auff die seytten legen/ sich dem Türcken huldigen und underwerffen/ in für einObrigkeit an und auffnemmen/ erkennen und ehren/ ihme den Rock/ Händ und Füß küssen/ für ihme niderfallen/ unnd ihme gleichsamb anbeten.

38 Osiander, *Christlicher Bericht*, 2:

> Derwegen will es ein hohe notturfft sein/ daß die Christen auffgemundert werden/ dann deren ein grosser theil/ auch under fürnemen Leuten/ der massen mit fleischlicher sicherheit vom Satan truncken gemacht worden sein/ daß sie gar starck schlaffen/ schnarchen/ unnd der ernstlichen Straffen Gottes so gar nichts empfinden/ daß man holtz (wie man im Sprichwort sagt) auff ihnen spalten möchte. Dise Leut (wie auch andere/ so dise Gefahr nicht verstehen/ oder nach notturfft behertzigen) muß man auffwecken: Damit sie sich das jenige fürnemen/ das zu abwendung des vorstehenden/ unaußsprechlichen Jamers dienstlich/ unnd zum eussersten notwendig ist.

39 Osiander, *Christlicher Bericht*, 21: "Wie mächtig hat uberhand genommen/ Neid und Haß/ Mißgunst und Rachgir/ da ein Nachbaur/ und ein Freund den andern/ umb eines worts/ oder (wie man im Sprichwort sagt) umb einer Heringsnasen willen/ ubergibt/ darüber ein Zanck unnd Rechtfertigung anfahet?" 22: "Wie sehr ist die Brüderliche Liebe erkaltet/ gegen den rechten armen unnd krancken Leuten? gegen denen man doch das Herz nicht beschliessen sollte?"
40 Schulze, *Reich und Türkengefahr*.
41 Scherer, *Rettung*, 13.
42 Ibid., 19.
43 Christoph Rosenbusch, *Declaration der untüchtigen/ unwarhafften Abfertigung/ Luce Osiandri Predicanten. Dadurch an Tag gebracht/ das sein Osianders Aufflagen/ damit er vermeynt der Jesuiter Unschuld zubeschwären/ noch wie zuvor/ falsche grundtlose Gedicht: Rosenbuschs aber Retorsion und Beweiß wider Osiander und seines gleichen Predicanten/ daß sie Blutgierig*

und Auffrürisch wider die Catholischen Ständt/ etc. beständig: und endtlich die Narrata/ so er Osiander auß Rosenbuschs Replica gezogen/ nit Lugen/ sondern Warheiten seyn und bleiben (Ingolstadt, 1588), 128:

> Dann solche Schmächwort richten nichts guts an/ sie pflanzen kein Liebe/ kein Sanfftmut/ kein Freundlichkeit/ kein Burgerliche liebliche Beywohnung/ sonder sie heben zwischen den Verwandten beyder Religion bey diser Stadt alles Vertrawen/ alle Freundschafft/ unnd alles Politisch Fridwesen auff/ sie machen die Obrigkeit verachtet und verhaßt.

And 129:

> Da ist alle Lieblichkeit/ alle Freundschafft unnd Verwandtnuß erloschen unnd nichts geachtet/ die Lieb ist ganz und gar erstorben/ und der Augenschein täglicher Erfahrung hats vor diesem zuerkennen egeben/ daß man auf jeder Preidg noch verbitterter/ und mit Grollen noch mehr angefüllet und besessen zu Hauß kommen. Ja wann man von der Communion gangen/ so hat man gespürt/ daß in gemein derjenig der best Christ zu seyn sich bedunken lassen/ welcher am meisten Widerwillens/ Neid/ Grollens und feindseliger Geberd/ in Augen/ in Wercken/ in Worten/ wider Catholische/ wider die Obrigkeit/ und diejenigen so zu derselben sich gehalten/ erzeigt hat.

44 Osiander, *Warnung* (1585), 7: "So seind auch ihre obgedachte Carmina uffs hefftigste geschärpfft/ und dahin gerichtet/ die Potentaten/ zu Verfolgung der Evangelischen Christen/ und ihr Blut zuvergiessen/ auffzubringen unnd anzuhetzen."

45 Ibid., 10:

> Und halten uns also nach dem Wort und Bevelch unsers Herrn Jesu Christi/ sovil uns in der Schwachheit des Fleisches müglich ist. Wann nun die Jesuiter ein Tropffen Christliches Geblüts/ und ein Fünklin des sanfftmütigen Geists Jesu jetten/ solten sie uns billich nit allein nit hassen oder verfolgen/ sondern von hertzen lieben/ und im fahl der not/ auch das leben für uns setzen/ wie Johannes in seiner Epistel lehret/ da er spricht: Wir sollen auch das Leben für die Brüder lassen.

46 This debate about trust has a larger background in the political culture of these decades, see Hannes Ziegler, *Trauen und Glauben. Vertrauen in der politischen Kultur des Alten Reiches im Konfessionellen Zeitalter* (Affalterbach: Didymos, 2017).

47 Scherer, *Triumph der Wahrheit*, 96.

48 Rosenbusch, *Antwort und Ehrenrettung*, 55.

49 Scherer, *Heer-Predig*, passim.

50 Ibid., Aii.

51 Thomas Sigebertus, *Eine schöne und tröstliche Rede/ Von dem Ungerischen und Türckischen Kriegswesen/ wie man sich drein schicken/ unnd es recht betrachten solle. Item/ Eine Vermanung zur Bestendigkeit wider den Türcken zu streiten* (Erfurt, 1595). See on Sigebertus also Schmidt, *Vaterlandsliebe und Religionskonflikt*, 258–260.

52 Schmidt, *Vaterlandsliebe und Religionskonflikt*, 258.

53 Karant-Nunn, *The Reformation of Feeling*, 60.

54 Osiander, *Christlicher Bericht*, 4:

> Zum andern/ will ich auch beständigen satten Trost/ auß dem Schatz des Göttlichen Worts/ herfür bringen/ durch welchen gestärckt/ und beherzt gemacht werden/ die jenige/ so entweder sich im Krieg/ wider disen mächtigen Feind wöllen gebrauchen lassen: oder aber/ die den Türcken so nahend sitzen/ daß sie diser grewlichen Bestiae/ gleich in den Rachen sehen: Oder aber/ die auch an weit entseßnen orten/ forchtsamer/ unnd verzagter seind/ dann billich die Christen/ welche auff Gott warhafftig vertrawen/ sein sollten.

55 Ibid., 2:

> Derwegen will es ein hohe notturfft sein/ daß die Christen auffgemundert werden/ dann deren ein grosser theil/ auch under fürnemen Leuten/ der massen mit fleischlicher sicherheit vom Satan truncken gemacht worden sein/ daß sie gar starck schlaffen/ schnarchen/ unnd der ernstlichen Straffen Gottes so gar nichts empfinden/ daß man holtz (wie man im Sprichwort sagt) auff ihnen spalten möchte. Dise Leut (wie auch andere/ so dise Gefahr nicht verstehen/ oder nach notturfft behertzigen) muß man auffwecken: Damit sie soch das jenige fürnemen/ das zu abwendung des vorstehenden/ unaußsprechlichen Jamers dienstlich/ unnd zum eussersten notwendig ist.

56 Ibid., 10:

> Darumb zubesorgen/ daß dise fleischliche Sicherheit/ da man halßstarrig in verthädigung abgöttischer und falscher Lehr unnd Religion/ nicht allein verharret/ sondern auch die arme Underthonen zu selbiger zwinget/ ein bösen Außschlag werde nemen: zum wenigsten (wann es wol gerhatet) uber die Personen/ welche mit solchem verhärten und verstockten Hertzen wider den Türcken ziehen.

57 Ibid., 19:

> Hie würdt vielleicht jemand sagen: Mit solchen worten und Erinnerungen/ würdt man nicht lustige und fraidige Kriegsleut machen: wann man ihnen will ein solche Forcht einstossen/ als ob sie dem Türcken kein abbruch thun mögen/ sondern under ligen müssen: Solche Prediger sollte man abschaffen/ oder ihnen das Maul stopffen. Antwort: Das verbiet mir Gott/ daß ich redliche Christliche Kriegsleut sollte wöllen verzagt machen (dann hernach an seinem ort/ will ich selbige trösten/ und auß Gottes Wort behertzt machen) sondern ich warne allein die jenigen/ so sich in disen wichtigen Handel/ der Leib und Seel antrifft/ nicht recht schicken wöllen. Und warne sie darumb/ damit sie nicht den Leib verliren: ihr Seel dem Teuffel auffopffern: jämerlich vom Türcken auffs Maul geschmissen werden/ und unserm geliebten Vatterland/ dem Teutschland/ einen unwiderbringlichen Schaden zuziehen.

58 Osiander, *Warnung* (1585), 10–14 and passim.
59 Ziegler, *Trauen und Glauben*, 94–104.
60 See for example Scherer, *Triumph der Wahrheit*, 96:

> Wer mercket/ ja greiffet hie nicht/ daß Osiander mit solcher Predig unnd Außführung vom Jurament unnd Eydspflichten/ die Catholischen wil verdächtig machen bey den anderen Ständen unnd Fürsten deß Römischen Reichs/ als ob sie uber dem gescjwornen Religionsfrid Eydbrüchig und Meineydig gedächten zuwerden/ und hinfurt weder Trawen noch Glauben mehr halten wolten. Darzu understehet sich Osiander den seinigen auff gut Müntzerisch ein groß Hertz/ unnd unerschrocken Mutz zumachen/ daß nemblich Gott bey ihnen seyn und stehen/ sie underm Schatten seiner Flügel beschirmen werde/ Glück und Sig verleyhen/ unnd uns Papisten schlagen.

61 Scherer, *Heer-Predig*, Ciii:

> Auß disen unnd dergleichen vilen andern Exemplen und Historien ist genugsamb abzunemmen/ das der schrecken und die zagheit/ den unglaubigen Heyden und Türcken gebüere/ unnd nicht den Glaubigen so ir zuversicht in den wahren Gott setzen und stellen. Begibts sichs aber das auch die Christen das zittern unnd die fluchtsucht bekommen/ ist solches für ein straff Gottes uber unser Sünd zuhalten.

62 Christoph Rosenbusch, *Antwort und Ehrerrettung auff die Ehrnrürig im Rechten unnd Römischen Reich verbottene Schmachschrifft/ Lucae Osiandri, die er intituliert/ Warnung vor*

der Jesuiter Blutdurstigen Anschlägen und bösen Practicken. Durch Christophorum Rosenbusch Societatis IESU (Ingolstadt, 1586), 66:

> Wie fürchtest du dir nit vor dem Gesatz Gottes/ das also sagt: Du solt kein Verleumbder auch Hader macher sein under deinem Volck? Bist du nit ingedenck was der H. Apostel Jacobus sagt: Hinderredet nit einander/ lieben Brüder. Wer seinem Bruder arges anchredet/ und vortheilet/ der hinderredet dem Gesatz/ etc. Wie trewlich vermanet Petrus die Christen mit disen worten: So leget nun ab alle Boßheit/ und alle Läst/ und Gleisnerey/ und Haß/ und alles Nachreden. Ursach hat der H. Geist durch den weißen Mann angezeigt/ der also spricht: Deßhalben hütet euch vor murmlen/ das euch keinen nutz bringt/ und verwahret ewre Zungen/ daß sie nit nachreden/ dann die Dunckelred wirdt nit ungestrafft hingehn: Aber der Mund der Lugen redet/ der tödtet die Seel.

Osiander, *Warnung* (1585), 17:

> Dieses hat das ansehen/ als ob lauter sanfftmut unnd Christliche Liebe und Bescheidenheit bei den Calvinisten zuverhoffen: Aber der Augenschein weiset viel ein anders im Werck auß/ da/ nämlich/ die Calvinische Kirchenrhät zu Heidelberg albereit reine Preidger unnd Schuldiener von ihren Diensten gestossen/ unnd die ubrigen täglich nichts anders zugewarten. Aber das ist alles lauter brüderliche Liebe/ und Christliche sanfftmut/ deren sich die Calvinisten stetigs rhümen.

63 Scherer, *Trewhertzige Vermahnung*, D:

> Wer kan alle Exempel erzählen/ deren von Türcken am Christlichen Adel und Potentaten geübten Crudelitäten unnd Tyranneyen/ darbey sie genugsam vor aller Welt zuerkennen geben/ wie sie den Christlichen Herren unnd Rittern gewogen/ unnd was für ein angeborne hässige Erbfeinschafft unnd verbittertes Blutdurstiges Gemüth sie gegen ihnen haben und tragen. Wie ist es dann müglich/ daß jemand vom Herren-Stand oder auß der Ritterschafft ainiges verlangen nach dem Türckischen Regiment in ihme fühlen oder empfinden soll/ Es wolte dann einer von freyen stucken mutwillig und verzweyfleter weiß selber den Straichen nachgehen/ und dem Schwerdt oder der Ruthen deß Henckers zulauffen.

64 Osiander, *Warnung* (1585), 10–4.
65 Scherer, *Rettung*, 3:

> Oder/ wie wann du/ und deines gleichen durch die heilige Schriff getroffen wurden/ die da sagt: Der Gottloß fleucht/ und niemand jagt ihn. Item: Was der Gottloß höret/ das schröcket ihn/ Und wann gleich frid ist/ dannoch besorgt er sich des Schwerts. Item: Sie förchten sich/ da nit zuförchten ist. Item: Das einer so verzagt ist/ das macht sein eigne Boßheit/ die ihn uberzeugt und verdambt/ und ein erschrocken Gewissen/ Versihet sich immer deß ärgisten.

And page 5f.:

> Ein jegliche Seel sey underthan der Obrigkeit. Dann es ist kein Gewalt dann von Gott/ was aber von Gott herkommet/ das ist ordenlich. Derhalben/ wer sich wider die Gewalt setzet/ der widerstrebet Gottes Ordnung/ die aber widerstreben/ die uberkommen ihnen selbs die Verdamnuß. Dann die Fürsten seynd mit denen/ die guts thun/ sonder den bösen zuförchten/ Wilt du dich nit förchten vor der Gewalt/ so thu guts/ so wirst du Lob von derselben haben/ dann er ist ein Verwalter/ oder Diener Gottes/ dir zum guten: Thust du aber böses/ so förcht dir/ dann er trägt das Schwert nit umb sonst/ sonder ist Gottes Diener/ unnd ein Rächer zur Straff uber den/ der böses thut.

66 Osiander, *Warnung* (1585), 11.
67 John 13:34–35.

68 Scherer, *Heer-Predig*, Ciii.
69 Osiander, *Warnung* (1585), 40f.
70 Scherer, *Heer-Predig*, Aii–Aiii:

> Auß diser instruction unnd fürgestecktem zill/ will ich auch nicht schreiten/ Sonder mein vorhabende Predig dahin ordnen und anstellen/ damit alle Obristen/ Haubtleuth/ Bevelchshaber/ und gemeine Kriegsknecht/ darauß ein dapffers Hertz fassen/ wider den Ertz unnd Erbfeindt deß Christlichen Namens und Glaubens wider den Türcken, dann ein unerschrocken und unverzagtes Hertz haben/ ist der fürnembsten unnd nothwendigisten stücken eins/ so zur Kriegsexpedition und Heerzug gehören.

S. Aiii: "Aber vor allen dingen gehört darzue ein Ritterliches künes Hertz/ und ein grosser Heldenmuet/ wo der nit ist/ sonderlichen in Obristen und Hauptleuthen/ wirdt gewißlichen nichts fruchtbarliches ausgerichtet/ sondern es ist alles umb sonst unnd vergebens." Osiander, *Christlicher Bericht*, 43f.:

> Wollen wir aber solchen glückseligen Sieg erlangen/ oder desselben geniessen unnd theilhafftig werden/ so muß man zu forderst die fleischliche Sicherheit/ unnd Gottloses Leben und Wesen mit allem ernst abschaffen und abstellen: Wir müssen unser Hoffnung und Vertrawen nicht auff unsere Kräfften und Vermögen/ oder auff Menschen Hülffe/ sonder allein auff den ewigen Allmächtigen GOtt stellen und bawen. Wir müssen ein Christlich Gottgefelig Leben führen/ und auß wahrem Glauben/ mit eiferigem/ bestendigem Gebet bey unserm Himmlischen Vatter/ umb Hülff und Beystand wider den Türcken anhalten/ und mit dem Gebet nicht nachlassen. Christliche Kriegsleute sollen (neben anruffung des Göttlichen Namens) ein Löwenmut fassen/ und gedencken/ daß sie fürs Vatterland/ für der Christen/ und ihr eigner Weiber und Kinder Zucht und Ehr/ und zu abwendung des Mahometischen verdamlichen Grewels streiten.

71 Adam S. Francisco, *Martin Luther and Islam: A Study in Sixteenth-Century Polemics and Apologetics* (Leiden/Boston: Brill, 2007); Gregory Miller, *The Turks and Islam in Reformation Germany* (London: Routledge, 2018).

Bibliography

Angel, Sivert. *The Confessional Homiletics of Lucas Osiander (1534–1604)*. Tübingen: Mohr Siebeck, 2014.

Bähr, Andreas. *Furcht und Furchtlosigkeit. Göttliche Gewalt und Selbstkonstitution im 17. Jahrhundert*. Göttingen: V&R, 2013.

Boettcher, Susan R. "German Orientalism in the Age of Confessional Consolidation: Jacob Andreae's Thirteen Sermons on the Turk, 1568." *Comparative Studies of South Asia, Africa and the Middle East* 24 (2004): 101–115.

Bremer, Kai. *Religionsstreitigkeiten. Volkssprachliche Kontroversen zwischen altgläubigen und evangelischen Theologen im 16. Jahrhundert*. Tübingen: De Gruyter, 2005.

Dingel, Irene and Wolf-Friedrich Schäufele, eds. *Kommunikation und Transfer im Christentum der Frühen Neuzeit*. Mainz: V&R, 2007.

Francisco, Adam S. *Martin Luther and Islam: A Study in Sixteenth-Century Polemics and Apologetics*. Leiden/Boston: Brill, 2007.

Gloning, Thomas. "The Pragmatic Form of Religious Controversies around 1600: A Case Study in the Osiander vs. Scherer & Rosenbusch Controversy." In *Historical Dialogue Analysis*, edited by Andreas H. Jucker, Gerd Fritz, and Franz Lebsanft, 81–110. Amsterdam: John Benjamins Publishing, 1999.

Grimmsmann, Damaris. *Krieg mit dem Wort: Türkenpredigten des 16. Jahrhunderts im Alten Reich.* Berlin/Boston: De Gruyter, 2016.

Haag, Norbert. "'Erbfeind der Christenheit'. Türkenpredigten im 16. und 17. Jahrhundert." In *Repräsentationen der islamischen Welt im Europa der Frühen Neuzeit*, edited by Gabriele Haug-Moritz and Ludolf Pelizäus, 127–149. Münster: Aschendorff, 2010.

Hanss, Stefan. *Lepanto als Ereignis: Dezentrierende Geschichte(n) der Seeschlacht von Lepanto (1571).* Göttingen: V&R, 2017.

Haug-Moritz, Gabriele and Ludolf Pelizäus, ed. *Repräsentationen der islamischen Welt im Europa der Frühen Neuzeit.* Münster: Aschendorff, 2010.

Hille, Martin. *Providentia Dei, Reich und Kirche: Weltbild und Stimmungsprofil altgläubiger Chronisten 1517–1618.* Göttingen: V&R, 2010.

Höfert, Almut. "Alteritätsdiskurse: Analyseparameter historischer Antagonismusnarrative und ihre historiographischen Folgen." In *Repräsentationen der islamischen Welt im Europa der Frühen Neuzeit*, edited by Gabriele Haug-Moritz and Ludolf Pelizäus, 21–40. Münster: Aschendorff, 2010.

Höfert, Almut. *Den Feind beschreiben. "Türkengefahr" und europäisches Wissen über das Osmanische Reich 1450–1600.* Frankfurt am Main: Campus, 2003.

Holtz, Sabine. *Theologie und Alltag: Lehre und Leben in den Predigten der Tübinger Theologen 1550–1750.* Tübingen: Mohr Siebeck, 1993.

Karant-Nunn, Susan. *The Reformation of Feeling: Shaping the Religious Emotions in Early Modern Germany.* Oxford: Oxford University Press, 2010.

Kaufmann, Thomas. "Protestantischer Konfessionsantagonismus im Kampf gegen die Jesuiten." In *Konfessioneller Fundamentalismus. Religion als politischer Faktor im europäischen Mächtesystem um 1600*, edited by Heinz Schilling, Elisabeth Muller-Luckner, 101–114. München: Oldenbourg, 2007.

Kaufmann, Thomas. *"Türckenbüchlein". Zur christlichen Wahrnehmung "türkischer Religion" in Spätmittelalter und Reformation.* Göttingen: V&R, 2008.

Kissling, Hans Joachim. "Türkenfurcht und Türkenhoffnungen im 15./16. Jahrhundert. Zur Geschichte eines 'Komplexes'." *Südost-Forschungen* 23 (1964): 1–18.

Krebs, Richard. *Die politische Publizistik der Jesuiten und ihrer Gegner in den letzten Jahrzehnten vor Ausbruch des dreissigjährigen Krieges.* Halle, 1890.

Lanzinner, Maximilian. *Friedenssicherung und politische Einheit des Reiches unter Kaiser Maximilian II. (1564–1576).* Göttingen: V&R, 1993.

Lorenz, Karl. *Die kirchlich-politische Parteibildung in Deutschland vor Beginn des dreissigjähriges Krieges im Spiegel der konfessionellen Polemik.* München: Beck, 1903.

Miller, Gregory. *The Turks and Islam in Reformation Germany.* London: Routledge, 2018.

Paintner, Ursula. *'Des Papsts neue Creatur'. Antijesuitische Publizistik im deutschsprachigen Raum (1555–1618).* Amsterdam/New York: Brill, 2011.

Reddy, William. *The Navigation of Feeling. A Framework for the History of Emotions.* Cambridge: Cambridge University Press, 2001.

Robert Pichl, "Scherer, Georg." *Neue Deutsche Biographie* 22 (2005): 689–690.

Rosenwein, Barbara. *Emotional Communities in the Early Middle Ages.* Ithaca: Cornell University Press, 2006.

Schilling, Heinz. "Die Konfessionalisierung im Reich. Religiöser und gesellschaftlicher Wandel in Deutschland zwischen 1555 und 1620." *Historische Zeitschrift* 246 (1988): 1–45.

Schmidt, Alexander. *Vaterlandsliebe und Religionskonflikt. Politische Diskurse im Alten Reich (1555–1648).* Leiden/Boston: Brill, 2007.

Schulze, Winfried. *Reich und Türkengefahr im späten 16. Jahrhundert. Studien zu den politischen und gesellschaftlichen Auswirkungen einer äußeren Bedrohung.* München: Beck, 1978.

Schott, Theodor. "Osiander, Lucas." *Allgemeine Deutsche Biographie* 24 (1887): 493–495.
Seebaß, Gottfried. "Osiander, Andreas." *Neue Deutsche Biographie* 19 (1999): 608–609.
Traitler, Hildegard. *Konfession und Polemik. Interkonfessionelle Flugschriftenpolemik aus Süddeutschland und Österreich (1564–1612).* Frankfurt am Main: Peter Land, 1989.
Ziegler, Hannes. *Trauen und Glauben. Vertrauen in der politischen Kultur des Alten Reiches im Konfessionellen Zeitaler.* Affalterbach: Didymos, 2017.

INDEX

Note: *Italic* page numbers refer to figures and page numbers followed by "n" denote endnotes.

actor-network theory (ANT) 234
Adrian VI, Pope 99
affective language 49–54, 61, 64
agency 231–235
Akhimie, Patricia 290, 304
Alessio, Matteo Pérez de 103
Alexander the Great 137; and loss of the flower-maidens 260–262; *Straßburger Alexander* 260, 270
Alexander VII, Pope 158
Alfonso II 96
Alfonso III 96–97
Americas 95, 96; Santiago Matamoros in 100–113, *102, 104, 106, 109, 110*
Amsler, Nadine 7
Amsterdam sex trade 81
Anderson, Benedict 10
anger in early modern Denmark, materiality of 176–184
animal emotion 250n40
animal sacrifice 232
Anisius, Michael 315
Anna, Maria 203
anxiety 51, 58–61
Apollonius of Tyrland, generic timeliness in 262–267
Appadurai, Arjun 234
Appel, Charlotte 176
Appiah, Kwame Anthony 1

appresentation techniques, bridging distances by 21–34
Aquinas, Thomas 55
Arbel, Benjamin 242
Aristotle 232
Arnold, John 49
Assumpção, Luís Afonso 113; 'Swimming Against the Red Tide' 113
Aston, Walter 204
Atocha, Virgen de 203
Augsburg Peace of 1555 312
authenticity of emotional expressions 34–37
avatar 28, 43n56
Ávila, Teresa de: *Vida* 200
Axelrod, Paul 141

Bähr, Andreas 312
Bakhtin, Mikhail 262–263
Baptista, son of Johannes van Doetecum 134
The Barbary Company 292–293
Barberini, Antonio 157
Bargrave, Robert 207
Barneville, Marie-Catherine Le Jumel de 202
Baronio, Cesare: *Annales ecclesiastici* 160
Bartel, Emily C. 300
Batavia 82–84
Battle of Lepanto 311

Battle of Monte Laturce (859) 96
Beck, David: 'Spiegel van Mijn Leven' 185, 187
Belton, Frances 219, 220
Belton, Henry 219, 221
Ben-Amos, Ilana Krausman 185
Bentham, Jeremy 242
Berryman, John: *Mary of Egypt* 276
Bhabha, Homi 7
Biblioteca Angelica, Rome 163–166, 167–168n30
Black Legend of Inquisition 198
Blackman, Morris 56
Blunt, Richard 291
Bonelli, Carlo 162
Book of Common Prayer 55
Bourdieu, Pierre 10
Bourk, Joanna 51
Bracciolino, Poggio 126, 129
Bradforth, John 205
British East India Company 243
Broadie, Nicholas Dean 6–7, 8
Broomhall, Susan 6, 9–10, 50, 61
Brown, Bill 234
Brown, George 18, 20
Brunel, Antoine de 204; *Voyage* 213n38
Bry, Johann Theodor de *124*; *Indiae orientalis* 134; *Voyages* 123
Buckley, John 21
Buckley, Sarah 20–24, 31, 38
Buddhism 252n61
Buono, Amy 95–96
Burton, Robert 159
Butler, Alban 155
Butler, Anne 20, 24–29, 31–34, 37

Callaghan, Dympna 294
Calvin, John 55
Calvinism 134
Camargo, Diego Muñoz 109; 'Alegoria de Cortez conquistador' 108; *Historia de Tlaxcala* 108, 111
Camino del Santiago 199
Camiño de Santiago 97
Cañari 105
Cantatrice, Anna 157
Cape of Good Hope 53
Cardonne, Don Frederic de 205, 207
Catechism 186
Catholicism 208–209; suppression of 74, 75
Catholic Reformation 135
Cervantes, Miguel 165n3
Chachapoyas 105
Chamberlain, George 57

The Character of Spain 205–206
Charles V 98, 100, 101
Cholmley, Nathaniel 60
Christianity 6, 126, 318; suppression of 88n3
Christian IV 173, 182
Christian, William 201
chrononormativity 4
Church of Santiago Apóstol, Málaga 99
Church of St Thomas 129
Clavell, Walter 51, 63–64
Clement VI 135
Clement VIII, Pope 155, 160
Cnoll, Pieter 84
Cock, Henri 207
Codex Casantense *131*
Coeman, Jacob 84
"Cogito, ergo sum" 4
Cohen, Jeffrey Jerome 264
Colborne, Henry 57–58
Collett, Joseph 53
colonisation 224
communities of feeling 234
Constantia 318
Conti, Niccolò 129
Convention of Peace and Amity between the United States of America and the Empire of Japan (Nichibei Washin Joyaku) 73
Cornwallis, Sir Charles 203
Coromandel Coast 52
Corpus Christi Procession 111, 125, 135–137, 142, 201, 204
Cortez 101, 103, 108
Cracow, Carel van 175
Croix, Edmond de la 197
Cromberger, Juan 101
Crown of Castile 100, 104
Cuelbis, Jakob (Diego) 206, 207
Curcio, Quinto 101
curiosity 73, 74, 79, 84–88
Cursio, Quinto: *De los hechos del Magno Alexandre* 101

Dandelet, Thomas 157
dansyoku 79
Darwin, Erasmus: *The Temple of Nature; or, the Origin of Society* 216
Das, Nadini 125–126
d'Aulnoy, Marie-Catherine 202–205, 207, 209; *Les Contes des Fées* 203; *Relation du voyage d'Espagne* 203, 211n17, 211n18, 212n33
Davis, Thomas 56
Deia (The Call) 114

Index **335**

Dejima 73, 74, 78–80, 83, 88n1; romping in 76–77; West beyond 84–87
Delmas, Adrien 50
Denmark, early modern: love and anger, materiality of 172–190, *174, 180, 188*
Deroux, Margaux 292, 294
Descartes, René 4
Desiderius Helmschmid 100
Deuteronomy 318
al-Dhahabī, Shams al-Dīn 236
Díaz del Catillo, Bernal 105; *True History of the Conquest of New Spain* 105
Dibbits, Hester 185
Diemeringen, Otto von 144n36
Dierks, Konstantin 43n54
Dirichs, Ryken 187
Discalced Trinitarians 155, 156, 158, 159, 161–163
Ditchfield, Simon 160, 166n18
Dixon, Peter 234
Doetecum, Johannes van 134
Don García de Osorio 99, 100
Don Pánfilo de Narváez 101
drama, as affective technology 200
Duke of Terranova 161
Dutch East India Company 6, 9–10, 48–64, 82
Dutchmen, and morality at home and abroad 80–83
Dutch Revolt 136–137

Edo Sanpu 74
Egmond, Florike 185
eighteenth-century transmaritime family correspondence 17–38
Eishi, Hosoda 79
Eitler, Pascal: *Emotional Lexicons* 235
Ekman, Paul 2
Elias, Norbert 207; *Civilizing Process* 1
Eller, Poul 176
Elliott, J.H. 38n3
'El primer Nueva coronica y buen gobierno' (Felipe Guaman Poma de Ayala) 105–107
embodied emotions 123–142
emotional arousal 280
emotional binaries 172
emotional communities 9–10, 50, 59, 200, 234, 249n24, 322, 322n15
emotional company 48–64
emotional expressions, authenticity of 34–37
emotional fraying 64
emotional integrity 22

emotionality 28, 29, 78
emotional language 320–322
emotional reactions 291
emotional regimes 200, 234
emotional register 290–306
emotional space 277
emotionology 10
emotions 2, 4–11; as cultural and personal engagement 3; in early modern world 231–247; impact on identity-building 3; in religious encounters 6; as social practices 10; temporalities 3–4; timeliness of 3–4
emotives 234
English East India Company 48–64
epistemic anxieties 50
epistolary space 18, 20, 39n9
epistolary conversations 19
Erstenberger, Andreas 318
European men 'at play,' portrayal of 77–80
Europeanness 5, 78
Europeans, in Japan 74–75

Fabricius, K.: *Holland-Danmark*, I–II 176
familiarity 30, 38
Fanshawe, Lady Ann 204
fear 320
Febvre, Lucien 2, 38n3
Felix of Valois 155
Fenner, W. 159
Ferland, Catherine 40n19
Forster, Georg 217–219, 222, 226; 'Cook der Entdecker' 218; *A Voyage Round the World* 218, 220, 221, 227n9
Forster, Johann Reinhold 216
Fort St. George 48, 49, 52, 56, 59, 62, 63
Four Horsemen of the Apocalypse 125
Frank, Graham 20, 24–31, 34, 37, 38, 42n49
Frederik II, King 173, 178, 187
Freeman, Elizabeth 3–4
French Wars of Religion 136
Frois, Luis 75, 86
Fudge, Erica 234, 235
Fuerch, Michelle A. 141

Galen, Johan van 175
Galle, Philips *138*
Galliano, Antonio 166n18
Gambino, José 113
Gammerl, Benno 8
Geary, Patrick J. 159–160
Genette, Gérard 259
Gerritsen, Anne 185
Gill, Andrew 56–57

336 Index

Gillies, John 292, 297–298
globalization 10
Godwin, William: *Caleb Williams* 222;
  Enquiry into Political Justice, An 221
Goethe, Johann Wolfgang von: *Faust* 276
Gonzales di Medina, Fray 153, 158, 163
Gonzales, Fra 161
Gospel of John 320
grand tour 20
Great Turkish War (1683–1699) 311
Grenier, Benoît 40n19
guilt 242–245
Guzman, Nuño de 112

Haag, Norbert 314
Habib, Imtiaz 292
habitus 10, 290, 292, 305, 306
Habsburg Empire 199
hadith 236
Hakluyt, Richard 292
Hammond, Henry 55
Harding, Sandra 234
harem 4; definition of 2
Harris, Bernard 299
Harris, Frederick 78
Harris, K.A. 161
Harris, Thomas 59
Harris, Timothy 57
Hasoda 90n46
Heemskerck, Maarten van 137, *138*, 139, *140*
Heinrichs, Willum 187, 272n40
Heroica Matamoros 112
Hess, Anders 179
Het Amsterdamsche Hoerdom (Amsterdam whores) 81
Heyne, Gottlob 217
Hillgarth, J.N.: *Mirror of Spain* 199
Hindu Jagannath temple, Odissa 123
Historia do Japam [História do Japão], 74–75, 86
Hodgeon, William 18
Hoff, Albert von 187
Hofreise 74
Hollænder, Berent 177, 178, 179, 181–184
Hollanders 80
hollandology 87
Holtz, Sabine 314
Holy Roman Empire 311–313, 315–317, 319, 324n29
Huber, Ludwig 218; *The Lonely Death Bed* 221
Huber, Therese: *Abentheuer auf einer Reise nach Neu-Holland* [Adventures on a Voyage to New Holland] 217–222; colonial projections of 216–226; *Die Familie Seldorf* 217
human–animal interactions 231, 239–241
Humbolt, Wilhelm von 217
Hunter, G. K. 302; *The Discovery of Witchcraft* 291–292
Hurayrah, Abu 237
Huygen, Jan 123

Iberian Peninsula 95, 97
identity: collective 6; communal 200, 208; confessional 201; construction 270; Dutch 87; emotion and 311–322; ethnic 111; European 82, 141; formation 184, 190; group 111; national 199; negotiation of 4, 10, 11, 190; politics 4; religious 199
identity-building 1, 3, 4, 8
Imagined Communities (Anderson) 10
Inchbald, Elizabeth 217
Indian ritual procession, European perspectives of 123–142
Ingrès, Paul 2–3
Innocent X, Pope 158
inquisition 48
interpersonal emotions 234
intimacy 29–31
Irving, David R.M. 125
Isaacsz, Pieter 175
Isidor of Seville 264

Japan: *Convention of Peace and Amity between the United States of America and the Empire of Japan* (*Nichibei Washin Joyaku*) 73; Dutchmen and morality at home and abroad 80–83; European men 'at play,' portrayal of 77–80; Europeans in 74–75; romping in Dejima 76–77; *shunga* 73, 77–82, 88; West beyond Dejima 84–87
Jesuit College, Vienna 314
Joannes, son of Johannes van Doetecum 134
Johnson, Walter 233
John the Baptist of the Conception 155
Joly, Barthélemy 197–198, 202, 205, 206, 208, 209; "Voyage" 209–210n3, 210n4, 211n32
Jordan, the first bishop of Kollam, Malabar Coast of India 126
Jordan of Catalonia 132; *Mirabilia* 126–127, 136
Josephus, Flavius 101; *De Bello Judaico* 101
joyful desire 280
Judaism 232; Rabbinic 232
Jyagarata bumi (Jakarta Letter) 84
Jyoken, Nishikawa 85; *Nagasaki yawagusa* 85

Kaempfer, Engelbert 86, 87
Kaislaniemi, Samuli 63
Kamen, Henry: *Imagining Spain* 199
Karant-Nunn, Susan 9, 200, 312–315, 318, 322
Kaufmann, Thomas 311
keesjes 76
Keiga, Kawahara 79, 90n48
Kello, Josh 38n1, 38n2
Kelsdatter, Ellen 187
Kiening, Christian 269
Kim, Lawrence 263
'King Sapor' 100
Kirklington 24
'Knight and the Devil' 100
Knights Templar 153
Koris, Joel 206
Koselleck, Reinhart 218: *Gleichzeitigkeit des Ungleichzeitigen* 4

Lach, Donald 38n3
Latour, Bruno 234
Lauridsen, Mads 179, 184
Lees, Clare A. 280
Lellis, Camillo de 156
Leo, John: *Geographical Historie of Africa, A* 299
Leupp, Gary P. 78
The Lies that Bind. Rethinking Identity (Appiah) 1
Linschoten, Jan Huygen van 137, 140; *Itinerario* 134; *Le vray miroir de la vie humaine* 137
Lipsius, Justus 318
London 17, 21, 24, 31, 35, 36, 48, 49, 57, 58, 62
London Council 48
longing, tokens of 184–189
Long Turkish War (1593–1606) 311, 312
Lopez, Aaron 21
Lordomanes 97
love 73–88, 125, 242–245, 262; in early modern Denmark, materiality of 172–190, *174, 180, 188*; relationship 85; tokens of 184–189
Loyola, Ignatius 200
lust 73–88
Luther, Martin 316, 321
Lyall, Alexander 179
Lyall, Frederik 179, 184

McCant, Anne 185
MacDonald, Robin 6
Machilipatnam 48–51, 54, 58, 60, 61

Magennis, Hugh: *The Old English Life of St Mary of Egypt* 276–288
Mahatma Gandhi 1
Mahler's Eighth Symphony 276
Mahr, Jørgen 179, 184
Mainwaring, Matthew 61
makurae 79
male-male eroticism (*nansyoku* or *dansyoku*) 79
Malpas, Jeff 287
Mandeville, John 125, 126, 128–132, 144n25; *Travels* 128, 130–131, *130, 131*
Manoncourt, Charles-Sigisbert Sonnini de 238
Marco Polo 128
Marino, John 157
Martyr, Peter 55
Maruyama 76
Maryland 33
Massimo, Camillo 153, 162
Matamoros Effect 100
Matsys, Quentin 276
Mattei, Marchese Girolamo 156
Mauricio, Miguel 103, 104
Mayo, Thomas 57
Meersbergen, Guido van 64
Melanchthon, Philippe 186
Mernissi, Fatima 2, 4; *Dreams of Trespass: Tales of a Harem Girlhood* 2
Mesoamerica 6
Mesquita-Cateral/Mosque-Cathedral 98
Metzendorff, J.C. 17–18, 20
Meurs, Jacob 186–187
Milne, Ester 19; *Technologies of Presence* 19
Miranda, Juan Carreño de 155; "The Mass of the Foundation of the Order of the Trinitarians" 166n16
Mohun, Richard 53
Montaigne, Michel de 242
Montanus, Arnoldus 75; *Gedenkwaerdige Gesantschappen der OostIndische Maetschappij aen de Kaiseren van Japan* (Memorable Embassies of the East Indies Company to the Emperors of Japan) 75
Moore, John 114; '*James the Greater: Interpreting the Interstices of Santiago as Peregrino and Matamoros*' 114
Moravians, religious community of 9
Moris, John: *Pearls of Eloquence, or The School of Complements, Wherein is Shewed a Brief Description of Beauty, Vertue, Love, and Eloquence* 35
Morning Chronicle 225
Morris, John 19, 20, 34–38

Morris, Thomas 56
Mullaney, Steven 200, 201
Muret, Jean 204, 209, 212n28, 212n30
Museum of Pilgrimages, Santiago de Compostela 111

nansyoku 79
Nationalsozialismus 1–2
Neostoicism 318
Neustadt, Heinrich von: *Apollonius von Tyrland* 263–264, 270
Nielsen, Hans 184
Nielsen, Morten 179–181
Nielsen, Philipp 8, 179
nihon-yuki 76
Nijenrode, Cornelia van 84
Nolde, Emil 276
Noldus, Badeloch 176
non-human animal emotions 231–233
Northern America 34
Nugent, Maria 7

O'Doherty, Marianne 141, 144n25
Odorico da Pordenone 126–129, 132
Ogborn, Miles 50
Ogier, Charles 173–175, 178, 190
O'Leary, Heather McStay 140
oppression 219, 277
oranda-yuki 76
Order of Santiago 98–99, 114
Order of the Fleece 101
Order of the Knights of St. John 153
Order of the Most Holy Trinity for the Redemption of Captives 153–156, *154*
Order of the Trinitarians 154, 155, 161
Osiander, Andreas 313, 316–320, 323n18, 325n38, 325n39, 328n62
Osiander, Lucas 313, 314, 315
Osuna, Francisco de: *Abecedario espiritual* 200
Oswald, John 243
Ottoman Empire 3, 237, 238, 311
Ovid: *Metamorphoses* 139; "The Story of Picus and Canens" 34
Oviedo, Gonzalo Fernández de 101; *Historia General de Indias* 101
Owen, Lewis: *Running Registre* 203–204

paiderasita (love of boys) 79
Paine, Thomas: *Rights of Man* 218
Palencia, Alonso de 101
Pamphilij, Girolamo 160
Panciroli, Ottavio 156, 166n20
Paolo da San Leocadio, Iglesia Arciprestal de San Jaime Vila-Real 97–98

Paravicini, Fray Hortensio Felix de 159
Paravincini, I.E. 30, 35, 37
Pathosformel 140
Paul V 160
Pedersen, Laurids 182; *Helsingør i Sundtoldstiden 1426–1887* 176
Pedersen, Oluf 179
Pendóndelos Zamorano 97
Peralta, Gastón de 101
Pereyns, Simón 101–103; *Virgen del Perdón* 103
Pernau, Margrit 8
Petrarch: *I Trionfi* 137
Philip III, Hapsburg King 105
Philippines 95, 103; Spanish activities in 59
Pieters, Isaac 175, 187
Pizarro, Francisco 105, 107–108
plagiarism 34–37
Pliny the Elder 264
Poma de Ayala, Felipe Guaman 105–108
Pontanus, Isaac 175
Portugal, public baptisms of Muslims and Jews in 6
Pory, John 299
Povinelli, Elizabeth A. 7; *The Empire of Love* 7
Pratt, George D. *139*
Prophet Muhammed 232, 245; cat of 235–239
Protestant Europe 199
proto-racism 293
Puckle, William 48–64; abuses in Machilipatnam, recording 52–58; report to East India Company 61–64

Qur'an 232, 233, 239, 245

Rabbinic Judaism 232
Ragona, Alfonso 206
Ramirez of León, King 115
rangakusha 87
Reconquista 95–97, 115
Reddy, William 3, 200, 234, 313
Richelieu, Cardinal 167n25
Riis, Thomas: *Should Old Acquaintance be Forgot… Scottish-Danish Relations c. 1450–1700* 176
Rise, Sarah 20, 32, 37, 43n65
Rittersma, Rengenier C: *Luxury in the Low Countries.* 185
Roberts, Lisa 85
Robinson, Mary 217
Rodrigo, Marchese di Castel 157
Roepete, I.E. 20
Rome, influence of Spanish in 156–157

Roper, Lyndal 49
Rosenbusch, Christoph 316, 325–326n43–44, 326n45, 326n54, 327–328n62, 327n55–57
Rosenvinge, Willum 175
Rosenwein, Barbara 3, 9, 10, 37, 50, 200, 234, 285, 322n15
Roux, Frederick 23–24
Royal Charles 56
Royal Council of Castilla 101
Royal James 56
Royster, Francesca T. 298
Rudolf II, Emperor 314
Ryan, Michael T. 38–39n3

Sachs, Anders 179, 184
Sacra Congregazione dei Riti 163
Sacred Congregation of Rites and Ceremonies 160
St. John of Matha, church of S. Tommaso, Formis 153–165; Order of the Most Holy Trinity for the Redemption of Captives 153–156; *sede vacante* 157–158; theft of the body 158–163, *162*
St Thomas (or São Tomé) 52
sakoku 74, 87, 88
Sande, Duarte de 75; *De Missione Legatorum Iaponensium ad Romanam Curiam* (The Mission of the Japanese Legates to the Roman Curia) 75
Santiago Mataindios (Saint James slayer of Indians) 95–115; in medieval Spain 96–100, *98–100*
Santiago Matamoros (Saint James slayer of Moors) 95–115; in Americas 100–113; in medieval Spain 96–100, *98–100*
Sawyer, John 239
Scheer, Monique 9, 10, 35, 36, 115, 200, 277, 290
Scheil, Andrew 278
Scherer, Georg 313, 315, 318–320, 325n32, 325n37, 327n60, 327n61, 328n63, 328n65, 329n70
Scheuchzer, Johann Jakob 86
Schultz, Hostrup: *Helsingørs Embeds-og Bestillingsmænd* 176
Schulze, Winfried 311
sede vacante 157–158
Sen, Amrita 59
Settei, Tsukioka 79
Seville 101, 103
sex education 77
sexual addiction 282
Sforza, Cavalier 157
Shah, Abul Hasan Qutb 52

Shakespeare, William: changing emotional register of blackness in 290–306; *Love Labour's Lost* 291; *The Merchant of Venice* 303; *Othello* 290, 299–306; *Titus Andronicus* 290, 291, 293–295, 299, 300, 305
Shehada, Housni Alkhateeb 232, 236
Shelley, Mary: *Frankenstein* 222
Shogun 74
shunga 73, 77–82, 88
shunpon 79, 82
Siebold, Philipp Franz Balthasar von 85, 87, 90n48, 91n73
Sigebertus, Thomas 318
Smith, Haig 55
Sobieski, Jacob 206
social emotions 234
Solis, Don Diego de 161
Sonnini, Charles-Sigisbert 244–245; *Travels in Upper and Lower Egypt* 244
South Asia 48
Soyer, Francois 6, 200
Spada, Giovanni Battista 157, 167n26
Spain: attachment to a warlike and racist Santiago, consequences of 113–115; medieval, Saint James the Apostle in 96–100; public baptisms of Muslims and Jews in 6
'Spaniards and Mesoamericans with Santiago Matamoros presiding' (Museo de las Culturas de Oaxaca, Mexico) 111
Spanish Discalced Trinitarian Order 153, 163
Spanish: activities in Philippines 59; influence in Rome 156–157
spirituality 6
Spriggs, Elizabeth 20, 33–34, 37, 38
Stearns, Carol Z. 3
Stearns, Peter 3
Stern, Philip 51, 53
Stevenson, Jane: *De Transitu Mariae Aegyptiace* 276–277
Stoler, Ann Laura 50, 51
Sunnah 232, 233, 247n4

Tafur, Pero 126, 129
Tarizzo, Don Antonio Francesco 154
Taylor, Joseph 59
temporalities 3–4, 7
Tenshokenou shounen shiseteu (shnen shisetsu, (*Embaixada Tensho*) or the Tensho Embassy) 75
Teresa of Avila 113
Teuscher, Simon 43n66
Texan Revolution 112

Thekla, Abbess 276
Thevet, André 137, 140; *Cosmographie universelle* 132, 133
Thirty Years War 312
Thoen, Irma: *Strategic Affection* 185
Tintoretto 276
Tokugawa Bakufu (*Shogunate*) 86
Tønnesen, Allan 175
Torquemada, Fray Juan de 103
Tourankanzu 90n48
Tournefort, Joseph Pitton de 238
Towers of Catoira 97
Trexler, Richard 112–113
Triumph of Caesar 125
Tuggett, Richard 32–33, 37, 38
Tympanum of Clavijo 97

Valdepeñas 155
Valera, Jerónimo 101; *Comentarii ac quaestiones in universam Aristotelis* 101
Van Gent, Jacqueline 5, 6
Vaughan, Virginia Mason 292, 293, 294, 297, 305
Vellusig, Robert 43n56
Vereenigde Oostindische Compagnie (VOC) 6, 50, 61, 74, 76, 77, 80–83, 85, 87
Vergil, Polydore: *On Discovery* 138
Vidal, Fray José 153, 158, 161, 163
Villars, Madame de 204, 212n31

violence 30, 50, 53, 57, 61, 97, 114, 125, 126, 129, 136–138, 158, 178, 221; cross-cultural 6; interpersonal 136; self-harming 135
Visconti, Vitaliano 165n1
Vivar, Rodrigo Díaz de 100
Volfing, Annette 260

Wakefield, E. G. 216–226; *Letter from Sydney* 217, 222–226
Wales, Samuel 61
Walsham, Alexandra 156
Warburg, Aby 140
Watt, Diane 280
Watts, Edward 20, 33
Whitehead, Thomas 54–56
White, Samuel 59
'The White Knights' 114
Wilson, Judith 219–220
Wittkover, Rudolf 264
Wollstonecraft, Mary 217
Worcester Art Museum, Massachusetts 100
Wright, Thomas: *The Passions of the Mind in General* 297
Wynne, Sir Richard 203, 204

Yale, Elihu 53
Young, Spencer 5
Yupanqui, Manco Inca 105

Zika, Charles 136

Printed in the United States
By Bookmasters